# Revolutionary Social Democracy

# Historical Materialism Book Series

The Historical Materialism Book Series is a major publishing initiative of the radical left. The capitalist crisis of the twenty-first century has been met by a resurgence of interest in critical Marxist theory. At the same time, the publishing institutions committed to Marxism have contracted markedly since the high point of the 1970s. The Historical Materialism Book Series is dedicated to addressing this situation by making available important works of Marxist theory. The aim of the series is to publish important theoretical contributions as the basis for vigorous intellectual debate and exchange on the left.

The peer-reviewed series publishes original monographs, translated texts, and reprints of classics across the bounds of academic disciplinary agendas and across the divisions of the left. The series is particularly concerned to encourage the internationalization of Marxist debate and aims to translate significant studies from beyond the English-speaking world.

*For a full list of titles in the Historical Materialism Book Series*
*available in paperback from Haymarket Books, visit:*
https://www.haymarketbooks.org/series_collections/1-historical-materialism

# Revolutionary Social Democracy

*Working-Class Politics*
*Across the Russian Empire*
*(1882–1917)*

Eric Blanc

Haymarket Books
Chicago, IL

First published in 2021 by Brill Academic Publishers, The Netherlands
© 2021 Koninklijke Brill NV, Leiden, The Netherlands

Published in paperback in 2022 by
Haymarket Books
P.O. Box 180165
Chicago, IL 60618
773-583-7884
www.haymarketbooks.org

ISBN: 978-1-64259-764-6

Distributed to the trade in the US through Consortium Book Sales and
Distribution (www.cbsd.com) and internationally through Ingram
Publisher Services International (www.ingramcontent.com).

This book was published with the generous support of Lannan
Foundation and Wallace Action Fund.

Special discounts are available for bulk purchases by organizations and
institutions. Please call 773-583-7884 or email info@haymarketbooks.org
for more information.

Cover art and design by David Mabb. Cover art is a detail of *Construct
29. Morris, Medway / Stepanova, Untitled Textile Design*. Paint and
wallpaper on canvas (2006).

Printed in the United States.

10 9 8 7 6 5 4 3 2 1

Library of Congress Cataloging-in-Publication data is available.

*For Leo Panitch*

# Contents

# Acknowledgements

For their help and critical advice along the way, many thanks to Lars Lih, David Walters, Danny Hayward, Wiktor Marzec, Krystian Szadkowski, Agata Zysiak, Kamil Piskała, Ivars Ijabs, Sami Suodenjoki, Paula Rauhala, Risto Turunen, Tauno Saarela, Marjaliisa Hentilä, Ralf Hoffrogge, Brian Porter, Zbigniew Kowalewski, Brendan McGeever, Charlie Post, Samuel Farber, Jake Blanc, Isabel Pike, Olivia Lichterman Gamboa, everyone in Bread and Roses-DSA, Jason Farbman, Bhaskar Sunkara, Micah Uetricht and the whole *Jacobin* crew, all those who housed me on my research trips, and the countless librarians and archivists upon whom I depended in Poland, Ukraine, Russia, Latvia, Finland, Germany, France, and the United States. Countless thanks to Galit Gun for all her love and patience, and for making my life so much brighter this past year. A very special thanks to John Riddell and Sebastian Budgen, without whose support and intellectual engagement this book would not have been possible.

Above all, I would like to thank my mother Lita and my father Alan – I couldn't ask for more loving parents or better political role models – and my brother Jake, my best editor and my best friend.

# Tables

Regions of the Russian Empire, 1897

MAP BY ALTES (CREATIVE COMMONS). CAPTIONS BY AUTHOR, USING MODERN DESIGNA-
TIONS, OF THE EMPIRE'S REGIONS THAT HAD THEIR OWN MARXIST PARTIES.

# Introduction

Activists for well over a century have debated what, if anything, from Russia's revolutionary experience should be emulated by socialists abroad. During this same period, historians have plumbed the depths of Moscow's archives, while sociologists have systematically compared the 1905 and 1917 upheavals with other revolutions. Yet the vast majority of these contributions share a common flaw: they have looked only at central Russia, instead of the empire as a whole.

The Russian Revolution was far less Russian than has often been assumed. Most inhabitants of imperial Russia were from dominated national groups – Ukrainians, Poles, Finns, Latvians, Jews, Muslims, and Georgians, among others. The same was true for most Marxists within the empire. But since these non-Russian socialist parties have been ignored or marginalised, the hegemonic accounts of revolutionary Russia remain at best one-sided and at worst deeply misleading.

More than a century after 1917, it is well past time to examine the development of working-class politics in Russia from an empire-wide perspective. By expanding our geographic scope to the imperial borderlands – including Finland, with its exceptional political freedom and autonomous parliament – this book challenges long-held assumptions about the Russian Revolution and the dynamics of political struggle in autocratic and parliamentary conditions.

Arriving at a more accurate assessment of this experience is not simply an academic affair: a critical engagement with the past remains an indispensable instrument for critically confronting the present. With capitalism's ongoing crisis and a renewed interest in democratic socialism across the globe, it is an opportune moment to return to old questions with fresh eyes. To quote historian Orlando Figes, 'the ghosts of 1917 have not been laid to rest'.[1]

## 1    Bringing in the Borderlands

Over four decades ago, Latvian scholar Andrew Ezergailis called for a break from the 'refusal to recognise that the revolution originated, developed, and

---

1  Figes 1997, p. 824.

matured in the Empire at large rather than in Petrograd or Moscow alone'.[2] Yet the study of revolutionary politics in Russia has remained marred by a myopic focus on the imperial centre.

This blind spot has been shared by academics and activists alike, reflecting the longstanding Russocentric tendencies of both. For much of the twentieth century, Russia was analysed as if it were an ethnically uniform nation-state. Numerous influential studies of the 1905 and 1917 revolutions and the development of Marxism under Tsarism have almost completely ignored non-Russian socialists and their parties. More frequently, the borderlands were given a brief mention, while the general account remained focused on central Russia.

After the fall of the Berlin Wall in 1989, increased scholarly attention to race and nationality led to an upsurge in academic research on the Russian Empire's periphery. Yet since this 'imperial turn' in the academy took place simultaneously with a stampede away from research on labour movements and socialist parties, the overwhelming majority of these newer works have continued to ignore the borderland Marxists, preferring instead to study subjects such as the formation of national identities.[3]

Socialist writings have likewise been limited by a narrow geographic and interpretative lens. Though a considerable literature on non-Russian Marxists was produced by leftist scholars in the Eastern Bloc, Bolshevism in central Russia remained the hegemonic empirical focus and analytical model. Socialist writers outside the Soviet Union and its satellite states paid far less attention to the non-Russian Marxists – if borderland socialists were mentioned at all, it was usually fleetingly in uncritical discussions of V.I. Lenin's support for national self-determination. In none of these works does the imperial periphery shift the authors' general account of Second International socialism or the struggles that led to the overthrow of Tsarism and capitalism in 1917.

These dominant interpretative trends have been exacerbated by the fact that most serious studies on non-Russian socialists, as well as the primary sources on which they are based, were written in not-widely-read Eastern European languages. As such, this history generally remains unknown beyond small circles of specialists. On the basis of my original research in Finnish, Latvian, Polish, Ukrainian, Russian, German, and French sources, the following study is the first to comparatively analyse the borderland Marxists and to demonstrate how their story obliges us to rethink socialist politics.

---

2   Ezergailis 1974, p. 77.
3   For overviews of the academic historiography, see Riga 2000, pp. 6–46, Weeks 2012, and Suny and Martin 2010, pp. 3–7.

TABLE 1    Marxist parties in the Tsarist Empire (1882 to 1907)[a]

| Organisation | Year founded | Peak membership |
|---|---|---|
| The Proletariat | 1882 | 2,000 |
| Polish Socialist Party – PPS | 1892 | 55,000 |
| Social Democracy of the Kingdom of Poland and Lithuania – SDKPIL | 1893 | 40,000 |
| Georgian Social Democracy – *Mesame Dasi* | 1893 | 20,000 |
| Lithuanian Social Democratic Party – LSDP | 1896 | 3,000 |
| General Jewish Labour Bund in Lithuania, Poland and Russia | 1897 | 40,000 |
| Social Democratic Party of Finland – SDP | 1899 | 107,000 |
| Revolutionary Ukrainian Party/Ukrainian Social Democratic Workers Party – USDRP | 1900 | 3,000 |
| Polish Socialist Party – Proletariat | 1900 | 1,000 |
| Latvian Social Democratic Union | 1903 | 1,000 |
| Armenian Social Democratic Workers Organisation 'Specifists' | 1903 | 2,000 |
| Bolshevik faction of the Russian Social Democratic Workers Party – RSDRP | 1903 | 58,000 |
| Menshevik faction of the Russian Social Democratic Workers Party – RSDRP | 1903 | 45,400 |
| Latvian Social Democratic Workers Party – LSDSP | 1904 | 23,800 |
| Muslim Social Democratic Party – *Gummet* | 1904 | 1,000 |
| Ukrainian Social Democratic Union – *Spilka* | 1904 | 10,000 |
| Estonian Social Democracy | 1905 | 10,000 |

a   This list includes the major organisations in Russia that explicitly called themselves Marxist, though a few began as neo-populist and/or revolutionary nationalist parties. Parties are listed by their most well-known title. Peak membership under Tsarism was reached by all parties between 1905 and 1907. Readers should note that membership numbers of underground parties in Tsarist Russia are notoriously unreliable, given the lack of clear member lists and the tendency for all groups to exaggerate their size. The relative strength of the organisations, however, is roughly accurate. The cited membership for the Mensheviks includes the Georgian Social Democrats and the Ukrainian *Spilka*, which, though largely autonomous, were formally affiliated with the Menshevik faction. The RSDRP was formally founded in 1898. The Bund was affiliated from start to finish, with the exception of the 1903–05 period, the Georgian Mensheviks affiliated in 1903, and the SDKPIL and LSDSP in 1906. This chart has been compiled on the basis of the following sources, in order by party: Blit 1971, p. 83; Żarnowska 1965, p. 457; Samuś 1984, p. 69; Jones 2005, p. 209; Sabaliūnas 1990, p. 114; Рафес 1923, p. 161; Soikkanen 1961, p. 338; Головченко 1996, p. 65; Targalski 1973, p. 39; Švābe 1962, p. 611; Багирова 1997, p. 232; Уткин 1987, p. 19; ibid.; Salda 2006, p. 209; my rough estimate, based on Агакишиев 1991; Риш 1926, p. 25; Arens 1976, p. 58.

The marginalisation of non-Russian radicals in the academic and activist literature does not accurately reflect their actual weight in imperial Russia, or their analytical importance for understanding the evolution of working-class struggle. Reducing the socialist movement under Tsarism to a bilateral Menshevik-Bolshevik conflict has obscured a far more dynamic picture: over a dozen Marxist parties debated, collaborated, split, and united throughout the empire. All, with the significant exception of the legal Finnish socialist party, were engaged in the unprecedented experiment of building a Marxist movement in underground political conditions. Indeed, imperial Russia's first Marxist organisation arose in Poland in 1882 – over twenty years before the emergence of the Bolsheviks and Mensheviks.

As Table 1 illustrates, borderland socialists were over-represented in Russia's leftist movements before 1917. In an empire where non-Russians comprised 58 per cent of the population, borderland parties represented over 75 per cent of organised Marxists. Up through 1917, the massive Finnish Social Democracy remained the single largest socialist party per capita in the whole world. And the experiences of the borderlands are vital for understanding the Bolsheviks and Mensheviks themselves, each of which had a considerable base among non-Russians.

Analysing the rise and unexpected fall of working-class politics in Russia's borderlands also helps explain the defeat of the most serious challenge ever mounted against global capitalism: the post-1917 international revolutionary wave, whose containment paved the way for the consolidation of bourgeois rule in the West and the subsequent emergence of Stalinist authoritarianism in Russia. For Marxists of the era, it was a tragic surprise that the imperial borderlands ended up constituting more of a barrier than a bridge to world revolution.

Revolutionary movements had remained stronger in the borderlands than in the centre for much of Tsarist rule. The first revolution in Russia advanced furthest in non-Russian regions such as Poland, Latvia, and Georgia, where general strikes, workers' insurrections, soldier mutinies, and rural rebellions culminated in the partial or complete seizure of power by working people in many locales.

Though St. Petersburg became the undisputed vanguard of the empire-wide movement after 1905, the borderlands again played a pivotal role in 1917 and in the subsequent civil war. Tsarism's overthrow in February unleashed a revolutionary wave that immediately engulfed all the country's regions and nationalities – within a span of months, most of the radical non-Russian parties allied with or joined the Bolsheviks in the fight for soviet power and international socialist overturn. Revolution was not just a central Russian affair. Even in relatively peaceful, parliamentary Finland, working people and socialists became

increasingly convinced that only a workers' government could offer a way out
of social crisis and national oppression.

At a decisive juncture in world history, Bolsheviks and Western capitalist
powers alike understood that Russia's periphery was a key battleground for the
expansion or containment of socialist rule. Brian Porter's recent monograph
notes the depth of the post-war anti-capitalist challenge:

> The old political, social, and economic norms were discredited and des-
> troyed. Today we call the events of 1917 'the Russian Revolution', but at the
> time there seemed to be a genuine possibility that it would turn out to be
> *the* revolution, the moment of creative destruction that would topple all
> the old centers of power and introduce a totally new world order.[4]

Between central Russia and the rest of the world stood the borderlands: if the
revolution triumphed in the empire's periphery, it could proceed to advance
across Western Europe and Asia. To quote a Latvian Bolshevik leaflet:

> From the Rhine to Vladivostock and from the Black Sea to Archangel on
> the White Sea the civil war rages. Soon it will break through the walls and
> ramparts raised by victorious Imperialism. ... A swift victory of the Soviet
> power in the whole of Latvia and its firm establishment there will itself
> be the surest means of throwing another burning torch into the revolu-
> tionary powder magazine of our opponents.[5]

Part of the reason why this vision did not materialise was that governmental
outcomes unexpectedly diverged across the empire in 1917–18. Why were anti-
capitalist governments established in certain regions but not others? To help
answer this puzzle requires examining the political evolution and competition
of socialist parties, especially following 1905. Up through Russia's first revolution, class struggle radicalism predominated everywhere except in Finland and
among Armenian communities. But in the wake of 1905's demoralizing defeat,
moderate socialists eventually became hegemonic in Ukraine, Georgia, Poland,
and among Jews. In Finland, however, the opposite pattern prevailed, with radicals displacing moderates after 1905. As outlined in Table 2, political outcomes
in 1917–18 corresponded entirely to whether radicals or moderates predominated in the socialist movement. Where radicals were hegemonic, they set up

---

4   Porter 2014, p. 66.
5   Cited in Popoff 1932, p. 51.

anti-capitalist governments. Where moderates predominated, they generally established coalition governments with bourgeois parties and often proceeded to invite foreign militaries to intervene in 1918. Ukraine and Poland – the two largest and most geo-politically strategic borderland regions – were particularly decisive defeats for the spread of revolution westward.

Making sense of the divergent political outcomes in 1905 and 1917–18 poses a challenge to the vast comparative scholarship on revolution, which has over-looked Russia's borderlands and minimised the causal impact of political parties. For instance, by treating Russia as a homogenous nation state, Theda Skocpol's sociological classic *States and Social Revolutions* does not acknow-ledge, let alone explain, the divergent outcomes of socialist politics and revolu-tionary struggle for the different nationalities of the Russian Empire in 1905 and 1917–18.[6] A broader geographic scope would require tempering her 'state-centric' structural account of revolution with an appreciation of social move-ment agency, particularly as concretised through competing party-building projects and the strategic decisions of socialist leaders.[7]

One of the key dynamics illustrated in the following chapters is the relat-ive autonomy of political parties and their importance for articulating popular interests.[8] This insight, properly understood, cuts against the prevailing mar-ginalisation of class analysis among both scholars and activists. While it is true that many different social relations and identities can spur political contention, it does not follow that all forms of collective mobilisation are equally effica-cious or that popular struggle is entirely contingent on discourse.[9] Economic exploitation makes possible, but does not guarantee, the emergence of a class-conscious and politically independent workers' movement – the presence and influence of parties seeking to polarise working people against capitalists is the crucial intermediary variable.

Unlike so many activists today, revolutionary social democrats consistently viewed their *raison d'etre* to be the promotion of working-class conscious-ness, organisation, and struggle. As the experience of the Tsarist Empire helps demonstrate, the crystallisation of workers into a politically coherent and hegemonic class depends to a significant degree on the existence of parties pushing in that direction. Exploring what this strategic project looked like

---

6  Skocpol 1979. In one of the few comparative analyses of borderland revolutions in Russia, Alapuro's (1988) account of Finland, Estonia, and Latvia similarly downplays party agency.
7  On the agency of socialist leaders, and the outcomes of their decisions, see Vössing 2017.
8  For recent sociological scholarship on political party 'articulation', see Desai 2002, Desai and Tuğal 2009, de Leon, Desai, and Tuğal (eds.) 2015, and Eidlin 2016.
9  Aminzade 1993.

in imperial Russia not only sheds light on the trajectories of workers' movements across the empire, it retrieves a tradition of *class* politics that has largely
been abandoned over recent decades, to the detriment of both labour and the
Left.

Imperial Russia, with its diverse regions, organisations, and outcomes, is a
historically unique laboratory for a comparative analysis of working-class politics, illustrating how workers' movements were shaped by parties as well as governmental regimes. The exceptional case of Finland – the only region of Russia
where the Tsar allowed political freedom, a democratically elected parliament,
and a legal labour movement – provides an especially rich comparison to reveal
the distinct dynamics of socialist politics in authoritarian and parliamentary
polities. Analysing the entirety of the Russian Empire makes it clear that the
presence of an autocratic regime was *the* single most important factor differen-
tiating the trajectory of Russia's underground socialists from their counterparts
across Europe.

Bringing in the history of the borderlands thus shines light on the failure
of post-1917 Leninist attempts to export an insurrectionary strategy and soviet
power to political democracies abroad. At the same time, the Finnish Social
Democracy's rise to power in 1918 lends credence to the democratic socialist
case that anti-capitalist rupture under parliamentary conditions likely requires
the prior election of a workers' party to the state's democratic institutions.

In other words, experience across the Russian Empire confirms the case of
sociological work positing that successful insurrectionary movements generally only arise under conditions of authoritarianism. Conversely, workers and
socialists in parliamentary contexts will tend to focus more on what Walter
Korpi labels 'the democratic class struggle': building class power and transforming society through electoral politics as well as union organising.[10]

## 2        Strategic Continuities and Ruptures

Broadening our lens to include all of the major socialist parties under Tsarism
obliges us to rethink long-held views on the nature and development of Marxism in the early Second International. Indeed, the problem of Russocentrism
is inseparable from a second deficiency in the existing literature: Bolshevik
exceptionalism. According to liberal and leftist accounts, the Bolsheviks under

---

10      McDaniel 1988, Goodwin 2006, Korpi 1983, Esping-Andersen 1985, and Vössing 2017.

TABLE 2      Political outcomes in imperial Russia

| Region/nationality[11] | Hegemonic socialist orientation[12] | Governmental outcome[13] |
| --- | --- | --- |
| **1905 Revolution** | | |
| Latvia, Poland, Georgia, central Russia, Ukraine, Lithuania, Jews, Estonia, and Azerbaijan | Radical | *Local seizures of power by workers and peasants* (1905), suppressed by Tsarist military (1905–06) |
| Armenia | Moderate | *Cross-class armed defence squads* |
| Finland | Moderate | *Cross-class government*, conquest of universal suffrage (1905–06) |
| **1917–18 Revolution** | | |
| Latvia | Radical | *Anti-capitalist government* (1917), overthrown by German intervention (1918) |
| Central Russia | Radical | *Anti-capitalist government* (1917), descends into civil war |
| Estonia | Radical | *Anti-capitalist government* (1917), overthrown by German intervention (1918) |

---

11    This table covers the 11 national groups and regions in the Tsarist Empire that had at least one Marxist party of their own.

12    This refers to the dominant socialist approach on the eve of the revolution (e.g. late 1916) and at its climax (e.g. late 1917), with the exception of Ukraine, where radicals generally predominated before, but not during, 1917. Note: radicals in regions like central Russia briefly lost hegemony early in 1917, but regained it quickly. 'Radical' refers to socialists committed to class struggle and a revolutionary break with capitalism. 'Moderate' socialists were those strategically or practically oriented to a bloc between working people and the upper class, an orientation that usually meant opposing the establishment of an anti-capitalist government.

13    Cross-class here refers to administrations that included bourgeois parties or that subordinated themselves to foreign capitalist powers. Listed outcomes are for the governments established in the main urban centres (e.g. Baku in Azerbaijan). For 1917–18, the governmental outcomes are from February 1917 up through the end of 1918. Note that cross-class regimes generally preceded anti-capitalist conquests of power in 1917 and that there were numerous localised power seizures by parties across the political spectrum. Post-1918 outcomes are not listed, since these were far more determined by the contingencies of military dynamics. As will be discussed further in the book's Epilogue, radicals received a second chance at wielding power following the retreat of German troops in November 1918; yet the new Soviet regimes in Latvia, Estonia, Lithuania-Belarus, and Ukraine – established with the help of the Red Army in late 1918 and early 1919 –

TABLE 2    Political outcomes in imperial Russia (*cont.*)

| Region/nationality | Hegemonic socialist orientation | Governmental outcome |
| --- | --- | --- |
| Finland | Radical | *Anti-capitalist government* (1918), overthrown by German intervention and civil war |
| Azerbaijan | Radical | *Anti-capitalist government* (1918), resigns after losing soviet majority |
| Lithuania | Radical | *Anti-capitalist government* (1918), overthrown by Polish army (1919) |
| Ukraine | Moderate | *Cross-class government* (1917), invites German-Austrian intervention (1918) |
| Armenia | Moderate | *Cross-class government* (1918) |
| Georgia | Moderate | *Cross-class government* (1918), invites German then British intervention |
| Poland | Moderate | *Cross-class government* (1918) |
| Jews | Moderate | *Cross-class government* (*support for*) (1917) |

V.I. Lenin's guidance set themselves apart from all other socialist parties of the era by breaking with the moderate socialist gradualism embodied in the German Social Democratic Party (SPD) and its leading theoretician Karl Kautsky. While the former historiographic school has framed this rupture as the genesis of Soviet totalitarianism, the latter has insisted that this strategic break was a precondition for the victorious October Revolution – as well as the programmatic foundation for rescuing Marxism from its supposed Second International defanging. A central thesis of this book is that neither interpretation can withstand scrutiny once non-Russian socialists are taken into account.

In most academic interpretations, the Bolsheviks under Lenin's tutelage substituted the elitist and violent conspiratorialism of the Russian revolutionary tradition for the theory and practice of Western social democracy. Orlando Figes claims that 'Bolshevism was a very Russian thing. Its belief in militant action, its insistence, contrary to the tenets of Hegel and Marx, that a revolution could "jump over" the contingencies of history, placed it firmly in the Russian

---

quickly collapsed under the combined weight of their ultra-left politics, popular discontent, and military counter-offensives. From late 1919 through 1921, Red Army intervention helped to re-establish Soviet regimes in Ukraine, Belarus, and Azerbaijan and to establish Soviet regimes in Armenia and Georgia.

messianic tradition'.[14] In this view, first pioneered by Lenin's factional opponents in 1904, the Bolshevik-Menshevik split was essentially a conflict between traditional Russian revolutionism and Western socialism.[15] Agreeing with this assessment, historian Abraham Ascher more recently has affirmed that the Bolsheviks lacked the 'Western orientation' adhered to by the Mensheviks.[16]

Marxist historiography has painted a similar portrait of Bolshevik distinctiveness, though it inverts the negative and positive signs in its assessment. According to this interpretation, only by breaking with the political model of the German Social Democracy and Kautsky's Marxism was Lenin able to build a party capable of leading the world's first successful socialist revolution. The starting point of this narrative, as in its academic counterpart, is the fundamentally non-revolutionary nature of 'Second International Marxism'.

Of the Bolsheviks' supposed innovations, the most commonly cited are their break with Kautsky's fatalism; their advocacy of an opportunist-free 'party of a new type'; or their novel conception of the state and revolution from 1917 onwards. For Tony Cliff, Lenin was 'totally wrong' to have looked to Kautsky as the leading exponent of revolutionary socialism in the pre-war years – this was simply a reflection of Lenin's 'long-standing illusions'.[17] According to Donny Gluckstein, 'although the [German Social Democratic] party was formally committed to revolution, under the intellectual guidance of Karl Kautsky it had abandoned this in practice'.[18] The proof of the non-revolutionary nature of Kautsky's Marxism, it is argued, was that Europe's major socialist parties supported World War One and opposed anti-capitalist overhaul in its wake.

Like in the prevailing academic literature, the existence of borderland Marxist parties is generally ignored in these works written by, and largely for, activists. The resulting effect is to give the impression that the Bolsheviks were alone in pursuing a path different from their counterparts in Western Europe. But even a cursory examination of the underground socialist parties in the Russian Empire illustrates the flaws in Bolshevik exceptionalism. Positions and practices long assumed to have been particularities of Lenin's faction were actually very common. The fact that there was no major Bolshevik stance that was not also shared by various non-Russian parties helps illustrate that no position on its own could lead directly to October 1917 – or, as anti-Communist scholars would have it, to Stalinism. There was no socialist silver bullet or original sin.

---

14    Figes 1997, p. 812.
15    Woytinsky 1921, pp. 48–9.
16    Ascher 1988, p. 187.
17    Cliff 1985, pp. 15, 20.
18    Gluckstein 2014.

A few examples, explained in detail later, should suffice here to demonstrate the trend. Rosa Luxemburg's famous 1904 critiques of Lenin's conception of centralism are almost always cited without any acknowledgement that her own party in Tsarist Poland was far more top-down and anti-democratic. Ignoring the radical anti-militarism of other leading borderland Marxist parties, it is often erroneously claimed that the Bolsheviks were the only major socialist party to oppose World War One, when in fact it was also opposed by the PPS-Left and the SDKPIL in Poland as well as the LSDSP in Latvia. And, finally, the fact that the Bolsheviks were not the sole party in the former Tsarist Empire to lead workers to power in 1917–18 has remained remarkably unacknowledged.

In the following chapters I will show that dominant academic and activist accounts have unjustifiably equated the Marxism of the Second International with moderate socialism. Both have overlooked the impact of the autocratic Tsarist context in pushing *all* illegally organised socialists down a very different path than their counterparts in Western Europe.

To today's readers, the category 'revolutionary social democracy' might appear to be a contradiction in terms. Yet up through 1917, this was the main self-identification used by 'orthodox' Marxists in the Second International to differentiate their orientation from the accommodationist political tendency that now is usually referred to as social democracy. Clarifying the content of *revolutionary* social democracy, of which Kautsky was the leading exponent, is thus essential for understanding the political orientation that enabled Russia's radicals to lead successful revolutions in and after 1917.

There were, of course, important evolutions in the politics of Marxism between 1882 and 1917. In particular, the 1905 revolution was a major turning point. But, on the whole, the approaches of imperial Russia's radicals reflected an implementation and development of orthodox Second International Marxism far more than a break from it. The roots of 1917 lie firmly in revolutionary social democracy.

Though Kautsky for the past century has been pegged as an advocate of fatalistic reformism, looking at his actual writings – rather than their prevailing caricatures – confirms why the 'Pope of Marxism' in this era was seen as the foremost defender of revolutionary socialism. Among all nationalities, Kautsky's pre-1910 works effectively served as the foundation for the Tsarist Empire's Marxist parties that stood on the furthest left of the political spectrum. Indeed, his influence over socialist politics was much higher in Tsarist Russia than in any other country, including Germany. This is a crucial point to stress from the outset, as Kautsky's theories have often been mistakenly blamed for the German Social Democratic Party's break from class struggle. Such interpretations fundamentally misdiagnose both the content of Kautsky's early orientation and the reasons for the SPD's degeneration.

In sharp contrast with the Russian Empire's illegal Marxist parties, the German Social Democracy came increasingly under the control of a caste of bureaucrats. As Kautsky lamented in 1909, the German party and union leaders 'have been so absorbed by the administrative needs of the huge apparatus that they have lost every broad view, every interest for anything outside the affairs of their own offices'.[19] For this unprincipled SPD leadership, it mattered little that its decision to support World War One in 1914 and head a capitalist government in alliance with the bourgeoisie after 1917 flagrantly violated the traditional stances promoted by Kautsky and the SPD as a whole. In the words of historian Hans-Josef Steinberg, the story of the German Social Democracy from 1890 to 1914 is 'the history of the emancipation from theory in general'.[20]

If political practice is the ultimate criteria for socialist theory, then revolutionary social democratic strategy should be judged by the practices of the parties that actually sought to implement it. To see what a party led by orthodox social democrats looked like in practice, one must examine the Tsarist Empire, *not* Germany. This holds for the underground parties in imperial Russia as well as the legal Finnish Social Democracy. For strong evidence of the anti-capitalist thrust of revolutionary social democracy, there is the incontrovertible fact that Kautsky's theories trained the Bolsheviks, Finland's Marxists, and the other socialists in the former Russian Empire who led the world's first victorious assaults on bourgeois rule.

Finland is an especially significant test case for analysing the ruptural potentialities of Second International 'orthodoxy' since the legal, parliamentary-oriented Finnish Social Democracy was the party under Tsarism that operated in the political context most similar to Western European democracies and Germany in particular. Finland's socialist movement closely resembled its German counterpart, but unlike the latter, the Finnish Social Democracy did not discard revolutionary social democratic politics. In early 1918, rather than propping up capitalist rule like the German SPD, Finland's socialists led workers to seize state power. Learning about Finland's forgotten socialist movement may be of considerable use in enabling Marxists to overcome a problematic tendency to overgeneralise Left strategy from the particular experience of the revolutionary movement in autocratic Russia, whose exceptional dynamics were largely determined by the absence of political freedom or parliamentary institutions.

An empire-wide lens shows that the differences between the Bolsheviks and Europe's social democratic parties were not the product of theoretical

---

19      Cited in Day and Gaido 2009, p. 52.
20      Steinberg 1967, p. 124.

ruptures from Second International orthodoxy. Conditions of Russian absolutism obliged Marxists of all nationalities to adopt a different approach from
their counterparts in Western Europe. In the following chapters we will see
that Marxist parties operating illegally under Tsarism adhered to many of
the strategic perspectives and organisational practices that have usually been
portrayed as distinct to Bolshevism by both its detractors and defenders. Up
through the 1905 revolution, each of these currents (including the Mensheviks)
engaged in violent armed revolutionary struggle; each broke from the organisational model of Western socialist parties; and each rejected blocs with liberals
and argued that only an independent working-class movement could lead the
democratic revolution to victory.

For the autocratic context of Russia, such stances were explicitly sanctioned
by orthodox social democracy, which made a sharp distinction between
strategy for countries with or without political freedom. Conditions under Tsarism clearly precluded any attempt to adopt the specific organisational structure or the political focus of the German social democratic model. In other
words, not only was orthodox Marxism much more revolutionary than is usually assumed in regard to capitalist democracies, but its stance for the absolutist
Russian context was particularly intransigent.

Both in the centre and the periphery of Russia, the absence of political freedom and parliamentary democracy mitigated against working-class moderation or the emergence of conservative labour bureaucracies. Tsarist absolutism,
in other words, facilitated the ability of the Russian Empire's socialist parties
to uphold their political radicalism. The growing gap between the militant programmes and the accommodationist practices of Western social democratic
parties could not be replicated in the same way under the Russian autocracy.[21]

As Moira Donald noted in her pioneering critique of the scholarly consensus,
'Bolshevism pre-1914 was not only not out of line with the orthodox left wing
of international Social Democracy, but in no major area did Lenin add anything of any weight that could be regarded as an original contribution to the
development of Marxist theory'.[22] Historian Lars Lih's watershed 2006 monograph *Lenin Rediscovered* decisively developed the case for the political continuity between early Bolshevism and orthodox Second International Marxism.[23] Though Lih's arguments remain in a minority within both academic and
activist circles, it is largely because of his iconoclastic research that there has
begun a serious re-examination of revolutionary social democracy.

---

21    Post 2013, p. 6.
22    Donald 1993, p. ix.
23    Lih 2006.

Acknowledging the radical nature of so-called 'Kautskyism' – as well as the congruence between the Bolsheviks and the empire's other radicals – does not require us to ignore real evolutions in Marxist politics from 1882 to 1917. Nor should we minimise the specificities and unique trajectories of each party in Russia. An underlying goal of this monograph is to reach a more accurate assessment of both the continuities *and* evolutions in socialist strategy up through the October Revolution. The latter were significant, though I will show that these strategic changes were quite different, and less politically foundational, than those referenced in most socialist and scholarly accounts.

Given the disparate regional contexts of the empire and the inherent challenges of concretising theory into practice, parties committed to the same overarching political principles could and often did diverge on the ground. Revolutionary social democracy was sufficiently flexible, and sufficiently open-ended, to be implemented and developed in different ways. Both Kautsky and his peers under Tsarism insisted that Marxism was a method, not a dogma; tactics and strategy, therefore, always had to be based on a hard-nosed appraisal of a concrete situation. And their respect for Kautsky notwithstanding, imperial Russia's socialist leaders did not refrain from adopting a distinct approach from him when they felt it was warranted by the particular conditions they faced.

At any given moment, there were considerable tensions within and between Marxist parties over how best to advance the working-class struggle. Translating strategy into tactics was always a challenge. An orthodox conception of the driving forces of the revolution did not provide easy answers to the questions posed day-by-day – or even hour-by-hour – in the whirlwind of political struggle. With the course of events so difficult to predict, the fine line between opportunism and a necessary compromise was not always clear.

The 1905 revolution in particular was a trial by fire. For the first time in world history, Marxist parties were faced with the challenging opportunity of participating in an actual workers' revolution. To quote Jewish socialist poet Dovid Einhorn: 'I do not know how others number the years. But I count them from 1905'.[24] In the aftermath of 1905, Kautsky and revolutionary social democrats across Russia reoriented their approaches on a variety of questions. Indeed, the conclusions drawn by different parties during the rise and eventual suppression of the 1905 upsurge set the stage for their subsequent approaches in 1917. As Teodor Shanin has observed, 'in the aftermath of the revolution's defeat

---

24      Cited in Frankel 1981, p. 134.

in 1905–07 in Russia, the primary issue was the capacity or failure to learn, unlearn, and relearn by its survivors'.[25]

Demoralised by the loss, leaders of a wide range of socialist currents – including the Mensheviks, Georgia's social democrats, the Jewish Bund, and Ukrainian social democrats – broke from the hitherto radical consensus and for the first time began to search for a bloc with the bourgeoisie. These post-1905 ruptures to the right were a major strategic turning point. As moderate socialists dropped their previous advocacy of working-class hegemony, they increasingly built ties with liberals and nationalists, setting the stage for the cross-class coalition governments that arose in 1917–18.

The empire's other Marxist organisations largely upheld their stances on the big questions of revolutionary strategy; on this shared basis, they organisationally and politically converged in 1917. Finland, as usual, was an exceptional case: participation in the 1905 revolution veered the then-moderate social democratic party to the left. Among the world's mass socialist organisations, the Finnish Social Democracy was unique in becoming more committed to orthodoxy *after* 1905, while most Western social democratic parties increasingly accommodated themselves to their respective regimes.

Some of the radicals' strategic modifications – for example, on how to build working-class unity – have been ignored in the literature. Other stances have incorrectly been assumed to constitute ruptures with Second International orthodoxy. This, as we will see, is the case regarding Marxist approaches to the imminence and strategic centrality of international revolution.

Numerous important issues have been misjudged. For example, it is often posited that the October Revolution was made possible by Lenin's novel 1917 re-conceptualisation of the state and revolution. In actuality, the key question in that year was whether Marxists would uphold the longstanding orthodox call for working-class hegemony or participate in coalition governments with liberal parties. Indeed, the question of alliances with liberals tended to overdetermine all the other major political debates in 1917. The ability of socialists to fight for agrarian reform, oppose the war, or champion workers' pressing economic demands was more often than not conditioned by their willingness to break from the political representatives of bourgeois interests. The real political innovators here were not the Bolsheviks and their non-Russian allies who fought for soviet power, but rather the Mensheviks and moderate borderland socialists who insisted upon the possibility and necessity of building a progressive bloc with capitalists in Russia and abroad.

---

25    Shanin 1986, p. 184.

In short, the interrelated limitations of Russocentrism and Bolshevik exceptionalism have distorted our understanding of the development of socialist politics in Russia and abroad. To effectively examine the evolution of working-class struggle – and to lay the basis for extracting lessons relevant for capitalist democracies today – requires that we combine an empire-wide analytical framework with an accurate assessment of revolutionary social democracy.

## 3     Method, Structure, Sources

This is a book about the politics of Russia's workers' movements, not high Marxist theory. Though socialists in imperial Russia did their fair share of describing the world, they were primarily focused on transforming it; theoretical treatises were almost always attempts to justify and elaborate the pre-existing approaches of their particular organisations on the ground. I focus on those core political stances that had a demonstrable impact on parties' interventions in working-class struggle.

It should be kept in mind that the most influential vehicles for spreading socialist politics among the broad mass of workers in the Russian Empire were not newspapers or theoretical journals but rather oral agitation and leaflets.[26] Nevertheless, studies of Marxist politics in Russia have for much of the past century tended to rely on a myopically close reading of Lenin's *Collected Works*. A distinct political portrait emerges when we expand our source base to include other socialist leaders and activists, local and regional party bodies, public speeches, and mass fliers.

To fruitfully examine revolutionary politics, textual analysis is necessary but insufficient because words and deeds were frequently distinct, even contradictory. Marxist historiography, unfortunately, has often assumed that socialist practice was always a direct result of theory. But concrete assessments of immediate circumstances and wagers on the likely course of events often counted just as much as ideological considerations. Furthermore, parties and their militants were subjected to significant centrifugal pressures that mitigated against the consistent upholding of their programmes. 'Firmness of principles alone', noted one Russian socialist in 1901, was not capable of 'preventing unprincipled vacillations'.[27]

---

26    Steenson 1991, p. 10.
27    Krichevskii 1901a [2015], p. 249.

This was especially the case with moderate socialists. By the 1890s, Marxism was fashionable in Tsarist Russia – verbal commitments to class struggle, revolution, and socialism were surprisingly common even among liberals and mainstream nationalists. Given the depth of popular radicalisation across Russia, right-leaning socialists in 1917 framed their practical acceptance of bourgeois rule in the most militant discourse possible. Ukrainian social democratic leader Volodymyr Vynnychenko, for instance, regretted that despite the Marxist declarations of his party in 1917, 'we in our *actions* were only republicans and democrats, not socialists'.[28]

Policy and action could diverge for the additional reason that parties operating illegally under Tsarism were highly decentralised in practice. Most organisations were headed by émigrés in Western Europe; a resolution passed in Paris or an article written in Geneva were not necessarily implemented on the ground in imperial Russia. Exiled revolutionaries, in turn, often failed to understand the dynamics inside the empire. Local cadre in all parties frequently clashed with, or simply ignored, their own party leaderships in exile. This dynamic was underlined by Bolshevik M.N. Pokrovsky in a 1926 letter to a fellow party historian:

> Your book takes the well-trodden path of the history of congresses, conferences, pre- and post-congress polemics. That is the way in which one could write the history of the party in our own days, when political initiative is centralised. But even in 1905, due to the objective circumstances, organisations on the ground had to be incomparably more independent.[29]

When I first began researching the borderland Marxists nearly ten years ago, I believed that traditional Leninist interpretations of revolutionary Russia were generally correct – my initial goal was to extend these accounts to make sense of developments in the imperial periphery. Researching and writing this book has substantially shifted my views, both historiographic and strategic, as it became increasingly clear that it was unhelpful to treat Bolshevism as a generalisable political model. Effective politics is always context specific and mass politics is a terrain of trade-offs and wagers, in which even the best formulas usually prove insufficient. As such, I have sought to produce an analytically critical and

---

28    Винниченко 1920, Vol. 2, p. 92.
29    Cited in White 1985, p. 342.

methodologically rigorous study that highlights the inherent dilemmas of socialist theory and practice, which arise in distinct forms under different political regimes.

To illuminate these dynamics, I have made extensive use of primary documents, particularly leaflets, newspapers, journals, pamphlets, and memoirs.
One of the reasons why a comparative account of imperial Russia's socialist
movements has not been attempted until now is that most researchers have
been able to read only one, or perhaps two, of the empire's many languages.
In contrast, this monograph is the product of my analysis of primary and secondary sources in eight languages: Russian, Ukrainian, Polish, Latvian, Finnish,
German, French, and English. In 2014 and 2015, I conducted research in 25
archives and academic libraries across Eastern Europe.[30] This work has been
complemented by my research in the holdings of libraries in Western Europe
and the United States.[31]

This study deliberately covers a wide geographic and time range to analyse the evolution of Marxist politics in the Russian Empire. Over 25 years
of history are addressed, from the founding of Poland's Proletariat party in
1882 up through 'the long 1917' – i.e. the Russian Revolution of 1917, the 1917–
18 revolutions in Finland and Ukraine, and the 1918–19 revolution in Poland.
The geographic scope of this study is also ambitiously broad. I analyse all 11
of the regions and nationalities that had their own Marxist parties under Tsarism: Finland, Latvia, Estonia, Poland, Lithuania, Jews, Ukraine, central Russia,
Azerbaijan, Georgia, and Armenia. And, as in any serious discussion of Second
International politics, this book deals extensively with Kautsky and the German
Social Democracy.

---

30    Finland: Työväen Arkisto, Työväenliikkeen kirjasto, Kansan Arkisto, Kansalliskirjasto, Edu-
    skunnan kirjasto, Helsingin yliopiston kirjasto, Tampereen yliopiston kirjasto, and Turun
    yliopiston kirjasto; Poland: Czytelnia Wydziału Zbiorów Historii Społecznej–Biblioteka
    Sejmowa, Archiwum Akt Nowych, Biblioteka Narodowa, Dokumenty życia społecznego-
    Biblioteka Narodowa, Archiwum Państwowe w Warszawie, Archiwum Państwowe w
    Łodzi, and Biblioteka Uniwersytetu Łódzkiego; Ukraine: Національна бібліотека
    України імені В.І. Вернадського and Корпус по вул. Володимирській Національної
    бібліотеки України імені В.І. Вернадського; Latvia: Latvijas Nacionālā bibliotēka,
    Viduslaiku un jauno laiku vēstures nodaļa-Latvijas Kara muzejs, Latvijas Valsts arhīvs,
    Latvijas Akadēmiskā bibliotēka, Latvijas Universitātes bibliotēka; and Russia: Российская
    национальная библиотека, Научная библиотека им. М.Горького СПбГУ.

31    Given the wide-ranging geographic and temporal sweep of this study, I have also fre-
    quently turned to secondary accounts for my source base. In particular, this is the case
    for those national groups such as Georgians, Armenians, Azeris and Lithuanians whose
    original primary documents I could not read. Throughout the following chapters I try to

There is only so much that one can examine in a single monograph. The following work in no way pretends to be a comprehensive account of all socialist parties in the empire, nor of the 1905 and 1917 revolutions and the labour movements that spawned them. Covering a broad geographic-linguistic span allows me to delineate major political patterns across the empire up through 1917, but it also has some obvious drawbacks. Greater breadth has necessarily cut into the depth of detail provided about particular events, parties, and personalities.

Space limitations have similarly made it necessary to focus on certain nationalities and political issues more than others. Poles, Finns, Jews, Ukrainians, and Latvians, for example, receive much more attention than Armenians, Estonians, or Lithuanians, who had a more limited impact on the revolutionary movement. Readers should also keep in mind that beyond the Marxist organisations examined in the following pages, there were other socialist organisations in all regions of the empire, including the influential neo-populist Socialist Revolutionaries, as well as smaller groups of anarchists. Finally, while I highlight some key socio-economic factors that shaped the stances of imperial Russia's social democrats, a systematic analysis of the interaction between social structures and political orientation lies beyond the scope of the project.

In the order that they appear chapter by chapter, this book examines the following topics: the ABCs of revolutionary social democracy; intellectual-worker relations; organisation building, electoral work, and mass action in parliamentary and autocratic polities; proletarian hegemony versus blocs with liberals; working-class unity; the party question; and, finally, the state and revolution under parliamentary and absolutist conditions. Far from being disconnected issues, the narrative of each chapter builds off those that precede it.

A few major political topics are not systematically dealt with. These include national liberation and the agrarian question, which are examined only in so far as they overlap with the book's central themes. The reason for taking this approach is not that these questions were less significant than those that I chose to discuss but rather that the political complexity of these issues and wide regional variations precluded chapter-length analyses.[32] Nevertheless, readers will quickly see that national and agrarian struggles appear frequently throughout the book, testifying to the fact that few aspects of revolutionary politics in imperial Russia were un-impacted by the multi-national and peasant-majority nature of the empire.

---

highlight some of the most important contributions from the scholarly literature on non-Russian Marxists, a body of work that deserves a much wider readership.

32    I have also already written extensively on Marxism and the national question in imperial Russia (see Blanc 2014a and Blanc 2016a).

Regarding terminology, many of the political categories used by Marxists of the era were highly contested. Divergent meanings could be given, for example, to terms like 'democratic revolution', 'revisionism', or 'orthodox Marxism'. Rather than resort to the inelegant method of keeping these terms in quotes throughout the text, I will use quotation marks only sporadically to draw the reader's attention to particularly controversial concepts.

City names in the empire varied considerably over time and between different nationalities. For the sake of simplicity, I have generally stuck with the prevailing term used under Tsarism (for example, Tiflis rather than Tbilisi). No political judgement is intended in my usage. And since national delineations within Russia were often fluid and contested before 1917, to help simplify this geography for the lay reader I anachronistically refer to the regions of the Tsarist Empire by their current denominations (e.g. Azerbaijan, Belarus, etc.). The exception here is my use of 'Russia' to refer to the entire polity ruled by the Tsar. The term 'Russian', however, will be more narrowly reserved for ethnic Russians and fully assimilated individuals from other national backgrounds.

For consistency, I have employed the most common transliterations of the names of socialist leaders. And in the hope of minimising the possible confusion created by the alphabet soup of party names, I refer to organisations by their most well-known title and acronym, despite the fact that these sometimes changed over time. For instance, I use the acronym SDKPIL for Rosa Luxemburg's party even though it was named the SDKP before it expanded to Lithuania in 1899; similarly, I refer to the post-1905 right wing of the Polish socialist movement as the Polish Socialist Party-Revolutionary Faction (PPS-FR), although it eventually began to refer to itself as simply the PPS. For further ease of reading, I often preface party acronyms with the nationality of origin – e.g. the Latvian LSDSP – even though national terms were included within most party names. Unless otherwise noted, dates are in the old Julian calendar up through October 1917.

# CHAPTER 1

# The Social Context

Like almost every issue involving the historical development of the Tsarist Empire, the date of its birth is subject to considerable dispute.[1] Many scholars make a case for the year 1552, when Tsar Ivan IV conquered the Muslim Khanate of Kazan. Over the following centuries, the Russian state expanded outwards in all directions: through military conquests and deals with local ruling groups, Tsarism largely displaced its neighbouring rivals, the Swedish, Persian, and Ottoman empires. By the time of the first census in 1897, Russia had expanded to rule over at least one hundred distinct ethnic groups and nationalities.

Covering one sixth of the world's landmass, Russia's population was the third largest in the world, after the British Empire and China. Russians were a minority: non-Russian peoples made up roughly 58 per cent of the population. The empire's ethnic Russian geographic core was hitherto surrounded by a largely non-Russian periphery, giving the latter a notable geo-political importance as gateways to both the West and East.

Capitalist modernisation – as measured in proletarianisation, literacy, and urbanisation – progressed unevenly across the empire during the nineteenth century. Imperial Russia was not a 'classical' form of colonial rule in which the metropole had a greater level of socio-economic development than the dominated periphery. Some nationalities, like the Finns, Poles, and Latvians, were indisputably more modernised than the Russians. Others, like most of the empire's Muslim peoples and the various nomadic or tribal groups in Central Asia, were significantly less so. Russians themselves were among the most unevenly developed groups, as they lived in deeply underdeveloped rural areas as well as the most advanced and industrialised cities.

Further complicating any neat categorisation is the fact that the Russian state itself stood in a semi-subordinate position to Western nations such as France and Britain. Largely reliant on foreign financial investment, Russia's socio-economic development was inseparable from the influence and interests of European capital. In 1905 as well as 1917, Russia's relations to Europe would prove to be a significant theme in the revolutionary drama.

---

1  There is an immense body of literature on the political and social development of the Russian Empire. For a good introduction, from which I have drawn for this chapter, see Kappeler 2001.

TABLE 3      Russia's ethnic-linguistic groups, 1897[a]

| Group | Percentage of population |
| --- | --- |
| Russians | 42 |
| Ukrainians | 17 |
| Poles | 6 |
| Belarusians | 5 |
| Jews | 4 |
| Finns | 2 |
| Germans | 1 |
| Lithuanians | 1 |
| Latvians | 1 |
| Estonians | 1 |
| Azerbaijani Turks | 1 |
| Georgians | 1 |
| Armenians | 1 |
| Others | 17 |

a   For a full listing of ethnic groups in Russia circa 1897, see
    Kappeler 2001, pp. 397–9. Note that in 1897 the census
    determined these groups through the criteria of native lan-
    guage. Kappeler, like most historians basing themselves on
    the 1897 census, lists ethnic Russians as comprising 44 per
    cent of the Tsarist Empire. But apart from the fact that the
    census appears to have undercounted Poles, it did not
    include the populations of the semi-autonomous regions of
    Finland, Bukhara, or Khiva (about six million people com-
    bined). My table has been adjusted accordingly.

The extent of national consciousness among non-Russian groups varied widely.
Poland and Finland after 1899 both had influential cross-class national movements, but these were exceptions. In the big cities, many native workers and
intellectuals assimilated themselves into Russian society, especially Ukrainians
and Jews. In the countryside, local or regional particularism reigned supreme;
national consciousness was low to non-existent. To quote scholar Liliana Riga:
'Most of the empire's inhabitants did not consider themselves in national
terms, particularly the nationalities' peasantries. Regional, religious, and local
linguistic identities were far more significant social forces than "nationality"'.[2]

---

2   Riga 2000, p. 84.

National identity and political nationalism among ethnic Russians were similarly weak.

Opposition to Tsarist Russification and state centralism was certainly present among non-Russians, especially in urban areas. But national separatism was virtually absent, with the partial exception of Poland. The following words of one Georgian populist leader were typical: 'by linking its fate to modern Russia, Georgia will sooner arrive at the best possible arrangement of its position than it would in union with or under the aegis of … any other European nation, let alone Turkey or Persia'.[3] Though the 1905 revolution witnessed a growth in national consciousness of borderland peoples, most demands remained limited to political equality plus national and cultural autonomy within Russia. Pushes for state independence only became a widespread political phenomenon following the October Revolution.

Ethnic Russians did not constitute a majority of the empire's population, but their social weight was higher than their population numbers might imply. First of all, political power was centred in the empire's capital, St. Petersburg, which was overwhelmingly Russian in composition. The importance of the capital (renamed Petrograd in 1914) gave both the Tsarist regime and the Russian Social Democracy a disproportionate influence over the empire's political life.

None of the other nationalities on their own were close in size to the Russians. Moreover, the Russian state, as well as wide layers of the population, viewed Ukrainians and Belarusians as subsets of a single ethnic-national 'Russian people', thereby undercutting the popular perception that Russians constituted a numeric minority in the empire. Also, Russians generally dominated the governmental administration, although this was often done in conjunction with local non-Russian elites. Russian was imposed as the language of instruction and government, thereby becoming the lingua franca for much of the non-Russian intelligentsia. Finally, widespread ethnic-class tensions between many non-Russians peoples mitigated against the emergence of any united anti-imperial front.

By the first years of the twentieth century, Tsarist Russia was mired in crisis. The preceding decades of state-sponsored capitalist development, much of which was financed by foreign lenders, had given rise to social forces that the autocracy was finding hard to keep in check. The empire's estate system – which ranked the population into distinct groupings (e.g. peasants, nobles, clergy, merchants) with delineated duties – was increasingly anachronistic. Respon-

---

3  Cited in Галоян 1976, p. 287.

TABLE 4      Russia's largest cities, 1897[a]

| City | Population | Region |
|------|-----------|--------|
| St. Petersburg | 1,264,000 | Central Russia |
| Moscow | 1,039,000 | Central Russia |
| Warsaw | 684,000 | Poland |
| Odessa | 404,000 | Ukraine |
| Łódź | 314,000 | Poland |
| Riga | 282,200 | Latvia |
| Kiev | 248,000 | Ukraine |
| Kharkov | 174,000 | Ukraine |
| Tiflis | 160,000 | Georgia |
| Vilna | 155,000 | Lithuania |

a   Kappeler 2001, p. 401.

ding in an improvised and ad hoc manner, Russia's absolute monarchy failed to chart a viable ideological and political course to navigate these new stormy seas. And imperial Russia's capitalist classes remained notoriously weak.

Industrialisation, initially strongest in Poland, began in the 1860s and took off across the empire in the 1890s. St. Petersburg and Moscow were by far the largest urban areas, but the borderlands also witnessed the rise of major metropolises. In fact, of the empire's largest cities, eight of the top ten were outside of central Russia, as were 12 of the top 18. Inevitably these towns became the economic, intellectual, and political hubs of their respective regions. As the saying went in Latvia, 'great roads, small roads, all lead to Riga'.[4] By the turn of the century, the spread of railways throughout Russia had linked together these regional economies and their populations.

With modernisation came the emergence of a large urban working class, mostly comprised of peasants who had come to the cities looking for employment, as well as the concentration of students and professionals in these same municipal centres. Across imperial Russia, urban workers and young intellectuals formed the core social base of the growing revolutionary opposition. Marxist organisations did not emerge among the various peoples under Tsarism – e.g. Belarusians and most Muslim ethnicities – that had neither a proletariat nor an intelligentsia, or that only had the latter.

4   Cited in Henriksson 1986, p. 181.

Unlike in the West, where socialists usually had to fight to separate the work-ers' movement from the tutelage of rival democratic formations, socialists in Tsarist Russia had a virtual monopoly in organised labour from its inception. In the absence of political freedom and parliamentary institutions, there was little space for a flourishing liberalism or its nationalist equivalents.

Capitalists in the empire generally remained atomised by region, national-ity, and industry; with the partial exception of Finland, most focused on private accumulation rather than on political intervention. Alfred Rieber observes that the few 'attempts to lay the foundations for a genuine bourgeois party in Russia' were 'abortive'.[5] Fear of the growing working-class movement tended to push capitalists further into the arms of the Tsarist state. As Polish historian Feliks Tych notes, 'the social profits which [the] bourgeoisie could expect to reap from a democratic, bourgeois revolution were out of all proportion to the dangers inherent in this revolution – a confrontation with the people's masses, which could become a threat to bourgeois rule'.[6]

Socialists dominated and often completely monopolised the anti-Tsarist opposition movement. In Georgia, as one observer noted, 'the Marxist idea remained as the only teacher of the popular masses'.[7] Particularly before 1905, and frequently well after, mainstream nationalists were isolated and relatively un-influential. On the whole, the relationship of forces between socialist and non-socialist oppositionist tendencies was generally even more favourable to socialism in the borderlands than in the centre – which is one reason why the 1905 revolution went furthest in the periphery.

In such a context, the main obstacle to the spread of socialist influence was rarely rival political ideologies or parties. Of greater consequence was working-class resignation, illiteracy, fear of state repression, inter-ethnic tensions, or popular 'hooliganism'. Perhaps the most serious ideological competitor was organised religion, obliging Marxists to duel with churches for the hearts and minds of working people. In turn, religious leaders widely criticised secularism and political radicalism. An assembly of Rabbis thus denounced socialism as contrary to the holy Torah, 'which has told us to obey its laws and the decrees of the government where we reside'.[8]

While religious sentiment remained widespread, the political influence of the main organised churches was remarkably limited, due in large part to their

---

5   Rieber 1982, p. 319.
6   Tych 1970, p. 161.
7   Woytinsky 1921, pp. 51–2.
8   Cited in Tobias 1972, p. 257.

close association with the status quo. Even in heavily Catholic Poland, as one scholar observes, 'the numerous social and political activities of the workers developed, with few exceptions, independently of [the church's] influence. The political organization of the working class evolved outside the church'.[9] Socialists across Russia frequently criticised religious institutions and leaders, but not popular religious sentiment as such. The Muslim Social Democratic Party-*Gummet*, for example, lambasted the Baku *ulema* for its subordination to the Tsarist state, but it never attacked the religion of Islam itself.[10]

Though the cities dominated Russia's political and economic life, the country's population was overwhelmingly rural. Modernising tides began to transform the countryside in the nineteenth century, though at a slower pace than in the cities. Serfdom was abolished in 1861, facilitating rural social stratification and mobility. Closer ties to urban life brought new ideas, as well as greater pressure to produce for the market. Such processes began to bear down on all regions, but rural capitalist development advanced furthest in Western borderlands such as Finland, Latvia, Lithuania, Poland, as well as in pockets of Ukraine. These regions witnessed the steady growth of capitalist agricultural production, with its market-dependent cultivation, sustained capital investment, use of new technologies, and often a growing reliance on rural wage labour.

With this overhaul came the emergence of large populations of landless peasants, who turned to wage work on the big landed estates or seasonal employment in the cities. For instance, German landlords in Latvia transformed their massive estates into market-oriented firms and by 1904 roughly 70 per cent of the rural population was landless.[11] Rural central Russia and most of Ukraine on the other hand remained immersed in small-scale peasant production. Less subjected to market compulsion and its resulting class dynamics, production here remained oriented to peasant consumption rather than the marketplace. Commercial ties were weaker and the size of the rural proletariat smaller; in central Russia, land was held and managed collectively through the village commune, an institution absent from almost all other areas of the empire.

At the turn of the century, rural areas saw significantly less protest than the cities. Landed nobles of all nationalities remained a central pillar of support for

---

9       Żarnowska 1991, p. 316.
10      Swietochowski 1978, p. 120.
11      Kalniņš 1956, p. 44.

the autocracy and decades had passed since the last major peasant rebellions in the 1860s. Though rural unrest erupted in Ukraine in 1902 and Georgia in 1903, the extent to which the peasant majority would link up with urban resistance remained an open question for most of the period before the first Russian Revolution, as well as the years following its defeat.

Russian absolutism attempted to stem the growing revolutionary tide through a mix of repression and reform. Which of these was emphasised varied greatly by region and by the whims of local governmental authorities. In comparison with the twentieth century's subsequent authoritarian regimes, Tsarist absolutism seems somewhat mild and ineffective. Indeed, the empire was surprisingly under-policed – in 1897, it had only 100,000 policemen, while France (which had a third as many people) had 142,000. All this, however, is hindsight. At the time, the Russian regime was widely, and not unjustifiably, perceived to be a brutal police state. Basic political liberties, popular suffrage, and a constitution were absent, obliging socialist organisations to operate illegally. The *Okhrana*, the Tsar's secret police, was tasked with infiltrating and exposing these organisations, leading to frequent mass arrests, imprisonment, and banishments to Siberia.

Major strikes frequently resulted in Tsarist massacres of workers, students, and socialists, a dynamic that legitimised armed responses both among radicals and broad layers of workers. In March 1902, for example, massive labour strikes erupted in the factories of the Transcaucasian port-town of Batumi, culminating in clashes with police resulting in 14 deaths, dozens of wounded workers, and 500 arrests. A partial list of the government's repressive toll during the summer 1903 strike wave alone includes Kiev (11 killed, 160 injured); the Transcaucasian railway (18 killed, 14 wounded); Batumi (two killed, two injured); and Nikolaev (18 wounded). In light of such horrors, it is not surprising that when Minister of the Interior V.K. Von Plehve was assassinated in 1904, 'almost everywhere, it seems, the reaction was one of joy and relief'.[12]

At the same time, the autocracy made a concerted effort to win popular support by allowing some legal publications (including 'Legal Marxist' journals), promoting state-sponsored trade unionism, and granting limited voting rights for the middle and upper classes for local government in parts of the empire. Finland was even allowed wide political freedom, national autonomy, and its own parliament, an exceptional context that allowed the Finnish socialist party to operate legally.

---

12      Judge 1983, p. 238. On the violence against workers in 1903, see Пушкарева 2011, p. 105.

Ultimately, Tsarism's approach proved ineffective. Its repression was not heavy enough to smash the revolutionary movement and its reforms were insufficient to ideologically and socially integrate the lower and middle classes into the polity. Repressive measures often proved to be counter-productive, as they tended to deepen the very dissent they were supposed to crush. In Georgia, one squire observed in his town that 'they have posted a gendarme there. Until he came nobody ever bothered about politics. Now there is nothing else talked of'.[13]

After a mass strike wave spread through Ukraine, Georgia, and Azerbaijan in the summer of 1903, a revolutionary explosion felt imminent across the empire. Social democrats (SDs) in Poland exclaimed that Russia was 'on the eve of a political revolution'. Marxists in Kiev noted that the recent general strike had come to the verge of barricade struggles across Southern Russia; only the lag of the movement in St. Petersburg and Moscow, they argued, had prevented the eruption of an anti-Tsarist empire-wide revolution.[14] For his part, Minister of the Interior Von Plehve had famously concluded that a 'small victorious war' was needed to divert attention from Russia's growing 'internal turmoil'.[15] The government wagered that its war against Japan, begun in February 1904, would rally the population around the regime. These hopes proved to be unfounded. Anti-war protests grew throughout the year, particularly in Poland and Latvia. And on the fateful day of 9 January 1905, government troops fired on peaceful demonstrators in St. Petersburg, unleashing a popular revolution throughout the empire.

## 1        The Workers' Movement

By only counting industrial workers, many Western historians have drastically underestimated the size of the working class in Tsarist Russia. But Second International Marxists did not narrowly conceive of the working class as factory labourers. Kautsky broadly defined the 'working class', or 'proletariat', as those who owned no property from which they could survive (factories, small businesses, land). This category thus included not only industrial workers, but also wage earners such as employees in commercial stores, service workers like barbers, waiters, and cab drivers, and even 'educated proletarians' like intellec-

---

13    Cited in Parsons 1987, p. 265. On political repression in Russia, see Daly 1998.
14    Cited in Кирьянов 1987, p. 210. On Kiev, see Кирьянов 1987, p. 179.
15    Cited in ibid.

tuals, teachers, and artists. Such a broad approach defined the perspectives and practices of SDs across the Tsarist Empire.[16]

Extensive research by Russian historians has concluded that only a minority of wage workers under Tsarism were employed in industry (manufacturing, mining, and construction). The majority were employed as agricultural labourers, transportation and communication workers, unskilled dayworkers, domestic servants, service sector employees, or clerks. When one includes non-industrial wage earners, the proletariat's empire-wide numeric total in 1897 was, according to some estimates, as high as 12–14 million – slightly less than 10 per cent of the total population. If one adds their families, a significantly higher percentage of the population could be said to be part of a broadly defined working class. Yet the largest sector of non-industrial workers were agricultural labourers, who were often engaged simultaneously in private farming and who usually remained aloof from the organised workers' movement.

Social democrats at the time justifiably considered that the working class was a social minority under Tsarism. The absence of a working-class majority, however, was less of a distinguishing feature of Russia than has often been assumed – many European countries were predominantly rural and non-proletarian up through the 1940s, making the conquest of electoral majorities for socialism far more difficult than initially anticipated, pushing most socialist parties to moderate their politics and to search for new allies.[17]

Like in Western Europe, the workers' movement in Russia was centred in the biggest cities. Here the concentration of workers gave them a social weight and potential political power that tended to make up for their relatively small numbers in the total population. Each city had its own ethnic and industrial specificities, shaping the contours of the local labour movement. Though central Russia was almost homogeneously Russian, in the borderlands national diversity was the norm in the cities and their working classes. Industrial and urban life here was generally stratified by ethnicity and nationality, as different groups usually lived in separate neighbourhoods and worked either in completely different professions or in distinct branches of the same industry.

Employees were frequently of a different nationality than their bosses and supervisors, thereby aggravating class struggles and giving them sharp ethnic dimensions. Russian dominance of local and regional government similarly gave clashes with the authorities in the borderlands a dual class-ethnic

---

16    See Blanc 2016b.

17    On the class structure of Russia, see Рашин 1958 and Иванова and Желтовой 2004.

character. Various borderland national groups such as Ukrainians, Georgians, Latvians, and Lithuanians did not have a native capitalist class and were ruled entirely by other ethnic groups. In the Baltic, for example, a German elite ruled over Latvian toilers. Conservative Baltic German writer Astaf von Transehe-Roseneck lamented that 'the fact that the "ruling class" belonged to a foreign nation' helped agitators to 'exacerbate the existing social contradictions'.[18] In Georgia, likewise, most factory owners were Armenian and most workers Georgian, leading one observer to note that 'no link united the representatives of capital to the popular masses and, consequently, they could not exercise any political influence over them'.[19]

In contrast, national relations in Ukraine – where the large cities were predominantly comprised of Russians, Jews, and assimilated Ukrainians – posed more of a challenge for class-struggle politics. According to one Ukrainian Marxist, the Russification of the urban ethnic Ukrainian working class 'isolated it culturally from the rural proletariat, which surely broke the unity of the labour movement in Ukraine and slowed its development'.[20]

Patterns of mobilisation and organisation for the different strata of the working class were surprisingly uniform across the empire. The inability of the Tsarist regime to effectively integrate workers ideologically or socially, the precarity of workers' organisations, and the absence of a parliament or a conservative labour bureaucracy all facilitated a strong tendency towards mass militancy and 'spontaneity' – i.e. actions initiated and led by workers independent of any formal labour organisations. Until 1905, worker struggles under Tsarism were generally local, small-scale, and 'economic' (directed at the bosses, not the state). Between 1895 and 1899, for instance, 95 per cent of strikes were waged around economic demands.[21]

These day-to-day struggles, initiated more often than not without any socialist agitation, constituted an indispensable bedrock for the growth of organised socialism. Though economic struggles were often about wages and working hours, demands for humane treatment and dignity were also prevalent. 'The first thing we want to do is remind the whole community and our employers that we are all human beings', declared labourers in Łódź.[22] Workers often demanded that management address them with formal pronouns, rather than the informal 'you' used for children and servants. Others fought for an end

---

18    Transehe-Roseneck 1908, p. 79.
19    Woytinsky 1921, p. 50.
20    Юркевич 1917, p. 31.
21    Кирьянов 1987, p. 84.
22    Cited in Karwacki 1972, p. 294.

to their physical revision and inspection by management, a practice that frequently led to the widespread sexual abuse of female workers.

These elemental struggles drove forward worker empowerment and radicalisation. One Jewish worker recalled her personal evolution after she and her co-workers confronted the factory owner's abusive wife: 'After recovering from the fight I felt that I was not alone and I felt the power of workers. Until then I thought that the owners could do whatever they wanted with us, but now I knew this was not so'.[23] Inna Shtakser's study of Jewish working-class activists' personal correspondences concludes that 'the primary emotion in all the sources was pride in the kind of people that they became. ... While the economic gains that often ended labour disputes were short-lived, the pride, self-respect and power achieved through solidarity with others endured'.[24]

Though most workers in the pre-revolutionary period remained aloof from Marxist organisations, a solid and growing core of working-class socialist activists emerged. Up through the 1905 revolution, workers' movements in the borderlands grew significantly stronger than their counterparts in central Russia. Of the street demonstrations in the empire from 1895 to 1900, for example, only three of 59 took place in central Russia, while 25 occurred in Poland, nine in the Baltic, nine in Ukraine, seven in Belarus, and six in Finland.[25] The wave of general strikes in the summer of 1903 was concentrated almost exclusively in 'the South' of Russia, i.e. today's Ukraine, Azerbaijan, and Georgia. And the non-Russian Marxist parties were usually much larger than their Russian comrades during this period – the Jewish Bund's membership, for example, was close to three times higher than all of the Russian social democratic organisations combined.[26]

By 1903–04, Polish, Jewish, Lithuanian, Latvian, and Finnish socialists had already moved beyond disconnected circles and had built parties centralised on a regional level, with tens of thousands of members. Reflecting the social and geographic distance between the various peoples living under the Tsarist state, these parties had arisen and cohered separately from each other. Russian SDs remained far smaller and more atomised. But their concentration at the economic and geographic nerve centre of the imperial regime – combined with the fact that Russian was the country's lingua franca – continued to give them a disproportionate influence over political life.

---

23  Cited in Shtakser 2014, p. 68.
24  Cited in Shtakser 2014, p. 148.
25  Kappeler 2001, p. 330.
26  Пушкарева 2011, pp. 198–201 and Андерсон 2010, p. 8.

Contrary to the common assumption today that the most oppressed strata of the population are the most revolutionary, labour and socialist organisations consistently drew their members from the top layers of the working class – the relatively skilled, literate, and well-paid. The proletarian cadre of SD parties under Tsarism were generally male artisans and skilled workers in industry. Only in the peak moments of mass upsurge did broader layers tend to enter into the revolutionary ranks. Noting this phenomenon, Lenin observed that the 'history of the working-class movement in all countries shows that the better-situated strata of the working class respond to the ideas of socialism more rapidly and more easily'.[27] Such views were taken for granted in this era since they accurately corresponded to political dynamics throughout the empire and Europe. Historian Ilga Apine notes that in Latvia, the region of Russia where the working class was best off materially, this relative advantage was not an obstacle to radicalisation:

> Latvian workers' active involvement in the revolutionary movement was not the result of poverty and despair. The vulgarised Marxist interpretation that the poorer you are, the more revolutionary you will be, was not confirmed by the Latvian experience. ... Educated, self-confident Latvian workers took part in the revolution because they did not accept injustice, the absence of political rights, and social and national oppression.[28]

The lowest strata of the labour hierarchy were generally the most difficult to organise, as higher precarity, stronger ties to the countryside, and lower literacy constituted significant barriers to collective organisation. Most social democrats, both men and women, thus concentrated their efforts on recruiting the upper layers of the working class. This dynamic, in turn, sometimes led to a condescending approach to the unskilled 'dark' masses of workers, particularly when they were of a different gender or ethnicity than skilled workers.[29] Building class unity in practice proved to be more difficult than proclaiming its necessity.

Often this hierarchical stratification overlapped with ethnicity and gender. Ethnic-Russian workers, for example, had a disproportionate weight in the empire's revolutionary struggle not only because of their location in the imperial capital, but also because they dominated the skilled occupations (metal-

---

27    Lenin 1899 [1960–65], p. 280.
28    Apine 2005, p. 11. On the vanguard role of the highest proletarian strata across Russia and beyond, see Jones 2005, p. 84, Acton 1990, p. 65, Glickman 1984, p. 156, and Post 2010.
29    Smith 1983, p. 200.

working, railroads, etc.) that served as a central social base for the workers' movement. Ukrainian and Muslim wage earners, as well as working women of all ethnicities, were usually relegated to the lowest rungs of the labour hierarchy and underrepresented inside the organised workers' movement. Cecilia Bobrovskaya recalled that during her time as an organiser in Baku, 'it never occurred to us to carry on work among [working women]; the job seemed such a thankless one. Besides, there was so much other work which we could barely cope with that agitation among the women was left for more favorable times'.[30]

The lower levels of the proletariat were almost always less organised, but this did not mean they were always less militant. Throughout the 1890s, for instance, female textile workers played a predominant role in the major mass strikes across imperial Russia. In May 1892, tens of thousands of unorganised Polish workers in the textile centre of Łódź, the 'Polish Manchester', struck against poor working conditions and national discrimination. They marched in the streets, sang patriotic songs, symbolically elected a tailor to be the 'Polish King', and clashed with the army and police, resulting in the deaths of hundreds of workers, and scores more wounded or arrested. Inspired by the 'Łódź Revolt', the Polish Socialist Party was formed later that year in Paris. The emergence of a mass workers' movement in the Baltic took a similar form: in May 1899 Latvia was shaken by the 'Riga Rebellion', an economic struggle of female textile workers that sparked city-wide strikes and violent confrontations with the armed forces.

In the face of such disturbances, key sectors of the Tsarist regime argued for a more proactive policy to integrate and appease the working class. The government soon allowed limited forms of apolitical labour organising such as mutual-aid societies, cultural associations, and state-sanctioned 'police-unions' led by gendarme chief Sergei Zubatov. But these concessions proved to be insufficient to effectively co-opt workers or their leaderships. After workers began to push these legal organisations beyond acceptable bounds, the regime shut them down.[31]

Because of these autocratic conditions, moderate social democracy among workers and their representatives tended to be much less prevalent than in Western Europe. As Edward Acton notes, the 'tsarist political system was the critical factor distinguishing the experience of the Russian working class from that of its western counterparts. The prospects of the working class embarking upon a reformist path in the pre-war years therefore depended upon the

---

30    Bobrovskaya 1934, p. 109. On women workers under Tsarism, see Glickman 1984.
31    On the early workers' movement and state policy, see Schneiderman 1976.

prospects for a liberalization of the political system'.[32] Russian absolutism facilitated the growth of proletarian radicalism to an unparalleled degree, creating exceptionally favourable conditions for promoting revolutionary socialism.

The absence of democracy significantly undermined any popular expectations that the interests of workers could be advanced within existing state institutions. A Tsarist functionary in Georgia typically lamented the congruence between socialists' class war doctrine and popular proletarian sentiment: 'this propaganda would not have such a strong influence if the evil family of socialist teachings didn't fall on such productive ground'.[33]

Autocratic conditions had a profound effect on the political orientation of imperial Russia's socialists. Workers and labour organisations did not face the same integrative pressures that bourgeois democracy placed upon their counterparts in the West. Elsewhere, the exigencies of winning office and passing pro-worker reforms in parliament led socialists to frequently moderate their demands or make compromises with non-socialist political currents. And though the formal stance of most Western socialist parties remained oriented to class struggle and revolutionary rupture, party practices, particularly in the leadership, tended to become increasingly oriented towards class accommodation and a gradual permeation of the existing state. As often is the case, practice preceded theory. In 1904, Rosa Luxemburg argued that bourgeois parliamentarism 'is the breeding place of all opportunist tendencies now existing in Western Social Democracy'. She concluded, however, that 'the situation is quite different in tsarist Russia' as 'there is no bourgeois parliament'.[34]

Top labour leaders in the West were not the only ones in the labour movement whose sights were set much lower than the revolutionary conquest of power. Moderate socialism found a ready social base among a broad mass of workers who understandably hoped that significant improvements in their lives could be achieved peacefully through building unions and working within the existing electoral system. In the decades before World War One, the steady growth of the workers' movement and the conquest of important democratic and economic gains appeared to make this a viable path.

But universal suffrage was still rare across Europe. Beyond France, Britain, and Switzerland, the influence of liberals over workers and society was still remarkably weak. Only after World War Two did robust welfare states, as well as routinised industrial relations, become the norm. Thus one should not exag-

---

32    Acton 1990, p. 70.
33    Cited in Jones 2005, p. 101.
34    Luxemburg 1904. For comparisons between levels of working-class integration in Russia and abroad, see Van der Linden 2003, pp. 23–41, and Vössing 2017.

gerate the extent to which workers were integrated into capitalism before 1914.[35] Organised mass radicalism was particularly pronounced in 'low inclusion' constitutional monarchies like Germany and Finland, where political freedoms and parliamentary powers were relatively restricted, a context that undercut pressures from above and below for class compromise while also enabling the space for socialists to accumulate organisational and electoral strength.[36]

Perhaps the most atypical aspect of Russia's labour movement was that there was no crystallised labour officialdom. As S.A. Smith notes, in Russia 'the absence of an entrenched labour bureaucracy enormously facilitated the development of a revolutionary socialist labour movement'.[37] If in times of social stability in bourgeois-democratic polities there was a relative congruence between the moderate views of labour leaders and the broad mass of workers, the same was not true at moments of intense class struggle. Numerous historians have documented how union and party officialdoms in Germany and beyond reacted to mass upsurges by dampening militancy and channelling workers into acceptable routines of parliamentarism and moderate tradeunionism. Across the world, such labour leaders played a significant role in propping up capitalist rule at its deepest moments of crisis.[38]

In contrast with Western socialist parties, illegal SD parties and workers' organisations in Tsarist Russia were highly unstable. Over and over, they were broken up by the Tsarist police and had to be rebuilt from scratch. This situation had major consequences for the fate of the revolutionary movement, as it prevented the emergence of a significant caste of full-time party, union, and parliamentary functionaries. Similarly, illegal conditions precluded parties in the empire from building a broad membership base of relatively unengaged members – a dynamic which provided labour bureaucracies in Western Europe with much of their internal rank-and-file base. Only in Finland, with its legal socialist movement, did a workers' party under Tsarism experience the growth of a large organisational apparatus of full-timers.

Faced with Tsarist absolutism, some Marxists occasionally opined that socialist 'opportunism' would never be able to take hold inside of Russia. As we will see in later chapters, such claims were overstated. Following the demoral-

---

35    On workers' movements across Europe, see Geary 1981 and Luebbert 1991.
36    For a useful comparative analysis of how Second International parties were shaped by
      their political regime's distinct levels of labour inclusion, see Vössing 2017.
37    Smith 1983, p. 104.
38    On the structural roots of labour opportunism, see Offe and Wiesenthal 1980.

ising defeat of the 1905 revolution, significant currents of moderate socialism *did* eventually arise. The ascension of right-leaning social democrats over their radical rivals in regions such as Poland and Ukraine illustrates an important point: the impact of an autocratic context on its own did not guarantee the continued hegemony of revolutionary socialism within the working class. But the absence of parliamentary rule and political freedom generally made social democratic parties in autocratic Russia more radical in both words and deeds than their sister organisations in the West.

## 2      The Unique Impact of Orthodox Marxism

Unlike in much of Western Europe, revolutionary social democracy was the accepted guide to action of underground socialist parties in Russia up through the 1905 revolution. Across the empire, socialist activists and leaders were deeply engaged with and committed to orthodox Marxism, the most influential exponent of which was Karl Kautsky.

It would be hard to exaggerate the exceptional extent of Kautsky's importance in Tsarist Russia, both in the centre and the periphery. As Moira Donald and Lars Lih have ably demonstrated, Kautsky had an enormous influence on Lenin and the Bolsheviks.[39] But this impact was just as strong among non-Russian Marxists and their parties. In the words of one Jewish socialist, Kautsky was 'in our eyes the direct heir and most authoritative interpreter of Marxism'. Kautsky himself noted that 'my most faithful readers' were in Tsarist Russia.[40] *Die Neue Zeit* (The New Age), the German-language theoretical review edited by Kautsky, was the single-most influential journal for the empire's SDs. And in the second half of 1905, at least 266,000 copies of Kautsky's works were published in the empire, the highest number of any political writer. According to another estimate, over a million of his writings were produced in Russia by 1907.[41]

Nowhere in the world, including in Germany, were Kautsky's writings more popular and influential than in the lands ruled by Russian Tsarism. The anom-

---

39    Donald 1993 and Lih 2006.
40    Kats 2012, p. 165; Kautsky cited in Donald 1993, p. 248. References to Kautsky are pervasive in the primary sources and serious secondary sources on Marxists across imperial Russia. For a small sample from the latter, see Waldenberg 1972, pp. 19–32, Steenson 1978, p. 274, Sabaliūnas 1990, pp. 25, 28, and Naarden 1992, p. 198.
41    Larsson 1970, p. 258.

alous nature of this development should be underscored since accounts of Second International Marxism generally overlook the heterogeneity of the era's social democratic parties. Far from being clear-cut products of a particular theory, workers' parties across the world were motley manifestations of the trajectories of the labour and radical movements in distinct countries, with a wide variety of political traditions, cultures, and experiences shaped by pragmatic adjustments to organising under distinct political regimes.

Throughout the nineteenth and early twentieth centuries, various tendencies of non-Marxist socialism (utopianism, co-operativism, Lassaleanism, Christian socialism, Blanquism, etc.), radical republicanism, anarchism, revolutionary nationalism, as well as the broader political influences of outside society, swirled together in different proportions inside the world's socialist movements. Most frequently, party members and leaders were vaguely defined social democrats, uncommitted to Marxist theory as such or revolutionary social democracy in particular. This political diversity was both a cause and reflection of the lower influence of orthodox Marxism outside of Tsarist Russia.

The parties of the Russian Empire, of course, also inevitably reflected the distinct contexts and traditions of their respective regions and peoples. But the influence of Marxist orthodoxy was generally much higher under Tsarism. Whereas socialist parties across Europe often traced their political roots and traditions back to the 1860s or 1870s, socialist parties under Tsarism were built from scratch in the 1890s and early 1900s – i.e. at a moment when Marxism was ideologically ascendant, often even fashionable. Most parties in the empire were founded on an orthodox basis and faced little in the way of radical competition. To quote Georgian Bolshevik Filipp Makharadze, 'among us the Marxist orientation did not have to struggle with any other kind of tendency for hegemony among the working class as took place in other countries'.[42] At the turn of the century, political nationalism was extremely weak, Russian populism had virtually collapsed, and strong liberal-democratic currents were absent.

In most European countries, the labour movement reflected the accumulated traditions of decades of artisan and craft organisation. By way of contrast, the rapid industrialisation of Tsarist Russia combined with absolutist conditions meant that its urban proletariat consisted mostly of recent transplants from the countryside lacking pre-existing experiences with politics and

---

42    Cited in Rieber 2015, pp. 20–1.

labour organisation. As the Revolutionary Ukrainian Party declared in 1903, 'the Ukrainian proletariat is strong and healthy because of its youth – and because it has no tradition'.[43]

The urgency of the anti-Tsarist struggle and the weight of revolutionary intellectuals inside these parties, moreover, promoted an intense engagement with Kautsky's writings. And state repression prevented Russia's illegal socialist parties from developing (unlike the German SPD) atheoretical bureaucracies and/or loose membership structures that included many workers relatively uncommitted to socialist politics. In the Austrian Social Democracy, by way of contrast, one activist complained of the 'custom that anyone who has a vague conception of what social democracy is, anyone who in some election fills out his ballot with the name of a social democratic candidate, anyone who comes to a meeting, who claps approval of the speaker and votes for the resolution, is without further ado a social democrat'.[44] For all of these reasons, the orthodox Marxism of the Russian Empire's illegal SD parties was relatively unalloyed.

Karl Kautsky's exposition of the 1891 *Erfurt Programme* quickly became the most widely read text in the international Marxist movement, training the first generations of organised SDs across the world. Virtually all parties in the empire modelled their platforms on it. In Latvia, for example, the *Erfurt Programme* constituted the essential political foundation for the birth of its social democratic party. In 1893, poet and socialist Jānis Rainis travelled to Zurich, then Berlin, and smuggled works of Marx, Engels, and Kautsky back into Latvia through a hidden compartment of his suitcase. Soon after, he published extensive excerpts of the *Erfurt Programme*, a document that, as scholar Ivars Ijabs has noted, 'served as the main ideological cornerstone of Latvian social democracy'.[45] Latvian SD leader Pēteris Stučka later recalled that 'there was agreement on the *Erfurt Programme* – and that was enough'.[46]

The Ukrainian Social Democratic Workers Party similarly adopted as its programme the entire theoretical section of the *Erfurt Programme*, declaring that it was 'the best and most complete expression of the theoretical views of the international revolutionary Social-Democracy'.[47] Eight separate editions of Kautsky's *Erfurt Programme* were published in Polish alone before 1911. And

---

43    Andriewsky 1991, p. 17.
44    Cited in Steenson 1991, p. 201.
45    Ijabs 2012b, p. 185. Rainis bragged that 'from my suitcase grew the Latvian socialist movement' (cited in Kalniņš 1956, p. 8). In Latvia and beyond, the *Erfurt Programme* referred to both the short 1891 SPD programme as well as the long exposition of this published by Kautsky the following year. I follow this usage.
46    Cited in Dauge 1958, p. 104.
47    Cited in Гермайзе 1926, p. 261.

like many other non-Russian socialist organisations in the empire, the first two theoretical works translated and published by the Jewish Bund were Kautsky's *Erfurt Programme* and Marx's *Communist Manifesto*.[48]

Kautsky's works were more widely read than those of the founding fathers of Marxism. In this period, the number of Kautsky writings published in the empire was roughly double that of Karl Marx and over five times the amount of Frederick Engels.[49] In Finland, the *Erfurt Programme* was published in 1899, while the *Communist Manifesto*, the first Finnish translation of Marx, only came out in 1906. One scholar's quantitative analysis of early socialist publications in Finland concludes that 'the first and foremost point to note is the subordinate position of Marxist classics in relation to Kautsky'.[50]

But the empire's socialists by no means considered themselves to be 'Kaut-skyists'. Rather they viewed Kautsky as the foremost defender of revolutionary social democracy, a tradition established by Marx and Engels and articulated by a range of subsequent socialists across Europe.

Kautsky was especially influential across imperial Russia because interest in revolutionary politics was particularly high. A socialist in Warsaw recalled his initial engagement as a teenager: 'There could still be no talk of Marx. I liked Kautsky ... because of his struggle against the revisionists and because of his defense of the historical necessity of the social revolution'.[51] In Tsarist Russia's borderlands, like in the centre, the *most* radical activists and parties turned to his strategies and sought to implement them in practice.

Kautsky's writings had more of an impact in the Tsarist Empire than in the German Social Democratic Party itself. Nevertheless, Kautsky's theories have frequently been framed as causing or reflecting the German party's abandon-ment of revolutionary politics, culminating in its support for World War One and its thwarting of the German Revolution. These later events have cast a long shadow backwards, seriously distorting the nature of the debates and dynam-ics of the years prior. The fact that Kautsky himself made a turn to the right after 1909, eventually bending to the SPD bureaucracy and reversing many of his former positions, has similarly obscured the radical content of his earlier strategy.

In 1957, Erich Matthias put forward the influential thesis that 'Kautskyism' was a reformist ideology largely responsible for the integration of the SPD into

48 Waldenberg 1972, p. 32 and Tobias 1972, p. 88.
49 Waldenberg 1972, p. 22.
50 Ehrnrooth 1992, p. 110.
51 Mendel 1989, p. 64.

capitalist society. This conception continues to be widely accepted today.[52] But it fundamentally misdiagnoses the content and evolution of Kautsky's politics and unconvincingly conflates them with the SPD's rightward drift. In reality, the German party's leadership, from at least 1906 onwards, was not comprised of 'Kautskyists', but rather of a strata of full-time functionaries who were dismissive of socialist theory in general and Kautsky's writings in particular. As Gilbert Badia has explained, 'the new leadership of the party (and in the unions even more so) demonstrated an indifference, indeed a growing mistrust towards "political theory" and towards those who brought it to the fore'.[53] By 1910, Kautsky's political influence in party summits was in sharp decline.

The German SPD bureaucracy's risk aversion combined with its distinct structural interests as a caste of functionaries, facilitated an unconscious adaptation to the bourgeois polity. In periods of relative social stability, the labour officialdom could balance its political moderation with ongoing support for class struggle within controlled parameters. But when the German ruling class required that the organised workers' movement support the war in 1914 and prop up the regime in 1918–19, top party and union leaders were unwilling to risk the consequences of opposition.

To blame the *theories* of 'Second International Marxism' for the degeneration of Western socialist *practice* obscures the deep social roots of this process as well as the salient fact that many European socialist party leaders by 1914 had already overwhelmingly rejected or discarded orthodox Marxism. Conversely, absolutist conditions bolstered the ability of socialist parties in imperial Russia to translate Kautsky's revolutionary theory into revolutionary practice.

## 3        Socialist Political Cultures

Before diving into the big strategic questions confronting the Russian Empire's socialist parties, it is useful to sketch out common aspects of their subcultures. A shared political programme formed the basis of all socialist organisations, but interpersonal dynamics also determined their internal cohesion and peri-

---

52    Matthias 1957. For recent articulations of this thesis, see, for example, Blackledge 2013.
53    Badia 1975, p. 140. For more on Kautsky's growing isolation from the leadership, see Steinberg 1967, p. 85, Gilcher-Holtey 1986, and Waldenberg 1972, *passim*.

odic factional ruptures. Involvement in Marxist organisations was arguably rooted as much in cultural and emotional dynamics as in high political theory.

Parties became friend groups, cultural associations, and revolutionary battle squads all at once. Socialists often lived with each other; revolutionary organisations frequently acted as surrogate families.[54] Marxist memoirists almost always recalled the importance of personal relations for getting recruited, with one activist noting that 'the reason [for joining one socialist party instead of another] was not always a well-thought out ideological difference, but simply ... which friends were the first to invite them to join their group'.[55] Helena Nicolaysen's study of personal networks among the empire's SDs has demonstrated the extent to which 'the formation of personal associations among socialists preceded and influenced individuals' commitment to Marxist ideology'.[56]

Youth was a major characteristic of these personal-political networks. For instance, a vast majority of Jewish militants arrested in Warsaw at the turn of the century were between the ages of 17 and 25. In Łódź, 63.4 per cent of the SDKPIL was under 28 years old; in the RSDRP, the single largest age subgroup was 20 to 24-year olds. Noting the difficulties in recruiting older workers, a militant in Łódź concluded that young workers were the 'most energetic, the most enlightened, the most revolutionary'.[57]

Unsurprisingly, the spread of socialism often took on dimensions of a generational conflict. Inside of the Russian intelligentsia, politicised student youth were usually revolutionary socialists, while older intellectuals tended to lean in more liberal directions. In 1903, Zionist leader Chaim Weizmann lamented this socialist influence: 'it is a fearful spectacle ... to observe the major part of our youth – and no-one would describe them as the worst part – offering themselves for sacrifice as though seized by a fever. ... Children are in open revolt against their parents'.[58]

The revolutionary upsurge also went hand in hand with artistic flourishing across the Russian state. Literature, poetry, and music all played key roles inside the socialist movement. At the rallies, demonstrations, and gatherings of most parties, songs were central – and in addition to international standards such as 'The Internationale' or 'The Marseillaise', parties had their own

54    Ury 2012, p. 105.
55    Kats 1956 [2012], p. 197.
56    Nicolaysen 1991, p. 27.
57    Samuś 1984, p. 70 and Ury 2012, p. 94. Citation from Samuś 2013, p. 317.
58    Weizmann 1971, p. 301.

particular songs and anthems. Meetings of the Jewish Bund would generally close with the singing of the party anthem, *Di Shvue* (The Oath), which began as follows:

> Brothers and sisters of work and need,
> All who are scattered like far-flung seed –
> Together! Together! The flag is high,
> Straining with anger, red with blood,
> So swear together to live or die! ...
>
> We swear our stalwart hate persists,
> Of those who rob and kill the poor:
> The Tsar, the Masters, Capitalists.
> Our vengeance will be swift and sure.

Hersh Mendel recalled how he got introduced to the Bund as a young working-class child in Warsaw, when his older sister started bringing home a new group of friends:

> They naturally went dancing every Sabbath as well, but their conversa-
> tions had nevertheless begun to touch upon other subjects. They talked
> about politics, about strikes, and above all sang revolutionary songs. The
> first song I heard them sing was the old Bundist *Shvue*. What an impact the
> *Shvue* had on me. Moreover, it was the first revolutionary song I had ever
> heard. So it was perfectly natural that I conceived of Bund and revolution
> as one and the same thing.[59]

For many radicals, artistic expression was seen as both a means and an end. Socialism was envisioned as a society that would liberate individual and collective human creativity from wage slave drudgery. According to Polish Marxist Julian Marchlewski, 'there will be a time when every man, without exception, will have the right to be human, to develop all of their abilities ... art will cease to be luxury, it will become an aspect of our daily lives, spreading into all areas of private and social life'.[60]

The struggle to reach this 'inspiring' and 'noble' goal was invariably painted in heroic colours. A seemingly endless stream of leaflets proclaimed that the

---

59    Mendel 1989, pp. 34–5.
60    Cited in Jakubowski 2007, p. 29.

'heroic proletariat' would topple 'villainous' Tsarism, then capitalism. In the words of Aspazija, Latvia's leading socialist poet, playwright, and feminist:

> When the hour strikes, all of those,
> Who were small, lowly, unknown,
> Come out into the open and become heroes.[61]

Ongoing Tsarist repression and state violence also transformed sacrifice and martyrdom into major themes. Funeral marches were a common form of mass political action. One typical Latvian SD leaflet proclaimed:

> The struggle for people's freedom requires from us now all of our energy, our blood, our lives. But we go in this battle boldly and joyfully because it will bring victory and liberation to all slaves and servants. A glorious revolutionary morning is dawning. There is no greater happiness in life than to join the ranks of the freedom fighters, to fight, and, if necessary, to fall under the social democratic banner. Victory, however, belongs to us![62]

Most parties had their own martyrs, whose sacrifices were commemorated and celebrated over subsequent years. The first Marxist party in the empire, the Proletariat, won itself a mythical status among Polish workers when its top leaders were arrested and hanged by the Tsarist state in 1886. While awaiting the gallows, party leader Stanisław Kunicki sent out from prison his moving final testament to his 'Brother Workers': 'We know what we are dying for, for what we gave our life. Now it is up to you, brothers, to ensure that we did not give up our lives in vain. Courage and perseverance!'[63] Party head Ludwik Waryński, in a collective letter with other prisoners, sent out a similar sentiment: 'Do not let the cause die, and if you have the strength, do not forgive the hangmen. Let the enemy know that working people, once awakened, will not cease to fight until victory'.[64]

Though orthodox socialists rejected the 'utopian socialist' conception of socialism as a moral rather than class-struggle project, Marxist mass agitation and political subcultures were deeply imbued with moral norms and rhetoric. Leaflets melodramatically appealed to the highest sentiments of workers and

---

61    Cited in Matiss 2000, p. 80.
62    Cited in Kalniņš 1956, p. 60.
63    *Przedświt*, January 1886.
64    Ibid.

simultaneously denounced capitalists and government officials as 'evil', 'tyr-annical', 'blood-suckers', and 'monsters'.[65] A common morality was shared by socialists across the empire. This collectivist ethos stressed that individual lib-eration and self-expression could only be won through collective struggle and organisation. Regarding early Finnish social democracy, Jari Ehrnrooth notes: 'The selfish individual must be suppressed in favour of the morally pure fighter for the international labour movement'.[66]

Because drinking, gambling, carousing, and brawling had long constituted major obstacles to socialist influence among working people, Marxists pushed back against what they saw as the vices of class society that disrupted the for-ward march of the revolutionary proletariat. Advocacy of alcohol temperance was a particularly longstanding theme, with the Tsarist Empire's monopoly on the distribution and sale of liquor only adding to its political thrust. 'In tsarist Russia the perception of temperant workers as troublemakers was pervasive enough that actual revolutionaries sometimes posed as drunkards in order to evade detection', notes historian Laura Phillips.[67]

In Finland, the labour movement and the Social Democracy in fact arose dir-ectly out of the temperance struggle, the most important pre-1905 Finnish mass movement. 'Workers want to be free of the fetters which weigh them down: capitalism and the liquor trade which it fosters', declared the Finnish labour newspaper *Työmies* (The Worker) in 1898.[68] In most periods, such sentiments were shared only by a relatively small layer of organised workers. During times of mass upheaval, however, they spread much further. In 1905, factory workers in Riga, for instance, decided to ban drinking – all breaches were fined up to three roubles, which were used to buy arms for the revolution. Attacks on liquor stores, including their physical destruction by arson, became a widespread fea-ture of the 1905 revolution, which witnessed at least 1,321 separate attacks on liquor stores and alcohol distributors across Russia.[69]

Of course, practice often diverged from these lofty ideals because socialist activists remained shaped by the society that they were seeking to overturn. To cite just one example of many: despite the Finnish socialist movement's strong opposition to liquor, several of its top leaders were themselves alcohol-ics, leading to numerous internal organisational conflicts. And while socialist collectivism and single-minded political dedication were powerful drivers for

---

65    On SD political cultures, see Samuś 2013 and Shtakser 2014.
66    Ehrnrooth 1992, p. 576.
67    Phillips 1997, p. 29.
68    Cited in Sulkunen 1990, p. 215.
69    Miške 1955, p. 16 and McKee 1997, p. 332.

revolutionary activism, they also had their downsides. Marxists were frequently caught up in excessive factionalism against rival radical currents, undermining the potential to build unity in action against the employers and the state. Internal party splits, likewise, almost always became deeply bitter and traumatising events with far-reaching repercussions. Virtually overnight, close friends could become enemies. One participant in the December 1904 split of the Revolutionary Ukrainian Party recalled that, 'the divergence in opinions proved to be deep. Long-time friends found themselves against each other. It was literally brother against brother, husband against wife'.[70]

Socialist and church subcultures were in many ways quite similar. Though Marxist organisations were consistently secular, in the process of seeking to displace religion as the main ideology of working people, they absorbed and leaned on key components of religious rhetoric and ritual. Revolutionary songs were set to the melodies of the most well-known spiritual hymns; socialist traditions, above all May Day, were often celebrated according to longstanding customs associated with the church. SD leaflets and mass agitation relied on religious metaphors and rhetoric. 'Faith', 'spirit', 'sacrifice', 'eternal glory', 'reckoning', and 'deliverance' were all common revolutionary tropes. A typical Polish Socialist Party leaflet declared that 'revolution is a great and holy work of liberation of the people from the shackles of slavery, the revolutionary act is a heroic sacrifice, an act of noble courage'.[71]

Religious groups and socialist organisations shared some key commonalities. At their best, each provided a supportive community, meaning in life, and hope for a better world to come. Their paths often parted ways, however, regarding the means to reach, and the nature of, this hoped-for future. As one Latvian socialist explained to a free night-class for workers in the 1890s, the crucial question was how to 'make these dreams a reality'.[72]

---

70   Cited in Гермайзе 1926, p. 256.
71   'Towarzysze robotnicy!', 22 May 1907, Odezwa Centralny Komitet Robotniczy Polskiej Partii Socjalistycznej (Lewicy) Warszawa, in Tych 1961a, p. 231. The socialist future was also not infrequently referred to as 'the Kingdom of Heaven'. See, for instance, 'Towarzysze Robotnicy!', 27 December 1905, Odezwa Komitet Centralny Pol. Par. Soc. 'Proletaryat', Warszawa (Dokumenty życia społecznego, Biblioteka Narodowa). For more on the overlap between socialist and religious cultures and discourse, see Chwalba 2007 and Ehrnrooth 1992, *passim*.
72   Cited in Millers and Stumbiņa 1965, p. 40.

CHAPTER 2

# Revolutionary Social Democracy: An Overview

A central goal of this book is to analyse how Marxists in imperial Russia addressed big strategic questions such as whether to bloc with liberals or how to build working-class unity. But to make sense of these debates requires that readers first understand the movement's overall project of class formation – an especially critical task given how many myths about Second International socialism continue to distort the literature. This chapter thus outlines the broad political framework of revolutionary social democracy in the years preceding the 1905 revolution. Describing the fundamental shared tenets of imperial Russia's early Marxist parties will lay the groundwork for our subsequent examination of their evolution on particular points of socialist strategy.

## 1    The ABCs of Revolutionary Social Democracy

The red thread tying together the central tenets of orthodox Marxism was a recognition of the class struggle and its political consequences. Revolutionary social democracy's fundamental planks can be summarised as follows:
– *Capitalism's socio-economic dynamics and periodic crises create the necessity and possibility of socialism;*
– *Workers of all nationalities have common interests, which are diametrically opposed to those of capitalists;*
– *The working class is the main social force with the interest and power to win democracy and overturn capitalism;*
– *The primary task of a socialist party is to promote the class consciousness and independent organisation of workers, and to merge socialism with the broader workers' movement;*
– *The historic duty of the working class is the conquest of state power, the abolition of the private ownership of the means of production, and the establishment of a worldwide classless society;*
– *Political liberty is needed for socialists to effectively organise and educate workers to fulfil their historic mission.*
These axioms were the political bedrock for revolutionary social democrats in Russia and beyond. A striking aspect of socialist leaflets across the empire is just how similar they were to each other in form and content – and just how often they repeated the ABCs of socialist orthodoxy. As such, these tenets were more

central to the mass agitation and actual practices of imperial Russia's rank-and-file SDs than the finer points of émigré theoretical polemics to which scholars have given undue weight.

For the empire's Marxists, the irreconcilability of the exploited and exploiting classes was an ever-present theme. 'Every nation and society's history ... is in one form or another the history of class struggle', declared *Kvali* (The Track), Georgia's first Marxist newspaper.[1] For its part, the Muslim Social Democratic Party-*Gummet* in Baku issued a leaflet along similar lines:

> Brothers, Muslim workers. Your life and position, like that of the workers of other peoples, is burdensome, hard, and monotonous because the capitalist owners and manufacturers exploit you and take away your earnings. The autocratic Russian Tsar, officials and police are supporters of the capitalists.[2]

Revolutionary social democracy was premised on the principle of working-class independence. Contrary to those who have portrayed Kautsky's theories as a force for integrating the workers' movement into the bourgeois polity, his battle against 'revisionism' between 1899 and 1910 was dedicated precisely to preventing the working class and its organisations from succumbing to class collaboration.[3]

Georgian SD leader Noe Zhordania fiercely polemicised with nationalists for promoting cross-class unity and the formation of a single national party. Attempting to get all social classes to peacefully collaborate, Zhordania wrote, was like herding 'a goat and a wolf into a single pen'.[4] This approach was the norm among Marxists up through the first Russian Revolution. A leading Jewish national-liberal, Simon Dubnow, thus lamented that the 'Bundists are devoted sons of only one "nation", the proletarian class. They never join with national parties for any common cause'.[5]

Flowing from orthodox Marxism's strategic orientation was the 'class criteria' axiom, i.e. the view that socialists must address politics from the standpoint of furthering the interests of the working class and its fight for state power. The Polish Socialist Party's founding congress in 1892 therefore resolved

---

1   Cited in Jones 2005, pp. 74–5.
2   Cited in Кузминский 1906, p. 47.
3   See, for instance, Waldenberg 1972, p. 496.
4   Cited in Jones 2005, p. 116.
5   Dubnow 1905 [1958], p. 208.

that 'the class position of the proletariat is the position of the Socialist Party'.[6] Its newspaper *Robotnik* (The Worker) declared: 'Our party is primarily a workers' party, its goals and demands are the expression of the interests of the working class: it leads the class struggle against the capitalists, and prepares and organises the masses for this'.[7] This class criteria informed Marxist approaches to *all* political questions. To quote Latvian socialist leader Pēteris Stučka, '[t]here is no absolutely correct tactics ... a change of tactics is a practical matter, the only boundaries of which are set by social democracy's ultimate goal and the proletariat's class interests'.[8]

This framework constituted a fundamental methodological point of divergence with other political tendencies. Non-Marxist socialists generally based their theories and strategies on ethical or normative criteria such as justice, equality, or freedom, rather than the exigencies of class struggle.[9] Nationalists, for their part, viewed the promotion of the nation as their starting point and goal. In Lithuania, nationalist liberals thus called upon sds to prioritise the interests of the nation over the interests of their class. Against such appeals, Lithuania's Marxists insisted that they defended only the interests of working people because 'representation of the whole nation is just a trickery'.[10]

According to orthodox social democrats, the inexorable and deepening contradictions of the class struggle could only be positively resolved through the workers' seizure of power. The pps declared that it set 'as its primary goal the conquest of political power for the proletariat and by the proletariat'.[11] And in the words of Latvian Social Democratic Union theoretician Miķelis Valters, 'the whole essence of socialism lies in the idea that the proletariat needs to acquire political power for its freedom'.[12]

According to orthodox Marxism, a socialist party should always propagate this 'final goal' (the socialist conquest of power) to the working class. Likewise, the party must always approach its immediate activities with this final goal in mind. Indeed, this was one of the main points of disagreement with the 'revisionism' promoted by German social democrat Eduard Bernstein, who argued that the spd was in practice a reformist party and, therefore, that it should drop its counter-productive emphasis on the revolutionary 'final goal'.

---

6      'Protokuł Zjazdu Paryskiego (Ostateczny)' [1892] in Wasilewski 1934, p. 32.
7      'Wyjaśnienie', *Robotnik*, 30 November 1894.
8      Cited in Šteinbergs 1977, p. 110.
9      See, for example, Suodenjoki and Peltola 2007, p. 58.
10     Cited in Udrenas 2000, pp. 396–7.
11     'Szkic programu Polskiej Partii Socjalistycznej' [1892] in Tych 1975, p. 252.
12     Valters 1905, p. 18.

For revolutionary SDs, the importance of stressing the final goal was not only that socialism could be established solely through seizing state power, but that this inspiring vision was needed to unify workers and to raise their fighting spirit against capitalism. Against Bernstein, SPD leader August Bebel declared: 'It is utterly false tactics to rob the party of its enthusiasm and of its willingness to make sacrifices by pushing its goals into the indefinite future'.[13] Marxist parties across imperial Russia rejected revisionism and proclaimed the final goal of socialism. Social democratic leaflets, which invariably concluded with a short list of slogans, more often than not ended with some version of 'Long live socialism!'

The proletariat's conquest of power, in their view, required a revolution. Rejecting Bernstein's advocacy of a gradual transition to socialism, orthodox Marxists argued that only through a revolutionary rupture could workers seize state power and overthrow capitalism because breaking the inevitable resistance of the ruling class could only take place through 'a decisive battle'.

An emphasis on the socialist final goal did not mean that socialists refrained from fighting for the immediate interests of workers under capitalism. To the contrary, they saw fights for economic demands and democratic rights as important for raising proletarian confidence, organisation, and class consciousness. The role of social democrats, they argued, was not to oppose these struggles, but to tie them to the fight for socialism. Indeed, connecting the immediate struggle with the final goal constituted the *raison d'être* of organised socialists. In 1899, Latvian SD leader Fricis Roziņš explained that Social Democracy was 'a workers' party because only socialism can free workers from capitalist exploitation and socialism can only expect to win if it rests on the working class'.[14] Social Democracy, Marxists endlessly repeated, represented the merger of socialism and the workers' movement.

As noted in the Introduction, the basic content of revolutionary social democracy has been widely mischaracterised over the past century. Here it may be useful to address four common myths that spill into the specific topics addressed in later chapters. First, contrary to what has often been claimed, none of the orthodox SDs in imperial Russia – including Lenin and the Bolsheviks – adhered to an elitist theory in which the working class should remain under the permanent tutelage of an enlightened socialist vanguard.[15]

---

13    Cited in Vössing 2008, p. 212.
14    Roziņš 1899 [1963–65], p. 70.
15    Alan Wildman, for example, argues that 'Bolshevism carried its banner high for the pure tradition of blatant elitism' (Wildman 1967, p. 190).

In reality, social democrats explicitly rejected the idea that the party could substitute itself for the working class. Given the uneven development of consciousness among working people, they argued, a revolutionary organisation necessarily began with only a minority of the class. But according to the prevailing 'merger' conception, the party would massively expand through a process of proletarian education, organisation, and action to eventually encompass the broad mass of workers and oppressed. Kautsky's *Erfurt Programme* declared that the 'socialist movement is nothing more than the part of this militant proletariat which has become conscious of its goal. In fact, these two, socialism and the militant proletariat, tend constantly to become identical'.[16]

According to orthodox Marxism, the party-class relationship, as well as the division of labour between mental and manual labour (and state and society), would be eventually eliminated through a dialectic of class struggle and socialist transformation. The party's task was to make itself superfluous. Until this goal was achieved, the role of organised socialists was not to act in the name of the working class, but to help lead it towards victory. As Polish SD leader Leo Jogiches put it, 'we are a mass party, we try to increase the proletariat's consciousness of its role, we can lead it but we cannot – and in no sense must we try to – be a substitute for it in the class struggle'.[17]

A second widespread misconception is that Kautsky adhered to an evolutionist and economic deterministic conception of Marxism, according to which socialism would arise as the inevitable result of blind economic forces. Like political scientist Sheri Berman, socialist writer Donny Gluckstein has recently written that using 'a completely mechanical interpretation of the argument in *The Communist Manifesto*, Kautsky insisted that socialists need do nothing but wait for events'.[18] Similarly, one recent Finnish scholar has argued that Finland's social democrats 'interpreted Marxism through the ideas of the German ideologist Karl Kautsky, who excluded any voluntary action and relied on the technical determinism of productive forces'.[19]

In point of fact, both Kautsky and his co-thinkers across imperial Russia and Europe emphatically rejected such conceptions. According to Kautsky, socialism could arise only from the 'the consciousness, will and struggle of the proletariat'.[20] While the socio-economic dynamics of capitalism formed the material basis for the class struggle and the eventual establishment of socialism, con-

---

16      Kautsky 1892 [1910], p. 183.
17      Cited in Nettl 1966, p. 567.
18      Gluckstein 2014; Berman 2006, pp. 12–13.
19      Siltala 2014, p. 60.
20      Cited in Larsson 1970, p. 53. See also Kautsky 1904 [2009], p. 223.

scious intervention by the proletariat and its party was needed to overthrow capitalist rule.[21] In the orthodox socialist view, history would help those who helped themselves.

Revolutionary social democrats certainly believed that proletarianisation and industrialisation were indispensable premises for the growth of the socialist movement. And their confidence in upholding an intransigent political strategy reflected a somewhat over-optimistic view, shared by Marx, that economic development was rapidly creating a solidly majoritarian constituency for anti-capitalism.[22] But Kautsky expressly rejected the idea that more capitalist development *necessarily* translated into stronger revolutionary movements. As such, he consistently contrasted the heroic militancy of workers in economically backwards Russia with the philistine moderation of the proletariat in industrialised and democratic England.[23]

The extent of the historiographical confusion about Kautsky's supposed fatalism can be seen in Marxist writer Michael Löwy's claim that Rosa Luxemburg's slogan 'socialism or barbarism' constituted 'a fundamental methodological break with fatalistic, Kautsky-type economism'.[24] In reality, the world-historic perspective of socialism or barbarism was first put forward in the Second International by none other than Kautsky himself. His *Erfurt Programme* declared that 'capitalist civilization cannot continue; we must either move forward into socialism or fall back into barbarism'.[25] According to Kautsky and other SDs, stressing the eventual triumph of the working class was necessary precisely to *encourage* activity – to foster the practical dedication of workers and socialists and to help them persevere through the ups and downs of class struggle. A PPS leader therefore argued in 1902 that 'the struggling masses' faith in victory is as important a factor for success as good weapons and good organization'.[26]

In socialist agitation, even quasi-religious declarations that history and the future were on the side of workers were meant to encourage proletarian activity rather than passivity. A Jewish Bund appeal proclaimed: 'Our war cry is "Death or victory!" We are sure of victory, we have faith in our triumph and we call on

---

21  Kautsky 1904 [2009], p. 223.
22  The persistence of middle classes and of working-class political moderation over the past century made it unexpectedly difficult to forge anti-capitalist majorities, posing major strategic dilemmas for democratic socialists (see Stephens 1979).
23  Kautsky 1902 [1916], p. 100.
24  Löwy 1976, p. 88.
25  Kautsky 1892 [1910], p. 118.
26  Karski 1902a, p. 419.

all those who, like us, thirst for freedom to give their support to us in this difficult hour'.[27] Awaiting possible execution, imprisoned Polish socialist leaders in 1886 likewise hoped to rouse their supporters to continue the fight in their absence: 'Look to the future with faith, because the future is ours, of our ideal. And you, comrades, bring closer its arrival through your work. Be steadfast and joyful'.[28] One need not agree with this rhetorical-political approach to understand its intended function.

A third common historiographic fallacy is that Marxists of this era were only interested in class exploitation, thereby dismissing the political agency of oppressed nationalities, women, and non-proletarian strata of the population.[29] One can justifiably criticise various aspects of early socialist stances on racial, national, and gender oppression, but the fact remains that revolutionary social democrats pushed for an undeniably broad anti-capitalist movement that would promote the struggles of (and seek to organise) a wide range of dominated groups, including non-industrial wage workers, housewives, youth, the unemployed, peasants, and nationally oppressed peoples.

The *Erfurt Programme* openly declared that socialists fought against 'not only the exploitation and oppression of wage-workers, but also every form of exploitation and oppression, be it directed against a class, a party, a sex, or a race'. A singular political orientation to the working class was explicitly rejected. Socialist parties, it argued, must increasingly become the representative 'of all laboring and exploited classes, or, in other words, of the great majority of the population'.[30]

This broad perspective was shared by revolutionary socialists across the Russian Empire. To cite just one example, Mammad Amin Rasulzade, the leading writer of the Muslim *Gummet*, declared:

> The Social Democratic organisation always fights for the happiness of the people and protects its interests. Waking humanity through the means of revolution, it aims to eliminate violence and oppression from the world, to free the poor and disadvantaged from the pressure of the exploiters and the state. It is the party of the people, humble, disadvantaged and disenfranchised.[31]

---

27    'Aux Citoyens libres du Monde entier', 26 October 1905, Comité central du 'Bounde' (Archiwum Akt Nowych, 19: 30/1–1).

28    *Przedświt*, January 1886.

29    See, for example, Federici 2013. For a reply, see Blanc 2016b.

30    Kautsky 1892 [1910], pp. 160, 211, 220. See also Kautsky 1906.

31    Cited in Агакишиев 1991, p. 83.

The question of how to most effectively promote national equality and liberation (discussed further below) was a major focus of many Marxist organisations throughout the Russian state, particularly in the borderlands. Women's equality was another consistent component of socialist politics. Social democrats across Russia, following the example of the *Erfurt Programme*, concretised their perspective in the following demands: universal suffrage without distinction of sex; the abolition of all laws that placed women at a disadvantage compared with men in matters of public or private law; free medical care, including midwifery; free education for both boys and girls; and legal equality for domestic servants. In the Finnish socialist newspaper *Kansan Lehti* (The People's Paper), party militant Alma Jokinen enthused: 'We live in a wonderful period of time. ... Women, who have always been subordinate, suddenly get the idea that they really are equal with the other sex'.[32]

Though implementation of this egalitarianism was uneven, such calls for equality did not remain on paper. At the turn of the century in Białystok, for example, when some male workers began to agitate and even use violence to expel females from the factories – on the grounds that low-paid women workers were driving down men's wages – the PPS responded with a campaign in defence of the right of women to work in the factory. Its leaflet exclaimed:

> We socialists demand equal pay for equal work for men and women and their complete equality! To save us from poverty, we don't need a fight against companions of work and misery, but a fight against government oppression and capitalist exploitation. In this struggle, the men must go hand in hand with women.[33]

Progress went furthest in Finland, which in 1906 became the world's first polity to grant full female suffrage. Confirming socialists' longstanding contention that the working class was the social force best positioned to fight all forms of oppression, it took a mass general strike in Finland and a socialist-led empire-wide revolution to wrest this watershed achievement.[34]

While socialists fought for important immediate demands around the rights of women and envisioned their liberation from 'household slavery' in the future, they were nevertheless shaped by patriarchal mores and practices. Party leaderships tended to be disproportionately made up of men and even those male socialists who actively supported women's political rights often

---

32   *Kansan Lehti*, 19 December 1905.
33   Cited in Korzec 1965, p. 238. On Russia's socialists and women's liberation, see Marik 2008.
34   Blanc 2017a. On the fight for women's suffrage across the empire, see Ruthchild 2010.

resisted efforts to make family relations more equitable in the here-and-now. The Finnish working women's publication *Palvelijatarlehti* (The Maids' Paper) lamented that many men supported women's rights, 'but only within the established limits. As soon as women's endeavours have anything to do with the emancipation of mothers from the chains binding her into home's narrow scope, then resistance is encountered'.[35]

That said, it would be ahistorical to judge the SDs by today's standards. In the wake of decades of increased female participation in the labour force, mass women's movements, and significant societal shifts in gender norms, it is far easier now to see their limitations. But judged by the standards of their time, early Marxists at their best were path breakers in the struggle for women's liberation.

Finally, there remains a widespread myth that Second International socialists generally treated Marxism as a dogma. Abraham Ascher's influential study of the 1905 revolution claims that the SDs were 'saddled with a dogmatic view of the historical process' and unable to 'cope with complexities they had not, and could not have, anticipated ... [T]he course of events in 1905 played havoc with the theories evolved by both groups of Marxists'.[36] Socialist writers, as we saw earlier, have also frequently put forward similar interpretations by claiming that the 'creative Marxism' of Lenin or Luxemburg constituted a break with Kautsky's wooden schemas.

Instances of doctrinarism did exist among the era's Marxists, as was true for all political currents. But, on the whole, the evolution of revolutionary social democracy in the years leading up to 1917 underscores the degree to which this strategy was flexibly transformed in response to novel developments in political life. For his part, Kautsky perpetually insisted that it was impossible to make hard and fast assertions about the future course of events. Social democrats in imperial Russia likewise affirmed that it was always necessary to transform revolutionary theory in response to new social and political developments. For Polish socialist Julian Marchlewski, Marxism was not a 'template', but rather a 'tool for creative work'.[37]

While social democrats sought to base their strategy on lessons of the past and their understanding of capitalism's economic tendencies, they also noted

---

35    E-a V-t. 1906, p. 29.

36    Ascher 1988, pp. 188–9.

37    Cited in Michta 1987, p. 7. In Kautsky's words, 'revolutions are, for everyone, rich in surprises and, above all, the proletariat develops in a literally unforeseeable manner during a revolution' (Karl Kautsky, 'Die Nationalitätenfrage in Russland', *Leipziger Volkszeitung*, 29 April 1905).

the unpredictability of political life. Russia's convulsions from the turn of the century onwards made this dynamic particularly evident. To quote one leader of the PPS, 'no one can know what will happen in the future, and by the same token, it is not possible to predict the fate of the future Polish revolution. In politics, however, the question is not of potentiality, but of probability'.[38] Divergent socialist tactics often reflected distinct projections about future developments. Politics, put simply, was always a wager.

Within a broadly shared strategic framework of revolutionary social democracy, all sorts of organisational and political differences could and did arise. Building an illegal Marxist movement in an absolutist context was an unprecedented historical experiment, obliging a large degree of trial and error. The answer to the question of what to do in the concrete circumstances of a given time and place was never obvious, with each major political turn of events posing new questions to address.

## 2   Strategy and Tactics in Germany and Russia

Social democrats saw the conceptions discussed above as valid internationally. But the orthodox consensus also crucially distinguished between strategy for parliamentary democracies and for absolutist regimes like Tsarist Russia.

Political freedom, they argued, constituted nothing short of the 'light and air' in which the organisation and education of the proletariat could grow strong enough to achieve its final goal. A typical Latvian leaflet declared: 'Only if it [political freedom] is conquered will the working class be able to grow the strength over time to crush the power of capital and introduce a socialist order'.[39]

A sharp distinction was made between countries with or without political freedom. As a result, a different approach was advocated for both. In countries with civil liberties and parliaments, revolutionary Marxists argued that social democratic parties should focus on patient and peaceful activities such as promoting socialist ideas through the press, building strong party organisations, running in elections to further spread the message, and building trade unions.

---

38   Karski 1902b, p. 6. Eminent Latvian socialist poet Janis Rainis captured this sentiment in a well-known revolutionary poem: 'The dices have been thrown. Now, go ahead, the whirlwinds!' (cited in Grumolte 2013, p. 102).

39   Cited in Kalniņš 1956, p. 34.

Legal tactics should be pursued if at all possible, to not give the regime a pretext to clamp down and destroy the accumulated power of working people before they were strong enough to defeat their enemies. Mass proletarianisation, the further growth of the labour movement, and capitalist crises would sooner or later pose revolution – and distinct tactics – as an immediate task. Until that point, however, it would be unwise to prematurely provoke government repression by engaging in unruly mass actions or breaking with bourgeois-democratic legality.

Kautsky and other revolutionary social democrats explicitly argued that the practice of persistently promoting proletarian education and collective association was revolutionary as long as it was consistently linked to the assertion of the party's final goals. Kautsky summed up this stance through the following maxim: 'avoid all possible provocation and yet always maintain the consciousness that we are a fighting party, conducting an irreconcilable war upon all existing social institutions'.[40]

In hindsight, it is fair to criticise Kautsky for sometimes overgeneralising international strategy from Germany's particularly 'low inclusion' context, where restrictions upon mass action – and transformative legislative reform – were significantly lower than in more democratic polities. The educationalism of patiently spreading the class-struggle gospel, and the downplaying of mass actions or parliamentary reforms, made more sense in a semi-authoritarian constitutional monarchy like Germany or Finland than it did in France or England.

But regardless of how one weighs the strength and limitations of orthodox Marxist strategy for parliamentary polities, the crucial point to stress here is that conditions in autocratic Russia precluded any attempt to adopt the organisational structure or political focus of the German Social Democratic Party. A strategy of patiently accumulating forces could not be implemented in a context where the state so frequently smashed attempts to independently organise workers. By necessity, socialists in underground Russia had to rely more on mass action tactics than their counterparts abroad.

Believing that the German SPD's 'tried and tested' approach would become possible following the overthrow of Tsarism, orthodox Marxists rejected calls to immediately overthrow capitalism in imperial Russia. Only in conditions of democratic liberty, according to this consensus, would socialists have sufficient political space to help organise and educate the working class for socialism. In 1903 Luxemburg thus argued that the 'working class cannot achieve wide-scale

---

40      Kautsky 1909a, p. 61.

organisation and consciousness without certain political conditions enabling open class struggle, that is without democratic institutions in the country'.[41]

No precise criteria was articulated for the level of proletarian strength and consciousness required for a socialist revolution. But presumably Russia's socialist parties would, upon winning political freedom, seek to build organisations at least as strong as the German SPD, a development that could be expected to take a significant amount of time in post-autocratic Russia. This argument was generally linked to affirming workers' self-emancipation as opposed to 'Blanquism', which sought to take power in the name of working people and *then* to use this state power to further workers' struggle for economic and social liberation. On these grounds Plekhanov, for example, in 1885 opposed the call for socialists to orient toward a direct seizure of power in Russia.[42]

For an autocracy like Tsarist Russia, revolutionary SDs saw that a distinct strategic orientation was required from that of their Western European peers. While stressing that democratic institutions allowed for the proletariat to grow its strength through organisation and education, Kautsky hastened to add: 'Only Russia is an exception'.[43] As Kautsky explained in 1904, the particular tactical stances he advocated for Germany were not necessarily relevant for the absolutist context of imperial Tsarism, where the workers 'find themselves in a state in which they have nothing to lose but their chains'.[44]

Faced with Tsarist absolutism, all SDs agreed that the most pressing political task was to win political freedom. They repeated this point *ad infinitum* in leaflets and articles across the empire. A joint conference of the empire's Marxist parties thus affirmed: 'We need to win political freedom so that on its soil we can conduct an even wider struggle against capitalist exploitation in the name of the great ideal of socialism'.[45] Socialist leaflets translated this two-stage perspective into the dual calls for 'Long live Political Freedom' (or 'Down with the Autocracy!'), followed by 'Long Live Socialism!'

For the reasons described above, both socialist perspectives *and* practices in imperial Russia were necessarily more stridently oppositional to the existing state than their counterparts in Western Europe. Consider the issue of armed struggle. Kautsky rejected a strategic orientation towards promoting armed proletarian insurrections in Western European democracies. Advances in military technology, he argued, had made modern armies too strong to be over-

---

41    Luxemburg 1903, pp. 23, 52.

42    Plekhanov 1885.

43    Kautsky 1909 [1996], p. 35.

44    Kautsky 1904 [2009], p. 215.

45    'Извещение о конференции' [1905] in Андерсон 2010, p. 401.

thrown through uprisings on the old nineteenth-century model of barricades and street fighting – instead, it was necessary to win over the troops of capitalist armies. Furthermore, Kautsky argued, workers in the West would generally seek to use existing democratic channels and freedoms to advance their interests. At the same time, Kautsky posited that a successful armed uprising could take place against the *Tsarist* state, since it was militarily weak and because the absence of political democracy tended to push workers towards armed confrontation.[46]

Sharing these assumptions, Marxists in imperial Russia uniformly advocated insurrectionary struggle to topple the state. From at least 1902 onwards, they openly called for armed struggle against the Tsarist regime. Noting that the absence of political freedom and parliamentary democracy precluded any hope for a peaceful or evolutionary change in Russia, the Revolutionary Ukrainian Party in 1902 concluded that only a violent revolution was possible: 'Ukrainian socialism, whether it wishes to or not, must ... become revolutionary socialism'.[47]

A sense of the actuality of revolution informed the strategies and practices of the empire's parties. Far from being an exceptional attribute of Lenin's political genius, understanding the immediacy and urgency of preparing for revolution was a widespread response to the rather evident crisis of Tsarist society and the rapid growth of an insurgent opposition. Socialists in Russia treated revolution as a pressing task because this was almost self-evident. From 1901 onwards – and often well before – radicals and literate observers of politics predicted that a revolutionary outburst was impending in Russia.[48]

Who would lead the struggle for political freedom in imperial Russia? On this question the pre-1906 socialist response was unanimous: the independent workers' movement. For the Latvian SDs, '[o]nly we, the workers, are able to overthrow the Russian autocracy. We will show that we are ready to fight for liberty and rights to the last drop of blood!'[49] All throughout Russia, SDs proclaimed that only the heroic working class could and should lead the struggle for a democratic order. Only after the disorienting defeat of the 1905 revolution did significant wings of socialists for the first time began to drop their support

46    Waldenberg 1972, pp. 361–2; Kautsky 1904 [2009], *passim*.
47    Cited in Boshyk 1982, p. 94.
48    'Our New Programme' [1902] in Harding 1983, p. 271. Socialists across Europe reached a similar assessment. In 1904, Dutch socialist Henriette Roland Holst wrote that the previous year's general strikes in Ukraine and Transcaucasia constituted 'the first formidable wave of the Russian revolution' (cited in Кирьянов 1987, p. 215).
49    Cited in Kalniņš 1956, p. 34.

for this strategy of proletarian hegemony. The issue of blocs with the 'bourgeois democracy' soon became the most consequential point of divergence in the empire's movement.

Notwithstanding periodic agitational affirmations that only workers could overthrow absolutism, the orthodox consensus was that the working class *would* find social allies in its struggle against Tsarism. The idea that all non-workers were 'one reactionary mass' was explicitly rejected by Marx, Kautsky, and other revolutionary SDs. Though the proletariat was the main and leading force of the anti-autocratic struggle, it should expect, seek, and welcome – but not depend on – support from all popular strata willing to combat Tsarism.

None of the Marxist parties at this time argued that workers should subordinate or hold back their independent movement for the sake of alliances with other social strata. It was stressed that the working class must at all times seek to maintain its political and organisational independence. As Kautsky declared in 1893, other groups such as peasants 'are most welcome to join us and to march alongside us, but the proletariat will always show the way'.[50] Polish Socialist Party leader Felix Perl wrote:

> although socialism comes from a purely proletarian standpoint, and although the working class is its core, its banner is the banner of all the oppressed, all those who are suffering. Especially today, when liberalism and bourgeois democracy have completely betrayed the cause of freedom, socialism is the focal point of all progressive currents, the leader of the whole vital opposition.[51]

Within this strategic consensus, there were ongoing debates over which non-proletarian strata could be expected to fight Tsarism and how best to relate to them. Students were one group that virtually all SDs in Russia agreed was a crucial ally of the working class. Attracted by the ideas of democracy and socialism coming from Western Europe, much of the young intelligentsia viewed the Tsarist state as an antiquated obstacle to social progress.

Indeed, most of the empire's SD parties arose from circles of radicalised students. Across Russia, student protests and demonstrations erupted from 1899 onwards, leading to mass expulsions, arrests, and violent confrontations. In 1901, for example, Kharkov student actions against the authorities led to the expulsion of the entire first-year class at one university, the banning of all stu-

---

50    Kautsky 1893 [2018], p. 157.
51    Perl 1894, p. 3.

dent general assemblies, and a widespread outcry across the empire. Adopting
the tactics of the workers' movement, students led strikes in all regions for better school conditions, university democracy, and eventually against the autocracy itself. As student and worker struggles mutually reinforced each other,
radicals throughout Russia advocated close collaboration between the two. In
the words of the 1903 empire-wide sd-led student congress: 'Let us go hand in
hand with the workers and together with them sooner or later we will deal our
common enemy the final mortal blow'.[52]

Given that the majority of the population in all regions of the empire lived
in the countryside, it is not surprising that peasants were also frequently projected as key allies in anti-autocratic struggle. Though there was considerable
debate over the extent to which Marxists should accommodate their demands
for land, social democrats in Russia generally agreed that peasants would be
a potentially important ally in the fight against Tsarism. In 1901, the SDKPIL
declared that while the party 'should be guided exclusively by the interests of
the proletariat', peasants could be 'temporary allies in the fight against the government'.[53]

Orthodox Marxists argued that the working class should support and ally
with peasants in so far as they fought the Tsar, but it could not depend on
them; proletarian organisational and political independence must at all times
be maintained. sds believed that the paths of the land-holding peasants and
the proletariat would eventually part ways in the struggle for socialism, as only
the latter had an interest in abolishing the private ownership of the means of
production. And since all orthodox Marxists posited that the peasantry was not
a socialist class, they rejected the left Socialist Revolutionary (sr) advocacy
of overthrowing capitalism in conjunction with Tsarism in the impending
revolutionary upheaval. Only through mass proletarianisation and industrialisation, Marxists argued, could the material preconditions for socialism be
established.[54]

Though imperial Russia's Marxists hoped for rural resistance to emerge,
work among the peasantry was generally not a priority. This urban-proletarian

---

52    Cited in Roobol 1976, p. 25. On the student movement under Tsarism, see Kassow 1989.
      The only partial exception to the revolutionary role of students in imperial Russia was
      Finland, where most students tended to remain linked to bourgeois parties.
53    'Stosunek partji do klas przejściowych' [1901], in Szmidt 1934, p. 275. In 1903, Kautsky
      responded as follows to the recent peasant uprisings in Ukraine: 'The revolution has noth-
      ing to fear from a peasant uprising, it can only bring about good things' (Cited in Weill 1977,
      pp. 178–9).
54    For useful general overviews of Marxist positions on the agrarian question in Russia, on
      which I have drawn for this section, see the discussions in Larsson 1970 and Shanin 1986.

focus was rooted in expediency as much as political orthodoxy; peasant resistance during the years before the first Russian Revolution was generally muted.[55] Given the relative lack of mobilisation, organisation, and education in the countryside, by the turn of the century only a minority of socialists, even within the neo-populist movement, advocated a focus on work among the peasantry. It was not obvious whether peasants would enter into the political struggle and what they would demand if they did.

Activity in the cities and among workers was more fruitful and easier to sustain than rural and peasant agitation; most political forces – from socialists to liberals to nationalists – were weak to non-existent among the peasantry in this period. In so far as SDs agitated in the countryside, it was usually among the rural intelligentsia (teachers, students, etc.) or agricultural wage workers. Success in these activities was very uneven. In regions where the core urban intelligentsia and working class were the same nationality as the surrounding rural population – particularly the Baltic, Finland, and Georgia – rural socialist work generally sunk deep roots. By way of contrast, urban SDs were isolated from the rural population in regions where the cities were islands of non-natives (Ukraine, Azerbaijan, Central Asia, Belarus, and Lithuania).

A partial turn by some Marxists towards sustained political work among peasants – and towards emphasising the importance of a worker-peasant alliance – began in 1903. The year before had witnessed historic rural uprisings in the Poltava and Kharkov regions of Ukraine. The spark for these revolts had been the widespread agitation of the Revolutionary Ukrainian Party, a party which had begun with an ideology close to that of the neo-populist Socialist Revolutionaries (SRs), but which by 1902 was in the process of transforming itself into an orthodox Marxist organisation. The year 1903 witnessed an even more impactful uprising, the 'Gurian Republic' in Georgia, which presaged later socialist-led peasant rebellions in China, Vietnam, and other colonised countries. Under the direct leadership of the local Georgian Marxist organisation, peasants in the region of Guria displaced the Tsarist authorities and established their de facto revolutionary rule, which lasted up through the end of 1905.

Yet Zhordania and his Georgian comrades' pro-active approach to peasant struggle was not the norm among the empire's SDs during the years preceding 1905. It would take the experiences of 1905 and 1917–18 to push wider currents of Marxists across the empire – especially those in borderland regions like

---

55     Shanin 1986, p. 146.

Poland and Latvia with greater rural class differentiation – to more consciously strive for an alliance with the peasantry and to deepen their support for radical agrarian reform.[56]

Before concluding this overview of orthodox social democratic strategy, it is necessary to touch upon the question of national liberation in imperial Russia, an immense and complex topic. A few key issues should be highlighted. To begin with, early Marxist parties in the empire shared critical points of agreement on the national question. All, for instance, took the class criteria as their theoretical starting point. The following statement by the Latvian Social Democratic Union – one of the borderland Marxist parties most focused on national liberation – was entirely typical:

> We are not nationalists, we are socialists. We will never forget that our first calling is to awaken, enlighten and liberate the working class from political and economic slavery. We address the national question only in so far as it is important for these goals.[57]

As historian Marek Waldenberg notes, 'the theoretical recognition of the subordination of national interests to the struggle for socialism' was common to all orthodox Marxists, though this did not preclude significant differences over how to best implement this approach in practice.[58] In the period before 1905, none of the empire's social democratic parties advocated the prioritisation of national over class demands, promoted national development as an end in itself, or supported cross-class national unity. All – including those least inclined to promote national demands – supported the struggle for political equality and fought, often arms in hand, against the pogromists and other reactionary forces. And all social democrats believed workers of distinct nationalities could and should unite for their common interests. 'We can never forget the unshakable truth that proletarians of different nations have a hundred times more in common with each other than they have with their own nation's bourgeois classes', explained Pēteris Stučka.[59]

In the years before 1905, the empire's organised Marxists generally shared a common strategic outlook on the basic questions of working-class independence, internationalism, and anti-Tsarist revolution. Their differences concerned how these goals could be reached effectively and how to incorporate

---

56    Tych 1970, p. 168.
57    Cited in Dopkewitsch 1936, pp. 24–5.
58    Waldenberg 1972, p. 584.
59    Stučka 1904, p. 6.

national liberation into the general revolutionary struggle. Of all the debates between Russian and borderland SDs, the conflict over party organisation was the most concrete and the most immediate. Before 1905, the predominantly Russian and Russified *Iskra* current led by Lenin and Julius Martov fought hard to build a single, centralised empire-wide Marxist party. Given the growing revolutionary upsurge, according to *Iskra* it was urgently necessary to connect the atomised circles into a powerful centralised All-Russian party capable of leading the rapidly rising tide of revolutionary struggle to overthrow the auto-cracy.[60]

Yet all of the borderland parties at this time – whether or not they organised one or more nationalities – rejected *Iskra*'s push for a single centralised All-Russian party.[61] Instead, they advocated a looser federal party to unite SDs across imperial Russia. A leader of Rosa Luxemburg's anti-nationalist SDKPIL, for example, argued: 'To accept these terms [*Iskra*'s organisational proposal] means agreeing to the destruction of our party, making her one of the local organisations of the Russian party, which given the state of the struggle in Russia would be detrimental to our movement'.[62] Likewise, Stučka, who many years later became the leader of Latvian Bolshevism, challenged *Iskra*'s view that greater organisational centralisation would always lead to greater political effectiveness. This was not necessarily the case, Stučka argued, because the Russian SDs were 'somewhat indifferent to the other nationalities in Russia' and did not often have a good understanding of the particularities of the borderlands.[63]

An analogous debate unfolded over the best form of state to replace the autocracy. *Iskra* called for a single centralised republic for the whole territory and generally opposed governmental federalism and national autonomy.[64] Though state separatism was overwhelmingly opposed by non-Russian Marxists (with the exception of the Polish PPS), most advocated different forms of broad national autonomy or federalism. 'Freedom and democracy in Russia are inconceivable without free peoples linked to each other solely through mutual alliances that are freely entered in to. Russia must be proclaimed as an

---

60    Lenin 1903a [1960–65], p. 460.
61    The only partial exception was the Georgian Social Democracy, which joined the RSDRP in 1903. Though their organisation was formally subordinate to the RSDRP leadership, in practice the Georgian SDs from 1905 onwards acted as a 'party within the party' that implemented its own line on crucial issues such as agrarian struggle, party organisation, terrorism, and the Duma. See Jones 2005.
62    'J. Marchlewski do Członków Komitetu Zagranicznego SDKPIL' [1903] in Tych 1962, p. 457.
63    Stučka 1904, p. 5.
64    Lenin 1903b [1960–65], p. 326.

association of free democratic republics', argued the Latvian LSS.[65] The Ukrainian Social Democratic Workers Party similarly demanded broad autonomy for Ukraine in a federal Russia. Opposing proposals to limit autonomy to administrative or cultural questions, it proposed a vision of national autonomy concretised in a legislative *Sejm* (parliament) with the power to control financial, agrarian, economic, educational, and cultural affairs.[66]

Scholars and socialists have overlooked the fact that it was the non-Russian Marxist advocacy of state federalism – not *Iskra*'s call for centralism – that was closest to the stance of Karl Kautsky. On this question, Lenin and his comrades were decidedly unorthodox. Kautsky's influential 1905 article on Russia's national question argued that the only way to avoid the secession of the empire's oppressed nationalities was for a democratic Russia to be transformed into 'a federal state, the "United States of Russia"'.

He cautioned that such a territorial solution could not resolve national oppression on its own, as it did not address the national minorities on these lands. In Russia – like in Austria, the Balkans, and Asia Minor – it was common for multiple peoples to live interspersed on a given territory, 'resulting in national questions that are incomprehensible for a Western European and unsolvable through Western European means'. Given this particular dilemma, Kautsky put forward the perspective of the Marxists in Austria as a plausible solution for Russia, arguing that 'a series of useful proposals have been made in Austria to combine the self-administration of regions with the self-administration of each nation, and in the Austrian social democratic party the two forms of autonomy are in practice implemented side by side with each other'.[67]

Within the RSDRP after 1905, former Iskraists – Bolsheviks and Mensheviks alike – eventually moved towards a federalist stance and away from many of their earlier positions on the national question. Though Lenin's evolution began in 1913, the fundamental turn in the practice of the Bolshevik current as a whole came in 1917–21, especially following the defeats of workers' revolutions in Lithuania, Ukraine, Latvia, Poland, Georgia, and Azerbaijan. In response to these setbacks, Bolsheviks in all levels and regions felt a need to more pro-

65    Cited in Dopkewitsch 1934, p. 21.
66    Порш 1907. Bundists developed their own particular case for national federalism. They argued that the establishment of political freedom and legal equality would not necessarily end the oppression of minority groups. Without collective rights and institutions for all peoples, national minorities would be subjected to de facto coerced assimilation, manifest in the inevitable pressures to adopt the culture of the majority (Медем 1904, pp. 34–6, 47).
67    Karl Kautsky, 'Die Nationalitätenfrage in Russland', *Leipziger Volkszeitung*, 29 April 1905.

actively and flexibly address non-Russian national aspirations. To help root the Soviet regime among non-Russian peoples, from 1921–23 onwards the Bolsheviks actively developed national cultures and languages, implemented state federalism, and promoted borderland Marxists to leadership positions in government.[68]

Soviet historians have argued that the Communists' post-1917 difficulties establishing Soviet rule in the borderlands could have been avoided had they not delayed in adopting Lenin's approach to national liberation.[69] This is a plausible counterfactual, particularly regarding Ukraine and Poland, where the leading radical socialists in 1917–18 tended to underestimate popular national sentiments, thereby undercutting attempts to build working-class hegemony. But apart from the fact that Lenin himself often continued to dismiss nationally oriented Marxists in Poland and Ukraine well after 1913, one should be cautious not to overstate the national question's causal impact.

During the 1905 revolution, theoretical differences between socialist parties over national issues were largely overshadowed by their general political agreement and collaboration in the fight against the autocracy. Though national oppression shaped the form and intensity of working-class movements, supraclass nationalism largely remained the purview of the intelligentsia and political elite in all regions of the empire. The same held true twelve years later. As Ronald Suny has shown, it was class concerns that primarily animated lower-class struggles in 1917 – even in the imperial borderlands, 'ethnic conflicts were far less frequent than social clashes throughout the first year of revolution'.[70] Pro-independence sentiment remained low.

Furthermore, the Bolsheviks were the empire-wide political current *most* supportive of the demands of dominated national groups during 1917. The Bolsheviks' alliance with non-Russian currents primarily broke down or solidified over anti-capitalist transformation, not the national question as such. An excessive focus on the national policies of Lenin and his comrades minimises the political agency of borderland socialists, obscuring the ways their strategic choices in the years leading up to Tsarism's overthrow – particularly on the advisability of blocs with bourgeois forces – determined their political practices.

In and after 1917, national struggles became inextricable from fundamental differences over whether the unfolding revolution(s) should remain within

---

68    On these developments, see Smith 1999 and Blanc 2016a.
69    Popov 1934, Vol. 2, p. 72.
70    Suny 1993, p. 75. See also Suny 1993, pp. 81–2.

bounds acceptable to the bourgeoisie at home and abroad. In the empire's periphery, as E.H. Carr long ago pointed out, conflicts over social revolution took on a national form: 'in whatever guise the battle was fought, the real issue was the life or death of the revolution'.[71] As such, one cannot analyse the development of revolutionary processes – including national conflicts – separate from the broader strategic questions confronting all of the empire's Marxists. It is to these questions that we now turn.

---

71      Carr 1950, p. 268.

# Intellectuals and Workers

The story of the revolutionary movement in Russia has often been told as one long conflict between workers and intellectuals. In this view, the socialist intelligentsia sought to impose its ideology and wardship over constituencies in whose name it claimed to speak. According to Bruno Naarden, 'the gulf between the workers and the intelligentsia was and remained wide and the history of the RSDRP could be described as a series of hopeless attempts to close this rift'.[1]

Historian Igal Halfin further contends that for Russia's Marxists 'the proletariat, in order to become a class "for itself", had to entrust itself to the intelligentsia's tutelage. ... All factions [of Marxists] accepted that, before history ended, the proletariat was to be tutored by one external agency or another'. Inspired by academia's 'discursive turn', Halfin argues that Marxism was a 'narrative' and a 'discourse of power' with no actual connection to 'the working class' as an 'empirical entit[y]' – what 'was real was the revolutionary discourse itself', the internal logic of which found its ultimate expression in Stalinist authoritarianism.[2]

Addressing such claims is a useful starting point for our discussion. If authors like Halfin and Naarden are correct, then the real subject matter of this book is not class formation and working-class politics but rather the discourse of socialism and the politics of the intelligentsia. This chapter, however, shows that there *was* a meaningful elective affinity between imperial Russia's workers and the social democratic parties that organised to express their interests and aspirations.

In both their sociological composition and their political orientation, the parties that came to lead the 1905 and 1917 revolutions were in fact *workers' parties*. Radical socialists of all nationalities shared a common vision that explicitly rejected intelligentsia tutelage over the working class. According to revolutionary orthodoxy, socialist transformation was impossible without the conscious and organised activity of the majority in the interests of the majority. If anything, social democrats of all backgrounds tended to be rather sceptical of intellectuals: it was precisely Marxism's emphasis on working-class self-

---

1   Naarden 1992, p. 115.
2   Halfin 2000, pp. 13, 16, 38, 112.

emancipation that validated and sparked ongoing debates over the influence of intellectuals inside the movement.

Unlike much of the Left today, Marxist currents were committed in theory and practice to making their parties as proletarian in composition and leadership as possible. Given the social disparities endemic to capitalist society, this was no simple task. Difficult questions arose concerning the relationship between the personal and political, relative privilege inside the movement, and how to build solidarity and camaraderie across real differences in social background. The ensuing tensions and controversies in many ways resembled today's debates around identity politics; a century ago, however, disputes tended to centre around class.

On the whole, Marxist parties across the Russian state were remarkably successful in their efforts to merge socialism with the workers' movement. In the early years, intellectuals played a significant role in this process, but, as we will see, the intelligentsia largely abandoned radical politics and became disillusioned with labour after the failed 1905 revolution. When working people again moved towards seizing power in late 1917, liberals and right-leaning socialist intellectuals this time generally stood on the opposite side of the barricades from organised workers. A lack of political confidence in the working class defined Russia's political moderates, not its radicals.

## 1      Intellectuals and the Tensions of Class Formation

Who exactly was referred to when Marxists spoke about 'the intelligentsia'? Though its precise boundaries were somewhat ambiguous, this concept generally was reserved for educated members of society who were at least somewhat critical of the status quo. Since Marxists called highly politicised labourers the 'workers' intelligentsia', the term intelligentsia as such carried with it a non-proletarian connotation.

Despite widespread historiographic claims about Marxist elitism, calls for the intelligentsia to free the workers were absent in the era's social democratic movements. According to orthodox socialists, since wage workers were the driving force towards their own self-liberation, intellectuals could, at best, help facilitate (but not substitute themselves for) this process. The ultimate goal, to quote one Ukrainian Bolshevik pamphlet, was 'to abolish the intelligentsia as a separate group by transforming all classes into intelligentsia'.[3]

---

3   Mazlakh and Shakhrai 1919 [1970], p. 76. See also Lenin 1894 [1960–65], p. 298.

For a typical exposition of the Marxist consensus, consider Polish Socialist Party theoretician Feliks Perl's 1894 article on the role of the intelligentsia in the socialist movement. Citing the precedent of German Marxist articles on this topic, Perl argued that while it was wrong to reject the participation of intellectuals in labour struggles, it was also erroneous to view intellectuals as 'the most important revolutionary factor ... the alpha and omega of social creativity, the force that has to pave the way forward for humanity'. He explained that such a 'cult of the intelligentsia' was a part of Russian Populism and Polish nationalism that modern-day socialists rejected. Intellectuals were far too numerically small and heterogeneous a social group to play any such role. Moreover, even radical intellectuals were often incapable of overcoming the 'bourgeois views and prejudices ... imposed by their upbringing' such as indiscipline and ambition. As such, they not infrequently 'disturbed the workers' movement with their disputes'.

Workers, in contrast, were 'the main, the most important, the most essential element of revolutionary struggle'. Because of their location in the relations of capitalist exploitation, they had the 'most interest' in overturning the current social order and the most power to do so: 'only the proletarian army can demolish the old world!'

At the same time, Perl polemicised against the view that intellectuals were 'always more harmful than useful' and that they should therefore be excluded from labour organising. The history of the international socialist movement, he argued, demonstrated the important and positive role that individual intellectuals could play, especially in the initial formative stages of labour organising. 'Even the biggest opponents of the intelligentsia [in the socialist movement] often have to admit that it is a necessary evil', he noted. In any case, only a minority of the intelligentsia was capable of breaking from its class roots. Workers' influence in the party must predominate:

> The core of the socialist party is the proletariat, but around it can and should be grouped other discontent and oppositional elements of society. The question is: whose influence will prevail and who will determine the character of the movement. We completely agree that it would be harmful if the influence of the intelligentsia, the petty bourgeoisie, and the peasantry prevailed. But with their consciousness and strong organisation, workers do not have much to fear on this account.

Perl concluded that individuals from any social background were thus welcome to join the socialist workers' movement, provided that they break from bourgeois ideology and biases. The condition for entering the movement was 'not whether someone has hard-worked and callused hands, or white and delicate ones, but whether they precisely understand the necessities of the time and, having gotten rid of any prejudices, honestly want to fight in the great proletarian army for the liberation of humanity'.[4]

This basic orientation was repeated over and over by Marxists throughout the empire. Political practice, nevertheless, was messier than theory. Programmatic commitments had to be concretised in political and organisational measures, the specifics of which were subject to tactical and organisational contestation.

Though there were some individual instances of latent or open elitism among Marxist intellectuals, it is significant that one finds in the sources far more examples of condescension by worker-militants themselves towards their unpoliticised peers, particularly when they were female, unskilled, linked to the village, and/or of another ethnicity. This dynamic was well captured in S. Ansky's 1907 fictionalised vignette of Jewish socialists, in which working-class militant Dovid pushes back against intelligentsia baiting by commenting that '[a]mong the workers themselves aren't there divisions, and sharp ones at that, between "superiors" and "inferiors" ...? Doesn't the worker who's read a dozen brochures preen himself and look down on the worker who hasn't read them?'[5]

Early socialist intellectuals in Russia were more likely to idealise workers than to disparage them. A belief in the potential power of workers to lead the revolutionary overthrow of world capitalism was one of the most fundamental tenets of Marxism and upon this conviction rested the whole project for which socialists dedicated – and often sacrificed – their lives. That this confidence in the revolutionary capacities of the working class could blend into romanticisation is unsurprising. S.A. Smith's study of Petrograd, for instance, observes that 'those intellectuals who joined the socialist movement idealised the proletariat, seeing in it the means whereby their own lives could acquire wholeness and purpose'.[6]

One important consequence of this romanticising tendency was the widespread belief that opportunism within the movement was primarily transmitted via the middle-class intelligentsia.[7] Identifying the main social base of moderate socialism as middle-class influence in the party reflected the SDs' confid-

4  Perl 1894, pp. 2–6.
5  Cited in Frankel 2009, p. 84. For more on the often condescending attitudes among 'conscious' workers towards their 'backwards' peers, see Smith 1983, p. 200, McDaniel 1988, pp. 206–7, and Tanni 2008, p. 59.
6  Smith 1999, p. 200.
7  Lenin 1904 [1960–65], p. 378.

ence in the revolutionary instincts of the proletariat. But, in addition to under-estimating the social roots of working-class moderation in the West, it also enabled problematic behaviours and blind spots in Russia.

Whenever sharp factional struggles broke out inside Marxist parties before 1905, each side almost always accused the other of reflecting alien class forces. Yet such accusations often had little to do with the precise social backgrounds of the opposing wings. In Latvia, for example, the LSDSP – which at the turn of the century was led by a small group of upper-class intellectuals – denounced its rival, the LSS, as an 'intelligentsia' and 'petty-bourgeois' party, despite the fact that its central leaders were both of proletarian origin and had been the Latvian socialist movement's earliest worker-organisers.[8] The same dynamic was manifest after the Bolsheviks and Mensheviks split in 1903. As the Russian socialist observer Vladimir Akimov noted in 1904, 'each claims that it is proletarian ... and each accuses its factional opponents of prejudices typical of intellectuals'.[9] Such claims, however, became far less common from 1905 onwards, as the explosion of popular participation and mass workers' organisation made it easier to test the relative representativity of different socialist currents by the extent to which they organised large numbers of workers.

Another weakness in the prevailing conception of intellectuals as the main source of opportunism was that it could obscure the danger of internal party bureaucratisation. Contrary to the expectations of orthodox Marxism, individual wage workers often became the most conservative bureaucrats once in paid party posts. This would become especially problematic after 1917, when Georgian Bolshevik Joseph Stalin's plebeian roots – his father had been a shoemaker and his mother a house cleaner – helped shield him from criticism as he cohered a bureaucracy of mostly non-intelligentsia apparatchiks.[10] But there were also earlier examples of similar processes across Russia and Germany. For example, many of the most conservative functionaries of the German SPD, such as Ignaz Auer and Fritz Ebert, were manual workers before climbing to the top of the party hierarchy. 'Colourless, cool, determined, industrious and intensely practical, Ebert had all those characteristics which were to make of him, *mutatis mutandis*, the Stalin of social democracy', notes historian Carl Schorske.[11]

In Finland, like in Germany, the moderate leadership of the Social Democracy was predominantly of proletarian origin, while the top radical lead-

8      On early Latvian socialism, see Menders 1959 and Henning 1986.
9      Akimov 1904–05, p. 314.
10     See, for example, Deutscher 1959, pp. 135–6.
11     Schorske 1955, p. 124.

ers were disproportionately intellectuals and students. In comparison with their middle-class comrades, Finland's working-class functionaries tended to become particularly materially dependent on the organisational apparatus. As one historian of the party notes, 'the strongest support for a peaceful parliamentary tactic came from the working-class old guard'.[12] After 1905, the Finnish SDP's swing to the left was marked by the displacement of these worker-leaders by a cadre of radicalised students (though the Finnish intelligentsia as a whole remained in the nationalist camp).

The tendency of intellectuals to romanticise workers was not a one-way street – many workers across Russia similarly idealised the intelligentsia, especially up through 1905. Intellectuals were seen as the embodiment of the culture and education from which working people had been systematically excluded. In the words of one worker from Odessa: 'We trusted the students more than anybody, and if a student said something it was holy. He is educated and knows everything, and no matter what party he belonged to, he always had influence'.[13]

Above all, positive proletarian sentiment towards intellectuals was rooted in the practical experience of revolutionary organising. Intellectuals often possessed particular skill sets – regarding publishing, public speaking, and political education – that were less frequently shared by other party members. Charters Wynn's study on Ekaterinoslav, the city in imperial Russia that experienced the sharpest conflicts over the role of intellectuals, notes that,

> recognizing their own inexperience, radical workers' attitudes toward party *intelligents* were often much more ambivalent than their complaints indicate. Workers felt insecure about their own oratorical and writing ability. Ekaterinoslav's artisans welcomed guidance from veteran members of Committees in other cities when they arrived.[14]

In the face of harsh working conditions and a brutal autocracy, working-class militants were eager to enlist and accept the help of anybody willing to join their struggle.

The absence of intellectuals often severely impeded the work of local committees. This was an acute problem for the Polish SDKPIL, which attracted

---

12    Kirby 1971, p. 92. Outside of the SDP's top leadership structure, there was no such line of social-political division, since the party ranks were overwhelmingly proletarian. One of the exceptional features of Finland in comparison with the rest of the empire was the absence of social radicalism among the intelligentsia as a whole.

13    Cited in Shtakser 2007, p. 158. See also Smith 1999, p. 200.

14    Wynn 1987, p. 226.

relatively few members from the intelligentsia. Bronisław Radlak's study on Luxemburg's party shows how its shortage of intellectuals was a 'chronic headache' that created serious ongoing difficulties.[15] And on an empire-wide level, winning preliminary support from the rural intelligentsia was usually the critical bridge for SD parties to establish a mass popular base in the countryside. In Latvia and Ukraine, for example, rural Marxist teachers were the pillar of establishing a strong socialist presence outside of the cities.[16]

Effectively implementing social democracy's strategy of working-class self-emancipation was not an easy task. But even in the pre-1905 period, when the influence and participation of intellectuals was at its height, the class composition of the empire's Marxist parties generally reflected their proletarian orientation. Over 70 per cent of the membership of the Latvian LSDSP, for example, was made up of urban and rural workers in 1904 – Stučka noted that the party faced a shortage rather than overabundance of intellectuals.[17] In parties with a stronger intelligentsia presence, workers still generally predominated. The PPS's Warsaw branch, for example, in 1903 was comprised of roughly 1,000 industrial workers, a few hundred artisans, and about a hundred intellectuals. Likewise, even in the period before 1905, workers were a majority of the membership of the RSDRP, one of the parties that initially faced the most difficulties in establishing a solid working-class base.[18]

Serious scholarly works on local party committees generally belie claims about perpetual worker conflicts with intellectuals. Gerald Surh's study of the workers' movement in the capital concludes that 'Petersburg workers at no time displayed universal sympathy or antipathy toward members of the intelligentsia'.[19] Relations between workers and intellectuals in the Marxist movements of imperial Russia could be marked by close comradely collaboration, sharp factional battles, or a wide range of dynamics in between these two extremes.

Personal trust generated through common struggle against capitalists and the state facilitated processes of political and personal inter-mingling within socialist parties, which tended to undercut the demonisation or romanticisation of the party's distinct social layers. 'Both social groups [intellectuals and

---

15  Radlak 1979, p. 157.
16  In contrast, the weakness of Iskraists in the countryside of central Russia was to a significant extent rooted in their inability to attract rural intellectuals away from the Socialist Revolutionaries (Seregny 1989, *passim*).
17  Dauge 1958, p. 298. In the SDKPIL, the number of intellectuals was even smaller: in Radlak's estimation it was roughly seven per cent of the party (Radlak 1979, p. 150).
18  Żarnowska 1965, p. 26 and Кирьянов 1987, p. 177.
19  Surh 1989, p. 241.

workers] would seek out the other for their own purposes; each would be shaped by the encounter', writes Heather Hogan in her monograph on Russia's metalworkers.[20]

Revolutionary politics was not a zero-sum game. More participation by intellectuals did not necessitate less participation by workers – to the contrary, Marxist intellectuals' primary focus was promoting the ever-wider mobilisation and conscious involvement of workers in political life, an arena from which they were generally excluded.

In an imperial polity deeply divided by social class, it was no small feat to have constructed organisations in which wage earners and intellectuals could collectively collaborate as comrades. Numerous socialist parties in the empire, moreover, never experienced any significant internal conflicts over the role of intellectuals. For instance, studies of the Polish Proletariat, the Polish SDKPIL, and the Latvian LSDSP attest to the depth of sustained collaboration in the party and the absence of any significant clashes. In organisations such as the PPS and the Georgian Social Democracy, conflicts over this issue were also relatively rare.[21] Since worker-militants in these currents were not shy about raising their political differences on a host of other issues, this silence in relation to the role of intellectuals is telling. Unless one assumes that all workers in these organisations were simply duped, it can be reasonably concluded that they did not see Marxist intellectuals as an obstacle to their self-emancipation.

Further evidence of the relative marginality of hardened anti-intelligentsia sentiment is the fact that the so-called Machaevists, the one radical current in the empire to make this their central political plank, remained a tiny and isolated grouping. According to the followers of radical Polish intellectual Jan Wacław Machajski, the intelligentsia was a new exploitative class whose material and political interests were contradictory with those of the working class. Social revolution, argued these Machaevists, could only take place if and when workers and peasants broke all ties with the intelligentsia. The main historian of Machajski notes that this vision met with little success: Machaevists 'were able to put forth only a few ephemeral groups in a few towns'.[22]

On the other hand, it is undeniable that various Marxist parties – notably the Bund and the RSDRP – did experience some very sharp conflicts over the role

20 Hogan 1993, p. 38. Surh notes that intelligentsia participation within the workers' movement was not necessarily at odds with proletarian self-activity: workers 'found no inconsistency in the notion that they could aspire to the utmost autonomy and at the same time seek and accept outside help' (Surh 1989, p. 406).
21 Naimark 1979, Radlak 1979, Шалда 1989, Żarnowska 1965, and Jones 2006.
22 Shatz 1989, p. 143.

of intellectuals before 1905. One such moment was captured in a letter from an Odessa Jewish socialist intellectual to her brother: 'There is absolutely nothing to do here. Whoever wants to work goes to another place, since the conditions here are such that any work is impossible. The workers here say: away with the intelligentsia, we will do everything by ourselves'.[23] The precise extent to which such sentiments were shared across Russia is hard to determine. Though factional battles leave a larger paper trail than periods of peaceful cooperation, it does not follow that the latter were the exception. Many participants in these movements recalled that conflicts over the role of intellectuals were marginal at best. 'I never found the workers unfavorable to the intelligentsia. Of course, there were individual cases, but I deny categorically that it was widespread', recalled *Iskra* leader Lydia Dan.[24]

The grievances of worker-militants were rooted in the real inequalities they experienced in social life as well as within the party. Socialist movements were marked by the pressures and norms of society at large. Most obviously, the fact that socialist intellectuals did not face the same material deprivations and exploitative relations as their proletarian comrades often created a reservoir of resentment. This merged easily with a tendency to be sceptical of the political judgement of non-proletarian members. When internal polemics arose between workers and intellectuals, the former could easily (and not necessarily without justification) challenge the opinion of the latter on the grounds that they lacked experience in working-class life.

It should also be also kept in mind that Marxism was fashionable among intellectuals across Russia up through 1905. For more than a few individuals, socialism was seen not as a guide to action for class struggle, but rather as a useful doctrine for analysing social, political, and cultural processes. Others were drawn to the socialist movement primarily out of anti-autocratic sentiment rather than a commitment to workers' struggles per se. A sense of this dynamic was manifest in the recollection of activist Nikolay Valentinov:

> With the optimism of youth we had been searching for a formula that offered hope, and we found it in Marxism. ... Marxism held out the promise that we would not stay a semi-Asiatic country, but would become part of the West with its culture, institutions, and attributes of a free political system.[25]

---

23   Cited in Shtakser 2007, p. 161.
24   Haimson 1987, p. 81.
25   Valentinov 1968, p. 23.

76

Instances of socialist intellectuals dropping their former radicalism added fuel to suspicion and bitterness. So too did Tsarism's unequal policy of repression. Working-class socialists captured by the gendarmes were generally subjected to worse punishment than their educated comrades, whose personal and family connections often provided some form of protection. And idolisation of educated socialists could quickly turn into its opposite. Jewish worker B.A. Breslav recalled that 'when I came into close contact with the intelligentsia in prison and exile, my initial idealization fast disappeared, and a strong reaction even set in against my original enthusiasm'.[26]

Above all, it was the intelligentsia's disproportionate weight in the movement's leadership that created the sharpest frictions. The fact that upper-class members had received an educational training gave them an ability to shape party policy disproportionate to their numbers. Even more importantly, they had more free time for political activity due to their profession, family support, or inheritance. In such a context, intellectuals were almost always over-represented inside party leadership structures. Workers in a Menshevik committee raised a common complaint: 'We want to be the masters in our workers' party, we don't want to carry out only the technical functions in it. It's time to bring an end to playing godparent, which has become such an established practice in the party that *intelligenty* easily make a career in it'.[27]

There was certainly evidence to substantiate such assertions, at least as it pertained to the top leadership structures of the Russian party. At the 1903 RSDRP Second Congress, for instance, only five per cent of the delegates were workers. Such disparities, however, were lower in its regional and local leadership structures. On a local level, where the overwhelming majority of party members operated, intellectuals tended to be in a minority in the coordinating structures. For instance, between 1897 and 1906, 67 per cent of the Bund's top leaders had received some form of higher education; yet among the second-level leadership, this number was only 33 per cent.[28]

Proletarian resentment towards socialist intellectuals was also fundamentally rooted in and validated by Marxism's heavy emphasis on the importance of the working class. Contemporary socialists such as Perl, and various scholars since, have noted that the very sense of class consciousness and class pride promoted by Marxist parties often rebounded internally against non-proletarian socialists – including the very individuals who helped politi-

---

26    Cited in Shatz 1989, p. 65.
27    Cited in Smith 1999, p. 193.
28    Elwood 1970, p. 297 and Woodhouse and Tobias 1966, pp. 344–5.

cise worker-members in the first place. And since all parties insisted that their organisations and leaderships should be as proletarian as possible, it was understandable that any perceived discrepancy between theory and practice could become the subject of sharp disputes.[29]

Like today's debates over gender and race, conflicts over the relationship between workers and intellectuals were the result of prevailing ideological conceptions, real demographic limitations in the movement, as well as factional initiatives to discredit political opponents. The complexities of the relationship between an individual's social location and their particular political perspective were not easy to navigate. All Marxists agreed that class relations shaped views and behaviour. At the same time, they saw that individuals from various backgrounds could become conscious Marxists and it was evident that not all workers shared the same political perspectives.

Conflicts over the role of intellectuals were almost always linked to broader political and organisational divergences. 'Worker opposition [to the intelligentsia] posed a serious threat only at those times when the socialist movement was undergoing organizational and tactical changes. Otherwise it remained only an irritant, albeit a persistent one', notes Ezra Mendelhson's study of the Jewish social democratic movement.[30] Marxist debates over whether to stress economic or political struggle in particular brought with them a flurry of anti-intelligentsia invective. Advocates of emphasising politics were subject to harsh critique since their stance downplayed the importance of workplace organising and specifically proletarian demands. In his memoir, Semen Kanatchikov recalls why he and other worker-militants in Saratov supported the stance of the *Rabochee Delo* current against those SDs who placed an exclusive focus on politics:

> We were pushed toward that position by the negative attitude of many prominent Social Democrats toward economic questions, and their inclination toward 'pure politics.' 'First let's overthrow the autocracy,' they would say, 'let's win our political freedom, and then we can see to your petty, material interests.' This negative and contemptuous attitude toward the workers' economic struggle offended us. We would then shift the disagreement to the arena of the relations between the workers and the intelligentsia, and we would attack the intelligentsia with harsh words.[31]

---

29   Perl 1894, p. 3 and Wildman 1967, pp. 108, 115, and 118.
30   Mendelsohn 1965, p. 282.
31   Kanatchikov 1929 [1986], pp. 204–5.

Rank-and-file opposition to the SDs' refusal to sanction individual terrorism against capitalists and state officials similarly led to sharp conflicts. In Berdichev, one working-class Bundist reported to a meeting that 'workers demanded that the *intelligents* be expelled from the leadership. Their reasons were that the leadership of the intelligentsia represses their initiative, that they [workers] cannot sufficiently prove themselves and that the intelligentsia is taking control of the movement and leaves no space for others to prove their abilities'. But when asked whether there were any tactical differences involved, the militant admitted that 'the workers' opposition ... supported economic terror and the Bund organization forbade participating in terror'.[32]

Debates over the intelligentsia were most heated at moments of factional struggle. Revolutionary social democracy's conception that socialist opportunism was in large part the result of middle-class contamination facilitated intelligentsia-baiting. Perl observed that it was rather 'easy to exploit resentment against intellectuals for demagogic purposes'.[33] Stučka similarly wrote that 'hounding against the intelligentsia is a quite ugly method, especially when it is used by intellectuals'.[34] That worker-militants were almost always found on all sides during internal and inter-party conflicts did not often deter the respective factions from claiming exclusive possession of the 'truly proletarian' mantle.

The problem of intellectual over-representation in party leaderships was widely acknowledged by Marxists, but there were no quick or simple solutions to resolving it. Attempts to completely exclude intellectuals from an organisation were exceedingly rare. Even Machaevists conceded that intellectuals who fully understood, and openly denounced, the exploitative role of the intelligentsia would be allowed to participate in their movement.[35]

To promote worker participation and leadership, various Marxist parties instituted forms of what we would now call affirmative action. To encourage proletarian participation, for instance, the Georgian SDs established stricter membership requirements for intellectuals than for workers.[36] Another common practice – implemented by the Polish Proletariat, the early Bund, and many pre-Iskra RSDRP committees – was to establish dual party organisations, one for workers, another for intellectuals. The rationale for such a structure was that it would allow workers to direct their own affairs, build their self-

32    Cited Shtakser 2007, pp. 166–7.
33    Perl 1894, p. 3.
34    Cited in Dauge 1958, p. 432. Subsequent historiography has confirmed that radical intellectuals were often the most vociferous intelligentsia-baiters (Avrich 1967, p. 49).
35    Halfin 2000, p. 189.
36    Jones 2005, p. 207.

confidence, and gain critical leadership skills. Intellectuals would take on only the secondary role of suppliers of propaganda and literature.

Other Marxist currents rejected such dual structures, arguing that contrary to their intended purpose they tended to reify a division of labour in which intellectuals were the thinkers and workers the 'do-ers' in the movement. *Iskra*, in particular, went on a sharp campaign to establish joint committees. In response to a query from a Georgian SD, *Iskra* leaders explained that their current 'completely rejects any distinction among SDs between *intelligenty* and workers'; leadership should pass to the 'most conscious and developed elements, regardless of whether they come from the workers or other classes or social strata'.[37]

It was hardly the case, as Abraham Ascher has claimed, that Lenin's conception of the party 'implied a commitment to permanent tutelage of the proletariat by the intelligentsia'.[38] To the contrary, Iskraists underestimated the difficulties in recruiting and promoting worker-leaders.[39] Their turn of the century campaign for joint committees, combined with their insistence on moving away from a focus on workplace struggle, created a significant amount of rank-and-file resentment and undercut efforts to integrate a new proletarian layer into the party leadership. In the course of 1905, top Bolsheviks – including Lenin – saw the need to drop their former 'class-blind' conception of building leadership. Instead, they now began instead to advocate forms of affirmative action to promote promising but unseasoned worker-militants to positions of responsibility.[40]

These ongoing internal debates ultimately reflected the fact that the Marxist movement could not immediately overcome society's prevailing division of labour. If it were possible for radical movements to have built islands of socialism within a sea of capitalism, there would have been no need for collective struggle and organisation to end class domination and the multifarious hierarchical relations that it engendered. Grappling with internal movement inequities was necessary, but instruments to overcome the old world could not be expected to fully prefigure the world-to-be.

---

37  Cited in Smith 1999, p. 186.
38  Ascher 1972, pp. 177–8.
39  Cited in Lih 2006, p. 421.
40  See, for example, Lih 2006, pp. 272, 531, 540–3.

## 2      Intellectuals and Workers (1905–17)

Revolutionary social democrats consistently sought to build parties of and
for workers, reflecting their commitment to a strategy of working-class self-
emancipation. This task was difficult in periods of political calm, when working
people tended to focus on their personal and familial affairs. But when workers
surged to the centre of political life, especially in 1905 and then again in 1917,
hundreds of thousands of them chose to join socialist parties and many millions of others followed their lead. That liberals and mainstream nationalists
generally garnered no analogous support underscores the extent of the elective affinity between imperial Russia's workers and the politics of the empire's
Marxist parties. Analyses that divorce political discourse from broader social
relations, or that assert an inherent antagonism between workers and socialist
intellectuals, cannot begin to make sense of such developments.

Across the empire, the experience of the 1905 revolution contradicts claims
that there was an insurmountable social abyss or perpetual political conflict
between the working class and intellectuals. As Gerald Surh has demonstrated,
'1905 was on the whole a period of rapprochement between workers and intelligentsia'.[41] With the notable exception of Finland – where the intelligentsia
remained generally hostile to socialism – such a dynamic was manifest inside
most Marxist parties as well as within the broader revolutionary movement.

This deepening alliance was reflected in, and made possible by, the political hegemony of radical socialism among both workers and the intelligentsia.
Though older intellectuals inclined towards liberal or progressive-democratic
politics, socialist students and teachers in 1905 were the most prominent wing
of the intelligentsia in the majority of imperial Russia's regions. Marxist borderland parties were hegemonic among urban and rural teachers (though not university professors). Within central Russia, the Socialist Revolutionaries reigned
supreme in the teachers' movement and its newly formed union, the All-
Russian Union of Teachers and Workers in Public Education. And revolutionary
socialist predominance was particularly deep amongst students. Samuel Kassow's empire-wide study of the student movement during the 1905 revolution
observes that 'the *studenchestvo* believed liberal politics connoted cowardice
and surrender'.[42]

The orientation of Marxists within the student movement was succinctly
articulated by the Union of Socialist Youth in Poland: 'Today, for both workers

---

41      Surh 1989, p. 241.
42      Kassow 1989, p. 251. Even in St. Petersburg, the city in the empire where liberals had their
         strongest presence, Surh notes that 'the attractiveness of the socialist parties to that part

and for the intelligentsia the place to gather is under the red flag of socialism ... Let us join with the struggle of the working class'.[43] This political project was facilitated in practice by the youthfulness of the revolutionary movement, as radical youth of all social backgrounds played a critical role in breaking down the divide between workers and intellectuals across Russia. Young workers, a Polish socialist publication typically noted, were 'the flower of the working class'.[44]

The mobilisation and radicalisation of wage earners and intellectuals fed off of each other throughout the year. All throughout the empire the high point of their convergence came in late 1905 when students occupied the universities and opened them to workers and revolutionary organisations, transforming them into public centres for mass assemblies, popular education, and the performances of radical plays, poetry, and music. A study of Kharkov recounts the impact of this joint student-labour activity:

> The great rallies of that month 'wrought profound psychological changes in the Russian working class', according to one official. Workers came face to face with students and *intelligenty*, who treated them as equals and even with deference. Social barriers tumbled into a common cause, into a cascade of demands for immediate and fundamental reform.[45]

But all this evaporated after 1905. After the Tsarist state crushed the popular upheaval in late 1905 and throughout 1906, a period of reaction set in that radically altered worker-intelligentsia relations. Disillusionment with the working class spread across intellectuals of all nationalities, as the failure of the revolution led many activists to conclude that their previous hopes in the power of the proletariat had been misplaced.

The old question of worker-intelligentsia relations within socialist organisations soon became a decidedly secondary concern for the simple reason that so few intellectuals remained. In a pattern that was widely repeated throughout Russia, top leaders of the Muslim *Gummet* – including its founder Mammad Amin Rasulzadeh – turned away from social democracy and became left-

---

of "student youth" that was politically active in 1905 was overwhelming, and constituted one the revolutionaries' great secret resources in the conquest of the masses' (Surh 1989, p. 258).

43    Cited in Kmiecik 1980, p. 213.
44    Samuś 2013, p. 317.
45    Cited in Hamm 2002, p. 63.

nationalists. Historian Ismail Agakishiyev notes that 'some of the members of the party began to look for other paths to freedom' after the 'workers did not meet [their] expectations'.[46]

One leading Ukrainian journalist vividly expressed the newfound demoralisation he shared with his intellectual milieu:

> As if a dream, the years of struggle for freedom have passed away and taken everything with it: hope and everything that one's soul had become so accustomed to within the short period of the liberation movement. ... Really, it is frightening to feel the will to live in one's self and yet not be able to live; it is frightening to lie down into a coffin alive.[47]

The Bund's 1910 report to the International lamented the 'mass exodus of intellectuals from party work' following 'the collapse of hopes for victory of the revolution'.[48] This pattern was repeated in all socialist parties within Russia. Students as well as teachers made a sharp turn away from radical politics. In her memoir, Latvian Marxist Klāra Kalniņa recalled that the 'youth, in particular the students, became passive. They lost their strong confidence and faith in humanity and the victory of the revolution, they did not believe in anything anymore'.[49]

This empire-wide 'flight of the intelligentsia' exacerbated the internal crises and decline of organised socialism. Local party committees decried the absence of militants able to write articles or organise study groups, resulting in ineffectiveness or paralysis. Some parties collapsed and vanished for good. In others, this vacuum was partially filled by a new layer of relatively inexperienced worker-activists. A 1909 police report in Latvia, for example, observed that 'currently in the party all the work is carried out by the workers themselves'.[50]

Though some intellectuals continued to participate in Marxist movements, the hegemony of revolutionary socialism inside of the intelligentsia was done for good. Among those individuals who did not fully retreat into their own private affairs after the 1905 revolution's defeat, many joined cultural, liberal, or nationalist organisations. Such milieus and parties often maintained (or established) personal and political ties with those socialists that made a shift to

---

46      Агакишиев 1991, p. 222.

47      Cited in Szuch 1985, pp. 30–1.

48      'Доклад о деятельности Бунда' [1910] in Савицкий 1997, p. 338.

49      Kalniņa 1964, p. 78. For this dynamic in the Lithuanian LSDP, see Sabaliūnas 1990, p. 95.

50      Cited in Шалда and Спруте 1992, p. 63.

the right after 1905, including the Mensheviks, the Jewish Bund, and the PPS-Revolutionary Faction in Poland, as well as much of the Ukrainian USDRP.

Marxist organisations that upheld the radical class struggle traditions of 1905 – such as the Polish SDKPIL, the PPS-Left, and the Bolsheviks – became particularly cut off from the intelligentsia. To quote Jewish Bolshevik cadre Cecilia Bobrovskaya: 'The intellectuals no longer placed their apartments at [our] disposal. The lawyers and doctors had ceased to sympathize with us. We Bolsheviks were not fashionable, for we had "failed".[51] Faced with this context, Bolshevik committees dropped *Iskra*'s former approach to party leadership, choosing now to take affirmative action to bring worker-militants into leadership even if they lacked much experience or political education.[52]

In contrast with the often intense pre-1905 hand-wringing about the role of intellectuals among underground socialists, the emergence of mass parties, unions, and soviets during 1905 and again in 1917 made it possible for imperial Russia's socialists to more clearly measure the extent to which they and their rivals actually represented workers, without having to impute this from discourse. After the Tsar's overthrow, hundreds of thousands of workers surged into socialist parties. While moderate socialists were able to consolidate and expand their proletarian base in regions like Georgia and Poland, over the course of 1917 workers tended to increase the organised strength of radicals in central Russia, Baku, Latvia, Estonia, and urban Ukraine. Among the Bolsheviks, notes Edward Acton, 'a clear majority of members were workers, with a substantial minority of soldiers and sailors, while members of the intelligentsia were relegated to a small minority. ... Far from being an exclusive clique of radical intellectuals, the Bolshevik party had become a mass workers' party'.[53]

This proletarianisation was manifest not only in the membership as a whole, but even the very top leadership level of Bolshevism. Most significantly, 52 per cent of the Bolshevik Central Committee members between 1917 and 1922 were from proletarian or peasant backgrounds. On a city-wide level, this percentage went up to 75 per cent or more.[54] In Finland, the intelligentsia remained overwhelmingly hostile towards, or wary of, the workers' movement in 1917–18. As one Finnish-Swedish conservative writer observed, 'the whole "intelligentsia"' saw the difference between a 'Western state of culture, law and order, and the

---

51    Cited in Elwood 1974, p. 64. To my knowledge, the only major SD organisation that maintained its hegemony over the politicised intelligentsia after 1905 was the Georgian Social Democracy.
52    See, for example, Stalin 1909 [1953–55], p. 156.
53    Acton 1990, pp. 193–4.
54    Smith 1999, p. 202 and Mandel 1984a, p. 253.

Eastern chaos of Russia'. Accordingly it insisted in 1917 that 'Finland must be plucked from out of the whirlpool of the Russian revolution'.[55]

Elsewhere in the empire, previously inactive socialist intellectuals returned to Left political activity after February 1917, but they generally did so without their previous confidence in the working class. In sharp contrast with 1905, only a small minority of intellectuals after the overthrow of the Tsar in February supported the fight for proletarian hegemony – by this time, liberals, nationalists, and right-leaning social democrats of various persuasions predominated inside the intelligentsia. Unlike their radical Marxist rivals, none of these currents thought that working people in Russia were capable of seizing and wielding state power for progressive social transformation. Attempts to rule without the bourgeoisie, they felt, could only lead to counter-revolution, civil war, and anarchy. For liberals, this lack of confidence in the working class was nothing new. But its pervasiveness among socialist intellectuals in 1917 constituted a major shift away from the traditions of 1905. Throughout 1917, the dominant criticism raised by radical workers against the intelligentsia was not that it lorded over the labour movement, but that it had abandoned it.

A Menshevik article in March voiced the prevailing worry about the spectre of Russia's undisciplined lower classes: 'a people that had lived in slavery for centuries could not suddenly become free and restrained'.[56] David Mandel's study of moderate socialist intellectuals during 1917 demonstrates that 'this fear of the *stikhia* – the "elemental", "benighted", "uncultured", "anarchistic" masses – is a basic motif in all the[ir] statements'.[57] Ukraine's leading Marxist party was similarly marked by such anxieties. In a self-critique of his party's class collaborationism, Volodymyr Vynnychenko of the Ukrainian USDRP later acknowledged that this approach arose to a significant extent because 'we were afraid of the "dark instincts" of the masses, we were frightened by their great simplicity, we lacked, moreover, sufficient enthusiasm. ... It was a major mistake and failure'.[58]

Analogous worries about working people were central to the politics of liberals of various non-Russian nationalities. Latvian left-liberals in May 1917, for example, argued that the revolution was threatened by the excesses of 'the dark millions of people who [are] completely unprepared for a Parliamentary life ...

55    Söderhjelm 1919, p. 87.
56    Cited in Galili y Garcia 1989, p. 144.
57    Mandel 1984b, p. 83.
58    Винниченко 1920, Vol. 1, p. 129. In fact, armed Ukrainian students played a determining role in crushing the attempts by Kiev's workers and Bolsheviks to seize power in early 1918 (Солдатенко 2007, p. 214).

It is sad to talk about the grave of freedom. But the anarchistic deeds of our day are digging the grave of our liberty!'[59]

Believing that workers and peasants in Russia 1917 were not yet sufficiently educated and organised to rule, the intelligentsia in most regions overwhelmingly opposed the October Revolution and the fight for soviet power. Many non-socialist intellectuals, particularly in central Russia, became disillusioned with democracy as such, even in the form of a Constituent Assembly elected by universal suffrage. Russian historian Lev Protasov has documented the intelligentsia's 'disenchantment with the prospects of popular rule in Russia' by late 1917: 'For the intelligentsia, the triumph of democracy had turned into a triumph of mob rule'.[60]

Given the subsequent descent of Russia into chaos, civil war, and Stalinism, it may appear that the fears of these intellectuals were vindicated. According to Bruno Naarden, the 'disastrous developments after 1917 were to show what would happen if state and society had to manage without the bourgeois elite'.[61] It is certainly true that the collapse of Russia's economic, social, and political institutions accelerated after the October Revolution. Running a state machine in a context of war and economic free fall proved to be significantly more difficult than anticipated.

But Naarden's critique obscures the extent to which the intelligentsia, by failing to support radical social transformation, itself facilitated Russia's tragic trajectory. In central Russia, this opposition took the form of opposing or actively sabotaging the new Soviet regime. In the borderlands, this was expressed generally through initiatives to secede from Russia under the aegis of a foreign power.

Vynnychenko's self-critique of the Ukrainian Social Democracy asked the key question: 'Wouldn't it have been better to have gone with the masses?'[62]

---

59    Cited in Ezergailis 1974, p. 216.
60    Protasov 2004, p. 260. Georgia constitutes a partial exception to this pattern. Here the intelligentsia continued to be overwhelmingly moderate socialist in composition and it maintained hegemony over the Georgian working class during and after 1917. This was only a partial exception, however, since the decision of the Georgian SDs to secede from Russia was directly tied to their fear of the 'anarchy' of Russian working people. Poland also did not completely fit with this pattern, since the leadership of the PPS-FR after 1914 was able to rebuild – and maintain – a strong (if far from uncontested) base among Polish workers. The PPS-FR's separatist orientation was longstanding, and thus constituted less of a break from past tradition in comparison with the Georgian Social Democracy.
61    Naarden 1992, p. 240.
62    Cited in Солдатенко 2007, p. 184.

As David Mandel notes, the scepticism of moderate socialist intellectuals was to a certain extent a self-fulfilling prophecy:

> Certainly, the generally low level of culture, especially political culture, was an important factor in the progressive elimination of soviet and party democracy and the ultimate rise of Stalin. But one must also ask if the [non-revolutionary] socialist intelligentsia, of course with important exceptions, did not help to ensure by its own actions that its fears would come true. ... Would it not have been more rational, even from their own point of view, as the bearers of culture, to throw in their lot with the masses and try to have at least some influence on the movement that was rolling forward with or without them?[63]

From the standpoint of moving towards democratic rule, the relevant problem in imperial Russia was not Marxism's supposed advocacy of intelligentsia tutelage over workers, but rather the post-1905 intelligentsia's doubts about the 'dark masses'. Contrary to the claims of anti-Communist historians, intellectuals generally played constructive roles in fomenting class formation up through 1905 and in the following years it was their under-representation in the mass workers' movement, rather than their alleged dominance over it, that proved to be most politically consequential.

It was precisely because orthodox SDs focused on building an independent workers' movement that the role of intellectuals had become a periodic cause of concern, though one that became less acute in Russia from 1905 onwards once workers began to predominate internally and once the emergence of mass politics made it easier to assess the rootedness of competing political currents. This confidence in the political capacities of workers – and a consistent strategic focus on organising the working class to speak in its own name – differentiated revolutionary social democrats not only from currents to their right, but also from recent generations of radicals for whom organised labour is, at best, just one good movement among many.

While the disputes described in this chapter were often similar in form to present-day polemics over identity, the debate on worker-intelligentsia relations had distinct strategic and practical ramifications. Working-class politics carried with it a particular emphasis on *uniting* working people independently of, and against, capitalists and ruling-class politicians. Moreover, because

---

63    Mandel 1984b, pp. 85–6.

this strategy hinged on bringing together individuals with few economic or social resources, it necessarily placed an especially high premium on building *organisation*. For this reason, in the era of the Second International many socialists came to understand that the actual representativity of contending activists and currents was best measured by whether or not they led organised mass constituencies and the relative strength of their organisations.

Such a focus on organising, as we will see in the following chapters, meant that socialist parties not only shaped the working class, they were also shaped by it. Often, this bottom-up influence was directly expressed through worker-militants in local and top-level party leaderships or intra-party deliberations. But the political agency of broader layers of working people also manifested itself indirectly through granting, or withholding, support to parties and their organising initiatives. In all corners of imperial Russia, many of the major tactical and strategic evolutions of organised Marxists were pragmatic responses to their successes or setbacks in cohering a socialist workers' movement. Class formation was always a two-way street.

CHAPTER 4

# Organisation, Mass Action, and Electoral Work

This chapter compares labour organisation and socialist strategy in underground Russia and parliamentary Finland to examine how governmental regimes shape working-class politics. How did the relative degree of political freedom determine the structure of social democratic parties? And how did socialists in different political contexts strategically prioritise building working-class organisation, promoting electoral and parliamentary work, or participating in disruptive actions such as strikes and protests?

On the first question, I contest the prevailing accounts of Bolshevik exceptionalism. Academic and activist historians have frequently claimed that the defining feature of the Bolshevik Party was its supposedly unique organisational structure. According to historian Geoffrey Swain, the essence of Bolshevism for Lenin was building a hierarchical and strictly centralised organisational structure: 'Party organisation was principal'. In Swain's view, the 'true Bolshevik form of party organisation was finally imposed on the party by Lenin in 1921'.[1] Many Marxists share a similar analysis – though they invert the negative and positive signs – by treating the so-called 'Leninist' organisational model as an essential bedrock for socialist success. An often-rigid organisational practice, based on a narrow conception of 'democratic centralism', became central to Stalinist and Trotskyist organisations alike throughout the twentieth century.[2]

Taking an empire-wide look at the underground Marxist parties of imperial Russia shows why it makes little sense to define Bolshevism by its organisational approach. All orthodox Marxists in Europe and Russia saw that conditions of absolutism precluded building a mass legal workers' movement along the lines of Western Europe's main socialist parties. Only in the exceptional case of Finland, with its legalised labour movement, was such an approach plausible in imperial Russia. Since Tsarism forced most socialists to operate illegally, a distinct type of structure was obviously needed.

Many organisational features that have long been portrayed as distinctly 'Leninist' – tight discipline, centralised leadership, professional revolutionaries, and the use of a newspaper as a collective organiser – were longstanding and widespread components of underground Marxist parties across the

---

1  Swain 1983, pp. xiv, 95. For a recent iteration, see Cohen 2017.
2  Post 2013, pp. 2, 6, 8–9, 14.

empire. Each of the illegal socialist organisations under Tsarism structurally resembled Bolshevism far more than the German Social Democracy. Moreover, police state conditions made it very difficult in practice for the empire's social democrats to consolidate themselves organisationally – goals of tight party centralisation were rarely implemented on the ground.

When open public activity and democratic functioning became possible in late 1905 and again after February 1917, almost all parties rapidly adopted organisational forms that were a far cry from their previous practices in the underground. I will show that, contrary to longstanding myths about the 'iron discipline' of Russia's radicals, the major organisational impact of autocratic rule upon socialists was that it made their party structures unconsolidated, decentralised, and fluid.

Without consolidated mass organisations – and in the absence of a legitim-ate parliamentary body – both workers and socialists across Russia focused on mass action to an unparalleled degree. The autocratic context obliged a distinct tactical emphasis from the German SPD's focus on strengthening working-class consciousness and organisation through legal, often electoral, means.

In Finland, unlike central Russia, such an approach *was* both possible and necessary. In a dynamic described by Walter Korpi as 'the democratic class struggle', where political opportunities existed for emphasising organisation building and electoral politics, it was rational for workers and their repres-entatives to seize them.[3] The experience of the Finnish Social Democracy, moreover, undermines claims that Kautsky's revolutionary social democratic strategy consisted of fatalistic parliamentarism masked by Marxist verbiage. This remains the dominant account not only of German socialism, but of Fin-land's movement as well.[4] Such conflations of Kautsky's strategy with moderate socialism, and the facile equation of Finnish and German Social Democracy, cannot help explain why the Finnish SDs overthrew capitalist rule in 1917–18 while the German party actively upheld it.

One should not assume that the mass action orientation appropriate in autocratic Russia could have been exactly replicated in parliamentary regimes like Finland or Germany. It is true that Kautsky's stress on the dangers of premature action in Germany dovetailed with the excessive tactical cautious-ness of the party and union leaderships. But not all those who advocated patiently accumulating forces for the 'final blow' were masking accomodation-ism with radical rhetoric or endlessly postponing action to a distant horizon.

---

3  Korpi 1983 and Vössing 2017.
4  Heikkilä 1993, p. 388.

Finland shows that it *was* possible for orthodox Marxists in parliamentary conditions to take decisive revolutionary action. As an empire-wide view demonstrates, there was no context-free socialist formula for effectively prioritising mass action, electioneering, or organisation building.

## 1 Socialist Organisation in Finland

As a point of comparison with the illegal socialist parties in Tsarist Russia, it may be helpful to begin by discussing the anomalous example of Finnish socialism. Due to its exceptional degree of national autonomy and political freedom, Finland was frequently treated by socialists and the Russian state alike as almost a separate country. Unlike every other socialist group in the empire, the Finnish Social Democracy operated as a legal, above-ground party. Social Democracy in Finland and Germany was similar in many ways: massively influential workers' parties were built up on the basis of a legalistic and parliamentary-oriented tactic of patiently educating and organising the proletariat.

Like Germany's Social Democracy, early Finnish socialists placed a particular stress on remaining within legal limits. This similarity cannot be explained primarily by a shared ideology, as the Finnish labour movement adopted this cautious approach well before it sought to emulate the German SPD's political-organisational model. Above all, this structural likeness reflected shared responses to comparably repressive political regimes.

It is crucial to underline that Germany and Finland were among the most anti-democratic and restrictive of Europe's polities. In both nations, civil liberties were sufficient to allow for a legal labour movement, but censorship restrictions were strong, and selective state repression of workers' leaders was consistent enough to impress upon workers and especially labour leaders a legitimate fear that their organisations would be disbanded at any moment were they to transgress the bounds allowed by the regime. While electoral campaigns and parliamentary debates provided an unmatched platform to spread the socialist gospel, the policy making powers of legislative bodies were seriously constrained by the imperial state.

This semi-authoritarian context created tactical dilemmas regarding repression for Finnish and German socialists that their counterparts in freer countries in Western Europe did not face to the same extent. At the same time, the restricted nature of democracy in Germany and Finland meant that the pull of practical parliamentary politics was significantly lower. In such a 'low inclusion' polity, it made sense to most organised workers and socialists to stress class intransigence and accumulate strength for the final battle, rather than throw the dice on risky mass actions or get mired in compromises in parliaments whose decisions could get easily overruled.[5] Marxist politics thus took on a strongly educationalist ethos, in which the accent was on building an organised proletarian subculture and patiently spreading the 'good word' of socialism, rather than focusing on promoting mass actions or winning immediate parliamentary reforms.

Though it eventually proved to be less relevant for regimes that were qualitatively more democratic or more authoritarian, the 'tried and tested' stance was remarkably effective in both Finland and Germany. By the eve of World War One, the German SPD had amassed around one million members, making it the largest socialist party in the world. It built up a dense subculture based around independent proletarian political, social, and cultural associations, from unions to sports leagues to singing groups. Like its electoral apparatus, its press machine was legion: local German socialist newspapers alone amassed a circulation of over a million by 1909.[6]

The dynamic was similar in Finland, though parliamentary campaigns only became possible after 1905. Reflecting a rational fear of Tsarist repression, as well as the virtual absence of orthodox Marxists in the early Finnish movement, any mention of socialism was at first purposefully avoided.[7] The initial title of the organisation adopted at its 1899 founding congress was the Finnish Workers Party – only four years later did the party change its name, to become the Finnish Social Democratic Party (SDP).

In sharp contrast with its illegal counterparts, the Finnish SDP built a massive network of organisational and cultural institutions, based around hundreds of urban and rural workers' halls.[8] Early party tactics consisted largely of educating workers through the press and building a strong proletarian organisational infrastructure, with an emphasis on cultural activities.

Clinging to its tenuous legality, the Finnish party from 1899 onwards manifest a strong legalism that eschewed tactics or policies that could potentially lead to the party's suppression. As Finnish historian Antti Kujala notes, 'nowhere in the Russian Empire ... was there another socialist party which was

---

5   On Germany's degree of democracy from an international comparative perspective, see Vössing 2008, pp. 184–224.
6   For a general overview of the SPD, see Steenson 1981.
7   See Marzec and Turunen 2018 for a useful comparison of the Finnish and Polish socialist movements.
8   Upton 1980, p. 10.

so moderate'.[9] The early Finnish party did not call for revolution, nor did it even call for a gradual working-class conquest of power. The main political demand raised was universal suffrage.[10]

The cautious approach of Edward Valpas – the leftist editor of the party's Helsinki daily newspaper *Työmies* (Worker) – was manifest in his stance on the national question. Since 1899, a national movement in Finland had arisen to resist the Tsarist government's efforts to roll back Finnish autonomy. As long as the workers' movement limited itself to propaganda and criticisms of the Finnish ruling class, the Tsarist regime tolerated it. But in 1903 and 1904, the deepening of the state's Russification campaign and the growth of the movement in defence of Finnish autonomy significantly narrowed the legal space granted to organised labour. Faced with a possible shutdown of *Työmies*, Valpas decided to do everything possible to conform to the new strict regulations.[11]

In response to increasing Tsarist repression and Russification during 1903–04, some tendencies of the Finnish workers' movement turned to illegal work – including the underground distribution of revolutionary literature and collecting arms for anti-Tsarist groups across imperial Russia. Such 'worker-activists', however, were the exception.

One major aspect of the Finnish party's cautious approach, particularly before 1905, was its lack of an empire-wide political perspective and its organisational disconnect from the empire's other socialist parties. To quote Kujala: 'The Party's ideology was not nationalistic at all but in action it was very ethnocentric. ... The existence of autonomy and political freedoms placed the Finns in a different position than all the other inhabitants of the Russian Empire who had *less to lose with revolution*'.[12]

Whereas underground militants elsewhere in Tsarist Russia generally advocated an empire-wide revolution, the early SDP pushed only for political demands affecting Finland proper. The Finnish socialist leadership understood that tying its activities to illegal anti-Tsarist parties could jeopardise the party's legal status.[13]

---

9    Kujala 1989, p. 326. On the early Finnish socialist movement, see also Kujala 1996 and Soikkanen 1961.
10   Before 1906, most workers, male and female, were not allowed to vote in elections to the Finnish Parliament.
11   Kujala 1996, p. 53.
12   Kujala 1989, pp. 324, 326, my emphasis.
13   One of the hallmarks of the party's left wing from 1904 onwards was its push to link up the Finnish working class with the empire-wide revolutionary struggle and Russian socialists in particular.

This caution also coloured how Finnish socialists approached mass strike action. Like Kautsky, Finnish socialists supported local labour strikes, but viewed general strikes as a potentially important but risky tactic. Such a measure, they argued, required a long period of preliminary organisational and educational build-up and it should only be used as a last resort. In 1899, Finnish socialist party leader Taavi Tainio thus explained that a general strike could be a useful tool down the road, but that it required many years of preparatory work to have any chance of success. Along similar lines, Edvard Valpas took a very sceptical stance on the short- and mid-term potential for general strikes in Finland. Because so many workers remained unorganised, he argued, such an action would easily be defeated. Only by first building strong trade unions would it be possible to organise a successful mass strike.[14] The experience of 1905 would shake up this conception for socialists not only in Finland, but across the Russian Empire and abroad.

## 2      Illegal Organising in Tsarist Russia

While political freedoms and legal labour organisations predominated in Finland, illegality was the norm for the rest of Russia's socialists. The empire's social democrats thus went down a very different path than their above-ground counterparts in Europe's parliamentary states. It was not difficult to see that key organisational features of Western Europe's mass socialist parties were inapplicable for a context of absolutist rule. Nor could Russia's socialists utilise electoral politics to build up their movements and organisations.

The Polish Proletariat, like subsequent generations of socialists in Russia, argued that open political activity was of course preferable to underground work, but that the latter was necessary when conditions allowed no other option.[15] 'We would like to breathe in the daylight, but we know how to work in the dark', noted one Latvian SD leader.[16]

At no point in the pre-war years did the Bolsheviks or borderland socialists argue that their form of party organisation should be replicated by revolutionaries in Germany or the rest of Europe. Rosa Luxemburg offers an illuminating case, especially because her views on party-building have so often been mistakenly counterposed to those of Lenin. Luxemburg's SDKPIL in Tsarist Poland

---

14      Heikkinen 1980, pp. 50, 55, 125.
15      Blit 1971, p. 62.
16      Roziņš 1905a [1963–65], p. 46.

shared all of the attributes that are generally said to be the distinct features of
Bolshevism – in fact, her party was consistently more disciplined, top-down,
and politically narrow. Yet during this very same period, Luxemburg did not
seek to transform the German SPD along such lines – nor did she even organise
a distinct political tendency in Germany until after 1914.[17]

In the face of the Russian police state, socialists could not attempt to build
up the dense organisational infrastructure and proletarian subculture of the
large Western social democratic parties, with their electoral campaigns, associated trade unions, workers' halls, cultural associations, and sports leagues.
Russia's underground SDs were obliged to improvise new methods to agitate
and organise workers despite the repressive conditions.

Without freedom of the press or association, and without the right to vote,
both workers and socialists turned to strikes and demonstrations to an unprecedented degree. Despite the very low level of labour organisation in imperial
Russia, proletarian upsurges shook the empire from the mid-1890s onwards. A
few statistics give a sense of this dynamic. Half of all Jewish industrial workers in the empire were involved in a strike between 1895 and 1904, roughly five
times the average percentage of strikers in Germany. According to a recent collective study by Russian scholars, the total number of strikers in Tsarist Russia
from 1895 to 1904 was over 1,343,000.[18] And the curve was clearly ascendant:
from 1895 to 1903, the number of strikes multiplied by 7.5 times. As historian
I.M. Pushkareva has observed, the actions of workers under Tsarism tended to
consistently surge ahead of both their level of organisation and their crystallised political consciousness.[19]

Though the autocratic government experimented at times with allowing
limited forms of collective workers' organisation, it never accepted a fully legalised labour movement. Loosely organised proto-unions in the form of strike
committees or mutual aid associations frequently arose, but they could not survive for long in the face of state and employer repression. This authoritarian
dynamic pushed Russia's labour movement down a distinct trajectory from its
Western counterparts in at least two fundamental ways. First, in the absence
of a legally recognised channel for collective bargaining, socialist parties were
faced with the opportunity and challenge of *directly* promoting workplace
struggles against the employers.

According to most socialists of the era, workplace activity was an arena of
intervention for unions rather than the party. Under the Tsarist state, however,

17    For a full discussion of these questions, see Blanc 2018.
18    Пушкарева 2011, p. 58.
19    Пушкарева 2011, p. 161.

this division of labour between a trade union movement dedicated to economic demands and a socialist party focused on politics was made impossible. Recalling her work promoting strikes in St. Petersburg in the mid 1890s, future Iskraist leader Nadezhda Krupskaya made the following observation:

> The method of agitation based on the workers' everyday needs struck deep root in our Party work. I did not fully appreciate how efficacious this method was until years later, when, living in France as a political emigrant, I observed how, during the great strike of the postal workers in Paris, the French Socialist Party stood completely aloof from it. It was the business of the trade unions, they said. In their opinion the business of a party was only political struggle. They had no clear idea whatever about the necessity of combining the economic with the political struggle.[20]

Secondly, the combination of Tsarist absolutism and high levels of mass militancy obliged imperial Russia's Marxists to engage with working-class spontaneity to an unprecedented extent. Such actions were not leaderless or necessarily uncoordinated – rather they were initiated and led, to greater or lesser degrees, by individuals and groups outside of any formal organisation.

Memoirs from the era are replete with anecdotes of how personal experience in such actions transformed workers' consciousness and confidence. To cite just one example, Fania Chizhevskaya, a young Jewish factory worker in Gomel, recalled the aftermath of being beaten by her bosses for challenging their abuse:

> During the fight all the workers got up and insisted that the factory owner's wife and daughter leave me alone, but they were so infuriated, they did not want to listen. Then Grisha Kagan, a worker from Lodz, ran over and pulled them away, releasing me from these furious wild animals. After recovering from the fight I felt that I was not alone and I felt the power of workers. Until then I thought that the owners could do whatever they wanted with us, but now I knew this was not so.[21]

It is tempting in hindsight to romanticise these spontaneous fightbacks. But there were compelling reasons why all orthodox SDs acknowledged their limit-

20   Krupskaya 1979, p. 19.
21   Cited in Shtakser 2007, pp. 84–5.

ations and why they felt a party was needed to provide them with more organisation, leadership, and purpose. On a local level, strikes were often defeated due to the weaknesses in workers' collective cohesion and coordination. Lacking a structure to represent the entire workforce, for example, various branches of a factory might counterproductively strike at different times, or with different demands.

Much of the drama of the labour movement under Tsarism consisted of attempts by SDs to catch up with the insurgent labour movement and to give it political leadership. Without sufficient preparation, strike funds, or broader organisational support, strikers often could not hold out and were either obliged to return to work defeated or were simply fired. The 1903 general strike in Baku, for instance, floundered from a lack of sufficient organisational and political coordination. The Baku RSDRP Committee reported: 'events overtook the Committee. Old history was repeating itself: organization lags behind the movement'.[22] The limitations of spontaneity were deemed to be even greater in regard to the anti-autocratic struggle, as revolutionaries felt that only a sufficiently concentrated and coordinated attack could topple the regime.

Underground party organisation and agitation likewise differed greatly from Finland and Germany. Given the difficulties of printing and distributing a party newspaper in illegal conditions, mass agitation fliers took on an importance unparalleled elsewhere in Europe. The real propaganda innovation of socialists in Russia was *not* the party newspaper, but rather their novel emphasis on leaflets, which were relatively easier to produce and distribute. Indeed, the average party flier remains our most accurate window into the mass politics promoted by Marxist parties in Russia. Pushkareva estimates that from 1895 through 1904 alone, between 1.7 and 2.2 million copies of leaflets were distributed in Russia.[23]

The absence of political freedom similarly impacted how and where socialists could meet. Assemblies were often held in the forests or countryside outside of the cities, disguised in the form of picnics, and meetings often had no option but to take place in restaurants or bakeries. Bundists, for their part, would organise a *birzhe* (exchange) on a given street or park, guarded by the party defence groups, in which members, sympathisers, and curious workers would meet to debate, share information, and socialise. A vivid description of the *birzhe* was penned by Jewish socialist writer S. Ansky:

22      Cited in Reichman 1977, p. 157.
23      Пушкарева 2011, p. 236.

All these working youngsters who have just left their airless factories, their dingy workshops, their shop counters, with no time to rest and often hungry, walk around here full of life and energy. One cannot but feel that in this compact area, in these few hundred square meters, is concentrated all the spiritual life of the working masses, all the poetry of their existence.[24]

Under absolutism, forms of protest like demonstrations took on especially subversive dimensions. May Day rallies became an important tradition and a test of strength against the regime. One Georgian activist recalled the elation caused in 1900 by the high workers' turnout to the first major May Day demonstration organised in Tiflis:

We were overwhelmed with joy. We cried, we embraced, we believed that there would be no more Tsarism. In the evening, when it was time to separate, we swore that the next year, on the same day, we would again unfurl our flag on the same city streets.[25]

The following year's May Day protest led to clashes with the gendarmes, forty-one arrests, and the military occupation of the centre city. The French consul in Tiflis reported that 'the emotion created in the city by the clash was very high'.[26]

Memoirs by socialists who organised under Tsarism are full of personal anecdotes that would have been unimaginable in conditions of political freedom. To cite one example, Hersh Mendel recalled how the absence of any open workers' parties in Warsaw made it difficult to find out how to join the movement: 'I had heard that socialists wore long hair, black-brimmed hats and black shirts. I took to the streets in search of people who looked like this. I walked around for hours but met nobody to fit this description'.[27] In Warsaw, one of the Polish Socialist Party's first public actions was to float a large wooden raft down the Vistula river covered in a banner of revolutionary slogans – 'Proletarians of all countries, unite!', 'Long live socialist Poland', 'Away with the autocratic government'. These Warsaw activists were immediately arrested afterwards, since gendarmes had infiltrated their local organisation.[28]

---

24    Cited in Frankel 2009, p. 77.
25    Quoted in Woytinsky 1921, p. 58.
26    Report of Alexandre Chayet 12 May 1901. NS 12 (Archives du Ministère des Affaires Étrangères).
27    Mendel 1989, p. 47.
28    Haustein 1969, pp. 140–1.

The stress that socialists in imperial Russia placed on the fight for political freedom reflected more than just a theoretical attachment to Marxist orthodoxy. Tsarist repression incessantly hammered this point home, as illustrated by this early Latvian Marxist proclamation responding to the 1897 incarceration of roughly eighty leading activists: 'The arrests taught us in the most persuasive language possible that one of the most important points in the Latvian Social Democratic programme must be: The overthrow of the tyrannical political order'.[29]

Since absolutism helped radicalise the working class, it is easy in hindsight to downplay its downsides for the development of organised labour. Time and time again, party committees were infiltrated and broken up by the Tsarist secret police. And though precautions were taken to make state infiltration more difficult, SDs realised that there was no way to completely immunise their organisations. Ongoing police repression imposed a strange rhythm to the activities of the empire's Marxists, who had to start their organising efforts virtually from scratch every few months. As the Bolsheviks' 1904 report to the Second International noted, it 'was considered a general rule that members of a local committee could not hold out for more than 3 to 4 months without arrests. It was considered something extraordinary if a party worker was able to work in one place for six to eight months'.[30]

Such a dynamic made it difficult to build a solid party infrastructure or cement a broad organisational base in the working class. Further damage was done by the regime's periodic murder of socialist leaders. One such militant was Georgian SD Lado Ketshoveli, the main Iskraist cadre in Baku, as well as the mentor to a young Georgian militant Ioseb Jughashvili, later known to the world as Stalin. Ketshoveli was shot in prison in 1903 after being tortured by state gendarmes and refusing to disclose the location of the socialists' printing press. Stalin concluded that '[u]nder the tsar's regime, any attempt genuinely to help the people put one outside the pale of the law; one found oneself hunted and hounded as a revolutionist'.[31]

The absence of open political life also meant that new party members often had little to no understanding of the differences between (or existence of) various socialist groups. To quote scholar Paweł Samuś, joining one socialist organisation rather than another 'was often a matter of chance, not choice'.[32] On the ground, organisations and political tendencies remained remarkably

---

29    Cited in Henning 1986, p. 55.
30    Лядов М. 1904 [1933], p. 9.
31    Cited in Kotkin 2014, p. 54.
32    Samuś 1975, p. 25.

unconsolidated. Militants loosely affiliated with different SD and SR currents frequently organised through amorphous shop-floor or city-wide committees unaffiliated to any political centre. As historian Michael Melancon argues, up through 1917 the 'plasticity of the boundary lines between the various groups suggests that Russian political parties had not yet achieved a high degree of definition; they were movements, operating in daunting circumstances, rather than parties'.[33]

Government repression also played an important role in shaping internal party debates, whose stakes were inevitably raised by the ever-looming threat of a state crackdown. A push for more open organising methods, for instance, could result in the arrest, banishment, and possible execution of the comrades involved. In such conditions, social democratic committees sometimes leaned towards excessive secrecy. No less significantly, periodic state persecution frequently determined the course of faction fights or inter-party feuds. Since the regime targeted a given city's leading militants, government crackdowns often allowed internal oppositions or rival parties to step into the resulting political vacuum.[34]

Constant government infiltration created a fair amount of suspicion and paranoia. Though most parties did their best to minimise the dislocating dynamics of such sentiments, Tsarist repression enabled the most hardened faction fighters to resort to unscrupulous methods to defeat their opponents. Rosa Luxemburg's organisational practices, for example, belie the almost-universal portrayal of her as a paragon of democratic politics. One particularly egregious method used by Luxemburg and her leadership team was to publicly disclose the real names of factional opponents who operated under pseudonyms, opening them up to state repression.[35]

A further result of the police state context was that all illegal Marxist parties were obliged to adopt conspiratorial organisational methods and to stress the importance of strict political discipline. In the words of the Latvian SD journal *Cīņa* (Struggle), 'the interests of the organisation must be placed above personal interests'.[36] To survive, radicals had to learn how to smuggle in or illegally print the party press; how to distribute leaflets and newspapers without getting immediately arrested; how to avoid (to the extent possible) state infiltration;

---

33  Melancon 1990, pp. 251–2.
34  For an example of this in Baku, see Suny 1972b, p. 381.
35  This method was used against PPS Marxist Kelles-Krauz in 1904 (Snyder 1997, pp. 184–5) and against internal SDKPIL rival Karl Radek in 1912 (Nettl 1966, pp. 586–7). See also Fayet 2004, p. 113.
36  Cited in Augškalns-Aberbergs 1929, p. 50.

how to shake off spies tailing individual militants; and how to organise underground meetings and assemblies without detection. The threat of the secret police also precluded keeping detailed member lists, one of the effects of which was that parties almost always claimed inflated membership sizes for themselves. Security precautions concerning membership rolls also made it more difficult to self-finance the organisation through individual dues, obliging most parties to rely heavily on fundraising among well-off supporters and immigrants in Western Europe and the United States.

Contrary to accounts that portray Lenin as initiating a novel form of underground party organisation, the *Iskra* tendency of which he was a co-founder repeatedly pointed to the Jewish Bund as a model for an efficient, centralised, and disciplined underground apparatus.[37] Indeed, the basic forms of conspiratorial work promoted by Iskraists had been pioneered by Bundists in Vilna; former Bund leader Julius Martov, in particular, played an important role in transmitting these lessons to the Russian movement. The Bund's organisational strength and cohesiveness was lauded by socialists across the empire, with one Bolshevik observing that 'nowhere is there such discipline as in the Bund ... [I]t has developed a strong organisational patriotism to defend the Bundist point of view, in which a decision of the Bund is defended whether or not they themselves personally agree with it or not'.[38] In his 1904 case for organisational centralism and discipline against the Mensheviks, Lenin again pointed to the Bund's exemplary organisational structure.[39]

Like most socialists in this period, the Bund built itself around its newspaper, *Di Arbiter Shtime* (The Workers' Voice). Far from being an invention of Lenin or *Iskra*, a conception of the newspaper as collective organiser was already common across imperial Russia. Though all socialist parties relied primarily on leaflets to get out their message to the broad mass of working people, each was also politically organised around, and associated with, their respective newspapers. Indeed, some parties were most commonly known by the title of their newspapers – Baku's Muslim Social Democratic Party, for example, was almost universally referred to as the *Gummet*, the name of its principal publication.

Promotion of the socialist press was also a central feature of the German SPD model. But under Tsarist absolutism, the challenge of writing, publishing, and distributing the party publication necessarily took on a distinct organisational

37    Weinstock 1984, p. 179 and Gitelman 1972, p. 39.
38    РСДРП 1905 [1959], p. 369.
39    Lenin 1904 [1960–65], p. 388.

importance, requiring a solid underground network of militants. Given the precarity of the local committees, often the party press was the main instrument capable of providing some form of organisational and political coherence.

To assure continuity despite the inevitable dispersions of local organisations in Russia, editors of the party press and the party leadership generally lived in exile. This geographic divide between émigrés and local cadre has been frequently overlooked by historians, but its impact was major. Parties inevitably became simultaneously top-down (as the central leadership and publications were concentrated in a small group abroad) and bottom-up (since the local committees often acted on their own initiative, by choice or by circumstance). Such a set-up was a necessary evil, often leading to major organisational tensions and political difficulties. Local committees frequently ignored or failed to receive instructions from abroad; top party leaders struggled to base their political projections on an accurate assessment of conditions in the empire. As such, it was easy for local militants to disregard the tactical line of the party leadership if they felt that the émigrés did not have a good grasp of local particularities. Similarly, there was a strong tendency for on-the-ground militants to dismiss party polemics and splits as reflecting the disconnect of émigrés from practical work. In turn, top party leaders frequently considered that their ranks were becoming so engrossed in local activity that they were losing sight of the big picture of revolutionary strategy.

A geographic-political gap between the top leadership and local bodies similarly facilitated a tendency for party factional disputes to crystallise around the axis of émigrés versus cadre based inside of the Russian Empire. Within the Polish Socialist Party, for instance, the faction fight culminating in the organisation's split began in 1902–03 when the party's main leaders inside of Tsarist Russia began pushing back against their émigré leadership's downplaying of mass struggle and its hesitancy to ally with Russian socialists. Given the relative disconnect between émigré leaders and local committees across imperial Russia, one cannot simply assume, as so much of the historiography has done, that the positions of émigré leaders – or even party congress resolutions – were necessarily implemented by their party's militants in the class struggle. This gap, combined with the constant dislocation of state repression, meant that the top structures of even the most formally centralised parties found it hard to steer their own organisations. Ironically, one of the main reasons why Russia's Marxist leaders emphasised centralism was that their organisations were so decentralised in practice.

*Iskra*'s ambitious organisational plan for a centralised empire-wide party – and its determined campaign to implement it – won many supporters among Russian socialists because RSDRP committees at the turn of the century were

particularly dispersed and poorly organised. The Iskraist party-building project was above all an effort of militants oriented to Russian-speaking regions
to overcome this *kustarnichestvo* (amateurism). Given the growing revolutionary upsurge, *Iskra* argued, it was urgently necessary to overcome organisational fragmentation. Only by connecting atomised circles into a powerful
party would it be possible to lead the rapidly rising tide of proletarian struggle
to overthrow the autocracy.[40]

Not all Russian SDs in the empire, however, agreed with *Iskra*'s drive towards
stricter centralism. Various RSDRP cadre and committees rejected what they
saw as an attempt to subordinate their organisations to an inflexible leadership, and they objected to *Iskra*'s method of sending outside cadre into local
committees to win them over. Thus *Rabochee Delo*, the RSDRP paper and political current that sought to articulate and justify the approach of such activists
and groups, claimed that *Iskra*'s approach to the local committees was dictatorial. Opposed to granting extensive powers to an émigré party leadership,
*Rabochee Delo* argued that while a centralised party was necessary, it should be
built from the bottom up and must grant considerable autonomy to its local
affiliates. Throughout 1902 and 1903, multiple RSDRP committees across Russia – including in important centres such as St. Petersburg – experienced sharp
factional resistance to *Iskra*'s push for organisational and political hegemony.[41]
These unresolved disputes would soon spill into the Menshevik-Bolshevik split
of 1903–04, the dislocating results of which largely reversed Iskraist efforts to
consolidate a centralised party.

Struggles for party democratisation and local autonomy tended to arise only
when they were tied to deeper strategic differences. Trotsky perceptively noted
in 1904 that 'to understand the difference on the organisational questions one
must go beyond them' by examining the underlying political divergences.[42]

On a local level, organisational and political questions were closely bound
up. Top-down conspiratorial structures were often uncontroversial as long as
there were no serious political disputes in the organisation, but they became
a problem when the ranks sought to reshape the local party orientation and
lacked adequate organisational channels to make their will felt. At such
moments of conflict, the existence of appointed (rather than elected) leaderships became a point of contention in the eyes of members seeking a political reorientation. Inside the RSDRP, for example, *Rabochee Delo*'s resistance

40      Lenin 1902a [1960–65], p. 248 and RSDLP 1903 [1978], p. 356.
41      Lih 2006, pp. 324, 458, 603, Akimov 1904–05 [1969], pp. 348–51, and Wildman 1967, pp. 213–
        53.
42      Trotsky 1904.

against Iskraist centralism was inseparable from its rejection of what it saw as *Iskra*'s underestimation of mass action and economic struggle. In turn, *Iskra*'s call for greater centralisation was tied to its desire to eradicate what it labelled as 'Economism' and amateurism from the local committees.

Concerning the internal organisation of party committees, orthodox socialists agreed that complete 'democratism' – the election of each local and regional party leadership post – was impossible in the face of Tsarist repression and infiltration. Though top party leaderships were generally elected by party congresses held abroad, democratic methods were impossible to consistently implement within Russia itself. That said, even the most top-down of the empire's Marxist parties continued to uphold various democratic norms common to the parties of the Second International. Cultivating a political culture of open and vigorous debate was seen as essential for the healthy development of the socialist movement. Crucially, this meant constant public discussion of party differences inside the socialist press (not just prior to party congresses), the expectation and legitimisation of internal party tendencies, and the publication of the minutes of all party congresses.

Experiences across imperial Russia highlighted the difficulties in determining the most suitable organisational form for a given time and place. Since effective party structures were so context specific, the organisational methods of local SD committees continued to be frequently determined on an ad hoc basis and thus varied widely by locale. In her detailed memoir of underground party-building, Jewish Iskraist Cecilia Bobrovskaya noted that,

> there were no definite forms of organization in Kharkov or anywhere in Russia, for that matter. Sometimes local committees were elected and sometimes appointed by the centre, and later supplemented by co-opted members. More often than not these committees were formed by some active revolutionary (or group of revolutionaries) in the city, who would establish strong contacts with the masses. He (or the group) would select a few capable comrades and these would declare themselves a committee.[43]

Few leading Marxists advocated either a purely democratic or a purely dictatorial party structure, and a wide spectrum of forms existed between these poles. Social democratic committees in Latvia, for instance, were occasionally but not generally elected – historian Detlef Henning notes that the local

---

43    Bobrovskaya 1934, p. 40.

leaders' 'commitment seemed to be authority enough'.[44] In Georgia, by way of contrast, there was a much stronger tradition of electing party committees, dating back to the mid-1890s. But the increase of Tsarist repression at the turn of the century led a growing number of local militants, including Stalin, to object to this method, since it made it easier for regime infiltrators.[45]

Some organisations and leaders raised the banner of organisational democracy but did little to implement it in practice. This was true both within Marxist parties and among their radical rivals. For instance, anarchists and ultra-left SR Maximalists denounced social democrats for their overly centralised, top-down organisations, which they saw as inhibiting the spontaneous creativity of the masses. Yet their own organisations were often no more democratic. Despite their programmatic insistence on decentralised, bottom-up organising, the SR Maximalists, for example, were dominated and run by a single charismatic leader, M.I. Sokolov.[46]

Such discrepancies were also manifest inside the Polish SDKPIL. On the basis of her famous 1904 polemic against Lenin's organisational proposals, Rosa Luxemburg has been almost universally upheld as a consistent promoter of party democracy against the supposedly authoritarian Bolsheviks. Yet, in practice, the SDKPIL was one of the least democratic socialist parties in the whole Tsarist Empire. Nettl notes that Luxemburg's 'own attitudes in the Polish party hardly bore out such demands for more "democracy"'.[47] Repeated internal oppositions arose to challenge the party line and its internal functioning, only to be slandered, isolated, and/or expelled through organisational manoeuvres by the SDKPIL leadership. In 1904, Stanisław Gutt, an anti-Luxemburg critic, resigned in protest from the party leadership, arguing that 'the triumvirate of Tyszka [Jogiches], Luxemburg and Dzierżyński does what it wants without coming to an agreement with the rest of the members'.[48]

A major reason why debates over permissible levels of party democracy and openness were so frequent is that the form and weight of Tsarist repression varied significantly over time and place. What worked at one point might not work later, and what failed in Moscow might succeed in Riga. On an empire-wide level, repressive policies underwent major ups and downs in the decades

44  Henning 1986, p. 73.
45  Parsons 1987, p. 324, Suny 1994, p. 162, and Jones 2005, p. 106.
46  Сапон 2009, p. 189. This dynamic was also manifest inside the anarchist movement. The anarchist Brotherhood of Free Communists, for example, split when its leader was denounced for 'dictatorial behaviour' (Avrich 1967, p. 115).
47  Nettl 1966, p. 288.
48  Cited in Blobaum 1984, p. 103.

prior to the 1905 revolution. During the 1870s, 1880s, and 1890s, the government underestimated the workers' movement and focused its repression on intelligentsia terrorists and non-Russian nationalists. The general trend in the last few years before 1905, however, was towards greater repression of socialists. But this often varied greatly year by year, or even month by month – the second half of 1904, for instance, was marked by relatively open conditions following the assassination of Von Plehve, the hated Minister of the Interior.

Concretising an appropriate organisational balance was always a challenge, particularly in the face of the inconsistency of labour mobilisations as well as uneven state repression. Practical politics was often as much about making distinct wagers on the likely turn of events as it was about ideological differences. A distinct organisational pattern emerged. Initially, local militants or parties as a whole would pursue a comparatively open organisational approach; this usually succeeded for a period, but would almost always lead to mass arrests. In response, a large swath of these militants would conclude that a more secretive stance was henceforth required. After the passage of time – or the eruption of mass struggle – a new layer of militants would subsequently push for a distinct emphasis and the cycle would begin again.

This was the dynamic at work in 1900 when Lenin, Martov, and their comrade Alexander Potresov took the initiative to found *Iskra*. These militants had begun their revolutionary careers emphasising mass agitation and semi-public organising in St. Petersburg. In late 1895 and early 1896, they and other local leaders were arrested en masse and, by the end of the year, the local committees had collapsed. Eager to avoid repeating this early experience, *Iskra* called for systematic conspiratorial techniques and an organisational infrastructure less prone to state repression. As was the case in the rest of the empire, this meant tightening up party centralisation and minimising internal democratic processes.

*Iskra*'s efforts to cohere an empire-wide party on this basis were nevertheless rejected by numerous RSDRP cadre and committees, which argued for the viability of more open organisational methods. Cecilia Bobrovskaya recalled the major tensions that *Iskra*'s organisational approach created in Kharkov: 'We were obliged to carry out the decisions of the committee blindly, since we had not the slightest share in their making. This ultra-conspiratorial state of affairs created serious dissatisfaction in our ranks'. Yet she went on to underline that this tension was caused neither by authoritarian inclinations on the part of local cadre, nor even by major strategic differences:

In the conflict between the Kharkov Committee and its periphery the latter did not accuse the former of bureaucracy and excessive privileges.

Both the centre and the periphery had but one privilege – that of being caught by the tsarist police, if not today, then tomorrow. The conflict was not due either to the evil intentions of the committee members, the unreasonable demands of the periphery or to the obstinacy of any one of its members, but simply to the fact that the workers' movement was growing apace in Kharkov while we still groped for the organizational channels through which our work was to be carried out.[49]

Geographically, the weight of police pressure was similarly uneven. The first sections of the *Okhrana* (the special gendarme branch directed at revolutionaries) were set up in the early 1880s only in Moscow, St. Petersburg, and Warsaw. Before 1903, Polish and Russian Marxists were generally subjected to the worst repression. Though some legal Marxist publications and independent worker associations were also permitted in these regions, they were much more restricted than elsewhere. In the rest of the borderlands during the crucial formative period of the 1890s, gendarmes frequently focused their fire on upper-class non-Russian nationalists and elites, who were mistakenly assumed to pose a serious threat to the regime. Thus, the early workers' movements in borderland regions such as Georgia, Latvia, Lithuania, and Belarus were subjected to less repression than their counterparts in Poland and central Russia.[50]

Borderland socialists generally succeeded in seizing the opportunity provided by early windows of comparatively less regime persecution in the 1890s and the first few years of the new century. In Latvia, the 'New Current' from 1893 onwards promoted socialism and Marxism in its legal newspaper *Dienas Lapa* (The Daily Page). These Latvian radicals were able to publish relatively freely on social questions because Tsarist censorship here was primarily concerned with combatting national separatism.

SD memoirs from Latvia are full of stories about the ageing censor A. Rupert, nicknamed the 'old turtle', whose knowledge of socialism was so minimal that he confused German socialist August Bebel with Swedish scientist Alfred Nobel.[51] The one term he always censored was 'Poland', which he invariably replaced with the official Tsarist designation 'Vistula lands'; a geological article about the earth's North and South Poles was for this reason changed by Rupert into 'the North and South Vistula lands'.[52] But when the militants associated

49    Bobrovskaya 1934, p. 40.
50    On the political-geographic dynamics of state repression in Russia, see Daly 1998.
51    Dauge 1958, p. 71.
52    Millers and Stumbiņa 1965, p. 38.

with *Dienas Lapa* began leading major strikes, the regime finally cracked down in 1897 and swept up the leading socialists. Henceforth, Latvian Marxism faced more repressive policies, though still not to the same degree as their Russian and Polish counterparts.

Early political developments were similar in Georgia. Police interference was relatively minimal in Georgia since the state focused on combatting local nationalist groups rather than the socialists. In fact, SD leader Noe Zhordania had polite relations with the local censor, who allowed the paper *Kvali* to more or less publish what it wanted, short of direct appeals to the masses for action. Though underground socialist militants in these years continued to be persecuted, *Kvali* was simultaneously able to propagate across Georgia a version of 'legal Marxism', with articles ranging from discussions of theatre, to reports on working conditions, to excerpts of the *Communist Manifesto*. The paper was eventually shut down by the regime in 1904.

Geographic unevenness in repression diminished throughout Russia after 1903, as the regime reacted violently to the spread of strikes in the periphery and the rapid growth of non-Russian Marxist parties. Accordingly, the *Okhrana* in 1904 set up new bureaus in Vilnius, Ekaterinoslav, Kazan, Kiev, Odessa, Saratov, Tiflis, and Kharkov. But the greater opportunities for legal work in these regions over the preceding period meant that within the Georgian and Latvian organisations there were greater traditions of above-ground activity.[53]

In contrast, Polish Marxists had received no such openings. Facing heavy state repression, the question of how open the movement could afford to be was a constant source of debate. The PPS leaned more on conspiratorial methods than its SDKPIL rivals, whose focus on mass economic struggle made it hard to uphold strictly secretive methods. Polish historian Jan Kancewicz notes that the PPS's early approach came at the expense of broad agitation among the working class. At the same time, the author underlines that a comparative analysis with Luxemburg's party in these years demonstrated the advantages of conspiracy.[54]

Luxemburg's party sought to balance underground methods with an emphasis on mass economic action and a semi-public organisational presence. Initially, during 1893–94, this approach proved to be a major success and the party was able to lead a variety of significant strikes and protests. But the public exigencies of mass agitation left the SDKPIL particularly vulnerable to state repression. In 1895, Luxemburg's party was entirely wiped out by the

---

53  Villari 1906, pp. 75–6, Jones 2005, p. 67, and Жордания 1968, p. 29.
54  Kancewicz 1984, pp. 169, 180.

regime. Kancewicz observes that these 'tactics and organisation, though fruitful in the long run, often led to the unmasking [of party militants], exposing them to repression. In conditions when the mass movement ebbed, this led the organisation to be broken up through the periodic mass arrests of 1894–95'.[55] Indeed, this experience in Poland was cited by Iskraists as evidence for why such methods were not advisable for the prevailing autocratic conditions. Lenin concluded that a strictly conspiratorial organisational core had to be separated from a broader layer of looser affiliated structures through which sDs could develop their mass work.[56]

## 3      The Bolshevik-Menshevik Split

The experience of the early PPS and SDKPIL illuminates the inherent dilemma that illegal Marxist parties faced in the empire. Greater organisational openness held the potential for building a broader proletarian base, but it made the party more vulnerable to state repression. More focus on conspiracy facilitated organisational continuity, but it risked isolating the organisation from the mass movement and creating a gap between party leaders and the rank and file.

Such organisational tensions, combined with the unevenness of state repression across the empire, were significant factors in the dynamics of the Bolshevik-Menshevik split that arose during and following the RSDRP's Second Congress. Yet most historiography on the split has generally failed to address, let alone explain, its geographic dimensions, i.e. why the Mensheviks became hegemonic in Transcaucasia and Ukraine, while the Bolsheviks found their roots in central Russia.[57]

As is well known, Lenin and Martov at the RSDRP's Second Congress in the summer of 1903 clashed on how to define who was a party member. After considerable debate, Martov's broader definition won the day with the support of the Bund, 'soft' Iskraists from Ukraine, and the former leaders of *Rabochee Delo*. The eventual party split, however, did not concern membership rules, but rather the composition of *Iskra*'s editorial board. Lenin's proposal for a three-person team (Plekhanov, Martov, and himself) was adopted against the push by the soon-to-be Mensheviks for maintaining a six-person board. Upon losing this vote, the Mensheviks (the Russian term for those in a minority) boycotted

---

55    Kancewicz 1984, p. 41.
56    Lenin 1902b [1960–65], p. 458.
57    For one of the few attempts to tackle this question, see Lane 1969.

the new party leadership body, setting into motion a split that would eventually percolate throughout imperial Russia.[58]

The particular debates at the Second Congress, however, played remarkably little role in the party division inside of Russia itself. For their part, the Bolsheviks maintained *Iskra*'s 'hard' organisational approach. Not surprisingly, the faction took root in areas that faced the most severe state repression, particularly the urban centres of central Russia. Early Menshevism, with its calls for more organisational autonomy and democracy, found its strongest base of support before 1905 in borderland regions that had stronger mass movements, that faced somewhat less restrictive political contexts, and that had longer autonomous SD organisational traditions.[59]

To be sure, the top Menshevik leaders were hardly advocates of strong organisational decentralisation or pure 'democratism'. And most RSDRP committees initially opposed the Mensheviks for an anti-democratic action: their refusal to abide by the collectively made decisions of the Second Congress. Bolsheviks affirmed that since their rivals had not raised any substantial differences of principle, their refusal to implement the decisions of the Second Congress was primarily due to having lost a majority of seats in the editorial board.[60]

Bolshevik leaders proposed to resolve the split by calling a Third Congress in which the decisions would be binding on all sides. The Mensheviks' refusal to go along with this proposal, in their view, again reflected a refusal to respect revolutionary discipline and the basic norms of any democratic organisation. These were well-founded charges, against which the Mensheviks never came up with a coherent rebuttal.[61] Given the compelling case of the Bolsheviks on this score, and the generalised membership opposition to organisational splits, the subsequent growth of Menshevism is a puzzle that merits serious analysis. By mid-1905, the Mensheviks had won over a majority within the RSDRP in both the centre and the periphery. Such a dynamic would have been inconceivable had there not been widespread internal discontent across the empire with key components of Iskraism and its continuation in the form of early Bolshevism.

Despite the Mensheviks' disrespect of Second Congress decisions, their call for more organisational autonomy and democracy played an important role in

---

58    The relative unimportance of the debate over membership definition was underscored by the fact that the Menshevik-led 1906 RSDRP 'reunification' Congress accepted without controversy Lenin's original formulation.

59    Martov 1904 [2015], p. 422. See the numerous documents in Mullin 2015 for the main Menshevik polemics following the Second Congress.

60    Martov 1904 [2015], p. 446. As the other resolutions cited by Martov likewise attest, the early support for the Bolsheviks across the empire primarily expressed such sentiments.

61    Lih 2006, pp. 500–3.

garnering the backing of key borderland RSDRP organisations, many of whom
had expressed significant divergences with the dominant *Iskra* line before and
during the Second Congress. Though the structural specifics of their proposals
remained hazy, in 1904 Martov and Trotsky also argued for overcoming Iskraist rigidity, criticised top-down organisational practices, and argued for more
autonomy for local committees.[62]

These issues were particularly important components of the factional developments in Ukraine and Transcaucasia. In their reports to the 1903 RSDRP
Second Congress, key committees from Ukraine had objected to *Iskra's* overly
polemical and 'inaccessible' content, stressed the importance of their regional
organ *Iuzhnii Rabochii* (Southern Worker), and argued that the Iskraist plan
to centralise the party around an all-Russian newspaper was 'unworkable and
undesirable'.[63] At the Second Congress, committees from 'the South' formed the
main base of support for Martov's incipient Menshevik faction, while Lenin's
wing received the backing of the central Russian committees. Likewise, the
southern committees almost uniformly pledged their support to the Mensheviks following the party split. Ukraine was henceforth a bastion of Menshevism –
only in Odessa did the Bolsheviks become the hegemonic RSDRP faction.[64]

The RSDRP's Caucasian Union had initially sided with the Bolsheviks on the
grounds that it was necessary to respect the democratic decisions of the Second
Congress. Yet by pushing for more internal party democracy, the Mensheviks were relatively soon able to displace their rivals both in Tiflis and nearby
Baku. In the latter city, during the mid-1904 anti-Menshevik faction fight, the
Bolshevik committee had expelled a small group of party members led by the
brothers Lev and Ilya Shendrikov. The Shendrikovs' new organisation soon initiated a campaign to mobilise the mass of unorganised workers and win the
party's ranks away from the Bolshevik committee, which they accused of being
overly conspiratorial and top-down. Refusing to recognise the legality of their
expulsion, the Shendrikov Committee – officially titled the Balakhany and Bibi-
Eibat Workers Organisation – continued to speak in the name of the party
and issue its leaflets under the RSDRP heading. It adopted the 1903 RSDRP
programme and constituted the core of what soon became the powerful Menshevik organisation in Baku.[65]

This orientation, combined with the Shendrikovs' push for mass strike
action, struck a responsive chord. By the end of 1904, the Shendrikov-led organ-

62     Martov 1904 [2015], p. 452 and Trotsky 1904.
63     РСДРП 1903 [1959], p. 549.
64     Lane 1969, p. 40, Martov 1904 [2015], p. 414, and Попов 1929, pp. 54, 64.
65     Keenan 1962, pp. 239–40.

isation had 4,000 members, while the Bolshevik-led RSDRP committee had 250.[66] Eva Broido, a leader of the town's Mensheviks, noted that the low level of repression in Baku helped explain this rapid success:

> Several districts and factory groups came over to us … simply because they were dissatisfied with the conditions in this particular Bolshevik organ-ization. … The fact that the Bolshevik 'Baku committee' did not allow democratic elections only weakened its influence. And the exaggerated and quite unnecessary secretiveness in which it shrouded itself was also a mistake. We fully proved it by our experience – we carried out elections in the factories very thoroughly and we openly electioneered among the masses, yet we remained comparatively unmolested by the police.[67]

The faction fight in Georgia followed a similar pattern. As we have seen, the local Marxist movement had a long history of relative openness. Significantly, the founding Caucasian Union conference in March 1903 had (against the line of *Iskra*) insisted that local committees should be elected rather than appoin-ted. Soon-to-be Bolshevik leaders Stalin and Misha Tskhakaia, however, argued that elections would open up the organisation to Tsarist infiltration. After the Second Congress, most of the top Menshevik-inclined Georgian leaders remained in jail or abroad, and the Caucasian Union pledged its support for the Bolsheviks. If there was ever a time for the Bolsheviks to have established a solid base in Georgia, this was it. The opportunity, however, was squandered. After a wave of arrests in January 1904, the Bolshevik-led Caucasian Union leadership decided to co-opt new members, including the unpopular Stalin. This decision marked a breach from the local norm – reaffirmed as recently as October 1903 – to let local committees choose their representatives. Next, the Caucasian Union disbanded Menshevik-leaning committees in the Georgian town of Imereti-Samegerelo. A widening chasm emerged between local committees and the Caucasian Union, the influence of which had largely eroded by late 1904.

It was in this situation that soon-to-be Menshevik leader Noe Zhordania returned to Georgia in January 1905. In the span of a few months, Zhordania managed to win over the vast majority of the organisation by campaigning for greater organisational democracy and worker participation. The Bolsheviks' failed attempt to dissolve the Tiflis Committee after it passed into Menshevik

66    Багирова 1997, p. 65.
67    Broido 1967, p. 90. On the low level of repression in Baku, see also Bobrovskaya 1934, p. 106 and Lane 1969, pp. 181, 187.

hands seemed to only further vindicate the charges of their rivals. Looking back at the reason for Bolshevism's rapid reversal of fortunes in Georgia, Bolshevik activist M.N. Leman admitted that the Caucasian Union had been particularly vulnerable due to its overly heavy emphasis on centralism.[68] Bolshevik leader Filipp Makharadze, likewise, attributed the demise to the 'personal influence' of Zhordania combined with the fact that 'certain Bolsheviks behaved tactlessly'.[69] From mid-1905 onwards, Bolshevism's public expression in Georgia became, to quote one Soviet historian, 'only a drop in the Menshevik sea'.[70]

By way of comparison, an insistence on strict centralisation and conspiratorial practices was far more widely accepted in the heavily policed regions of central Russia. And since this region had no equivalent of *Iuzhnii Rabochii*, there was less of an institutional basis for local SDs to push for regional autonomy from the top party leadership. Apart from St. Petersburg – where the newly formed Menshevik committee emerged as the leading RSDRP organisation in 1905 – the Bolsheviks remained preponderate in the imperial centre during and well after 1905.[71]

## 4      The First Mass Strike Debates (1903–04)

Only after the 1903 strike upheavals did the tactic of general strikes come to the fore of debates among imperial Russia's Marxists. Until this moment, the empire's socialists had largely ignored the issue. The prevailing conception was that such an action was off the table for the foreseeable future since it required a very high level of preliminary proletarian collective association and consciousness.

In a 1900 polemic against Polish anarchists, Leon Wasilewski of the PPS thus dismissed the relevancy of mass strikes in Europe and in Poland. After invoking the recent resolution of the Second International congress, he explained that such a tactic was particularly unrealisable in Poland since 'our country is deprived of almost all the conditions [political freedoms] allowing for the preparation of a general strike'.[72] In 1901, Stalin likewise affirmed that 'the organ-

---

68    Cited in Jones 2005, p. 124. On the split of the Georgian Social Democracy, see Jones 2005, pp. 104–28.
69    Cited in Jones 1984, p. 128.
70    Cited in Jones 1984, p. 221.
71    On the geographic concentration of the factions, see Lane 1969, pp. 40–1.
72    Wasilewski 1900, p. 20.

isation of a general strike is a very difficult matter even in Western Europe, but in our country it is quite impossible'.[73]

Before 1903, only a small minority of SDs in imperial Russia put forward a more positive approach. In a 1900 pamphlet on labour movement tactics, Stučka envisioned a growth of strikes over immediate issues empowering workers to eventually initiate a general strike: 'Without such small strikes, the working class will never be able to reach the high level of self-confidence necessary to make possible a general strike across Russia'.[74]

This conception began to gain greater traction after the 1903 summer strike wave. As Menshevik leader Fyodor Dan wrote in 1905, this work stoppage upsurge was the 'dress rehearsal' for the revolutionary upsurge two years later.[75] Virtually all of the major urban centres in Ukraine and Transcaucasia, as well as some towns in the Northwest, were paralysed by city-wide strikes. By all accounts, spontaneity weighed heavier than purposeful socialist leadership. The fact that these actions had shaken Russian society despite an extremely weak level of proletarian organisation was hard to square with the orthodox view that general strikes could only take place after extensive preliminary organisational preparation.

For their part, mass action-oriented Marxists framed the 1903 strikes as a confirmation that revolution was imminent, that workers in Russia radicalised primarily through experience in struggle, and that the main task of SDs was to lead disruptive actions towards the overthrow of Tsarism. The SDKPIL, for instance, argued that the strike wave showed that 'only the mass struggle is able to revolutionise the masses and lead them to fight, to victory'.[76]

Early Menshevism took a similar approach. In *Iskra*'s first issue after being taken over by the Mensheviks in November 1903, it published an article by Vera Zasulich in which she analysed the lessons of the recent upsurge. Citing the correspondence of a participant in the Kiev events, she lauded the mass participation, solidarity, and discipline of the strikers in spite of their lack of organisation. In Western Europe, she stressed, 'despite a half-century of the socialist

---

73  Stalin 1901 [1953–55], p. 28. The following year, Lenin similarly opposed the programmatic advocacy of general strikes, arguing that the absence of democratic rights in Russia prevented SDs from preparing them (Lenin 1902c [1960–65], p. 168). He added: 'To declare that strikes are "the best means of developing class-consciousness" is also absolutely incorrect' (ibid.).

74  Stučka 1900 [1976–78], p. 59.

75  Дан 1904 [1905], pp. 1–2. The French consul in Odessa reported that the general strikes in 1903 'marked a whole new era in the internal life of the country' (cited in Carrère d'Encausse 1980, p. 431).

76  'Konferencja białostocka', *Czerwony Sztandar*, February 1904.

movement, of organisation and political freedom, there have never been any strikes like this'. Zasulich concluded that 'life itself' demonstrated that 'as long as the revolutionary movement is growing, "spontaneity" in this regard will always develop into organisation'.[77] Along similar lines, the Mensheviks' 1904 report to the Second International's Amsterdam Congress stressed the importance of the 1903 general strikes in raising proletarian consciousness: though the actions themselves were often defeated, the 'proletariat tangibly felt its power'. In Fyodor Dan's 1905 introduction to the republication of this report, he proudly noted that it had highlighted the forms of workers' action, notably the general strike, that had become central to the development of the revolution.[78]

Socialists in Russia who prioritised organisation and education also saw the 1903 strikes as a confirmation that the revolution was imminent. But their analyses generally omitted a discussion of the transformative dynamics of mass action, emphasising instead that Marxists must concentrate on directly strengthening their party organisations. For instance, Wasilewski wrote in 1903 that while the 'mood of the masses everywhere was extremely revolutionary' during the recent general strikes, the revolutionary organisations were generally unable to provide leadership to the actions. His conclusion was that the Russian socialists had to 'as quickly as possible form a uniform and unified command for the [revolutionary] army, which already exists, which is just waiting to be led against the Tsar'.[79]

To illustrate how the increasingly distinct orientations on labour action between Bolsheviks and Mensheviks could be translated into practice, it is helpful to examine Baku's December 1904 general strike, the most important working-class struggle to erupt in imperial Russia before the revolution. A sense of this event's significance can be gleaned from the fact that Soviet historiography falsely claimed that Stalin himself had led the strike. According to Lavrentiy Beria's 1935 hagiographical account,

> In December 1904, under the leadership of Comrade Stalin, there was a huge strike of the Baku workers, which lasted from December 13 to December 31 and ended with the conclusion of a collective agreement with the oil magnates, the first collective agreement in the history of the Russian labour movement. The Baku strike was the beginning of the revolutionary upsurge in Transcaucasia.[80]

77    В. Засуличъ, 'О чемъ говорятъ намъ іюльскіе дни?', *Искра*, 25 November 1903.
78    Дан 1904 [1905], pp. 1–2, 36.
79    Wasilewski 1903, my emphasis.
80    Beriia 1949, p. 49.

Apart from these fabrications about Stalin – who was not even in Baku during December 1904 – Beria's quote is accurate enough about the moment-ousness of the action. Yet far from leading this struggle, the Bolsheviks were bypassed by it. To build towards a general strike, in October 1904 the proto-Menshevik Shendrikov committee had begun agitating and organising among the city's tens-of-thousands of oil workers. Bolsheviks in Baku actively opposed this call for a general strike, arguing among other things that workers were insufficiently organised. In a public leaflet, they denounced their rivals for advocating 'the principle of the general strike'. Such a stance, the Bolsheviks insisted, was 'sharply divergent' both with the programme of the RSDRP and the latest resolution of the Second International Congress in Amsterdam, which had condemned the anarchist campaign for a general strike and declared that 'strong organisation' was a precondition for a mass strike 'if it, one day, were found to be necessary and useful'.[81]

The *Shendrikovsky* countered these charges on the eve of the strike. Their response affirmed that given the build-up of proletarian anger in Baku, if the party did not seek to lead a strike immediately 'the workers would do this spon-taneously' in a disorganised manner. Bolshevik calls to push back the strike until workers were better organised (e.g. by stockpiling food reserves) were simply unrealistic: 'if Russia's workers had to think of their reserves before launching a strike, they would never have launched a single one'.[82] In response to the Shendrikov committee's appeal, the general strike began on 13 December. Its size – involving roughly 50,000 wage workers of all nationalities in Baku – and its level of coordination were unprecedented both in the region and empire-wide.

Though the Bolsheviks reversed their opposition to the strike the day before it began, their organising efforts were no more successful throughout the action than they had been during its lead up. Trained more in conspiracy than agit-ation, they fared poorly in the arena of open public struggle. Among other limitations, their militants tended to be weak in skills like public oratory neces-sary for leading mass actions. As local Bolshevik leader and participant Cecilia Bobrovskaya recalled, 'the trouble with the Baku Committee was that it adop-ted a somewhat academic approach to the working masses'.[83] After two and a half weeks of striking, the employers eventually caved and the workers won all their demands. Building off this historic victory, the Baku Mensheviks retained their leadership over the city's working class in 1905, directing it by the year's

81    Cited in Невский 1930, pp. 340–1.
82    Cited in Keenan 1962, p. 246.
83    Bobrovskaya 1934, p. 108.

end into an open revolutionary offensive against the Tsarist state. The Bolsheviks, on the other hand, remained marginal. It would take the experience of 1905 for Baku's Bolsheviks to fully assimilate a key insight: under Tsarism, experience in mass struggle was necessary not only to empower workers, but also to root the party in the class and to educate its cadre in the art of leading disruptive collective actions. The extent to which a focus on mass action and general strikes was also relevant for contexts beyond autocratic Russia soon became one of the main debates in the international socialist movement.

## 5      Mass Action and Organisation in 1905

Contrary to any hopes of building a strong and disciplined proletarian army under Tsarism before engaging in general strikes and insurrections, the revolution unfolded as an undeniably volcanic affair. The empire was shaken in 1905 by 13,000 strikes with over 2.7 million participants.[84] Throughout the year, mass actions generally preceded and spurred the growth of proletarian collective association and conscious political radicalism – to quote one historian, 'organisation structures lagged behind workers' consciousness'.[85] In turn, the ability of socialists to influence the course of events and win leadership depended on their participation in these spontaneous upheavals.

Working-class mobilisation surged so rapidly that radicals had a hard time catching up. Workers who had previously been reluctant to engage in collective struggle and organisation – usually those at the bottom of the labour hierarchy – streamed into action. Strikes spread far beyond artisans and skilled workers in the factories. Professions that took strike action in 1905 included farm labourers, hairdressers, musicians, drugstore attendants, servants, lighthouse keepers, hospital staffs, maids, waiters, firemen, teachers, salesclerks, newspaper sellers, cab drivers, theatre troops, and even synagogue workers. In this new class-conscious spirit, socialists in Moscow published a newspaper by and for white-collar workers, proclaiming that 'although we wear clean starched linen, we are only slaves, just like those smoke-blackened and dusty proletarians'.[86]

Different strata of workers pushed forward at different times and in different ways, reflecting uneven levels of organisation, consciousness, and social location. Through the empowering experience of struggle, some of the least organ-

---

84      Surh 1989, p. 51.
85      Sutton 1987, p. 140.
86      Cited in Kaplunovskiy 2007, p. 205.

ised workers could in a matter of days become among the most combative. For instance, the strikes of Baku's Muslim oil workers in May and July were so large that they surged past the ability of the *Gummet* to provide organisational leadership. Indeed, during the May strike, the militancy of Muslims outpaced all other ethnic groups; they 'went ahead of everyone', noted *Gummet*-Bolshevik leader Sultan Majid Efendiev.[87]

In Finland, high society was particularly scandalised by the participation of their female maids in labour strikes, which shattered paternalistic notions of servants as members of the host family and represented the direct intrusion of the labour movement into their homes. In daily mass meetings in a Helsinki elementary school courtyard, thousands of maids came together to formulate their demands. According to the president of the servant's union Miina Sillanpää, one week of general strike had transformed working women 'more than what could have been promoted in ten years of peaceful conditions'.[88]

All across the empire, socialists marvelled at the speed of proletarian radicalisation acquired through the experience of struggle. Latvian Marxist Fricis Roziņš observed that in a revolution 'people feel more alive, think more deeply, and rapidly reach a consciousness that in other times would take decades to arrive at'.[89] A correspondent of the SDKPIL described the January general strike in the Dąbrowa Basin mining region as follows: 'only the revolutionary storm can purify the public atmosphere and in one fell swoop raise the people to a level of true civilisation and heroism'.[90]

The overarching trend over the course of 1905 was for mass actions to inspire not only workers' radicalisation, but also their self-organisation. Factory committees, unions, parties, and workers' councils grew increasingly strong in all regions of imperial Russia, particularly following the October Manifesto. By late 1905, an unprecedented number of workers were organised in one form or another. Yet throughout the year the breadth of popular action nevertheless outpaced organisational growth and cohesion. Socialists – particularly the best organised parties like the Latvian Social Democracy or the Bund – were sometimes able to initiate and coordinate mass actions from start to finish. But labour struggles often broke out well before parties or other existing workers' associations were sufficiently strong to guide them.

A militant of Rosa Luxemburg's SDKPIL explained: 'it must be said emphatically that despite our preparations, this movement has outgrown the strength

---

87    Cited in Агакишиев 1991, p. 122.
88    Sillanpää 1906, p. 34.
89    Roziņš 1905b [1963–65], p. 10.
90    'Jeszcze o strejku powszechnym w Zagłębiu Dąbrowieckiem', *Z Pola Walki*, 29 March 1905.

of all organisations, its turbulent and hot stream poured past the organisational boundaries and spilled over all over the country'.[91] How to move from this elemental struggle to a conscious and coordinated assault against the regime constituted the major challenge for Russia's revolutionaries. After noting the largely spontaneous nature of the strikes, one early 1905 SDKPIL editorial concluded: 'Now it is time for the second phase of the revolution, the phase in which the social democracy ... strives to steer the mass movement as much as possible and gain control over the impending revolutionary events'.[92] No Marxists believed that unorganised mass upsurges on their own would be sufficient to topple Tsarism.

The profusion of relatively spontaneous strikes, demonstrations, and armed clashes in 1905 made it difficult for social democrats to convince workers to hold off from action. For example, Trotsky recalled that in November the St. Petersburg Soviet leaders were obliged to go along with a push by workers to institute an eight-hour-day from below: 'If it [the Soviet] had shouted "Halt" to the masses, from considerations of "realpolitik," they simply would not have complied and would have rebelled against it. The struggle would still have broken out, but without its leadership'.[93] Such popular explosions obliged Marxists throughout Russia to orient towards spontaneous actions to an unprecedented degree.

Socialists were not always able to steer the course of popular resistance. Generally they achieved more success in the borderlands than in central Russia, where SD organisations were weakest on the eve of 1905 and throughout the year. Consider the extent of socialist organisation inside the Tsarist army: eleven of the fifteen social democratic military bodies established before the summer of 1905 were established by non-Russian Marxist organisations. Especially strong military work was developed by the Bund and the Latvian LSDSP, as well as (to a lesser extent) the Georgian SDs and the Polish SDKPIL.[94] Among the faction-torn and overstretched RSDRP, this work was generally neglected until very late in the year, which had significant repercussions upon the revolution's outcome.

In late November-early December 1905, as historian John Bushnell notes, 'mutinies effectively deprived civil authorities of control over ten of the nineteen cities of the Russian empire with a population over 100,000': Moscow, Ekaterinoslav, Kharkov, Tiflis, Baku, Riga, Łódź, Saratov, Kazan, and Rostov-on-

---

91    Cited in Kiepurska 1967, pp. 73–4.
92    'Pod znakiem Socjaldemokracji', *Czerwony Sztandar*, March 1905.
93    Cited in Anweiler 1974, pp. 56–7.
94    Bushnell 1977, pp. 191–3.

don.[95] But Russian SDs were unable to take advantage of (let alone guide) the soldier rebellion. A top organiser of the RSDRP military work castigated the 1906 London Congress of the RSDRP for the party's lacklustre approach to 'agitation work in the army':

> This work is not organized well, it's not professional. A lot of revolutionary energy in the army is lost. We do not connect our military organizations. And many times we lost chances to utilize this great force in a planned manner. When the armed uprising flared up in Moscow, an artillery unit was eager to go to Moscow [to help the revolution], but we did not know about it and did nothing to put this force to any use.[96]

Significantly, the missed opportunities of 1905 convinced even anarchist leaders to push for the formation of an anarchist party so that the ruptural potential of revolutionary crises would not again be squandered.[97] Such calls for reorientation, however, went unheeded. Due in part to its inattention to organisation, the anarchist movement remained a surprisingly marginal force across Russia.

Difficulties in providing leadership during the revolution were rooted in various objective and subjective dynamics. One was perpetual Tsarist repression, particularly before October. Party committees continued to be broken up, militants arrested, workers and leaders killed. In such conditions, it often proved easier for SDs to call for demonstrations or strikes than to coordinate them once they were underway. And while the popular upsurge put the regime on the defensive and created significantly more space for broad organising, it was not until the October–December 'Days of Freedom' that socialists could openly organise and agitate. Making the transition from underground work to mass action, moreover, was not an easy task for many activists, particularly those that had been most focused on underground organising and propagandising. Ekaterinoslav's Bolsheviks in August 1905 thus lamented their inability to meet the challenges posed by the new period: 'arming the masses, organizing the masses, leading mass action ... [the *komitet*] was not able to respond to such tasks'.[98] Winning leadership over mass struggle proved to be more difficult than many SDs had initially anticipated.

---

95     Bushnell 1985, p. 107.
96     Cited in Petrovsky-Shtern 2001, p. 222.
97     Gooderham 1981, pp. 129–30.
98     Cited Wynn 1992, p. 182.

Another important obstacle was that the broader labour movement grew more rapidly than the revolutionary parties. Despite their numerical weakness, socialists generally set the tone of the revolution as a whole and their political impact was felt far beyond party ranks. Yet the fact that even the strongest of the socialist parties had memberships in the tens of thousands on the eve of the revolution, made it a challenge to provide organisational and political direction to an upsurge of millions. The extent to which action preceded consciousness in the revolution is well-illustrated by the fact that the major surge in recruitment to most parties occurred in 1906–07. In other words, most workers did not decide to join Marxist parties until many months after the high tide of the revolution had already been reached.[99]

On the potentially controversial issue of general strikes, the big story of 1905 was that social democrats across the empire overwhelmingly supported and participated in such actions. At least four waves of general strikes shook the empire in 1905: in the wake of Bloody Sunday, in July, in October, and in late November-early December. Orthodox SDs played important roles in supporting and spreading all of these, though the extent to which they were able to directly lead them varied considerably. In neighbouring Germany, by way of contrast, it was controversial even to discuss this tactic.

This widespread Marxist support for general strikes in Russia testifies to the strong mass action traditions in the empire's revolutionary parties, as well as the ability of their cadre to flexibly adjust to the exigencies of collective struggle. Georgia's Mensheviks thereby stressed the 'enormous educational' impact of general strikes on working people and highlighted the need to 'use this tool' for 'revolutionising' the not-yet fully politicised layers of the class.[100] Praising mass strikes, Latvian SDs likewise declared in December 1905: 'Now the proletariat of Russia has taught the proletariat all over the world how to use the heavy, deadly weapon of the working class: the general strike'.[101]

Finland, as was so often the case, witnessed a different dynamic. Relatively peaceful for much of 1905, Finland's labour movement initially reflected its isolation from the rest of the empire, its context of relative political freedom, and the correspondingly moderate orientation of the SDP. The party leadership's hesitant approach to mass strikes persisted well into the fall. Indeed, the SDP prevaricated for almost two weeks before joining, under pressure, the historic general strike begun in central Russia in late October.

---

99    On the peak moments of recruitment, see the citations to Table 1 in the introduction.
100   'О всеобщей стачке' [1905] in Тютюкин 1996, p. 130.
101   'Krievijas proletariāts un Krievijas valsts', *Pēterburgas Latvietis*, 17 December 1905.

The strike in Finland only began after Finnish railway workers spontaneously walked off the job on 30 October. Despite its late start, the 'Great Strike' in Finland proved to be a watershed moment for the working class, both in the cities and in rural areas. All strata of the wage-earning population participated – even the Finnish police joined in. Contrary to Kautsky's earlier predictions, the general strike in Finland was neither a final decisive battle for state power, nor did it lead to the destruction of workers' organisations.[102]

The Great Strike was a major turning point in the course of the Finnish Social Democracy. With the subsequent influx of tens of thousands of newly radicalised workers, a strong counter-current arose within the party ranks oriented towards class struggle and mass action, specifically strikes and (to a lesser extent) armed struggle through the vehicle of the newly established 'Red Guard' militia. Numerous conflicts between the old SDP leadership and this militant rank and file arose throughout 1906. Kujala notes that these workers' 'mental world was pervaded by the belief in the omnipotence of the mass movement'.[103]

In 1906, this effervescence culminated in the participation of a minority of radicalised Finnish workers and Red Guard members in the ill-advised July 1906 Sveaborg Rebellion initiated by Russian soldiers stationed outside of Helsinki. The soldiers' mutiny broke out in a premature, spontaneous fashion, and it was easily crushed by the Tsarist authorities. The rebellion's bloody defeat dampened the enthusiasm of Finnish working people – as well as radical SDP leaders – for mass action, at least in the short-term. Soon after, the Finnish workers' movement returned to its reliance on 'tried and tested' tactics, which included a strong emphasis on electoral politics after the conquest of universal suffrage in 1906.

Nevertheless, the Great Strike marked the first eruption in Finland of a new tradition of mass action, which was henceforth more firmly incorporated into the strategic vision of SDP Marxists. In a 1906 editorial titled 'Parliamentary Struggle is Good, but Not Enough on its Own' the young orthodox SD current led by Otto Kuusinen thus declared: 'The general strike, both a political and economic general strike, is one of our tools of struggle, alongside parliamentary struggle. We have actually experienced that it is an excellent weapon when used at a suitable time'.[104]

---

102    On the Great Strike, see Tikka 2009 and Heikkinen 1980.
103    Kujala 1989, p. 316.
104    Kuusinen 1906, p. 338.

6        Party Organisation and Mass Action (1906–14)

The extent to which Marxists in Russia viewed top-down and conspiratorial organisation as, at best, a necessary evil was illustrated by their transformation in 1905. Relatively freer political conditions were won from below by the revolutionary upsurge, allowing almost every Marxist party in the Tsarist Empire to take strides towards internal democracy and open functioning. This was particularly the case after the Tsar issued his famous 'October Manifesto', which promised to significantly extend democratic rights. For the next two months, governmental authority all but vanished. Describing these 'days of freedom', one Jewish socialist recalled that:

> People completely lost their fear of police intervention, which, incidentally, made less and less appearance on the streets. People who, a short time ago, had avoided any gathering like the plague, began stopping anywhere a crowd gathered. They would try to grasp the gist of the conversation and then, without realizing it themselves, begin to speak and fume.[105]

All across imperial Russia, local committees were increasingly elected by the ranks and party structures were opened up to new members with little political or organisational training. In Riga, to cite one example, the hitherto tightly organised LSDSP signed up 40,000 members at a mass rally of over a hundred thousand workers and students in late October.[106] It was in this period that the term 'democratic centralism' first arose. This concept has often been wrongly assumed to have been invented by Lenin's current, but in fact it was coined by the Mensheviks in November 1905. It referred neither to the top-down monolithic organisational approach later associated with Stalinism, nor even to the method of 'freedom of discussion, unity in action'. At the time, it referred simply to the act of electing leadership structures and openly discussing all major party issues. As Latvian SD leader Pēteris Stučka noted in 1906, 'democratic centralism as dubbed by the Russians' meant 'electing [the leadership] from the bottom', rather than 'building the leadership from the top'.[107]

The Bund and the Bolsheviks – two of the hitherto most top-down currents in Russia – were no exception to this pattern of organisational democratisation. Lenin and his comrades had always argued that the party should function

---

105    Kats 1956 [2012], p. 79.
106    Dauge 1958, p. 222. For the democratisation of the Ukrainian Social Democracy, see Boshyk 1981, p. 308.
107    Stučka 1906 [1976–78], p. 284.

openly and democratically when political conditions allowed it.[108] The only major Marxist party in the empire that refused to significantly democratise itself during the revolution was Luxemburg's SDKPIL. In 1906, the party rejected all motions by rank-and-file leaders to make concessions to democratic functioning; instead it deepened its centralising tendencies by adopting a new party structure that granted unprecedented powers to its émigré leadership. The SDKPIL was henceforth run in an exceptionally authoritarian manner by Leo Jogiches and Feliks Dzierżyński – a situation that would have been impossible without Rosa Luxemburg's consistent backing and ideological support.[109]

Elsewhere in the empire, organisational democratisation advanced throughout late 1905 and early 1906. But after the decisive retreat of the revolution in 1907, the government's repressive onslaught resulted in tens of thousands of socialists going back into the conspiratorial underground, thrown in jail, or exiled abroad. Marxists in Nikolaev, Ukraine, lamented that the newfound fear of infiltration and arrest was 'an extremely noxious poison which seeps into all the pores of the organization, kills all its tissues, and eventually paralyses its activities'.[110] An empire-wide economic slump further dampened labour militancy, as workers feared to take action lest they be replaced by the unemployed. Though some of the conquests of the revolution remained – e.g. various legal labour unions were allowed to function – the arrests of socialist leaders, the breakup of committees, and the subsequent escape of militants abroad decimated all socialist parties between 1907 and 1911.

Repression after 1905 was especially severe in borderlands such as Latvia, Poland, and Georgia, where the revolution had been the most militant. In Latvia, about 3,000 workers, peasants, and intellectuals were killed by the regime in the wake of the revolution, while another 10,000 were imprisoned or forced abroad. Georgia witnessed a similar number of casualties and victims. And though Poles only made up six per cent of the population, a quarter of the death sentences for revolutionaries were issued in Poland.[111]

In the face of widespread anti-Jewish pogroms in 1905 and 1906, as well as the decline of traditional artisanal industries, many Jewish socialists immigrated abroad, as did Jewish workers generally.[112] A. Litvak, a member of the Bundist central committee, described the party's decline as follows:

---

108    Cited in Lih 2013.
109    Blobaum 1984, pp. 34–5, Strobel 1974, *passim*, and Blanc 2018.
110    Cited in Elwood 1974b, p. 52.
111    Běržiņš 2000, p. 399, Bushnell 1977, p. 140, and Kappeler 2001, p. 334.
112    Penkower 2004, p. 205.

> During the entire summer of 1907, we spoke of a crisis in all our organ-
> izations. We discussed and searched for the reasons. Already in 1908
> there was nearly no one with whom to talk about the crises. One after
> another, the organizations had either crumbled or fallen into a deep
> winter sleep.[113]

In this period, the most critical organisational task was simply to survive. Some
parties – including the Ukrainian USDRP and the Armenian 'Specificists' –
maintained continuity as loose literary circles. Many parties did not survive at
all. The Muslim *Gummet*, the Ukrainian *Spilka*, the PPS-Proletariat, the Latvian
LSS, and the Estonian Social Democracy were wiped out in the 'period of reaction'. Tsarist repression was the immediate cause of the disappearance of these
organisations, but there were also political roots to why some organisations survived and not others. Among those groups that disappeared, defections of key
party leaders into private life – or into the RSDRP, the SRs, or the nationalist
camp – meant that cadre were lacking to rebuild their repressed party structures.

Reversing the pre-1905 geographic pattern of Tsarist repression, St. Petersburg became the city in the empire with the most space allowed for organising.
As Swain notes, in the pre-war years 'it was only in Petersburg that a really
thriving legal labour movement survived'.[114] One reason for this was that the
capital was somewhat shielded from the most brutal forms of repression by
the presence of a new State Duma, a form of popular representation conceded
by the Tsar in October 1905. This was a sham parliament that did not fundamentally transform Russia from an autocracy to a constitutional regime.[115] As
socialists incessantly pointed out, the Duma disenfranchised huge segments of
the population (particularly from non-Russian peoples), it had no real power,
it was repeatedly dispersed at the whim of the Tsar, and it operated in an
empire deprived of basic political freedoms. Nevertheless, Duma representatives, including socialists, were generally given legal immunity and were able to
use the institution as a platform to propagate their ideas and support workers'
struggles.

Though openings were significantly greater in St. Petersburg than elsewhere,
Marxists throughout the empire sought to combine illegal work with attempts
to utilise the new opportunities provided by the Duma and those labour uni-

---

113  Cited in Zimmerman 2004, p. 233.
114  Swain 1983, p. ix.
115  Vössing 2008, pp. 165–6, 460–5.

ons that remained.[116] From 1907 onwards, discussions arose within all socialist currents and parties about the most appropriate combination of illegal and legal work. The so-called 'liquidationist' conflict revolved around the relative importance of these two forms of work and the organisational relation between the two. Within the RSDRP, the most right-wing Mensheviks were based in St. Petersburg and explicitly sought to counterpose legal workers' organisations to a functioning socialist underground.

But particularly in the borderlands, where repression remained higher than in St. Petersburg, the indispensability of the illegal organisations was obvious to virtually all SDs. The dissolution of underground party structures was thus overwhelmingly rejected even by those SD currents that had made a political turn to the right after 1905, like the Jewish Bund and the Georgian Mensheviks.[117] At the same time, all Marxist parties agreed that legal opportunities, limited and tenuous as they were, provided an important lever and cover for socialist mass work. During the new rise in the labour movement from 1912 through 1914, socialists across Russia began utilising these opportunities to rebuild their party organisations. By this time, organisational debates were mostly overshadowed by more significant political questions.

Despite a sharp upsurge in labour militancy after the April 1912 massacre of mineworkers in the Siberian town of Lena, socialist parties across the empire remained remarkably organisationally weak and uncoordinated. The dislocating impact of the counter-revolutionary onslaught, the collapse in financial and political support from the intelligentsia, and ongoing state repression significantly undercut attempts to build organisational coherence. On the whole, Marxist parties were even more decentralised than they had been in the pre-1905 period.

In the face of this atomisation, it is significant that the Bolsheviks did not seek to repeat *Iskra*'s old campaign to build a tightly centralised empire-wide party. After 1905, Lenin's current prioritised political debates over organisational ones, demonstrating a more realistic assessment of the degree of centralisation achievable in Tsarist Russia and a more flexible approach to the autonomy of local committees.

---

116 The only significant exception was the Polish Socialist Party-Revolutionary Faction, which, in its efforts to focus on separatist struggle, boycotted the Duma and abstained from the legal labour movement. Against its rival's one-sided insistence on conspiracy, the PPS-Left affirmed the need for participation in the mass workers' movement, in both its legal and illegal iterations.

117 Jones 1984, pp. 276–8 and Mendel 1989, p. 53.

In short, there is a wide gap between the actual historical record and claims about a deeply disciplined and centralised Bolshevik organisation. Despite facing brutal autocratic conditions, every underground Marxist current in the Tsarist Empire, including the Bolsheviks, functioned with a degree of local initiative – and open political debate – exceeding almost all Leninist parties of the twentieth century, even when the latter operated in conditions of political freedom.[118]

Given the underground socialist parties' severe organisational limitations in all regions, the ability of Marxists to promote or lead mass actions largely devolved to the initiative of their militants on a shop-floor level. Thus the PPS-Left noted in 1913 that the recent strike movement in Poland was largely spontaneous, 'even though there was no lack of people who have had an impact on the masses'.[119] An internal gendarme report in Łódź the following year similarly observed that at 'the present time there is no news of any strikes led by socialist parties, although it is likely that the strikes in particular factories are led by members of the socialist parties'.[120] This dynamic was no less true for the Bolsheviks. One Baku Bolshevik recalled that the successful intervention of their militants in the 1914 strikes was possible 'despite the wretched condition of our forces'.[121]

All of the socialist currents were constrained during the 'period of reaction' to limit their activities mostly to propaganda and to defending their rapidly shrinking organisations. But with the post-1911 upsurge in the labour movement, the radicals – Bolsheviks, the Polish PPS-Left and SDKPIL, the Latvian LSDSP, etc. – picked up where they left off in 1905–06. Each consistently supported and participated in the tumultuous strike wave that erupted in the last few years before WWI.

As before, radicals remained the hegemonic political force within the labour movement empire-wide, despite their serious organisational limitations. St. Petersburg had by this time become the vanguard of the working-class struggle. In 1912–13, the capital alone was responsible for 40 per cent of strikers in Russia.[122] Yet other cities also moved in the same leftwards direction, particularly those with large metalworking factories, which were bastions of labour milit-

---

118    Myth-making about Bolshevism's supposedly longstanding 'iron discipline' began during the Russian Civil War, generating an organisational model problematically followed by subsequent generations of socialists. For a discussion of this evolution, see Riddell 2013.

119    Cited in Petz and Karwacki 1990, p. 123.

120    Cited in Karwacki 1964, p. 197.

121    Стопани 1923, p. 21. See, also, Haimson 1989b, p. 531.

122    Haimson and Petrusha 1989, p. 118.

ancy from 1912 up through 1917. When the Tsar declared war in the summer of 1914, St. Petersburg was on the verge of insurrection, Riga was not far behind, and most other big urban centres of the empire were swept up in a rising tide of worker action as well. Orthodox Marxists were again at the fore. In Latvia, the LSDSP was completely dominant. In Poland the PPS-Left was the leading current, as was Bolshevism in central Russia, Estonia, Baku, and urban Ukraine.[123]

Unlike their liberal counterparts, leftist historians have noted that radicals were by far the most influential current in the workers' movement on the eve of the war.[124] But the analytical importance of this fact has largely been elided. The hegemony of radicalism in the pre-war period undercuts the still-widespread view that a marginal but programmatically pure Bolshevik party was able to transform itself into a mass party over the course of a few short months in 1917. Such a story may be comforting for small socialist organisations that imagine that their marginality will somehow come to an end at a moment of revolutionary crisis, but it does not conform to the facts about Russia. Unlike in most of Western Europe, autocratic conditions led radicals to predominate within Russia's labour movement for almost the entirety of its existence. Had revolutionary socialists across Russia not already accumulated significant mass influence under Tsarism, it is highly unlikely that they would have been serious contenders for power after its overthrow.

Like in 1905, organised Marxists in 1912–14 sought to give direction to the diffuse groundswell of labour militancy and they once again stressed the importance of general strikes. The PPS-Left thus declared in 1912: 'Our old weapon – the

---

123　On SDs in the pre-war upsurge, see Ripa and Apine 1964, Kasprzakowa 1965, Bonnell 1983, Arens 1976, Попов 1925, and Elwood 1974b. The one major exception to the hegemony of radicals was Georgia, where the relative absence of pre-war labour militancy in the region may help explain the ability of the region's Mensheviks to maintain and solidify their hegemony against rivals to their left (Suny 1994, p. 178). Soviet historians have attributed Menshevik dominance to the prevalence of the petty bourgeoisie and small-scale industry in Georgia. It also should be kept in mind that Georgia's Mensheviks remained to the left of their central Russian counterparts, a dynamic which undercut the ability of pre-war Bolsheviks to differentiate themselves and challenge for leadership. It seems that the relatively lower level of class antagonisms in Georgia during 1917–21 facilitated the continued hegemony of the Georgian SDs and the remarkably successful implementation of their moderate socialist project (Suny 1990, p. 343).

124　The 1912–14 wave of labour militancy in imperial Russia has also tended to be ignored or downplayed in liberal historiography, which has often treated the October Revolution as an accident of history born solely from the turmoil of World War One. Noting that the Russian Empire was on the verge of a revolutionary crisis by the summer of 1914 would seriously undercut that narrative. (For a classic discussion, see Haimson 1964, pp. 620–4).

general strike – again has proven its power and strength'.[125] As in preceding years, the pre-war upsurge itself was predominantly spontaneous. A 1913 PPS-Left report noted that 'this year's strikes usually broke out without the strikers' consulting with any organisation, without preparation, and without having first created a strike committee to lead the strike. In some factories, workers walked out of work and only then formulated demands'.[126] This pattern held true even in St. Petersburg, with its relatively developed legal trade union movement. Ad hoc workplace committees provided the main form of organisational structure for the strikes and shop-floor protests.

Not all Marxist currents in the empire maintained their previous emphasis on mass action. Under the impact of the post-1905 reaction, various SD organisations turned to the political right, including the Mensheviks, the Bund, the Ukrainian Social Democracy, and the Polish Socialist Party-Revolutionary Faction. And these moderate socialists' post-1905 class-collaborationism translated into a very different method of appraising mass action than their radical rivals. As would be the case over the years to come, the prioritisation of education, organisation, or action was inseparable from broader political issues.

By the eve of the war, the relative weight that Mensheviks and Bolsheviks placed on actions like strikes was the reverse of their respective positions in 1904. As early as 1907, Menshevik leaders began accusing their Bolshevik rivals of adopting the 'direct action' methods of the syndicalists.[127] Haimson notes that by the eve of the war, 'the chief focus of the conflicts between Bolsheviks and Mensheviks became the proper use to be made of the strike weapon itself'.[128]

Across the empire, moderate SDs tended to move away from mass action after 1905. The heavy prioritisation of these currents on legal work and, above all, their search for an alliance with liberals pushed them steadily away from their earlier focus on collective disruption. Instead, they focused their efforts on Duma elections, the legal workers' press, cultural activities, and building open trade unions.

After 1907, for instance, the Bund sought to establish cultural-educational societies to promote socialist ideas among workers. Yet repression soon undermined the viability of their project. As Vladimir Levin has documented, 'socialist directors of such legal institutions stood before a choice: either maintain strictly socialist content and risk closure by the authorities, or provide less

125    'Walka zawrzała nanowo', *Robotnik*, July 1912.
126    Cited in Orzechowski and Kochański 1964, p. 270.
127    Williams 1986, p. 84.
128    Haimson 1989a, p. 26.

socialism and more education and culture. Ultimately, the demand for education marginalized the socialism'. Bundists then turned to broader cultural associations to promote their politics, yet the results were meagre. These organisations, Levin notes, became 'clubs for the intelligentsia, whose role in the development of Jewish culture, especially of Yiddish literature and theatre, was very important'. But they had 'little impact on the Jewish population as a whole' and did not ultimately help rebuild the Bund or the Jewish workers' movement.[129]

Among the Mensheviks, 1905's crushing defeat sapped much of their former enthusiasm for mass action. A turn towards prioritising education and organisation was further deepened by their new strategic orientation towards establishing a bloc with the bourgeoisie, leading the Mensheviks to reject what they now saw as the excessive and irrational spontaneity of Russia's working-class movement. In an important 1910 article in Kautsky's journal *Die Neue Zeit*, Martov set out the new Menshevik strategy in a polemical response to Rosa Luxemburg's call to spread Russia's mass action focus to the West.

According to Martov, the exact opposite development was needed. The tried and tested method of Western European socialists, he argued, was henceforth possible and necessary for contemporary Russia as well. In his view, it was no longer justified to make a strategic exception for Tsarist Russia's socialists when it came to the prioritisation of political education and disciplined organisation. Events in 1905, he argued, demonstrated that 'enthusiasm alone' was not enough for victory. The time was past for mass strikes without 'sufficient preparation, without wide and strong organisations'. He concluded that 'Russian Social Democracy spoke too eagerly "Russian" even when the social conditions of Russia had already advanced so much that they could speak "European"'.[130]

But because Tsarism continued to repress workers' associations and restrict their ability to effectively promote workers' interests, the Mensheviks' desired approach had little space to flourish. And their wager that workers could, through disciplined struggle and strategic alliances with liberals, conquer greater democratic freedoms under Tsarism proved to be ill-founded. As such, the Mensheviks' organisational-educational focus was widely rejected from below in the 1912–14 upsurge. Indeed, the main forces of moderate social democracy – the Mensheviks, the Bund, and the PPS-FR, and class-collaborationist Ukrainian SDs – were decidedly secondary actors in workers' struggles on the eve of the war.[131]

---

129   Levin 2007, p. viii.
130   Martoff 1910, pp. 907–19.
131   The main exception was the still-influential Georgian Social Democracy.

Only in Finland did it prove possible for socialists to effectively implement the tried and tested strategy. The regime's brief 1903–04 experiment in anti-labour repression had ended by 1905, facilitating the Finnish Social Democracy's explosive growth to over 100,000 members by 1907. By restoring Finnish autonomy and conceding universal suffrage (though not local democratic governance) in 1906, the embattled Tsarist regime hoped to quell unrest in Finland in order to more effectively concentrate its forces on putting down the revolution in the rest of the empire. Once the 1905 revolutionary wave had ebbed, the Russian authorities in Finland again began introducing some targeted anti-labour sanctions and increased occasional restrictions on the SDP. In 1910–12, for example, some demonstrations and rallies were banned in Finland and a few party leaders were even briefly imprisoned for contempt of the Tsar.[132] But the political freedoms and parliamentary powers granted remained at a qualitatively different level than the rest of Russia.[133]

After radicals swept into the SDP party leadership in 1906, the Finnish Social Democracy upheld the party's longstanding cautious tactics. Now, however, it infused them with a sharp insistence on class independence and a clearer affirmation of the 'final goal' of socialism, including in its parliamentary campaigning. Buoyed by successful electoral efforts, the tried and tested approach was spectacularly successful in Finland: by 1907, the SDP had transformed itself into the largest socialist organisation per capita in the world.

Yet not all members of Finland's Social Democracy agreed with this downplaying of mass action. Indeed, at multiple party congresses it was forcefully challenged by SDP leader Kaapo Murros, the new leftist editor of Tampere's *Kansan Lehti* magazine from 1907 through 1909. Murros had after 1905 immigrated to the United States, where he had grown sympathetic to the syndicalist Industrial Workers of the World. Upon returning to Finland, Murros emphatically argued in the press and at the SDP congresses that the party should make a turn towards mass action by building militant trade unions to initiate workplace disruption against the bosses and eventually the capitalist system as a whole. But, as Finnish scholar Jari Ehrnrooth notes, in 'party circles the proposals of Murros received no support at all'.[134]

It is significant that not only right-leaning party leaders but also other leftists and SDP rank-and-file militants rejected Murros' push for a strategic reorientation. By all indicators, the Finnish party's cautious strategy corresponded

---

132  Carrez 2008, p. 311.
133  On post-1905 repression in Finland, see, for example, Carrez 2008, p. 211.
134  Ehrnrooth 1992, p. 567.

to the rational calculations and sentiments of most SDP members during a non-revolutionary period in a low inclusion parliamentary polity. For the particular constraints and opportunities of Finland's semi-authoritarian political regime, a slow-but-steady organisational, educational, and electoral focus made sense. And in July 1916 the Finnish Social Democracy made history by becoming the first socialist party in any country to win a majority in parliament. As we will see below, the democratic mandate of the 1916 elections proved to be a crucial legitimising factor for the SDP throughout the 1917–18 revolution.

## 7       War and Revolution

With the declaration of war in August 1914, the Tsar put a temporary end to the growing labour upheaval and curtailed the limited freedoms of the preceding years. As described further in later chapters, Russia's borderland socialist movements were often profoundly shaped by the war, whose impact on the relationship of forces between radicals and moderates – and on their political orientations – was perhaps second in importance only to the 1905 revolution's defeat.

Entry into World War One not only deepened state repression, it radically overhauled the political and industrial geography of borderland regions such as Poland, Lithuania, and Latvia. Faced with a German invasion in 1915 (and the subsequent occupation of Poland and Lithuania), whole industries and hundreds of thousands of workers were uprooted. As many as half a million people in the Baltic alone fled to central Russia; among the Poles, the number was upwards of one million. Petrograd, the centre of a wartime production boom, gained an unprecedented level of economic and political centrality.

By 1917, there were hundreds of thousands of Polish, Latvian, Lithuanian, and Estonian wage labourers working in the factories of central Russia and Ukraine. Among these were thousands of non-Russian socialists, many of whom would go on to play critical roles in 1917, including in the capital. Represented in the Petrograd Soviet were not only all the Russian socialist parties, but also the Jewish Bund, the Latvian SDs, and the three wings of Polish socialists. With the geographic dispersion of these and other borderland Marxist organisations during the war came closer integration into the RSDRP and its competing factions.[135]

---

135    White 1990 and Манусевич 1965. Various Soviet-era historians pointed to partial de-industrialisation in Poland as a reason for the hegemony of conciliatory socialists during the Polish Revolution of 1918–19. Though there is likely some truth to this, workers in Poland nevertheless remained militant and, as a point of comparison, radicals remained

February 1917 marked a definitive turning point regarding the organisational question for all Marxist parties. Virtually overnight, Russia became the freest country in Europe, allowing the empire's socialists, including the Bolsheviks, to abandon the underground's conspiratorial and undemocratic norms. The impact of the previous decades of autocratic rule, however, continued to hang over the revolutionary movement's organisational dynamics. After February, all socialist currents attempted to crystallise new party structures over the span of a few short months, in the heat of the revolution. As such, they remained remarkably unconsolidated.

Socialist parties in 1917 tended to be decentralised, regionally fragmented, and fluid, often with only a tenuous hold over their new mass memberships. This was especially true for non-Russian socialist organisations, which were often still reeling from the geographic dispersion imposed by the war. Regarding the Bolshevik current in 1917, historian Edward Acton writes: 'Far from being highly centralized and disciplined ... it could barely keep track of the local party organizations which sprang up in the course of the year. ... Formal policy directives issued from the centre were followed only in so far as they corresponded to local Bolshevik opinion'.[136]

As another historian has observed, 'if the Bolshevik cause had depended on its organizational capacities, its prospects were very dim in October 1917'.[137] That the Bolsheviks were somewhat better organised than their moderate socialist rivals is not saying much. Moreover, the organisational edge of the Bolsheviks was first and foremost rooted in their cohesion on the big political questions of the day: the war, proletarian hegemony, soviet power – and mass action. In 1917, like in years prior, political rather than organisational questions determined the fate of social democratic currents.

After a brief moment of united activity to take down the Tsar in February 1917, socialists in Russia generally reverted to their longstanding strategic approaches towards mass action. For their part, right-leaning SDs pushed patient proletarian organisation and education. Now that political freedom reigned, they argued, it would finally be possible to build a 'European' labour movement in Russia. This stance was true to the spirit of the German SPD's tried and tested tactics, but its advocacy cannot be explained solely by ideology, seeing as one of the defining attributes of moderate social democrats in

---

hegemonic in Latvia, which also experienced a dramatic decline of industry during the war.

136   Acton 1990, p. 194. See also Service 1979, pp. 3, 62 and McDaniel 1988, pp. 389–90. On this dynamic in Ukraine, see, for example, Бош 1925, p. 4.

137   Cited in Acton 1990, p. 195.

1917 was their disregard for Marxist theory and their break with key orthodox axioms concerning blocs with liberals and coalition governments with capitalist parties. Indeed, it was precisely because of their class collaborationism that so many moderates sought to hold back what they saw as a precipitous upsurge.

In 1917, as had been the case in previous years, it was the conciliatory socialists, not the radicals, who tended to demonstrate a distrust of mass mobilisation. Among most Ukrainian SDs, for example, an emphasis on organisational discipline and political education reflected their desire to channel working people into a cross-class project of nation-building. Undirected plebeian action threatened to implode the national-democratic front in Ukraine and it risked an undesirable rupture with the Russian Provisional Government. In response to July's food riots in Kiev, the newspaper of the Ukrainian SDs criticised the rioters for 'having no plan, no ideological slogans'; according to the article, these were simply 'a series of unnecessary, rash actions'.[138]

Though this hesitancy in large part reflected the Ukrainian Social Democracy's prioritisation of the push for national autonomy, it was simultaneously linked to the party's view that winning Ukrainian rights needed to pass through a negotiated settlement with the Russian government. As Ukrainian scholar O.Yu. Vysotskyy has recently pointed out, 'one of the major factors that led to the defeat' of the Ukrainian SDs was that they envisioned winning their political project 'not so much through the support of the masses, but rather through an agreement with the Russian Provisional Government'.[139]

Unlike in Ukraine, the insistence of Mensheviks and Bundists on tried and tested tactics in 1917 was not linked to the national question. In addition to reflecting a sincere political desire to emulate the strongly organised mass labour movement of Western Europe, this stance also reflected a hope to maintain an alliance with liberals. With the overthrow of Tsarism and the conquest of political freedom, it seemed to the Bundists and Mensheviks that it would now be possible to effectively construct the cohesive and disciplined labour movement that had been blocked under Tsarism. If workers surged into premature mass militancy, they would throw the liberals into the arms of reaction, thereby imperilling the political freedom needed to build a lasting and powerful labour movement.

As historian Ziva Galili y Garcia has demonstrated, the Mensheviks 'clung to their belief in the efficacy of educational and organizational work'. In a March 1917 article titled 'Anarchism and Organisation', the currents' newspaper

138    Cited in Солдатенко 2007, pp. 138–9.
139    Висоцький 2004, p. 76.

*Rabochaia Gazeta* (Workers' Newspaper) warned of the danger that anarchist orientations 'could again cast their shadow on our revolution, as they had
in 1905–6'.[140] In Georgia, as elsewhere, the Mensheviks thus promoted class
organisation rather than action in their hopes of building a strong labour movement capable of pressuring but not alienating the liberal bourgeoisie.[141]

   In the first months of the 1917 revolution, moderate socialists received widespread – indeed, unprecedented – support among working people. With the
advent of political freedom, there were no longer serious obstacles towards
building mass workers' associations and spreading the socialist message – in
such conditions, the tried and tested approach became more plausible than
ever before. Workers and peasants initially hoped that the government could be
peacefully pressured to meet their demands and, in the soviets and trade unions, radical internationalists almost invariably found themselves in a minority. Yet the deepening economic crisis, the capitalist counter-offensive against
the gains won in February, and the inability of the Provisional Government to
meet workers' pressing demands quickly turned working people in Russia back
towards militant tactics.

   Strikes, wildcat workplace disputes, unauthorised demonstrations, and land
seizures arose across Russia. The key patterns and radicalising dynamics of the
1905 labour movement largely repeated themselves. Strikes, while strongest in
the capital, spread like wildfire.[142] Working-class organisation and politicisa-
tion also grew as the struggles progressed, a dynamic now facilitated by the
absence of Tsarist repression. Unions, parties, and soviets exploded in size.
But as numerous scholars have demonstrated, from an international comparative perspective Russia's 1917 revolution was distinctly marked by a low level
of organisational cohesion and a high level of proletarian spontaneity.[143] The
overwhelming majority of labour conflicts, observed one metalworker leader
in June, 'arise and proceed in their first stages without the knowledge of the
trade union organizations'.[144]

   To keep the Provisional Government afloat in the face of an increasingly
militant working class, Mensheviks and other class-collaborationist currents
were obliged to call on workers to hold back their struggles and demands. 'All

---

140   Cited in Galili y Garcia 1989, pp. 143–4.
141   Jones 1992, pp. 258–9.
142   On the dynamics of strikes across Russia in 1917, see Koenker and Rosenberg 1989.
143   See, for example, the discussion in Koenker 1981, pp. 364–5 and McDaniel 1988, pp. 326–
      47. McDaniel notes that 'worker organizations could not make of the young Russian labor
      movement anything like a labor army' (McDaniel 1988, p. 335).
144   Cited in Devlin 1976, p. 179.

Mensheviks theoretically shared this emphasis on organization', notes Galili y Garcia. But it was particularly the most class-collaborationist Mensheviks who 'looked on the new organizational opportunities as a means of restraint' over workers.[145]

Yet by the autumn, class-collaborationist socialists across the empire were losing their short-lived control over mass labour organisations. Rather than acknowledge that working people were making a rational choice by turning towards mass action and its radical advocates, moderates dismissed these developments as the product of popular ignorance, peasant immaturity, and Bolshevik manipulation.[146] More perceptively, one Menshevik member of the Provisional Government admitted in 1918 that 'much of what the Bolsheviks did later could and should have been done by the provisional government' – yet such action was not taken because the 'basic and fatal characteristic' of the administration had been its opposition to 'the creativity of the lower classes'.[147]

Free of any orientation towards an alliance with liberals, revolutionary social democrats – of which the Bolsheviks were now the most influential current – consistently promoted and participated in the workers' upsurge. Neil Harding's well-known study of Lenin's political thought has detailed how a commitment to mass initiative lay at the heart of his revolutionary strategy throughout 1917.[148] But this approach was not Lenin's personal invention. Bolsheviks as well as their non-Russian allies consistently promoted bottom-up action in all regions, stressing that collective disruption and the creativity of working people was the motor driving the revolution forward, as well as the basis for building a new state of and for working people. Indeed, from February onwards – well before Lenin's return in April – Bolsheviks disputed the moderates' contention that a prolonged period of proletarian education and association was necessary before working people could seize power. This stance has often been overlooked in the literature, but it was central to the events of 1917.

In a revealing article on 21 March, Stučka made the case for why revolutionary Marxists in the Russian Empire rejected the view that 'first there must be a long period of social freedom and only then can one start a serious struggle for socialism', which would mean 'postpon[ing] socialism itself for many years'. The transformative impact of revolutionary struggle, he insisted, could allow Russia's workers to rapidly reach socialist conclusions without an extended

---

145    Galili y Garcia 1989, p. 144.
146    Cited Gitelman 1972, p. 95. See also Acton 1990, p. 165.
147    Cited in Lande 1974, p. 21.
148    Harding 2009.

phase of patiently accumulating strength under conditions of political freedom: 'it should be noted that six months in the life of a revolution equals the
same as decades of peaceful development'.[149] This dynamic, combined with
the imminent international revolution, put socialist overhaul on the immediate political horizon.

Concerning labour movement tactics, Bolshevik labour leader V.P. Miliutin
argued as follows at the party's April conference:

> It is not enough to talk only about propaganda and education: even when
> we are in a minority, we not only propagandise, but also take action ... [I]n
> this era, life dictates definite mass actions and it requires that we provide
> these actions with definite leadership.[150]

Latvian SD leader Fricis Roziņš elaborated on this mass action approach and
its strategic implications, explaining that 1905 showed that revolutions could
erupt virtually overnight and that working people could be rapidly transformed
through participation in struggle. An emphasis on mass action, Roziņš posited, constituted a strategic break with the older social democratic tradition: in
his view, this approach was '[o]ne of the most important features of the new,
revolutionary socialism'.[151]

Against liberal and class-collaborationist socialist accusations that Russia's
internationalists were promoting 'anarchism', Zinoviev replied that '[a]ll these
cries ... are dictated by a dead, official, bureaucratic view on what a revolution
is'. His conclusion was to the point:

> Self-initiated actions are inevitable. ... We propose to organise these
> actions, to systematise them, to consider and conduct them in a planned
> manner, relying on the majority of the population. We are the only ones
> really fighting against anarchy.[152]

Zinoviev was justified in disputing accusations of anarchism. Without continual efforts to preserve and strengthen party and mass organisation structures in the face of intense centrifugal pressures, revolutionaries would not
have been in a position to independently shape the course of events in 1917.
By way of comparison, anarchists in Russia remained inattentive to strength-

---

149   Stučka 1917a [1976–78], p. 128.
150   РСДРП (большевиков) 1917a [1958], pp. 87–8.
151   Roziņš 1917 [1963–65], p. 298.
152   [Г. Зиновьев], 'Об "анархии"', *Правда*, 4 May 1917.

ening their organisations, severely undercutting their ability to constitute an alternative leadership pole. As Russian historian Vladimir Sapon has noted in his otherwise sympathetic survey, 'the organisational question turned out to be an insurmountable obstacle for anarchists ... an All-Russian anarchist party remained an unrealised dream'.[153]

Though Russia's Marxists strategically oriented to labour spontaneity, they consistently sought to lean on this to raise working-class consciousness and build organisation. Nor did the Bolsheviks launch into action at every possible opportunity, regardless of the relationship of forces. At critical junctures in 1917, the party leadership in Petrograd sought to prevent what it saw as premature action since the rest of the empire was not yet supportive of soviet power. For example, during the July Days armed demonstrations in the capital, the cautious approach of Bolshevik leaders clashed with party rank and filers who were over-eager to plunge into militant battle. These attempts by Bolsheviks and allied radicals in 1917 to hold back mass action until a more favourable moment must be underlined, since Leninist writers have too often posited that only supposedly 'fatalistic' Marxists like Kautsky or the Finnish SDs ever put the brakes on collective action.[154]

Tactical debates took on different forms in the various regions of the empire. In Petrograd, the workers' movement was generally a few steps ahead of the rest of Russia. As such, Bolsheviks in the capital from February onwards sought to hold back the city's workers from attempting a seizure of power before this could be accomplished on an All-Russian level. In July, the dam burst early, as radicalised workers and party ranks – against the judgement of the local party leadership – swept the Bolshevik Petrograd committee into supporting an ill-advised armed demonstration. Burned in July, workers and party cadre in the capital up until the October Revolution were cautious about calling any mass actions that could lead to another premature outbreak.

Bolsheviks in other cities were not confronted with an analogous dilemma of holding back the mass movement so that the rest of the empire could catch up. Consistently, they not only participated in but also initiated mass actions and general strikes throughout the year. Unlike in Petrograd, the months of September and October across Russia were marked by a revolutionary SD-backed upsurge of economic and general strikes. Over forty city-wide strikes shook the empire in September and October, compared to 14 in the spring. In the Donets Basin, Moscow, and beyond, the October Revolution was the

---

153   Сапон 2009, p. 277.
154   See, for example, Hart 2018.

culmination of a mass strike wave promoted by the Bolsheviks and internationalists over the opposition of the moderates.[155]

The seizure of power by working people across much of the empire in late 1917 constituted the climax of the preceding months and years of popular insurgency. Despite relatively low levels of working-class organisation, the weakness of the Russian bourgeoisie and the Provisional Government's lack of political legitimacy and repressive capacity opened space for rebellious workers to fill the political vacuum.

Nevertheless, the cumulative impact of mass action made October possible, not inevitable. Even faced with a relatively weak ruling class, the conscious intervention of organised Marxists proved to be necessary to help workers overcome the various obstacles on their road to power. In other words, without the impact of a sufficiently influential party, the potential energy of the popular upsurge would not have become kinetic. Historian John Marot has argued that 'in times of revolution, free political activity – the action of parties – is the determining determination'.[156]

A comparative empire-wide lens suggests this point's plausibility. Militant mass labour struggles did not culminate in the same outcome in all areas. In important regions such as Georgia and Ukraine, radicals failed to win the leadership of the revolution and the soviets failed to take power. Class-collaborationist socialists opposed the October Revolution, reflecting their longstanding view that working people in Russia were unprepared to rule society on their own.[157] During and following October, right-leaning leaders of the Mensheviks, Ukrainian SDs, and Bundists insisted that the 'Bolshevik coup' was an anti-Marxist aberration plunging Russia into 'anarchy'. Rather than a step towards socialism, October reflected nothing more than Lenin and Trotsky's dictatorial manipulation of the unconscious, impatient, hungry masses.

Bolsheviks and allied socialists denounced these claims.[158] Like his comrades across the empire, Baku Bolshevik leader Stepan Shaumian in November emphasised the centrality of working-class initiative:

---

155    Mandel 1984a, p. 310, McDaniel 1988, p. 319, Koenker and Rosenberg 1989, pp. 520–1, and
       Koenker 1989, pp. 141–2. Noting the uneven development of this mass action wave on the
       eve of October, Trotsky wrote: 'The most peaceful city of all, perhaps, was Petrograd' (Trotsky 1932 [2008], p. 610).

156    Marot 2012, p. 139.

157    Raleigh 1986, p. 268.

158    Шаумян 1917 [1958], pp. 111–12. Subsequent historians have confirmed the radicals' claims
       about the depth of proletarian support for soviet power across Russia and the extent to
       which this stance reflected a rational choice by working people. See, for example, Suny
       1972a, Acton 1992, and Rabinowitch 1976.

The direct and definite democratic policy which the Soviet undertakes today, free from obstacles and obstructions, I hope, will arouse the spontaneous activity of the members of the Soviet and of those masses of the population which invested them with their confidence. The slight loss [of the moderate socialists] will be made up by the general inspiration, by the awakening of selfless activity of those healthy and powerful creative forces of the lower classes that up to this time have slumbered because they did not have room to make their appearance.[159]

In light of the subsequent rise of Stalinism, the Bolsheviks' wager on self-activity appears somewhat over-optimistic. A reliance on mass action and the weakness of collective organisation – not to mention stable parliamentary bodies – facilitated revolutionary mobilisation in the post-February effervescence, but it made working-class governance that much harder, particularly in conditions of economic free fall.

On the whole, Bolsheviks and their non-Russian allies tended to underestimate the difficulties of post-capitalist state administration. Mass participation was no panacea for effective revolutionary governance and, furthermore, high levels of soviet participation proved difficult to sustain after October. By early 1918, mass actions by desperate Russian workers and peasants were increasingly directed *against* the new government, leading many Bolsheviks now to lament the absence of stronger traditions of disciplined organisation and socialist consciousness among the country's workers.[160]

## 8      Mass Organisation and Action in Finland: 1917–18

Finland's 1917–18 revolution constitutes a unique case study for analysing orthodox Marxist politics in a revolutionary process under parliamentary conditions. In a polity with longstanding legal labour organisations and parliamentary institutions, most Finnish socialist leaders – including the radicals – remained committed to prioritising proletarian organisation and electoral work. And while focusing on mass action proved to be indispensable for revolutionary practice in the rest of the Russian Empire, the Finnish experience shows that there was no universal 'one size fits all' approach for the most effective socialist balance of working-class association, education, and action.

---

159    Cited in Suny 1972a, pp. 163–4. See also McDaniel 1988, p. 392.
160    Rosenberg 1985 and Acton 1990, pp. 204–8. The Communist International (1920) nevertheless persisted in arguing that in all countries the 'most important method of struggle of the proletariat against the bourgeoisie … is above all mass action.'

In contrast with Germany and much of Western Europe, where labour bureaucracies actively combatted mass action in order to conserve their organisations, top Finnish SDP leaders sought to implement Kautsky's old vision of patiently accumulating forces for the final revolutionary blow. As such, their politics and practices in 1917–18 pose a serious challenge to those who dismiss the anti-capitalist potential of revolutionary social democracy.[161]

The SDP had seized the available openings to raise class consciousness via popular associations and sustained electoral work, culminating in its 1916 parliamentary victory. The strength of its organising, and the legitimacy granted by its electoral majority, gave the party sufficient leverage to face off with Finland's powerful and well-organised bourgeoisie. Indeed, one historian has recently argued that it was primarily the 'exceptionally far-reaching [degree of] organisation' in Finland that led to its civil war.[162] Building upon the preceding decades of socialist organising, 1917 witnessed a further mushrooming of Finnish labour associations. For instance, from 1916 to late 1917 the trade union movement grew from 30,000 to 165,000 members and the party from 52,000 to well over a hundred thousand. In the most novel development, unskilled workers surged into the organised labour movement in 1917, marking a departure from years prior.[163] Pertti Haapala sums up this process:

> The party [was] exceptionally strong and powerful, the best-organized political force in Finland. The membership peaked at 110,000 in 1917, and regular meetings were organized in close to 1000 Workers' Halls. The party and its local associations created a lively subculture of papers, books, festivals, cultural activities, and sports. It is self-evident that the organization of the Red Guards and the Red civil organization in 1918 were based on the organizational structure and activity of the previous years. Ironic or not, the choirs and playhouses were the backbones of the volunteer army.[164]

But coexisting with the Finnish labour movement's institutional strength was a significant growth in mass action after February 1917. As *Työmies* observed in April: 'in the political activity of the working class a new form of action, direct mass action, is coming to support and assist the former, purely parliamentary form'.[165] Facing a deepening social crisis and the looming threat of hunger,

161	For a recent debate on this question, see Hart 2017 and Blanc 2017b.
162	Cited in Alapuro 2018, p. 10.
163	Suodenjoki and Peltola 2007, pp. 212–13.
164	Haapala 2014, p. 32.
165	Cited in Upton 1980, p. 57.

many hitherto peaceful and patient Finnish workers took direct action to an unparalleled degree. Strikes shook urban and rural Finland from the spring onwards. Noting the 'weakening of the hitherto carefully observed discipline and rules of conduct', historian David Kirby explains that 'the cautious and well-tried tactics of the union official were increasingly cast aside'.[166] As the food crisis deepened, workers – often working women – began breaking into stores and warehouses to seize provisions. Finally, the Red Guard self-defence units set up or sanctioned by the party and unions began to assert themselves as an autonomous and militant expression of radicalised workers.

According to the Finnish bourgeoisie – a well-organised class with a long history of institution building – the SDP was actively pushing society toward anarchy and collapse. Conservative writer Henning Söderhjelm's first-hand account of the revolution describes the popular upsurge in Finland after February 1917 as follows:

> Pure mob-rule developed with unexpected swiftness. ... The proletariat no longer begged and prayed, but claimed and demanded. Never, I suppose, has the working-man, but especially the rough, felt so puffed up with power as in the year 1917 in Finland.[167]

Within the Finnish Social Democracy there existed all shades of opinion on mass action. Socialist MPs, class-collaborationist SDP functionaries, and trade union officials were adamant about the need to put a stop to what they saw as undisciplined popular disorder. In their view, efforts to promote peaceful organised activities were being fatally undermined by anarchistic forces interested only in direct action. Throughout the year, SDP moderates exhorted working people to join organisations and respect their directives rather than engage in reckless combat. The continued efforts by this small but influential minority to halt the mass movement frequently led to clashes with an increasingly radicalised rank and file. One socialist leader lamented that union 'functionaries were threatened, even attacked, if tactics were not in line with the workers' own ideas'.[168]

The party's orthodox Left took a different stance. Though it also focused its efforts on the parliamentary and trade union arena, it saw the mass movement as useful for generating pressure to push through a platform of radical reforms

---

166    Kirby 1971, p. 219.
167    Söderhjelm 1919, p. 20.
168    Cited in Kirby 1917, p. 219. For an influential right-leaning SDP leader's accusation of anarchism against the orthodox party Left, see Huttunen 1918, pp. 25, 52, 70, 77–8.

against the opposition of the capitalist class. Concerned not to lose their influence over the increasingly militant wings of Finnish workers, Finland's leading revolutionary SDs supported – or at least went along with – the surge from below. Söderhjelm perceptively noted the political roots of the SDP's general refusal to put a brake on the proletarian upsurge:

> The leaders of the Labour Party might, of course, have done much to stop this movement which, for every week that passed, assumed more plainly the character of arbitrariness and violence. But they did not. The reasons for this were many. In part they were not able, and in part they were not willing to interfere with the violent agitation of the masses. *This would have demanded co-operation with the bourgeoisie, and such co-operation was not desired.*[169]

Both the strengths and potential limitations of the SDP's approach became evident in the climactic moments of the revolution. The anti-democratic dissolution of Finland's socialist-led parliament by Finnish and Russian elites in the early fall enraged large numbers of workers and socialists. By October, the crisis in Finland – and across the Russian Empire – had come to a boil.

A radical flank of Finnish workers in the city and countryside, particularly those linked to the Red Guards, angrily demanded that the party seize power. Violent clashes bubbled up across Finland. But moderate SDP leaders remained wary of abandoning the parliamentary arena since a turn to revolutionary mass action risked destroying the considerable organisational and political gains of the labour movement over the preceding years. Others to their left believed that a moment of revolutionary action was necessary, but that it should be pushed back until the working class was better organised and better armed. In late October, SDP leader Kullervo Manner thus argued that the party should attempt to hold off a revolutionary uprising until there was a more favourable relationship of forces:

> We cannot avoid the revolution for very long. ... Faith in the value of peaceful activity is lost and the working class is beginning to trust only in its own strength. ... If we are mistaken about the rapid approach of revolution, I would be delighted.[170]

---

169    Söderhjelm 1919, p. 19, my emphasis. See also Upton 1980, pp. 58–9 and Carrez 2008, pp. 497, 502, 540.
170    Cited in Upton 1980, p. 133.

After the Bolsheviks led Petrograd's workers to power in late October, it seemed that Finland would be next in line. Deprived of the military support of the Russian Provisional Government, Finland's upper class was dangerously isolated. Russian soldiers, stationed in Finland by the tens of thousands, supported the Bolsheviks and their call for peace. 'The wave of victorious Bolshevism will give our socialists water under their mill, and they are certainly able to start it turning', observed one Finnish liberal.[171]

The far left of the SDP, as well as the Bolsheviks in Petrograd, implored Finnish socialist leaders to immediately take power. But the party and trade union leadership prevaricated. It was unclear to anybody whether the new Soviet government could last more than a few days. In this climate, socialist leaders were justifiably worried that a defeated revolution would destroy the considerable accumulated gains of the movement over the previous years – Finnish workers had more to lose than their peers elsewhere in the empire. Moderate socialists clung to the hope that a peaceful parliamentary solution could be found. Some radicals argued that the seizure of power was both possible and urgently necessary. Others agreed with the need to take power, but felt that such a task first required the support of a united party leadership. Most leaders wavered.[172]

Unable to come to an agreement on seizing power, the SDP instead called a general strike on 14 November in defence of democracy against the counter-revolutionary bourgeoisie, for workers' urgent economic needs, and for Finnish sovereignty. Contrary to historiographic claims about the SDP's purported passivity and fatalism, the party actively initiated proletarian action on a massive scale. The strike call explained that bourgeois intransigence had 'forced the workers to take the path of mass action'.[173] In a further call to battle, the party press underscored that whereas the 1905 Great Strike had been directed against the Russian Government, this was the first general strike in Finland ever aimed 'against the native exploiting classes'.[174]

The response from below was overwhelming – in fact, striking workers went further than the strike appeal itself. Finland ground to a halt. In a few locales, SDP organisations and Red Guards occupied strategic buildings and arrested bourgeois politicians. It seemed that this insurgent pattern might soon be

---

171 Cited in Upton 1980, p. 140.
172 The SDP's head in Turku warned on 30 October that 'the dissatisfaction directed towards the bourgeoisie can be directed also against us, if we do not decisively assume the leadership of the rising mass movement' (cited in Siltala 2014, p. 76).
173 Cited in Suodenjoki and Peltola 2007, p. 246.
174 Cited in Kiiskilä 2010, p. 75.

repeated in Helsinki. Nevertheless, the party and union leaders ultimately hesitated to make a decisive turn to revolutionary rupture. Though Otto Kuusinen,
the SDP's top revolutionary social democrat, had raised the potential of seizing
power in late October and early November, he too rejected widespread calls to
transform the general strike into an armed uprising.

In subsequent chapters we will examine the multiple reasons why SDP
leaders missed what in hindsight appears to have been the most favourable
moment for revolution. Kuusinen argued in a 1918 Communist pamphlet that
this had been a 'historical error' and that the party's 'natural tendency to
delay the revolutionary explosion' was rooted in an understandable but flawed
desire 'to protect and conserve its [democratic and organisational] conquests'.
The result was that the revolution was 'postponed till a time when the bourgeoisie [was] better prepared for it than they were in November'.[175] Finnish
scholar Juha Siltala has similarly argued that November constituted an important missed opportunity for revolution.[176]

On the whole, these points are well taken. Finland's bourgeois forces certainly took advantage of the two months after the November strike to build
up their troops. But such political developments are far clearer in hindsight
than they were at the time. There was no way of knowing during the general strike whether a more favourable moment for taking power might subsequently present itself. And far more than purely ideological considerations
were at play. Petrograd's Bolsheviks, too, had at various moments in 1917 sought
to prevent what they considered to be a premature seizure of power. Moreover,
in Baku, the Bolsheviks hesitated to seize power in October and ultimately
waited for another six months before doing so.[177]

There is no way of demonstrating with any certainty that a revolution in
November would have been more successful than what occurred two months
later. During November's general strike, upper-class forces were more poorly
organised and had fewer arms than in January; conversely, in November the
Red Guards too were poorly organised and the SDP was deeply divided. A push
by the most radical wing to seize power would likely have led the party to
split down the middle, potentially preventing the labour movement from seiz-

---

175    Kuusinen 1919, pp. 8–9. Though insights can be gleaned from Kuusinen's self-critique, this
       was a one-sided polemic published to win cadre to a new Communist Party. Moreover,
       it was written during his brief conversion to an ultra-left, anti-parliamentary strategy of
       Left Communism, an approach he and the Finnish Communist Party abandoned by the
       following year. As such, it was hardly a balanced self-assessment.
176    Siltala 2014, p. 76.
177    Suny 1972a, pp. 147–233.

ing and holding onto power across Finland since many workers would have abstained from any revolutionary action not explicitly sanctioned by their mass organisations.

Yet the most radicalised workers across Finland were incensed at what they saw as an unnecessary retreat in November, leading a significant minority to lose confidence in the SDP leadership. Many frustrated socialist militants looked for arms and turned to direct action, largely through the vehicle of the Red Guards. The bourgeoisie likewise prepared for civil war by building up its White Guard militia and turning to the German government for armed support. For their part, the Bolsheviks encouraged Finland's socialists to end their vacillations and initiate a bold fight for power.

Despite the rapid breakdown of Finland's social cohesion after November, many SDP leaders persisted with fruitless parliamentary negotiations. Yet this time the party's orthodox left wing stiffened its spine and declared that any further delay would only lead to disaster. Yrjö Sirola, one of the SDP's orthodox leaders, insisted that the party must now take revolutionary action since the masses could no longer be held back: 'we cannot deprive workers, who have taken the revolutionary path, of hope ... [W]e must go along with them'.[178]

The SDP's late 1917 temporising gave radicals time to win the party leadership to support the establishment of a workers' government. Through a long series of internal battles in December and early January (discussed in later chapters), Kuusinen, Sirola, and the other party radicals eventually won out. In late January, the SDP translated its revolutionary words into deeds. To signal the start of the revolution, party leaders on the evening of 26 January 1918 lit a red lantern in the tower of the Helsinki Workers' Hall. Over the next days, the SDP and its affiliated workers' organisations seized power in all the large cities of Finland. Explaining the party's actions, on 28 January *Työmies* declared that while organisational and parliamentary efforts had 'great value and importance', they 'are not enough'. At a certain moment in the development of the struggle for proletarian liberation, it was necessary to 'pass to the road of revolutionary battle'.[179]

The Finnish Social Democracy's seizure of power in January 1918 demonstrated that orthodox Marxism could be concretised into a pro-active break from capitalism. SDP leaders' insistence on class independence ultimately helped them overcome their caution about general strikes and revolutionary struggle. True to revolutionary social democracy's longstanding perspec-

---

178    Cited in Upton 1980, pp. 172–3. See also Hodgson 1967, pp. 68–9.
179    Cited in Kiiskilä 2010, p. 104.

tive for non-autocratic regimes, patient organisation and education, and a strong parliamentary focus, eventually led to anti-capitalist action. To quote sociologist Risto Alapuro: 'the worker movement was able to delay the outbreak of the revolution to the point where it conceived the takeover as a defensive act. The postponement was made possible by the strong tradition of associational organisation'.[180] Though Alapuro downplays leadership agency, compared with the rest of the empire the role of socialist leaders was *especially* important in Finland because of the labour movement's strongly organised nature. Elsewhere in Russia, the relative weakness of party structures precluded their top leaderships from exercising the same degree of political sway.

The historical record, in other words, does not support the frequent assertion that Finland's 'defensive Kautskyists' were swept into the revolution despite their fundamental reformism.[181] Claims about the party's purported fatalism are difficult to square with the fact that the SDP launched a general strike in November and an armed revolution in January 1918. Moderate SDP leader Evert Huttunen was right to observe in 1918 that though the SDP's leftist leaders could have sought to prevent the uprising, 'they did not do it. To the contrary, they contributed to the revolutionary action by stirring up the crowd for the "decisive battle", as the party's proclamations so well demonstrated'.[182]

This chapter has shown how working-class organisational structures and tactical priorities were shaped by a regime's degree of political freedom and parliamentary democracy. Autocratic conditions prompted underground Marxists to orient to mass actions like strikes and demonstrations far more than their counterparts abroad. The strategic perspectives and organisational practices of illegal SD organisations under Tsarism could not be mechanically transposed to low inclusion parliamentary polities like Finland or Germany, where organisational and electoral openings were much greater, where spontaneous militancy and strike waves were less common, and where the bourgeoisie was stronger.

Contrary to Leninist assumptions that the Russian Revolution constituted an internationally replicable model, experiences across imperial Russia show that the transformation of the proletariat into a class for itself could take many different forms and sequences in different political contexts. There was no universal socialist formula for the correct balance of organisation, propaganda,

---

180    Alapuro 2018, p. 11.
181    For a further elaboration of this argument, see Blanc 2017b. For a standard account of Finland's 'defensive revolution', see Alapuro 1988.
182    Huttunen 1918, pp. 97–8.

and action – or parliamentary and extra-parliamentary activity – since this depended not only on the conjuncture, but also on the degree of regime democratisation as well as the strength of one's opponents. And for that same reason, it would be wrong to assume that the educationalist emphasis and tactical intransigence of Finnish and German Marxists, who operated in decidedly undemocratic parliamentary polities, are precisely replicable in advanced capitalist welfare states, where risks for mass action are lower and where the possibilities for transformative legislative reforms are higher.

Under relatively democratic regimes, socialists cannot realistically hope to win a popular majority through a strategy hinged on preaching the socialist gospel and organising an isolationist working-class subculture like in Finland – let alone a strategy that minimises electoral politics in the hope of eventually leading a volcanic wave of disruptive mass actions like in central Russia. Effective socialist strategy will necessarily look different in an autocracy, a low-inclusion parliamentary regime, or a democratic welfare state. For radicals in capitalist democracies, experience has shown that the central strategic task, and the key political dilemma, is how to fight – both inside and outside the state – for transformative reforms in ways that open up, rather than close off, avenues for organising workers to overcome capitalist domination.

But as the experience of the Second International clearly demonstrates, the growth of mass workers' organisations also necessarily increases bureaucratic and conservative tendencies. Labour opportunism is not primarily caused by leaders' moral or political failings, but rather by the structure of class relations: faced with the immense power of the capitalist class, workers' organisations (and especially their full-time leaderships) tend to become more conservative as they grow in strength, because the potential costs and risks of disruptive action – which are already high for a heterogeneous, relatively powerless group like workers – increase once organisations have more to lose.[183] Socialists engaged in mass politics have no way to avoid confronting these dilemmas. Finland's revolution, however, underscores that they are not always insurmountable.

Especially since successful workers' revolutions in parliamentary conditions were exceedingly rare in the twentieth century, Finnish Social Democracy's contributions should not be overlooked. The SDP for almost two decades patiently accumulated its forces, which it ultimately deployed for revolutionary action in early 1918. In contrast, German Social Democrats proved to be unable to push beyond capitalist rule at the moment of truth. Contrary to pre-

---

183   On these dynamics, see Offe and Wiesenthal 1980.

vailing scholarly and socialist interpretations, this default did not arise because socialists followed Kautsky. In Germany, labour's leaders abandoned orthodox Second International Marxism. In Finland, like central Russia, they implemented it to overthrow capitalist rule.

# CHAPTER 5

# Working-Class Hegemony

Academics and activists have tended to assume that the defining political divide within the Russian revolutionary movement concerned issues such as intelligentsia-worker relations, party organisation forms, or parliamentary versus soviet democracy.

None of these interpretations are borne out by the historical evidence. By examining how Marxists approached strategic alliances with liberal parties and capitalists before 1917, this chapter will argue that the most decisive political dividing line in the Russian Empire was whether or not to fight for the 'hegemony of the proletariat'. In both parliamentary and autocratic conditions, socialist parties and tendencies in imperial Russia that upheld this strategy pushed for a government of working people in and after 1917. And those parties that dropped this perspective after 1905 became absorbed into coalition regimes with the local bourgeoisie or they placed themselves under the aegis of an imperialist power.

With the early exception of Finland, socialist parties under Tsarism overwhelmingly adhered to revolutionary social democracy's intransigent class struggle commitments up through the first Russian Revolution. Pushing for socialists to head the urban-rural insurgency, Marxists insisted that liberals were incapable of effectively leading the fight for democracy or for the social demands of peasants, workers, and other dominated sectors. The following axiom, as affirmed by the Bund in 1900, was incessantly repeated: 'the political freedom needed by Russia's proletariat can be won only by the proletariat itself'.[1] Crucially, no early social democratic party argued that the working class should subordinate or temper its independent struggle for the sake of a bloc with liberal currents, considered to be vacillating at best or treacherous at worst.

Despite the centrality of this strategic question, many historians have gravely mischaracterised the stance of revolutionary social democracy. Historian Geoffrey Swain, for instance, writes that 'the notion that the proletariat might play a hegemonic role in the bourgeois revolution was not something that orthodox Marxists could easily accept'.[2] This claim, as we will see, inverts reality.

One of the main reasons why radical socialists in Russia and Europe saw Karl Kautsky as their theoretical leading light was that he was the most influential

---

1  'Доклад цк Бунда' [1900] in Андерсон 2010, p. 107.
2  Swain 2006, p. 28.

proponent of class conflict. Indeed, a principled insistence on class independence was *the* defining tenet of Marxist orthodoxy in the eyes of both its supporters and detractors. As Bolshevik leader Grigory Zinoviev noted in a laudatory 1909 defence of Kautsky's approach:

> The issue of the relation of the proletariat to the bourgeoisie (both liberal and democratic), of possible blocs and agreements with it, of the growth or the blunting of contradictions between it and the proletariat, and so forth, has for a long time been the central point of dispute between Marxists and revisionists in all countries.[3]

In this chapter's concluding section, we examine how the early consensus on the issue of the hegemony of the proletariat broke down after 1905. Henceforth, advocating ongoing blocs with bourgeois parties and capitalist governments became the determining line in the sand for the empire's social democrats. An autocratic context, on its own, did not guarantee the political predominance of radicals inside the workers' movement; relatively contingent processes of political articulation – particularly how socialist parties responded to the defeat of Russia's first revolution – became especially important. Demoralised in the wake of 1905, various Marxist parties and currents in the empire made a marked turn to the right. Above all, this was manifest in abandoning their formerly antagonistic approach to bourgeois liberalism. In so doing, they were breaking from, not affirming, the longstanding position of revolutionary social democracy and the hitherto hegemonic radicalism of imperial Russia's workers' movements.

But in Finland, the opposite pattern prevailed: orthodox Marxists won the leadership of the previously moderate Social Democratic Party following the radicalising upheaval of 1905. Under their stewardship, Finland's socialist movement resisted efforts to build cross-class national unity, thereby laying the basis for the sharp class conflicts of 1917–18. In Finland, like in underground Russia, the years between 1906 and 1916 proved to be a political crucible for socialist strategy because the divergent approaches to proletarian hegemony that crystallised in this period set the stage for how social democrats responded to the upheavals of 1917.[4]

---

3   Zinoviev 1909. In this chapter, as throughout the book, I use the terms 'class independence' and 'class collaboration' to refer to relations between workers and capitalists (as well as liberal parties). Supporters of working-class hegemony usually advocated proletarian alliances with non-capitalist classes.

4   Chapters Eight and Ten examine how proletarian hegemony was approached during the revolution(s) of 1917–19.

1        Analysing Liberalism

Before beginning our discussion, a few terminological clarifications are needed. Second International Marxists generally saw 'liberals' (a political current) as representatives of 'the bourgeoisie' (a social class). It was assumed that the former spoke for the latter. Thus, the terms 'the bourgeoisie' or 'the capitalist class' were frequently used as synonyms for liberal politicians and parties. As historians have since demonstrated, the extent to which liberals actually sociologically or politically represented the capitalist class (or fractions thereof) was more varied than SD agitation implied. In terms of class composition, many of these parties were primarily based in the middle-class intelligentsia and professions. Russia's main liberal group, the Kadets, for instance, only became a direct political expression of Russian capitalists after the 1917 February Revolution.[5]

Who exactly were the liberals? The era's Marxists used this term as a shorthand for a wide range of non-socialist political tendencies whose long-term goals were limited to establishing some form of constitutional rule on the basis of the private ownership of the means of production. But readers should keep in mind that liberals in Russia were a politically and ethnically heterogeneous group. In the borderlands, for example, non-Russian liberalism usually took on a nationalist form, which tied the project of national affirmation to the attainment of a constitutional government across the whole of Russia. Put differently, up through 1917 most non-Russian liberals were nationalists and most nationalist parties were liberal. Readers confused by these terminological questions can console themselves with the fact that such ambiguities were very much a defining part of the political life of the era. Socialists knew they were against the bourgeoisie, yet it was not always clear who (if anybody) represented this class politically.

Prior to the defeat of the 1905 revolution, the issue of blocs with liberals was a decidedly secondary debate among Marxists in most regions of the empire. Far more energy was spent on disputing tactics in the workers' movement, the national question, relations with other socialists, forms of underground party organisation, or the use of terror. One of the main reasons for this lack of controversy across Russia was the ideological sway of revolutionary social democracy, with its unambiguous advocacy of proletarian hegemony. But there were also key contextual factors that merit consideration.

---

5   On Russian liberalism, see Timberlake 1972.

Liberals were so lacking in influence in most regions of the empire that the issue of how to relate to them was frequently a secondary question before 1905. Often they were simply ignored. This weakness, in turn, partly reflected the peculiarities of the Tsarist context. The absence of democratic freedoms and parliamentary institutions prevented liberals from expanding their influence beyond relatively small groups. And absolutist conditions made revolutionary political solutions attractive to broad sectors of the population, including the middle-class intelligentsia, at least up through 1905. As Lenin noted, 'political activities' in Russia could only be practiced by 'political offenders'.[6]

In order to function, political parties had to do so illegally – outside of Finland, no liberal parties were formally founded before the expansion of democratic freedoms in October 1905. In the preceding years, liberals generally existed as loose trends linked to specific legal newspapers or institutions of local self-government. The first political parties founded in the borderlands as well as the imperial centre were almost always socialist, allowing them to establish mass roots well before any competitors. Georgian SD Grigol Uratadze recalled that 'when we started work among the Gurian peasants we faced no opposing parties or groups with a set programme and corresponding organisation. ... The peasantry saw and knew only our Social-Democratic organisations'.[7] Even if socialists had rejected the strategy of working-class hegemony, it would have been hard to find any bourgeois political current to which the proletariat could potentially subordinate itself.

Nationalism, in both its liberal and authoritarian iterations, was surprisingly weak. 'The embryonic working classes of Russia's peripheries remained ambivalent about nationalism in most cases and expressed their political consciousness through ethnic socialist movements', notes Ronald Suny.[8] Even in regions like Poland where national consciousness was most pronounced, organised nationalism's influence on the working class was low. In 1903, Poland's nationalists, the National Democrats, lamented that Polish workers were divided from the other strata of the nation because of their lack of 'tradition' and 'divisive foreign influences' (i.e. socialism). They thereby insisted upon the need to develop among workers a 'national feeling' and a 'sense of union with all of society' in order to undercut the attractiveness of 'the slogans of class struggle and the international unity of the proletariat'.[9]

---

6   Lenin 1905a [1960–65], p. 397.
7   Уратадзе 1968, p. 89.
8   Suny 1993, p. 29. Only in Poland, and pre-1905 Finland, did nationalists have any major organisational base and influence among working people.
9   Cited in Porter 2000, pp. 151–2.

The tendency of nationalists to accommodate themselves to the Tsarist regime similarly undercut their popular echo and precluded them from taking sharp oppositional stances. Before 1905, nationalist currents mostly confined themselves to literary and cultural activities – for all their stress on the importance of national development, nationalists usually demanded *less* national sovereignty than their socialist competitors. Non-Russian activists interested in fighting for national liberation against Tsarism overwhelmingly joined the borderland socialist parties. Unlike in later years, the national question was not a significant spur towards class collaborationism.

Throughout Russia, socialists generally faced no serious rivals over their working-class and student base. With a few exceptions, liberals – including liberal nationalists – were absent among the lower classes, creating a distinctly open political field for Marxists to work in. To quote one Baltic contemporary, 'the Lettish [Latvian] proletariat knows of no inspirational idea besides socialism. The Lettish worker, if at all politically minded, is inevitably a Social Democrat'.[10] And since the neo-populist Socialist Revolutionaries were important players only in central Russia and Ukraine, Social Democracy held a virtual political monopoly in much of the empire before 1905.

With the notable exception of Finland, liberalism was especially weak in the non-Russian periphery. The autocracy's paranoia about national separatism had led it to place more severe restrictions on non-Russian elites than their ethnic-Russian counterparts. For much of the 1890s and the early twentieth century, the regime half tolerated working-class movements in various borderland regions, as it saw these as a means to undermine non-Russian middle and upper classes.

One particularly important expression of this geographic-political unevenness concerned the issue of local self-government. In the hope of winning popular support through liberal concessions, the regime in 1864 allowed the creation of *zemstvos*, bodies elected by limited suffrage to decide on local concerns of education, health, transportation, and agronomy. These bodies were based in central Russia and they formed much of the basis for the rise of its liberal movement. In contrast, *zemstvos* were more limited or banned in most non-Russian regions.[11] This lack of institutional space for liberalism and its nationalist expressions in the periphery became even more pronounced with the rise of the Tsarist Russification campaigns in the 1890s, which increasingly pushed out non-Russians from city and regional state apparatuses.

---

10    Cited in Page 1959, p. 17.
11    On the *zemstvo*, see Emmons and Vucinich 1982.

Russian liberalism, for all its weaknesses, was in fact one of the strongest representatives of this political tendency under Tsarism. 'In St. Petersburg the liberal intelligentsia played a more prominent oppositional role after 1901 than it did in most other parts of the country', notes Gerald Surh.[12] If borderland Marxists in these years had anything positive to say about liberals, it generally came in the form of contrasting the irrelevance and/or cowardice of non-Russian liberals to their relatively more vital ethnic Russian (and Russified) counterparts. As one Jewish Bolshevik put it, 'Jewish liberals were such flabby, colorless loyal citizens that even the most inveterate Menshevik couldn't put any stake on them. By comparison with Jewish liberalism Russian liberalism looked revolutionary'.[13] Similarly, the SDKPIL's newspaper wrote in 1904 that 'Russian liberalism fights with absolutism. And what does Polish liberalism do? It and the entire "national" Polish intelligentsia hides its moral support for Russian absolutism under proud phrases about national identity'.[14]

Socialist intransigence towards the bourgeoisie was rooted in a specific socio-political analysis of this class and its liberal representatives in modern capitalist society. According to Marxist orthodoxy, capitalists were inextricably caught between a desire to extend their power vis-à-vis absolutism and a fear of the working class. From this contradiction flowed liberalism's political indecisiveness.

Liberals might periodically support progressive demands, as the bourgeoisie had an objective interest and desire in extending its political power through some form of constitutional rule. But the dominant trend, SDs argued, was for bourgeois forces to waver and abandon the fight for democracy in the face of a growing workers' movement. This overriding dynamic thereby precluded the viability of systematic long-term collaboration between socialists and liberals. As Kautsky declared in 1903, 'today we can nowhere speak of a revolutionary bourgeoisie', arguing that the Russian bourgeoisie 'has already adopted the reactionary turn of mind of the bourgeoisie in the West'.[15]

This antagonistic approach to capitalists and liberals was almost universally shared by early SDs across the empire, a consensus reflecting the ideological influence of Second International orthodoxy as well its congruence with the political stances taken by Russia's liberals. Though historians have often accused the Tsarist Empire's Marxists of elitism, this shortcoming was without

---

12    Surh 1989, p. 98.
13    Cited in Holmes 2008, p. 27.
14    Cited in Kiepurska 1967, p. 58.
15    Kautsky 1903 [2009], pp. 176, 184.

a doubt far more evident among their non-socialist political rivals. Roberta Manning's comment on Russian gentry liberalism is no less relevant for its non-Russian equivalents:

> All too many gentry liberals, like their conservative counterparts, tended to regard the workers and peasant masses as little more than childlike creatures, moved mainly by irrational passions and desires. This patronizing attitude towards the masses of the Russian people, which after 1905 would often be tinged with fear and distrust, was the prime reason why Russian liberalism failed to fulfil 'the historic task' that many have rightly or wrongly attributed to it.[16]

Reflecting their general scepticism about the 'maturity' of the mass of working people, and their hesitancy to openly challenge monarchic rule, a large number of liberals in this period did not call for granting the vote to the lower orders. For example, the Association of Finnish Women led by the internationally famous women's rights activist Alexandra Gripenberg called to extend suffrage only to upper-class women. Working women, she believed, were ignorant and prone to vice; they therefore had to be guided by their morally superior upper-class sisters.[17] Terrence Emmons has summarised the hegemonic pre-1905 liberal constitutionalist outlook on political democratisation as follows:

> Constitutional reforms would be granted from above under pressure from the educated elements of society, without revolutionary violence. ... A constituent assembly elected by universal direct suffrage, however it might come to be convened, involved (to use a phrase often employed in zemstvo constitutionalist circles in those years) too great a 'leap into the unknown' to have any appeal to the moderate reformist mentality.[18]

In addition to this cautious liberalism, there also existed from 1902 onwards a more democratic current among Russian liberals. Assembled around former socialist Peter Struve's illegal newspaper *Osvobozhdenie* (Liberation), this tendency would go on to play an important role in late 1904 and 1905. These Russian 'Liberationists' – sometimes referred to as the 'democratic intelligentsia' – generally believed in universal suffrage, advocated more confrontational (though

---

16    Manning 1979, p. 54.
17    Hinkkanen and Lintunen 1997, p. 204.
18    Emmons 1977, pp. 73–4.

non-violent) tactics against the autocracy, and supported working with socialists. Yet a desire to maintain a front with the moderate liberals led the Liberationists to frequently tone down their politics for the sake of maintaining
liberal unity. Historian Abraham Ascher notes 'the discrepancy between the
rhetoric of the left liberals and their political behavior'.[19] In this period, as in
subsequent years, the relatively oppositional words of these democratic liberals were inconsistently matched by their deeds.

It was thus understandable that Marxists denounced liberals from a variety
of angles and on a range of issues. Bourgeois subordination to absolutism was
a central line of critique. Typical in this respect was PPS leader Jozef Pilsudski's assertion that 'liberalism in all of Europe has betrayed everything there
was to betray, has sold out everything it had to sell'. In the face of the growing
socialist movement, it 'is ready to give up on its own freedom, ready again to
surrender to the whip of absolutism, as long as this whip lashes the workers'.[20]
For the PPS, the task of saving 'the country from the suicidal policy which our
upper class and petty bourgeoisie have imposed on us' required that socialists
'ensure that the masses of workers achieve the proper political consciousness,
thus they must maintain their independent political organisation'.[21] Polemi-
cising with Rosa Luxemburg's argument that the Polish bourgeoisie's loyalty to
the Russian state was primarily due to economic benefits, party theoretician
Kazimierz Kelles-Krauz argued that this was in fact 'far less due to the Russian
markets than fear of disorders, of revolution'.[22]

Similarly, the Latvian Social Democratic Union denounced not only the
Baltic German rulers but also the small Latvian upper class, which it saw as
politically timid and nationally accommodationist to Tsarism. 'Each nation
must overcome its own bourgeoisie', concluded the organisation's theoretician Miķelis Valters.[23] In the borderlands, the non-socialists' deference to the
regime was often reflected in an apolitical focus on promoting national culture.
The Revolutionary Ukrainian Party thus lambasted local liberals for myopically concentrating on language issues and ignoring political questions.[24] Early
Latvian socialists likewise rejected the dominant cultural nationalism of the
Riga Latvian Association:

19    Ascher 1988, p. 58.
20    [Jozef Pilsudski] 'Nasze hasło', *Robotnik*, 15 August 1895.
21    'Szkic Programu Polskiej Partii Socjalistycznej' [1892], in Tych 1975, p. 251.
22    Kelles-Krauz 1905 [1907], p. 252.
23    Valters 1905, p. 19.
24    Boshyk 1981, pp. 275–6.

> Why does *jandaliņš* [a folk dance] have so deep and sacred a meaning, and why is it to be regarded as better than a polka or a waltz? Our great nationalists know very well how worthless this foolery is; however, they clearly understand that as long as people's attention is attracted by this adoration of the past, as long as people's minds are occupied by empty and blind self-glorification, their own position remains secure.[25]

Though SDs insisted that they would support the bourgeoisie in any concrete steps it took against the regime, they never tired of pointing out that liberals at best demanded a constitution for Russia while socialists fought for a republic. This liberal support for a constitutional monarchy constituted a fundamental divide. As Latvian Marxist Pēteris Stučka noted in 1904, 'bourgeois circles are not raising their voice for a democratic republic'.[26] Affirming the orthodox consensus, Kelles-Krauz wrote that the capitalist class, threatened by the growing labour movement, had ceased to fight for political democracy.[27]

In the eyes of imperial Russia's Marxists, not only the demands but also the methods of liberalism were far too moderate. While liberals relied on petitions and literary activities to pressure the Tsar into granting a constitution, socialists pushed for anti-Tsarist mass mobilisation, culminating in an armed uprising. A Bund leaflet declared that 'Russian liberals have never tried to take an open stand against absolutism, they have never tried to fight for political freedom with arms in hand'.[28] Indeed, armed struggle came to constitute a crucial divide. Arguing that liberals refused to take serious anti-Tsarist action, one socialist quipped that they preferred to 'feed on the chestnuts others have picked out of the fire'.[29]

## 2       Tactics Towards Liberals

Turn-of-the-century socialist debates inside of Russia took place within a context marked by the emergence of sharp strategic polemics inside the Second International. This conflict between orthodox and revisionist socialists in Germany, according to many scholars and socialists, simply concerned questions

---

25    Cited in Ijabs 2012b, p. 184.
26    Stučka 1905a [1976–78], p. 122.
27    Kelles-Krauz 1905 [1907], pp. 252, 256–63.
28    'Opozycja liberalna a proletarjat', December 1904, Centralny Komitet 'Bundu' (Archiwum Akt Nowych, 19: 30/1–1).
29    Cited in Kujala 1988, p. 96.

of theory.[30] Historian Dick Geary has developed this line of thought by claiming that 'though certainly not intentionally, Kautsky too was a "revisionist"'.[31]

In reality, there *were* important divergences between these contending currents concerning immediate political practice, especially on whether to seek a bloc with the bourgeoisie. Eduard Bernstein's insistence on dropping the party's 'final goals' was linked to his push for the German Social Democracy to overcome its longstanding intransigence. If the SPD were to downplay its calls for socialism, Bernstein argued, liberals would then be more willing to collaborate and take a firmer oppositional stand against the German regime.[32]

Kautsky agreed that periodic agreement with liberals on this or that point of action might be possible, but he insisted that SDs must always maintain an independent orientation and openly attack all the betrayals and prevarications of bourgeois democrats. He thus rejected claims that working-class power could be advanced by seeking an alliance with one wing of the bourgeoisie against the other. Class intransigence, rather than compromise, was paramount.[33] Both workers and socialists in Germany remained overwhelmingly committed to this orientation, in large part because the exceptional weakness of German liberalism and the low inclusion nature of the regime significantly undercut incentives to compromise.[34] Since class independence, hostility to bourgeois liberalism, and the espousal of the final goal of socialism continued to be the dominant political line within the German SPD for many decades, it is hard to accept claims about the early party's purported revisionism.

The German Social Democracy's internal debate over alliances with liberals was important for imperial Russia not only by way of political example, but also because Germany's moderate socialist leaders called on socialists under Tsarism to join with liberals in a common front. Throughout 1904 and 1905 a major polemic on this issue raged between Kautsky and the editors of the important German socialist daily *Vorwärts* (Forward). While Marxist orthodoxy posited that the exceptional circumstances of Tsarist absolutism allowed for novel tactics regarding issues like organisational structures and armed struggle, this exceptionalism did *not* carry over to the question of class collaboration. Kautsky defended the refusal of social democrats under Tsarism to bloc with liberals – given the deep political divide between the two, he argued, a 'Liberal-

30    Schorske 1955, p. 22.
31    Geary 1987, p. 14.
32    Luxemburg 1900 [2004], pp. 154, 160.
33    Kautsky 1905 [2018], p. 259.
34    On the relative weakness of German liberalism from an international comparative perspective, see Vössing 2008, p. 191.

Socialist Alliance' was simply an 'ineffectual pose'.[35] Interestingly, liberals were frequently the sole defenders of Bernstein's ideas within the Tsarist Empire.[36]

Like Kautsky, orthodox socialists in Russia opposed tying the proletariat to the bourgeoisie in the name of a common struggle against absolutism. Were liberals to fight against the Tsar, so much the better. But were they to refrain from this battle, or stop half way, the working class must be prepared to continue fighting until victory. Temporary agreements on concrete actions and demands with other parties (representing other classes) were acceptable, but the proletariat should never self-limit itself for the sake of such an agreement. 'Any permanent alliance or bloc with the bourgeois democrats is impossible', declared the Ukrainian USDRP.[37]

This strategic consensus did not preclude significant practical disagreements. Chief among these concerned predicting how strong a liberal opposition might arise and how far it might go against Tsarism under pressure from below. It was impossible to foresee this with any great degree of precision. Yet according to orthodox Marxist strategy, socialists should remain strategically intransigent no matter what the liberals did or did not do. The influential Vilna SD pamphlet 'On Agitation' thus posited that whether or not there would be 'conflicts between the government and Capital is of course an important question, but in either case it would not change the direction of our work. Either way, the most important thing is for the working class to be conscious and understand its interests, that it not become a tool of the bourgeoisie'.[38]

Of course, it was no simple task to concretise a sharp class orientation while simultaneously supporting other opposition movements. The dividing line between a strategic bloc and tactical unity in action around a particular point of agreement was not always clear. Despite formal affirmations of orthodoxy, socialist collaboration with bourgeois parties on common demands and projects could, consciously or subconsciously, lead groups to bend to their temporary allies. But before 1905 it was relatively easy to uphold an intransigent class line in practice since liberals were usually such an insignificant force. The real test of support for proletarian hegemony did not come until later.

Given the general weakness of bourgeois parties throughout Russia, socialists faced significant rivals for popular support only among four nationalities in the pre-1905 period: Poles, Jews, Finns, and Russians. As we will see, the reactionary policies of Jewish and Polish nationalists made the question of how to

---

35    Kautsky 1905, p. 714.
36    See, for instance, Kmiecik 1980, p. 105 and Surh 1989, p. 132.
37    Boshyk 1981, p. 315.
38    Кремер 1894 [2010], p. 27.

deal with them a rather uncontroversial issue for socialists. In contrast, the relatively oppositional stance of liberals in Finland and central Russia prompted
serious tactical debates.


## 3    The Bund versus Zionism (1897–1904)

The Jewish Bund was the first Jewish political party in the world, the leading combatant against anti-Semitism in Russia, and the largest revolutionary
organisation in Russia before 1905. Unfortunately, it has been unjustifiably
portrayed in most Marxist historiography as synonymous with narrow nationalism. According to Georgi Plekhanov, Bundists were no more than 'Zionists
afraid of seasickness'.[39]

But the early Bund was in reality an orthodox Marxist organisation dedicated
to class struggle and internationalism. Far from being nationalists, Bundists
were fiercely anti-Zionist and declared themselves to be Zionism's 'mortal
enemy, its angel of death ... its grave-digger'.[40]

Founded in Basel, Switzerland in 1897, the Zionist movement led by Theodor
Herzl pushed for the creation of a Jewish state in Palestine and it sought to
win the favour of imperial governments abroad to achieve this goal. Bundists
initially ignored the Zionists, as their influence among Jewish workers under
Tsarism was almost non-existent. But by 1901, the growing expansion and influence of Zionism among both students and workers obliged a response. In
May, a Bundist declaration announced that Zionists and social democrats were
'unconditional enemies between whom there are no points in common'.[41] Later
that year the Bund's congress resolved to expel all Zionists from the Jewish
workers' movement. From this point onwards, 'the Jewish street' was wracked
by an ongoing clash between the two currents, leading in one case even to an
armed battle in Ekaterinoslav's main synagogue.[42] In the words of Chaim Weizmann, chairman of the World Zionist Organization:

> Our hardest struggle everywhere is conducted against the Jewish Social
> Democrats (the Judischer Arbeiterbund of Russia and Poland) ... Saddest

---

39    Cited in Frankel 1981, p. 255.
40    Cited in Marten-Finnis 2000, p. 54. On the Bund's stance on the national question, see
      Tobias 1972 and Blanc 2016a.
41    'Воззвание ЦК Бунда к Еврейской Интеллигенции' [1901], in Андерсон 2010, p. 154.
42    Wynn 1992, p. 159. The term 'the Jewish street' was widely used at the time as a synonym
      for the Jewish community.

and most lamentable is the fact that although this movement consumes much Jewish energy and heroism, and is located within the Jewish fold, the attitude it evidences towards Jewish nationalism is one of antipathy, swelling at times to fanatical hatred.[43]

For the Bund, this was an irreconcilable conflict between socialism and nationalism. In the words of one Bundist, 'the starting points of our views – for us: class; for them: nationalist – are fundamentally different, and from this ultimately flows all the other differences'.[44] Whereas the Zionists advocated Jewish national unity, Bundist leader Medem explained that 'solidarity of the whole nation means giving up the class struggle, means peace between proletariat and bourgeoisie, means spiritual and material enslavement of the proletariat'.[45] According to the Bund, a class orientation required a commitment to internationalism, which it counterposed to Zionism's 'religious bigotry' and 'national chauvinism'. In response to Plekhanov's accusations of semi-Zionism, the organisation replied that 'anybody even slightly familiar with the history of the Bund' knew that it had always stressed the importance of the non-Jewish workers' movement and that it had always sought to actively assist and unify with it.[46]

Bundism was based on the principle of *doykayt* (hereness), according to which Jewish workers should fight for emancipation wherever they already lived. Rejecting Zionism's notion of eternal anti-Semitism, the Bund argued that fighting against Jewish oppression was in the mutual interest of workers of all nationalities and it denounced the plan for a Jewish state in Palestine as 'utopian and impractical'.[47] Zionism, it insisted, led in practice to 'servility to the autocratic government'.[48] In turn, Zionists replied that the Bund 'and its pernicious activities bear the blame if so much blood is needlessly spilled in Russia and if the government has worked its suspicion of the Jews up to the point of persecution'.[49]

The extent of this 'servility' became particularly evident in July 1903. Theodor Herzl, the founder of Zionism, took the initiative to meet with Vyacheslav von Plehve, the Tsar's anti-Semitic Minister of the Interior, widely

---

43   Weizmann 1971, pp. 305, 307.
44   'Отчет о V Съезде Бунда' [1903] in Андерсон 2010, p. 336.
45   Медем 1904 [1906], p. 18.
46   'Из Доклада М.С. Гуревича' [1905] in Савицкий 1997, p. 216.
47   'Отчет ЦК Бунда IV Съезде' [1901] in Андерсон et al. 2010, p. 178.
48   'Отчет о V Съезде Бунда' [1903] in Андерсон 2010, p. 337.
49   Cited in Tobias 1972, p. 249.

considered to have instigated a pogrom four months earlier in the town of
Kishinev. Herzl made the case to Plehve that only Zionism could end the Jewish
'defection to the Socialists'.[50] Plehve accepted Herzl's proposal for the Russian
government to aid immigration to Palestine and facilitate the work of Zionist
organising in Russia, as it would 'lead to the diminution of the Jewish population in Russia'.[51] Eager to remedy the damage done to Tsarism's international
image by the recent Kishinev pogrom, Plehve requested Herzl's assistance in
preventing criticism of Russia at the upcoming international Zionist congress –
a request that he enthusiastically implemented.[52]

Herzl's open alliance with the Tsarist regime led to a major split in Russia's Zionist movement. In 1903 and 1904, Zionism's labour wing broke off from
the mainstream movement, resulting in the creation of Socialist-Zionist parties
combining a call for a Jewish state as a long-term goal with class struggle tactics
and anti-Tsarist revolutionism in the Russian Empire.[53] Cross-class nationalism
from this point on was largely absent as a viable contender for the sympathies
of the organised Jewish working class. After 1903, the struggle for the hearts and
minds of Jewish workers would, like with most nationalities in the empire, take
place primarily between different socialist parties.

## 4      The PPS and the National Democrats Before 1905

Like with the Bund, the Polish Socialist Party's Marxist credentials have often
been denied. One typical socialist account, for instance, argues that the PPS
believed that 'the struggle for Poland's national independence from Russia
took precedence over every other struggle, including the class struggle'.[54] Such
claims, however, do not conform to the historical record.

The PPS, the largest socialist organisation in Poland, promoted both class
struggle and national independence. Its founding 1892 programme declared

---

50      Herzl 1960, p. 1526.
51      Judge 1983, p. 108.
52      Ibid.
53      See Tobias 1972, pp. 248–54 and Weinstock 1984, pp. 238–77. The contradiction between the
        colonial project of Zionism and the revolutionary class-struggle thrust of many Socialist-
        Zionists in Russia was manifest in the future evolution of the movement. The main
        Labour-Zionist organisation, Ber Borochov's *Poalei Zion*, went on to play a central role
        colonising Palestine under the leadership of David Ben-Gurion. In contrast, major wings
        of the Socialist-Zionists after 1917 became Communists and dropped their call for the col-
        onisation of Palestine.
54      Lewis 2000, p. 52.

that only the proletariat could defend the Polish nation and win national independence because the Polish upper class had capitulated to the occupying power. Calls for cross-class unity were explicitly rejected: 'Our upper classes use the banner of national unity to fight the increasing consciousness of the toiling masses. This banner is everywhere contradicted by the existing social relations'.[55]

At the same time as the PPS pushed for national independence, it advocated unity and collaboration between workers of different nationalities within Poland and across the empire, including with Russians. An 1894 editorial in the party's newspaper *Robotnik* (The Worker) counterposed a class struggle perspective to hollow patriotism: 'The principles of the Polish Socialist Party are known. Our party is primarily a workers' party, its goals and demands are the expression of the interests of the working class: it leads the class struggle against the capitalists, and prepares and organises the masses for this'.[56]

That said, significant internal divisions over how to synthesise and balance class and national demands existed from the party's inception.[57] From 1893 onwards, what I will refer to as the PPS Centre was led by separatist socialist Jozef Pilsudski, a young Pole from the Lithuanian town of Vilna who edited the PPS's underground newspaper *Robotnik*. The Centre remained hegemonic until 1903, after which the PPS in Poland itself, though not yet in exile, came under the leadership of the party's new orthodox Marxist Left, known as the *Młodzi* (the Youth). The latter, as we will later see, stressed that Polish freedom could only be won through mass action and a revolutionary alliance with Russian workers.

The crucial point to underline here is that there was a general consensus among *all* wings of the PPS against blocs with the Polish upper class and the nationalists. Given the accommodation of the native bourgeoisie to Tsarist rule, it was understandable that cross-class nationalism held little appeal for PPS militants, including those like Pilsudski who were most focused on the separatist struggle. In 1896, Pilsudski, for example, declared that 'the class struggle in

---

55  'Szkic Programu Polskiej Partii Socjalistycznej' [1892] in Tych 1975, p. 250.

56  'Wyjaśnienie', *Robotnik*, 30 November 1894.

57  Though social democracy was accepted as the programmatic basis of the PPS from its inception, it was the most heterogeneous of the major Marxist parties in the empire before its 1906 split. The PPS Centre, for whom the fight for independence was largely a self-evident response to foreign occupation, had an ambiguous relationship to revolutionary social democracy. Most of its leaders were socialists with, at best, a superficial commitment to orthodox Marxism, rooted largely in Marx's support for Polish independence. In hindsight, the most nationalistic elements of the PPS were political precursors to the revolutionary nationalist currents (often self-described socialists) that became hegemonic in so many anti-colonial struggles across the world in subsequent decades.

the interests of the workers, the fight against all governments that are tools in the hands of the propertied classes – this today is the indispensable foundation of our tactics'.[58]

Advocates of class collaboration did not join the PPS, but rather Roman Dmowski's National Democrats (NDs), the *actual* Polish nationalists. In his founding 1893 political manifesto, *Nasz patriotyzm* (Our Patriotism), Dmowski summarised his vision as 'the general principle that every political act by every Pole, regardless of where it is performed and against whom it is directed, must have in view the interests of the whole nation'.[59] In these early years Dmowski was a left populist who projected independence as a long-term goal, but argued against armed struggle to achieve it. In practice, the NDs focused on cultural activities and combatting Russification in the schools and the countryside. By the eve of 1905, however, the NDs had undergone a hard turn towards the right. Arguing that Jews, socialists, and Germany were the major threats to Poles, the National Democrats had become increasingly anti-Semitic, authoritarian, and accommodationist to the Tsarist state. The NDs also became more elitist towards Polish workers, stressing the need to discipline and ideologically purify the lower orders.[60]

Relations between the Polish Socialist Party and the National Democrats deteriorated in the years before 1905. In 1893 and 1894, when the NDs were still left populists, the two currents had collaborated closely. Various members of the PPS were even dual members of both organisations, which sparked one of the first major clashes between the Left and Centre in the PPS. Orthodox PPS militants successfully pushed to break this bloc with the NDs and prohibit dual party affiliation. Thus the 1895 Polish Socialist Party congress banned its members from belonging to any other parties and unanimously reaffirmed that the PPS was 'based on the principles of the class struggle, it does not compromise with other classes and parties'.[61]

Relations between the PPS and the NDs continued to worsen as the latter became more politically conservative and turned away from the fight for Polish independence. In 1904 Leon Wasilewski – one of the PPS Centre's main writers and a close comrade of Pilsudski – published a major critique of the NDs ironically titled *Nasi nacjonaliści* (Our Nationalists). Wasilewski denounced the National Democrats' chauvinism towards other nationalities, their refusal to fight for independence, and their preaching of national unity in a society riven

---

58       [Jozef Pilsudski] 'W Rocznicę', *Robotnik*, 9 February 1896.
59       Dmowski 1893 [1938], p. 247.
60       On the NDs, see Porter 2000 and Fountain 1980.
61       'Uchwały III zjazdu Polskiej Partyi Socyalistycznej' [1895] in Malinowski 1907, p. 147.

by class divisions.[62] Later that year, after the start of the Russo-Japanese war, Dmowski personally travelled to Japan to dissuade the Japanese government from accepting Pilsudski's proposal for it to fund the Polish revolutionaries' efforts to topple the Tsarist regime.[63] By 1906, the conflict between the NDs and the PPS had deteriorated to the point of violent armed struggle, in which dozens lost their lives. Dmowski and Pilsudski remained bitter lifelong rivals. Thus, as on the Jewish street, the hard right-wing politics of Polish nationalists by 1905 prevented socialists from considering them to be potential partners against Tsarism or for national liberation.

In the absence of upper-class allies in Poland, PPS debates on independence revolved around the question of allies among other nations. Given the Tsarist occupation's forces – over 240,000 troops, a third of the Tsar's peacetime army, were stationed in Poland – no PPS leaders believed that independence could be won by the efforts of the Polish working class alone. The party consensus was that Poles needed help from other nations, but the question of which allies to seek out remained in dispute. Would assistance come from the West or the East, from workers' parties or bourgeois governments, from wars or revolutions?

During the early period, all PPS factions upheld an open-ended view on this topic, refusing to place all their strategic eggs in one basket. Three possible scenarios existed for how a secessionist uprising could succeed: a political crisis or revolution in the Russian Empire; a war between Western governments and Tsarism; or a revolution in Germany or Austria. How the PPS should strategically orient to these possibilities was a critical axis of the internal conflict that culminated in the party's eventual split.

One of the defining characteristics of the PPS Centre was its tendency to downplay the potential of the Russian revolutionary movement and the strategic need to ally with it. Linked to this scepticism of the Russian movement was the Centre's orientation towards allying with foreign governments to win Polish independence. This was not a novel stance. Poland had long been seen as the vanguard of the fight against the Tsarist state, which was considered to be the bulwark of reaction across Europe. The Polish national movement had throughout the nineteenth century looked to Western European 'democracy' – i.e. Republican governments and the labour movement – as its main allies. It was assumed that a war would eventually break out between the Tsarist autocracy and Western democracies, in which the latter would support the Polish liberation struggle. Marx and Engels throughout their political careers

---

62    Wasilewski 1904.
63    Fountain 1980, pp. 115–37.

were open and active advocates of this perspective – a fact that the PPS Centre repeated against its internal and external critics. On the Polish question, the party Centre painted itself as a hardline defender of Marxist orthodoxy.[64]

Notwithstanding its formal Marxist credentials, this orientation was hard to synthesise with the PPS's advocacy of class independence. As such, the party's approach to the national question was increasingly rejected as both unprincipled and impractical by the new generation of Left PPS militants. By 1903–04, the *Młodzi* were in control of most PPS organisations based in Poland and they soon began pushing in a different direction from Piłsudski's exile leadership. In late 1903, for instance, the *Młodzi* argued that the summer's general strike wave represented the 'symptoms of an inevitable revolution', in which the main ally of the Poles would be the Russian proletariat.[65] This new orientation was articulated most forcefully in PPS leader Marian Bielecki's *Zagadnienia Rewolucji* (Revolutionary Questions). Agreeing with Kautsky on the need for unity with Russian workers, Bielecki argued that Polish socialists must tie the struggle for proletarian and national emancipation to the impending revolution in the Russian Empire. Advocating Polish independence as a Western outpost against Tsarism was simply 'outdated' – basic principles of democracy were a 'sufficient justification' for the reconstitution of a nation 'torn into several pieces'.[66]

During this period, the PPS Centre's approach to foreign governments was mostly theoretical since Western governments, unlike after 1914, showed no inclination to ally with the Polish liberation struggle. Help was only slightly more forthcoming from the Japanese government, which in 1904 rejected Piłsudski's ambitious request to fund widespread Polish armed struggle against the Russian state.[67] These intrigues with the Japanese regime were kept secret from the party, as Piłsudski knew that the left of the PPS would be opposed.[68]

The significance of this internal political conflict over class allies and national goals lies beyond its impact on the PPS split. In many ways the divergences within the Polish Socialist Party foreshadowed socialist debates that swept across the Russian periphery after the October Revolution. As will be shown in our concluding chapter, in Poland and the other borderlands that separated from Russia after 1917, the moderate socialist road to national independence passed through collaboration with foreign powers and away from working-class hegemony.

---

64    Wasilewski 1902, p. 324.
65    Flis 1903, p. 349.
66    Bielecki 1904a, pp. 201–2.
67    Fountain 1980, pp. 134–6.
68    Żarnowska 1965, p. 115.

5    Class Independence in Finland

Scholars have generally portrayed the Finnish Social Democratic Party as politically analogous to the moderate socialist parties of Western Europe. According
to Finnish sociologist Risto Alapuro, the Finnish SDP was 'a big, Western-type,
non-revolutionary Social Democratic worker movement'.[69] But this assertion
obscures both the unique trajectory of Finnish socialism and the politics of
revolutionary social democracy. We will see that it was precisely by becoming *more* committed to orthodox Second International strategy that Finland's
socialists set the stage for workers' revolution in 1917–18.

Whether or not to form a bloc with the bourgeoisie consistently constituted
the most important conflict within Finland's workers' movement. And if there
was one issue that defined Marxist orthodoxy, it was an insistence on class independence.

In the years before 1905, Finland's labour movement was politically eclectic
and decidedly non-orthodox, like many of its socialist counterparts across
Europe. Noting the Second International's 'rich diversity in terms of ideology,
national identity, and historical experiences', historian Kevin Callahan explains
that 'European socialism was really a hodgepodge of varied national working-
class parties fractured by internal and external pressures'.[70]

Before the radicalisation of 1905, revolutionary SDs were a rarity and class
collaborationism was common in Finland. The organised Finnish workers'
movement had been founded in 1883 by paternalistic members of the upper
classes seeking to 'uplift' the working class, to integrate it into the Finnish
national community, and, thereby, to prevent the emergence of a socialist
movement. In an era when liberalism was weak to non-existent throughout
Russia, the Finnish capitalist class held unparalleled political hegemony within
the workers' movement.[71]

Led by Viktor Julius von Wright – a liberal nationalist and furniture indus-
trialist – the early workers' associations promoted education and moral self-
improvement, rather than class struggle, let alone revolution. Workers and
employers, Wright declared, had common interests. Through mutual understanding it would be possible to boost living conditions and productivity
without strife.

69    Alapuro 2011, p. 142.
70    Callahan 2001, p. 5.
71    On the political and social roots of this early Finnish upper-class influence, see Alapuro
      1988.

Upper-class tutelage was first undermined in 1896, after a string of bitter labour strikes in Helsinki. Under the slogan 'cut loose from the bourgeoisie', servile labour leaders were pushed out by the rank and file. In July 1899, the Finnish Workers Party was founded, signalling a step away from direct political subordination. Though it was a watershed moment, it hardly signified the end of class collaborationism. N.R. af Ursin, the party's new leader, was a nobleman who espoused an eclectic mix of nationalism and evolutionary socialism.[72] The party's early politics were decidedly non-Marxist: the most widely read works were translations of British socialist Robert Blatchford's *Merrie England* and Edward Bellamy's utopian novel *Looking Backwards*.[73]

Even when the party changed its name and adopted a social democratic programme in 1903, the actual influence of Marxism remained low. Despite this formal programmatic adoption, most party leaders and members in this period remained unorthodox and the workers' movement in many Finnish cities and rural regions continued to engage in organisational, political, and cultural work with upper-class Finns.

This approach reflected a pragmatic adaptation to circumstances and prevailing Finnish national traditions, rather than a theoretical commitment to Bernstein's revisionism. In fact, the revisionist debate of 1898–1903 did not take place in Finland, as neither orthodox nor revisionist socialists had any serious proponents in these years. Pertti Haapala's study of the industrial town of Tampere has demonstrated that the local party organisation's moderate practice emanated from a lack of doctrine rather than socialist revisionism.[74] Indeed, Bernstein's seminal 1899 revisionist work, *The Preconditions for Socialism*, was not translated into Finnish until 1910.[75]

Unlike orthodox social democrats across Russia, Finland's Social Democracy at this time did not adhere to a strategy of proletarian hegemony. 'On the whole, the [Finnish] Socialist Party's relationship to bourgeois parties was vague and indistinct', notes historian Reijo Heikkinen.[76] Given this eclectic pragmatism, the extent of ongoing co-operation varied greatly by city. Helsinki had the sharpest tradition of class struggle, while collaborationism prevailed in Tampere, Turku, and Oulu. Reflecting the party's moderation, the Workers Party's leadership was based in Turku, a bastion of collaborationism, rather

72    On Ursin and the early years of Finnish socialism, see the discussion in Rahikainen 1986.
73    Soikkanen 1961, p. 175.
74    Haapala 1986.
75    Soikkanen 1975, p. 136.
76    Heikkinen 1980, p. 90.

than the Finnish capital of Helsinki. A running conflict between these cities'
socialist leaders persisted through 1905.

Low engagement with Marxist theory did not mean an absence of political
debates over the issue of blocs with capitalist forces. This controversy, however,
took place primarily in the context of a national struggle against Tsarist Russification. From 1899 through 1917, the fundamental divisions between the left
and right of Finnish socialism centred on the question of whether or not to
collaborate with the bourgeoisie in the fight for Finland's autonomy.

Of all the lands of the Tsarist Empire, Finland had long been allowed the
most self-government and political freedom. Annexing Finland from Sweden
in 1809, the Tsar granted his new dominion extensive political autonomy and
cultural freedom, though the Russian regime maintained ultimate authority.
As an autonomous Grand Duchy, Finland preserved its own constitution and
most governmental functions – including military, industrial, financial, educational, and agricultural policymaking – were governed by Finns through their
autonomous Senate. An elected Finnish Diet also existed, though only a very
small percentage of the population was allowed to vote and its powers were
limited.

In February 1899, the region's Tsarist authorities headed by Nikolay Bobrikov
began to undermine Finland's special autonomous status in an attempt to bring
its laws and administration more in line with the rest of the empire. Over
the next five years, Bobrikov abolished Finland's separate army, heightened
press censorship, imposed the Russian language in schools and government,
and rolled back Finnish political autonomy. Protests quickly emerged, led by
middle- and upper-class Finnish 'constitutionalists', a coalition of liberal
nationalists committed to non-violent 'passive resistance' (boycotts, petitions,
etc.) to restore Finland's autonomy. Though an influential group of conservative 'Old Finns' urged continued compliance and collaboration with the Russian
regime, the exceptional feature of the early Finnish capitalist class was its general willingness not only to challenge the Tsarist state, but to actually organise
and mobilise lower-class Finns in such a direction.[77]

This effort to activate the population reflected both the Finnish bourgeoisie's
exceptional confidence in its own strength, its nationalist conception of the
fundamentally united nature of the Finnish people, and a paternalistic belief
in its duty and ability to guide the lower classes. Many workers and farmers
were at first sceptical of the battle for autonomy, which was initially seen as a
movement of the Finnish elite to defend its old privileges. This ambivalence,

---

77    On the early 'constitutionalist' movement for Finnish national autonomy, see Huxley 1990.

however, was seriously undercut in 1901 when the Russian government initiated the conscription of Finns into the Tsarist army. And within a few years
the national movement had completely escaped the control of its initiators. 'By
starting the passive resistance, the traditional political elite of Finland destabil-
ised authority among the vast masses of the population and unwittingly paved
the way for the spread of socialism', explains Antti Kujala.[78]

All labour leaders in Finland supported the re-establishment of Finnish sovereignty and the founding 1899 programme of the Workers Party declared that
the protection of Finland's autonomy was a precondition for advancing worker
interests. According to the party's conception of 'proletarian patriotism', the
working class was the best and most consistent defender of the Finnish nation.
But the question of whether to unite, and on what basis, with Finnish constitutionalists against Russification became a continual conflict within the labour
movement.[79]

The major exponent of building a bloc with the constitutionalists was Yrjö
Mäkelin, a former shoemaker who had risen to the top of the party in Tampere
and edited the local labour publication *Kansan Lehti* (The People's Paper).
Close alliances with the bourgeoisie had long marked the city's workers' movement, with local SDP leaders consistently running on the electoral lists of
upper-class parties. In Mäkelin's view, it was necessary to advance national and
working-class struggle simultaneously, but the fight for autonomy was the most
urgent task – only after reconquering it could the 'internal' class struggle within
Finland be fully unleashed. In his opinion, the necessity to flexibly adapt to
local conditions meant that Finnish socialists should not try to copy political
models from abroad (e.g. Germany) or adhere to a rigid political programme.

Mäkelin was attached to the national cause and actively built the constitutionalist movement in conjunction with bourgeois parties. Like the Finnish
upper class generally, he was disappointed in what he perceived as the insufficient nationalism of Finnish workers, whose prioritisation of socio-economic
struggles was seen by Mäkelin as a reflection of political ignorance. In this
context, he and the Tampere party leadership refused to support the push of
landless sharecroppers (crofters) in the surrounding countryside for land, as
doing so would have led to a break with Finnish nationalists. By downplaying the fight against Tsarist national oppression, Mäkelin declared, SDP leftists
were subordinating themselves to the Russian regime.[80]

---

78    Kujala 1989, p. 18.
79    Heikkilä 1993.
80    On Mäkelin, see Tanni 2008 and Suodenjoki and Peltola 2007, *passim*.

The party leader most opposed to Mäkelin and his national collaborationism was Edvard Valpas, editor of Helsinki's labour newspaper *Työmies* (The
Worker). Valpas had been won over to orthodox Marxism while attending the
1903 Dresden congress of the German SPD, which famously accepted and codi-
fied Kautsky's stance against revisionism. Valpas returned to Finland committed to spreading the 'good word' of orthodox social democracy. As his biographer notes, Valpas was 'generally hostile to everything that departed from
the pure Kautskyist doctrine'.[81]

Though he supported the demand for Finland's national autonomy, Valpas
rejected prioritising it over the class struggle. His pioneering 1904 pamphlet
*Mikä menettelytapa? työväenliikkeen taktiikasta* (What Policy? Workers' Movement Tactics) denounced Mäkelin and class collaborationism in the harshest
political and sociological terms. Valpas described Mäkelin's wing as a bought-
off labour elite that stood in awe of the culture and privileges of the upper
class and that preferred to maintain its privileged relationship with Finnish
elites rather than fight for working people. Arguing that workers must 'completely rely on their own strength', Valpas made a case for why the German SPD
model of class intransigence was also relevant for the Finnish context. Instead
of an ongoing alliance with the bourgeoisie – 'a flagrant violation' of principle –
the labour movement must consistently maintain an independent orientation.[82] Along similar lines, a 1903 pamphlet on women and the vote by Hilja
Pärssinen – the anti-liberal socialist leader of the Finnish Working Women's
Association – made the case for irreconcilable class conflict. Bourgeois women,
she wrote, wanted only equality with upper-class men, while women workers
wanted the vote to pass laws, such as a prohibition bill, to improve their material conditions.[83]

Valpas, Pärssinen, and others on the left of the Finnish Social Democracy
particularly emphasised the need for the workers' movement to fight for universal suffrage, a demand – as they repeatedly noted – that was not supported
by any of the other parties in Finland. Indeed, the vote was one of the central
points of contention between workers and the upper class. As was true elsewhere in the empire and Europe, much of the Finnish elite felt that workers
were not yet mature enough for full suffrage – such a democratic experiment,
in their view, threatened to give too much power to the lower class. For constitutionalists, the national struggle aspired to return to the pre-1899 status

81   Sario 1968, p. 79.
82   Valpas 1904, pp. 12, 46, 50–1, 62–73.
83   Pärssinen 1903, p. 6.

quo, which meant maintaining a Finnish parliament based on a narrow franchise that effectively disenfranchised the majority of urban and rural working people.

In broad outlines, these remained the basic terms of debate that would be repeated in the Finnish socialist movement up through 1905. While both sides affirmed the need to combine the class and national struggle, moderates accused their opponents of harming the national cause by dogmatically rejecting necessary alliances. In turn, orthodox Marxists derided their opponents for damaging the independent workers' movement by subordinating it to their class enemies.

Though Valpas' non-cooperation stance had often been rejected in the first years of the movement, it gained more adherents in 1904 as the Finnish workers' movement began to radicalise in response to the Tsarist government's clampdown on its activities. The SDP's 1904 congress marked an initial victory for Valpas, as it nominally adopted his stance for the upcoming elections and rejected Mäkelin's proposal to let each locality choose for itself how to relate to the constitutionalists. This 1904 decision, however, was rooted above all in the party membership's reaction to the recent refusal of bourgeois parties to accept their demand for universal suffrage, rather than a commitment to orthodoxy per se.[84]

And despite this 1904 resolution, much of the party outside of Helsinki continued to closely collaborate with the Finnish upper class.[85] Many chapters simply ignored the 1904 congress decision; Mäkelin, for instance, soon ran for office on a constitutionalist slate. The Finnish Social Democracy's heterogeneous approach towards the upper class continued throughout 1905. But, as we will discuss further below, the late-year proletarian upsurge led to a major overhaul in the party's political perspective as well as its leadership in 1906.

---

84  As Soikkanen notes, 'the political situation ... rather than Kautskyite ideology, won the day for Valpas' line' (Soikkanen 1978, p. 358).

85  Not all of this collaboration was along the lines pushed by Mäkelin. A militant wing of the party, the 'worker-activists', in late 1904 and 1905 collaborated in underground activities (such as the smuggling of illegal proclamations and even arms) with the Finnish Activist Party, a left split from the constitutionalists in 1904 that advocated armed resistance against Tsarism. This alliance, however, proved to be ephemeral: the Finnish Activist Party dissolved soon after 1905, once Finnish autonomy was restored. On Finnish Activism and socialists, see Kujala 1988 and Kujala 1989.

## 6    Early Russian Marxism and Liberals

The leading theoretical founders of Russian Marxism – Pavel Axelrod and Giorgi Plekhanov – advocated a proletarian hegemony strategy that was particularly optimistic about the bourgeoisie's anti-Tsarist potential. In part, this stress on the progressive nature of the capitalist class stemmed from their perceived need to combat the political influence of Russian populism, with its pro-peasant, anti-capitalist view that Russia should move directly towards a social revolution without a long intervening period of political democracy and capitalist development. As leaders of the Emancipation of Labour Group, a tiny but widely read Russian exile circle founded in Switzerland in 1883, Axelrod and Plekhanov argued that while Russia's economic and cultural backwardness meant that the upcoming revolution could not move beyond establishing a democratic capitalist order, it would have to be led by the working class to succeed.

Axelrod appears to have been the socialist responsible for coining the term 'hegemony of the proletariat'. And in 1899, Plekhanov famously declared to the 1889 Paris Congress of the Second International: 'The revolutionary movement in Russia will triumph only as a working-class movement or else it will never triumph!'[86] At the same time, each of them argued that Russian liberals were a necessary ally in the anti-Tsarist struggle. Axelrod was particularly insistent on this point:

> In Russia ... where the working class is still very young, where it is only in the process of separating itself from the masses who for centuries have vegetated in barbaric ignorance and slavery, the vast majority are still on too low a cultural level to be able to emerge – within the chains of absolutism – as a conscious revolutionary force without the direct and indirect help of the bourgeoisie.[87]

Axelrod argued that while the anti-bourgeois stance of Kautsky and the SPD was appropriate for the German context, the semi-feudal conditions of Tsarist Russia meant that it was both possible and necessary for the proletariat to successfully push liberals to support a constitution. The independent workers' movement, in his view, would constitute 'a lever pushing all the enemies of absolutism into an organised attack upon it'.[88] Marxists could expect (and

---

86    Cited in Day and Gaido 2009, p. 32.
87    Cited in Ascher 1972, p. 138.
88    Cited in Ascher 1972, p. 135.

should seek) support from Russian liberalism in the fight for political freedom, while simultaneously promoting the independent organisation of the working class and instilling in it a clear sense of its overall antagonism with capitalist interests. Significantly, both Axelrod and Plekhanov argued at various times that workers should be prepared to self-limit their struggle so as to not frighten off the liberals from joint action against Tsarism – a line of argument that became a central component of post-1905 Menshevism.[89]

As early as the 1880s, Plekhanov and Axelrod's strategy was attacked by rival Marxist currents in Russia. For instance, the leaders of the Tsarist Empire's first Marxist party – the Polish Proletariat, founded in 1882 – argued that it was a dogmatic mistake for Plekhanov to assume that Marx's strategy in 1848 was still relevant for the particular conditions of the modern Russian state. Against Plekhanov, leaders of the Proletariat responded that 'today the bourgeois has played its role and the proletariat is the only progressive element'.[90]

The nascent SD current around Julius Martov and V.I. Lenin was also more anti-liberal than the Emancipation of Labour Group. These two young militants began their joint revolutionary work together mobilising workers in St. Petersburg in the mid-1890s along the lines laid down by the influential Jewish SD pamphlet *On Agitation*. Both Lenin and Martov were critical of Axelrod's stance on liberalism, which in their view overestimated its progressiveness and vitality. At best, they believed, cowardly liberals might be compelled to 'march along in the rear'.[91] In turn, Axelrod considered that the strategy of *On Agitation* – with its focus on mass action and workplace struggle – constituted a regression to anarchism that would only leave the proletariat dangerously alienated from upper-class allies.[92]

Despite their differences with the Emancipation of Labour theoreticians abroad, Martov, Lenin, and their comrade Alexander Potresov decided to link up with them to harness their prestige and literary abilities to further the project of building an all-Russian party capable of centralising the anti-autocratic struggle. Regarding liberalism, the newly founded *Iskra* current represented a middle ground between the early radicalism of Martov and Lenin and the more moderate Emancipation of Labour stance. Criticism of liberals became more

---

89    Ascher 1972, p. 138. Plekhanov similarly warned against scaring off liberals in his case for achieving an alliance with the oppositional bourgeoisie (Larsson 1970, p. 171).

90    St. 1884, pp. 25–6. This line of critique was continued as early as 1896 by the PPS, which directly challenged Axelrod's belief in the democratic potential of the propertied classes under Tsarism (Najdus 1973, p. 42).

91    Ascher 1972, p. 169.

92    Pipes 1960, p. 333.

common and Axelrod's argument that bourgeois support was *indispensable* for democratic transformation was minimised. At the same time, however, both Lenin and Martov toned down their former anti-bourgeois radicalism.

*Iskra* consistently stressed the possibility and importance of liberal-proletarian joint work against Tsarism and advocated the need for Marxists to support the growth of liberalism in this direction. Like the Emancipation of Labour Group, *Iskra* also de-emphasised strikes and economic struggles, pushing instead for a focus on workers leading a broader multi-class anti-Tsarist movement. According to Lenin's 1902 *What Is To Be Done?*, 'the Social Democrats must go among all classes of the population'.[93] From an empire-wide perspective, Iskraists were one of the orthodox SD currents with the most optimistic approach to liberals, an ongoing criticism raised by their main Russian SD rival, *Rabochee Delo*, which accused *Iskra* of overestimating the progressiveness of capitalist forces, underemphasising specifically proletarian action and organisation, and advocating an 'opportunist' tactic of lending support to liberals.[94]

The question of whether to bloc with the progressive bourgeoisie eventually became the central point of divergence between the Mensheviks and Bolsheviks – but only *after* the defeat of the Russia's first revolution. Before 1905 most social democrats inside the empire and across Europe considered that, given the absence of any clear principled differences, the RSDRP's 1903 split was unwarranted. Many believed that it was largely a personal squabble among émigrés. As a RSDRP leader in Ukraine admitted, 'one must say that at the time this split was incomprehensible not only to the working masses, but also to the higher-up [party] groups'.[95] The following 1904 comment by Latvian SD leader Pēteris Stučka was typical: 'For we who are watching from the sidelines, it is difficult to understand this "brotherly war," which is still going on in the press of the two organisations, because we do not see any important difference in principle that seriously distinguishes the two factions'.[96]

## 7     Working-Class Hegemony (1905–16)

In recent years, academic historiography has tended to downplay the radical and proletarian content of the first Russian Revolution. According to Beryl Williams, 1905 'was a popular movement more concerned with dignity, freedom

---

93    Lenin 1902b [1960–65], p. 422.
94    Akimov 1904–05 [1969], pp. 53–4.
95    Cited in Friedgut 1994, p. 125.
96    Stučka 1904, p. 1.

and civil rights than with class hatred and socialism'.[97] A peaceful constitutional evolution for Russia, claims Abraham Ascher, could have been cemented had all sides (the government, the liberals, and the socialists) shown 'wisdom' by compromising with each other during the year.[98] In short, these scholars see the first Russian Revolution as legitimate and democratic, unlike October 1917.

But such a counterposition of the two revolutions is misleading. Popular radicalism, class war, rural uprisings, and armed clashes were central to 1905, prompting many political moderates to denounce what they felt to be an irrational and violent eruption of mob rule that threatened to destroy culture, property, and civilisation. Writing of 1905, Latvian nationalist Ernest Blanks exclaimed:

> Whoever has experienced the horrors of the Russian Revolution can only hope that other nations will avoid the fate of this scourge. Happy is the nation whose social, political and national development can take place in the normal course, i.e., without external and internal wars – revolutions – a natural evolution where all conflicts are resolved by minds, not by guns.[99]

If anything, socialists were more consistently committed to working-class hegemony in 1905 than they were twelve years later. As outlined in the introduction (see Table 2), radical Marxists were almost always at the head of the workers' movement during Russia's first revolution, unlike in 1917–18. Over the course of 1905, it was only in Finland and Armenia that moderate socialism prevailed.[100] Across the empire, radicals led the workers – and workers led the revolution.[101]

Since the prevailing stance in 1905 towards proletarian hegemony followed the longstanding orthodox position, a few examples here should suffice to reit-

---

97    Williams 2005, p. 50.
98    Ascher 1988, p. 344.
99    Blanks 1930, p. 31.
100   As in Table 2, these generalisations pertain to the eleven national groups and regions in the empire that had at least one Marxist organisation of their own.
101   Faced with Ottoman empire oppression and violent inter-ethnic clashes between Azeris and Armenians in 1905, the nationalist-oriented, moderate socialist Dashnak party became hegemonic in the Armenian community – a position it maintained up through and after the formation of an independent Armenian state in 1918. Significant groups of Armenians also joined three radical organisations oriented to class struggle: the RSDRP, the (formerly nationalist, now proto-Marxist) Hunchak party, and the Bundist-influenced Armenian Social Democratic Workers Organisation 'Specifists'. On the evolution of the Armenian national and revolutionary movements, see Ter Minassian 1983.

erate the content of the consensus. No social democrats claimed that capitalists could lead the revolution to victory. As Fricis Roziņš wrote in 1905, due to its weak and 'cowardly' nature, 'the Russian bourgeoisie is unable and unwilling to win a great revolution'.[102] One Bund leaflet from early October in Minsk gives a good sense of the general tenor:

> To battle, comrades! Onwards to merciless, mortal battle against the autocracy! Let the bourgeoisie and its representatives – the liberal parties – go to meet the new plans of the Tsar, let them rush to the Duma, away from the revolution. We are not alone – with us are the poor and oppressed of Russia. Death to Tsarism! Death to the executioners-murderers! Long live the revolution! Long live the democratic republic! Long live socialism![103]

This confidence in proletarian hegemony was both a reflection of and contribution to the unfolding revolution, which was driven forward throughout the year by urban proletarian mobilisation. The largest Polish peasants' organisation thus affirmed that 'when the revolution sounded its bells to call each oppressed soul into battle, the first who stood in line was the factory worker'.[104] As had been the case in the preceding period, in 1905 the political influence of liberals was only truly significant among Russians and Finns. In every region other than Poland, non-socialist currents remained basically absent from organised working-class movements. And in Georgia, Latvia, Lithuania, Ukraine, and Finland, Marxists also became the dominant political tendency in the countryside during 1905 and 1906.[105]

Workers from nationalities that had previously remained uninvolved in the labour movement surged into struggle. A noteworthy development along these lines emerged in Baku, where widespread assumptions about Muslim indiffer-

---

102    Roziņš 1905b [1963–65], p. 20.
103    'Прокламация Минского социал-демократического комитета Бунда' [1905] in Савицкий 1997, p. 199.
104    Cited in Kmiecik 1980, p. 84.
105    See, for example, Balkelis 2011, Zimmerman 2004, p. 216, Махарадзе 1927, p. 126, Surh 1989, p. 243, Schwarz 1967, p. 319, Apine 2005, Федьков 2007, and Alapuro 1988, p. 121. In Poland, the NDs were able to build a base in the working class, but their influence continued to significantly trail behind the socialists. Socialist-led mass workers' organisations in Poland had over three times the number of members as their rival nationalist associations (Żarnowska 1991, p. 315). Elsewhere in the empire, a minority strata of workers – invariably the least organised, most downtrodden – participated in anti-Jewish pogroms, but there was no significant crystallisation of right-wing nationalist organisation inside the working class (Lambroza 1981 and Weinberg 1993).

ence to class politics were contradicted by the course of events. In marked
contrast with prior years, Muslim workers in Baku struck in large numbers
beginning in 1905. As local Communist historian Akhmed Akhmedov documented in his long-forgotten 1926 monograph, some of the most remarkable
of the multifarious actions during the late-year upsurge were the *Gummet*-led
mass rallies of Muslim labourers in November and December 1905. Bringing
together thousands of participants from the outskirts of town, *Gummet* leaders exhorted their constituents to get organised and to maintain and deepen
their participation in the revolutionary struggle.

At the 4 December rally in Baku, R. Zeynalov for instance spoke about the
power of the working class, insisting that no help could be expected from
the capitalists. He concluded with a chant denouncing the bourgeoisie and
the Muslim upper class. Accordingly, the rally approved by popular acclaim a
two-point resolution expressing the support of Muslim workers for the anti-
autocratic struggle and announcing their decision 'to organise themselves' into
a Muslim-proletarian organisational bureau because 'only the workers themselves can improve their situation'.[106] Mammad Rasulzadeh, the *Gummet*'s
main theoretician, pointed to this upsurge as evidence for why it was necessary to reject calls for cross-class unity:

> It is said that to the Muslim his religion is more valuable than any class
> struggle. Turks are united only under the name of being Turks. They are
> alien to the class struggle, others said. But all subsequent events have
> proved just the opposite. The facts have convinced the public that the
> most developed section of Muslims is not alien to universal ideas.[107]

In all regions, the influence of workers' parties spread far beyond workplaces.
Marxists, for example, led major battles to reduce rents in Warsaw and to
provide relief for the unemployed in Baku. One Bundist recalled the new influence of the party's *birzhe*:

> Divorce, dowries, a falling-out between business partners, a swindled
> speculator, a shamed girl, a family dispute, the complaints of a servant
> girl about her employer – all sorts of matters were brought there, and it
> was impossible to refuse help, to say that it would be better to go to the
> rabbi.[108]

---

106   Ахмедов 1926 [2002], pp. 242–9.
107   Cited in Багирова 1997, p. 37.
108   Cited in Tobias 1972, p. 309.

Developments in Ukraine constituted a unique concretisation of the strategy of working-class hegemony. Unlike in 1917, Ukrainian and Russian radicals found a way to unite despite the region's daunting ethnic-class structure (Russianised cities surrounded by a Ukrainian countryside). During 1905–06, the single largest Ukrainian party of any political tendency was the Ukrainian Social Democratic Union, better known as the *Spilka* (Union), which had arisen in early 1905 after the Revolutionary Ukrainian Party (RUP) split over how to formulate an orthodox Marxist stance for the region, given Russian socialists' leadership over Ukraine's urban labour movement.

This dilemma had confronted the RUP ever since its creation in 1900. At the turn of the century, the organisation had advocated a somewhat amorphous, rural-oriented populist socialism. It thus declared: 'Without renouncing work among the industrial workers, where agitation has already been established by Russian, Polish and Jewish socialists, the RUP mainly addresses the village'.[109]

But in 1903–04, the RUP's new orthodox Marxist leadership under Mykola Porsh had pushed for the party to abandon its prior focus on Ukrainian peasants and, instead, concentrate its efforts on organising ethnic Ukrainian workers. Only by building a strong Ukrainian labour movement in the cities, he argued, would it be possible to forge political unity between Ukraine's rural and urban working people. This was a plausible orientation, but in practice it met with little success due to the marginality of the urban Ukrainian proletariat and its low level of national consciousness. Most class-conscious workers in the cities, including ethnic Ukrainians, persisted in joining the RSDRP and the SRs.[110] Porsh's current – renamed the USDRP in 1905 – remained marginal.

The wing of the RUP that would go on to form the *Spilka* argued that the main task of Ukrainian SDs was to mobilise and organise Ukrainian rural masses as a constituent part of the Russian Social Democracy. Since the urban working class would be the leading force in the impending revolution, they argued, 'Ukrainian revolutionaries, in the interests of the general economising of revolutionary forces, should above all go to the village'.[111] Upon splitting from the RUP, the *Spilka* affiliated to Menshevik-led RSDRP organisations in Ukraine.

By leading rural strikes and struggles during 1905 and 1906, the *Spilka* surged to 10,000 members, turning right-bank Ukraine – with its large market-oriented estates and massive rural semi-proletariat – into one of the empire's most militant concentrations of rural resistance. This *Spilka*-Menshevik alliance illustrates that though Ukraine's ethnic-class relations were a political obstacle for

---

109   Cited in Гермайзе 1926b, p. 309.
110   Boshyk 1981, p. 283. See also Andriewsky 1991, pp. 89–90.
111   Меленевський 1923, p. 131.

implementing a strategy of proletarian hegemony, they were not necessarily an insuperable one.[112] That a similar alliance was not forged during the Ukrainian Revolution of 1917–21 was not an inevitable consequence of social structure.

In 1905, socialists across the Russian Empire churned out leaflet after leaflet hammering home the same basic message: Only the organised working class could overthrow Tsarism, win the burning social demands of working people, and establish a democratic republic, thereby enabling the subsequent struggle for socialism. In the words of Pēteris Stučka, 'the proletariat is fighting for bourgeois political freedom against the bourgeoisie itself'.[113]

If anything, SDs tended to exaggerate liberalism's political servility, at least during the first nine months of 1905, the highpoint of liberal opposition under Tsarism. Indeed, moderate Russian scholars such as Victor Leontovitsch today chastise their ideological predecessors in 1905 for having gone too far in supporting the revolution.[114] Throughout imperial Russia, most liberals demanded a constitution, praised the workers' movement, supported non-violent resistance, and generally refrained from attacking the radicals.

After 'Bloody Sunday' in January, liberalism's democratic wing gained traction at the expense of more moderate factions. Hoping to lead a broad cross-class front to win a constitution, Russian liberals raised the slogan 'No Enemies on the Left' – an approach culminating in their active support for the late October general strike that obliged the Tsar to make significant political concessions. In February, Luxemburg wrote that the liberal nobility and professions were 'marching along behind' the revolutionary proletariat, as part of 'a great army of fighting people, one people, against Tsarism'.[115] In contrast with the anarchists, no revolutionary social democrat voiced opposition in principle to specific joint efforts with bourgeois democrats around concrete actions in the anti-Tsarist struggle. But the predominant orthodox view throughout 1905 was that the paths of the proletariat and the bourgeois opposition would part ways well before the convocation of a Constituent Assembly to establish a democratic republic – a demand, as we have seen, that was not generally raised by liberals.

This prediction was confirmed by developments later in the year. On 17 October, under pressure from the ongoing general strike and the threat of army mutinies, the Tsar issued the October Manifesto in the hope of restoring calm to the country. Liberals in all regions claimed victory, withdrew from the mass

---

112    On the *Spilka* in 1905, see Федьков 2007, Boshyk 1981, and Риш 1926.
113    Stučka 1905a [1976–78], p. 131.
114    Leontovitsch 2012, p. 226.
115    Luxemburg 1905.

struggle, dropped their support for workers' strikes, and concentrated their hopes on the upcoming Duma elections.[116]

Socialist parties and the workers' movement, in contrast, became increasingly militant. The Tsar's hope that the October Manifesto would quell the revolt sorely underestimated the depth of popular and socialist radicalism. SDs declared that the revolution was *not* over and that an armed uprising was still needed to destroy the autocracy and establish a democratic republic. The day after the Tsar's declaration, the PPS in Warsaw, like its socialist counterparts elsewhere in Russia, thus issued a proclamation denouncing the 'fraudulent manifesto' as 'a piece of paper that is wrapped around the whip, the Cossack's sabre, the executioner's noose'.[117] Lithuanian SDs similarly responded by distributing a flier calling for armed insurrection to 'depose that treacherous blood-smeared tsarist government!'[118]

Finland, which had been relatively calm for most of the year, was finally swept up in the revolution. Inspired by the general strike that had spread across Russia, Finnish railway workers walked off the job on 30 October, setting into motion the single most important event for the Finnish workers' movement before 1917. By the next day, all of Finland was on strike, and effective power passed into the hands of strike committees and armed guards. In many cities, constitutionalists and socialists closely collaborated during the first days of the 'Great Strike' and a spirit of Finnish national unity was widespread.

Despite the efforts of constitutionalists and moderate SDP leaders to build a united national front, the weight of their political differences began to break it apart. Even Mäkelin's collaborationist *Kansan Lehti* journal later acknowledged that the strike had begun with patriotic unity but was transformed within a few days into class struggle.[119] By the end of the Great Strike, Finland's armed guards – which had originally been cross-class in composition – had broken down into rival socialist and nationalist bodies, foreshadowing the dynamics of the 1918 civil war.

Whereas the liberals primarily demanded the restoration of pre-1899 constitutional legality, the labour movement (including its moderate wing) fought for universal suffrage and a unicameral parliament, which it argued must be established through the convocation of a Finnish Constituent Assembly. The latter demand was rejected by the Finnish bourgeois parties, which insisted that any constitutional changes must be implemented through the existing state struc-

---

116   Ascher 1988, p. 231.
117   Cited in Kiepurska 1974, p. 203.
118   Cited in Udrenas 2000, p. 304.
119   Tanni 2008, p. 113.

ture. On 4 November, the Tsar's historic 'November Manifesto' repealed the Russification of Finland and re-established the pre-1899 status quo. But the Manifesto did not guarantee that the new Finnish parliament would be elected by the whole population. Any new changes to the constitution would thus be made by the unrepresentative Finnish government, not a truly democratic assembly.

With their main demand achieved, Finland's constitutionalists now pushed for an end to the strike. The radicalised ranks of the SDP desired to continue the strike until these demands were won, but the party's moderate leadership called off the action on 6 November, pledging, however, to subsequently continue the fight for its demands. Working people across Finland responded to the end of the strike by denouncing the 'betrayal' of the Finnish upper class. Labour had initiated and led the general strike, yet liberals played a decisive role in ending it before workers' demands for full suffrage and a Constituent Assembly had been met. A typical post-strike workers' resolution concluded: 'Now we have come to realise clearly that the Finnish exploiting class, the bourgeoisie, is worth no better than its brothers in other countries'.[120]

This turn of events constituted a major setback for Mäkelin and his collaborationist line within the SDP.[121] Against calls for national collaboration, an emblematic article in the labour press now affirmed that 'class hatred is to be welcomed, as it is a virtue'.[122] Such sentiments did not remain on paper. In 1906, an unprecedented wave of strikes, protests, and mass suffrage meetings erupted across Finland. Under pressure from below, in 1906 the Finnish elite and the Tsar conceded to the labour movement's demand for universal suffrage, thereby transforming Finland into the world's first polity with full suffrage for women.[123]

Elsewhere in the empire, the course of the class struggle surged towards insurrection in late 1905. Though the Tsar's concessions were sufficient to spur a liberal retreat, they simultaneously set off an unprecedented working class, peasant, and soldier upsurge. In late November and early December this culminated in mass mutinies and armed insurrections in most regions of imperial Russia. A December general strike call by the empire-wide railway workers'

---

120    Cited in Tikka 2009, p. 138.
121    Suodenjoki and Peltola 2007, p. 101. The rhythms of this turn toward orthodoxy, nevertheless, varied by region. For example, class polarisation had long been strongest in Helsinki, while collaboration between the workers' movement and upper-class parties lasted somewhat longer in Tampere after 1905.
122    Cited in Soikkanen 1961, p. 233.
123    Blanc 2017a.

union declared: 'We are not alone, the urban proletariat, the laboring peasantry, and the conscious parts of the army and fleet have already risen up for popular freedom, for land, and for liberty'.[124]

Mensheviks and Bolsheviks alike fought for proletarian hegemony throughout 1905. Most socialist scholarship on the revolution has mistakenly claimed that the Mensheviks believed capitalists would lead it and that workers should therefore not aspire to win leadership or seize power.[125] A more nuanced version of this story acknowledges that the Mensheviks acted in a revolutionary manner in late 1905, but claims that this was simply due to pressure exerted from below by the upsurge.[126] Both of these accounts fundamentally distort the historical record. An accurate assessment of Menshevism in the first Russian Revolution shows that orthodox socialists in imperial Russia abandoned the fight for proletarian hegemony only *after* the defeat of the 1905 revolution, thereby breaking with the revolutionary social democratic consensus.

Though the Mensheviks were certainly one of the empire's orthodox Marxist currents with the highest hopes in liberals, throughout 1905 they still maintained a firm strategic and practical commitment to working-class leadership of the revolution. Martov's 27 January response in *Iskra* to the outbreak of revolution was emblematic: 'in one powerful blow the Petersburg proletariat secured for the whole empire-wide proletariat its class position: liberator of the nation, the class position of truly possessing hegemony in national affairs'.[127] The Mensheviks consistently affirmed their traditional Iskraist emphasis on unity in action with bourgeois democrats from the standpoint of working-class independence and hegemony, simultaneously supporting and criticising their temporary allies.

At no point during the year did the Mensheviks drop their longstanding position that the working class must lead the democratic revolution; nor did they claim that the proletariat should subordinate its struggle to maintain a bloc with its allies. Iuri Denike – a Bolshevik militant in this period – later recalled that the Mensheviks 'were always for it [attacking the liberals], and criticized them no less sharply than the Bolsheviks – even more artfully'.[128] One scholar's study of the Mensheviks in Georgia likewise concludes that though 'they were ready to cooperate with the bourgeoisie on a state wide level ... locally they

---

124   Cited in Reichman 1987, p. 289.

125   Conrad 2006a.

126   See, for example, Bobravaskaya 1934, p. 141.

127   Cited in Тютюкин 2002, p. 107. See also Хомерики and Рамишвили 1905, p. 25 and Редакция 'Искры' 1905.

128   Cited in Haimson 1987, p. 279.

were immersed in the social question, which invariably put them on a collision course with the liberals'.[129] Relations with liberals did not constitute a significant dividing line separating Menshevik and Bolshevik practice.

It is true that émigré theoreticians Axelrod and Plekhanov continued in 1905 to admonish socialists to not scare off the liberals. Foreshadowing the dominant post-1905 Menshevik position, Axelrod argued that the proletariat must be prepared to sacrifice its own political needs were these to come into conflict with the liberal bourgeoisie. For Plekhanov, socialist 'tactlessness' towards the liberals was 'most harmful' for the revolutionary cause.[130] But their stances hardly reflected or defined the Mensheviks' approach during the first revolution in Russia. Biographers of Axelrod and Plekhanov note that each stood on the far-right wing of the Russian Social Democracy and were largely ignored by Menshevik cadre throughout 1905. During the year, in fact, Plekhanov left the Menshevik faction and criticised its excessive radicalism.[131]

On the other hand, Menshevism as a whole generally held higher hopes for the progressive potential of liberals than other orthodox Marxist currents in the empire. This stance diverged less in its analysis of the immediate role of the liberals (and the appropriate tactics towards them), than in its more optimistic expectations in liberalism's future potential. Upholding the traditional position of *Iskra*, Martov explained that 'we have the right to expect that sober political calculation will prompt our bourgeois democracy to act in the same way in which, in the past century, bourgeois democracy acted in Western Europe, under the inspiration of revolutionary romanticism'.[132]

Events up through October 1905 seemed to justify Menshevik hopes in a vigorous Russian liberalism. But true to their conception of proletarian hegemony, Mensheviks adjusted their tactics when liberals deserted the anti-Tsarist struggle in late 1905. In Georgia, for example, the Mensheviks dropped any remaining hope in the local liberals after Tsarist troops killed 60 workers and wounded hundreds during a 29 August mass assembly inside Tiflis city hall. A Menshevik leaflet declared:

> Comrade workers! Here is a lesson taught to you by blood. The liberals howl about political freedom, about the indisputable rights of the people; however, when the people itself demands its own rights and begins a struggle for these rights, the cowardly and timid liberals run away from it,

129    Megrian 1968, p. 94. See, likewise, Jones 1984, p. 114.
130    Donald 1993, p. 86 and Plekhanov cited in Тютюкин 2002, p. 109.
131    Baron 1963, pp. 265, 268–70, 277–8.
132    Cited in Davidson 2012, p. 201.

concealing themselves in their comfortable homes, but the people are left
behind to be driven away by the cossacks and police. This bloody lesson
will leave an imprint on your memories together with the timid liberal
bourgeoisie which always betrays the people. Down with the cowardly
liberals! Long live social democracy![133]

This orientation was generalised across Russia following the October Manifesto.[134] Denouncing the liberals as 'traitors', the first issue of the new Georgian
Menshevik-Bolshevik newspaper *Skhivi* (Ray) declared: 'Every revolution in the
past has stopped halfway. The bourgeoisie which led the revolution forward did
not need to take it to its end ... The proletariat too ... was not developed enough
class-consciously. Today things are different ... [T]oday a conscious working
class is fighting which already knows the aim of the revolution'.[135]

During the Russian Revolution's peak in late 1905, Mensheviks across the
empire pushed for armed insurrections and fought for state power side by
side with Bolsheviks and non-Russian radicals.[136] Contrary to the polemical
claims of Bolsheviks and later Marxist historians, this undeniable radicalism
was hardly an ephemeral response to pressure from below. Rather, it fit squarely
within the Mensheviks' longstanding strategic outlook, which was reversed
only following the 1905 revolution's defeat. Later developments in the empire
and across Europe would show that the general tendency of moderate socialists during times of revolutionary upheaval was to oppose, rather than begrudg-
ingly go along with, attempts by working people to seize power.

## 8      Proletarian Hegemony and Liberals (1906–16)

The liberals' retreat after the October Manifesto was widely seen as a betrayal
of the liberation struggle.[137] This abandonment of the anti-autocratic mass
movement, combined with the unexpected depth of the rural upsurge – which
spread throughout 1906 – hardened most SDs' anti-liberalism and deepened
their strategic consideration of the peasantry. For the Bolsheviks, Stalin now
bluntly declared that the liberal bourgeoisie was not 'an ally of the prolet-

---

133    Cited in Megrian 1968, p. 152.
134    Getzler 1967, p. 110.
135    Cited in Jones 1984, p. 115.
136    Кураев 2000, pp. 61–2, Sutton 1987, p. 479, and Jones 1984, pp. 208–9.
137    Shanin 1986, p. 200. Likewise, see Hogan 1993, p. 151.

ariat'.[138] Pre-1905 social democracy's somewhat open-ended approach to the potential allies of the hegemonic working class was increasingly replaced by a more defined stance: since liberals in Russia were *not* a driving force for democracy, the main empire-wide social ally of the proletariat could *only* be the peasants, and rural workers in the case of Poland, Latvia, and Finland where rural class differentiation was more advanced.[139]

Kautsky's classic 1906 piece 'The Driving Forces of the Russian Revolution and its Prospects' reflected and legitimised this new orientation. He argued that the bourgeoisie 'does not constitute one of the driving forces of the present revolutionary movement in Russia and to this extent we cannot call it a bourgeois one', concluding that '[w]ithout the peasants we cannot win in the near future in Russia'.[140]

Explicitly hinging the revolution on a proletarian-peasant alliance was not a new approach; it had been pioneered by the SRs and advocated by various SD currents during the first year of revolution. But after 1905 it became a more widely accepted component of revolutionary social democracy across imperial Russia. A Polish Socialist Party editorial in September 1906 thus declared that the peasantry was (after the proletariat) the 'second-most important revolutionary element, which in the ongoing fight against the autocracy must play a decisive role; without it the complete victory of the revolution is impossible to imagine'.[141] Pointing to the example of the Menshevik-led 'Gurian Republic' in Georgia, Trotsky similarly wrote:

> Kautsky speaks of Social Democracy in terms of revolutionary leadership of the peasantry. In that respect he merely describes the situation that already exists in the Caucasus. Guria is the finished model of revolutionary relations between the peasantry and the party of the proletariat.[142]

---

138  Stalin 1907a [1953–55], p. 4.
139  On the roots of the Finnish SDs' remarkable rural influence, see Alapuro 1988, pp. 40–51. While orthodox Marxists during 1905–07 came to see the Russian and Ukrainian peasantry as a revolutionary force whose demands for land confiscation and distribution should generally be supported, they simultaneously argued that this approach remained irrelevant for borderlands such as Poland, Finland, and the Baltic where rural class differentiation was more advanced (Kautsky 1906 [2009], pp. 586–7 and Waldenberg 1972, p. 369). Along these lines, both the Latvian and Polish SDs were granted exceptions to the RSDRP's land redistributionist agrarian programme when they affiliated to the Russian Social Democracy in 1906. Marxist hesitancy to distribute land to the peasants in the Baltic and Poland played a major role in undercutting radical hegemony after 1917 (Kowalski 1978).
140  Kautsky 1906 [2009], pp. 605–6.
141  'Zgodne działanie żywiołów rewolucyjnych a SDKPIL', *Robotnik*, 4 September 1906.
142  Trotsky 1906a [2009], p. 578.

To sum up, by 1906–07 the orthodox conception of the hegemony of the working class had become consistently more dismissive of Russia's liberals and more supportive of peasants as allies. Not all Marxists, however, stuck with this approach after the defeat of the revolution. For socialists of all nationalities and backgrounds, the victory of Tsarism was experienced as a brutal blow on both a political and personal level. The mass movement's collapse and violent governmental suppression of socialist committees demoralised militants throughout the empire. Hersh Mendel, a Jewish Bundist, recalled the mood:

> It became dark and misty in tsarist Russia in the second half of 1907. It was like being on a boat, cutting through thick fog on a murky night. And you stand and look, to see whether you will recognize a sign, a ray of light. But all efforts are in vain. The darkness oppresses you and fills you with a heavy sadness.[143]

At the same time as socialists were getting thrown into prison or fleeing to exile, the Tsar gave liberals and nationalists an unprecedented opportunity to assert themselves publicly. The experience of the revolution had finally enabled the regime to understand which social forces constituted the main threats to its rule: from 1906 onwards it consciously targeted socialists and labour-militants while providing liberals access to wider freedoms and opportunities in the press and the new State Duma. No longer was labour the unchallenged centre of oppositional political life. By relying on these new platforms, moderate political currents for the first time became serious rivals to socialists. In central Russia, the liberal Kadet Party from 1906 onwards used its predominance in the elected State Duma to assert itself as the official opposition to the regime. Nationalist political currents, mostly liberal in character, similarly blossomed in the borderlands. Sociologist Liliana Riga notes that 'though they were still some way from being "mass movements", nationalists now had to be explicitly countered by socialists'.[144]

It was in this context that various hitherto orthodox Marxist parties – or major currents within them – for the first time began to drop their advocacy of working-class hegemony. Events seemed to have disproved orthodox strategy. Describing conditions in 1907, Polish Marxist Julian Marchlewski observed that 'the reaction has triumphed, the popular mass has been knocked down ... It has been plunged into apathy, it has lost faith in its own forces, this hero from

---

143    Cited in Levin 2008, p. 111.
144    Riga 2000, p. 451.

1905, the working people'.[145] In such conditions, moderate socialist arguments seemed increasingly pertinent. Their new case was straightforward: Workers had not proven to be strong enough to overcome Tsarism – therefore successful anti-autocratic struggle required an alliance with liberals.

On this point, the Mensheviks were empire-wide trendsetters. After the defeat of the December 1905 uprisings, most top Menshevik leaders began to reverse their previous advocacy of working-class hegemony. In their view, the proletariat's isolation from (and opposition to) liberals was responsible for the revolution's defeat. Not surprisingly, Plekhanov and Axelrod were the first to draw what would eventually become the dominant Menshevik balance sheet and strategic reorientation. In late December, only days after the insurrections were violently put down, Plekhanov proclaimed that recent events showed that the proletariat's 'power was insufficient for victory'. Overcoming Tsarism, he concluded, was impossible as long as workers were isolated from bourgeois society.[146]

Though this analysis of the 1905 defeat was not immediately taken up by all Menshevik leaders, by 1907 it was incorporated into their general orientation.[147] Even left Mensheviks such as Martov openly rejected Kautsky's insistence on class intransigence and accused him of bending to syndicalism.[148] To be sure, Menshevik affirmations of the need for proletarian political independence remained common and within their heterogeneous current there existed a variety of approaches towards liberalism in Russia. But, on the whole, the prevailing Menshevik position from 1907 onwards constituted a break from the strategy of proletarian hegemony. Leopold Haimson observes that 'Menshevism did not really begin to take shape as a distinct political movement, and especially as a political culture, until after the collapse of the great revolutionary expectations of 1905, and the searing criticism and self-criticism that this revolutionary maximalism generated within the Menshevik camp'.[149] For the first time, Bolsheviks and Mensheviks were now divided by fundamental strategic differences.

Ironically, the Mensheviks' novel orientation to liberals took place at a moment when the latter were making a definite turn to the right throughout Russia. In January 1906, Kadet leader Pavel Miliukov declared that revolutionaries had de facto aided Tsarism by insisting on the 'childish goals of "armed

145   Cited in Sobczak 2009, p. 580.
146   Plekhanov 1905.
147   Martov et al. 1907.
148   Zinoviev 1909.
149   Haimson 1987, p. 8. See also Shanin 1986, pp. 218–19.

uprising" and "a democratic republic".[150] By the end of 1906, the liberals' previous flirtation with the Left and mass struggle had been abandoned for good.
Even more than in the pre-1905 period, fear of a new revolutionary upsurge
outweighed liberals' desire for a constitutional regime. Until early 1917, liberal
parties limited themselves to calls for reform while refraining from engaging in
subversive action.

In 1906, Menshevism's push for a bloc with the bourgeoisie was widely rejected by imperial Russia's Marxists. Despite the defeats of the December insurrections, it was still initially hoped that the revolution had only suffered a temporary setback and that it would soon rebound. A majority of social democratic
parties continued to affirm a stridently anti-liberal approach; most explicitly
rejected the Menshevik stance. It was not a polemical flourish when Luxemburg noted in 1906 that 'the Menshevik comrades have not yet been able to
persuade anyone of the correctness of their views'.[151]

In this context it was unsurprising that Bolsheviks pushed hard during the
year for the RSDRP to accept into membership the Jewish Bund, the Polish
SDKPIL, and the Latvian LSDSP, while the Mensheviks remained reluctant.[152]
Indeed, it was because of the entry of these borderland Marxists into the Russian Social Democracy that the Mensheviks lost their initial majority at the
subsequent 1907 party congress in London. At this meeting, SDKPIL leader Leo
Jogiches described the Mensheviks' strategy as a dogmatic construct divorced
from reality: there was no revolutionary bourgeois democracy in Russia, nor
was there any reason to expect that such a force might emerge in the future.[153]

Along similar lines, in 1906 Symon Petliura – a top Ukrainian SD leader who
in 1920 became the nationalist head of the anti-Communist Ukrainian People's
Republic – published a glowing review of Lenin's pamphlet denouncing the
Menshevik approach. Agreeing that recent experience had shown that the liberals 'cannot carry the revolution forward', Petliura affirmed that Lenin's 'view
of the Russian Revolution is the same that is held by all revolutionary Social-
Democrats'.[154]

From late 1906 onwards, however, once it became clear that the revolution
had suffered much more than a temporary setback, a growing number of bor-

---

150  Cited in Ascher 1988, pp. 326–7. Similar turns to the right were the norm among non-
     Russian liberals and nationalists. On Latvia and Finland, for instance, see Bēržiņš 2000,
     p. 431 and Kujala 1989, p. 313.
151  Luxemburg 1906a.
152  For the discussion and resolutions on the merger with the Bund, for instance, see РСДРП
     1906, pp. 422–56.
153  Jogiches 1907.
154  П–ра. 1906, p. 74.

derland socialist parties abandoned the strategy of proletarian hegemony. Of these, the most important, apart from the Georgian Mensheviks, were the Jewish Bund, the PPS-Revolutionary Faction, and more unevenly, the Ukrainian USDRP. These political reorientations – and the ensuing inter-party competitions for leadership of the socialist movement – had a significant impact upon the course of the revolution in 1917, underscoring the causal importance of political parties and the relatively contingent strategic decisions of party leaders. A very brief sketch of the pre-war evolution of these three organisations should suffice to illustrate how moderate socialism crystallised in the borderlands, as socialist leaders drew new strategic conclusions from the suppression of the revolutionary upsurge.[155]

The Bund broke from its previously militant approach in early 1907, eventually becoming a close ally of the Mensheviks and sharing many of their strategic perspectives. Henceforth, Bundists sought to balance class struggle politics with ongoing collaboration with liberals, Russian and Jewish alike (though not the Zionists).

Various contextual factors help explain this unexpected political evolution, including mass pogroms in Ukraine and Poland, the Bund's precipitous fall from hegemony in Jewish political life, the deepening crisis of the artisanal economy in Russia, and the growing waves of Jewish emigration abroad. But, as with other parties in the empire, it was above all the demoralising defeat of the revolution that prompted a political reorientation among Bundist leaders.

Historian Vladimir Levin has documented 'the feeling of weakness' that came to pervade the Bund in 1907. This perception stood in sharp contrast with the 'state of near euphoria' of 1905, when it had seemed that socialists 'enjoyed almost absolute control on the "Jewish street"'. Though there remained a significant left wing inside the Bund, as inside the Mensheviks, Bundist leaders now generally dropped their 'militant anti-bourgeois line' in favour of an orientation towards class collaboration within local Jewish community structures:

> At the beginning this idea found only a weak echo among party activists, even giving rise to disagreement and opposition. After many years pursuing class politics and aspirations for a revolution which would change the existing order immediately, it was very hard to adapt to the plane of small-scale community affairs, where it was necessary to cooperate with 'class enemies'.[156]

---

155    For more on this dynamic, see Shanin 1986.
156    Cited in Levin 2004, pp. 143, 145.

Within the Polish Socialist Party, the issue of working-class hegemony became one of the fundamental lines of division between its Left and Centre. Throughout 1905, the Left's insistence on internationalism and class intransigence was dominant in the PPS, culminating in the party's December 1905 call for a workers' general strike and armed uprising in solidarity with the Moscow insurrection. Immediately following the crushing of the December uprisings, Ignacy Daszyński – the moderate leader of the PPS's sister organisation in Austria and a close ally of the PPS Centre – issued a controversial 'Open Letter' to the party in Russia. In this document he argued that the PPS's excessive focus on class struggle and blocs with Russian socialists had alienated key potential allies in the patriotic Polish camp, thereby undercutting the potential for a successful cross-class separatist uprising. This analysis and orientation was rejected by the orthodox PPS Left, which maintained a firm majority of the party, expelling the increasingly proto-nationalist PPS Centre in late 1906.

As the head of the newly founded PPS-Revolutionary Faction (PPS-FR), Pilsudski insisted that the failure of 1905 demonstrated that all political efforts had to be concentrated on building a cross-class paramilitary force to conquer independence. To this end, 'even an alliance with a bourgeois party' was deemed permissible.[157] By 1914, the year Pilsudski's military efforts prompted him to leave his own party, the PPS-FR's orientation had led to its virtual disappearance from the Polish workers' movement.

On the eve of the war, other PPS-FR leaders deemed it necessary to rebuild a base inside the working class. Though they continued to ally with Pilsudski, most of the remaining PPS-Revolutionary Faction leadership did not agree with his complete abandonment of the workers' movement and socialist politics.[158] Rejecting both the strategy of proletarian hegemony and calls for 'national unity', the PPS-FR after 1914 came to adopt a strategy it called the 'consolidation of democratic forces'. Essentially, this meant organising workers as part of a bloc to win Polish independence together with Pilsudski's militarist-nationalist Foreign Legions plus Polish peasant and bourgeois democratic parties – but, crucially, not the conservative National Democrats.

The new PPS-FR leadership sought to displace the radical PPS-Left and SDK-PIL from their longstanding position at the head of Poland's labour movement. After Pilsudski's departure, the PPS-FR took advantage of its radical rivals' disunity and their refusal to support the fight for independence, enabling it to

---

157    Cited in Garlicki 1988, p. 139. The author notes the 'far-reaching political consequences' of
       this new stance for the trajectory of Pilsudski and the PPS-FR (ibid.).
158    On the PPS-FR from 1906 through 1914, see Ładyka 1972.

rebuild a base in the Polish working class by leading strikes and labour fight-backs during the war, while simultaneously raising the flag of national independence. From 1915 onwards, the PPS-FR began to make important inroads within the working class by fighting for workers' immediate interests and by participating in trade union activity under the new German imperial occupation of Poland.

The party tempered this militancy, however, with support for Pilsudski's leadership in the fight to achieve an independent Polish state. As such, together with Pilsudski, the PPS-FR supported the German and Austrian occupying governments in World War One, with whom they closely collaborated in the hope of winning Polish independence against Russia.[159] Indeed, the PPS-FR was the only major socialist party in the Russian Empire to overwhelmingly support the war.[160]

After the defeat of 1905, much of the Ukrainian Social Democracy similarly dropped its support for proletarian hegemony. For example, in a reversal of its stance on blocs with bourgeois parties, many USDRP committees in 1907 established electoral agreements and/or common lists with Ukrainian and Russian liberals.[161] That said, the organisation remained more politically heterogeneous than the previously mentioned moderate socialist parties. Gauging the precise strength of its radical and moderate wings is difficult due to the USDRP's organisational implosion between 1907 and 1917. While the top literary bodies that officially spoke in the name of the USDRP remained primarily controlled by

---

159   On the PPS-FR, and its Austrian sister party (the PPSD), during World War One, see Holzer 1962, pp. 17–41.

160   Anti-war stances among socialists were far stronger in Russia than in most of Europe, partly due to the widespread opposition to Tsarist rule even among Russia's moderate socialists. Homogeneously orthodox SD currents such as the PPS-Left, the SDKPIL, the Bolsheviks, and the LSDSP consistently opposed World War One from the outset. Though open support for Russia's military participation was undercut by the existence of the Tsarist autocracy, most other socialist parties in the empire were divided over how to approach the war, with some currents calling to support it once Tsarism was eliminated. Large (often majoritarian) anti-war wings existed in all such organisations, and these gained increasing strength from 1916 onwards. On imperial Russia's Marxists during the war, see Tych 1960, Riddell 1984, pp. 131–4, Galili y Garcia 1989, pp. 38–43, Heikkilä 1993, p. 391, and Солдатенко 2007, pp. 65–6.

161   Павко 1999, pp. 136–7. The Lithuanian LSDP underwent a similar evolution after 1905. By 1914, the party was deeply divided over the question of blocs with Lithuanian liberals (see Sabaliūnas 1990, pp. 96, 139–46). During the war and the 1917 revolution, anti-liberal LSDP radicals allied with the Bolsheviks, while moderate Lithuanian SDs blocked with liberal nationalists. The LSDP split into Social Democratic and Communist parties in March 1918 (White 1971, p. 189).

leftists, the more diffuse bulk of intellectuals who considered themselves party members abandoned their former militancy.

The political trajectories of Symon Petliura and Volodymyr Vynnychenko, the two most influential leaders of the Ukrainian Social Democracy in 1917, are emblematic of this turn away from orthodox Marxism. As late as 1906, Petliura openly supported the orientation of Lenin and the Bolsheviks, but by 1908 he became disenchanted with the prospects for independent class struggle in Ukraine and Russia. Moving to St. Petersburg, he joined an intellectual literary milieu dominated by Ukrainian and Russian liberals. As editor of the legal journal *Ukrayinskaya Zhizn* (Ukrainian Life), Petliura now advocated a decidedly non-revolutionary line centred on promoting Ukrainian cultural autonomy with liberals and progressives of all nationalities. Like the Russian Kadets to which they were allied, Petliura and *Ukrayinskaya Zhizn* openly supported the Russian government's entry into World War One, arguing that this alliance with the French and British regimes would facilitate Russia's gradual democratisation and the promotion of Ukrainian rights.[162]

Vynnychenko moved in a similar direction, though he upheld the core tenets of orthodox Marxism for longer and remained more sympathetic to radicalism than Petliura. For most of the period before 1914, Vynnychenko focused on literary activities (in both the Ukrainian and Russian languages) and was associated with the left of the USDRP. When the war broke out, he was initially sympathetic to the anti-war internationalism of the Ukrainian SDs headed by leftist Lev Yurkevich. Yet Vynnychenko soon moved away from the party's left and instead came to associate most closely with Petliura's *Ukrayinskaya Zhizn*. As the main political and organisational leader of the USDRP in 1917, Vynnychenko would continue to pursue a relatively class-collaborationist Ukrainian national project throughout the year.[163]

Given that Ukrainian independence later became such a controversial political issue, it is worth noting that the moderate turn of these Ukrainian SD leaders did not make them any more disposed to support separation from Russia. If anything, their turn to the political centre led them to become *more* accomodationist to Russian liberals and the Russian state. Both Petliura and Vynnychenko rejected the call for independence and denounced the Union for the Liberation of Ukraine, a marginal circle of socialists and ex-socialists who during the war years sought to win Ukrainian independence under the aegis of the Austrian and German regimes.[164]

---

162  Верстюк 2004, pp. 116–17 and Солдатенко 2007, pp. 76–80.
163  Солдатенко 2007, pp. 59–66.
164  On the Union for the Liberation of Ukraine, see Smolynec 1993.

After 1905, the fight to preserve the USDRP's commitment to revolutionary social democracy was led by Lev Yurkevich. Though he is remembered today mostly for his polemics with Lenin over the national question, his major political contribution was to insist that the Ukrainian working class uphold a strict strategy of proletarian hegemony and reject any blocs with Ukrainian, Russian, or German-Austrian rulers. In Yurkevich's view, only through independent class struggle in alliance with workers of other nations would the Ukrainian working class be able to win its national and social liberation. He opposed blocs with liberals of any nationality and denounced the war, as well as those Russian and Ukrainian socialists who supported it.

As a supporter of broad national autonomy for Ukraine within Russia, Yurkevich emphatically rejected any collaboration with the Central Powers and declared that separatism 'cannot but become transformed, in the current intense atmosphere of antagonism between the "great powers", into an imperialist war combination'.[165] Though Yurkevich's wing of the USDRP spoke in the name of the party as a whole, its influence on the ground is unclear. From 1912 onward, most Ukrainian revolutionaries joined the rural-oriented Ukrainian Socialist Revolutionary Party (UPSR), which in 1917 became the single largest, as well as the most radical, Ukrainian party.[166] The potential for a radical Ukrainian SD-SR alliance in 1917 was tragically undercut by Yurkevich's death en route to Ukraine from Geneva after the February Revolution.

In marked contrast with their moderate rivals, various Marxist currents maintained a homogenous commitment to proletarian hegemony after 1905. Most prominent among these forces were the Polish SDKPIL, the PPS-Left, the Latvian LSDSP, and the Bolsheviks. It would be redundant here to reiterate their stances, which consisted of the longstanding axioms of revolutionary social democracy. Suffice it to say that these currents in Russia maintained their confidence in the working class in the face of extremely difficult circumstances. This was no small achievement, since during the period of reaction many forces succumbed to demoralisation and dispersion.[167]

In 1911, Latvian SD Jānis Jansons-Brauns implored workers and party supporters to understand that the current era 'claimed more moral strength, endurance and bravery' than ever before. It was easy to fight for one's ideals when victory

---

165    Юркевич 1917, p. 23. See also Smolynec 1993, pp. 25–7 and Заводовський 2006.

166    On the UPSR, see Бевз 2008.

167    I have not been able to identify any consistent contextual factors explaining why these parties, rather than others, upheld a class struggle approach following the revolution's defeat; further research on this question could prove fruitful.

seemed near, 'but true heroism is displayed when our side has been suppressed for a period'. Arguing that 'history still has more pages in its book', Jansons-Brauns concluded his piece optimistically: 'The future belongs to us!'[168] For his part, SDKPIL leader Julian Marchlewski in late 1907 called upon the readers of *Czerwony Sztandar* to reject the idea that working people 'had been knocked down forever'. Since 'the masses will once again be awakened' it was necessary to keep raising the red flag: 'Persevere! Do not let your spirits fall!'[169]

In contrast with these orthodox parties, the Finnish Social Democracy after 1905 was predominantly, but not homogeneously, committed to proletarian hegemony. Had Finland not been part of the Tsarist Empire, it is likely that the SDP would have evolved down a similar path as most Western socialist parties, in which party bureaucratisation and parliamentary integration relegated orthodox currents to an internal minority by the eve of World War One. Yet, unlike every other legal socialist party in Europe, Finnish socialists directly took part in the 1905 revolution, a radicalising experience that swerved the party to the left. The Finnish Social Democracy was the only major socialist party in Europe to become *more* orthodox after 1905.

In the wake of 1905's Great Strike and the subsequent unrest across Finland, much of the SDP's old guard was voted out of leadership. In its place came a new group of young revolutionary social democrats, the *Siltasaarelaiset*, committed to implementing a strictly orthodox perspective premised on a rejection of any blocs with the upper class. They declared:

> The lesson learned from hard experience is that when we build a union with the bourgeoisie, we dig our own grave. ... The clearer class boundaries become, the wider the gap between the poor and the bourgeoisie, the closer we get to our goal and the victory of all progress. The class struggle must always be the guiding principle of our actions.[170]

Interest in Kautsky's writings surged after the Great Strike, a dynamic reflecting both the active pedagogical efforts of the young radical cadre and the radicalisation of the party's rank and file. As one Finnish socialist leader noted, 'it is not an exaggeration to say that no socialist from abroad is as well known in Finland as Kautsky, nor has any other had an influence on the Finnish labour movement equal to his'.[171] Under the new party leadership, no electoral alli-

---

168    Cited in Kalniņš 1956, p. 168.
169    Cited in Sobczak 1980, p. 681.
170    Cited in Soikkanen 1961, p. 233.
171    Cited in Waldenberg 1972, p. 21.

ances with the bourgeoisie were allowed. In the 1907 election, the first after the Tsar's 1906 concession of universal suffrage to Finland, the SDP ran a completely independent slate and won 37 per cent of the seats in parliament – the highest score of any party.

Though orthodox social democracy became the official doctrine of the SDP from 1906 onwards, a significant wing of the party's leadership remained committed to class collaborationism. Moderate socialist leaders continued to argue that Finland's status as a dominated nation meant that proletarian unity with Finnish capitalists against Tsarism was both possible and necessary. The main enemy and oppressor of Finnish workers, they declared, was Tsarist feudalism.

Such voices became louder when the Tsarist government began a new offensive against Finnish autonomy in 1908. Faced with this 'second period of oppression', SDP moderates, including Mäkelin and Ursin, pushed for a renewed bloc with Finnish nationalists. Scores with the Finnish bourgeoisie, they argued, could be settled only after the defeat of the Tsar's renewed programme of Russification; refusing to collaborate in defence of national autonomy meant siding with the Russian government. An overly strict insistence on class struggle, in their view, reflected a doctrinaire regurgitation of German Marxism that failed to account for the concrete realities and practical exigencies of Finnish political life. Though open defenders of these positions were in the minority, a significant layer of the party's parliamentary fraction, bureaucratised organisational apparatus, and diffuse party membership were either indifferent to or opposed to revolutionary social democratic strategy.[172] The Finnish party remained less homogeneously orthodox than its radical counterparts such as the Bolsheviks, the Latvian LSDSP, or the Polish PPS-Left.

Finland's orthodox socialist leaders for the most part succeeded in preventing a return to a collaborationist line – and the anti-democratic nature of the regime aided their intransigence. Because the Tsar after 1906 frequently dissolved the Finnish parliament and blocked proposals to democratise local government, pressures from above and below upon socialists to make compromises to pass reforms were relatively low. As historian Hannu Soikkanen notes,

> The continual dissolutions of the *Eduskunta* [parliament] cut the ground from underneath any such [revisionist] cause, since no useful legislative reforms could be produced and the emphasis was shifted to election cam-

---

172    Soikkanen 1978, Heikkilä 1993, *passim*, and Carrez 2008, pp. 262, 305–6, 408–9.

paigns, in which all the parties vied with each other for votes. Repeated electoral campaigns focused attention on the basic issues which divided the parties.[173]

SDP party congresses in 1909, 1911, and 1913 affirmed a strictly anti-liberal stance, emphasising the inevitability and desirability of the intensification of the class struggle. And, unlike in the pre-1905 period, the party generally concretised this orientation in practice. In response to the SDP's newfound intransigence, as well as the 'anarchy' of 1905–06, Finland's liberals and nationalists made a major shift to the political right. David Kirby notes that 'the [SDP's] rejection of any sort of alliance with the bourgeois parties had the effect of pushing those parties into a more entrenched form of conservatism than had previously been the case. ... [T]he erection of class barriers by the SDP produced a counteraction and the radicalism of the bourgeois parties tended to disappear'.[174]

All of these countervailing tendencies impacted the trajectory of Finland's Social Democracy. On the one hand, the existence of a significant wing of leaders seeking (or potentially open to) a rapprochement with the bourgeoisie would shape the course of Finnish socialism in 1917. As will be discussed in later chapters, many party and union officials, as well as rank-and-file workers, succumbed to calls for national unity immediately following Tsarism's overthrow. In turn, the wavering of the SDP's orthodox wing that year was to a significant extent rooted in an attempt to push forward a class struggle line without provoking a party split.

On the other hand, it would be hard to exaggerate the impact of the deep polarisation between the SDP and the representatives of Finland's elite. Scholars have documented how the party's class-struggle line from 1906 onwards shaped the actions and orientations of both sides in the revolution of 1917–18.[175] The radicalism of the labour movement in 1917 cannot be divorced from the Finnish Social Democracy's longstanding line of enforced class isolation; post-1905 efforts by moderates in each camp to rebuild lasting collaboration ultimately failed in the face of the prevailing intransigence. As such, there are solid reasons to reject historian Anthony Upton's influential claim that the 'SDP was a true paper tiger; for all its class-war truculence it threatened nobody and was no danger to the survival of Finnish bourgeois society'.[176]

---

173    Soikkanen 1978, p. 356.
174    Kirby 1971, p. 129. See also Heikkilä 1993, p. 390.
175    Salkola 1985, p. 284.
176    Upton 1980, p. 15.

In both autocratic and parliamentary conditions across imperial Russia, the single most decisive strategic question for socialists was whether to antagonise or appease the bourgeoisie. Though Tsarist absolutism bolstered the strength of a radical approach, the latter's continued hegemony within the workers' movement was not guaranteed by the political context, as can be seen in the divergent ways parties responded to the defeat of the first Russian Revolution.

The post-1905 political re-orientation towards liberal elites by Mensheviks, Bundists, Ukrainian SDs, and the PPS-FR constituted a significant break from hegemonic anti-capitalist traditions in their regions – and it set the stage for their class collaborationism in and after 1917. The final three chapters of this book will demonstrate in detail that blocs with bourgeois forces tended to determine the other major political questions of the revolution. We will see that the ability of socialists to oppose the war, meet the pressing economic demands of workers, or implement agrarian reform was largely conditioned by their willingness to politically break from the bourgeoisie. Currents that had begun to orient towards liberals after 1905 generally continued this stance in 1917. Mensheviks and Bundists allied with the Kadets and propped up the Provisional Government. The PPS-FR remained embroiled in Pilsudski's military-nationalist coalition. Despite more radical traditions, the USDRP built a bloc with Ukrainian nationalists, and then turned to German imperialism.

In contrast, those parties that homogeneously upheld working-class hegemony following 1905 put forward remarkably similar lines in 1917. Following the Tsar's overthrow, the Latvian LSDSP, the Polish SDKPIL, the PPS-Left, the Bolsheviks, and orthodox wings within the other SD parties all continued to reject alliances with the liberals; they demanded a break with all native and foreign bourgeoisies; they opposed support for (and entry into) the liberal Provisional Government; and they fought for the establishment of a government of working people as the first step towards world socialism. So too did the SDP establish workers' rule in parliamentary Finland.

The divergent trajectories of socialist organisations across the empire after 1905 are hard to explain without taking into account the political choices made by party leaders, especially following the first Russian Revolution's defeat. As we will see, socialists in 1917 generally championed the approaches that they had defended ever since 1905's demoralising fallout. In other words, currents that upheld revolutionary social democracy's approach to blocs with capitalists found themselves on the same side of the barricades during and after the October Revolution.

On the question of working-class hegemony, there was a clear line of continuity between the Comintern and its Second International antecedents, as well as between Marxist politics in authoritarian and democratic contexts.

Summing up socialist strategy in 1920, Grigory Zinoviev explained that the 'most important question for all countries' was simply that 'we do not support the bourgeoisie, as it is the enemy'.[177]

---

177    Cited in Zinoviev and Martov 1920 [2011], p. 134.

# CHAPTER 6

# Working-Class Unity

One of the dynamics that differentiates working-class politics from other forms of political articulation is its emphasis on uniting working people across their myriad of divides. Far from being an arbitrary discursive divergence, this focus is a response to the structure of capitalist social relations. Since isolated workers – brought together from a wide variety of backgrounds by their shared employment relationship – are generally powerless against capital, it is only through uniting and organising that they can defend themselves effectively. Coalescing such a heterogeneous group of people is made possible by, but is never the automatic product of, a shared class location.[1] Whether the task is to lead a strike, establish a trade union, or fight for state power, the central challenge for labour organisers has always been how to bring together otherwise atomised workers for their collective interests.

The theme of unity was front-and-centre in the very first leaflet ever produced by a Marxist party in the Russian Empire. Issued by the Polish Proletariat in 1882, the declaration concluded: 'Unity, that is all we need. Unity and more unity, and the future and happiness will belong to us. ... "All for one, one for all", that is our slogan!'[2] The same viewpoint was later expressed by *Iskra* in theoretical rather than agitational terms: 'The necessary condition for the success of the struggle of the proletariat is the unification of all their forces'.[3] Yet strategies to unite workers have fallen out of political fashion and the question of how Second International parties pushed for labour unity has been mostly ignored in the literature.

In this chapter I will show that orthodox Marxists initially conceived of the social democratic party as the highest force for, and expression of, workers' unity. According to this view, there should only be one workers' party, to which all mass workers' organisations would be politically and organisationally tied. Proletarian unity could thus be achieved primarily through the Social Democracy. This orientation – which I call 'monopolism' – was plausible in Germany, but it proved ill-suited for autocratic Russia, where multiple relatively small socialist organisations co-existed.

---

1  On the collective action dilemmas posed by working-class heterogeneity, see Offe and Wiesenthal 1980.
2  Cited in Naimark 1979, pp. 109–10.
3  Cited in Krichevskii 1901b [2015], p. 256.

Many revolutionary social democrats under Tsarism initially attempted to implement the orthodox, monopolistic model. But in practice this approach tended to undercut the effective coordination of mass activity and it led to excessive factional battles. Over the course of many years, and particularly in response to the 1905 revolution, Russia's revolutionary SDs began to accept the need for unity in action between different political tendencies within the labour movement. Accumulated experience in this same period also led socialists to eventually accept the formation of non-party mass organisations – trade unions, federal committees, and soviets – to coordinate struggles and organise the wide strata of workers who did not belong to any parties.

This method became an almost universally accepted component of Marxist practice in imperial Russia after 1905. Indeed, collaborative efforts and united front mass organisations would prove to be critical for the successes of radical socialists in 1917. By pushing for workers' unity against the bourgeoisie, and by constantly fighting for leadership within non-party mass organisations, Bolsheviks and their allies were able to lead working people to power in key regions of the former Tsarist Empire.

Ultimately, the degree of workers' unity achieved in 1917 was one of the truly exceptional features of the Russian Revolution. By way of comparison, Europe's post-war revolutionary wave was defeated in part because labour movements were deeply fractured by splits between Social Democrats and Communists. An inability to cohere a united working-class fightback was also a significant cause of the defeat of Poland's 1918–19 revolution. As before, class formation depended on workers' unity. But in a post-war context marked by unprecedented partisan divisions among working people, the united front tactics pioneered by Marxists under the Tsarist autocracy took on a new strategic importance.

## 1      United Front Practices Before 1905

Before the creation of Communist parties following the Russian Revolution, most countries had only a single workers' party. For this reason, the question of unity in action between different socialist organisations could not be posed in pre-war Germany, nor in most of Europe.[4]

---

4  Finland also had only one workers' party up through 1918, which is why the Finnish Social Democracy will not be discussed in this chapter.

For the early German Social Democracy and its orthodox leaders, the main vehicle for workers' unity was the party itself. In the words of Rosa Luxemburg, 'the unity of the labour movement flow[s] from this organisation'.[5] According to the prevailing merger narrative, the party and its socialist programme would expand outwards to eventually encompass the mass of working people. The organised and conscious SPD members of today thus represented what currently unorganised and backwards workers would look like tomorrow.

Marxists did not view this merger as an automatic process resulting inexorably from economic developments. To the contrary, they insisted that such an advance required the conscious intervention of SDs every step of the way. The social democratic party's consistent stress on the final goal of socialism was seen as an indispensable means to unify workers both in the short and long-term, beyond their various sectional, national, religious, and geographic divisions. As Kautsky argued, the political goal of a socialist future was not a superfluous or romantic vision, it had 'the great practical task of preserving the unity of the proletarian movement'.[6]

The tendency of workers and unions to remain divided from their peers through narrow and isolated particularism could only be overcome by spreading the common final goal of socialism.[7] Flowing from this conception of the party as the guarantor of proletarian unity was the orthodox view that non-party mass organisations (unions, etc.) should be tied to the party and politically subordinate to it. Only this party guidance could guarantee that the workers' movement would maximise its power against the capitalists and avoid breaking off into various feuding groups.[8]

In hindsight, this strategy was shaped by the particular experience of the German Social Democracy more than its advocates realised at the time, reflecting an extrapolation of the SPD's remarkable growth since the early 1890s. Likewise, insisting on party control of mass labour organisations expressed the German Left's opposition to the attempts by moderate union officials to buffer themselves from party pressure.

Experience after 1914 and 1917 would lead Marxists in Germany and beyond to drop this conception, replacing it with an orientation to push for unity in action between different workers' parties and organisations. But in Russia, this break from social democratic orthodoxy began at a much earlier date in response to the lived exigencies of the mass movement.

5   Luxemburg 1906b.
6   Kautsky 1901, p. 69.
7   Cited in Waldenberg 1972, p. 500.
8   Schorske 1955, pp. 50–1 and Waldenberg 1972, p. 382.

Achieving working-class unity in Tsarist Russia was a daunting task. The organisational weaknesses of the workers' movement and the existence of various socialist parties vying for influence were challenges not generally faced by their counterparts in Western Europe. By 1905 every region and every large nationality in Russia had multiple underground socialist organisations in operation, none of which paralleled the reach or influence of the German SPD. It was this context that prompted many, though not all, of the empire's SDs to eventually find novel ways of collaborating across party divisions inside the labour movement.

Partly because of the tension between such novel practices and orthodox Marxist theory, united front tactics were unevenly implemented before 1905. Nevertheless, their reproduction across Russia demonstrated the extent to which experience in struggle pushed groups towards collaboration. Michael Melancon, one of the few Western historians to have studied this question, sums up the dynamic:

> [P]arties and factions did not completely sacrifice their independence, but at all levels they informally coordinated activities and, at key times, resorted to official inter-party arrangements ... [R]evolutionary leaders and activists of all outlooks regularly met together to work out joint approaches to important problems; this process found concrete expression in the innumerable joint declarations and proclamations they issued and in the strike committees, social organizations, soviets (1905), [and] armed detachments.[9]

Promoting strikes, particularly when these went beyond the confines of a single workplace, was one common form of joint activity. Historian I.M. Pushkareva, for example, charts how SDs, SRs, and other activists frequently collaborated in cities throughout imperial Russia. To call such actions, local militants not uncommonly issued united leaflets – e.g. from the 'Joint Committee of the RSDRP and the SR Party'.[10] Demonstrations were also often organised together by different groups. In April 1903, for instance, the Ukrainian RUP planned a demonstration jointly in Kiev with the SRs and SDs. That same year, the SDKPIL and the Bund in Łódź called a major anti-government demonstration to protest the recent pogrom in Kishinev. The result was a violent clash with the police, leading to the arrest of many militants. Armed self-defence actions against the

9    Melancon 1990, pp. 239, 251.
10   Пушкарева 2005, pp. 158–9.

pogromists – though usually initiated by the Bund – were also generally organised in conjunction with SDs of other nationalities.[11]

Not all forms of socialist cooperation were directed toward mass action. For example, PPS and SDKPIL émigrés such as Esther Golde and Cezaryna Wojnarowska built a non-partisan 'Red Cross' to give financial assistance to the victims of Tsarist repression and their families.[12] Socialist organisations also commonly sought to help other groups smuggle in literature to the empire, or even to print their publications if the latter lacked their own local press. In Odessa, for instance, the RSDRP group supplied literature to anarchists who were organising quarry workers.[13] In fact, some Marxists involved in such underground activities simultaneously worked for different groups. Future Bolshevik leader Josep Piatnitskii, to cite one example, organised the illegal transport of literature for the Bund, the PPS, as well as *Iskra*. Like many other underground socialists at this time, he had no clear partisan affiliation: 'If I were asked to what organization I then belonged I could not answer as definitively as I could [now]'.[14]

Joint socialist efforts were driven not only by the need for coordinated struggle against employers and the regime, but also by the unique political culture engendered by Tsarist repression. Prisons in particular were an important space where militants formed personal bonds across party divisions. The memoir literature is full of anecdotes about endless political discussions and growing comradeship between political prisoners. Often these personal ties would carry over once they were released, setting the stage for closer collaboration between local committees and parties. Georg Strobel notes in his history of the SDKPIL that 'personal acquaintances were often more important than lengthy negotiations between official delegations'.[15]

A desire to promote working-class unity was a central reason why so many workers and militants objected to what they perceived as socialist hyperfactionalism. There was a fine line between debating political differences and engaging in attacks that needlessly undermined potential collaboration on points of agreement. Striking workers in Ekaterinoslav called on leaders of the different parties to stop their infighting so as 'to unite against our common

11    Boshyk 1981, p. 205, Samus 1984, p. 65, and Tobias 1972, pp. 224, 229.
12    Kasprzakowa 1988, p. 63. Due to their opposition to collaboration with the PPS, Luxemburg and the SDKPIL leadership ended the project after 1902.
13    Schneiderman 1976, p. 296.
14    Cited in Riga 2000, p. 181.
15    Strobel 1974, p. 328.

enemy'.[16] *Iskra* in particular was often accused of excessive polemics against its rivals. For example, a 1901 'Joint Letter' issued by activists inside Russia argued that '*Iskra*, in the heat of controversy, at times forgets the truth and, picking on isolated unfortunate expressions, attributes to its opponents views they do not hold, emphasises points of disagreement that are frequently of little material importance, and obstinately ignores the numerous points of contact in views'.[17]

A desire to uphold or achieve united action also animated the widespread opposition of local committees to splits within their parties. After 1903 this would be a major reason why local RSDRP militants were so reticent to follow their party leaders in cementing a Menshevik-Bolshevik organisational rupture. Contrary to much Marxist historiography, such sentiments cannot be explained away as 'conciliationism' or as a reflection of an ideological commitment to building a politically amorphous 'party of the whole class'.

In many cities, the 1903–05 split indisputably damaged the RSDRP and the workers' movement generally. For example, Bolsheviks in the capital explained in 1905 that the 'struggle against the Mensheviks completely disorganised the work of the Petersburg Committee. The workers often, without joining the Mensheviks, left the organisation altogether'.[18] In his case for unity between the two currents, one Bolshevik militant concluded that 'Lenin did not understand the extent to which unity was necessary for action in Russia'.[19]

The desire to promote joint activity on the ground sometimes even led to the complete merger of local socialist organisations. In 1901 and 1902 such amalgamations took place between SRs and SDs in important cities including Saratov, Kharkov, and Kiev. In fact, the subsequent hyper-factionalism of *Iskra* against its SR rivals arose largely from the perceived need to clearly differentiate the two tendencies, to reverse the mergers, and to prevent them from spreading.[20] As was so often the case, the degree of factional heat from above was often inversely proportional to a tendency from below to gloss over political disagreements for the sake of practical activity.

Such local mergers across the empire usually reflected a real underestimation of substantial political differences. Particularly since the ideological and strategic foundations of the various parties were frequently hazy among the

---

16    Cited in Wynn 1987, p. 244.

17    Cited in Lenin 1901 [1960–65], p. 314.

18    РСДРП 1905 [1959], p. 544.

19    Piatnitski 1931, p. 198. It is important to note, however, that this hyper-factional style inside the RSDRP predated Lenin, with Plekhanov and Axelrod pioneering this no-holds-barred polemical approach (Larsson 1970, p. 151).

20    Haimson 1987, p. 477 and Melancon 1990, p. 240.

rank and file, many members concluded that there was no need for multiple competing socialist groups. Such pragmatic 'merger-ism' between politically incompatible factions and parties was in part a consequence of the absence of a consistent united front orientation among the empire's revolutionaries. Since socialist organisations inconsistently agreed to collaborate despite ideological differences, it is understandable that militants seeking to build unity frequently saw amalgamation as the only viable solution.

While most SD committees in Russia maintained their organisational and political autonomy, they were generally more disposed than their émigré leaderships to collaborate with others. Melancon notes that 'whereas revolutionary leaders manoeuvred gingerly around this thorny question, local activists plunged right in'.[21] But the degree of cooperation between activists varied greatly by city and over time. Big cities such as St. Petersburg, Kiev, and Warsaw saw some of the sharpest faction fights; united front efforts in these areas were only sporadic. In contrast, socialists in smaller provincial towns – as well as certain larger cities such as Kharkov, Łódź, and Odessa – more consistently worked together across party lines. Historian Jeremiah Schneiderman notes that in Odessa, '[i]deological differences among the social democratic groups and between the Social Democrats and their rivals did not prevent them from acting in common on the more practical matter of organizing economic and political agitation. The Odessa revolutionary underground groups evinced none of that sectarian narrowness so characteristic of political life among the émigré socialist leaders'.[22]

Collaborative socialist efforts in imperial Russia arose well before any attempts were made to theoretically articulate a united front strategy. Theorising the need for unity in action between different workers' parties was off the table as long as orthodox Marxists were convinced that there should only be one party for one working class. Indeed, the absence of the term united front (or any equivalent) before 1917 is illustrative of the prevailing political assumptions. Significantly, when the slogan 'march separately, strike together' was raised by SDs in these years, it was in reference to joint activity between parties of different classes (e.g. liberals, SRs, and SDs) to take down Tsarism.[23]

Despite this theoretical blind spot, a few socialist parties by the eve of 1905 had issued limited resolutions regarding political coordination. The Socialist Revolutionaries were among the earliest advocates of collaboration and in 1902

---

21     Melancon 1990, p. 241.
22     Schneiderman 1976, p. 296.
23     Baron 1963, p. 263, Tobias 1972, p. 283, and Lenin 1905c [1960–65], p. 164.

they advocated the creation of a loose empire-wide coordinating structure for all of Russia's socialist parties to promote 'agreement of action'.[24]

Among Marxists, the Bund was one of the most vocal advocates of united front tactics, as these aligned with its conception of national-party federalism. In 1903, a Bundist case for a federal Marxist party thus argued such a structure would enable 'coordination and unity of action' between SD organisations of different nationalities.[25] This approach was most effectively implemented in Latvia, where in 1902 the Bund and Latvian SDs set up a Federal Committee in Riga to bring together the city's diverse working class. The responsibility of the Federal Committee was to coordinate socialist activity in multi-national work-places; organise actions, strikes and demonstrations; issue common proclamations; manage joint work among students, teachers and soldiers; and run the illegal smuggling and distribution of literature. On all other issues, the national SD organisations were independent.[26]

In much of the empire, the Bund remained the most vocal Marxist advocate of unity in action. Nevertheless, its efforts went hand-in-hand with a dogmatic insistence on building separate Jewish proletarian organisations in all regions, even in places like Ukraine where strong RSDRP groups among Jewish workers already existed. The Bund's controversial expansion to 'the South' after 1902 proved to be particularly divisive, leading to sharp mutual recriminations.[27]

For its part, the PPS leadership initially insisted that it would only collaborate with other currents if they supported Polish independence. From 1903 onwards, this became a major point of contention between the party Centre and the Left, since the latter aimed to work with the Bund, the Russian SDs, and the SDKPIL. Reflecting the ascendancy of radicals within the Polish Socialist Party, its early 1905 congress gave the green light to cooperation with the Bund, the SDKPIL, and other socialist parties on the specific issues around which they agreed.[28]

*Iskra*'s approach was ambiguous. As noted above, many local RSDRP committees eagerly collaborated with other groups. Such efforts, however, were inconsistent. For example, rather than taking part in political demonstrations initiated by the Latvians SDs and Bundists, Iskraists in Riga held their own smaller actions instead. In 1902, the Ukrainian RUP criticised Iskraists for fail-

---

24    Melancon 1990, p. 240.
25    Cited in Peled 1989, pp. 66–7.
26    On the Federal Committee, see Dauge 1958, p. 196, Kalniņš 1956, p. 39, and Шалда 1982. Russian SDs had participated in the Federal Committee in 1902, but from 1903 onwards they boycotted it.
27    See, for example, Weinberg 1993, pp. 74–5.
28    Żarnowska 1965, p. 185.

ing to co-operate with other political groups locally. Indeed, during the 1903 summer strike wave, SDs in Ekaterinoslav rejected the SR proposal to form an ad hoc committee to call and organise a general strike. As a result, each group eventually called for the general strike to begin on a different day, leading to tremendous confusion among the city's workers.[29] A recent study likewise notes that the SDs in the Don region fought bitterly to prevent SRs and anarchists from participating in the local labour movement because 'the Social Democrats considered themselves to be the only political force that had the right to speak on behalf of workers and express their interests'.[30]

Such tensions in *Iskra*'s approach found a theoretical expression at the RSDRP's 1903 Second Congress. The delegates passed a resolution denouncing the SRs as a 'bankrupt' bourgeois-democratic faction whose actions were 'detrimental' to the proletarian and the anti-Tsarist struggle. The text only permitted 'partial agreements with them in particular instances of struggle against Tsardom, the conditions of such agreements to be subject to supervision by the Central Committee'.[31] Though the main point of contact with the SRs was in the urban labour movement, collaboration was framed as (and limited to) cross-class anti-Tsarist struggle. In other words, the 'true' proletarian party accepted working with the SR 'bourgeois-democrats' against the autocracy, but not against the employers. The main practical consequence of this 1903 resolution was that it alienated the Socialist Revolutionary party leadership, which called for limiting coordinating efforts outside of Russia until the resolution was rescinded.[32]

The ambiguities of *Iskra*'s stance on collaboration within the labour movement were also evident in its relations with national SD organisations like the Bund and the Latvians LSDSP. Though joint work with such parties prevailed in some locales despite their differences over the national question, in other places Iskraists refused to collaborate with their rivals. In Latvia, for example, Iskraists boycotted the Federal Committee after 1903, declaring that 'the Riga workers' movement must be concentrated in one leading committee ... This must be a non-national organisation and this can only be the RSDRP'. They announced that the path towards proletarian unity required 'stepping up the fight against the national organisations' and winning the Latvian working masses directly to their party.[33]

---

29    РСДРП 1905 [1959], p. 588, Boshyk 1981, p. 178, and Wynn 1987, pp. 235, 249–50.
30    Васьков 2005.
31    RSDLP 1903 [1978], p. 21.
32    Kujala 1988, p. 115.
33    Cited in Apine 1974, p. 136.

Riga's Bolsheviks and Mensheviks spent much of 1905 in futile efforts to raid the membership of the Latvian LSDSP. In response, the Latvian SDs publicly declared that in Riga 'the Russian comrades, big ones [Bolsheviks] and little ones [Mensheviks] alike, have behaved like pigs'.[34] Even usually uncritical Soviet historians noted this sectarianism: 'The fundamentally correct line of the Riga Committee of the RSDRP was implemented with a certain dogmatism; the Committee lacked tact and flexibility in relation to the LSDSP'.[35]

Of all the socialist tendencies in imperial Russia, the leadership of the SDKPIL was the most consistently opposed to united front practices. As Antti Kujala has observed, it 'reacted to the question of collaboration between the social democrats and the other revolutionary parties and opposition movements the least favourably of any party within the whole of the Empire'.[36] Though the Luxemburg leadership's rigid adherence to the monopolistic SPD model was impeccably orthodox, the roots of this stance had as much to do with (anti-PPS) factionalism as high theory. For many years, the SDKPIL's top leaders opposed joint work with either the PPS or the Bund, on the grounds that each were 'nationalist' organisations. In 1904, some leaders of the SDKPIL such as Jogiches began taking a more flexible stance towards cooperation with the Bund, while continuing to assert that any collaboration with the PPS was forbidden. This insistence on excluding the PPS defeated the Warsaw Bund's ongoing efforts to build joint demonstrations and strikes between the four socialist parties in Poland.[37]

## 2      Workers' Unity and the 1905 Revolution

As in previous years, 1905 was marked by collaborative efforts between different socialist tendencies as well as frequent failures to promote unity in action across party divides. Examples of the former can be found in all cities and between all socialist parties. In Ukraine, for instance, the Bund and RSDRP committees closely coordinated their activities throughout the revolution. Their early initiatives included calling joint strikes and demonstrations; later in the year, these efforts expanded to include self-defence against pogroms and armed struggle against the state.[38] In Riga, the Federal Committee – jointly led by

---

34    'Rīga' [Anon.], *Cīṇa*, 2 August 1905.
35    Apine 1974, p. 136.
36    Kujala 1988, p. 166.
37    Kiepurska 1974, p. 141.
38    See, for example, Равич-Черкасский 1923, p. 26 and Hamm 1993, p. 188.

Bundists and Latvian SDs – deepened its roots among workers of all nationalities, leading multi-national strikes, successfully combatting pogromists, and
organising joint work inside the army.

The Bolsheviks' April 1905 congress resolved that the Central Committee and
local committees should 'make every effort to reach agreement with national
Social Democratic organizations with the aim of coordinating local work'.[39]
Reflecting their emphasis on building a broad anti-Tsarist revolutionary
upsurge under SD leadership, the Bolsheviks were also increasingly eager to
collaborate with the SRs and their non-Russian equivalents in the anti-Tsarist
struggle (if not always in the labour movement). To mark the half-year
anniversary of Bloody Sunday, St. Petersburg's SRs, Mensheviks, and Bolsheviks jointly called for strikes. United actions and initiatives between SDs and SRs
spread throughout Russia, though the latter regretted that this only took place
locally and not empire-wide. In contrast, the PPS and SRs reached a formal all-
Russian accord: throughout 1905 they jointly organised conferences, coordinated revolutionary work in the army, and issued common proclamations.[40]

Despite the acrimonious Bolshevik-Menshevik split, multiple committees
refused to let the faction fight impair their organising efforts. Comradely cooperation in cities such as Kharkov, Nikolaev, and Saratov was consistent
throughout 1905. In the words of Bolshevik cadre Osip Piatnitsky, 'I could
not understand why seemingly petty disagreements should interfere with our
working together, especially since new fields of action had opened up after the
[1903] Congress'.[41] Reflecting a widespread desire for unity, as well as a generalised sense that the actual political differences were insufficient to merit
an organisational split, in November–December 1905 the local cadre of both
factions in all regions imposed a merger of the RSDRP over the heads of their
émigré leaderships.

In almost all corners of the empire, the revolutionary upsurge during the
last three months of 1905 was marked by a deepening of united front practices.
Multiple general strikes from October onwards pushed socialists towards closer
collaboration. Indeed, many of the 'dual power' institutions during late 1905
arose directly out of the strike committees created during the October general

---

39    'On the Attitude Toward the National Social Democratic Organizations' [1905] in Elwood
      1974a, p. 64.
40    Kujala 1988, p. 165, Melancon 1990, pp. 241–2, and Megrian 1968, p. 76. This close collab-
      oration with the SRs – a project led by Pilsudski and the PPS Centre – placed PPS leftists
      in a bind. They had long advocated closer collaboration with Russian socialists, but they
      sought above all an alliance with Russian Social Democrats (Kelles-Krauz 1905, p. 167).
41    Piatnitsky 1933, p. 60. See also Sanders 1987, p. 169.

strike. Another impetus for increased collaboration was the urgency of build-ing self-defence groups to protect workers' organisations and Jews from state violence and pogromist terror. Support for armed self-defence, for example, facilitated a practical rapprochement between the Bolsheviks, the Bund, and the Latvian SDs in Riga. Similarly, a push for fusion between the Menshevik and Bolshevik committees in Odessa came primarily from workers active in anti-pogrom activities.

Finally, socialists organising within the Tsarist army across imperial Russia built mass non-party organisations to coordinate their subversive activities in late 1905, and even more so in 1906. Virtually all major armed uprisings in 1905 were organised as joint efforts, not (as many Marxists had previously assumed) under the banner of the social democratic party.[42] Historian Helena Nicolaysen notes that cities with the strongest united front practices were generally the most militant during 1905.[43]

Despite these trends, the extent to which socialists forged a workable unity remained uneven across Russia. When a general strike spontaneously broke out in Odessa in May 1905, SDs were unable to put aside their differences for the sake of unity in action: a proposal to form a common strike committee was accepted but never got off the ground due to Bolshevik-Menshevik infighting. The ability of activists to guide the June strike in Ekaterinoslav was likewise undercut by the focus of SRs and SDs on denouncing each other. And in Octo-ber, the Russian SDs in Odessa rejected the appeal of the Bund, anarchists, and SRs to jointly organise the impending general strike – only the RSDRP, they insisted, should lead the action.[44]

Poland was the region with the most difficulties in cohering a united front. Early in 1905, even limited cooperation between the PPS and SDKPIL was rare to non-existent. This inability to achieve unity in action was mostly caused by the intransigence of the SDKPIL, which argued that programmatic differences between it and the PPS precluded any contact or cooperation. Calls for general strikes to protest Bloody Sunday were thus issued by different parties on dif-ferent days and the Warsaw Bund's proposal to form a joint PPS-SDKPIL-Bund strike committee floundered because Luxemburg's party refused to coordinate with the PPS. In the Dąbrowa Basin mining region, January's strike was marked by bitter fights in which both parties fought to monopolise leadership over the action. SDKPIL militants even went so far as to seize the flags of their rivals.[45]

---

42      Melancon 1990, p. 242, Weinberg 1993, p. 206, Шалда 1982, and Bushnell 1985, *passim*.

43      Nicolaysen 1990, p. 332.

44      Weinberg 1985, pp. 217–18, 265–6 and Wynn 1987, pp. 272–3.

45      Żarnowska 1965, pp. 162, 198 and Kałuża 2005, pp. 44–5.

The Bund's persistent efforts to build tri-party coordination in Warsaw floundered throughout the year. Many strikes and demonstrations in 1905 were marred by sharp inter-party clashes (or by boycotts from rival parties), impeding the ability of revolutionaries to provide guidance to these mass actions. Within the PPS, leftists encouraged joint coordination between the parties, but they came up against the dual intransigence of their SDKPIL rivals as well as the reluctance of Pilsudski's Centre.[46] PPS leftists in the Dąbrowa Basin reported in November 1905 that when they proposed the formation of a 'joint revolutionary committee' to the SDKPIL branch, it 'refused because of [its insistence on] "the purity of social-democratic political tactics"'.[47]

From the fall of 1905 onwards, the 'Military Revolutionary Organisation' in Warsaw led by PPS leftists proposed to the SDKPIL that they coordinate activities inside the army and form a joint military organisation. But these initiatives were consistently rejected by Luxemburg's party. The PPS's Russian language soldiers' newspaper in May 1906 decried the fact that the SDKPIL had still provided 'no significant reasons for this stubborn refusal to work together in the common cause of revolutionising the broad masses of the soldiers'.[48]

Nevertheless, like in the rest of the empire, Poland witnessed a spontaneous push for unity by the insurgent working class in 1905. Particularly outside of Warsaw, Poland's four socialist parties – the SDKPIL, PPS, Bund, and PPS-Proletariat – began to jointly coordinate strikes, demonstrations, and self-defence on a city-wide level, frequently at the initiative of the Bund. Yet time and time again, the top SDKPIL leadership intervened to put an end to these united fronts, declaring that programmatic differences precluded coordination with the PPS.[49] To cite one of many examples: after the SDKPIL in Łódź reached an agreement in late 1905 to jointly organise an anti-government strike with the PPS (as neither had sufficient influence to organise one on their own), the SDKPIL's top leadership intervened to annul the accord, eventually prompting various cadre to resign in protest of what they called the 'bureaucratisation' of their party.[50] Some influential SDKPIL figures even became members of the PPS in protest against the Luxemburg leadership's refusal to sanction united actions. Dissident SDKPIL organiser Stanisław Gutt wrote in 1905 that 'if the

46    Samuś 1984, p. 129, Żarnowska 1965, pp. 162, 198, and Strobel 1974, p. 242.
47    'Z prowincji – Zagłębie Dąbrowskie', *Robotnik*, 24 November 1905.
48    'Хроника', *Солдатская Доля*, 25 May 1906.
49    Kiepurska 1974, p. 143, Michta 1987, p. 143, and Żarnowska 1965, pp. 243, 324.
50    Michta 1987, pp. 142–3.

proletariat today falls in battle, moving in separate groups rather than as a compact batch, we will be to blame and we will in the future have to answer seriously to history'.[51]

In all regions of Russia, effectively building workers' unity also posed the question of how to relate to mass non-party organisations such as trade unions. On this question, orthodox theory and the German precedent provided ambiguous guidelines. According to the longstanding conception of Kautsky and other revolutionary SDS, unions – which represented only particular proletarian strata – must be connected to and guided by the party, which was a superior instrument because it represented the class as a whole and its final goal. At the same time, however, unions in Germany remained formally independent; the guidance of the SPD was largely implemented through party members in union leadership.

This set-up in Germany posed few problems initially, but it became increasingly strained from 1905 onwards, as moderate union officials attempted to assert their political independence from the SPD, which they saw as too radical. At the precise moment the 1905 revolution broke out, Kautsky, Luxemburg, and other German leftists were engaged in an increasingly bitter battle to (re)assert SPD dominance over the unions.[52]

In Russia, various Marxist organisations – most notably the PPS and the Latvian LSDSP – built trade unions that were neither structurally tied to their party nor based on their programme. They argued that socialists should seek to guide unaffiliated unions through the influence of party members. In their view, to affiliate or subordinate these mass organisations to the party was unnecessary (given the possibility for SDS to provide leadership organically) and counter-productive (since it could alienate non-party workers). As Stučka argued, it was not a question of getting the unions to affiliate to the party or recognise its programme, but rather of the political 'spirit that guides the trade unions'. The task of Marxists was to fight for a class struggle orientation, against 'an insular, narrow-minded' trade unionism oriented towards limited sectoral demands and class collaboration with the employers.[53] Both the PPS and the LSDSP successfully implemented this militant, non-monopolist approach. By consistently initiating and building non-party unions, each remained the leading Marxist current in their regions' powerful trade union movement during the 1905 revolution and again in the 1912–14 upsurge.[54]

---

51    Cited in Sobczak 1988, p. 64, see also p. 65.
52    Steenson 1981, pp. 79–110.
53    Stučka 1906b, p. 196.
54    Kochański and Orzechowski 1964, Karwacki 1972, and Lapa 1992.

Other sds in the empire, such as the Bund and the SDKPIL, promoted 'party unions' that were politically, organisationally, and/or financially tied to the Social Democracy. Though their precise organisational structures varied, such unions generally paid a percentage of their membership dues to the party and officially accepted its leadership or programme. This approach was in line with the monopolistic axioms of Marxist orthodoxy – particularly in its strongest articulations against the German union bureaucracy – if not the actual organisational precedent of the German labour movement.

Given the Bund's political and organisational hegemony on 'the Jewish street' during 1905, it implemented this vision relatively successfully. As historian John Holmes has noted, during 'the Revolution Jewish unions usually accepted these [monopolistic] conditions'.[55] Nevertheless, this advocacy of party unions resulted in some internal and external opposition. In October, for instance, large groups of workers in the town of Vitebsk who belonged to no party, or who were members of other socialist organisations, fought against the Bund's efforts to establish party unions in their industries. And within the influential Union of Jewish Tanners, Bundists were able to push through a resolution formally subordinating the body to the Bund, but only after sharp conflicts with other socialists. These political clashes even led to physical brawls.[56]

Such tensions were prevalent in Poland. Most Western historians and socialists have unsurprisingly ignored the SDKPIL's promotion of party control over the unions, since this stance directly contradicts prevailing myths about Rosa Luxemburg's supposed 'spontaneism'. But the SDKPIL's advocacy of party unions was especially detrimental in Poland, where four orthodox Marxist parties operated inside the workers' movement. Such a context was ill-suited for strict monopolism.

Unlike the German SPD, or to a lesser extent the Jewish Bund, the SDKPIL did not have sufficient influence to make a monopolistic approach viable. Bitter battles ensued from the efforts of the SDKPIL to create its own unions in industries where other unions already existed. Kochański and Orzechowski's study of the Polish labour movement highlights that the ensuing divisions 'negatively impacted the effectiveness of the entire working class'.[57] Luxemburg's

55   Holmes 2008, p. 27.
56   'Борьба вокруг профсоюзов в Витебске' [1905] in Савицкий 1997, pp. 230–1 and Holmes 2008, pp. 27–8.
57   Kochański and Orzechowski 1964, p. 74. Polish historian Władysław Karwacki notes that the party's union policy 'prevented it from impacting the broad masses of workers'. SDKPIL unions thereby tended to involve only the party's members and close periphery (Karwacki 1972, p. 60).

party openly acknowledged that such divisions played a detrimental role in the development of the class struggle – but, in its view, organisational unity in the trade unions could only be achieved once there was ideological cohesion under the banner of the SDKPIL. By casting off the social-patriots in the PPS, it argued, workers in Poland would be able to effectively join together against the bosses and the autocracy.[58]

Compared to the Polish SDs, Bolsheviks were better able to flexibly adjust to the dynamics of mass struggle. Within the RSDRP, there were initially a wide range of views on party-union relations in early 1905. As one member recalled: 'This was a period when directives of the Party center on the question of trade unions were still weak ... Party thinking was itself still searching for more productive paths for its work, testing various methods'.[59] Some Menshevik organisers had attempted to establish party unions in the first months of 1905, but they quickly dropped this approach in response to strong resistance by unaffiliated workers.[60] Henceforth the Mensheviks adopted an orientation like that of the LSDSP and PPS. Combined with their greater attention to economic demands, the Mensheviks' advocacy of non-party unions was a critical reason why they predominated over the Bolsheviks in the trade union movement during the first Russian Revolution.

Among the Bolsheviks, different views and practices regarding non-party mass organisations co-existed during 1905. Advocacy of party unions lasted longer among the Bolsheviks than their rivals. In April, Bolsheviks unsuccessfully attempted to build a party union on the railways and this stance was advocated as late as October in Odessa and November in Moscow. Some Bolshevik cadre, such as future Menshevik historian B.I. Nikolaevksi, even switched their factional allegiances over this issue. Nevertheless, the approach of Bolsheviks shifted over the course of the year in response to the same sorts of difficulties encountered by the SDKPIL and the Bund. By the end of the year, Bolsheviks had generally dropped their attempts to build party unions, though the long-term goal of eventually winning the existing unions to the programme and membership of the RSDRP often persisted.[61]

While trade unions represented the organisational crystallisation of workers' unity in a given workplace or industry, late-year institutions of dual power – soviets and Federal Committees – constituted an even broader class-wide

58    Kochański and Orzechowski 1964, pp. 105–8.
59    Cited in Reichman 1977, p. 334.
60    Bonnell 1983, p. 156.
61    Reichman 1977, pp. 341–3, 353, Bonnell 1983, pp. 153–60, Чернявский and Фельштинский 2013, McDaniel 1988, p. 441, and Schwarz 1967, pp. 147, 153–65.

united front. The soviets, i.e. workers' councils, were a novel form of organisation that arose largely out of the October 1905 strike committees. Lenin's
influential 1917 vision of soviets as the institutional basis for a workers' state has
obscured how socialists actually saw the role of these institutions in 1905 and
1917. Though councils ended up wielding various levers of proto-governmental
power when Tsarist authority collapsed in late 1905, their intended function
was simply to coalesce the various components of a given town's working class.
SDs and SRs of all nationalities, independent radicals, and unaffiliated workers all came together in the councils – liberals, however, were consciously
excluded. Oscar Anweiler notes that 'the first soviets were founded because
workers desired unity and leadership in their splintered struggle, and not
because they wanted to seize political power ... Frequently boundaries between
a simple strike committee and a fully developed council of workers deputies
were fluid'.[62]

One of the novel aspects of the council form was that delegates were mostly
chosen through elections in workplaces, giving these organisations a bottom-
up, participatory character. That said, it is worth noting that representatives
were elected (or selected) by a wide variety of methods. Sutton's empire-wide
study of the 1905 soviets notes that 'the method of election was executed on
an ad hoc basis. ... By and large, the process of elections was incidental to the
activities of the soviet in so much as once the decision had been taken to form
a soviet, elections took place with haste or deputies already representing workers took their place in the soviet'.[63] Unions and parties were also frequently
granted direct representation.

All Russian SDs at the time regarded this new form of organisation as an ad
hoc expedient to overcome the weakness of the RSDRP. As such, soviets only
arose in regions where the Russian Social Democracy was the main political
current: central Russia, Ukraine, and Azerbaijan. The Mensheviks argued that
while the fundamental vehicle for uniting the proletariat should be the party, in
the given circumstances some transitional form of broad non-party organisation was necessary to represent the broad strata of revolutionary workers who
remained unaffiliated to the RSDRP. According to Martynov:

> The coexistence of two independent proletarian organizations – a Social
> Democratic Party organization and another one that is officially nonpar-
> tisan, though influenced by the Social Democrats – is an abnormal phe-

---

62    Anweiler 1974, pp. 39, 47. See also Weinberg 1985, p. 341.
63    Sutton 1987, pp. 144, 146.

nomenon that must disappear sooner or later. When we recommended the creation of organs of the revolutionary self-government of the proletariat [soviets], we considered this form of organization as something provisional and temporary.[64]

In his view, soviets were a transitional vehicle for revolutionary struggle as well as a first organisational step towards a mass social democratic party.

Mensheviks therefore consistently opposed Bolshevik proposals in 1905 to have the soviets adopt the programme of the RSDRP and recognise its leadership. Such a step, according to the Mensheviks, would abort the soviet's *raison d'être* as a unifying body for all workers. Were the structure to lose its non-party status, it would alienate the broad mass of unorganised workers as well as those belonging to other socialist organisations.[65] This did not mean the soviets should be apolitical, or that Marxists should avoid leading them. As one Menshevik explained in Kiev, because 'the most conscious workers' were SDs, their co-workers would naturally tend to elect them to represent their interests.[66]

As noted above, Bolsheviks were initially hesitant about non-party organisations, soviets included. This allowed their factional rivals to take the lead in establishing and leading workers' councils even in cities like Moscow where the Bolsheviks were the hegemonic current inside the RSDRP.[67] In St. Petersburg, home of Russia's pioneering and most influential soviet, the Bolsheviks did not prioritise working within the body. Historian Anne Morgan notes that the city's Bolshevik committee instead 'worked on organizing its local district Party committees and forming armed detachments of workers. Particularly after the arrest of the first Soviet, it abdicated from any leadership role in the second Soviet, which then was dominated totally by Mensheviks'.[68]

Like with the trade unions, Bolsheviks held a wide range of opinions on the workers' councils. Between October and December 1905, they heatedly debated this issue in their press. A 27 October statement from the St. Petersburg-based Central Committee leadership laid out the currents' official approach towards what it called 'politically vague and socialistically immature workers' organizations'. Arguing that such bodies risked halting the forward political progression

---

64    Cited in Anweiler 1974, p. 70.
65    Кураев 2000, pp. 52–61.
66    Cited in Sutton 1987, p. 448. See also Weinberg 1985, p. 340.
67    Engelstein 1982, p. 163 and Sutton 1987, *passim*.
68    Morgan 1979, p. 109.

of the proletariat, thereby subordinating it to the bourgeoisie, the leadership explained that the task of SDs was to 'persuade such organizations to adopt the program of the Social-Democratic Party as the party in accord with the true interests of the proletarian masses'. Were the body to reject the party's programme, SDs should resign from it and denounce its 'anti-proletarian character'. But were such a body to abstain from any decisions to adopt a political programme, SDs should remain within it, proving 'the absurdity of such political leadership and amplifying their own program and tactics'.[69]

Notwithstanding the variety of perspectives within the Bolshevik ranks – including some non-monopolistic stances nearly identical to that of the Mensheviks – St. Petersburg's Bolshevik leaders attempted to convince the Soviet to accept the programme of the RSDRP in late October. But this proposal was firmly rejected by the delegates – including even by some Bolshevik activists. Soon the St. Petersburg Soviet's non-party model was replicated by newly founded councils elsewhere in the empire. In Baku and Moscow, the Bolsheviks responded by opposing the establishment of these non-party bodies.[70]

Despite their political reservations, Bolsheviks nevertheless actively participated in the existing councils across the empire once they were set up. Bundists in Ukraine and St. Petersburg underwent a similar evolution. Initially they refused to recognise the soviets, which they saw as potential obstacles to the political influence of the Social Democracy. Nevertheless, these Bundists accommodated themselves to the new institutions.[71]

United front coordinating structures in late 1905 did not take the form of councils in areas where the Russian Social Democracy was either not the main Marxist party, or where the RSDRP was particularly hegemonic, such as Tiflis and Kharkov. Since socialist organisations were especially influential in borderland regions such as Latvia, Georgia, Belarus, and Lithuania, the dominant form of united working-class authority here became Federal Committees that brought together representatives of the various socialist parties. In these areas, Marxists felt that soviets would be superfluous, since the mobilised mass of working people were already organised into or around socialist parties by the end of the year. Similarly, in Bundist strongholds such as Vilnius and Minsk,

<hr />

69    'Letter of October 27' in Ivancevich 1967, p. 188. Disagreement over this stance on the soviet led one of the Bolsheviks' top leaders in St. Petersburg, the Armenian Marxist Bogdan Knuniants, to join the Menshevik faction (Haimson 1987, p. 201). See also Morgan 1979, pp. 101–4.
70    Suny 1972a, p. 40 and Bonnell 1983, p. 176.
71    Симчишин 2007, p. 127, Hillis 2010, p. 406, and Sutton 1987, p. 105.

Federal Committees that united different socialist parties became the central late-year institutions of dual power. Given the strength of their hold on Tiflis workers, Georgian Mensheviks in late 1905 established a Strike Committee bringing together all of the city's socialist organisations as an organ of revolutionary coordination and de facto governmental authority. The same approach was taken in the Federated Council of Kharkov.[72]

Despite their structural differences, the commonality between the soviets and these Federal Committees was that each arose to unite and coordinate the various currents of working-class struggle at a moment of peak revolutionary upsurge. This function, in turn, transformed these bodies into embryonic institutions of revolutionary government, usurping state functions from a weak and delegitimised Tsarist state. Both types of united front organisations constituted a novel development unforeseen by Marxist orthodoxy, with its monopolistic assumptions. Unsurprisingly, the importance of such structures for both armed uprisings and revolutionary government remained outside Kautsky's field of vision. His famous 1906 pamphlet on the driving forces of the Russian Revolution did not mention these forms of organisation and it projected that a victorious revolution would likely mean that the Social Democratic Party as such would take state power in Russia.[73]

Poland was the only major region of the empire in which Marxists proved incapable in 1905 of cohering a class-wide united front organisation. Despite the almost unparalleled militancy of the region's working class, no institutions of dual power arose in the late-year upsurge. On 27 December 1905, as the empire was engulfed in general strikes and insurrections, the PPS-Proletariat issued a call for Poland to follow the lead of central Russia by establishing workers' councils. The party argued that this was the only feasible way to overcome the 'tremendous damage' done by the prevailing disunity in the Polish workers' movement:

> On the banners of all socialist parties is inscribed the slogan: 'Proletarians of all countries unite!' However, it is easy to write this slogan – but to achieve it is harder. ... In [Tsarist] Poland there are as many as four different socialist organisations, and each cry: 'Follow us, for only we can lead you to the Kingdom of Heaven' ... [But] there is only one way to defeat the government: it is our solidarity and unity in action. ... [To achieve this unity requires] a Council of Workers' Deputies, which will include

---

72    Апине 1965, p. 88, Jones 2005, p. 193, Nicolaysen 1990, p. 341, and Remeikis 1963, p. 50.

73    Kautsky 1906 [2009], pp. 605, 607 and Larsson 1970, p. 263.

representatives from all factories, plants, and professions, and the representatives of all the socialist parties.[74]

This proposal was denounced by the SDKPIL. It issued a leaflet declaring that the call for councils in Poland 'could only create confusion in the revolutionary ranks and harm the workers' cause'. The purpose of the Soviet in central Russia, the SDKPIL claimed, was not 'to unite workers of different parties', but rather to 'link up the social democratic party to the unconscious, dark, inert mass'. Councils could not 'remedy the evil' of the division of the Polish workers' movement, because the proletariat 'must have one programme and one class party' and because 'without a programme it is impossible to struggle against the Tsarist government or struggle against the capitalists'. The statement concluded that unity and victory could be achieved through explaining to workers that only the SDKPIL represented their 'real demands and interests'.[75]

This rejection of soviets by Luxemburg's party was not a particularly distinguishing or controversial stand in Poland. The Bund and the PPS also opposed the formation of such a body, which they saw as superfluous given the strength of Poland's Marxist parties.[76] What made the SDKPIL's approach uniquely controversial was not its opposition to the formation of a workers' council, but rather its rejection of coordination between the existing Marxist parties. Unlike in other regions with strong party organisations, no Federative Committee was formed in Poland.

The SDKPIL's monopolism and its anti-PPS factionalism remained the main stumbling block. Consider the case of the Dąbrowa Basin mining region, a bastion of the radical left and the area of Poland where the revolution advanced the furthest. In November, the local Tsarist authorities were effectively overthrown and replaced by institutions of revolutionary government. Though the PPS and the SDKPIL had long been the largest and most influential parties in the region, they nevertheless lost the leadership of the movement at this crucial moment to the National Democrats. As Adam Kałuża's study of these events has detailed, the fundamental cause of this surprising political development

---

74    'Towarzysze Robotnicy!', 27 December 1905, Odezwa Komitet Centralny Pol. Par. Soc. 'Proletaryat', Warszawa (Dokumenty życia społecznego, Biblioteka Narodowa).

75    'Samozwańcza Rada Samozwańczej Komisji', 12 February 1906, Odezwa Komitet Warszawski Socjaldemokracji Królestwa Polskiego i Litwy, Warszawa (Dokumenty życia społecznego, Biblioteka Narodowa). Contrary to this leaflet's assertion, the soviets in St. Petersburg and beyond *did* unite different socialist parties (the various wings of the RSDRP, the Socialist Revolutionaries, non-Russian Marxists, etc.).

76    Sujecki 1996, p. 43.

was the SDKPIL's refusal to sanction any coordination with the Polish Socialist Party – despite the fact that the regional PPS branch was led by the party's far left. A local PPS declaration to mineworkers reported on the SDKPIL's rejection of its proposal to establish a 'joint Revolutionary Committee' to 'coordinate revolutionary action':

> Every conscious and thinking worker sees that the only power that can defy the Tsarist bayonets is the concentrated force of labour solidarity. Resistance to this collaboration is a grievous sin committed against working people! ... The refusal of the Social Democratic Committee stands in glaring contrast to the stance of the vast majority of conscious socialist workers.[77]

In this context, the local ND group – an anomalously left-populist branch of the current – seized the moment and filled the political vacuum. It raised a call for popular and proletarian unity to overcome 'party disputes and quarrels' between the socialists and it thus proposed the immediate formation of revolutionary-democratic institutions to replace Tsarist governmental structures.[78]

Elsewhere in Poland, Marxists maintained their hegemony over the working class and revolutionary struggle in late 1905, but they were no more capable of cohering a united front. Various Polish socialists, as well as subsequent historians, argued that this inability to sufficiently overcome party divides for the sake of coordinated action was a primary cause of the defeat of the 1905 revolution in Poland.[79]

In the other regions of Tsarist Russia, the years following 1905 were marked by a nearly universal Marxist acceptance and implementation of united front tactics. Accumulated experience during the first revolution had hammered home the indispensability of joint work with other SDs, SRs, anarchists, and independent radicals. As such, the monopolism and uneven commitment to collaboration manifest by social democrats in the preceding period virtually disappeared. Though the strategy of the united front was not formally articulated until after 1917, its associated practices had by this time already become the norm across Russia.

---

77   Cited in Kałuża 2005, pp. 177–8.
78   Cited in Kałuża 2005, pp. 180–1.
79   See, for example, Potkański 2008, p. 253.

## 3    Implementing the United Front (1906–18)

It is unnecessary here to elaborate in detail the socialists' post-1905 joint activities, which upheld and spread the collaborative practices described above.[80] But a few particularly significant developments should be highlighted. First of all, Marxists stopped attempting to prevent SRs, syndicalists, and anarchists from organising in the working class. A St. Petersburg Bolshevik recalled that SRs and SDs during the pre-war upsurge implemented 'all concrete measures in the factories together' upon joint decision by party activists (or in a broader workers' meeting if an initial agreement could not be reached). Melancon has shown that equivalent methods within the workers' movement were the norm across the empire, culminating in the jointly led general strikes and near-insurrections in the summer of 1914.[81] A recent study of radical parties in the Urals before the February Revolution describes a similar dynamic: 'Despite a number of ideological and theoretical differences between the SRs and the Bolsheviks, the "left bloc" in the Urals was the single most active political force up through the February Revolution of 1917'.[82]

In the wake of 1905, Russia's Marxists also eventually dropped their efforts to build party unions and monopolise mass organisations. This evolution took somewhat longer to become the norm than an acceptance of inter-party unity in action, despite the fact that the only way to form legalised trade unions after 1905 was for these bodies to be unaffiliated to any party. The Bund, for example, had begun as early as 1906 to build autonomous unions in various industries, but it only formally dropped its programmatic support for party unions in 1910. Bundist leader Vladimir Medem noted that 'the conclusion was reached that formal domination by the political party over the unions interfered with their activity. ... It was necessary to see that they should become permeated with the socialist spirit without, however, using methods tantamount to automatic dictation'.[83] For their part, the Bolsheviks after 1905 also began to increasingly participate in and build unaffiliated unions, which by 1912 had become the norm. Indeed, Bolsheviks and allied radicals in 1913–14 overwhelmingly won the leadership of the unions, which became important bastions for militant workers and the growing strike wave.[84]

---

80    Joint electoral campaigns for and collaboration within the Duma, did, however, constitute a novel form of inter-party socialist collaboration between 1906 and 1914 (Melancon 1990, p. 245).

81    Cited in Melancon 1990, p. 248. See also McKean 1990, p. 89.

82    ГаБдулнаков 2004, pp. 6–7.

83    Medem 1923 [1979], p. 476.

84    Bonnell 1983, pp. 391–406.

Regarding monopolism, however, Marxist practice advanced further than theory. Though their post-1905 collaborative practices implicitly acknowledged that the Social Democracy could no longer seek to hold exclusive leadership within the workers' movement, the RSDRP nevertheless continued to assert itself as the sole proletarian party. While *Iskra*'s 1903 claim that SRs were 'detrimental' to the labour and revolutionary struggle was dropped, a 1907 Bolshevik-initiated resolution encouraging an SD-SR alliance persisted in claiming that the latter were petty-bourgeois democrats with whom collaboration was only relevant for democratic, anti-Tsarist struggle. This framework was, to say the least, one sided. The Socialist Revolutionary Party remained deeply embedded in Russia's working class – roughly 46 per cent of its members were workers in 1905–07. Furthermore, the SRs in 1907–14 organised primarily in the urban proletariat and it was here that the bulk of SR-SD collaboration took place.[85]

Reflecting this theoretical gap, Marxists still had no vocabulary or articulated strategy for collaboration between political currents inside the workers' movement. Soviet historiography, as well as the much more limited Western literature on inter-party collaboration in Russia, has obscured this fact by anachronistically conflating the concept of a 'left bloc' with that of a workers' united front. But the former term – used only occasionally by socialists at the time – referred to joint anti-Tsarist political work by Marxists and populists, particularly in relation to the State Duma. In other words, the 'left bloc' embodied the political expression of a worker-peasant alliance for democracy. The category 'left' was virtually never used as a frame for proletarian unity because it blurred class lines, which was anathema to orthodox Marxists of the era. Moreover, collaboration within the labour movement was much less formal and more action-oriented than implied by the concept of a 'bloc'. Unity was focused on concrete actions, initiatives, and demands, not a common political platform.

The post-1905 rightward turn of moderate socialists across imperial Russia also created some novel collaborative dynamics. As Melancon notes, 'two separate socialist blocs emerged – right and left – which sometimes allied together, sometimes did not'.[86] In the pre-war upsurge, the main point of divergence between these blocs was whether to mobilise for militant class struggle or to organise workers as part of an alliance with liberals. Indeed, the concrete politics of radical Marxists and left populists from 1906 onwards were often

---

85    On workers and the SRs, see Rice 1988 and Melancon 1984.
86    Melancon 1990, p. 251.

much closer to each other than they were to the right wings of their respective parties. For instance, SR-Maximalists, Left SRs, anarchists, and Bolsheviks
worked closely inside the Baltic fleet, a strategically central radical strong-
hold.[87]

The politics of anti-liberal factions within borderland Marxist parties such
as the Ukrainian USDRP, the Lithuanian LSDP, and the Jewish Bund were (despite ongoing differences on the national question) similarly closer in practice to
radical SD parties than they were to class collaborationists in their own organisations. For example, the Jewish Bund in Poland remained led by leftists and
it upheld the party's old strategy of proletarian hegemony after 1905, unlike in
the rest of the empire. Polish Bundists worked closely with the PPS-Left and
(to a lesser extent) the SDKPIL to promote strikes, anti-Tsarist action, anti-war
agitation, as well as resistance to the German occupation during the war. Elsewhere in Russia, however, Bundists generally became an integral part of the
Menshevik axis, which was also now closely allied with the right SRs.[88]

United front practices eventually also became hegemonic among radicals in
Poland, though this evolution was more protracted and contentious than elsewhere in the empire. For its part, the PPS, which became known as the PPS-Left
in 1906, made the fight for a united workers' movement central to its orientation. It argued that to effectively combat the bosses and take down Tsarism
required unity in action, non-party mass workers' organisations, and a united
empire-wide social democratic party.

In contrast, the SDKPIL leadership for many years continued to uphold its
longstanding insistence on party unions and its opposition to coordinating
with its rivals. In a 1910 polemic against the PPS-Left's call for proletarian unity
in action, Luxemburg affirmed that 'the unity of the workers' movement is actually possible, durable and serious within the whole state, as within our own
country, only when it is founded on the unity of basic principles of programme
and tactics. Only a unity of spirit can create unity of action and deepen the
class struggle'. She concluded that PPS-Left members who sincerely wanted to
promote labour unity should join the SDKPIL.[89]

The Luxemburg leadership's opposition to united front policies became
a central point of contention during the party's post-1905 crisis. From 1906
onwards, multiple oppositions arose against SDKPIL émigrés to demand,
among other things, a change of the party's position on the unions and the

---

87    Longley 1978. See also Melancon 1990, pp. 247–50.
88    Mendel 1989, pp. 64–79, 120–5, Levin 2007, Levin 2008, and Морозов 1998.
89    Luxemburg [Anon.] 1910, 'O druzgocącej krytyce zdruzgotanej partii', *Czerwony Sztandar*,
      20 June 1910.

PPS-Left. In 1909, the SDKPIL leadership pushed out an internal opposition led by long-time cadre Stanisław Trusiewicz, who called for unity with the PPS-Left and the end of party unions.[90] The SDKPIL's Warsaw Committee soon after became the fulcrum of a more widespread opposition. Though much of its conflict with the party's émigré leaders concerned their dictatorial organisational methods, the issue of the united front was also an important component of the deepening division. Against Luxemburg's stance, the Warsaw-led oppositionists sought to collaborate with the PPS-Left and they pushed back against the SDKPIL's insistence on building party unions.

In 1912, the SDKPIL émigré leadership unilaterally declared that the Warsaw Committee was dissolved. But the oppositionists across Poland refused to submit, resulting in the split of most committees away from the party's old guard. In a December 1913 letter to the International Socialist Bureau demonstrating that Luxemburg's leadership had lost almost its entire base of support in Poland, the Warsaw and Łódź SDKPIL committees declared that 'Rosa Luxemburg and her "party leadership" represent at most a Berlin émigré group, but they have nothing to do with the workers' movement in Poland'.[91]

Following this split, the bulk of the SDKPIL began to work with the PPS-Left and to participate in unaffiliated trade unions during the 1913–14 upsurge in Poland. After having lost the majority of its members in Poland, Luxemburg's émigré leadership finally began in 1914 to readjust its position on party unions and collaboration with the PPS-Left.[92] Testifying to this new approach, the PPS-Left, the Bund, and both wings of the SDKPIL opposed Russia's entry into the war in August 1914 by issuing a joint declaration calling for revolutionary proletarian struggle to defeat the war, the Tsar, and the capitalist system.[93]

By 1917, both moderate and radical socialists across imperial Russia had come to consistently practice united front methods. The February Revolution constituted a high point of this approach. For a brief moment, all wings of socialists in the capital came together to coordinate the offensive that finally toppled the Tsar. As Bolshevik leader Alexander Shlyapnikov noted: 'With the existence of a whole multiplicity of groups and party organizations, the growth of the revolutionary movement demanded unity of action from these organizations'.[94] Throughout the rest of the year, a desire by working people for the

90    On Trusiewicz, see Michta and Sobczak 2004.
91    'An Das Internationale Sozialistische Bureau', 1 December 1913, Warschauer Komitee, Łódźer Komitee SDKPIL (Archiwum Akt Nowych, 9/VII–36).
92    Karwacki 1964, p. 211, Kasprzakowa 1965, p. 213, and Strobel 1974, p. 460.
93    'Do proletariatu Polski' [1914] in Tych 1975, pp. 491–5.
94    Shlyapnikov 1923.

continuation of unity between socialists and workers' organisations remained constant. This sentiment was above all concretised through the creation of soviets across Russia, which served as the primary organisational vehicles to cohere working people.[95]

Faced with a strong desire from below for a united fightback, socialist parties across Russia invariably framed themselves as the best defenders of working-class unity. Yet the political basis for united action remained contentious. Early in 1917, the broad push from the rank and file for unity, combined with the euphoria of toppling the autocracy, placed intense pressures on radicals to bend to the prevailing class conciliationism. Moderate socialists insisted that achieving workers' unity required that leftists drop their intransigent attitude towards the liberals – and more than a few Bolsheviks and other radicals bent to this pressure in March. Yet the 'honeymoon' moment of broad socialist collaboration ended remarkably quickly. In April, sharp conflicts erupted over stopping the war. Henceforth the empire-wide socialist movement reverted back to its preceding line of division: competition between class-struggle radicals and class-collaborationist moderates.

A one-sided focus on the Bolsheviks in 1917 has obscured the fact that their practical interventions in political struggles were rarely carried out separately from other radical socialists. Throughout the year, joint work was the norm between all 'internationalists', i.e. those organisations and tendencies committed to a consistent struggle against the national and international bourgeoisie. Key players in this informal alliance included Marxist organisations such as the SDKPIL, the PPS-Left, the LSDSP, as well as anarchists and SR-Maximalists. It also generally included unaffiliated activists and the left wings of parties led by more moderate forces such as the Socialist Revolutionaries, the Mensheviks, and the numerous non-Russian social democratic parties.[96]

The Bolsheviks became the most influential current within the Left not only because of their organisational strength and their strategic implantation in Russia's capital, but also because of their ability to effectively implement a united front approach. This marked a definite contrast with 1905. This time around, Bolsheviks decisively eschewed monopolism – unlike in the first revolution, there was no debate over whether to participate in and promote non-party mass organisations such as the soviet. Likewise, they consistently

---

95    McDaniel 1988, pp. 375–6, Koenker 1981, p. 190, and Lande 1974, pp. 12–13.
96    Стариков 2004, Сапон 2009, Дементьев 2013, and Тарасов 2017. John Riddell is one of the rare non-Russian scholars who has highlighted the importance of the Bolsheviks' united front tactics in 1917. See Communist International 1922 [2011], p. 10.

joined and built unaffiliated labour unions. As in previous years, collaboration was particularly central to activities within the workplace and its mass organisations (factory councils and trade unions), as well as in the military.

Though strategic differences with moderate socialists meant that they frequently clashed on specific political issues, neither the Bolsheviks nor other internationalists dropped their push for other socialists to break with the liberals, in order to establish the widest possible class-struggle front. When practical opportunities arose for united action between radical socialists and forces to their right, internationalists seized on the opportunity. While this was the case throughout the year, its most important manifestation was the joint struggle of all socialists and workers' organisations against General Kornilov's attempted coup against the Provisional Government in August. Broad ad hoc bodies open to any individual and organisation willing to fight Kornilov were established virtually overnight.

A typical 29 August appeal by the Kiev Bolshevik committee declared that the 'seriousness of the moment demands complete unity of action, resistance, courage and discipline' to defeat the counter-revolutionary threat.[97] The Bolshevik leaflet in Petrograd articulated the same sentiment: as 'a united family, with firm ranks, hand in hand, all as one man, meet the enemy of the people, the betrayer of the Revolution, the assassin of liberty!'[98] Across the empire, this united resistance movement's defeat of the Kornilov coup constituted perhaps the most important turning point in the political fortunes of internationalists in 1917. A minority on the eve of the coup, Bolshevik militants came to the fore of the anti-Kornilov mass struggle and soon after became the most influential Marxist current across Russia.

The concept of the united front has sometimes been narrowly framed by subsequent generations of socialists as a tactical expedient in conditions of defensive struggle or a manoeuvre to expose 'misleaders'. But the experience of 1917 illustrates the important strategic dimensions of consistently fighting for working-class unity. Consider the Bolsheviks' articulation of the fight for political power. It is often overlooked that for most of the year the demand 'All Power to the Soviets' concretely meant the establishment of a government led by Mensheviks and Socialist Revolutionaries. A Bolshevik editorial in September explicitly addressed the Mensheviks and SRs: 'You want a united front with the Bolsheviks? Then break with the Kerensky government, support the Soviets in

---

97   Cited in Любовець and Солдатенко 2010, p. 206.
98   'Appeal of the Central Committee and the Petrograd Committee of the Bolshevik Party'
     [1917] in Chamberlin 1935, p. 463.

their struggle for power, and there will be unity'.[99] Much of the internal debate inside the Bolshevik current in the fall of 1917 concerned the tactical dilemmas posed by the refusal of SR and Menshevik leaders to end their alliance with the bourgeoisie.

Though most Mensheviks and SRs continued to reject soviet power, the October Revolution was nevertheless a multi-party affair. As historian Konstantin Tarasov's recent study has shown, the 'slogan "All Power to the Soviets!" became the unity rallying slogan of the left-radical parties and groups'.[100] Since the October Revolution has so often been portrayed as a Bolshevik coup, it is important to highlight that it was led by alliances between the empire's radicals in the centre as well as the periphery. As Donald Raleigh explains, the 'October Revolution was not so much a Bolshevik Revolution as a triumph of all radical groups that had broken decisively with those elements that supported further coalition with the bourgeoisie'.[101]

In Petrograd and elsewhere, the armed bodies that organised the seizure of power were almost always multi-party committees associated with the local soviets.[102] Had Bolsheviks across Russia operated on their own in the armed struggle, or fought for bodies other than the multi-party soviets to take power, it is very unlikely that they would have succeeded in October or in the coming months. In Transcaucasia, notes Ronald Suny, 'the greatest attraction of the Bolsheviks was their identification with soviet power. Not the party, but the party's role as the most articulate voice of the local soviet, guaranteed Bolshevik power in Baku'.[103]

## 4    Disunity in Europe and Poland

The relative weakness of moderate socialists in Russia was a critical factor in preventing their opposition to soviet power from derailing the revolution by containing and dividing the working class. Indeed, the hegemony of class collaborationism in Russia lasted only for an ephemeral six months in 1917. In contrast, the strength of moderate socialism during Europe's post-war revolu-

99    Stalin 1917 [1953–55], p. 326.
100   Тарасов 2017, p. 9.
101   Raleigh 1986, p. 323.
102   See, for example, Mawdsley 1978, p. 102 and Rabinowitch 1976, p. 239.
103   Suny 1972a, p. 170. Diane Koenker likewise concludes that 'the unifying potential of the Bolshevik party alone may not have been sufficient to rally the fragmented workers of Moscow' (Koenker 1981, p. 186).

tionary wave proved to be a far greater obstacle toward cohering proletarian unity around an independent class axis.[104]

In a comparative study demonstrating how autocratic conditions combined with capitalist social relations make possible the rise of insurrectionary workers' movements, Tim McDaniel concludes that what differentiated Russia from elsewhere was not so much the depth of working-class support for socialism. In various other revolutions of the twentieth century, he notes, a popular desire for socialist transformation was if anything more widespread. Rather, the 'distinctiveness of Russia lies in the weakness of moderation within the labor movement and, correlatively, the lack of serious internal splits'.[105]

Confronting the hold of moderate socialism, and building unity on a class-struggle basis, thus proved to be far more of a challenge for revolutionaries in Western democracies than it was in Russia. From 1914 onwards, class-collaborationist leaderships and debilitating political divisions remained the norm across Europe. But even in the lands of imperial Russia one can find important examples of how the hegemony of right-leaning social democrats, combined with Marxist ultra-leftism, impeded the achievement of workers' unity. The fate of post-war Poland is a case in point. When it came to the united front and socialist class collaborationism, the aborted 1918–19 Polish Revolution resembled Western Europe much more than the other areas of the former Tsarist Empire.

By combining the fight for workers' immediate interests with a call for national independence, the Polish Socialist Party-FR during World War One displaced its radical rivals from the head of the labour movement. Unlike in Russia on the eve of the February Revolution, in Poland the moderates were unquestionably the most influential socialist force in early November 1918. Despite the PPS-FR's relative militancy during the war, it remained committed to building a broad multi-class front under the hegemony of Pilsudski's military-nationalist armed forces. Prioritising the achievement and defence of an independent Polish state above all else, PPS-FR leaders actively sought to prevent a working-class conquest of power, which they felt would lead to Poland's re-submission to Russia.[106]

Workers' councils quickly spread across Poland during the first weeks of November 1918. But instead of participating in these, the PPS-FR set up entirely separate councils explicitly dedicated to supporting Polish independence and

---

104   See, for example, the discussion on German socialism's disunity in Carsten 1972.
105   McDaniel 1988, p. 316.
106   Though the official title of the organisation by 1918 was the Polish Socialist Party, I use the acronym PPS-FR for the sake of expositional clarity.

the newly created Polish national government. Working-class unity, the PPS-FR argued, could only be established upon this political basis. But the creation of two separate groups of councils critically undermined the main purpose of council organisation, namely the unification of all the organised and unorganised tendencies of the workers' movement. Polish workers – including much of the radicalised PPS-FR rank and file – reacted negatively to this establishment of alternative councils. Throughout November 1918, pressure from below mounted on the party to agree to a merger. By early December, seeing that they risked losing their popular influence if they did not heed this call for unity, the PPS-FR leaders reluctantly agreed to merge their workers' councils with the other councils across Poland.[107]

The PPS-FR leadership, however, did not resign itself to accepting the united framework of these new bodies. Since the PPS-FR did not have a decisive majority of the delegates – almost half were Polish Bundists and Communists – it sought to paralyse then eliminate the councils. At the same time, the PPS-FR also continued to reject united actions with the Communist Party, recently founded through a merger of the PPS-Left with the SDKPIL. One Polish Bundist leader recalled the dynamic:

> During the short time of the councils' existence, the PPS Right Wing (Fraction) continually undermined their activities, and did everything in its power to limit the councils' role to an adjunct to the Polish government. The rapid demise of the soviet chapter of the Polish labor movement was as much due to this internal enemy as to the open pressure by the government.[108]

In May 1919, the PPS-FR leadership, over the objections of leftists in its own ranks, decided to split the existing councils on the grounds that the Communists did not support Polish independence. This controversial and deeply disorienting action effectively put an end to the council experiment across Poland.

Polish Communists denounced this move as a 'crime'.[109] As they had done over the months prior, Communists argued that the PPS-FR was consciously dividing the working class to avoid a socialist revolution. To quote one party statement, the goal of the PPS-FR was 'to break up the Councils of Workers' Delegates, thereby preventing them from initiating broad mass action and revolu-

---

107   On the PPS-FR and the councils in Poland, see Sacewicz 2014 and Holzer 1962, *passim*.
108   Nowogrodzki 2001, p. 21.
109   Cited in Sacewicz 2014, p. 293.

tionary struggle. This tactic results from the PPS's agreement with bourgeois political parties, from its selling out of workers' interests for the benefit of the Polish counter-revolution'.[110]

The PPS-FR claimed that the unfortunate division of the workers' movement was the fault of Communist 'splitters', whose minoritarian opposition to Polish independence and ultra-radical stances against parliamentary democracy created needless conflicts. In response, Poland's Communists attempted to present themselves as the main defenders of coordinated working-class activity against the capitalists and right-wing nationalists.[111] Yet strong tendencies towards ultra-leftism undercut the Communists' effectiveness and their mass appeal. Instead of consistently calling on their moderate rivals to break with capitalist forces, Poland's Communists – in part due to the anti-PPS factional legacy bequeathed by Luxemburg – focused on denouncing the PPS-FR for its 'betrayals' and 'counter-revolutionary' machinations. However justified such characterisations may have been, they were ill-suited for gaining a hearing among the majority of Polish workers who looked to the PPS-FR to promote radical social transformation.

Though the Polish Communists felt themselves to be upholding the banner of Bolshevism, their approach diverged from the actual orientation of Bolsheviks in 1917. The Bolsheviks focused their agitation on calls for moderate socialists to break from the liberals, especially early in the year when a strong majority of workers still had confidence in the SR and Menshevik leaders. Up through the conquest of power in late October, the Bolsheviks consistently pushed for these groups to end their alliance with the bourgeoisie and jointly establish an anti-capitalist, multi-party socialist government.

Yet in 1918–19 the Polish Communists, like many of their radical counterparts across Europe, failed to articulate an analogous united front approach on the crucial question of governmental power. Partly due to their caricatured understanding of the lessons of 1917, Polish Communists denounced parliamentary democracy, underestimated the popular roots of moderate socialism, and optimistically wagered that the radicalised Polish masses would quickly flock to their banner. Only in 1922–23 did the Polish Communist Party finally adopt the strategy of the united front and fight for a multi-party 'workers' government' comprised of the various political tendencies representing working people in Poland.[112] But in Poland, as in most other countries of Europe, the brief opening for anti-capitalist rupture had already closed by this time.

---

110   Cited in Sacewicz 2014, p. 288.
111   Sacewicz 2014, pp. 249–50, 282.
112   Komunistyczna Partia Robotnicza Polski 1923 [1968].

The case of Poland dramatically illustrates that social crises, state collapse, and mass proletarian radicalisation did not inevitably lead to the downfall of moderate socialists, the rise of Marxists, and successful working-class revolutions. In 1917–18, such conditions created a favourable context for radicals to expand their influence and contend for state power. But the result of the revolutionary struggle was by no means preordained by the social structure. Deep social crisis, state collapse, and labour insurgency were necessary but insufficient conditions for anti-capitalist rupture in imperial Russia. At least one other factor was needed: socialist parties that were sufficiently influential, radical, and tactically flexible to help the working-class majority effectively unite to break with capitalist rule.

The debilitating division of organised labour in Poland was replicated across Western Europe after the war, as the Comintern pushed for splits from the Second International in every country. Were the political benefits of this drive ultimately worth the costs? Organisational ruptures allowed for revolutionaries to better cohere themselves as a political alternative. Yet the ensuing divisions, exacerbated by the Communists' high bar of radicalism for membership and their virulent attacks on their rivals, played a debilitating role within the broader labour movement.

The existence of multiple competing workers' parties was a new phenomenon, disorienting a wide swath of the European working class in the years after 1917. Social Democrats blamed the division on the Communists; and the Communists reciprocated in kind. But overcoming their conciliatory rivals – and uniting working people on a class-struggle basis – proved to be harder than many revolutionaries had anticipated.

Widespread ultra-leftism in the early Communist movement was both a cause and an effect of these difficulties. Significant numbers of workers and activists veered far to the left in response to the catastrophe of World War One, the unexpected capitulations of Social Democratic leaders, the excitement of the October Revolution, and the one-sided polemics of the early Comintern against reformism and parliamentarism. Across the world, radicals of the era often had only the haziest knowledge of the actual experience of Bolshevism – the lessons of 1917 were frequently reduced to revolutionary intransigence, not least of which was a denunciatory approach to moderate socialists.[113]

In imperial Russia's borderlands, the adoption of such an orientation in 1918–19 did serious damage to efforts to root new Soviet regimes among work-

---

113    See, for example, Broué 2005 and Communist International 1921 [2015].

ing people and, in so doing, spread the revolution westwards. Consider, for example, this early 1919 declaration by Communist Party leaders in Lithuania and Belarus explaining why they were excluding all other parties from their newly established Soviet regime:

> Because at the present time only the Lithuanian and Belorussian Communist Party not only in words, but in fact, stands for the dictatorship of the proletariat; the other socialist parties, although they claim to be for soviet power, constantly vacillate between the Soviets and the Constituent Assembly, or some other organ of power, thus deceiving the population. The Central Committee of the ... Party finds it impossible in setting up the Provisional Revolutionary Government to enter into negotiations with those parties.[114]

Among the various problems with this approach, it should be pointed out that single-party soviets were essentially a contradiction in terms, evacuating the united front *content* from the workers' council *form*.

Across the empire in 1905 and 1917, it was the multi-tendency, unitary nature of the councils that gave them their democratic legitimacy. Unsurprisingly, Bolshevik political ascendancy largely took the form of winning leadership of the soviets and other united front mass organisations like the unions as well as factory committees. And though critiques of rival socialists were certainly not absent in Bolshevism's 1917 propaganda, their ability to win mass influence was in large part due to the fact they were – in both words and deeds – the most consistent force pushing for unity against the bourgeoisie.

Not only were the tactics of the Bolsheviks in Russia more flexible than presumed by early Communists, but non-autocratic political contexts abroad necessitated a more patient approach to working with and overcoming moderate socialism, i.e. the current henceforth known as Social Democracy. Democratically elected parliaments, entrenched labour bureaucracies, and strong capitalist classes were phenomena that Marxists within most of the Russian Empire had simply not faced. In such conditions, the process of cohering workers as a united anti-capitalist force was significantly more difficult, and their radicalisation necessarily more uneven and protracted.

Beginning with Lenin's 1920 pamphlet '"Left-Wing" Communism: An Infantile Disorder', Comintern leaders began adjusting their perspectives accordingly. This reorientation culminated in the 1921–22 adoption of the strategy of the

---

114  Cited in White 1971, p. 193.

workers' united front, according to which Communists were mandated to push for unity in action with all other currents of the labour movement, including through the election of a multi-party 'workers' government' to the existing state. Contrary to what some writers have claimed, this was not merely a new tactic in response to a temporary lull in the revolutionary offensive.[115] Rather, it constituted a significant, if embryonic, re-articulation of Communist strategy for political democracies, premised upon a novel assessment of the social weight and durability of moderate socialism within the working class, the legitimacy of the parliamentary arena, and the unevenness of class formation.[116]

Fighting for multi-party class unity, however, stood in contradiction with the practice of one-party rule in Russia and it was eventually marginalised by the rise of Stalinism, which imposed a new form of top-down monopolism upon the international Communist movement. Nor did working-class unity become a practical priority for much of the Trotskyist Left, whose social marginality often led to political sectarianism. Even when genuinely desiring to construct united fronts, a strategic focus on building 'Leninist parties' led both Stalinist and anti-Stalinist radicals to frequently place their party-building projects above the interests and cohesion of the labour movement as a whole.

The diffusion of this 'party of a new type' model, and its lack of congruence with Bolshevism's actual practices, will be discussed further in the following chapter. But Leninists were hardly the only socialists to undermine the political unity of working people. As Social Democrats throughout the past century integrated themselves into the status quo, they became decreasingly interested in bringing together workers as a class and they often focused more political fire on leftists than capitalists. To be sure, Social Democratic parties and governments in Scandinavia from the 1930s onwards charted a distinct, and remarkably successful, strategy of uniting and organising working people through transformative reforms to the labour market as well as universalistic welfare programmes. Yet by the 1980s this exceptional project stalled out in the face of heightened capitalist opposition.[117]

Over recent decades, the task of uniting workers has been further marginalised, with much of the Left, radicals included, abandoning a view of the organised working class as the central social agent for transformative change. Even when tied to calls for coalitions, treating the workers' movement as just one good movement among many can lead to accepting rather than effectively tran-

---

115   For an example of this interpretation, see Hallas 1985.
116   On the early strategic articulation of the united front approach, see Communist International 1922 [2011].
117   On Scandinavian Social Democracy, see Esping-Andersen 1985.

scending existing divisions. Moreover, it discards the main instrument through which class-wide consciousness has historically been forged: an independent workers' party. For these reasons, how to build working-class unity is a strategic question that remains remarkably underdeveloped – and the decline of class politics has become to a significant extent a self-fulfilling prophecy.

# The Party Question

One of the founding myths of 'Leninism' – as well as the academic literature on the Russian Revolution – is that the Bolsheviks broke from the prevailing party-building model of the Second International.[1] According to this account, orthodox Marxists like Kautsky advocated a politically amorphous 'party of the whole class', while the Bolsheviks from 1903 (or 1912) onwards sought to build a 'vanguard party'. Unlike the German SPD, this 'party of a new type' would cohere only the most advanced layers of the working class – 'opportunists' would not be allowed within its ranks.

Most scholars see the Bolsheviks' supposedly novel party model as a key contributor to the creation of a totalitarian state.[2] For their part, Leninists argue that the victorious October Revolution in Russia demonstrates the superiority of this new form of organisation. Evidence of the old SPD model's deficiency is that German radicals found themselves tragically unable to provide a political alternative to the Social Democrats during the German Revolution of 1918–19.

Such accounts have a long lineage. The influential 1938 'Short Course' history of Bolshevism edited by Stalin declared that a precondition for the Bolsheviks' victory was that they formed an independent party from the Mensheviks in 1912:

> The Party strengthens itself by purging its ranks of opportunist elements – that is one of the maxims of the Bolshevik Party, which is a party of a new type fundamentally different from the Social-Democratic parties of the Second International ... If the opportunists had remained within the ranks of the proletarian party, the Bolshevik Party could not have come out on the broad highway and led the proletariat, it could not have taken power and set up the dictatorship of the proletariat.[3]

Trotskyists have affirmed the same basic analysis. One recent article, for example, claims that Lenin from 1903 onwards sought to build a party of the militant workers' vanguard, while Kautsky pushed instead for a 'party of the

---

1  For a typical academic account, see, for example, Elwood 1974a, pp. 146–7.
2  Mawdsley 2003, p. 8.
3  Stalin 1938.

whole class' founded upon 'unity in the sense of breadth rather than unity in the sense of ideological cohesiveness'. According to the authors, understanding and upholding Lenin's 'distinct theory of revolutionary organisation' remains 'the only way to overthrow capitalism'.[4]

This chapter argues that the prevailing academic and activist interpretation is irreparably flawed. I demonstrate this by critically examining the actual stances and practices of the German SPD, the Finnish SDP, the Polish SDKPIL, and the Bolsheviks. We will see that the traditional account distorts orthodox Marxism's conception of a revolutionary party and misstates the reasons for distinct socialist trajectories in Germany and Russia.

Contrary to the standard story, I show that all pre-war revolutionary SDs, Kautsky included, agreed that the Social Democracy should cohere only the most advanced layers of the class on the basis of a clear Marxist programme. That the German SPD diverged in practice from this theory was due to the unexpectedly strong emergence of class collaborationism within Germany's labour movement, *not* a different party model.

In Russia, autocratic conditions produced a weak social basis for moderate socialism, facilitating the efforts of revolutionary SDs to build and maintain relatively homogenous Marxist parties. Radicals in imperial Russia built *in practice* the types of parties envisioned *in theory* by Marxist orthodoxy. We will see that an empire-wide perspective demonstrates that traits long assumed to be distinct to Bolshevism were in fact common across the Russian state. Despite the Second International's strategic injunction that there should only be one socialist party for one working class, the existence of multiple competing organisations was the norm under Tsarism.

Our discussion then turns to Poland. Rosa Luxemburg's hyper-orthodox SDKPIL shows that organisational demarcation from rival socialists did not necessarily translate into more effective revolutionary politics. Though Luxemburg failed to organise a distinct Marxist current within Germany, her party in Poland was consistently more 'Leninist' than the Bolsheviks. Believing that the most important criteria for Marxist politics in Poland was opposition to national independence, Luxemburg's organisation split from the Polish Socialist Party in 1893 and in later years it continued to refuse to merge with the revolutionary Marxist PPS-Left. The ensuing difficulties of Poland's socialist movement underscore a critical point: assessing which political differences were permissible inside a revolutionary party or current was a challenging

---

4   Corr and Jenkins 2014. See also Cliff 1975 and Blackledge 2011.

question to which no a priori formula could provide an answer. Even if one consciously sought to exclude crystallised opportunists, it was not self-evident who should be counted under this category.

The experience of Finland's Social Democracy further contradicts Leninist claims that the fatal flaw of Second International leftists was that they remained inside reformist mass workers' parties instead of splitting from them. The successes of orthodox Marxists in Finland were made possible *because* they worked within and transformed the Finnish Social Democracy. Despite the fact that it was one of the most conciliatory socialist parties in Europe before 1905, radicals were eventually able to lead the Finnish SDP to seize power in January 1918. To be sure, operating in a common organisation with class-collaborationist forces and a relatively diffuse membership was no easy task for Finland's revolutionary social democrats, who at times bent to their right-leaning comrades. Nevertheless, the Finnish experience largely vindicates the ruptural potentialities of the traditional orthodox Left orientation towards party-building.

This chapter's final section demonstrates that the organisational trajectory of Bolshevism was much more complicated than has been acknowledged in the historiography. When it came to working in a joint party, Bolsheviks stood somewhere between the aforementioned Polish and Finnish examples. Not only did Lenin explicitly agree with the SPD model, but Bolshevism for most of its existence constituted a tendency within a much broader Russian Social Democracy. The 1903 split was initiated first and foremost by the Mensheviks and its damaging impact on the course of the 1905 revolution seemed to confirm the traditional orthodox opposition to organisational splits. Beginning in 1912, Lenin pushed for a break from the Menshevik 'liquidationists', but his intransigence was rarely implemented in practice; not until the summer of 1917 did the establishment of distinct Bolshevik committees become the norm across Russia. Had the Bolsheviks prematurely broken from the RSDRP, their ability to cohere a working-class majority in 1917 would have been far less likely. Put simply, the rise to hegemony of radical socialists in underground Russia, like in parliamentary Finland, depended on participating in and building a broader workers' party.

## 1      The German SPD Model

Since the moderate trajectory of the German SPD has so often been attributed to a particular theory of the party, it is necessary to begin by clarifying the actual stance of orthodox Marxists. Well before 1917, all revolutionary social democrats – including Kautsky, Lenin, and Luxemburg – were committed to the goal of building a cohesive and disciplined Marxist party that included only the vanguard of the class.

The *Erfurt Programme* argued that given the proletariat's uneven political development, the party must necessarily begin as a fighting minority of the working class. Whereas mass organisations like unions should seek to represent all workers irrespective of their political beliefs, the party was constituted by the narrower strata of the proletariat that understood its final, socialist, goal.

This orientation did not remain only on paper. Anarchists, for example, were expelled from the Second International in 1896. And in Russia all orthodox SD parties – bolstered by the explicit backing of Kautsky abroad – rejected the periodic proposals of peasant-based Socialist Revolutionary leaders to merge Russian socialists into a single party.[5]

Orthodox SDs insisted that to successfully lead workers to power, a party must adhere to a common revolutionary programme. Kautsky argued that workers' parties should be based on 'definite Marxian Socialism, the theory of the proletarian class struggle as deduced from the study of capitalist society'. According to orthodox strategy, workers needed an independent party; this party should be committed in theory and practice to Marxism; and if the existing mass workers' party was not yet firmly Marxist, then orthodox SDs should patiently work within it to transform it in that direction.[6] Crucially, unity was declared to be essential not only for the party's programme, but also its action. Kautsky thus argued in his influential 1899 *Anti-Bernstein* that '[p]arty unity is based on the uniformity of its tactics'.[7] Through a process of open, democratic discussion and internal discipline, the party had to uniformly implement its collective decisions.

It is certainly true that the German Social Democracy, especially from 1905 onwards, began to diverge from this projected model of what would later be termed a 'vanguard party'. Moderate party leaders could lean for internal support on a diffuse rank and file that was often uncommitted to orthodox socialism and whose links to the party were sometimes no stronger than having voted for it in the previous election. Kautsky, however, did not overlook or accept this growing 'opportunism' in Germany or abroad. Indeed, the greater part of his writings between 1899 and 1909 were dedicated to combatting class-collaborationist tendencies and their theoretical proponents.

---

5   Kautsky 1892 [1910], Waldenberg 1972, pp. 347–8, 554–8, Lih 2006, Kautsky 1905, and Кирья-
    нов 1987, p. 46.
6   Kautsky 1909b. For further discussion, see Blanc 2016c.
7   Cited in Gronow 2015, p. 164. See also Kautsky 1905 and Waldenberg 1972, pp. 264–5.

Denouncing revisionism and its push to abandon revolutionary goals, Kautsky called upon its defenders such as Bernstein to leave the SPD. Indeed, he repeatedly criticised them for not doing so. At the same time, Kautsky opposed expelling them as long as their criticisms remained only at the level of discussion, not political practice; he argued that the SPD's method of freedom for discussion and unity in action must be upheld since an unnecessary split in the party would only help the forces of reaction. This view – stemming in part from the party's experience of debilitating factionalism in the 1870s – was shared across the board in the German Social Democracy.[8] As long as the SPD upheld its revolutionary programme, and as long as the revisionist minority implemented the decisions of the majority, then the party's revolutionary intransigence and the unity of its practice would be upheld.

Subsequent events would show that these perspectives significantly underestimated the extent of the political decay inside the SPD and the political danger posed by the growing labour bureaucracy. Kautsky was content to let the organisational side of the party be headed by his friend and (more accomodationist) comrade August Bebel.[9] Party radicals from Kautsky to Luxemburg accordingly made few efforts to build up an organisational base within the SPD or its leadership. To address the problems posed by the growth of revisionism, Kautsky, Luxemburg, and their allies stressed the need for theoretical clarity, party discipline, political education, organisational centralisation, and uniform tactics, particularly to make the moderate minority submit to the revolutionary majority. As such, radicals supported the SPD officialdom's push in 1905 to concentrate more power in its hands. In their view, this would be a step towards isolating the revisionists and subordinating moderate union leaders to the party.[10] It was a major miscalculation.

---

8    Steenson 1978, p. 127, Waldenberg 1972, pp. 552–3, 590–6, Schorske 1955, p. 194, and Thalheimer 1930. Contrary to what is often claimed in Marxist historiography, the SPD did in fact expel various leading members whose opportunist actions went against the party line. See, for example, Guettel 2012, p. 470 and Schorske 1955, p. 254.

9    Gilcher-Holtey's study of Kautsky's role in the SPD demonstrates that his influence was predicated on the unofficial 'mandate' granted to him by the party leadership headed by August Bebel. Ultimately, this separation from decision-making structures made him structurally dependent on the party leadership (Gilcher-Holtey 1986; see also Steenson 1978, p. 38).

10   The very disciplinary powers granted to the officials in 1905 were later directed against the SPD's left wing. As Schorske notes, radicals in 1905 'could scarcely realize that the centralized organization and the bureaucratic executive which they now sanctioned – partly as a weapon against revisionist federalism – would soon turn against them' (Schorske 1955, pp. 122–3; see also Waldenberg 1972, p. 559).

In hindsight, German leftists clearly misdiagnosed the main internal threat. As scholar Gerhard Ritter notes, 'revisionism was but a pale reflection of [the labour bureaucracy's] reformist practice'. Party officials 'determined the character of the party, which essentially became a workers' party of pragmatic practicos'.[11] Kautsky was not unaware of the dangers posed by the growth of this officialdom. But, as his biographer Marek Waldenberg explains, 'he did not appreciate their intensity'.[12] Like Lenin and Luxemburg, Kautsky argued that the deepening of the class struggle would eventually oblige conciliatory leaders in the SPD to radicalise or be cast aside. He wrote in 1903 that the impending political crisis in Germany would 'force the leaders of opportunism either to renounce opportunism or to join one of the less dangerous parties ... where they actually belong and to which they will be pulled when the comfort of social democracy comes to an end, and it does not merely pass out [electoral] mandates, but also demands sacrifices'.[13] Waldenberg notes that this 'conviction was very widespread' but 'as it turned out, it was deceptive and disastrous'.[14]

Orthodox Marxists' erroneous appraisal of the social base and political trajectory of moderate socialist leaders facilitated their failure to build a cohesive current within the SPD, capable of challenging for leadership. By way of comparison, Kautsky felt that it was necessary to establish a distinct organised Marxist tendency inside the opportunist British Labour Party.[15] The main weakness in the German radicals' approach was that they, like virtually all socialists of the era, underestimated the extent to which bureaucratised but programmatically Marxist parties such as the German SPD were analogous to the British Labour Party. Germany's Left failed to see that the strategy Kautsky advocated for Britain – i.e. the organisation of a coherent Marxist current within a mass workers' party – might be relevant for the continent as well.

Without a solid organisational base, SPD radicals were marginalised as the party's top layers drifted to the centre. In 1909, for the first time in his career, Kautsky found himself isolated from, and at odds with, the SPD apparatus, including Bebel. Testifying to the rightward turn of the leadership, the party officialdom sought to censor the most militant passages from Kautsky's 1909

---

11    Cited in Badia 1975, p. 437.
12    Waldenberg 1972, Vol. 2, p. 661.
13    Cited in Steenson 1978, p. 130. Lenin made the identical argument (Lenin 1910 [1960–65], pp. 311–12). Luxemburg likewise shared this view (Luxemburg 1906b).
14    Waldenberg 1972, p. 554.
15    Kautsky 1909b. Lenin supported this orthodox orientation (Lenin 1908 [1960–65], p. 235).

pamphlet *The Road to Power*. Waldenberg underscores the brutal predicament
that the leadership's new approach created for Kautsky:

> He faced the dilemma of either taking up the struggle with the [oppor-
> tunist] trends and moods dominating more and more in the decisive links
> of the structure of the workers' movement or of more or less thoroughly
> adapting to them. If he chose to fight it would mean losing the position of
> the official party ideologue and theoretician which he had enjoyed almost
> a quarter century and to which he was extremely attached. Moreover he
> was not used to 'swimming against the tide', he was then almost 60 and
> was a very tired and nervously exhausted man.[16]

Faced with this unexpected challenge, Kautsky eventually conceded to the
party apparatus. In late 1909, he acquiesced to many of the SPD officialdom's
demands regarding his pamphlet and, more importantly, he henceforth began
to distance himself from the radicals. Soon after, he sought a rapprochement
with both party and trade union officials and from 1910 onwards proceeded to
reverse many of his stances on fundamental political issues, including blocs
with liberals, participation in capitalist coalition governments, and the international imminence of socialist revolution. As early as 1913, imperial Russia's
revolutionary social democrats – from Lenin and the Bolsheviks to Kuusinen
and his orthodox Finnish comrades – had become critical of their theoretical
mentor.[17]

  Unlike Kautsky, Luxemburg and her SPD allies upheld their longstanding
political positions and continued to push back against the German Social
Democracy's rightward drift. In this struggle, however, the German Left still
limited itself to waging polemics in the party press and during party congresses.
Only after the SPD leadership supported the war in 1914 did German radicals
finally begin to organise themselves as a current to fight for hegemony within
the party. And it would take another four years before they established themselves as a distinct party, the Communist Party of Germany.

  These delays in cohering Germany's radicals played a detrimental role during the 1918–19 revolution, during which the Left found itself too dispersed to
provide a clear alternative to the Social Democrats. Yet this limitation cannot be
solely explained by orthodox Marxism's ideological commitment to maintaining party unity. As seen in Kautsky's writings on Britain, there was no inherent

---

16    Waldenberg 1972, p. 661.
17    Carrez 2008, p. 395 and Waldenberg 1972, pp. 176–8.

reason why German's radicals could not have organised themselves as a more cohesive and combative *internal* SPD tendency. Furthermore, the deep political, social, and cultural attachment of workers to the German Social Democracy undercut the viability of an organisational rupture, at least for most of the period up through 1918. As future Communist leader August Thalheimer noted, opposition to a split remained widespread among even leftist worker-militants well into the war; a premature break from the SPD risked isolating the revolutionaries from the bulk of radicalising workers. In turn, German leftists still held out hope that they might be able to seize back the party from the right wing:

> In 1914–15, we did not exclude the possibility of being able to still raise the flag of revolution within the Social Democracy and cleansing it of opportunist elements. Only gradually did we become convinced that within this old framework there was nothing more to expect, nothing more to gain. One must be clear, however, that inside the Social Democratic Party ... the idea of a split met with the most difficult obstructions and the most grave hesitations among even the most progressive workers.[18]

The degree of organisational separation eventually implemented by the Bolsheviks and generalised by the Comintern after 1917 was not necessarily possible in the pre-war German Social Democracy. Outside of Russia, the weight of working-class moderation, the popular attraction of parliamentary openings, and the existence of strong workers' parties posed distinct political opportunities and obstacles.

An international comparative perspective is illuminating. As early as 1901, orthodox Marxist leaders such as H.M. Hyndman in Britain and Daniel De Leon in the United States began systematically insisting upon splits from 'opportunists' in their countries and in the Second International. Their warnings about the dangers of moderate socialist leaders were prescient. But experience demonstrated the practical limitations of pushing for a 'party of the new type', especially in the pre-war period. When Marxists in the Second International did not participate in their country's existing workers' parties – e.g. in Britain and Holland, where the orthodox Left founded its own separate organisation in 1909 – they built only small sects.[19]

---

18   Thalheimer 1930. See also Broué 2005, pp. 71–2.
19   For early proto-Leninist arguments, see Hyndman 1901, pp. 451–5 and Daniel De Leon, '"Tight" and "Loose" Organization', *New York Daily People*, 7 January 1901. On Holland, see Gerber 1984, pp. 263–80.

The Comintern's push after 1917 to cohere mass revolutionary parties through splits with Social Democrats was made possible by a particular historic conjuncture: the growth of broad workers' parties over the preceding decades, the historic capitulation of Second International leaderships in 1914, the Russian Revolution, and the post-1917 revolutionary wave across Europe. In response to these watershed events, large wings of the traditional socialist parties – not infrequently even their majority – sought to affiliate to the Communist International. In the absence of similar political preconditions, a path of immediate organisational splits would likely have led to self-imposed marginalisation.

Each of Europe's influential Communist parties of the era emerged from mass splits within the Social Democracy or from the radicals' effective conquest of the leadership of these very parties. Moreover, in exceptional countries like the US, Canada, and Britain where there were no mass workers' parties or where Marxist forces remained weak, the Comintern counselled them to build – or, in the case of Britain, to join – broader labour parties, within which they could work as a distinct organised tendency.[20] As we will now see, the experience of Finland's Social Democracy shows that there was nothing inherently misguided about working to transform a moderate workers' party into an instrument for revolution.

## 2      Finland's Social Democracy

The relatively heterogeneous practices and politics of the German Social Democracy were replicated by the Finnish SDP more than any of its illegal counterparts in imperial Russia. But while revolutionaries became increasingly marginalised in the German party, in Finland the opposite dynamic occurred. Following the 1905 upheaval, orthodox Marxists fought for and captured most of the Finnish party leadership, thereby setting the stage for workers' revolution in 1917–18.

Before 1905, a commitment to Marxist politics within the ranks and leadership of Finland's Social Democracy was remarkably low. Unlike in the rest of the empire, members of the early Finnish party did not join individually; instead, they were automatically included through their membership in affiliated mass workers' associations such as unions or cultural clubs. Historian

---

20      On the Comintern and its internal debates, see Broué 1997. On how the Comintern belatedly convinced US radicals to fight for a Labor Party, see Blanc 2014b.

Hannu Soikkanen notes that most members were 'quite passive'.[21] As one Finnish study has demonstrated, it was often not even clear who was a member of the party.[22]

On a political level, Finland's orthodox Marxists made up only a small minority of the leadership and membership before 1905 – vague labour politics, Christian socialism and pacifist Tolstoyism prevailed. The party's objective was often framed as simply the promotion of workers' material interests and the extension of democratic rights, rather than the expropriation of economic and political power from the bourgeoisie.[23] The party's political eclecticism, in turn, was facilitated by, and rooted in, its decentralised organisational structure. Each Finnish city's SDP chapter tended to put forward whatever line it saw fit, as did the various independent labour newspapers loosely associated with the party.

As we have seen, the 1905–06 upheaval marked a turning point for Finnish socialism, prompting the SDP to undergo a major overhaul in its political perspectives and its organisational leadership. Soikkanen notes that 'the Great Strike tended to make the Kautskyite concept of the socialist revolution and the emphasis upon the class struggle more acceptable to the great majority of the party's active supporters'.[24]

While orthodox Marxists in Germany mostly remained unwilling or unable to fight for organisational leadership before 1914, this pattern was not repeated in Finland. Beginning at the November 1905 party congress in Tampere and especially at its August 1906 congress in Oulu, most of the conciliatory old-guard leadership around Mäkelin and Ursin was pushed out of office. Mäkelin was replaced as editor of *Kansan Lehti* and his 'national line' became a marginal and discredited position within the party. Influential SDP leader Matti Kurikka – whose eclectic commitment to utopian socialism and theosophism placed him on a collision course with the party's Marxist left – was kicked out of the party entirely. Long-time orthodox leader Edvard Valpas was elected as the new SDP chairman by an overwhelming majority. And reflecting this change in orientation, the central party leadership was moved from the moderate town of Turku to the more militant Helsinki.[25]

After 1905, the SDP's evolution was shaped by a cohort of young radicalised leaders known as the *Siltasaarelaiset*, in reference to the island neighbourhood in Helsinki where they were based. Their most prominent intellectual,

---

21    Soikkanen 1961, p. 284.
22    Saastamoinen 2005, p. 14.
23    Cited in Suodenjoki and Peltola 2007, p. 58.
24    Soikkanen 1978, p. 356.
25    Soikkanen 1961, p. 283.

Otto Kuusinen, is remembered today for his role as the founder of Finnish Communism and as a top leader in the Comintern. But in the pre-war period Kuusinen was known as 'the little Kautsky', reflecting his pioneering theoretical expositions of revolutionary social democracy for the Finnish context.[26] In alliance with Valpas, the *Siltasaarelaiset* fought to get the party in all regions of Finland to commit itself both in theory and practice to Marxist orthodoxy. Towards this end, they founded, and organised themselves around, Finland's first revolutionary social democratic publication, *Sosialistinen Aikakauslehti* (Socialist Journal).

The rise of the *Siltasaarelaiset* in the SDP leadership after 1905 both reflected and contributed to the party's radicalisation. Soikkanen writes: 'In the competition for leading offices in the labour movement in 1906–1907, the younger generation was able to ensure its dominant position by this appeal to the intellectual giants, especially Kautsky'.[27] One expression of the new weight of revolutionary social democracy inside the SDP was the fight against party leader J.K. Kari, an influential champion of class collaborationism who had joined the Finnish national government in November 1905. In response to Kari's controversial act, Kuusinen led a successful offensive at the 1906 Oulu congress to expel him from the SDP. True to orthodox theory, Kari's breach of party politics in *action* was widely seen as warranting expulsion.

In a further effort to cohere the party along revolutionary social democratic lines, the Oulu Congress overturned the SDP's previously loose organisational rules and established a more centralised and disciplined structure. Right-leaning leaders subsequently decried the party leadership's alleged 'autocratic' muzzling of 'heretical' views through overly strict political intransigence and institutional discipline.[28] Kautsky's vision of an orthodox party enforcing its political will over an opportunist minority in its ranks was implemented significantly more effectively in Finland than in Germany.

In a balance sheet of the 1906 Oulu Congress, Kuusinen argued that it marked a breakthrough for the SDP. Until this moment, he argued, the Finnish party had been mired in a 'still rather vague and immature stance'. In his view, this had been a phase of political development analogous to the British Labour Party or the moderate Swedish Social Democracy. But now, Kuusinen argued, the SDP was breaking from its previous ambiguities: 'The Oulu Congress took a clear class struggle position'.[29]

---

26    On Kuusinen, see Carrez 2008.
27    Soikkanen 1978, p. 359.
28    Huttunen 1918, p. 23.
29    Kuusinen 1906 [1981], pp. 345–7.

Despite these victories, the *Siltasaarelaiset* were well aware that the party and its leadership were far from being homogeneously committed to revolutionary social democracy. Their ongoing insistence on party unity and discipline reflected a conscious effort to keep class-collaborationist socialists from implementing an orientation contrary to that of the majority. The conciliatory wing still held a significant amount of power in the SDP – and subsequent experience would show that it was not resigned to accepting the new line or the new leadership. One such leader typically declared in 1906 that the party's propaganda should be less directed towards 'inflaming class hatred'.[30] In the radicalised context opened by the 1905 revolution, such calls went over poorly with the party ranks and were rare. Most socialist advocates of 'national unity' in this period took a backseat and bided their time.

In the decade between 1907 and 1917, social and political developments somewhat undercut the radical turn of the SDP and the clear dominance of orthodox Marxists. The ebbing of revolutionary unrest across Russia and Finland cooled the membership's militancy. Parliamentarism and bureaucratisation, with their moderating pull, soon made themselves felt in Finland. The existence of a significant moderate tendency within the SDP did not reflect a mistaken party model, it expressed the fact that moderate socialism still had a much deeper social base in parliamentary Finland than elsewhere in the autocratic Russian Empire. For Finnish radicals, there was no organisational shortcut to overcoming the specific challenges of operating inside a legal labour movement and intervening within a parliamentary regime.

After 1906, the revival of a class-collaborationist party minority was facilitated by the unprecedented importance of parliamentarism in Finland's political life. This dynamic was not just evident among the party's elected socialist representatives: after the SDP's tremendous electoral gains in 1907, and the exhaustion of the mass upsurge, much of Finland's working class understandably hoped that the existing elected institutions could be utilised to meet their demands. But socialist MPs, including those from the *Siltasaarelaiset*, were especially subjected to upper-class social and ideological influence, as well as political pressures to reach compromises with other parties. The social advantages bestowed upon working-class MPs further cemented the SDP's parliamentary fraction as a bastion of moderation. As historian Maurice Carrez notes, 'an important part of the parliamentary group was nostalgic for a "Yrjö Mäkelinist" line and only unwillingly accepted submitting to the official "class orientation"'.[31]

---

30    Cited in Soikkanen 1961, p. 254.
31    Carrez 2008, p. 350.

The party's rapid organisational expansion after 1905 brought with it a significant increase in SDP bureaucratisation. The rapid growth of the Finnish Social Democracy led to the crystallisation of a layer of full-time functionaries to run the party apparatus, staff its newspapers, and organise its electoral campaigns. As David Kirby notes, 'instead of the enthusiastic but ill-informed agitator, the party could now call upon over a dozen local newspapers, party schools, and paid organisers responsible to the central executive to reach the faithful'.[32]

Joining the officialdom became a path of upward mobility for more than a few talented Finnish workers. Historian Anthony Upton writes that after 1905, the 'SDP quickly developed into a bureaucracy within which local initiative was not encouraged ... The ordinary workers could suspect that the party leaders had created comfortable lives for themselves ... hobnobbing with the gentry and adopting bourgeois habits, and ignoring their followers, except when they needed the votes'.[33]

Finland's labour officials manifested many of the accomodationist tendencies common to this social layer, but they never had the same decisive political impact as in Germany. Of the contextual sources explaining this distinct trajectory, perhaps the most important was the legacy of the 1905 revolution, whose radicalising reverberations persisted in shaping the Finnish socialist movement in subsequent years. The relative lack of authority of the Finnish parliament due to the veto power and continued interference of Russian authorities was also an important factor undercutting moderate socialism.

The weakness of Finland's union movement was another source of this divergence. After 1906, a wing of Finnish union leaders pushed for a collaborationist, explicitly 'revisionist' line within the labour movement and the SDP. But since the Finnish Social Democracy remained far stronger than the unions, the political influence of the latter's leadership was limited.[34] By way of contrast, the union bureaucracy in Germany constituted the vanguard of the SPD's accomodationist turn.

Lastly, the political agency of the *Siltasaarelaiset* should not be underestimated. Without the conscious intervention of revolutionary SDs, the course of Finnish labour history could easily have moved in another direction. Given Finland's strong traditions of national unity and the pressures for collaboration produced by the renewed 'Russification' offensive begun in 1908, it was not

---

32  Kirby 1971, p. 205. For more on the bureaucratisation of the SDP, see Alapuro 1988, p. 125, Ehrnrooth 1992, pp. 361, 491, and Soikkanen 1961, pp. 277–8.

33  Upton 1980, p. 11.

34  Riihinen 1975, pp. 138–44 and Soikkanen 1978, p. 354. See the latter for a discussion of the relative weakness of revisionism in Finland.

inevitable that the Finnish Social Democracy would uphold class independence after the revolutionary euphoria of 1905–06 died down. Unlike in Germany – where Kautsky, Luxemburg, and their closest comrades refrained from fighting for organisational hegemony – the cohort of young orthodox Marxists in Finland led by Kuusinen engaged in a sometimes bitter battle for control over the party apparatus from 1906 onwards.

Indeed, the Finnish Social Democracy after 1907 was riven by constant internal factional-political struggles between the party's three main tendencies: the orthodox left, the class-collaborationist right, and an amorphous centre that vacillated between the party's two more coherent poles.[35]

Despite their repeated ideological victories at SDP congresses during the 1906–16 factional struggles, the *Siltasaarelaiset* switched back-and-forth multiple times from being a leadership majority to a minority. Inside the parliamentary fraction, Finnish radicals frequently found themselves in a minority: for example, in 1910 the collaborationist practices of a majority of socialist MPs openly contradicted the party's orthodox line. Incensed leftists criticised their parliamentary comrades; but it was only after the following year's SDP congress restricted the MPs' freedom of action that the latter fell into line.[36]

Moderate socialists never regained hegemony over the party, but a vacillating centre took back control at various junctures. Without a decisive hold over the SDP, orthodox leftists after 1907 often felt obliged to ally with the centre against the party's crystallised class collaborationists. This factional relationship of forces led revolutionary SDs like Kuusinen to become more conciliatory, as they sought to maintain Finnish socialist unity against the bourgeoisie and hoped to prevent the SDP centre from siding with the social democratic right.[37] By embroiling itself in these intra-apparatus disputes, the *Siltasaarelaiset* were better able to shape party policy, though the integration of so many radicals into the party officialdom also somewhat tempered their militancy.

In 1917, as in the preceding years, class-collaborationist socialism continued to have a deeper social and institutional base in Finland than in the rest of autocratic Russia. Any analysis of Finland's left wing must situate their approach within this particular context. The internal organisational dilemmas of Finland's Marxists in 1917–18 were to a significant extent rooted in their attempt to push forward a class struggle line without provoking a split in the party.

Implementing this strategy was no easy feat – sometimes it led the *Siltasaarelaiset* into a conciliatory approach, in which principles were fudged for the

---

35    On the SDP's post-1905 factional developments, see Carrez 2008, *passim*.
36    Carrez 2008, pp. 301–9, 330.
37    Carrez 2008, p. 300.

sake of party unity. Consider, for example, the April debates on political power following the February Revolution. Fearing a debilitating division within the party, much of the SDP left, including Kuusinen, eventually went along with the entry of social democrats into a 'national unity' Finnish government in April 1917. At the same time, however, Finland's leftists refused to participate in the new government – moreover, they refused to take political responsibility for it (or its socialist leaders) and they persisted in pushing forward class struggle policies. And under pressure from Finnish Marxist political initiatives against the Russian Provisional Government, as well as the pressure of working-class mass action, the SDP as a whole broke from the coalition government in August.

A similar pattern of relative conciliationism followed by class intransigence marked the SDP's approach to the fight for political power during the revolution's climax. To a large extent, the prevarications and tactical heterogeneity of *Siltasaarelaiset* leaders in November 1917 reflected their view that a successful proletarian seizure of power in Finland required that the party leadership as a whole be won to this objective.[38] Inside SDP leadership bodies as early as October 1917, Kuusinen had raised a call for Finnish workers to seize power. Yet an influential minority of parliamentary and union officials remained opposed to revolutionary rupture. In his 1918 critique of what he saw as the SDP's ultra-left adventurism, the influential moderate socialist MP Evert Huttunen thus congratulated the socialist Parliamentary Group for being 'the main obstacle' to the push for a seizure of power in late 1917.[39]

These contradictions came to a head during the November general strike. On 16 November, the General Strike Council in Helsinki voted to seize power. But when conciliatory union and SDP leaders denounced this decision and resigned from the body, the council beat a retreat that very day. It resolved that 'since such a large minority was of a different opinion, the Council could not at this time promote the seizure of power by the workers, but would work on to increase the pressure on the bourgeoisie'.[40] The strike was soon after called off.

Various authors have argued that this aborted seizure of power was the decisive missed opportunity of 1917. Kuusinen pioneered this case in his 1919 balance sheet of the revolution, a decidedly ultra-left pamphlet aimed at winning socialists to the new Finnish Communist Party. He argued that the Finnish left's 'historical error' at the moment of truth was rooted in a hope 'to avoid splitting the S.-D.'s into two opposite camps'. Acknowledging the potential dam-

---

38    Carrez 2008, pp. 626–7, 635. Carrez's monograph details the *Siltasaarelaiset*'s heterogeneity during the main debates of late 1917.
39    Huttunen 1918, p. 71.
40    'Meeting of the Revolutionary Central Council, 16 November' in Kirby 1975, p. 196.

age of a split at that critical juncture, he nevertheless concluded that 'for the real progress of the working class movement, and for the strengthening of the class-war, this internal rupture could not but have been of service'.[41]

Kuusinen's certainty about the viability of an organisational rupture in late 1917 is questionable. There was a strong minority of militant workers in Helsinki eager to push for a seizure of power, but this does not mean that the bulk of the party and union members would have followed Finnish radicals in a split at this moment. Whereas party loyalties and institutional structures were relatively weak in central Russia, allowing for rapid shifts in organisational allegiances during 1917, the SDP for decades had been the political home, church, school, and cultural centre for tens of thousands of Finnish workers. Without the political legitimacy bestowed by the SDP's official sanction, successfully taking power in Finland would have been hard to accomplish, even if the *Siltas-aarelaiset* had been more decisive.

Whether the benefits of preventing a split outweighed the costs of delaying the revolution is an open, and ultimately unanswerable, question. As it turned out, the plausibility of the SDP left's chosen approach was manifest over the two months following the general strike. Through a series of sharp internal debates in December and January, the *Siltasaarelaiset* overcame its own internal hesitations and divisions – and then proceeded to overcome its class-collaborationist internal rivals. Faced with a deepening bourgeois counter-offensive, and the spread of semi-spontaneous proletarian actions across Finland, the *Siltasaare-laiset* in conjunction with the Red Guards led the party as a whole to fight for power in late January 1918.[42] In light of this conscious political struggle waged by the SDP left, it is hard to accept Anthony Upton's claim that 'the Finnish revolutionaries were in general the most miserable revolutionaries in history'.[43]

The adherence by workers and party leaders to the unity of the Finnish Social Democracy proved to be a double-edged sword. On the one hand, it pushed radicals towards conciliationism throughout 1917; on the other, it made it much more difficult for the SDP right and centre to oppose the creation of a Red Government in 1918. While a few of the most class-collaborationist socialist leaders openly distanced themselves from the armed uprising, a large majority of the party leadership supported the revolution in late January 1918.

For some centrist leaders this stance was taken grudgingly – nevertheless, the evolution of the SDP leadership towards armed anti-capitalist rupture was

---

41    Kuusinen 1919, pp. 9, 11–12.
42    For the most in-depth account of these internal SDP struggles and the role of Kuusinen in particular, see Carrez 2008, pp. 628–62.
43    Upton 1980, p. 150.

undeniable. The moral and political basis of this turn was poignantly illustrated in a letter by moderate socialist leader Anton Huotari to his eldest daughter written a few weeks into the civil war. Asking her to take responsibility for the family were he and his wife (also a socialist activist) to be killed, Huotari explained why the two of them had supported the seizure of power: 'Though we had some doubts in regards to the current armed struggle, we considered that we owed the movement the whole of our working capacity once the decision to struggle for state power was taken. We have grown up with the social-democratic movement and our duty calls on us'.[44] Only after the Reds were defeated in the civil war did the Finnish Social Democracy finally split, with the revolutionary (Communist) and moderate (Social Democratic) wings breaking apart in late 1918.

To sum up: Finnish orthodox Marxists from 1903 to 1918 played an indispensable role in transforming one of the most right-leaning socialist parties in Europe into a vehicle capable of leading workers to power. The evolution of the Finnish SDP disproves the influential argument of sociologist Robert Michels that an 'iron law of oligarchy' necessarily leads mass organisations to come under the control of conservative bureaucrats. Rather than an 'iron law', bureaucratisation was a strong tendency whose political effects could be potentially overcome by countervailing factors such as the pressure of mass struggle and the conscious intervention of party radicals within the organisation, including inside the officialdom itself.

By way of international comparison, the Finnish experience also undercuts the common Leninist assertion that the crucial mistake of Second International radicals outside of Russia was their participation in the same parties as reformists before 1914. Indeed, Finland illustrates in a positive manner that orthodox Marxists could provide effective revolutionary leadership by participating in a broader workers' party that included entrenched moderate leaders within its ranks. In Finland, the persistent efforts of the *Siltasaarelaiset* to fight for organisational and political hegemony, combined with a mass radicalisation from below in both 1905 and 1917, helped prevent Finland's Social Democracy from travelling down the same road as the German SPD.

At the same time, the delays and hesitations that shaped so much of the 1917–18 Finnish Revolution were inseparable from the political heterogeneity of the Finnish Social Democracy. But this was not the result of mistaken socialist theory. The existence of an influential mass workers' party, the inherent tensions of intervening within parliamentary bodies and a legal labour movement,

44    Cited in Suodenjoki and Peltola 2007, pp. 254–5.

and the associated weight of socialist moderation inside Finland and across Europe, created opportunities and obstacles that were not present to the same degree for imperial Russia's underground Marxists.

One can criticise the excessive conciliationism of the *Siltasaarelaiset*, but there is little reason to believe that they would have been more politically successful had they attempted to split from the SDP. Apart from the fact that they were not organisationally or politically cohesive enough to have seriously considered this option, such a drastic move would have cut them off from the majority of Finnish socialist workers, who continued to look to the Finnish Social Democracy as their main political home and political expression. The existence of an entrenched mass workers' party meant that radicals in Finland, like in Germany, could not have simply replicated the organisational model of the Bolsheviks. Different governmental contexts required different paths towards building a party capable of effectively leading workers to break with capitalist rule.

3      The Normalcy of Splits in Underground Russia

In earlier sections we saw that the German Social Democracy increasingly diverged in practice from the party model envisioned by revolutionary social democrats. But it must be kept in mind that socialists across Russia and beyond had a rose-tinted view of the SPD before World War I. Only after the German Social Democracy's infamous capitulation on 4 August 1914 did radicals realise the extent to which class collaborationism had taken hold within the German workers' movement.

Imperial Russia's Marxists sought to replicate the cohesive party of the *model* articulated by Kautsky – and, in practice, they built organisations that resembled the orthodox conception more than the German SPD itself. Conditions in Russia set the empire's socialist parties down a very different path from their legalised counterparts abroad. Absolutism prevented Russia's illegal Marxist organisations from developing entrenched party bureaucracies or loose memberships of relatively uncommitted members. And the obvious risks of associating with an illegal organisation tended to keep memberships numerically smaller and more consistently radical than in Western Europe.

This relative political consistency, in turn, was further deepened by the high level of class militancy in Russia as well as the unparalleled attention of imperial Russia's SD leaders to orthodox Marxist strategy. This degree of cohesion certainly should not be overstated. In all regions of the empire, Marxist parties frequently accepted anybody who would join them; knowledge of socialist theory by rank-and-file members remained very uneven; and concretising the appropriate political-programmatic limits of a social democratic party (or an internal tendency) was a constant source of tension. Nevertheless, socialist parties in Russia remained significantly more politically cohesive, and radical, than their counterparts abroad.

Despite the weakness of moderate socialism in Russia, and despite the orthodox view that there should only be one unified proletarian party in every country, the existence of multiple socialist organisations was the norm under Tsarism. On this question, as on so many others in the scholarship, a presumed particularity of the Bolsheviks was actually common across the empire. Among the Poles, for example, there were three distinct parties that raised the banner of Marxist orthodoxy; among the Latvians and Ukrainians there were two. After 1903, the Bund faced at least four different Jewish socialist organisational rivals, some of whom considered themselves to be more 'orthodox' than the Bundists.

The RSDRP itself never came close to bringing all the non-Russian SD parties under its umbrella. And in addition to these intra-Marxist divisions, we should also highlight the importance of the Russian Socialist Revolutionary party, as well as their allied non-Russian socialist parties across Russia like the Ukrainian SRs and the Armenian Dashnaks. It was thus standard for a given city under Tsarism to have two to four (and often more) socialist parties organising local workers. Indeed, the Finns were the only nationality in the empire that had a single united socialist party.

The prevalence of competing socialist organisations in Russia seriously undercuts the myth of Bolshevik uniqueness. In light of these examples, it is hard to accept the idea that the RSDRP's split was primarily due to Lenin's factionalism and his unparalleled commitment to ideological demarcation. Social and political conditions in autocratic Russia clearly mitigated against the construction and maintenance of a single unified socialist organisation, even within a particular region and/or nationality. The prevalence of socialist splits can be attributed to a combination of the following socio-political factors: the difficulty in stabilising solid party infrastructures and institutions while operating underground; the tendency of émigré political leaderships to exacerbate factionalism; the political intensity of the revolutionary period; the strategic and organisational dilemmas generated by the national and agrarian questions; the intense engagement of party leaders with revolutionary theory; and, finally, the founding of the empire's SD parties at the height of the international revisionist controversy, which prompted widespread (and often unfounded) charges of opportunism against rivals.

The political and organisational content of early socialist splits varied widely by region and time – there was no one general pattern before the February

Revolution. Nor did each organisational break prefigure the divisions that arose in 1917. Indeed, one of the striking features of party ruptures in the period before 1905 is that none revolved around what would become the primary strategic line of division within Russia: whether to bloc with the 'progressive bourgeoisie' or promote the hegemony of the proletariat. Only after the defeat of the 1905 insurrections did serious divisions over this question arise. Currents that continued to homogeneously adhere to working-class hegemony – including the Bolsheviks, the PPS-Left, the SDKPIL, and the LSDSP – generally remained united in 1917 and supported the fight for a workers' (and peasants') government. In contrast, those parties that entered 1917 advocating, or split on, blocs with liberals were generally hostile towards soviet power.

Analysing the relative political narrowness or broadness of each SD party in Russia or the content of each organisational split is a task beyond the scope of this chapter. So to illuminate some of the trends and tensions of orthodox theory and practice concerning party unity in the Tsarist underground, our discussion will be limited to two cases: the Polish SDKPIL and the Bolsheviks.

## 4      The Split of Polish Socialism

Because Rosa Luxemburg was a Marxist leader in both Germany and Russia, an analysis of her stances on party organisation is especially revealing. Based on her German writings, most academics and activists have claimed that there were fundamental strategic differences between her conception of the revolutionary party and that of Lenin. Luxemburg, it is widely argued, remained wedded to the Second International's view that the party should embrace the whole class, not just its vanguard, and that revolutionaries should not organise apart from reformist socialists. According to this analysis, Luxemburg (unlike Lenin) refused to organisationally break from opportunists, hoping in vain that the impending revolutionary upsurge would sweep them away.[45]

The basic flaw in such an interpretation is that it cannot account for Luxemburg's party in Poland. Indeed, the SDKPIL shared all of the attributes that are generally said to be the distinct features of Bolshevism: organisational separateness from moderate socialists, political intransigence, ideological cohesiveness, and tight centralisation. In many ways, the SDKPIL was closer to the presumed 'Leninist model' than the Bolsheviks themselves.

---

45      Harman 1982, p. 95.

The fact that both Luxemburg and Lenin's parties in Tsarist Russia looked very different than the German SPD was not due to a break with orthodox Marxism – each saw their parties as an implementation of this strategy under absolutist conditions. At no point in the pre-war years did either Lenin or Luxemburg argue that their form of party organisation in imperial Russia should be replicated by revolutionaries in Germany or the rest of Europe. Moreover, the absence of political freedom created a completely different relationship of forces between moderates and revolutionaries inside Russia's socialist movements. As such, the tough question posed in Germany and across Western Europe of how a Marxist minority could effectively overcome entrenched and widespread moderation within a mass socialist party did not generally confront radicals operating in autocratic Russia.

It is justified in hindsight to criticise Luxemburg and other SPD radicals for failing to organise Germany's left wing as a distinct current before 1914. But it does not follow that this error reflected a strategic divergence with Lenin on party-building. While one can find isolated passages in Luxemburg's German writings that seem to downplay the distinction between the party and the class, or that argue against organisational splits from opportunists, such approaches were not reflected in SDKPIL practice. Nor were they present in Luxemburg's Polish writings.

The theory and practice of Luxemburg's Polish party demonstrates that her well-known debates with Lenin did not reflect any consistent strategic divergences. Even within a shared orthodox framework, all sorts of concrete differences were inevitable over how best to politically proceed in the specific conditions of Tsarist Russia. While Luxemburg advocated the organisational unity of Mensheviks and Bolsheviks from 1904 through 1917, she simultaneously rejected any organisational merger between the SDKPIL and the PPS-Left, despite the fact that the latter was a revolutionary Marxist party significantly to the left of the Mensheviks. Indeed, Luxemburg's organisation was far more consistent than the Bolsheviks when it came to remaining separate from those it considered to be opportunists. Some Polish scholars have even claimed that the PPS-SDKPIL split pioneered the later worldwide bifurcation of the socialist movement into Communists and Social Democrats.[46]

Readers will recall that Luxemburg's party was born from an 1893 break with the PPS over the national question. To call for Polish independence, Luxemburg argued, was a reactionary manifestation of non-proletarian nationalism. A truly social democratic party in Poland could never support this demand.

---

Whatever one might think about this stance, the critical point to underscore here is that no clear criteria existed for what constituted a 'splitting issue' that precluded participation in a joint socialist party. After 1911, many radicals, including Luxemburg, would denounce the Bolsheviks for pushing to split the RSDRP over what they saw as differences that could co-exist within a single Marxist party.

In Poland from 1893 onwards, the Luxemburg leadership engaged in an untiring campaign to discredit the PPS and dislodge it from a position of influence within the workers' movement. Indeed, the 1903 merger negotiations of the SDKPIL with the RSDRP largely revolved around the former's desire to isolate its factional rivals. In Luxemburg's words, 'joining the Russians' was simply 'an anti-PPS measure'.[47] As Antti Kujala has noted,

> whenever the RSDWP and PPS showed signs of burying their differences, the SDKPIL returned to the theme of the need to achieve the formation of a united social democratic party. As the danger receded, it contented itself with merely talking about the necessity of increased inter-party collaboration.[48]

For its part, *Iskra* deferred to its prestigious Polish comrades when it came to the issue of a RSDRP merger with the PPS.[49]

Luxemburg's anti-PPS factionalism also had important repercussions inside of Germany's workers' movement. In May 1898, Luxemburg moved from Switzerland to Germany with the conscious goal of winning SPD leaders to support her wing of Polish socialism against the PPS. As I have detailed elsewhere, she succeeded in achieving this goal by 1903 in large part by blocking with the increasingly conservative party bureaucracy against the PPS's radical sister organisation in Prussian Germany. Through gaining the confidence of the party hierarchy in this fight against 'Polish separatism', Luxemburg successfully established herself as the SPD's arbiter on Polish and Russian affairs.[50]

In the coming years, Luxemburg and other SDKPIL émigrés would systematically utilise their political prestige and connections to German and Russian socialist leaderships to prevent the PPS from joining Russia's Social Democracy.

---

47    'List R. Luksemburg do Warskiego' [1903] in Szmidt 1934, pp. 390, 396.
48    Kujala 1988, p. 114.
49    Kujala 1988, pp. 108–9 and Najdus 1973, p. 180.
50    Blanc 2018.

In 1906, with the support of the Bolsheviks, the SDKPIL demanded and won this veto power as a precondition for its entry into the RSDRP. Thus the PPS-Left's repeated post-1906 requests to join the empire-wide party were successfully blocked by Luxemburg's group.[51] Despite Lenin's serious differences with Luxemburg over national self-determination, and the PPS-Left's declaration of support for Bolshevik strategies, the Bolsheviks remained allied to the SDKPIL rather than the PPS-Left.

The irony of Luxemburg's intransigence is that the Polish Socialist Party was on the far left of imperial Russia's socialist movement from at least 1903 onwards. In 1906, PPS leaders announced their support for the Bolsheviks' revolutionary politics, declaring that the Mensheviks were moderates whose tactics led to the subordination of workers to bourgeois liberals.[52] Later in the year, the PPS expelled Pilsudski's proto-nationalist wing. In addition to confirming the party's radicalism, this organisational rupture further underscores the nature of the revolutionary social democratic party model. Like with Kari's expulsion in Finland, PPS leftists argued for expelling Pilsudski on the grounds that he had broken in *action* with party decisions, in this case by refusing to subordinate the combat squads and their activities to the democratically elected party leadership. PPS leftists declared that a 'party cannot have two programmes and two tactics'.[53]

Aiming to affiliate with the Russian Social Democracy and to overcome the disunity of Polish Marxism, in 1907 the PPS-Left eliminated the demand for independence from its political programme and called for a merger with the SDKPIL. Polish independence, PPS-Left leaders now argued, while a desirable long-term goal, was not an immediately realisable objective. Therefore Poland's socialists should unite regionally and they should cement their organisational unity with other nationalities across Russia. The remaining differences with the SDKPIL, according to the PPS-Left, were not sufficient to prevent organ-

---

51  Kasprzakowa 1965, *passim.*

52  'Walka kierunków w łonie Rosyjskiej Socjalnej Demokracji', *Robotnik*, 4 July 1906. In part because the Bolsheviks continued to ally with the SDKPIL against the PPS-Left, the latter's support for the Bolsheviks cooled after 1907. The PPS-Left henceforth situated itself in the 'non-factional' revolutionary social democratic camp that included most other borderland parties and Leon Trotsky. During the pre-war upsurge, the PPS-Left rejected the Mensheviks' call for an alliance with liberals, but argued that the Bolsheviks had not fully broken from a semi-sectarian stance towards the mass workers' movement and other SD organisations. The PPS-Left's ongoing efforts to unify the Polish Marxist movement particularly clashed with the top Bolshevik leadership's post-1911 drive to effectuate an empire-wide split inside the RSDRP. During the war, top leaders of the PPS-Left allied with Martov's Menshevik-Internationalists (Tych 1960, Kasprzakowa 1965, and Strobel 1974).

53  'Kierownicy t. zw. Frakcji Rewolucyjnej', *Łodzianin*, 22 February 1907.

isational unity within a single revolutionary Marxist party in Poland.[54] From 1907 onwards, the PPS-Left emphatically pushed for the organisational merger of Poland's Marxists.

Yet Luxemburg was no less hostile to the PPS-Left than she had been towards the PPS under Pilsudski's leadership. For Luxemburg, dropping the demand for independence was insufficient because real Marxists understood the historical impossibility of ever achieving an independent Poland.[55] Therefore she denounced the PPS-Left as 'a group of bankrupt social-patriots, who had to break with their own past, but who cannot find the way to a social democratic position'.[56] To become real Marxists, she affirmed, members of the PPS-Left would have to repudiate their 'opportunist' leadership and join the SDKPIL. Luxemburg's 1908 justification for intransigence towards the PPS-Left could easily be mistaken for something written by Lenin at his most strident:

> The fact is that the existence of a strictly class proletarian party – that bases its principles on a theoretical understanding of its activities, that knows no compromise on tactics, that is inflexible in the application and defence of the whole of its views, that is inaccessible to any half-bred and half-hearted shades of socialism – has an effect and impact far beyond its own organisation. It constantly weighs on the other factions and shades of socialism, and on the whole workers' movement. How many charges were thrown against the 'intransigent' Guesde-ists in France for their decades-long rejection of unification with all other socialist groups! History proved them right – it was shown that the strength of a socialist party consists not in superficially cobbling together a plethora of members, nor in opulent cashboxes or an abundance of rubbish party leaflets, but rather in the stability and clarity of its views, in the concordance and spiritual unity of its ranks, in the concurrence between its words and deeds.[57]

As discussed earlier, the SDKPIL leadership's opposition to a rapprochement with the PPS-Left was increasingly rejected by the ranks and local leaders of the party after 1906, culminating in the break of the SDKPIL majority away from Luxemburg's émigré leadership in 1911. But after their split from the Luxemburg group, the dissident Warsaw Committee and its supporters surprisingly failed

---

54   Kasprzakowa 1965, p. 57.
55   Luxemburg 1908.
56   Luxemburg [Anon.] 1910, 'O druzgocącej krytyce zdruzgotanej partii', *Czerwony Sztandar*, 20 June 1910.
57   Luxemburg 1908, p. 62.

to move forward towards a merger with the PPS-Left. This refusal was partly the result of empire-wide factional dynamics that had little to do with politics in Poland itself. In their fight against the Luxemburg leadership, SDKPIL oppositionists allied themselves with Lenin, who at this very moment was engaged in a bitter struggle to split the RSDRP. As such, moves towards organisational unity with the PPS-Left were shelved.[58]

After the arrest of top leaders on both sides of the SDKPIL faction fight, the Polish Social Democracy reunited in 1916. And like in previous years, the SDK-PIL continued to reject the PPS-Left's proposals for a merger. As had been the case since 1903, to quote Nettl, '[u]nity could come only if the PPS capitulated and went out of existence'.[59]

SDKPIL intransigence put the PPS-Left in a political bind. How to square its push for Marxist unity and national liberation became particularly challenging after 1914. In the face of the social turmoil and geo-political openings of WWI and the German occupation, Polish separatist sentiment spread to an unprecedented degree in the population at large.[60] From 1915 onwards, key PPS-Left cadre led by Antoni Szczerkowski in Łódź accordingly called on the party to bring back its demand for Polish independence, arguing that a working-class struggle for an independent Poland had again become viable. If Marxists did not raise this demand from an anti-capitalist perspective, they argued, it would be effectively monopolised by the PPS-Revolutionary Faction and its allies. The majority of the PPS-Left leadership, however, rejected this proposal, agreeing instead only to vaguely project the 'broadest possible independence' as a long-term programmatic goal.[61]

Everybody in the PPS-Left understood that agitating for national separation would preclude the possibility of merging with the SDKPIL and the RSDRP. In this context, rather than fight for independence, the PPS-Left continued to affirm a relatively hazy call for self-determination and national liberation through workers' revolution. This refusal to actively fight for independence in a period of growing separatist struggle, plus Polish radicals' disunity, was a critical factor enabling the rise of the PPS-FR. By tying the struggle for independence to workers' immediate interests, moderate socialists during the war overcame the former hegemony of radical Marxists in the Polish labour movement. After years of attempting to change the party line, Szczerkowski and the

58  Kasprzakowa 1965, pp. 232–3 and Strobel 1974, p. 423.
59  Nettl 1966, p. 283.
60  On the First World War as the turning point in the 'Polish question', see Biskupski 1990. For the impact of the First World War on Polish Marxists, see Tych 1960 and Najdus 1980.
61  Szczerkowski 1923.

pro-independence opposition within the PPS-Left reluctantly defected to the PPS-FR in 1918. Though they openly argued that the PPS-FR insufficiently upheld class independence and internationalism, Szczerkowski and his comrades felt that they could be more effective by constituting themselves as one of the elements of its far-left minority.[62] Poland's revolutionary socialists were thereby fractured into four separate parties (including the Polish Bund) on the eve of the Polish Revolution.

The 1917–18 upheavals in Russia, Germany, and Austria imploded the occupying states, leaving a power vacuum in Poland and unleashing an explosive radicalisation of workers and peasants. In the wake of the announcement of Polish independence on 7 November 1918, over a hundred workers' councils, as well as armed Red Guards, sprung up across Poland. The country was engulfed by instability. Ruling-class disarray, soldier mutinies, general strikes, and local armed battles posed the spectre of anti-capitalist rupture. But despite these favourable revolutionary conditions, Polish Marxists were unable to lead the working class to power.

Though party leadership decisions were only one factor shaping the turn of events, it is plausible that a different outcome would have been possible had a pro-independence revolutionary social democratic party existed inside the workers' movement. Instead, the SDKPIL and its anti-separatist strategy came to dominate the early Polish Communist Party at this pivotal moment. And, despite this, the Bolsheviks upheld their alliance with the SDKPIL. During 1917 and 1918, hundreds of SDKPIL militants living in St. Petersburg joined the Bolsheviks and the new Soviet state, often receiving top leadership posts. Anti-independence stalwart Feliks Dzierżyński entered the Bolsheviks' Central Committee in August 1917. And the new Soviet government's Department for Polish Affairs – a section of the Commissariat on Nationalities led by Joseph Stalin – was headed by Julian Leszczyński, a SDKPIL leader who used this position to agitate against Polish separation and national self-determination.[63]

Though the PPS-Left remained more rooted in Poland than Luxemburg's party, it too had militants organised in central Russia. In 1917, its party branches inside of Russia raised the perspective of imminent world socialist revolution and they fought hard against the war, the liberals, and the Provisional Government. Though various local PPS-Left groups across Russia were close to the

62   Karwacki 1964, pp. 378–81, 411–14.
63   Dzierżyński would soon go on to head the Soviet secret police (the 'Cheka'). Leszczyński became Stalin's main agent inside the Polish Communist Party. For his successful purges of the 'Trotskyites', Leszczyński was rewarded with a promotion to party head in 1929 – a post he retained until he perished in 1937 during Stalin's Great Purge.

Bolsheviks, for most of 1917 the organisation's top cadre in Petrograd were allied to the radical Menshevik-Internationalists led by Martov. They refused to affiliate to Martov's current, however, because it rejected their calls for it to break from the pro-war, class-collaborationist Menshevik 'defencists'.

After supporting the demand for a multi-party 'homogenous socialist government' in the fall, the PPS-Left in December 1917 officially declared its support for the October Revolution and the new Soviet regime. Nevertheless, the subsequent requests of PPS-Left groups in Russia to affiliate with the Russian Communist Party were rejected on the grounds that the PPS-Left had failed to fuse with the SDKPIL.[64]

As had been the case since 1906, by leaning on the leverage provided by the Bolsheviks, the SDKPIL was able to ensure that the PPS-Left would either have to dissolve itself or remain excluded from the international Marxist movement. Faced with this alternative, in the fall of 1918 the PPS-Left decided that the urgent need to form a united Communist Party in Poland outweighed its ongoing political differences with the SDKPIL. As a result, in December 1918 the PPS-Left co-founded the new Communist Party together with the SDKPIL, on the basis of the latter's anti-independence platform. After 25 years, Rosa Luxemburg's group had finally overcome its PPS rivals.[65]

Luxemburg's final action in the Polish socialist movement was to give her approval from Berlin to the founding programme of the new Polish Communist Workers Party, which in late 1918 declared that 'the Polish proletariat rejects all political slogans such as autonomy, independence, self-determination'.[66] Such a stance proved to be a major political liability at a moment when most Polish working people were euphoric about the conquest of state independence.[67] Dzierżyński later argued that the 'error made by us (former SDKPIL members) was rejecting Polish independence. ... Negating independence completely, we thus lost the struggle for an independent Soviet Poland'.[68]

The failure of Luxemburg's current to lead the 1918–19 Polish Revolution to victory helps demonstrate that, contrary to Leninist accounts, the existence of a distinct party of revolutionary socialists did not guarantee a successful working-class conquest of power.[69] Luxemburg's Polish party lacked

---

64    'List Sekretariatu Sekcji i Grup PPS-Lewicy w Rosji do CK RKP(b) w sprawie wstąpienia PPS-Lewicy do RKP(b)' [1918], in Wydziału Historii Partii KC PZPR 1956, p. 162.
65    On the PPS-Left's unification with the SDKPIL, see Strobel 1974, pp. 651–87.
66    'Sprawozdanie ze Zjazdu Organizacyjnego KPRP. Zjednoczenie SDKPIL i PPS Lewicy', 16–18 December 1918, Warszawa (Dokumenty życia społecznego, Biblioteka Narodowa).
67    Marchlewski 1920, p. 28.
68    Cited in Warski 1929 [1966], p. 611.
69    Poland was not unique in this regard. John Riddell explains, for example, that 'in the early

neither organisational independence from moderate socialists, nor a homogenous commitment to revolutionary Marxism. But it was unable to play a
mass leadership role analogous to the Bolsheviks, despite the relatively favourable conditions for workers' revolution in post-war Poland.[70] In the end, the
refusal of the SDKPIL to unite with the PPS-Left until late 1918 – and only after
it accepted Luxemburg's opposition to Polish independence – was one of the
contributing causes of the Polish Revolution's defeat.


## 5        The Bolshevik-Menshevik Split

No faction fight in the history of the socialist movement has been so extensively covered and so widely misunderstood as the Bolshevik-Menshevik split
of 1903. Academics and activists have produced an immense amount of literature on this topic, much of which has wildly distorted the actual content of
the division. The underlying analytical flaw in the bulk of this literature is that
it frames 1903 as the genesis of Communism and Social Democracy. In most
scholarly accounts, the split marked the emergence of an elitist band led by
the proto-dictator Lenin, whose anti-democratic orientation was rejected by
the Western-oriented Mensheviks.

Marxist historiography, beginning with the post-1917 writings of the Bolsheviks, has flipped the value signs in this interpretation, while maintaining its
fundamental contours. Accordingly, 1903 constituted the conscious, or at least
embryonic, formation of a disciplined and centralised 'vanguard party', which
was rejected by the 'social democratic' Mensheviks.[71]

Such claims, however, are contradicted by the historical record. The 1903
split arose from underlying tensions within the *Iskra* project. From 1900
onwards, Iskraists fought hard to establish their ideological and organisational
hegemony over the RSDRP party committees. But neither Lenin nor other leaders of *Iskra* argued for expelling or excluding their factional rivals. According
to Lenin, a party majority had the right to build a relatively homogenous leadership and to have its decisions implemented; a minority simultaneously had

Comintern it was said that the Bulgarian party was the closest to Bolshevism outside Soviet
Russia. But actually the Bulgarians' record in the revolutionary crisis of 1918 and thereafter
was quite poor' (personal correspondence with author).

70    Historian Bernard Stone argues that '[i]n no other country were conditions more favorable for a communist take-over than they had been in Poland in the wake of the collapse
of the Central Powers' (Stone 1965, p. 456).

71    Read 2005, p. 66, Trotsky 1930 [1970], p. 24, Lenin 1920 [1960–65], p. 162, and Gluckstein
2014.

the right to express and promote its views in the party and its press. As George Haupt has noted, 'the existence of multiple opinions, currents, and tendencies ... and their freedom of expression, was for [Lenin] like all social-democratic leaders something normal, natural'.[72] That said, *Iskra*'s combative polemics and organisational drive against other RSDRP currents was not always conducive to establishing or maintaining joint party structures.[73]

Organised with the goal of cementing the unification of the RSDRP around *Iskra*'s perspectives, the 1903 Second Congress surprisingly culminated in the implosion of the *Iskra* current itself.[74] Blaming their former comrades for the damaging split in the summer of 1903, both sides argued that party unity remained possible and necessary – but only on their stipulated conditions. Nobody argued for the exclusion of the other from the RSDRP. But each faction rapidly produced a plethora of heated polemics, the hyperbolic content of which has led subsequent scholars and socialists to grossly exaggerate the underlying issues in dispute.

Early Menshevik émigré justifications for the split concentrated on demagogic attacks against Lenin, who they claimed was a power-hungry dictator.[75] For their part, Lenin and other Bolsheviks unconvincingly argued that their hitherto close comrades virtually overnight had succumbed to opportunism.

Given that the split had taken place over apparently minor organisational issues, it is not surprising that most militants initially responded with exasperation and bewilderment. A large number concluded that the division was the product of personal squabbles among émigrés. Scholars and memoirists agree that opposition to the factional feud – and confusion about its content – was widespread well into 1905. In Saratov, worker-militant Semën Kanatchikov noted that '[n]ews of the disagreements between Lenin and Martov on organizational problems reached the people here, but their meaning was poorly grasped and absorbed. People here didn't want a schism in the Party'.[76]

72    Haupt 1963, p. 39.
73    In his even-handed study of early Russian Marxism, Larsson came to the following conclusion: 'The campaign conducted by Iskra's staff must in actual fact be considered dishonest to a great extent. They attributed opinions to several of their opponents which those opponents had never expressed and they continuously, and apparently consequently, refused to pay attention to the opinions which their opponents actually did present' (Larsson 1970, p. 151).
74    Richard Mullin's dissertation convincingly details the extent to which the 1903 split reflected the Mensheviks' adaptation to (and eventual convergence with) the militants of *Rabochee Delo* and *Iuzhnii Rabochii* (Mullin 2010).
75    See, for example, Тютюкин 2002, p. 84.
76    Kanatchikov 1929 [1986], p. 368. Kautsky argued in his private correspondence that the

A major reason for the confusion was that neither side put forward a political (as opposed to organisational) case until 1904. The initial debates were mired in what Trotsky described as 'scholastic debates on the organisational questions' that 'dulled the senses of the whole Party'.[77] Historian Leopold Haimson notes that only many months after the 1903 division did the Mensheviks seek to find 'some doctrinal grounds upon which to base their opposition'.[78]

In this context, the rhythm and depth of the initial split on the ground in Russia varied considerably. Factional identification remained low among the party ranks in most cities across the empire. Few local committees split in 1903 or even during much of 1904. In Transcaucasia, for example, the local Bolshevik leadership in 1904 attempted to keep news of the party division under wraps in the hope of avoiding a rupture locally. In Ekaterinoslav and St. Petersburg, the party committee divided just days before Bloody Sunday in 1905. An organisational break did not take place in many key centres including Moscow and Riga until mid-1905. And cities such as Kharkov, Nikolaev, and Saratov never experienced major factionalism – relations between SDs who identified with the different wings remained comradely.[79]

Conciliationism was widespread in both RSDRP wings, including within the top Bolshevik leadership. During this period, as in later years, it is impossible to assess the dominant Bolshevik approach towards rival socialists primarily by reading Lenin's *Collected Works*. Indeed, the degree of anti-Menshevik intransigence on the part of Lenin – with his strong anti-conciliationist tendencies and his one-sided 'stick-bending' method of polemics – was often inversely proportional to the degree of non-factionalism among the rest of the Bolsheviks. In 1904 and the first half of 1905, top Bolsheviks including Leonid Krasin and M.G. Tskhakaya pushed back against anti-Menshevik factionalism and insisted on the possibility and necessity of rapid party re-unification. At the 1905 Bolshevik congress, the Kharkov committee likewise emphasised the absence of strong factional feeling or disputes on the ground, noting that their committee distributed the publications of all RSDRP currents.[80]

---

split reflected the isolation of RSDRP émigré leaders from practical work in Russia, making them obsessed with high theory. Expressing his hope that the ranks of the RSDRP would replace the leaders of both wings, he wrote to his comrade Victor Adler in 1905 that in Russia '[n]ow *we need action* and organization, not criticism and theory' (cited in Ascher 1967, p. 104). See also Akimov 1904–05 [1969], p. 314 and Jones 1984, p. 92.

77    Trotsky 1904.
78    Haimson 1955, p. 183.
79    Jones 2005, p. 118, Wynn 1987, p. 230, Sanders 1987, p. 169, Lane 1969, p. 101, and Hamm 2002, p. 64.
80    Glenny 1970, pp. 198–201 and РСДРП 1905 [1959], pp. 339–41, 349–52.

In numerous areas of the empire, however, the faction fight became bitter. But contrary to the historiographic myth that 1903 constituted Lenin's embryonic effort to build a 'party of a new type', it was almost always the Mensheviks who initiated a split in party organisations. In St. Petersburg, Odessa, Riga, Tiflis, and Baku, organisational battles were ferocious and all sides subsequently acknowledged that the 1904 rupture gravely damaged the RSDRP's political influence.[81] As Georgian Bolshevik Filipp Makharadze later acknowledged, 'without a doubt, the disagreements within and, then, the division of the party into two factions largely bore damage upon the development of the revolution'.[82]

Though the main fallout of the 1903 split was the RSDRP's loss of sway among ethnic Russian and Russianised workers, it also significantly hindered efforts to unify the empire's Marxist organisations of different nationalities. In 1904, the Latvian LSDSP affirmed that any push for a merger with their organisation would have to wait until the factional war between the Bolsheviks and Mensheviks was resolved.[83]

The RSDRP's organisational rupture hobbled various local committees in 1904 and 1905. A 1904 Bolshevik report complained to the Second International that 'the positive work of the Party is being hampered more and more' by the split.[84] Reports from St. Petersburg, Riga, and Ekaterinoslav to the Bolsheviks' 1905 congress laid out how factionalism had paralysed the committees and alienated workers just as the revolution had begun.[85] Non-Russian Marxist parties implored their Russian comrades to overcome what they saw as an unjustifiable and (to quote the PPS) 'scandalous' organisational rupture for the sake of the greater interests of the revolutionary struggle.[86]

Some significant practical differences between Bolsheviks and Mensheviks emerged during 1904–05, particularly regarding mass action as well as economic versus political demands. But these were differences primarily of emphasis and the two currents still agreed on the strategy of proletarian hegemony and the need for an armed anti-autocratic uprising.[87] Likewise, Bolshevik militants inside the labour movement evolved in the same general direction as

---

81      РСДРП 1905 [1959], p. 588, Jones 1984, pp. 104–28, Sanders 1987, pp. 168–9, and РСДРП 1905
        [1959], pp. 544–5.

82      Махарадзе 1927, p. 90.

83      Editorial appendix in Stučka 1904, p. 10.

84      Лядов 1904 [1933], p. 82.

85      РСДРП 1905 [1959], pp. 544–5, 593, 621–6.

86      Redakcyja 1905, p. 323.

87      Тютюкин 2002, p. 153.

their RSDRP rivals during the course of 1905. A real political convergence thus underlay the successful empire-wide drive in October–November 1905 by the RSDRP ranks and local cadre to immediately re-unify the party from below.[88]

In light of the two factions' re-unification in late 1905, it is worth asking whether the 1903 split had been either justified or principled. While much of the reorientation towards mass action advocated by Mensheviks in 1904–05 was vindicated by events, it is likely that they could have more successfully pushed for this as a tendency within a united RSDRP. Both sides stoked the factional fires, but the particular damage Menshevik leaders inflicted on the RSDRP by initiating the split likely outweighed their positive impact in the realm of tactics and strategy. A turn towards mass action was severely undermined by the ensuing factionalism, which drew cadre energy inwards. To quote St. Petersburg Bolshevik Secretary S.I. Gusev: 'workers were awaiting direction from our party ... but we wasted three quarters of our strength and time on the fight with the Mensheviks'.[89]

The emergence of separate organised factions after the Second Congress set into motion a dynamic that crystallised into a far more programmatically justifiable political split after the defeat of the 1905 revolution. Yet it is not clear that the 1903 rupture was a necessary precondition for the RSDRP's later bifurcation. Indeed, the experience of the early Menshevik-Bolshevik fight, combined with the political congruity of the two factions by late 1905, led many party militants to conclude that further organisational splits and hyper-factionalism must be avoided at all costs. The post-1905 surge of RSDRP 'non-factionalism' across the empire – often dismissed in socialist historiography as a dogmatic attachment to orthodox Marxism's supposed advocacy of a broad party – was rooted in this concrete experience.[90]

In the wake of the first Russian Revolution, scepticism and hostility from below to party splits and excessive factionalism became more widespread than ever, despite the fact that the actual strategic differences within the RSDRP were now becoming much more profound. One SR perceptively argued in 1909 that the Bolsheviks were like the 'boy who cried wolf': their 'too frequent' denunciations of the Mensheviks over the past years meant that people 'ceased

---

88   See, for example, Попов 1929, p. 57 and Morgan 1979, pp. 53, 76, 217.
89   Cited in Sanders 1987, p. 169.
90   The most common argument of non-factional Marxists after 1905 was simply that excessive factionalism undercut the party's effectiveness in action. See, for example, Trotsky 1907 [1994], p. 87.

to believe it' when they heard these same critiques today.[91] Trotsky likewise affirmed that the Bolsheviks had blunted the knife of polemic by brandishing it too much.[92]

Non-factionalism remained hegemonic inside the Russian Social Democracy for most of the pre-war period. This is especially evident when one takes into account the three borderland parties that affiliated to the RSDRP on a non-factional basis in 1906 (the SDKPIL, the Bund, and the LSDSP). In the face of this prevailing mood, it was difficult for Lenin and his closest allies to push for a definitive organisational split from the Menshevik 'liquidators' after 1912, even though the latter had made a sharp turn towards class collaborationism.

At risk of oversimplifying the post-1905 RSDRP's labyrinthine faction fight, the genesis of the 1912–14 divisions can be briefly sketched out. After 1905, Bolsheviks and Mensheviks functioned as distinct (if internally heterogeneous) ideological-political currents within an organisationally united RSDRP. From mid-1906 onwards, the party experienced growing conflicts over the organisational and political issues described in previous chapters. Despite serious efforts by all tendencies to build a united party – and despite the strong influence of conciliators within all wings – factional cleavages deepened between Mensheviks and Bolsheviks. One result was that maintaining functioning RSDRP leadership structures became a challenge after 1907, due as much to Menshevik intransigence as Lenin's initiatives.[93] By 1911, the top RSDRP leadership structures had imploded, sparking an array of efforts by various internal tendencies to re-cohere the party.

Developments were far muddier on the ground in Russia than abroad. Political delineations were weaker, non-factionalism remained widespread, and a scepticism bordering on hostility to émigré leaders was pervasive. To quote one Odessa worker in 1910:

> Every common worker was astonished at this fight between the two factions; astonished and alienated, since as workers we thirsted for active work but were forced to waste our energies on endless and useless polemics ... about whether Lenin said this or Martov said that.[94]

RSDRP committees remained united organisationally, if not politically, and the rebirth of a fighting workers' movement in 1911 provided a further impetus

---

91    Сапон 2009, pp. 472–3.
92    Trotsky 1907 [1994], p. 87.
93    Шелохаев 2008, pp. 15, 31.
94    Cited in Elwood 1970, p. 300.

to re-solidify the party. Nevertheless, the atomised state of the post-1907 Russian Social Democracy, plus the difficulties in coordinating illegal and legal work, meant that militants in the same city organisation nevertheless could often function independently from each other – or even at cross-purposes. And though the vast majority of SDs in imperial Russia affirmed the need to maintain illegal organisations – a stance unanimously confirmed at the January 1910 RSDRP Plenum – the influential liquidationist group headed by Alexander Potresov in St. Petersburg asserted that underground work was 'the figment of a diseased imagination'.[95]

It was in this context that Lenin and his closest Bolshevik comrades in the summer of 1911 began an organisational drive that culminated in the controversial January 1912 Bolshevik-led Prague conference. Though the majority of non-Bolshevik tendencies were not present in Prague, the conference nevertheless spoke in the name of the RSDRP as a whole and elected a new Central Committee. Rival currents denounced Prague as an illegitimate assembly that constituted a 'clear attempt at usurping the party banner'.[96] Against their detractors, the Bolsheviks replied that the Prague meeting was both constitutionally legal and politically necessary.

Lars Lih has shown that Lenin and the Bolsheviks in 1912 remained strategically committed to the German SPD model and that the Prague conference was not a purely Bolshevik meeting in design or in fact.[97] The organisers of the conference framed the event as non-factional and invited a wide range of other organised tendencies to participate: all three of the non-Russian SD organisations affiliated to the RSDRP, Trotsky's *Pravda* group, Plekhanov's 'Party-Mensheviks', the ex-Bolshevik *Vpered* group, and the Georgian Mensheviks. The goal was to end the RSDRP's impasse by solidifying a liquidationist free, multi-tendency party.[98]

Of the many non-Bolshevik invitees, only the Kiev and Ekaterinoslav committees led by Party-Mensheviks ended up participating. The Party-Menshevik delegates fought for their own political perspectives and they were elected to the new Central Committee. Moreover, the Prague conference neither called for a split in the RSDRP nor did it exclude most Mensheviks. It only affirmed that the group of liquidationists organised around the *Nasha Zaria* and *Delo Zhizni*

95    Cited in Jones 2005, p. 206.
96    'On the Prague Conference' [1917] in Elwood 1974a, p. 158.
97    Lih 2012a.
98    For the full minutes, as well as preparatory documents and correspondence, of the 1912 Prague conference as well as the rival 'August Bloc' conference in Vienna, see Шелохаев 2008.

journals 'has once and for all placed itself outside of the party'.[99] Lenin and his comrades argued that this expulsion did not contradict orthodox Marxist norms about tolerating political minorities so long as they respected majority decisions. Over and over, the Bolsheviks argued that the liquidationists had not only broken in practice with the unanimous 1910 Plenum decision to uphold illegal work, but they were acting against the very *existence* of the party, which under Tsarism must necessarily include underground organisation. In regard to the wide array of non-liquidationist, non-Bolshevik tendencies in the RSDRP, the Prague Conference posed a sharp alternative: work with us in re-cohering a united party or side with the liquidationists.

To be sure, Lenin's approach reflected an uncompromising streak and a willingness to risk organisational rupture that was not consistently shared by all Marxists of the era.[100] Yet as I have shown in earlier sections, such attributes were not uniquely 'Leninist' and in numerous instances – e.g. the 1903–05 RSDRP split or Luxemburg's anti-PPS crusade – they could be decidedly counterproductive.

Prague established a predominantly (not exclusively) Bolshevik Central Committee, but it took many more years before an analogous organisational cleavage became the norm within Russia. The importance of the Prague conference was *not* that it immediately constituted a Bolshevik party, but that it set into motion the orientation and structures that allowed Bolsheviks to build an independent mass party around their leadership.

Recognising the complex and drawn-out nature of the RSDRP split is not a secondary matter of historiographic quibbling. Claims that Lenin and his comrades broke from the rest of the party at Prague necessarily lead to a distorted analysis of post-1912 dynamics, obscuring the fact that it was the Bolsheviks' continued participation within a broader workers' party that enabled them to become politically hegemonic.

From 1912 onwards, key Bolshevik cadre, particularly in the capital, fought to build a clear political-organisational pole within imperial Russia. Yet their approach on the ground was sensitive to the rank and file's desire to maintain party unity. For the most part, Bolsheviks continued to function as an organised faction fighting for hegemony within the RSDRP's multi-tendency political archipelago. Their main publication was *Pravda* (The Truth) – an explicitly non-factional legal newspaper published jointly with Party-Mensheviks – that called for 'unity at all costs'.[101]

---

99    'On Liquidationism and the Group of Liquidators' [1917] in Elwood 1974a, p. 156.
100   Le Blanc 2014, p. 188.
101   Cited in Lih 2012a.

This stance was not a political ruse. Lending credence to the Bolsheviks' assertion that the liquidators were the real splitters, the first major rupture in the unity of the St. Petersburg RSDRP came at the initiative of right-wing Mensheviks, who in August 1912 established the newspaper *Luch* (Ray) as a rival to *Pravda*.[102]

As would be true in the following years, organisational rupture went furthest in the capital. An unparalleled concentration of liquidationists and Bolsheviks, combined with the unique explosiveness of the city's 1912–14 strike wave, helped clarify in practice the concrete political differences between these competing tendencies. Unlike its rival publications, *Pravda* upheld an intransigent class line, steadily winning it the support of Petersburg's radicalising workers. It is significant, however, that throughout the pre-war upsurge militant party members and workers generally did not self-identify as Bolsheviks, but rather as supporters of *Pravda* rather than *Luch*. Similarly, the election of Pravdaists to the leadership of the capital's trade union movement came through the vehicle of non-factional, class-struggle slates jointly built with left Mensheviks and non-factional SDs. Despite the generalised support for *Pravda*'s political line, Bolsheviks barely had anything resembling a coherent city-wide organisation. On the shop floor level – where the bulk of political organising took place – factional lines remained hazy.[103]

Efforts to build a united RSDRP under Bolshevik hegemony were widely disputed, including by *Pravda* supporters. Many SDs continued to criticise Bolshevik leaders for preventing what they still saw as a viable project of uniting all RSDRP tendencies. As long as the minority submitted to the majority, they argued, unity was feasible. Others like the influential non-factional St. Petersburg *Mezhraionka* group – founded by former Bolshevik cadre and other radicals in 1913 – rejected the possibility of unity with liquidationists, but felt that exaggerated factionalism was preventing a merger of the empire's revolutionary Marxists.[104] There was some truth to this. For instance, without demonstrating much knowledge about the particulars of the Polish workers' movement, Lenin denounced the PPS-Left in 1913 as 'not Social-Democratic *at all*'.[105] Generally, Lenin and the other Bolshevik 'hards' pushing for an immediate break with the liquidationists tended to underestimate the distinct rhythms of party polarisation in Russia's provinces and periphery, where there were

102    Swain 1983, p. 155.
103    Elwood 1974b, p. 230, Melancon 1990, p. 248, and Swain 1983, p. 183.
104    Thatcher 2009.
105    Lenin 1913 [1960–65], pp. 63–4.

far fewer crystallised class collaborators and where the strike wave had not advanced to the same level of militancy.

Outside of St. Petersburg the process of division remained incipient and convoluted. Indeed, the capital was the only city where Bolsheviks ran a separate slate in the late 1912 Duma elections – elsewhere they were elected on united platforms with the support of Mensheviks and non-factional SDs.[106] Joint Bolshevik-Menshevik committees still predominated in the provinces and borderlands. Sometimes these committees were in line with the letter and spirit of Prague. In Kiev, for instance, the Central Committee-affiliated RSDRP committee was led by Party-Mensheviks, including important future Bolshevik cadre such as Giorgi Piatakov. Hardly puppets of Lenin, these Kiev militants pushed against the Bolshevik leadership on a range of important issues in subsequent years, including on the national question and the viability of a proletarian-peasant government in Russia.[107]

Elsewhere, local Bolshevik leaders went further than their émigré leadership had projected in maintaining organisational unity. In Georgia, the Bolsheviks conciliated with their rivals, functioning as a minority tendency in joint committees with mainstream Mensheviks.[108] The Bolshevik-led Baku Committee remained united and, against the decisions of the Prague conference, called for a joint electoral campaign with right Mensheviks in the Duma elections. Historian I.S. Bagirova observes that 'in the national borderlands, and in Azerbaijan in particular, the final split in 1912 did not happen'.[109]

In St. Petersburg there was also much more conciliationism than Lenin hoped for, leading to considerable internal debate and tension. By the summer of 1914, Bolsheviks had taken some initial steps to fuse together a distinct revolutionary social democratic current, but political and organisational delineations within the Russian Social Democracy remained tangled and fluid. As one old Bolshevik quipped in the capital: 'We believe [in Prague] as Protestants do; we are prepared to pray on Sunday, but every other day of the week have to sin'.[110]

Only after considerable internal conflict was the émigré Bolshevik leadership able to convince Bolshevik MPs to split from their joint parliamentary fraction with the Mensheviks in November 1913. For their part, Moscow's Bolsheviks in June 1914 affirmed that though they agreed with the politics promoted by

106    Swain 1983, pp. 150–7 and Багирова 1997, p. 55.
107    On the pre-war Kiev Committee, see Солдатенко 2004, pp. 34–53.
108    Jones 2005, pp. 178–9, 221.
109    Багирова 1997, p. 55.
110    Cited in Swain 1983, p. 155.

the Central Committee, in their view it was necessary to call for a new RSDRP congress open to all factions that accepted illegal party work. In the last month before World War One, the Tsar's secret police lamented the resurgence of rank-and-file efforts to reunify the party.[111]

Before discussing the subsequent evolution of the RSDRP, it is worth considering the convergence of the Latvian Social Democracy and the Bolsheviks because this experience further demonstrates that there was no one-size-fits-all approach to effectively building a revolutionary party. And the Latvian organisation was hardly a marginal force: from 1912 through the February Revolution, it was the single largest underground Marxist current in the empire.[112] For their leading role in the October Revolution and the civil war, Latvia's SDs became known as the 'midwives of the revolution'.[113]

After 1905, the Latvian LSDSP consistently upheld political radicalism and organisational non-factionalism. But on the basis of its experiences working within the conciliatory 'August Bloc', it concluded by late 1913 that an organisational split from the Russian liquidationists was necessary. About half of the organisation's top leadership had by this time become politically close to the Bolsheviks, while the rest of the organisation remained non-factional. How to proceed in these circumstances was the central topic of debate at the Latvian organisation's tense January 1914 Fourth Congress in Brussels. Lenin personally attended and spoke at the assembly, in the hopes of convincing the LSDSP to affiliate with the Central Committee. Though Latvia's Bolshevik supporters won a slim majority of the leadership at the congress and disaffiliated from the August Bloc, they nevertheless refused to heed Lenin's call. Affiliation to the Central Committee, they argued, would likely result in a needless split of the LSDSP, which remained organisationally united and free of liquidationism.[114]

Following the congress, Lenin criticised the Latvian SDs for not having broken fully from what he saw as conciliationism. But as historian Vitālijs Šalda notes, the 'flexible tactics of the Bolsheviks in Latvia' were vindicated by subsequent events.[115] Rather than forcing through a split at this early juncture, Latvia's Bolshevik supporters raised the banner of organisational unity. During the war, they proceeded to consolidate their influence through the party structures and their control over the party press. Not until July 1917 did the Latvian Social Democracy decide to affiliate with the Bolshevik-led Central Committee.

---

111    Elwood 1972, Swain 1983, p. 177, Bonnell 1983, pp. 425–8, and Longley 1978, pp. 43, 350.
112    Ezergailis 1974, p. 7.
113    Solzhenitsyn 1973, p. 72.
114    Ripa and Apine, pp. 158–72, Ezergailis 1967, pp. 239–47, and Шалда 1989, pp. 93–148.
115    Шалда 1989, p. 148.

By this time, the differences between the RSDRP factions had become much clearer to all and Latvia's Bolsheviks succeeded in bringing over the LSDSP virtually en toto. But even after this affiliation, Latvia's Bolsheviks did not expel the Latvian Menshevik minority that remained in their organisation. Only in May 1918 was there a final organisational split with these Mensheviks.[116]

Upholding party unity, in short, was a powerful political weapon that could be effectively wielded by radical socialists no less effectively than moderates. In later years, Latvian Menshevik leader Fēlikss Cielēns argued that the 'biggest mistake' in his political career was having not pushed to cohere an independent organisation after Lenin's allies won the LSDSP majority in 1914. Without their own political expression, he lamented, Latvia's non-Bolshevik socialists had missed their opportunity to act as a viable alternative during the 1917 revolution.[117] In this sense, the difficulties of Latvia's Menshevik minority were not unlike those of leftists in the German SPD. For internal socialist minorities, there was never an easy solution to the dilemma of risking isolation from the mass of party members for the sake of establishing an independent political apparatus.

Like in Latvia, the split of the RSDRP after 1914 was protracted and uneven. Service notes that during the war the Bolsheviks 'had still not formed a fully separate party of their own'.[118] Whereas Mensheviks and SRs were divided between 'internationalists' and 'defencists', the Bolsheviks' homogenous commitment to class struggle politics set them apart from other participants in central Russia's anti-war bloc. Yet the large number of internationalist Mensheviks and non-factional SDs in Russia, combined with the urgency of organisational coordination in the face of the regime's sharp wartime repression, continued to mitigate against splits in RSDRP committees outside of Petrograd.[119]

Per the usual dynamic, divisions among émigré leaders were much deeper than among their comrades within Russia. Lenin after 1914 called for a complete organisational separation of revolutionaries from moderate socialists and vacillating 'centrists'. He and many others of the era saw this stance as marking a break with longstanding Marxist tradition.[120]

For the first time, leading Bolsheviks now argued that aspects of their particular organisational structure – namely, their split from 'opportunists' – should

---

116    Kalnins 1956, pp. 191–2, Ezergailis 1974, *passim*, and Ezergailis 1983, pp. 23–4, 79.
117    Cielēns 1961, p. 385.
118    Service 1979, p. 36.
119    Melancon 1990, p. 250.
120    Lenin 1915a [1960–65], p. 257.

be emulated internationally.[121] As such, I am unconvinced by Lars Lih's contention that this stance stood in continuity with orthodox Marxism.[122] Indeed, few political innovations proved to be as controversial as Lenin's call to split the Second International and its national affiliates. Before the October Revolution, even many of the most radical internationalists – including those opposed to the participation of class-collaborationist socialists inside the Marxist parties of Russia – remained reluctant to push through a definitive split in the old International.[123]

The Bolsheviks' worldwide call for opportunist-free revolutionary parties was not just a conjunctural response to the betrayals of the old leadership. This orientation was inextricable from a novel analysis of the social roots, weight, and role of socialist opportunism.[124] In 1916, Zinoviev noted that Marxism's approach to this critical issue had evolved: 'Naturally, the socialists long ago recognized the reactionary role of the labor bureaucracy, but not quite so clearly as they did after the salient lesson of August 4, 1914'. He argued that the Social Democratic leaders' capitulations were rooted in deep social processes, not 'a consciously perpetrated sell-out of the workers' interests'. Consciousness, he argued, 'is conditioned by existence, not vice versa. The entire social essence of this caste of labor bureaucrats led inevitably, through the outmoded pace set for the movement in the "peaceful" pre-war period, to the complete bourgeoisiefication of their "consciousness"'.[125] Polish Bolshevik supporter Karl Radek spelled out the strategic conclusions of this new analysis:

> Before the war we already knew that this policy [class collaborationism] was incompatible with socialism. But we thought that it resulted merely from the illusions of the leaders and that it would fade away under pressure of heightening class contradictions. Experience has shown that we were wrong. ... No matter how you dance around the question, a split is unavoidable.[126]

---

121   Lenin and Zinoviev 1915b [1960–65], p. 329.
122   Lih 2012b.
123   See, for example, the initial hesitations of the PPS-Left regarding a definitive international organisational split (Tych 1961b).
124   Lenin 1915a [1960–65], p. 244.
125   Zinoviev 1916. Zinoviev's novel analysis of bureaucratism intermingled with ill-founded theories about the supposed existence of a broader labour aristocracy corrupted by imperialist 'super-profits'.
126   Radek 1916 [1984], pp. 464, 467.

The political basis for Marxist organisational unity in Russia and abroad remained a point of sharp debate as Russia entered into 1917. In the wake of the February Revolution, the political dynamics inside RSDRP committees showed that most Bolshevik leaders and activists at this time did not consider a distinct Bolshevik party to be either desirable or necessary. Within all wings of the Russian Social Democracy across the empire, factional allegiances were still weak and hopes for a united revolutionary RSDRP remained widespread. In the spring of 1917, at least half (and probably more) of the RSDRP committees in Russia remained joint Bolshevik-Menshevik organisations.[127] As had been the case since 1914, there was a general internal Bolshevik leadership consensus against organisational unity with 'defencists', i.e. pro-war, class-collaborationist socialists. At the same time, there was considerable debate over how – and on what basis – to organisationally unite with left Mensheviks and non-factional internationalists.

Various writers have claimed that Bolsheviks advocated a merger with all Mensheviks before Lenin's arrival in April 1917. But in fact the vast majority of Bolshevik leaders in Russia explicitly opposed a merger with any defencist Mensheviks.[128] On 8 March 1917, even the Kiev Bolshevik organisation – a bastion of former Party-Mensheviks who would soon after lead a struggle against Lenin's 'April Theses' – declared: 'Full ideological and organisational separation from the social-chauvinists is [due to the need to fight the bourgeoisie and the war] therefore one of the main tasks of the Party'.[129]

Throughout March and April, Bolsheviks debated how broad or narrow the desired party of united internationalist Marxists should be. One of the most substantive yet understudied debates on organisational unity before Lenin's return took place at the first Moscow Bolshevik city-wide conference on 3–4 April 1917. Historian A.V. Sakhnin notes that the Moscow Bolsheviks 'had to decide on the question of unification independently, without the intervention of Lenin'. Sakhnin concludes that the 'symmetry' of the approaches taken in Petrograd and Moscow 'shows that the matter in both capitals was determ-

---

127   See, for example, Snow 1977, pp. 15–16, 43, 76–80, Oppenheim 1972, pp. 112–13, Najdus 1967, p. 172, Lysenko 2003, p. 51, Попов 1929, pp. 110–11, Бурджалов 1971, *passim*, and Шляпников 1925 [1994], pp. 205–8.

128   A.V. Sakhnin's recent study, based on extensive primary material, observes that 'almost none of the Bolshevik leaders spoke in favour of the unification of all Social-Democrats; they limited the scope of a possible unification to internationalists' (Сахнин 2010, p. 120). Contrast this with John Marot's unfounded claim that the perspectives of Mensheviks and 'Old Bolsheviks' were so similar in March that the latter looked to a 'reunification' with the former (Marot 2014, p. 163).

129   'Резолюция о текущем моменте' [1917] in Манилова 1928, p. 467.

ined by objective tendencies in the political environment in general and in the development of the Bolshevik Party in particular, and not the personal efforts of the party leader'.[130]

At the meeting, a small minority of Moscow militants argued in favour of an unconditional merger with the Mensheviks on the grounds that the pressure of the class struggle would inevitably oblige both factions to unite against capital. When one of these members announced that the division of the RSDRP had been caused by the secret police, the rest of the delegates let loose a barrage of protests and shouts of 'Down with them!' Like in Petrograd, advocates of unity at all costs were so marginal among the Bolsheviks that they saw the writing on the wall and immediately thereafter joined the Mensheviks.

A larger group of Moscow Bolshevik militants argued against a merger with *any* Mensheviks. In their view, all Mensheviks were traitors to the workers' cause, with whom unification would be 'a lie' that could only result in a new split. One delegate explained that it was impossible to unite with the Mensheviks because 'the present-day Mensheviks' now supported defencism. Conciliatory socialist advocates of unity, he argued, were 'wolves in sheep's clothing'.[131] But the vast majority of those present, including the top local Bolshevik leaders, supported a third position: unity with internationalist Mensheviks who agreed to a shared programme and platform concerning the major issues of the day, such as the war and the Provisional Government. Feliks Dzierżyński, present at the meeting as a representative of the SDKPIL, argued in favour of unity with those Mensheviks who agreed on fighting the war and the Provisional Government. Expressing the general sentiment, one Bolshevik leader concluded: 'We offer to unite with the revolutionary Mensheviks'.[132] A resolution along these lines was passed by the delegates.

Similarly, the late April Bolshevik empire-wide conference voted to reject organisational unity with the Menshevik majority that supported the war, the Provisional Government, and class collaboration. At the same time, the conference resolved that 'rapprochement and unification with groups and tendencies which really are internationalist [e.g. the Inter-District Committee] is necessary on the basis of a break with the policy of petty bourgeois betrayal of socialism'.[133]

---

130    Cited in Сахнин 2010, pp. 207, 210.
131    Cited in Сахнин 2010, pp. 208–9.
132    Cited in Сахнин 2010, pp. 209–10.
133    'On Uniting with the Internationalists against the Petty Bourgeois Defencist Bloc' [1917] in Elwood 1974a, p. 220.

Despite the unevenness of the Bolsheviks' organisational separation from the Mensheviks on the ground, their possession of some semblance of a distinct state-wide organisation was a critical advantage over Martov's Menshevik-Internationalists, who refused to organisationally split away from their defencist Menshevik comrades.[134] These organisational gains and delimitations provided Bolsheviks with the means to take the lead in coalescing a majority of RSDRP internationalists over the course of 1917.

The party that led the October Revolution, however, was not simply the product of the numeric expansion of the Bolshevik current. In addition to the fact that Bolshevism itself contained a wide variations of tendencies, Georges Haupt and Jean-Jacques Marie have shown how the Bolsheviks – including their organisation's top leadership – underwent a fundamental transformation in 1917 due to their unification with other Marxist currents: 'These revolutionaries were not simply absorbed by Bolshevism in 1917'.[135] An ability to avoid the crystallisation of a rigid, self-perpetuating leadership team was one of the secrets of Bolshevik success.

Moreover, far from insisting on the acceptance of all stances defended by their current since 1903, Bolsheviks in 1917 proposed organisational unity to all those SDs who stood against the Provisional Government, opposed the war, and called for a political break with the bourgeoisie. Robert Service notes that the 'Bolsheviks were not the jealously exclusive political sect of popular mythology; they were really much closer to being a catch-all party for those radical Social-Democrats who agreed about the urgent need to overthrow the liberal-dominated cabinet, establish a socialist government and end the war'.[136]

On this relatively ecumenical basis, the Polish SDKPIL, the Latvian LSDSP, and the Lithuanian SDs affiliated with Bolshevik-led RSDRP structures over the first half of 1917. Yet far from dissolving themselves into the latter, they retained the broad organisational autonomy of their local committees and leadership bodies; moreover, these currents frequently upheld important differences with the Bolsheviks on fundamental issues ranging from the national question to the

---

134    Israel Getzler notes that Martov's insistence on remaining in the Menshevik group 'boomeranged on his own Menshevik Internationalist faction, many of whose Petrograd members went with Larin – he claimed to have taken 1,000 workers with him – when he joined the Bolsheviks in late August in protest, as Martov put it, "against our coexistence with the defencists"' (Getzler 1994, p. 434).

135    Haupt and Marie 1974, pp. 22–3.

136    Service 1979, p. 49. See also Haupt and Marie 1974, pp. 22–5.

peasant struggle. Significantly, both the Lithuanian and Latvian organisations up through 1918 continued to include significant wings of Mensheviks within their ranks.[137]

Convinced through experience that the bulk of left Mensheviks were unwilling to break from the defencists, Trotsky and the *Mezhraiontsy* amalgamated with the Bolsheviks at the July–August Sixth Congress of the RSDRP. This crucial meeting was framed as, and seen by, Bolsheviks and revolutionary SDs across imperial Russia as constituting a unification congress of RSDRP internationalists, not the dissolution of other tendencies into the Bolsheviks. A wing of Menshevik-Internationalists also joined at the Sixth Congress, though to the disappointment of all (including Lenin) Martov was not among them.[138]

Outside of Petrograd and Moscow, the process of the Bolshevik-Menshevik split remained even more convoluted and drawn-out. Sharp political polarisation spread within the joint RSDRP committees after April, but a majority of Bolshevik cadre still held back from organisational separation. Partly this reflected a hope that the Mensheviks could be pushed or convinced to break with the bourgeoisie.[139] The widespread local refusal to immediately split away from joint committees in 1917 did not necessarily imply political moderation. Consider, for example, the case of the radical Ruienskaya RSDRP committee, which on 12 March 1917 demanded that the soviets take the full reins of governmental power. At the same time, it called for 'the merger of all the social democratic forces in Russia'. In its opinion, this unification 'should be based on the principles of revolutionary social democracy and the total subordination of the minority to the decisions of the majority'.[140]

Staying in joint committees was often simply a tactical question. Many Bolsheviks considered it a mistake to leave united committees before the political differences on the major issues of the day were clear to most party members. Such an act, they affirmed, would only needlessly marginalise radicals.[141] Experience across Russia demonstrated that this was an accurate judgement in many instances. For example, an attempt by a group of ultra-left Bolsheviks in Siberia to split from united committees in the spring was a resounding failure. In contrast, the rest of the region's Bolsheviks decided to remain in the joint

137 White 1990, Remeikis 1963, pp. 69, 78–80, 93, Najdus 1980, pp. 412–19, and Ezergailis 1974, *passim.*
138 Thatcher 2009, 'On Party Unification' [1917] in Elwood 1974a, p. 260, Service 1979, p. 49, and РСДРП (большевиков) 1917b [1958], pp. 69–72.
139 Service 1979, p. 53.
140 'Сообщение Руиенской социал-демократической' [1917] in Латвияс кп цк Партияс вēстурес институтьūц 1963, pp. 23–4.
141 See, for example, Raleigh 1981, p. 199 and Бурджалов 1971, pp. 256–7.

RSDRP bodies and win them over – which they did successfully over the coming months.[142] On the basis of similar examples, historian Edward Acton writes:

> For all Lenin's tactical skill, the notion that it was his flawless guidance which brought the party to victory is misleading. More than once the party's flexibility and the rank and file's readiness to respond more closely to the popular mood than to instructions from above saved the Bolsheviks from the potentially damaging consequences of tactical decisions made at the centre. Widespread working-class hostility to factionalism, for example, encouraged party activists to ignore the official decision in April to sever links with Mensheviks and abandon 'joint' Bolshevik-Menshevik committees. In many areas it was only once the Mensheviks' identification with the policies of the Provisional Government had brought home the profound differences between the two social democratic parties that the break was made.[143]

As Acton notes, the single most important turning point in the 1917 separation of the RSDRP came when moderate socialists entered into the Provisional Government in May. Political divides now turned into organisational splits across Russia. In Georgia, for instance, the Bolsheviks broke away in June, arguing that the Mensheviks advocated revolutionary defencism, failed to see the capitalist class as counter-revolutionary, and rejected granting all power to the soviets. In Baku, the minority of defencist Mensheviks split away on opposite grounds. Similar summertime splits occurred in Nikolaev, Poltava, Minsk, and Krasnoyarsk, among other important proletarian centres. Crucially, these ruptures frequently pitted defencists against all the internationalists (Bolsheviks, left Mensheviks, non-factional revolutionary SDs, and non-Russian currents). United RSDRP committees affiliated with the (Bolshevik-led) Central Committee were thereby established.

Yet in much of the rest of the empire, the first organisational splits only came in the fall. Various important RSDRP committees – including in Odessa, Omsk, Riazan, and Penz – broke up in October itself. And in Mogilev, Vologda, and elsewhere, an organisational break only occurred after the October Revolution.[144]

---

142   Snow 1977, pp. 79–81, 121–2. In the face of such an approach, it was often the Mensheviks across Russia who took the initiative to split local committees during 1917.

143   Acton 1990, p. 147. See also Snow 1977, p. 122.

144   Jones 1984, p. 320, Suny 1972a, pp. 95–7, Дементьев 2013, p. 204, Bojcun 1985, p. 290, Манусевич 1965, p. 146, Lande 1974, p. 12, and Najdus 1967, p. 198.

Given the relatively wide range of currents associated with the Bolshevik-led RSDRP, and the grey areas of its organisational genesis, it is not surprising that there was considerable confusion about what to call it in 1917.[145] Up through the fall, Bolsheviks and Mensheviks both spoke in the name of the RSDRP – the official name of the Bolshevik leadership was still simply the Central Committee of the Russian Social Democratic Workers Party. This dynamic has been obscured by the tendency of historians to refer to 'the Bolshevik Party', even though this term was only very rarely used by radicals in 1917. No less anachronistic are historiographic references to the 'RSDRP (b)', a title projected backwards by Soviet historians even though it does not appear in the texts or speeches of the period.[146] As late as the July–August 1917 Sixth Congress of the party, local branches affiliated with the Bolsheviks overwhelmingly persisted in calling themselves simply committees of the RSDRP. And the term Bolshevik was conspicuously absent in either the names of their organisations or their party pronouncements.[147]

The relative absence of factional identification in 1917 was not a tactical manoeuvre. Rather, it reflected the fact that Bolsheviks saw themselves – and *acted* – as an orthodox Marxist current seeking to unite all class-struggle SDs in a joint party under a common platform.

The empire-wide experiences of 1917 show that political leadership by organised Marxists was critical for successful anti-capitalist revolutions. Yet developments outside of central Russia should caution us not to over-generalise lessons from the history of the Bolsheviks alone.

In this chapter we saw how Poland demonstrated that narrower political contours for a socialist party did not guarantee success. Finland, likewise, illustrated that the presence of moderate socialists in a broader party did not automatically lead to the hegemony of class collaborationism. The advisability of mergers or splits – and the viability of narrower or broader programmatic bases for a party – depended on concrete conjunctures and the relationship of forces between moderates and revolutionaries. Finnish radicals were able to take over and transform a non-revolutionary party; that their German counterparts failed to do the same did not mean that this strategy was inherently flawed. Similarly,

145    In the April 1917 debates, Lenin had pushed to change the RSDRP's name to the Communist Party. But Lenin's call was not accepted since Bolshevik cadre insisted that the term Social Democrat continued to be an attractive one to radicalised workers in Russia, unlike in the rest of Europe where it was associated with support for the war.
146    Тарасов 2014, p. 4.
147    РСДРП (большевиков) 1917b [1958], pp. 319–90. See also Lih 2012c.

the PPS-Left's push to unify Marxist organisations in Poland was reasonable – but analogous efforts inside the RSDRP after 1906 were probably doomed to fail.

Bolshevism's convoluted genesis hardly confirms widespread Leninist assumptions that the secret to Marxist success was a refusal to participate in the same party as right-leaning social democrats. Splits were sometimes fruitful, other times not. For instance, the 1903–05 Bolshevik-Menshevik rupture was mostly counterproductive, unlike the slow 1912–17 breakup of the RSDRP into separate organisations.

For those seeking to generalise from the experience of imperial Russia, the most significant political lesson is that the rise of the Bolsheviks as well as the *Siltasaarelaiset* in Finland was made possible by patiently organising as a Marxist tendency within a broader workers' party. Poland, in turn, showed that the establishment of a moderate-free party was not a political panacea.

Though Russia's radicals did not radically break with revolutionary social democratic strategy, there *were* important evolutions within their party-building approaches before the October Revolution. A novel appraisal of the role and weight of opportunism in political democracies, for instance, was a significant theoretical change for the international socialist movement after 1914. And the capitulations of labour officialdoms during the war convinced many revolutionaries to more consistently and coherently organise themselves as a distinct current, capable of challenging for leadership. This shift, however, not infrequently pushed radicals after 1917 to excessively emulate the party 'model' – and strategic orientation – that they believed had been vindicated by the October Revolution.[148]

Contrary to a common Leninist view that the Bolsheviks discovered a timeless formula for socialist political-organisational demarcation, the available evidence hardly demonstrates the need to maintain discrete parties of revolutionaries at all times and places. To the contrary, in autocratic as well as parliamentary contexts across imperial Russia, the influence of Marxists hinged on their ability to be the best builders of a wider workers' party. Proactively promoting class formation and working-class unity through a multi-tendency political instrument subjected socialists to a variety of moderating pressures and strategic dilemmas. But that was a necessary trade-off for anchoring their project in the class as it actually was, not as they wished it might be.

148    For a critique, see Miliband 1989, pp. 61–7.

# CHAPTER 8

# Democracy, the State, and the Finnish Revolution

Ever since the publication of V.I. Lenin's influential polemic *The State and Revolution* in 1918, Karl Kautsky's views on this topic have often been equated with gradualism and parliamentarism. Lenin's pamphlet has cast a long shadow backward, leading many academics and activists to assert that the fatal flaw in Second International Marxism was a reformist approach to socialist transformation.

To quote radical scholar Paul Blackledge, 'the practice of these [non-Bolshevik Second International] socialist parties was informed by an important break with Marx's theory of the state'. Kautsky is castigated for this detour into 'social democratic reformism' since he 'subordinate[d] all politics to parliamentarianism such as to effectively excuse the way German social democracy became tied to the German capitalist state in the decades leading up to 1914'.[1] Whereas the Bolsheviks were able to lead workers to power because they were 're-armed' in April 1917 with Lenin's new theory of state and revolution, the German SPD thus entered into – and propped up – the capitalist state in 1918–19.

Such critiques are premised on a fundamentally inaccurate account of orthodox Marxism's approach to the capitalist state and socialist revolution. As the 1917–18 Finnish and Russian revolutions attest, revolutionary social democracy proved to be a sufficiently radical political foundation for imperial Russia's socialists to lead the twentieth century's first anti-capitalist seizures of power.

This chapter examines orthodox Marxist approaches to democracy, the capitalist state and socialist revolution under parliamentary conditions. Though we review the perspectives of Marxists across Russia, as well as Germany, our focus is on Finland as this was the only part of Russia with a democratically elected parliament and political freedom. The book's final two chapters, in turn, will analyse how socialists operating elsewhere in the empire articulated and implemented the orthodox Marxist strategy on state and revolution for the exceptional context of Tsarist absolutism.

Revolutionary social democrats in the Second International explicitly rejected the view that capitalist states were neutral instruments capable of being wielded for gradual socialist transformation. According to orthodox

---

1 Blackledge 2011 and Blackledge 2013. See also Gluckstein 2014.

Marxists, political democracy was severely curtailed under capitalist parliamentary regimes due to the economic power of big business, the growth of unelected governmental bureaucracies, and the spread of state militarism. To establish genuine parliamentarism and a real democratic republic, in their view, required not only the overthrow of monarchies, but also profound governmental democratisation and the dissolution of the state's existing armed bodies. As such, the proletariat's struggle for political democracy – i.e. the radical restructuring of the current state – would constitute a bridge between today's struggles and the fight for anti-capitalist rupture.

According to Kautsky and his comrades, it was an illusion to believe that socialism could be reached simply by winning a parliamentary majority and through a piecemeal conquest of state institutions – only a revolution could break the hold of the bourgeoisie. No less importantly, orthodox Marxists were opposed on principle to the establishment of liberal-socialist coalition governments. After the overthrow of Tsarism in February 1917, this became perhaps the most decisive socialist conflict over political power in both Finland and central Russia.

The history of the Finnish Social Democracy, as we will see, disproves widespread claims about the opportunism of 'Second International Marxism'. Indeed, the experience of the Finnish Revolution of 1917–18 in many ways confirms Marxist orthodoxy's traditional view on state and revolution. On this question, like so many others, the Finnish SDP constitutes a better case for examining the theory and practice of revolutionary social democracy than its bureaucratised sister party in Germany.

Through patient class-conscious organisation and education, Finnish socialists won a parliamentary majority in the 1916 elections. After Tsarism's overthrow in February 1917, orthodox SDP leaders sought to use Finland's parliament and their popular electoral mandate to push through a series of radical democratic and social reforms. In response, Finnish and Russian ruling elites arbitrarily dissolved Finland's parliament, setting the stage for a socialist-led revolutionary uprising in January 1918. To quote Finnish scholar Risto Alapuro, the 'ballot box did not prove to be the coffin of revolutionaries, as so often has been argued. In Finland's case the ballot box turned out to be their cradle'.[2]

---

2   Alapuro 2011, p. 143.

## 1    Critique of Bourgeois Democracy

It is ironic that Kautsky is today associated with a gradualist vision of social-ist transformation, since for many decades his contemporaries justifiably saw him as the foremost advocate of the exact opposite position. In the early Second International's ongoing debates between 'orthodoxy' and 'revisionism', Kautsky was without a doubt the most influential theorist of a ruptural anti-capitalist approach. When practical tensions emerged between the exigencies of parlia-mentary compromise and the long-term project of class intransigence, Kautsky consistently opted for the latter.

'Revisionists', in contrast, were pragmatists and gradualists. Put briefly, they were more consistently focused on winning immediate reforms and they believed that social justice could be reached through the existing parliament, the extension of democratic rights, and the steady spread of public services, co-ops, and working-class organisations. A slow transition towards socialism would take place without the need for extra-parliamentary mass action or a rupture with state institutions and the capitalist class. In other words, in con-ditions of political freedom and parliamentary democracy there was no need for a revolution.[3]

For reasons discussed in earlier chapters, moderate socialism did not gain a wide base of support in Russia. Though the empire's Marxists were often quick to charge their factional opponents with revisionism, political debate on the transformation of (or participation within) capitalist states was not directly rel-evant to the context of Tsarist absolutism. In the absence of political freedom or parliamentary democracy, each of the early illegal Marxist parties agreed that the existing state had to be smashed through violent revolution. In 1903, the Polish Socialist Party noted that, unlike in Western Europe, 'the socialist parties of all nationalities in Russia agree that the first step must be to lead a violent revolution to clear away the main obstacle – Tsarism'.[4]

Reading pre-1918 history through the lens of Lenin's *The State and Revolution* has problematically obscured the main political debates in the Russian Empire. There were no major conflicts between Marxists over the gradual transforma-tion of the Russian state, because all orthodox social democrats saw the need to violently overthrow Tsarist absolutism. Until February 1917, the main contro-versy on state power in imperial Russia was between the socialist call to win a democratic republic through armed struggle and the liberal advocacy of estab-

---

3    Steger 1997b.
4    A.W. 1903, p. 247.

lishing a constitutional monarchy through peaceful pressure tactics. Only after the Tsar's overthrow and the establishment of the Provisional Government did the question of how to relate to a bourgeois regime become a pressing issue. And, as we will see in the next chapter, the autocratic legacy weighed heavy even after the toppling of Tsarism in February 1917, as Russia remained without a parliament or a democratically elected government.

It was only in the autonomous grand duchy of Finland – the one region of the Russian Empire with a legitimate parliament, political freedom, and a legal socialist party – where moderate socialist state perspectives were influential and a question of practical politics under Tsarist rule. Before the 1905 revolution, orthodox Marxists were a rarity and class collaborationism was widespread, with the founding 1899 programme of the Finnish Workers Party even eschewing any call for the conquest of power. Instead, its leaders declared the need to 'strive for participation in the power in the communal and state field'.[5]

Party chairman N.R. af Ursin insisted that evolution, not revolution, was the only viable path for progressive social change. Another important early Finnish socialist leader, Taavi Tainio, claimed that all social democratic parties in the world stood by purely legal means and oriented towards passing reforms through parliament. This early generation of Finnish socialist leaders categorically rejected the use of violence to reach a new society.[6]

Such gradualist views were rejected by orthodox Marxists across imperial Russia and Europe. Capitalist democracies, in their view, fell far short of being fully democratic and truly parliamentary regimes. Pēteris Stučka posited that no Western democracy had implemented anything beyond 'incomplete' political freedom.[7] One central reason for this was that the influence of the capitalist class undermined the democratic political process. As long as industry remained in private hands, political democracy would necessarily be stunted by the ruling rich.[8]

No less contradictory with democracy was the growth of the state bureaucracy. Revolutionary SDs argued that the increased power of the executive branch and non-elected governmental bodies was significantly undermining democratically elected parliaments. In a 1903 article on the political relevance of the 1871 Paris Commune, PPS theoretician Stanisław Mendelson explained that modern representative bodies could no longer impose their will on the

---

5   Cited in Martin 1971, p. 248.
6   Rahikainen 1986, Soikkanen 1961, p. 103, Kujala 1995, p. 140, and Soikkanen 1961, p. 253.
7   Stučka 1905a [1976–78], p. 128.
8   Kautsky 1905 [2018], p. 177.

executive branch or check 'the growing power of the state'.[9] Ten years earlier, Kautsky likewise argued that 'one of the most important tasks of the working class in its struggle for the achievement of political power is not to eliminate the representative system, but to break the power of government vis-à-vis the parliament'.[10] To combat political bureaucratisation, the *Erfurt Programme* – as well as subsequent orthodox Marxist party programmes in Tsarist Russia – called for the election of *all* state officials and the establishment of broad local self-government.[11]

Orthodox Marxists underscored another major threat to democracy: the massive expansion of the state's armed forces, a phenomenon referred to at the time as 'militarism'. In 1904, for example, Marian Bielecki of the PPS argued that the 'ominous growth of militarism' precluded the peaceful utilisation of Europe's bourgeois democratic regimes for socialist transformation.[12] Indeed, the fight against militarism played a prominent role in Marxist strategy across Europe and Russia. All orthodox socialist parties in the Tsarist Empire prominently demanded the dissolution of the standing army and its replacement by a militia. The Revolutionary Ukrainian Party's 1903 minimum programme typically proclaimed that 'we must destroy the present standing army and establish a people's militia'.[13]

Given the anti-democratic nature of modern governments, Kautsky concluded that most existing state forms and institutions – with the important exception of democratically elected parliaments – could not be utilised by a proletarian government for socialist transformation:

> The proletariat, as well as the petty bourgeoisie, will never be able to rule the state through these institutions. This is not only because the officer corps, the top of the bureaucracy and the Church have always been recruited from the upper classes and are joined to them by the most intimate links. It is in their very nature that these institutions of power strive to raise themselves above the mass of the people in order to rule them, instead of serving them, which means they will almost always be anti-democratic and aristocratic.[14]

---

9   Mendelson 1903. See also Stučka 1905a [1976–78], p. 100 and Kautsky 1905 [2018], p. 222.

10   Kautsky 1893 [2018], p. 155.

11   Kautsky 1892 [1910] and, for example, 'Latviešu Sociāldemokrātiskās Strādnieku Partijas Programa' [1904] in Latvijas KP CK Partijas Vēstures Institūts 1958, p. 13.

12   Bielecki 1904a, p. 157.

13   Гермайзе 1926, p. 171.

14   Kautsky 1905 [2018], pp. 191–2.

Put simply, revolutionary social democrats denounced all existing capitalist states for being insufficiently democratic. And in their place, orthodox Marxists called for the establishment of democratic republics.

The concept of a republic has become associated over the past century with bourgeois democracy and the simple absence of a monarchy. But for revolutionary social democrats, republicanism was a radical and ultimately anti-capitalist perspective. Unlike post-1917 Leninist followers of *The State and Revolution*, orthodox Marxists saw local governments and parliaments elected by universal suffrage as pivotal working-class conquests that could and should become cornerstones of governance under workers' rule.

Similarly, they placed a central strategic focus on running in elections and fighting to democratise the current regime, with the goal of increasing the political strength and confidence of the working class. Though they were suspicious of practical parliamentary compromises, rather than attempt to delegitimise the entire existing state, revolutionary social democrats sought to lean on and expand the power of its elected representative bodies to undermine both big business and unelected anti-democratic state structures.

At the same time, orthodox SDs argued that 'real parliamentarism' could only be established once workers took power, since the powers of existing parliamentary bodies were so significantly curtailed under capitalism.[15] In the 1906 words of the Georgian Marxist newspaper *Akhali tskhovreba* (The New Age): 'There exists no democratic republic anywhere in Europe today'.[16] Kautsky likewise argued that although the American and French governments claimed to be republics, they were not so in reality. Far more than simply eliminating the monarchy, a true republic meant radically restructuring the entire political regime by dissolving the standing army, electing all state officials, devolving administrative powers to local self-government, and subordinating 'all members of representative bodies to the control and discipline of the organised people'.[17]

Under the influence of Lenin's *The State and Revolution*, many writers have incorrectly claimed that the goal of building a government on the model of the 1871 Paris Commune was rejected by Second International socialists. But calls to emulate the Commune were raised well before 1917. In 1903, for example, Stanisław Mendelson's long piece on the Paris Commune concluded that the Parisian workers' regime 'illustrated the path down which the political devel-

15   See also Stučka 1905a [1976–78], p. 129.
16   Cited in Van Ree 2000, p. 35.
17   Kautsky 1905 [2018], p. 225 and Kautsky 1905 [2018], p. 259.

opment of all societies must go'.[18] Arguing that no Western republic 'is democratic in the proper sense of the word', Latvian socialist Jānis Bērziņš-Ziemelis explained that the socialist ideal was a republic on the model of the Paris Commune.[19] And during the 1905 revolution, SDs across Russia, from Trotsky to Stalin, declared that the Paris Commune demonstrated the form that the dictatorship of the proletariat should take.[20]

Historian Ben Lewis' pioneering research has demonstrated that Kautsky was no exception when it came to pointing to the Paris Commune.[21] As a model for 'the ideal of the democratic republic', Kautsky's 1904–05 essays on this topic explicitly highlighted the Commune as a template for socialist governance.[22] Kautsky cited and praised Marx's 'classical description' of the Commune, with its famous call for the 'destruction of the state power': 'While the merely repressive organs of the old governmental power were to be amputated, its legitimate functions were to be wrested from an authority usurping preeminence over society itself, and restored to the responsible agents of society'.[23] Unlike Lenin after 1917, however, Kautsky upheld Marx's vigorous advocacy of universal suffrage.

To be sure, prior to late 1917 the specific form to be taken by 'the dictatorship of the proletariat' was not a central topic of discussion. But on the crucial point of militarism, orthodox state perspectives were clear and consistent: all revolutionary social democrats insistently called for the breakup of the existing military machine. This consensus has received surprisingly little attention by scholars and socialists, even though the question of state and revolution ultimately comes down to which social class can wield a monopoly of violence in society. A myopic historiographic focus on the terms of debate set by Lenin in 1917 regarding state forms – parliamentary or soviet, centralised or decentralised, with or without the old state functionaries – has obscured the longstanding orthodox Marxist stance on the military. Yet this was hardly a secondary topic, because, to quote Kautsky, the army was 'the most important' means of rule.[24] As Marx had stressed, and Kautsky

18    Mendelson 1903.
19    Cited in Treijs 1981, p. 188.
20    Stalin 1906–07 [1953–55], p. 368 and Trotsky 1905 [2009], p. 518.
21    See, for example, Lewis 2011. I would like to thank Lewis for allowing me to quote from an advance copy of his translated collection of Kautsky's writings on republicanism (Lewis 2018).
22    Kautsky 1905 [2018], p. 286.
23    Kautsky 1905 [2018], p. 214.
24    Kautsky 1905 [2018], p. 224.

positively reiterated, the demand for the standing army's elimination and its replacement by a popular militia was 'the first decree of the [Paris] Commune'.[25]

Revolutionary socialists saw the growth of militarism as one of the fundamental trends of modern capitalism and *the* major threat to democracy. A call to arm the people and end the standing military was therefore a central plank in the *Erfurt Programme* and for the German SPD in general.[26]

German revisionists called on the party to drop this stance, prompting a major debate between Kautsky and his opponents in *Die Neue Zeit* during 1899. These early attempts to reverse the party's anti-militarist stance failed. But by the time of the German Revolution of 1918–19, the SPD had definitively shelved the orthodox position. Historians have documented how the German SPD responded to the outbreak of the workers' and soldiers' uprising in November 1918 by defending and upholding the German military over the following months.[27] Without this Social Democratic support, German capitalism may not have survived.

Experience in 1905 and 1917 in Russia would also show that breaking up the ruling class military machine constituted a necessary component of establishing *any* form of workers' government. While Lenin and his comrades' later views on the form of proletarian and peasant rule – in regard to utilising old state functionaries, levels of centralisation, the role of parliamentary institutions, etc. – evolved quite dramatically during and after 1917, the political constant underlying all of their stances was that the state's existing repressive apparatus must be eliminated.[28] This remained the party's orientation well after the October Revolution.[29]

Unlike in the rest of Russia, it took the socialist movement in Finland many years to adopt an orthodox approach to militarism. When the Finnish Work-

25    Kautsky 1905 [2018], p. 213.
26    Stargardt 1994, pp. 45–6 and Luxemburg 1899 [1971], p. 147.
27    Broué 2005.
28    'On the Provisional Government' [1917] in Elwood 1974a, p. 205.
29    The influential 1919 Communist treatise *The ABC of Communism* explained: 'Since the main strength of the government resides in the army, if we wish to gain victory over the bourgeoisie the first essential is to disorganize and destroy the bourgeois army' (Bukharin and Preobrazhensky 1919 [1970], p. 128). Significantly, the call in Lenin's *The State and Revolution* to immediately smash the old (non-military) state bureaucracy had been dropped by this time. The authors explained: 'Of course the new power takes over some of the constituent parts of the old, but it uses them in a different way' (ibid.). See also 'The Workers' Government' [1922] in Communist International 1922 [2011], p. 1159.

ers Party was founded in 1899, its moderate programme omitted any calls for a militia or ending the standing army.[30] In 1903, the Finnish party's first programmatic step towards revolutionary social democracy was reflected in its formal adoption of the orthodox Marxist opposition to a standing army. Nevertheless, revolutionary social democratic positions remained a definite minority within the SDP until 1906.

Stances on the army and armed struggle became a pressing issue for the first time in Finland during the 1905 Great Strike, which witnessed the creation of a 'National Guard' and its rapid split into contending bourgeois and proletarian defence squads. Soon after, the SDP – under pressure from below and from the orthodox *Siltasaarelaiset* – approved the official founding of a Finnish workers' militia, the *punakaarti* ('Red Guards'). Testifying to their historic importance, it was from the Finnish *punakaarti* that the Russian Red Guards of 1917 took their name.[31]

In 1906, the *Siltasaarelaiset* aimed to bolster the ideological case for the thousands-strong Red Guards and they sought to explain how such groups fit into revolutionary social democratic strategy. That year, Otto Kuusinen wrote an important article on popular militias and his young orthodox comrades translated and published August Bebel's classic 1898 pamphlet, 'Not a Standing Army, but a People's Army!' Whereas the SDP's moderate wing argued against the use of violence on principle and rejected an orientation towards a revolutionary rupture, the *Siltasaarelaiset* loudly affirmed the orthodox Marxist rejection of pacifism and perpetual gradualism.[32]

This radicalism was not merely rhetorical. In addition to their support for the Red Guards, Kuusinen and other *Siltasaarelaiset* leaders in mid-1906 founded a clandestine revolutionary body to distribute arms, print and publish illegal material, and collaborate with the RSDRP. The goal was to help prepare for an impending empire-wide revolution and to give an organised expression to the inclinations of a growing minority of radicalised workers and soldiers in Finland to push for revolutionary action.[33]

The upswell came to a head in July 1906, when a rebellion of Russian soldiers broke out in the Sveaborg naval base outside of Helsinki. Russian SDs and SRs operating at Sveaborg had been jointly planning a mutiny for months, but the action spontaneously broke out ahead of schedule. A few hundred of the

---

30    Suomen Työväenpuolueen 1899, p. 30.
31    Salkola 1985, p. 103.
32    Kuusinen 1906, Soikkanen 1961, p. 332, and Carrez 2008, pp. 190–1.
33    Kujala 1981 and Carrez 2008, pp. 203–4.

most militant Finnish Red Guards took up arms in support, but the mutiny was ill-timed and poorly organised. The Finnish SDP leadership did not call for participation in the action, which it accurately judged to have little chance to succeed. Historian Antti Kujala sums up the dynamic as follows: 'Through their impatience the soldiers ruined their initially modest chances for success, just as happened in many other individual military disturbances. ... The Sveaborg rebellion was crushed after having lasted less than three days'.[34]

The regime's violent suppression of a premature armed rebellion left a significant imprint on Finland's orthodox Marxists – Kautsky's stress on the importance of preliminary organisational build-up and his warnings about the dangers of precipitous action seemed to be vindicated. In the years following the crushing of the Sveaborg rebellion, the *Siltasaarelaiset* placed an increased tactical stress on parliamentary, educational, and organisational activities. Nevertheless, they continued to affirm that the path of Finnish workers to liberation passed through a revolution that would have to resort, if necessary, to force.[35]

SDP members and leaders were highly critical of the limitations of the Finnish parliament. In the labour press, they highlighted the democratic deficiencies of Finland's elected representative body in comparison with Western Europe's parliaments – not to mention a socialist parliamentary republic. The Russian regime dissolved the Finnish parliament on multiple occasions and vetoed numerous legislative acts – e.g. the establishment of compulsory education and the election of local governments, which would have allowed socialists to win decision-making power on a local level.[36] Even legislation regulating working conditions was unable to get through. Soikkanen rightly points to these anti-democratic restrictions and the Tsar's frequent dissolutions of parliament as a major reason why 'revisionism' and class collaboration failed to grow deep roots in Finland:

> The blocking of legislative reform by the autocracy prevented the introduction of several important measures which could have significantly strengthened the reformist case. The Emperor's unwillingness to give his assent to the legislation reforming the structure of local government denied local leaders and party activists the opportunity to play a part

---

34    Kujala 1989, pp. 323–4.
35    Soikkanen 1978, p. 348.
36    Singleton and Upton 1988, pp. 97–102. For the post-1906 SDP debates on how to relate to the Finnish parliament, see Carrez 2008, *passim*.

> in local decision-making ... [which is] almost essential as the first step
> towards a reformist policy.[37]

It was only after the overthrow of Tsarism in February 1917 that most workers
and socialists felt that the Finnish parliament finally had the power to usher
in deep social transformation. Nevertheless, Finland's elected representative
body from 1907 through 1916 was qualitatively different than the Russian State
Duma, the sham parliament set up by the Tsar in the rest of the empire after
1905. First of all, the existence of basic political freedoms and the fact that Finland's parliament was elected by universal suffrage gave it considerable legitimacy in the eyes of the population. Furthermore, unlike the Duma, Finland's
parliament did succeed in passing some significant social legislation, including
most importantly the tenancy act of 1909 that obliged big landowners to pay
their tenant farmers when the latter made improvements to the farms. Finally,
the parliament's constant battles to affirm its autonomy against the Tsarist state
provided it with continued mass popular support despite its relatively weak
record in implementing reforms.[38]

Before we turn our attention to orthodox conceptions of socialist revolution,
it is worth underlining that the revolutionary social democratic perspective on
republican democracy contradicts the claim that Second International Marxism envisioned no bridge between its minimum and maximum programmes.
Historian Pierre Broué, for instance, argued that 'this separation was to dominate the theory and practice of social democracy for decades'.[39] There is much
merit to this criticism in regard to moderate socialists and bureaucratised
labour leaderships. But orthodox social democrats did in fact articulate what
would later become known as a 'transitional' approach. They argued that given
the increasingly anti-democratic orientation of the bourgeoisie, the fight for
political democracy would place the working class on a collision course with
not only constitutional monarchies, but with capitalist rule itself.[40]

According to orthodox SDs, the most ambitious democratic planks of the
minimum programme such as the elimination of the standing army could most
likely only be won through socialist revolution. PPS leader Maksymilian Horwitz noted in 1906 that a 'large number of the demands of the minimum programme consciously violate ... the principles of the current capitalist state'. In

---

37    Soikkanen 1978, p. 356. Local democratic governance was also restricted in Germany,
      where socialists were generally banned from election to executive office.
38    On Finland's parliament between 1907 and 1916, see Tuominen 1958.
39    Broué 2005, p. 17.
40    Kautsky 1893 [2018], p. 169.

his view, the full implementation of political republicanism 'will not be possible before the complete abolition of capitalism'.[41] Against Rosa Luxemburg's argument that Polish independence should not be demanded because it was unachievable under the current system, Kautsky replied that by the same logic the SPD would have to drop its demands for a democratic republic and the election of all state officials.[42] Marxists, he insisted, should raise demands like the establishment of an armed militia, notwithstanding their likely incompatibility with the current order.[43] In short, the fight for democracy constituted a revolutionary bridge between today's struggles and the working-class conquest of power.

## 2      The Socialist Revolution

Contrary to what has often been claimed, orthodox social democrats did not argue that parliaments under capitalism could be utilised for a gradual transition to socialism. This was especially true in Germany, where the existing parliament was given so few powers that it could barely pass significant national reforms, let alone legislate a break from capitalism.

Marxists repeatedly lambasted the belief that all it would take to get to socialism was electing a socialist majority to the existing state. In a 1906 editorial titled 'Parliamentary Struggle Is Good, But Not Enough On Its Own', Otto Kuusinen polemicised with his socialist SDP rivals who 'unilaterally' focused on parliamentarism. Against this orientation, Kuusinen insisted that electoral campaigns and parliamentary activity did not make 'subversive activity' unnecessary. The purpose of parliamentarism, like trade unionism, was above all 'to prepare [the proletariat] for the final social revolution'.[44]

The 1900 programme of the SDKPIL succinctly summed up the orthodox consensus:

> The state today is an organisation which is at the service of capital, its every move is dictated by the interests of capital; governments today only implement the will of the capitalist class. The task, therefore, of the working class must be to abolish this form of state, to wrest the state from the hands of capitalism, to transform it in such a way so that it can begin to

---

41      Horwitz 1906b, p. 7.
42      Kautsky 1896, p. 514.
43      Kautsky 1898, p. 724.
44      Kuusinen 1906, p. 339.

serve the interests of the people. Only by breaking the political power of capitalism ... can workers attain their goal: the abolition of exploitation, ensuring the welfare of the entire mass of working people.[45]

Rejecting Bernstein's advocacy of a gradual transition to socialism, orthodox SDs argued that solely through a revolutionary rupture could workers seize state power and overthrow capitalism. Such a break was required to defeat the resistance of the ruling class 'through a decisive struggle'.[46]

The existence of a democratically elected parliament did not negate the need for revolution since the bourgeoisie even in democratic capitalist regimes would very likely resort to force to prevent or annul the election of a socialist government through parliament. A moment of rupture should therefore be expected – and prepared for. Arguing against a leading SPD revisionist, Kautsky asked:

> Does he expect the exploiters to look on good-naturedly while we take one position after another and make ready for their expropriation? If so, he lives under a mighty illusion. Imagine for a moment that our parliamentary activity were to assume forms which threatened the supremacy of the bourgeoisie. What would happen? The bourgeoisie would try to put an end to parliamentary forms. In particular it would rather do away with the universal, direct and secret ballot than quietly capitulate to the proletariat. So we are not given the choice as to whether we shall limit ourselves to a purely parliamentary struggle.[47]

Marxists across the Tsarist Empire praised Kautsky's influential 1902 pamphlet *The Social Revolution* for initiating a serious socialist discussion on the proletarian conquest of power.[48] Kautsky's tract was almost immediately translated, republished, and illegally distributed by Russia's Marxist parties. The working class, *The Social Revolution* affirmed, could free itself and all the oppressed only through seizing *all* political power and dissolving all anti-democratic institutions. A gradual conquest of power, he argued, was impossible.[49]

---

45    'Zjazd Zagranicznych Grup SD' [1900] in Szmidt 1934, p. 185.
46    Kautsky 1909 [1996], p. 5.
47    Kautsky 1908, p. 456. For an articulation of this argument in 1898, see Kautsky 1909 [1996], p. xxxii.
48    See, for example, Kelles-Krauz 1904, p. 560.
49    Kautsky 1902 [1916], p. 19.

What form would the socialist revolution take? On this question, Second International Marxist orthodoxy upheld an open-ended approach. Kautsky consistently argued that 'we do not know how the process of the conquest [of power] will take place; it will take different forms depending on the different countries'.[50] And though Kautsky's stress on parliamentarism carried with it the assumption that socialist overturn required the ability to win an electoral majority, in the pre-war years he did not promote a strict parliamentarism according to which socialists could only take power after having first won a majority in parliament. Indeed, one common revolutionary scenario projected by Kautsky was that capitalists would stop elections from taking place if it looked as if they would give socialists a parliamentary majority – Social Democracy in such a context would presumably be justified therefore in defensively seizing power and *then* subsequently confirming a mandate for socialist transformation through universal suffrage elections.[51]

In 1918, Lenin argued that the 'evasiveness' of Kautsky's views on state and revolution 'benefited and fostered opportunism' and 'resulted in the distortion of Marxism and in its complete vulgarization'.[52] A more balanced assessment of the strengths and weaknesses of revolutionary social democracy, however, requires acknowledging the potential benefits of strategic flexibility. Given the lack of precedent for a successful nation-wide workers' government, it was reasonable that Marxist conceptions of socialist revolution were vague. Furthermore, early socialist orthodoxy's open-ended strategy for the transition to socialism stands in positive contrast with the rigid parliamentarism and legalism of moderate social democrats, not to mention Leninism's dubious projection of soviet power as the universal mode of working-class rule.[53]

While refraining from detailed prescriptions for social revolution, revolutionary social democracy was consistently associated with a belief in its prox-

---

50    Kautsky 1906, p. 161.

51    Waldenberg 1972, pp. 409–11, 530–1. Experience over the twentieth century did not generally confirm this prediction about how capitalists would seek to prevent socialist transformation. Rather than abrogate democratic rule to *prevent* the election of a socialist government, ruling elites have generally sought to use their economic and bureaucratic power to pressure elected officials to remain within acceptable bounds. In the rare instances that socialists nevertheless proceeded to push radical transformation, only then did ruling-class forces resort to efforts to topple the new administration through economic or military means. On these dynamics and their strategic implications for electing a government to implement anti-capitalist change, see Miliband 1989, pp. 79, 195–6, 224–31.

52    Lenin 1917a [1960–65], p. 480.

53    On Kautsky's post-1909 evolution towards a more rigid parliamentarism, see Waldenberg 1972, Vol. Two.

imity and actuality: a continual point of contention between Kautsky and Bernstein was the latter's insistence that the proletariat was far too immature to
conquer power any time in the foreseeable future. Kautsky replied that revolution could happen much sooner, as it was impossible to formulate precisely
how organised the proletariat must be before it could overthrow capitalism. It
was no accident that the November 1905 inaugural issue of the Finnish revolutionary SD journal, *Sosialistinen Aikakauslehti*, highlighted precisely this aspect
of orthodoxy – and Kautsky's writings in particular – to its readers.[54]

Would the socialist revolution be peaceful or violent? According to orthodox
Marxists, this depended on circumstances. While moderate socialists insisted
that it was impermissible for the Social Democracy to ever take up arms or
promote violence, revolutionary SDs expressed their preference for a peaceful
revolution, but argued that the working class must be prepared to use violent
means if necessary.[55] Kautsky noted that capitalists would not forego violence
even if workers did: 'For those who renounce in advance the use of violence,
what remains beyond parliamentary cretinism and statesmanlike cunning?'[56]

This did not mean that revolutionary social democrats advocated violence or
oriented towards armed insurrection in bourgeois democracies. By organising
a general strike and winning over the military's rank-and-file soldiers, Kautsky
argued, a peaceful socialist transformation was possible.[57] Whether working-
class revolution would in fact result in violence could not be predicted, as this
largely depended on the response of the ruling class. Either way, workers would
need arms to win:

> Now, as in the past, Marx's saying remains true: force is the midwife of
> any new society. No ruling class abdicates voluntarily and nonchalantly.
> But that does not necessarily mean that violence must be the midwife of
> a new society. A rising class must have the necessary instruments of force
> at its disposal if it wants to dispossess the old ruling class, but it is not
> unconditionally necessary that it employ them.[58]

Flowing from these perspectives, revolutionary social democrats declared from
at least 1903 onwards that under no circumstances should socialists seek to

---

54    Anon. 1905, pp. 17–20.
55    Kautsky 1902 [1916], pp. 98–9.
56    '9 June 1902' in Adler 1954, p. 405.
57    Kautsky 1902 [1916], p. 88.
58    Kautsky 2009 [1904], p. 247.

participate in a capitalist government. State power could not be shared by the exploited and exploiters due to the depth of their class antagonism. Crucially, orthodox Marxists opposed the establishment of joint coalition governments with bourgeois parties. The significance of this opposition can hardly be overestimated, as it was precisely this issue that proved to be the central governmental question after Tsarism's overthrow. Chapter 10 will show that divergences over participation in a coalition regime with the bourgeoisie constituted *the* fundamental dividing line between moderates and radicals on the question of state power during 1917.

The Second International's ongoing debate on coalition government began in 1899. That year, following the anti-Semitic Dreyfus Affair in France, socialist Alexandre Millerand joined the French cabinet in the name of saving the Republic against the threat of the right wing. Moderate socialists like French leader Jean Jaurès defended Millerand on the grounds that democratic gains could best be maintained through an alliance with liberals. They framed such social democratic participation in government, moreover, as a first step in the gradual transformation of the state in a social democratic direction.[59]

A heated international struggle immediately erupted between orthodox and revisionist socialists over Millerand's 'ministerialism' and its strategic implications. Radicals vehemently argued against the possibility of a piecemeal conquest of power. After multiple years of conflict and controversy, orthodox socialists finally secured the adoption of their position in Germany and in the Second International. The 1903 German SPD Dresden congress and the 1904 Amsterdam congress of the International adopted a historic resolution, written by Kautsky, banning socialists from seeking entry into *any* capitalist administration.[60]

In a series of essays on Marxism and the republic written in 1904–05, Kautsky elaborated on the strategy underlying this resolution. Since many of the key points of these articles have already been cited above, here I will highlight Kautsky's pioneering – and prophetic – analysis of the indispensable role of socialist opportunists for propping up the capitalist state at a moment of crisis.

---

59    Frölich 1940, p. 81.
60    Secrétariat Socialiste International 1904, pp. 114–15. The 1903 Dresden and 1904 Amsterdam resolutions marked a harder line than the initial positions of Luxemburg, Plekhanov, and Kautsky. In their earliest contributions to the debate, each of these leaders opposed Millerand's entry into the French government and rejected the possibility of a non-revolutionary road to socialism. But initially they did not absolutely preclude the possibility for socialist participation in capitalist administrations in 'exceptional' circumstances (Larsson 1970, p. 149, Luxemburg 1899, and Waldenberg 1972, p. 308).

Kautsky argued that the roots of Millerand's entry into executive government lay in the weak French bourgeoisie's inability to rule without the support of socialists:

> There was now only one way of exploiting the proletariat's power for bourgeois ends – to win the socialist parliamentary deputies to carry out those bourgeois policies which the bourgeois republicans had already become too weak to carry out by themselves. Since they could no longer kill off socialism, they sought to tame it and make it subservient to them.[61]

Kautsky similarly pointed to moderate socialist Louis Blanc's decision to side with the French government against the 1871 Paris Commune. He concluded that anybody who 'does not possess the courage and abjuration to join the fighting proletariat against the bourgeoisie wholeheartedly and break all ties with it can eventually, notwithstanding his proletarian sympathies, all too easily be pushed onto the side of the proletariat's opponents at the decisive moment'.[62]

Whether to follow the path of Louis Blanc and Alexandre Millerand's ministerialism would become the defining political issue across the Russian Empire following the February 1917 revolution. Yet in the preceding years, the possibility of a socialist entry into executive government was precluded by the existence of Tsarism. Only in Finland was this debate posed as an immediate issue – and on this question the moderate and orthodox wings of Finnish socialism clashed repeatedly. Praising Millerand's entry into the French state as a positive example, Yrjö Mäkelin and other conciliatory activists in the party encouraged socialists to participate in a national Finnish government.[63]

In response, orthodox leader Edvard Valpas in 1904 denounced the idea of a coalition government between socialists and bourgeois forces. The experience of Millerand, he argued, clearly demonstrated that it was 'a deception' to believe that joining a capitalist cabinet would further the workers' cause – in practice, it could only serve to shield the state from independent working-class struggle.[64] This became a burning practical issue when SDP party leader J.K. Kari joined the Finnish government in the winter of 1905, culminating in a dramatic confrontation between the party's radical and moderate wings. At the August 1906 Oulu Congress, Kuusinen and his orthodox comrades succeeded in convincing the delegates to expel Kari from the SDP. The decision to join a

---

61    Kautsky 1905 [2018], pp. 279–80, my emphasis.
62    Kautsky 1905 [2018], p. 210.
63    Soikkanen 1961, p. 109.
64    Valpas 1904, pp. 60–3.

bourgeois government, Kuusinen declared, contradicted the central tenets of socialism and had not been agreed upon by the party.[65]

The debate emerged again after the 1907 parliamentary elections, in which Finland's Social Democracy won 37 per cent of the votes. Though short of a majority, the SDP was nevertheless by far the largest party in parliament. This electoral success prompted what historian Maurice Carrez refers to as 'a ministerialist offensive'.[66] Right-leaning SDP leaders such as Tainio and Ursin again raised a call for socialist entry into a national Finnish government. But Kuusinen and the *Siltasaarelaiset* pushed back hard against this proposal, which gained little traction in part because of the relative lack of power granted by the Tsar to Finland's democratically elected institutions. In such a context, for most socialists and organised workers, it made little sense to compromise on class independence. In a long series of articles and speeches, the *Siltas-aarelaiset* denounced Finnish revisionism and argued for the relevancy of an orthodox intransigent stance. Buoyed by popular disappointment in Finland's constrained parliament, SDP leftists won the debates and, in so doing, further popularised the ideas of orthodox Marxism.

Over the coming years, repeated calls by moderates to push for a Finnish 'national unity' government were defeated by the SDP leadership. Not until the overthrow of Tsarism did this debate re-emerge inside the Finnish Social Democracy.

## 3       The State and Revolution in Finland (1917–18)

Revolutionary socialists have generally assumed that the October Revolution in Russia vindicated the new political strategy articulated by Lenin's *The State and Revolution*, with its call to 'smash' the capitalist state and establish a 'commune state' in its place. In Chapter 10, we will see that Lenin's novel orientation in fact played relatively little role in shaping Bolshevik policy for most of 1917. But there is a more basic reason to question the prevailing account: there was neither a parliament nor a capitalist state in Russia to smash.

The February Revolution's insurrection broke up an autocratic monarchy, leaving a political vacuum that was tenuously filled by an unelected Provisional Government and the newly created councils of workers and soldiers. Both before and after February 1917, Russia's political arena was thus fundament-

65     Carrez 2008, pp. 198–9 and Kirby 1971, pp. 85–8.
66     Carrez 2008, p. 213 and Soikkanen 1961, p. 268.

ally different from the parliamentary regimes of Western Europe. Finland was the sole region of the empire that approximated the conditions facing Marxists in Europe's parliamentary countries, particularly 'low inclusion' constitutional monarchies like Germany and Austria. As such, the experience of the Finnish Social Democracy in 1917–18 is our closest point of comparison for assessing orthodox Marxist approaches to revolution under a parliamentary state.

News of the February uprising in nearby Petrograd came as a surprise to Finland. But once the rumours were confirmed, Russian soldiers stationed in Helsinki mutinied against their officers and declared their allegiance to the Petrograd Soviet. With the support of Russian soldiers, the old police force was virtually dismantled by Finnish workers in the largest cities, though not the countryside. Popular militias of Finnish workers' organisations were immediately set up and Russian administrators were thrown out. Conservative writer Henning Söderhjelm bemoaned the loss of the state's monopoly of violence in towns like Helsinki and Tampere: 'It was the express policy of the [Finnish] Labour Party to destroy the police entirely. ... The "people" felt no confidence in this institution, and in its stead local corps for the maintenance of order were established – a "militia," the men of which were to belong to the Labour Party'.[67]

Throughout the year, the Finnish labour movement's insistence on preventing the re-establishment of a regular army or police force edged the revolution towards anti-capitalist rupture. In early 1917, however, Finnish society was swept up by a widespread desire for national unity to reverse the previous years of Russification and to win autonomy from the new Russian Provisional Government. Following the Tsar's overthrow, all regions of the empire were marked by a mood of euphoria and class collaboration. Centrist SDP leader Oskari Tokoi recalled the dynamic in March:

> There was peace in the land and a spirit of hope, and both the cabinet and the Diet settled down to their tasks in a mood of mutual trust. It seemed as if all the suspicion, incrimination and schism which had prevailed among the parties, so often hampering the course of legislation and government, had vanished, and that everybody wholeheartedly wanted to work for the common cause and country.[68]

In this spirit, conciliatory SDP leaders broke with the party's well-known opposition to participation in bourgeois governments. In March, they insisted upon

---

67    Söderhjelm 1919, p. 20. See also Kirby 1971, pp. 203–4.
68    Tokoi 1957, p. 138.

forming a cabinet with Finnish liberals and the centrist peasant party, the Agrarians. After long and contentious negotiations, Tokoi came up with a draft agreement in late March to form an administration composed of six socialists and six non-socialists.

In Finland, like elsewhere in Russia, orthodox Marxists at this moment were subjected to tremendous pressures – from conciliatory socialists and from working people – to tone down or hold back their independent line for the sake of unity. In the face of these centrifugal forces, the left wing of the SDP did not put forward a cohesive alternative. Some leaders argued for the formation of a Red (purely socialist) government. Others like *Työmies* editor Edvard Valpas declared that because participation in a bourgeois government violated the principles of the party and the International, it was necessary to remain in strident opposition outside the administration.

Other revolutionary SDs such as Kuusinen and his closest comrades bent to the prevailing mood for coalition. One of the main reasons they rejected the proposal to immediately establish a Red Government was that it would likely split the party and the workers' movement – the first instance of a year-long pattern of making concessions in hope of preserving the unity of a heterogeneous party.[69] Though Kuusinen and his allies personally refused to participate in the coalition and disclaimed any political responsibility for it, they ultimately did not oppose its formation. For their part, Valpas and other SDP leftists denounced this decision to collaborate with the upper class – participation in any capitalist government, they argued, was a 'betrayal'.[70]

The hegemonic SDP line early in the year was that the new government would be supported solely in so far as it responded to the workers' needs. Socialists inside and outside of government would have to keep up their pressure, to oblige non-socialist ministers to cede to the popular will for democratic and social reform. Were the regime to come under the sway of the bourgeoisie and reject these demands, at that point the workers' representatives should be prepared to resign.[71] Two years later, Kuusinen offered a sharp self-critique of this early-year drift towards conditional class collaboration:

> This spring-time liberty fell for us like a gift from the skies, and our party
> was overwhelmed by the intoxicating sap of March. The official watch-

---

69    For the early 1917 SDP debates on forming a government, see Matikainen 2017, pp. 69–84. See also Carrez 2008, p. 483.
70    Cited in Carrez 2008, p. 485. See also Upton 1980, p. 30.
71    Kirby 1971, pp. 179, 340.

word had been that of independent class struggle, i.e., the same which German Social Democracy had put forward before the war. During the reactionary period it was easy enough to maintain this position; it was not exposed to any serious attack, and resistance on the part of the Socialists of the Right could not manage to make itself felt. In March the Party's proletarian virtue was exposed to temptation and to fall into sin.[72]

For the first half of 1917, the SDP leadership, including the *Siltasaarelaiset*, placed a particular emphasis on working within parliament, in which the party had won a majority in the 1916 elections. The Tsar, however, had not allowed it to meet due to wartime exigencies. After February 1917, the existence of a democratically elected parliament and a strong parliamentary tradition posed challenges that socialists did not face in the rest of the empire. Understandably, the popular legitimacy and political leverage generated by a socialist parliamentary majority were not gains that Finland's SDs were willing to forego lightly.

The absence of a bourgeois armed apparatus, moreover, seemed to provide an unparalleled opportunity for socialists to utilise parliament to push through a series of urgent political and economic reforms. These included, most importantly, the democratisation of the state and a wide range of economic improvements for urban and rural working people. To quote Kuusinen: 'At this moment the path of Parliamentary Democracy seemed cleared to an extraordinary extent, and wide vistas opened themselves out before our working-class movement'.[73] Given the existence of a socialist-led parliament in 1917, it is hardly surprising that Finnish workers' councils played only a very secondary role in political life.[74]

Finland's class-collaborationist honeymoon was short-lived. Unlike the Mensheviks and other moderate socialists across imperial Russia, the Finnish Social Democracy did not commit itself to a strategic alliance with the bourgeoisie even after some of its leaders joined a coalition government. The new government established in March was quickly caught between the dual intransigence of the SDP and the Finnish upper class; the preceding years of

---

72  Kuusinen 1919, p. 1.
73  Kuusinen 1919, p. 2.
74  A workers' council was formed in Helsinki and served as an organisational base for some of the capital's Finnish radicals. But, as Kirby notes, 'it in no way approximated to the role and position of the soviets in Russia' (Kirby 1971, p. 207). There was also a Russian soldiers' soviet in Helsinki, which played an important role within the debates of the Baltic fleet and the empire-wide revolution. For the most part, however, it did not intervene in the development of the Finnish Revolution.

polarisation continued to weigh heavy, mitigating against personal or political rapprochement.[75] Bourgeois hopes that the Social Democracy would significantly temper itself upon entry into coalition were quickly dashed. Söderhjelm's testimony gives a sense of this disillusionment:

> One would have thought that the Labour Party ought to have been satisfied [with its new influence in government] ... and should now have entered upon a sober and dignified policy. But this was by no means the case. ... Even if the Labour Party thus observed a certain dignity in its most official conduct, it still continued its agitation policy against the bourgeoisie with unwearied zeal.[76]

A political commitment to independent class struggle remained hegemonic inside the Finnish Social Democracy. Oskari Tokoi – the middle-of-the-road SDP leader who headed their governmental group – recalled the impossible situation this created for the socialist ministers:

> That faction of the old membership which had originally objected to participation in the government now began more and more insistently to attack the government and its measures designed to maintain law and order. It was a strange situation. The Social Democratic was the largest party, with a majority in the Diet and in the cabinet. Yet, reverting to its former traditions, it was placing itself in opposition to its government. The position of the Social Democratic cabinet members became very difficult, for they did not have the political backing they needed. ... The bourgeois ministers knew they had their parties behind them, but the Social Democratic ministers had no such assurance.[77]

Finnish liberals, nationalists, and capitalists responded by denouncing the organised labour movement as a menace to order and Western civilisation. In the eyes of the Finnish upper class, their country's workers had become blinded by the 'Russian infection' of mob rule.[78] Carrez notes that Finland's conservative elite never resigned itself to 'sharing power with a political formation that it saw as the devil incarnate. The growth of popular demands, moreover, gave the situation an apocalyptic allure. How to end this nightmare was the ques-

---

75    Salkola 1985, p. 284.
76    Söderhjelm 1919, pp. 16, 18–19.
77    Tokoi 1957, p. 141. See also Kuusinen 1919, p. 3.
78    Söderhjelm 1919, p. 83.

tion of questions above all for the old rightist circles that were traditionally conciliatory [with the Russian regime]'.[79] From the spring onwards, representatives of the Finnish upper class insistently demanded that the local militias be replaced by a regular police force – in fact, this was the very first major conflict to roil the coalition government. But throughout the year the SDP as a whole, with only a small group of right socialists dissenting, remained intransigently opposed to disarming the popular militias. True to orthodox Marxism's principled advocacy of an armed people, the party resisted the establishment of a bourgeois armed apparatus of any kind.[80]

The extreme left of the SDP – which at this time included Valpas, as well as a small circle of Finnish Bolshevik sympathisers – continued to denounce the coalition government as a breach of the party's social democratic principles.[81] On this issue, the *Siltasaarelaiset* were initially more reserved. Nevertheless, their initiatives to fight against the Russian government were soon pivotal to breaking up Finland's coalition government.

The summertime conflict revolved around the ongoing subordination of Finland to the Russian state. In March, Petrograd had repealed the Tsar's Russification measures, but it refused to accept the Finns' initial proposal to expand their autonomy. Provisional Government head Alexander Kerensky said that while he was not opposed to this proposal in principle, it could not be immediately granted, lest the other national groups in the empire demand the same. The Finns would thus have to wait and make their proposal to an All-Russian Constituent Assembly.

Under the leadership and initiative of Kuusinen, the SDP refused to acquiesce and decided instead to launch a major campaign for Finland's sovereignty. This push led Finland's socialists to reach out to Russian socialists, including those active among the large number of radicalised Russian troops still stationed in Finland. Of all the Russian political parties, only the Bolsheviks granted their support to the SDP's efforts. Looking to preserve law and order and aiming to reach a negotiated agreement with the Provisional Government, the Finnish right wing balked at the socialists' increasingly intransigent approach as well as their alliance with Russian radicals.

Finland's SDs saw the fight to win independence – or, earlier in 1917, at least full national sovereignty – as a central axis of the working-class struggle for democracy and social change. Leftists argued that by eliminating the interference of the Russian government over the internal life of Finland, the SDP would

79    Carrez 2008, p. 549.
80    Tokoi 1957, p. 139, Alapuro 1988, p. 153, and Upton 1980, pp. 59–60, 63.
81    Kirby 1971, p. 180 and Carrez 2008, pp. 528–9.

be able to use its parliamentary majority and its control of workers' militias to push through an ambitious programme of political and social reforms. One Finnish socialist leader announced in July that 'hitherto we have been obliged to fight on two fronts – against our own bourgeoisie, and against the Russian Government. If our class war is to be successful, if we are to be able to gather all our strength on one front, against our own bourgeoisie, we need Independence, for which Finland is already ripe'.[82] For their own political and economic reasons, Finland's right-wingers and liberals also favoured a push for strengthening Finnish autonomy; this perceived commonality of national interests served as the initial political foundation for the coalition government. But Finland's non-socialists were not willing to turn to revolutionary measures to achieve this national goal – nor did they generally go as far as the SDP in calling for full independence.

The fight against the Russian government and the Finnish elite came to a head during the 'July Days' unrest in the Petrograd. Believing that the Provisional Government would be immediately overthrown or overhauled in the face of workers' semi-spontaneous uprising in the capital, the SDP majority in the Finnish parliament proposed the landmark *Valtalaki* (Power Law) which unilaterally proclaimed full Finnish sovereignty; the Russian government's jurisdiction was acknowledged only in foreign and military affairs. Opposed by conservative Finnish MPs, but hesitantly supported by the centre, the *Valtalaki* was approved in parliament on 18 July.

Kerensky's regime, however, managed to hold on to power in July. Buoyed by its temporary victory over the Bolsheviks, the Provisional Government immediately rejected the validity of the *Valtalaki* and threatened to occupy Finland were this decision not respected. But Finnish socialists refused to back down or renounce the *Valtalaki*. At this point, Finland's liberals and conservatives seized the moment. Hoping to isolate the SDP and put an end to its parliamentary majority, they opportunistically proposed to Kerensky that he dissolve the Finnish parliament. Finland's bourgeois leaders openly denounced 'the irresponsibility and class selfishness of our socialist party, which has ... pushed our internal state of affairs to the brink of anarchy ... we must hold new elections, which must bring an end to socialist rule here'.[83]

Not for the last time would power trump patriotism for a ruling elite in imperial Russia. With the backing of the Finnish upper class, Kerensky's unelected administration pushed through the dissolution of the empire's only elected

---

82    Cited in Söderhjelm 1919, p. 22.
83    'The Finnish Parties in Electoral Pact' in Kirby 1975, p. 182.

parliament – an act supported by the Menshevik-SR leadership of the Petrograd Soviet.[84] Russian liberals and Social Democrats would later cite the Bolsheviks' disbanding of the Russian Constituency Assembly in January 1918 as an instance of indefensible authoritarianism, but their own actions hardly testify to a consistent commitment to the principles of republican democracy.

The dissolution of the Finnish parliament marked a point of no return in the nation's political life. All sides had thrown down the gauntlet. Hitherto peaceful Finland swerved towards a revolutionary conflagration. Finland's Social Democracy denounced the native bourgeoisie for colluding with the Russian state to trample upon Finnish national rights and democratic institutions. Disbanding Finland's parliament, the party press declared, was 'a blow against Finnish democracy'.[85] The party now broke from the experiment of coalition: in mid-August the Finnish Social Democracy ordered all its members in the administration to resign.

New parliamentary elections took place in October. Declaring that the elections were illegitimate, Finland's SDs nevertheless tactically took part in them – an approach reflecting both their hesitancy to break from the parliamentary arena as well their accurate perception that workers were going to overwhelmingly vote in any case. Finland's non-socialists narrowly won a majority in the elections, leading the SDP to reiterate its insistence that the election had been illegal from the start and that it had only been won through electoral fraud.[86]

With the end of the SDP's parliamentary majority and its exit from government, Finland's bourgeois parties pushed in September and October to abolish the people's militias. Upper-class forces simultaneously began setting up their own paramilitary forces to re-establish order and defend themselves against the 'prevailing anarchy'.[87] This 'anarchy' was not a figment of their imagination. As early as May, groups of radicalised workers had begun establishing their own defence squads to supplement the broader popular militias. Facing a rapidly polarising context, the SDP and the Finnish trade unions decided in early October to form a Workers' Security Guard, i.e. Red Guards, in all cities and towns. Their 20 October call to set up the Guards explained that since 'the bourgeoisie is now feverishly arming itself against the labourers in order to stifle their most important endeavours for reform, the leaders are of the opinion that in self-defence, and to provide against all contingencies, the labourers

---

84    On the *Valtalaki* and the ensuing conflicts, see Upton 1980, pp. 84–101.
85    Cited in Kiiskilä 2010, p. 55.
86    Carrez 2008, pp. 585–6.
87    Söderhjelm 1919, p. 24.

should immediately raise corps of Guards all over the country'.[88] By November, the Guards numbered in the tens of thousands.

Though the Red Guards were comprised of SDP members and were formally subordinated to the party and unions, these bodies frequently took autonomous action in the last months of 1917. They quickly became one of the main organisational vehicles for the most militant party members, who sought to use the Guards not just to defend workers against the elite but also to drive forward the revolution and overcome what they saw as the hesitations of the party leadership.[89]

Though there was sometimes considerable friction, the SDP leadership consistently supported the Red Guard movement. This support was an important practical consequence of the party's prevailing approach to violence: while it desired a peaceful revolution, it would resort to arms if necessary. *Kansan Lehti*, the party's paper in Tampere, declared: 'Conscious social-democratic workers have never admired violent occurrences. For us, civil war is particularly terrible. But social democracy cannot forbid its members from armed activity when things can no longer be solved otherwise'.[90]

The hegemonic party stance on breaking with legal tactics was analogous. The SDP press explained in October: 'Social democracy wants legality, but it will not allow itself to be killed in the name of legality'.[91] To defend the democratic mandate given by Finland's working people in 1916, the party argued, required combatting the current illegitimate parliament and the capitalist class generally. As Tokoi declared in a mid-October speech: 'labourers had other means of power besides the ballot to bring home their claims. It was necessary to stand firm, and fight for the victory of the revolution when the right moment had come'.[92]

On a programmatic level, each of these axioms remained hegemonic inside the SDP throughout 1917. So too was the general platform for which the party was fighting, which it summed up as 'Bread and Justice'. By the fall of 1917, the Finnish Social Democracy foregrounded two issues in particular: the fight against hunger and for political democracy. To prevent mass starvation and secure the basic material survival of working people, socialist leaders insisted that it was necessary to establish Finland's sovereignty against Russia and to

---

88    Cited in Söderhjelm 1919, p. 30.
89    On the Red Guards, see Salkola 1985. For the dynamics in Tampere, see, for example, Suodenjoki and Peltola 2007, pp. 238, 247.
90    Cited in Suodenjoki and Peltola, p. 244. See also Kiiskilä 2010, p. 95.
91    Cited in Kiiskilä 2010, p. 62.
92    Cited in Söderhjelm 1919, p. 30.

deepen real political democracy. This meant, among other things, disbanding the bourgeois armed guards, accepting Finnish independence, dissolving the illegally elected parliament, and electing a Sovereign Constituent Assembly based on universal suffrage.[93]

This remained the party's platform up through and after the January 1918 revolution as well as the subsequent establishment of a Red Government. Perhaps the most significant evolution was that the demand for national independence became redundant after it was won in December 1917. Following the Bolshevik-led seizure of power in Petrograd, the Finnish bourgeoisie reversed its previous alliance with the Russian state. Eager to win the armed support of Germany and isolate Finland from the 'Russian infection', the new government declared itself independent on 6 December. Wary of giving Finland's elite any potential nationalist ammunition against Russian imperialism, the Bolsheviks (unlike their liberal and moderate socialist predecessors) immediate recognised Finland's national claims, in the hopes that this stance would facilitate the SDP's fight for power.[94] Though less central than in previous months, the national question nevertheless continued to shape the class struggle inside of Finland: both sides painted themselves as liberators of the nation and both accused their rivals of subordination to foreign powers – Germany and Russia, respectively.

Finnish Social Democracy's various wings intensely and endlessly debated political strategy and tactics in the fall of 1917. After the November general strike, right-leaning socialists began to openly make their case against taking power. Fundamentally, the debates came down to the question of whether the current situation made it necessary and possible to turn from legal activity to an armed revolution to establish a workers' government.

Not until January 1918 did a majority of the party leaders come to support the latter option. Yet even in the preceding months the SDP simultaneously rejected the continued, and increasingly shrill, ultimatums raised by its moderate social democratic minority. According to these leaders, it was necessary to discipline the Red Guards and denounce their violent acts. Indeed, from November through January, the debate over how to relate to the Guards was second in importance only to that of the question of state power proper. The orthodox left successfully defeated the repeated calls of the party right for the SDP to publicly condemn Red Guard 'terrorism' or to clamp down on its activities.[95] Though Kuusinen and the *Siltasaarelaiset* were critical of some of

93    Upton 1980, p. 135.
94    On the SDP's approach to national independence, see Ketola 2017.
95    See, for example, Huttunen 1918, pp. 79–95 and Upton 1980, pp. 223–5. Right socialist MP

the autonomous armed actions of the Red Guards, these SDP leaders felt that armed self-defence and the necessity of a united fight against the bourgeoisie obliged the party to defend the Guards and maintain a close alliance with them. Moderate SDP party leaders at the time and in later years pointed to this stance by the *Siltasaarelaiset* as a decisive step towards civil war.[96]

To what extent did the SDP's delay in taking revolutionary action reflect its strategic perspectives? For a minority of conciliatory SDP leaders, it is clear that their opposition to revolution was neither tactical nor conjunctural. Throughout the year they employed strictly parliamentary means and they sought to forge a governmental alliance with non-socialists. At the November 1917 party congress, Seth Heikkilä put forward a resolution against seizing power signed by 18 moderate SDP leaders, openly articulating their principled opposition to taking power. This was a politically consistent stance – but it was not one rooted in orthodox Marxism. As we have seen, one of the defining attributes of conciliatory socialists in Finland, as across Europe, was precisely their longstanding rejection of revolutionary social democracy. In lieu of Marxist theory, their eclectic socialism absorbed elements of liberal politics and their practice tended to adapt to liberalism's political apparatuses. Furthermore, underlying the conceptions and actions of the SDP right was a deep distrust of the 'anarchic' mass of unorganised workers, a stance analogous in many ways to that of Finland's elite towards the working class as a whole.[97]

In contrast, orthodox SDP leaders had always argued that promoting working-class interests through legal and peaceful tactics would have to be superseded by militant, extra-parliamentary struggle when the situation required it. And by the fall, most of the preconditions set by orthodox Marxists for anti-capitalist rupture were present in Finland. These included the existence of a massive Social Democracy, the achievement of a socialist parliamentary majority, and a concerted campaign by bourgeois leaders against democratic institutions. In the eyes of SDP leaders, there was thus no principled or programmatic reason to oppose the conquest of power by revolutionary means, particularly after Finland's parliament had been dissolved. Indeed, events had developed remarkably closely to a revolutionary scenario long predicted by revolutionary social democrats: socialists had won a parliamentary

---

Matti Paasivuori even went so far as to vote for more funding for the bourgeois police force in January 1918 (Hentilä 2013, p. 185).

96 Siltala 2014, p. 82 and Huttunen 1918, pp. 18–20.

97 For moderate socialist denunciations of mass 'anarchy' and its *Siltasaarelaiset* enablers, see, for example, Huttunen 1918, pp. 2, 18, 81, 86.

majority and attempted to pass deep structural reforms, leading a capitalist minority to anti-democratically move against parliament, thereby generating a revolutionary opening.

Leaders of the *Siltasaarelaiset* were hardly of one mind over how to proceed in late 1917. Earlier we saw that the hesitations of Finland's orthodox SDs reflected their attempts to prevent a debilitating party split, as well as a desire to hold back the revolutionary explosion until the working-class movement was stronger and better organised.[98] No less important were their uncertainties about the unstable and rapidly evolving political situation. Of the questions that weighed on the minds of all Finnish party cadre, the following were most prominent: How would the stationed Russian soldiers react to a Finnish workers' revolution? Did Finland's working people have enough weapons to take power and hold on to it? If Finland went down the revolutionary road, would the German government invade? Could the new Soviet government in Petrograd last more than a few weeks? And would it be able to provide armed support for Finnish workers?[99]

Ideology was only one factor shaping the decisions of party leaders: it was not easy to assess the concrete political situation, particularly in such a tumultuous moment. No matter how revolutionary one's politics, wagering on the most opportune moment for the 'final battle' was an extremely challenging task. An analogous debate, it should be pointed out, also consumed the Bolsheviks in the fall of 1917 in Petrograd. And in various parts of the empire, the Bolsheviks did not attempt to take revolutionary action in October given what they saw as still-unripe conditions on the ground – in Baku, for instance, the party waited until March 1918 to seize power.[100]

The course of Finland's civil war – which ended in the massacre of tens of thousands of Finnish workers – would demonstrate that many of the left's

---

98  Another factor explaining SDP hesitancy was that a sense of political duty to spark international revolution – prevalent in the strategy of revolutionary SDs elsewhere in the empire – was relatively weak among Finnish SDs. In part, this stance reflected the long-standing insularity of the Finnish labour movement; it was also facilitated by Finland's relative marginality in European geo-politics and its non-participation in World War One. A workers' seizure of power in Finland would not likely have the same detonator impact as in central Russia or key borderland regions like Poland or Ukraine. Only after taking power did the question of the spread and promotion of international revolution become a central part of Finnish SD politics. For this increased internationalism, see, for example, Söderhjelm 1919, pp. 150–1, Kiiskilä 2010, p. 130, and 'The Appeal of the Finnish Red Government to International Socialism' [1918] in Kirby 1975, p. 228.

99  On how these questions affected the SDP's approach during late 1917, see Kuusinen 1924 [2016], p. 385, Blanc 2017b and Carrez 2008, *passim*.

100  Suny 1972a, p. 146.

initial doubts were not unfounded, particularly in regard to the danger of German military intervention and the inability of the Russian Bolsheviks to deliver on their promises of armed support. Without any substantial military backing from the Bolsheviks, the isolated Finnish Reds were outgunned by the German-backed counter-revolution and crushed beginning in April 1918.[101]

Regardless of how we measure the merits of the Finns' revolutionary wager with the benefit of hindsight, the key point to underscore here is that by January 1918 Kuusinen and other key leaders of the *Siltasaarelaiset* had concluded that a workers' seizure of power was now necessary – a stance fully in line with the revolutionary social democratic strategy they had promoted since at least 1905.

The Finnish Social Democracy in late January declared that workers had to take power to defend democracy against capitalists. From start to finish, Finland's SDs defended their actions through defensive formulations. As the party press incessantly insisted in the days before the uprising, working people had been forced to resort to arms by the anti-democratic, violent actions of a capitalist minority: 'Things have reached the stage where it is necessary to fight, where only fighting [is possible]. Working people are aware that they are not in any way to blame for the civil war. The bourgeoisie bears the historic responsibility for this'.[102] Upon taking power, Finland's insurgents and the new Red Government similarly justified their actions on defensive grounds: revolution had proven necessary since the native elite, in conjunction with foreign imperialism, had led a counter-revolutionary 'coup' against workers' conquests and democracy.[103]

This turn to anti-capitalist rupture did not require a break from revolutionary social democratic strategy: Finland's socialist leaders in 1918 remained ideologically committed to orthodox Marxism's traditional stance on universal suffrage, parliament, and republicanism. And true to the Finnish SD's longstanding push for real parliamentary democracy, the new Red Government adopted a constitution establishing the type of radical democratic republic long envisioned by orthodox Marxists.[104]

That the calls and justifications for Finland's armed workers' uprising were made in defensive terms has led numerous writers to claim that the SDP was pushed into revolution against its political will, unlike the Bolsheviks. According to one recent account, 'SDP leaders were forced into an insurrection faced

---

101    On the Finnish Civil War, see Tepora and Roselius 2014 and Smele 2017, pp. 58–60.
102    Cited in Kiiskilä 2010, p. 92.
103    Kiiskilä 2010, pp. 98, 101–4, 134–7, 153, 156, 158.
104    'Die Verfassung Finnlands' in Eliel 1920, pp. 153–69.

with the potential of imminent violent reaction'.[105] Finnish scholar Juha Siltala has similarly explained the apparent aberration of 'Kautskian' support for armed revolution: 'For the Kautskian leadership of the Finnish Social Democratic Party, supporting a revolution would have been an anomaly given their belief in the laws of gradual historical progress. But they saw counterrevolution as a threat to their promised reforms'.[106] And historian Anthony Upton claims that the SDP's defensive approach was a 'prime cause' of the revolution's defeat since 'a defensive revolution is a contradiction in terms'.[107]

Such assertions have little empirical or analytical merit. As we will see in subsequent chapters, the October Revolution itself was also a 'defensive revolution' and the Bolsheviks similarly cast their politics in defensive terms. In class struggle, as in war, the line between defensive and offensive actions is often blurry or non-existent. Casting blame onto the bourgeoisie for the onset of Finland's civil war was factually justified and, most importantly, it was a pivotal method to win over those workers and wavering leaders that were still hesitant to support revolutionary struggle.

Adhering to such an approach did not mean the Finnish SDP was somehow unwittingly forced by circumstances to make a revolution. The irony of such accusations of SDP 'fatalism' is that these analyses themselves are deeply fatalistic. By denying the political agency of the party and its leadership, such accounts problematically assume that certain objective circumstances on their own are sufficient to compel socialists to lead a workers' revolution. But subsequent international experience has demonstrated that moderate socialist apparatuses have generally responded to the spread of right-wing reaction and mass action by deepening their alliances with the liberal bourgeoisie, rather than breaking them – the main role of class-collaborationist socialists at moments of deep social crisis has historically been to actively prevent anticapitalist ruptures, not passively lead them. Without an accurate assessment of the politics of revolutionary social democracy and the role of party leaders, it is impossible to understand why the German SPD helped crush its proletarian insurgency, while Finland's revolutionary SDs ultimately led working people to power.

One can criticise this or that tactical decision of SDP leftists, but the big story of Finland in 1917–18 is that the actions of orthodox Marxists demonstrated the ruptural potential of revolutionary social democracy. This point must be

---

105   Hart 2018.
106   Siltala 2015, p. 14. For similar accounts, see Alapuro 1988 and Upton 1980.
107   Upton 1980, p. 265.

underscored, since for close to a century activists and academics have argued that Kautsky and the Second International's flawed conception of state power necessarily resulted in their subordination to bourgeois rule. Such claims have obscured the fact that orthodox Marxist strategy was dismissed by socialist party leaders in the West, while in Finland, like in central Russia, it continued to serve as a guide to action.

A political abyss separated the politics of the *Siltasaarelaiset* from that of the moderate socialist leaderships that helped prop up capitalism during the post-war revolutionary wave. This dynamic was evident in their divergent positions on anti-capitalist rupture generally and it was made poignantly clear by the German SPD's open opposition to Finland's revolution.

Germany's leading Social Democrats not only failed to support the Finnish Revolution – they openly backed the German state's subsequent invasion in 1918.[108] Finnish orthodox leader Yrjö Sirola's trenchant public response to the German SPD officialdom put the gulf between their politics into sharp relief:

> We Finnish Social Democrats declare before the whole world: There is no villainy to which the German social patriots are not prepared to commit. ... That the German government provoked civil war in order to support the power politics of the privileged, to acquire the lion's share of the plunder – that is natural. ... But that those who call themselves Social Democrats take the responsibility for this and seek to apologise for it by declaring that we (German social patriots) had to intervene with weapons against [Finland's] democracy, that is not natural.[109]

Revolutionary social democracy was put to the test by the Finnish Revolution. After many years of accumulating electoral strength, in 1917 Finland's SDs – true to their longstanding strategic perspectives – fought to radically democratise the state and they responded to a reactionary bourgeois offensive by initiating a revolutionary struggle for republican democracy and workers' rule.

In a twentieth century where anti-capitalist ruptures were almost exclusively witnessed in authoritarian polities, Finland's revolution stands out as one of the exceptional instances of workers seizing power under a parliamentary regime. Part of the reason why this example was so rarely repeated was that the post-1917 rise of Leninism and Social Democracy led most socialists to aban-

---

108    Kirby 1971, p. 363. In yet another illustration of his post-1909 turn to the right, Kautsky also opposed the Finnish Revolution (Soikkanen 1975, p. 215 and Kirby 1971, pp. 168–9).
109    Sirola 1918 [1918], pp. 105–6.

don efforts to push towards revolutionary transformation by expanding republican democracy. As such, socialists today would do well to reclaim radical republicanism.

Of course, it does not follow from this that the approach of Kautsky and Finland's Marxists can be simply transposed to today's advanced capitalist democracies. Because they organised under decidedly low inclusion parliamentary regimes, it was significantly easier for German and Finnish radicals to build a mass base for strict class intransigence.

In high inclusion parliamentary polities, socialist parties face significantly stronger moderating incentives, both from below and from above. Where there is more space to use democratic institutions to pass transformative reforms, workers are generally less inclined to adopt revolutionary solutions and socialists have to confront the dilemmas of parliamentary compromise and the challenges of anti-capitalist governance under a capitalist economy. In such conditions, pushing for intransigent revolutionary politics, without in the process becoming a marginal sect, has proven to be a far more daunting task than expected.[110]

The main reason why there has never been a successful socialist revolution in an industrialised democracy is not that socialists have lacked resolve, patience, radical leaders, or good strategies. Capitalism has survived primarily because the power of employers, combined with the intractable strategic dilemmas facing leftists under capitalist democracies, makes winning socialism very difficult. To take on such a powerful ruling class, mass disruption is necessary yet far from sufficient. Workers, above all, need to dramatically scale up their organised power. But how can socialists help build powerful workers' organisations without these becoming excessively conservative? And how can socialists forge electoral majorities and pass transformative reforms without excessively moderating their politics in the process? If there were easy answers to these questions, socialism would have been established a long time ago. For the as-yet-unsolved question of how to move beyond social democracy to socialism, Second International orthodox Marxism can only be a starting point, not the final word.

---

110   On these issues, see Stephens 1979, Korpi 1983, Esping-Andersen 1985, Miliband 1989, and Panitch, Gindin, and Maher 2020.

# The Autocratic State and Revolution: 1905

The 1905 revolution was famously described by Lenin as the 'dress rehearsal' for 1917. Yet the study of socialist stances on the state and revolution during 1905 remains plagued by myths and misconceptions. Understanding the orthodox Marxist approach is essential for any serious attempt to analyse the course of political struggle in 1905 and the evolution of revolutionary social democracy up through 1917. Without this, it is hard to make sense of why the 1905 revolution became a potentially existential threat to the autocracy *and* the bourgeoisie – or how the Bolsheviks came to become the leading current of a multi-national radical bloc in so many regions of imperial Russia over the course of 1917.

A highly politicised historiography has claimed that there was a major rupture between orthodox Second International Marxism and the position taken by the Bolsheviks in 1917. Liberals and socialist writers, for instance, have wrongly argued that the Bolsheviks' push in 1917 for a proletarian and peasant government in Russia constituted a radical departure from the prevailing socialist orthodoxy.[1] Though Mensheviks were quick to claim that the Bolsheviks had broken with Marxism by succumbing to 'anarchism' or 'maximalism', I will show that it was the moderates' class-collaborationist politics after 1905 that constituted a true political rupture from revolutionary social democratic strategy and Russia's hitherto radical traditions. For the politics of orthodox and moderate socialists alike, strategic continuity rather than rupture remained the dominant dynamic from 1907 onwards.

In this chapter we will see that Marxists across Russia by 1905 supported directly taking state power. The hegemonic orthodox perspective by 1905–06 can be summed up as follows: Only the working class can lead the democratic revolution to victory. Such a task entails far more than simply winning political freedom – it requires the armed destruction of the existing state, the formation of a provisional revolutionary government, the granting of the social demands of workers and peasants and the establishment of a democratic republic. Since liberals and the bourgeoisie will not support this project, workers and their allies must establish a revolutionary dictatorship to push through radical transformation and to crush the counter-revolution

---

1 See, for example, Trotsky 1924 [2016], pp. 92, 95–6 and Slusser 1987, p. 54.

that will inevitably arise. Objective conditions in the lands ruled by Tsarism preclude the direct establishment of socialism, but as the impending revolution could likely spark workers' revolutions in the West, such developments abroad would enable socialist transformation in Russia.

In late 1905, organised workers and Marxist parties came perilously close to turning this vision into a reality across the empire. In many borderland areas, they *did* in fact seize power. And twelve years later, their traditional orthodox strategy proved to be sufficiently relevant to serve as a common political foundation for the Bolsheviks and non-Russian SDs who fought to put all power into the hands of the soviets.

1      State Power and Marxist Strategy in 1905

Before 1905, few underground socialists under Tsarism had sought to articulate how the strategy of proletarian hegemony should be implemented on a governmental level in the forthcoming revolution. Workers would lead the struggle towards a democratic republic, but what kind of political authority should *immediately* replace Tsarism was largely left unanswered. Yet even in this early period, the orthodox consensus pointed in the direction of the conquest of power by working people.

As we have seen, Marxists across Russia advocated a socialist-led armed uprising to topple Tsarism. Though it was not always clearly spelled out, a successful armed uprising meant de facto seizing power – replacing one social group's monopoly of violence with another. As Trotsky argued in 1905, 'in a decisive victory of the revolution, those who led the proletariat will be awarded the power'.[2] In this sense, debates in imperial Russia on the issue of a provisional revolutionary government concerned whether the proletariat and its party should immediately give away or hold on to the reins of authority upon leading an armed insurrection. Events in February 1917 would confirm this dynamic in a negative sense, when the Menshevik and SR leaders of the Petrograd Soviet voluntarily handed political power to liberals following the successful February uprising.

By 1905, virtually all of the illegal social democratic parties in the empire were firmly oriented towards promoting an anti-Tsarist insurrection headed by the working class and its political representatives. Indeed, they argued that it was solely through such an act that a democratic republic could be estab-

---

2   Cited in Anweiler 1974, p. 88.

lished – peaceful protest could, at most, lead to a constitutional monarchy. In the words of the Ukrainian *Spilka*, 'only a rebellion, an uprising with arms in hand, can win a National Constituent Assembly'.[3] Mensheviks also pushed towards this objective, arguing in *Iskra* that the 'weapon of criticism cannot replace the criticism of weapons'.[4]

Throughout 1905, autocratic Russia's social democratic parties fought for an armed proletarian-led democratic revolution – and they came within a hair's breadth of succeeding. Given the refusal of liberals to orient to insurrection-ary struggle, the Marxists' insistence on this point constituted a fundamental point of divergence. So long as the autocracy continued to rule, this orientation towards socialist-led armed uprisings largely determined practical revolution-ary politics. As such, it outweighed the distinct stances taken by SDs through-out 1905 regarding the constitution of (and potential proletarian participation in) a provisional revolutionary government.

Though the advocacy of insurrection pointed towards taking state power, there was not an orthodox consensus concerning provisional revolutionary government in Russia, at least not prior to the climax of late 1905. Indeed, at no point before the revolution did Kautsky or most other Marxists in Tsarist Russia seriously examine the question.

Before the October Manifesto, a majority of Marxist parties and leaders in the empire abstained from articulating a position on the question of post-autocratic power. This approach did not necessarily imply political moderation or an adaptation to the bourgeoisie. Pro-insurrection, anti-liberal currents such as the LSDSP in Latvia, the PPS, the Jewish Bund, and the SDKPIL in Poland all said little about the question about provisional revolutionary governance for the bulk of 1905.

Among borderland Marxists, the one major exception to this agnosticism came from Latvian SD leader Pēteris Stučka. Though his party as a whole had not yet taken a position on the issue, Stučka's important mid-1905 pamphlet *Polistika Briviba* (Political Freedom) made a strong case that a victorious demo-cratic revolution necessarily required the establishment of a provisional pro-letarian government: 'For the revolution to win, it *must* be led by the conscious proletariat; if it wins, then naturally the reins of the provisional government will be in its hands'.[5]

But for other borderland Marxists in the empire, it initially appeared that the heated Bolshevik-Menshevik émigré debates over a provisional revolutionary

---

3   Федьков 2007, p. 39.
4   Редакция 'Искры' 1905.
5   Stučka 1905a [1976–78], p. 99.

government were just another manifestation of excessive polemical factionalism without immediate practical ramifications. At the Bund's congress in early
October, Vladimir Medem argued that 'the question of a provisional government is interesting, but not burning'.[6] Bundist leader Vitaly Yudin made a case
against immediately adopting a position on the topic: 'this question is theoretically very complicated, and I think that when we face it in practice, then we
will be able to solve it correctly'.[7] Thus the Bund's October 1905 congress postponed taking a position on the issue. For his part, Latvian Marxist theoretician
Fricis Roziņš similarly explained that while SDs would have to respond to post-
Tsarist political life from a class struggle platform, for the time being that was
'all a grey mist'.[8]

Only inside the factionalised RSDRP – or at least among its top leadership –
was the question of provisional government a major point of conflict before
October. Bolsheviks advocated a 'democratic dictatorship' of workers and peasants to lead the revolution to victory. Stalin thus argued in a 1905 polemic
against the Mensheviks that, '[w]e proletarians should not only take part in the
present revolution, but also be at the head of it, guide it, and carry it through
to the end. But it will be impossible to carry the revolution through to the end
unless we are represented in the provisional government'.[9]

Trotsky and his collaborator Parvus made a similar case. But whereas the
Bolsheviks left the question of the relative weight of the working class in the
revolutionary regime open ended, Trotsky and Parvus explicitly argued that a
viable provisional government would have to be led by the Marxist party – representatives of the peasantry and revolutionary petty-bourgeoisie would also
participate in the new power, but as supporting partners.[10]

While the positions of Trotsky and the Bolsheviks in 1905 have been extensively discussed by socialists and scholars, the early stance of the Mensheviks
on state power remains understudied and misunderstood. One-sided Bolshevik
polemics combined with Menshevism's post-1905 rightwards turn have
obscured what Lenin's rivals actually said and did during the first Russian
Revolution. Contrary to common myth, it is not the case that the Mensheviks opposed a conquest of power by working people. Towards their goal of an
empire-wide socialist-led insurrection, the Mensheviks' mid-year conference

---

6    'Протоколы и резолюции VI съезда Бунда' [1905] in Андерсон 2010, p. 562.
7    Ibid.
8    Roziņš 1905b [1963–65], p. 27.
9    Stalin 1905 [1953–55], p. 144.
10   Trotsky 1906b [1969], p. 70, Larsson 1970, pp. 284–92, Day and Gaido 2009, pp. 254–6, and
     Lih 2012d, pp. 439–44.

explicitly advocated the 'partial or episodic seizure of power and the formation of revolutionary communes in one city or another, or in one region or another'.[11] The model for this 'revolutionary self-government', they explained, was the Paris Commune. Due to this stance, combined with the Mensheviks' advocacy of insurrection, Lenin in 1909 thus quietly acknowledged that his rivals throughout 1905–06 had in actuality pushed for a revolutionary provisional government.[12]

At the same time, top Menshevik theoreticians in 1905 generally argued that Marxists in the empire should not aspire to participate in a state-wide provisional government after the victorious final uprising. Since the Russian Revolution did not seek to overturn capitalism, they argued, a working-class party should not aim to enter a provisional government in coalition with non-socialists and within the framework of bourgeois social relations. Such an approach, they claimed, could only lead to a repeat of the damaging ministerialism of Millerand in France; Lenin's stance, they claimed, was a petty-bourgeois tactic and clear opportunism. The political independence of the working class therefore would be better served by remaining in 'extreme revolutionary opposition' to a post-autocratic provisional government.[13] Unlike in later years, this Menshevik stance on the state in 1905 was explicitly tied to the need to promote (rather than restrain) proletarian insurgency: 'We do not say to the proletariat: retain your revolutionary impulses so that you don't somehow find yourself prematurely in power'.[14] And were the new post-autocratic government to become an obstacle to the further development of the revolution, they asserted, it must be overthrown by the working class: 'That is part of the revolutionary ABC'.[15]

For all its radicalism, this stance was not without significant ambiguities and shortcomings. Why should power be seized locally and regionally but not state-wide? In addition, the comparison of the Bolshevik approach to Millerandism was unconvincing – the Bolsheviks advocated a revolutionary regime of workers and peasants, not minority socialist participation in a capitalist coalition government.[16] Finally, underlying the Menshevik approach was a questionable hope in the emergence of a strong progressive bourgeoisie in

11  'On the Seizure of Power and Participation in a Provisional Government' [1905] in Elwood 1974a, p. 73.
12  Anweiler 1974, p. 68 and Lenin 1909 [1960–65], p. 372.
13  Мартынов 1923, Редакция 'Искры' 1905, 'On the Seizure of Power and Participation in a Provisional Government' [1905] in Elwood 1974a, p. 73, and Larsson 1970, pp. 340–3.
14  Редакция 'Искры' 1905.
15  Cited in Larsson 1970, p. 353.
16  Lenin 1905d [1960–65], p. 23.

Russia. It is unsurprising that this Menshevik view on provisional state power was not shared by other s D s across the empire in 1905.[17]

If this were all the Mensheviks had to say about their perspectives for revolutionary government, then it would be generally accurate to affirm that they opposed socialist participation in the post-Tsarist state. But throughout 1905, the Mensheviks openly argued that the working class must be ready to seize and hold on to full political power if the revolution spread to the West or if the liberal bourgeoisie failed to live up to its historic mission.[18]

While what one might call the Mensheviks' 'Plan A' was proletarian opposition to a capitalist provisional government, they clearly and consistently argued for a 'Plan B' if a democratic bourgeoisie did not emerge. In such a case, the Mensheviks argued, it would be necessary to establish a working-class, anti-capitalist regime in Russia that would seek to spread the revolution westwards. In March 1905, Martov thus argued that 'should all the strong bourgeois-revolutionary parties wither without having bloomed ... the proletariat will not be able to turn its back on political power'.[19]

Like Trotsky, the Mensheviks rejected the conception (shared by both Kautsky and the Bolsheviks) that some form of ongoing 'democratic dictatorship' of working people was possible under capitalism in Russia. Arguing that the state must either uphold or destroy capitalism, Martov declared that 'if [the proletariat] as a class comes to power, it cannot but lead the revolution on, it cannot fail to strive for Revolution in Permanenz, for an outright struggle with all of bourgeois society'.[20]

In light of this strategy, it is clear that the Mensheviks' response to what Martov called 'the betrayal of bourgeois liberalism' following the October Manifesto was neither a surprise nor simply a concession to pressure from below.[21] During the peak of the revolution in November and December, Menshevik leaders in Russia openly aligned themselves with Trotsky. To quote the 7 November editorial of their jointly published paper *Nachalo* (The Dawn): 'It is entirely possible that in the event of a protracted civil war our revolution, which began as a democratic revolution, will end as a socialist revolution'.[22]

---

17    For a mid-1905 critique of the Menshevik stance, see, for example, Stučka 1905a [1976–78], p. 99.

18    'On the Seizure of Power and Participation in a Provisional Government' [1905] in Elwood 1974a, p. 73.

19    Cited in Schwarz 1967, p. 11. See, also, 'On the Seizure of Power and Participation in a Provisional Government' [1905] in Elwood 1974a, p. 73.

20    Cited in Schwarz 1967, p. 11. See also Редакция 'Искры' 1905.

21    Cited in Казарова 1999, p. 149 and Larsson 1970, p. 345.

22    Cited in Ascher 1988, p. 287. See also Larsson 1970, p. 339.

Across the empire, socialist parties generally followed a similar post-October evolution towards state power, though most did not go as far as the Mensheviks and Trotsky in projecting anti-capitalist revolution. Liberalisms' abandonment of the mass movement in October and the emergence of proletarian dual power for the first time obliged concrete political answers to questions about establishing a popular authority.[23] In almost all regions, orthodox SDs dropped their previously open-ended stances on post-autocratic governance and explicitly called for all power to be placed in the hands of socialist-led provisional revolutionary governments on a local and state-wide level. Consequently in December the SDKPIL issued a leaflet calling on working people to fight to 'seize governmental power, to create a revolutionary government, which will proclaim a people's republic across the state and convene a state-wide Constituent Assembly'.[24] A PPS proclamation issued on 13 December likewise elaborated on the form and concrete tasks of such a regime.[25]

Russia's Marxists incessantly affirmed that only the working class could lead the democratic revolution all the way to the end. Indeed, for many socialists this dynamic was precisely what they were referring to by the phrase 'permanent revolution'.[26] In November 1905, for example, the PPS made a case for the working class to immediately conquer state authority, arguing that it must win and consolidate as much power as possible to carry the revolutionary transformation of society as far as it could go.[27]

Following the defeated uprisings of December 1905, Kautsky and revolutionary SDs across imperial Russia began to elaborate their strategies for establishing revolutionary provisional power. In 1906, Kautsky published a highly influ-

---

23  Faced with the experience of 1905, even some anarchists in Russia began to drop their former view that, to quote one Georgian anarchist leader, 'revolutionary government always plays an anti-popular role' (cited in Avrich 1967, p. 107). As Vladimir Sapon has demonstrated, wings of anarchists began to move away from this traditional opposition to all state authority in the wake of 1905, a process culminating in the entry of a significant number of anarchists into the Soviet government in 1917 and 1918 (Сапон 2009).

24  Cited in Samuś 2013, p. 308.

25  'Towarzysze! Obywatele!', 26 December 1905, Odezwa Centralny Komitet Robotniczy Polskiej Partii Socjalistycznej (Dokumenty życia społecznego, Biblioteka Narodowa).

26  In 1905 and 1906, the term 'permanent revolution' did not (outside of Trotsky's writings) generally carry the connotation of passing from a 'democratic revolution' to a 'socialist revolution'. Usually it referred to a process through which the hegemonic proletariat would lead the democratic revolution all the way to the end, over the opposition or hesitations of liberals and other non-socialists (Stučka 1905b [1976–78], p. 143, Редакция 'Искры' 1905, Schwarz 1967, p. 247, and Lih 2012d).

27  Kmiecik 1980, p. 70.

ential article 'The Driving Forces of the Russian Revolution and Its Prospects', which declared that 'it is very possible that in the course of the revolution victory will fall to the Social Democratic Party and social democracy does very well to hold out this prospect of victory to its supporters because you cannot struggle successfully if you have renounced victory in advance'.[28]

In a certain sense, Kautsky's stance contradicted the general revolutionary Marxist opposition to proletarian participation in national executive governance under capitalism. Indeed, this argument was raised at the time by Mensheviks against the SPD theoretician.[29] Nevertheless, Kautsky argued that the Russian Revolution should be viewed as an exceptional case, in which models from the West could not be mechanically copied. Reflecting on the apparent paradox that a democratic revolution would likely 'bring social democracy to power temporarily', Kautsky explained:

> We should do well to remember that we are approaching completely new situations and problems for which no earlier model is appropriate. We should most probably be fair to the Russian revolution and the tasks that it sets us if we viewed it as neither a bourgeois revolution in the traditional sense nor a socialist one but as a quite unique process which is taking place on the borderline between bourgeois and socialist society.[30]

While Kautsky refrained from predicting the particular institutional forms that such a post-autocratic government might take, the Bolsheviks elaborated their vision. They declared in 1906 that the soviets and other forms of mass self-organisation that had emerged post-October were the 'embryonic forms of a new revolutionary authority'.[31] This early call for soviet power is important to note, since it has often been wrongly assumed that the Bolsheviks' demand for 'All Power to the Soviets' in 1917 constituted a rupture from their previous position.

In 1906, non-Russian socialists also published their first major strategic documents on provisional power. A piece by the PPS explained why the party supported the 'consistently revolutionary' position of the Bolsheviks and not that of the Mensheviks, which 'essentially boils the role of the working class down to the role of an auxiliary army for the liberal bourgeoisie'. On the issue of provisional governance, the PPS declared: 'Only the iron hand of working people can

---

28    Kautsky 1906 [2009], p. 605.
29    Naarden 1992, p. 226.
30    Kautsky 1906 [2009], p. 607.
31    Lenin 1906 [1960–65], pp. 155, 157.

purify Russia from the remnants of despotism and repair the damage caused by Tsarism. ... The call for the revolutionary dictatorship of the proletariat and the rural people is the correct slogan, as it completely fits the current revolutionary situation'.[32] That same year, Rosa Luxemburg similarly published a long pamphlet laying out the need for a provisional working-class government to defeat the counter-revolution, implement the core demands of workers, and guarantee the convocation of a Constituent Assembly.[33]

In contrast, most Menshevik leaders after 1905 broke from their previous approach to seizing state power – i.e. they dropped their 'Plan B'. Despite the decisive retreat of liberals from the revolutionary struggle, the Mensheviks' overriding post-1905 stance crystallised into a dogmatic insistence on the feasibility of class collaboration for winning democracy and an inflexible opposition to Marxist participation in post-autocratic governance. On an empire-wide level in 1906, however, the Mensheviks remained a decisive minority on these questions.

In short, Kautsky and revolutionary socialists across the imperial territory during 1905 and 1906 were openly orienting towards establishing a socialist-led revolutionary government to radically democratise political and social relations. A state-wide lens confirms the conclusion of Reidar Larsson's overlooked study of Marxism in Tsarist Russia: 'those who did not concentrate on a Socialist seizure of political power in Russia deviated from "orthodox Marxism"'.[34] Ultimately, this strategy of proletarian hegemony to establish a government independent of the upper class defined the political orientation of revolutionary social democracy in Russia. Both in 1905 and 1917, this fundamental strategic consensus far outweighed the continued theoretical differences over the projected weight of the proletariat in such a revolutionary government – or the degree of social transformation it could realistically promote before the eruption of world revolution.

## 2 The Practice of Revolutionary Government in 1905

The fact that absolutism had banished workers from the formal political arena greatly facilitated the growth and legitimacy of institutions of dual power across imperial Russia.[35] It is necessary to briefly discuss the late-1905 prac-

---

32    'Walka kierunków w łonie Rosyjskiej Socjalnej Demokracji', *Robotnik*, 4 July 1906.
33    Luxemburg 1906a, pp. 4–5.
34    Larsson 1970, p. 358.
35    Anweiler 1974, p. 52.

tices of revolutionary governance, as the experience of these months established a political precedent that was revived in 1917. Had the December 1905
armed uprisings succeeded, the existing organs of popular power would likely
have been granted full state authority. As such, an examination of the politics
and practices of these embryonic institutions of revolutionary rule can give us
a glimpse of the type of government that would have immediately replaced the
autocracy.

After the October Manifesto, revolutionaries seized partial or complete control of numerous cities and rural areas throughout the Russian Empire. The
Bund, usually in alliance with socialists of other nationalities, assumed de facto
or complete power in various towns. In the Zolotonosha region of Ukraine,
the Bund seized state authority after leading a mass of torch-wielding peasants to demolish the police station, free prisoners from the jail, and destroy
the regime's records on owed taxes and debts.[36] To quote historian Jonathan
Frankel, 'the concept of the "hegemony of the proletariat" was considered an
appropriate description of the actual situation in a number of largely Jewish
cities'.[37]

Ekaterinoslav and the surrounding mining towns in Ukraine also came
under workers' rule in December. Power was assumed by the Fighting Strike
Committee (FSC) composed of representatives of the unified RSDRP committee, the Bund, the SRs, Anarchist-Communists, and the Railroad Union. Proclaiming itself to be the executive branch of the new revolutionary government, the FSC established free cafeterias, provided healthcare and medicine at
no charge, and distributed essential goods such as kerosene and matches. Poor
and unemployed workers were instructed to cease paying rent to their landlords.[38] The revolution proceeded even further in the nearby city of Novorussia,
where the soviet conquered full power for most of December and proclaimed
a Novorossiysk Republic.[39]

In Baku, the Tsarist security forces lamented that the new Menshevik-led
Soviet 'took power into its own hands and turned itself into an organ of provisional revolutionary government'.[40] Baku's Soviet in 1905 intervened to oblige
employers to meet the wage demands of oil workers. And, like in the rest of the
empire, its authority went far beyond the workplace. The Soviet, for example,
pressured merchants to lower their prices for basic necessities, announced that

36   Bushnell 1985, p. 106 and Риш 1926, p. 42.
37   Frankel 1981, p. 144.
38   Wynn 1987, p. 348 and Sutton 1987, p. 377.
39   Anweiler 1974, pp. 61–2 and Равич-Черкасский 1923, p. 17.
40   Cited in Lane 1969, p. 190.

tenants need not pay their full rents, established a system of people's courts, and built communal dining halls and soup-kitchens for the hungry.[41]

In Georgian towns such as Poti, Sukhumi, and Kutaisi, SD committees took full governmental control. In the regional capital of Tiflis, dual power prevailed. Deposed authorities in Georgia reported to St. Petersburg that 'under threat of death' all police had been disarmed and replaced by a workers' militia; all administrative functions were now carried out by the socialists.[42] And a local Tsarist official reported the following about the situation in his region: 'the Social Democratic Party is trying to concentrate the reins of government in its hands ... [A]ll the police have been removed ... and police service and maintenance of the trains is being carried out by their administration ... [I]n a word, anarchy, tyranny, mob law, boycott, and strikes under the leadership of the various parties'.[43]

Of all imperial Russia's regions, it was in Latvia that revolutionary governance went furthest. During and following the October strike, power in Riga was largely assumed by the Federal Committee, which united the LSDSP and the Bund, as well as smaller groups of German, Lithuanian, and Estonian SDs. Denouncing the 'infamous activities' of the Federal Committee, the Baltic German conservative writer Astaf von Transehe-Roseneck called this 'a strange alliance: the youngest and the oldest nation [Latvians and Jews]' joined together on the basis of their mutual 'fanaticism'.[44]

The powers and prerogatives of the Committee were manifold: setting rents, taxes, and prices; assuming judicial authority through revolutionary tribunals and administering justice; controlling the railways, postal service, and telegraphs; intervening in workers' disputes with employers; and maintaining order through armed workers' militias. The German consul lamented that, apart from the small city centre, Riga had 'fallen entirely into the hands of the revolutionaries'.[45] In late November, the Tsarist regime's attempt to impose martial law in Latvia was immediately beaten back by a new general strike. Transehe-Roseneck described this period of de facto revolutionary rule as the proletariat's 'Reign of Terror in Riga in November and December 1905'.[46]

Latvia's rural areas also experienced decisive revolutionary overhauls. By December, new democratically elected revolutionary governments were set up

---

41    Sutton 1987, pp. 375–6, 409.
42    Jones 1984, pp. 211–12.
43    Cited in Jones 1984, p. 172.
44    Transehe-Roseneck 1908, p. 102.
45    Cited in Benz 1989, p. 231.
46    Transehe-Roseneck 1908, p. 110.

in 94 per cent of Latvia's parishes. In Tukums, a militia of 3,000 rural workers and peasants led by the local LSDSP branch arrested the police and kicked
out the stationed troops, seizing the weapons from the armoury. Militias soon
established their armed authority in rural regions, leading most Baltic German
nobles to flee to the cities or to Germany. Those who attempted to resist were
mostly 'smoked out': during the Latvian revolution of 1905, over 40 per cent of
the landlords' manors were burnt down or destroyed.[47] The head of the Latvian
garrison reported to the Tsar in November that 'various regions have been abandoned to their fate. Almost all the landlords' estates have been plundered. Some
landlords and their families are forced to seek refuge in the city, some hide in
the forests'.[48]

For the purpose of our discussion, three points about these incipient forms
of revolutionary governance should be highlighted. The first is that although
institutions of popular power arose in both the countryside and the city, the
latter was undeniably politically decisive. Due to a shortage of reliable army
units, the Tsarist regime pulled its troops from rural areas, largely abandoning any attempts to control the countryside by late November. '[V]illages filled
with rebels and a half wild population are not dear to Russia', explained one
army major.[49] Across the political spectrum, everyone knew that the fate of
the revolution, i.e., the question of state power, would be decided in the big cities. The hegemony of the working class in the revolutionary process – and in
its nascent institutions of state power – was an accomplished fact despite the
proletariat's numerical weakness.

From the standpoint of socialist strategy, the embryonic forms of revolutionary governance gave Marxist currents a significantly higher political weight
than they might have had in a universal suffrage election, where their influence would be offset by the votes of Russia's rural majority as well as moderate
workers uninvolved in the labour movement. Later, this became perhaps the
decisive reason why workers' councils were so central to post-1917 Communist strategy. Winning a majority of working people organised into councils was
a more easily attainable benchmark for revolutionary-democratic legitimacy
than gaining a preliminary electoral majority of the entire population under
conditions of capitalist rule, particularly since so much of the population in
Russia and across Europe – not to mention Asia, Africa, and Latin America –
were non-proletarian.[50]

---

47    Apine 2005, pp. 29, 42 and Bērziņš 2000, p. 381.
48    Cited in Bērziņš 1986, p. 144.
49    Cited in Fuller 1985, p. 145. See also Bushnell 1985, pp. 106–7.
50    Most other socialists responded to this same majoritarian dilemma by slowly shedding
    strict revolutionary intransigence (Stephens 1979 and Esping-Andersen 1985).

Second, the institutions of popular democracy in Russia were distinctly more participatory than the existing parliamentary regimes in Western Europe. Though the particular forms varied widely from city to city, these revolutionary institutions relied on and embodied the direct involvement of working people in political life. Since the existing state apparatus and bureaucracy was clearly unusable for revolutionary ends, the insurgents were obliged to create new authoritative bodies from below. Making representatives recallable at any time allowed for a great degree of popular accountability. And the fact that representation depended at least to a certain extent on active participation incentivised passive workers to engage.

But given the tendency of radicals throughout the twentieth century to fetishise soviets – or to judge post-October 1917 Bolshevism by impossibly high standards of popular governance – it is important to note that even in 1905 these bodies reflected many of the limitations of direct democracy. Though there was no formal separation of powers in these organisations, in practice none of the soviets in 1905 were able to dispense with institutional structures that resembled traditional executive and legislative branches. On this question, Anweiler notes:

> As a rule the soviets were headed by an executive committee of several members ... which took care of the day-to-day business. As against the general assembly of deputies, the 'parliament,' the executive embodied the 'government,' as it were. ... The rush of events required quick decisions by the Executive Committee, which then sought approval from the soviet after the fact. The Executive Committee of the St. Petersburg soviet also composed proclamations and appeals – usually by Trotsky's pen – which were then ratified and proclaimed at soviet plenary sessions.[51]

The extent to which councils and their equivalents constituted a higher form of democracy than traditional parliamentarism depended on the degree of popular participation in these bodies and the rank and file's ability to exercise effective control over their representatives. The democratic promise – as well as the potential substitutionist dangers – of this informality and reliance on mass participation would become evident in the course of 1917 and subsequent years, when it became difficult to sustain the requisite levels of popular involvement.[52]

---

51    Anweiler 1974, p. 54.
52    For a discussion of how Bolshevism's post-1917 slide towards authoritarianism was aided

The third critical point to underscore is that although most Marxists in the empire rejected the idea of overthrowing Tsarism and capitalism simultaneously, the late-year revolutionary movement nevertheless began to pose a threat to capitalist rule itself. SDs were not consciously seeking to establish a socialist regime to overturn capital, but their efforts to establish a democratic government already stood in contradiction with capitalist prerogatives. In November, the German consul in Moscow predicted that 'serious disturbances with an anticapitalist thrust' were imminent.[53] Late 1905's situation of dual power put into sharp relief the inherent tensions within the orthodox strategy of proletarian hegemony in a 'democratic revolution'.

As long as the Tsar remained in power, the thrust of the revolutionary struggle would be directed against the autocracy rather than the bourgeoisie as such. Most socialists throughout Russia explicitly rejected the view that the current revolution could transcend capitalism, at least not before Western workers' rule. Nor did any Marxist parties at this time call for the organs of revolutionary self-government to assume power permanently. Authority would provisionally pass into the hands of working people after the victorious uprising, but the establishment of a Constituent Assembly and republic were consistently declared to be the governmental end goals of the current revolution. Given the proletariat's minority status in Russia, institutions elected by universal suffrage were presumably incompatible with working-class government.

Yet the course of revolutionary struggle in 1905 and the social democrats' insistence on proletarian hegemony had nevertheless led to a situation with real anti-capitalist potentialities. The aspirations of working people and their organised representatives were certainly not limited to changes in government.

Upon assuming partial or full governmental power in November and December, the workers' soviets and Federal Committees began encroaching on the power of business owners. For much of the industrial elite, November and December 1905 was experienced as a moment of mob rule. Embryonic revolutionary governments often interceded on workers' behalf in conflicts with employers, obliged price freezes or reductions on merchants, set taxes, imposed alcohol prohibition, lowered or cancelled the payment of rent, and sometimes even began providing free essential goods and services to the public. Various soviets threatened to destroy the property of local traders who refused to obey their edicts during the general strike. Strategic industries in the struggle against Tsarism were the most frequent victims of dual power. Labour organisations,

---

by Lenin's over-optimistic hopes, from *The State and Revolution* onwards, in the possibilities for an immediate transition from capitalism to direct democracy, see Miliband 1970.

53    Cited in Ascher 1988, p. 307.

for instance, frequently banned or boycotted counter-revolutionary publications or took over capitalist printing facilities to produce their proclamations.[54]
Given their social centrality, railways across the empire were seized and put
under workers' control during December.[55]

By late 1905, wide layers of the population believed that imperial Russia
stood on the brink of *social* revolution. Though none of the Marxist parties in
the empire advocated immediate anti-capitalist revolution, they were nevertheless the main political current responsible for encouraging a 'levelling spirit'
among the working class. The SDs' calls to overthrow Tsarism and win the central demands of working people – from the eight-hour day to the distribution
of land – raised hopes and expectations from below that 'the day of reckoning had come' in which the poor would get their fair share. It is significant
that Marxist mass agitation did not frame socialism as a distant prospect, but
rather portrayed political freedom as a necessary step in the fight to expropriate
the expropriators. Consider the following leaflet issued by the Bund's central
committee: 'Only truly freely chosen representatives of the people, vested with
sovereignty, will be able to re-create the whole system, to sweep away the old
one and introduce a democratic republic. And in the atmosphere of free institutions, we will deploy all our forces and move with accelerated steps towards
the realisation of socialism'.[56]

Taken on its own, such an orientation could easily be linked to a vision of
fast-approaching anti-capitalist revolution. For the average worker receiving a
socialist leaflet, the general impression received was *not* that socialism was a
faraway prospect, but simply that it was *first* necessary to overthrow Tsarism.[57]
Marxist theoretical journals and party congress resolutions certainly discussed
the obstacles to socialism constituted by Russia's majority peasant population,
but this line of argument was virtually absent in party leaflets and agitation,
which aimed at inspiring working people to take militant action.

Some socialist activists went further. In the words of one rank-and-file member of a SD battle squad, 'I had a gun and I felt that I could begin an armed
fight for socialism at once'.[58] Another socialist worker voiced a similar sentiment: 'whatever the party programme might say, we workers, if we are going
to shed our blood, it will be at once for freedom and for socialism'.[59] While

---

54    Sutton 1987, pp. 353–5, Rice 1988, p. 28, and Prevo 1988, p. 210.
55    Sutton 1987, pp. 357–8, Prevo 1979, p. 251, and Wojtasik 1981, p. 191.
56    'Прокламация ЦК Бунда "1 мая"' [1906] in Савицкий 1997, p. 250.
57    'Kapitala atriebšanās' in Latvijas KP CK Partijas Vēstures Institūts 1955, p. 75.
58    Nicolaysen 1990, p. 271.
59    Cited in Preobrazhenskii 2006, p. 296.

such arguments were made by only a small minority inside the Marxist movement, the fact that they appeared in all corners of the empire is significant.
Advocacy of immediate social revolution even emerged in Finland, a region
in which both workers and the Social Democracy had hitherto been relatively
disinclined towards radicalism.[60]

Because of the anti-capitalist orientation of workers and Marxists in late
1905 and their estrangement from liberals, it is unlikely that a successful
socialist-led armed uprising would have resulted in passing power to a bourgeois opposition, as it did in February 1917. In contrast with events twelve years
later, there were no Marxist currents in December 1905 oriented towards a bloc
with liberals or willing to hand off power immediately following an uprising. All
social democratic parties in imperial Russia, with the exception of the Finns,
at this time firmly opposed the establishment of a coalition government with
the bourgeoisie. And liberals were organisationally and socially weaker in 1905
than they were in 1917, making their potential assumption of power in most
regions of the empire hard to imagine.

The experience of late 1905 showed that in imperial Russia the dynamics
of a democratic revolution led by orthodox Marxists threatened to undermine
capitalist rule. Even though most workers and revolutionary socialists in 1905
did not fully foresee this dynamic, their actions and strategies nevertheless pro-
pelled it forward. The following 1906 argument by Trotsky was both an accurate
extrapolation from the recent experience of embryonic workers' government
and a realistic anticipation of the October Revolution:

> No matter under what political flag the proletariat has come to power, it is
> obliged to take the path of socialist policy. It would be the greatest utopi-
> anism to think that the proletariat, having been raised to political dom-
> ination by the internal mechanism of a bourgeois revolution, can, even
> if it so desires, limit its mission to the creation of republican-democratic
> conditions for the social domination of the bourgeoisie.[61]

## 3       Socialist Transformation in Russia

A large majority of imperial Russia's social democrats explicitly rejected the
view that the current revolution should seek to eliminate capitalism in Russia,

---

60    Cited in Järvinen 1983, p. 173. See also Kujala 1989, p. 322.
61    Trotsky 1906b [1969], pp. 101–2. My emphasis.

at least not prior to victorious socialist overturns in the West. The latter caveat, to be sure, was hardly a minor one: we will see below that orthodox SDs from 1905 onwards put the potential reciprocal effects of international revolution at the heart of their strategic vision. Yet orthodox Marxists overwhelmingly rejected the idea that the Russian Revolution could take steps towards socialism prior to Western workers' rule.

In 1905, Lenin asserted that an immediate socialist overturn was an 'absurd and semi-anarchist' idea.[62] Similarly, even when orthodox SDs invoked the phrase 'permanent revolution' and argued that the Russian Revolution should not be considered 'bourgeois', they simultaneously asserted the impossibility of directly transcending bourgeois social relations.[63] The main objections put forward in 1905 remained the same as in previous years: First, workers in Russia were not conscious and organised enough for socialism – therefore, a preliminary period of political freedom was needed. Second, workers were too numerically weak – the peasantry, a non-socialist class, constituted the majority of the population, thereby precluding attempts to successfully move to collectivist production. Though Marxist theorists sometimes tied these two points together, it is important to distinguish between them, as they had different implications for the timing and prospects of social revolution in Russia.

By far the most frequently raised Marxist axiom against socialist transformation was that a preliminary period of political freedom was required, so that workers could become sufficiently conscious and organised to permanently rule society. The orthodox case was succinctly affirmed by the PPS in 1906:

> The aim of the workers of all countries is through the organised proletariat to conquer political power (the dictatorship of the proletariat) and use it to carry out a social revolution, i.e., to abolish the private ownership of the means of production and make them the common property of the whole society. This objective can be achieved only through a decisive battle with the possessing classes. To prepare for such a huge task, the proletariat must build its strong and cohesive organisation, rise intellectually and culturally, and [prepare itself] to govern its own affairs. All these preliminary conditions for socialist revolution can be realised only in a democratic republic.[64]

---

62    Lenin 1905b [1960–65], p. 28.
63    Редакция 'Искры' 1905, Schwarz 1967, p. 247, Lih 2012d, and Luxemburg 1906c, p. 41.
64    Robotnik 1906 [1961], p. 95. See also Lenin 1905b [1960–65], p. 29 and Kautsky 1906 [2009], p. 605.

Marxist orthodoxy generally projected a high (if vaguely defined) bar for the level of proletarian organisation and education required for successful socialist transformation. Yet no precise criteria existed for just how conscious and organised the working class had to be.

If the determining variable factor in the fight for socialism was just the political-organisational strength of workers and their party, then nothing prevented social democrats from immediately commencing the fight for socialist revolution once political freedom was won. The tempo was not predetermined; the interval between the two ruptures need not be long. And, in a certain sense, this is precisely what occurred in 1917.

The second orthodox Marxist axiom against anti-capitalist overturn in imperial Russia was that socialist construction could not take place in a majority peasant country. Kautsky and orthodox Marxists across imperial Russia consistently asserted that since peasants as a class were committed to the private ownership of the means of production, the revolution underway could not plausibly introduce socialism.[65]

Tied to this view of the peasantry as a barrier to socialism was the question of democratic institutions elected by universal suffrage. All Marxists before 1917 assumed that representative institutions based on majority rule and universal suffrage would be integral components of a workers' state. In this context, it is understandable that many SDs argued that socialism could not be established until the working class made up a majority of society. Luxemburg explained in 1906 that workers in Russia were 'not strong enough at this time' to establish socialism because 'the proletariat, in the strictest sense of the word, constitutes a minority in the Russian empire. The achievement of socialism by a minority is unconditionally excluded, since the very idea of socialism excludes the domination of a minority'.[66]

On a theoretical level, these economic-agrarian arguments far more categorically precluded an imminent socialist revolution in Russia than the political freedom criteria. If workers first had to constitute the majority of the population, then it was understandable why Plekhanov concluded in 1901 that the democratic and socialist revolutions would 'of necessity be separated by a significant period of time'.[67]

The most consistent strategic alternative to this stance came from Trotsky. He agreed with the orthodox Marxist assessment that the peasantry was an

---

65    Kautsky 1905 [2018], p. 230 and Kautsky 1906 [2009], pp. 606–7. See also Stalin 1905 [1953–55], p. 142 and Šteinbergs 1977, p. 98.
66    Luxemburg 1906a.
67    Cited in Larsson 1970, p. 156.

obstacle towards socialist transformation and lasting workers' rule. In his view, a workers' government could not survive in a predominantly peasant country. Trotsky, however, argued that measures beyond capitalism, namely the expropriation of large capitalist enterprises, could be taken – indeed would *have to* be taken – by a workers' government despite the existence of a peasant-majority population. He posited that a workers' conquest of power did not require that the 'overwhelming majority of the population' be committed to socialist transformation. Rather 'the conscious revolutionary army of the proletariat must be stronger than the counter-revolutionary army of capital, while the intermediate, doubtful or indifferent strata of the population must be in such a position that the regime of proletarian dictatorship will attract them to the side of the revolution and not repel them to the side of its enemies'.[68]

Even if it wanted to, Trotsky argued, a transformative workers' government would not be able to remain within bourgeois property relations. Kautsky had repeatedly made this case for the context of Western Europe, but Trotsky was the first to argue for its applicability to Russia as well.[69] His point was not that the democratic revolution could be 'skipped', but rather that its successful implementation pushed beyond capitalism. By promoting and recognising the peasants' expropriation of the landed estates, this workers' government would initially be able to win the support of the large mass of peasants. Yet the inevitable cooling of the revolutionary fervour of the peasantry combined with the rising struggle of the rural proletariat against the peasant landowners, would eventually turn the agrarian masses against the new regime. Given these contradictions, Trotsky concluded that the survival of a Russian workers' government and the construction of socialism depended on the spread of socialist revolution to the West.[70]

The differences between Trotsky's theory and that of other Marxists of the era have far too often been exaggerated. Some of their critical points in common, such as advocacy of a proletarian government in Russia, have already been touched on in earlier sections. Here our focus will turn to their shared conception of the imminence and reciprocal nature of the international revolution. This orientation became a decisive component of revolutionary Marxism across the empire after 1904, thereby paving the way for SDs well before 1917 to reject the idea that socialist transformation in Russia had to be postponed until a distant future.

---

68    Trotsky 1906b [1969], pp. 85, 88.
69    Trotsky 1906b [1969], p. 100 and Kautsky 1904 [2009], p. 199. Contra Kautsky, subsequent experience – e.g. of Sweden's Social Democracy – showed that Left governments *could* challenge the status quo without overthrowing capitalism (Korpi 1983).
70    Trotsky 1906b [1969].

## 4 International Revolution

In some ways the stance of the empire's Marxists came full circle between 1882 and 1917. Indeed, world revolution was a central strategic component of the sole Marxist party in the empire to predate the birth of social democratic orthodoxy: the Proletariat, founded in Poland in 1882. Imbued with a revolutionary enthusiasm that proved in hindsight to be markedly over-optimistic, the Proletariat believed that the world social revolution was fast approaching.[71] Tied to this perspective, leaders of the Proletariat argued that the Russian autocracy and capitalism should be overthrown at the same time.

Party leader Ludwig Warynski declared in 1883 that the 'dictatorship of the proletariat will be the first act of the revolution' in Russia.[72] In his view, the social revolution must necessarily be international because neighbouring capitalist states would inevitably seek to crush the first nation to initiate socialist transformation. With its stress on the spread of world revolution, the Proletariat was largely unconcerned with the issue of the Russian Empire's material 'ripeness' for socialism – instead it focused its efforts on mobilising workers and peasants towards the direct seizure of political *and* economic power. The party's widely distributed 1883 manifesto to the peasantry declared: 'The land belongs to those who plough it. The factories belong to those who work them. So join the fight and bring sooner our common victory over our enemies'.[73]

In an 1884 polemic against Plekhanov's rejection of the seizure of power as an immediate task, the Proletariat invoked the writings of Marx to affirm that not all countries had to follow the path of Western capitalism. If the revolution in Russia was linked to revolution in the West, Marx argued, then both could proceed directly to socialism.[74] Proletariat leader Stanislaw Mendelson argued that Plekhanov's 'fanatical polemicism' against the populists had prevented him from 'carefully reading' Marx's writings.[75]

This orientation to international revolution was not upheld by most subsequent social democrats in Russia and Europe. In the early (pre-1905) writings of orthodox SDs, workers' revolution was framed largely as a discrete process occurring within the bounds of individual countries. A discussion of the

---

71  [Tadeusz Rechniewski] 'My i Rząd', *Proletariat*, 1 May 1884.
72  [Ludwik Waryński] 'My i Burżuazja', *Proletariat*, 20 October 1883.
73  'Do Pracujących Na Roli: Komitetu Centralnego Socyalno-Rewolucyjnej Partyi', 24 June 1883 (Archiwum Akt Nowych 305, 1, 1).
74  St. 1884, pp. 25–6.
75  Mendelson 1887, p. XIII.

international reciprocity of revolution was noticeably absent in the *Erfurt Programme*. The same was true in the early works of Axelrod, Plekhanov, Lenin, and Trotsky.[76]

Kautsky pioneered a break from this perspective in the early years of the twentieth century. Rather than looking at world politics simply as the sum of discrete countries, each with their own separate internal battles, Kautsky in 1903 argued that the growing interconnection of the globe meant that 'no country, and least of all a capitalist country, moves along the path of its domestic development solely as a result of its own internal driving forces. Outside influences, and above all the effects of class wars in foreign countries, become almost equally important for its class struggles'.[77]

Developing these insights, Kautsky the following year articulated an argument that would soon become central to the perspectives of revolutionary Marxists across Europe: proletarian revolution would likely break out in world capitalism's weakest link, the Tsarist Empire. In a context marked by an illegitimate and repressive state as well as a relatively weak bourgeoisie, the small-but-powerful working class in Russia was poised to lead a radical transformation of the entire social structure. And while under-developed economic conditions precluded a direct socialist revolution, the establishment of workers' rule in Europe could allow Russia to move straight towards socialism.[78]

From this international perspective, the economic 'ripeness' of a given country was superseded by the potentialities of international revolution. When socialist transformation was envisioned from a worldwide angle, it became possible to foresee political dynamics abroad enabling even a 'backwards' country like Russia to 'skip' past years of capitalist development.

Kautsky's argument was not simply that European socialism could profoundly influence revolutionary developments in Russia, but also, inversely, that the revolution in Tsarist Russia would accelerate social revolution in the West. In the particular chain of revolutionary events predicted by Kautsky in 1904, Russia's borderlands would act as a bridge towards socialist revolution in the German, Austro-Hungarian, and Ottoman Empires. All three of these states, Kautsky noted, ruled over nationalities that were also dominated by Tsarism, such as Poles and Ukrainians. Revolution among the Tsar's oppressed nationalities would likely spark both proletarian and national liberation upheavals in these neighbouring states. These national-proletarian movements of the Tsar-

76    Larsson 1970, pp. 175, 224.
77    Kautsky 1903 [2009], p. 183.
78    Kautsky 1904 [2009], p. 219.

ist borderlands could lead not only to the break-up of the German and Austrian Empires, but directly to proletarian revolution in the West.[79]

On the basis of their experience during Russia's first revolution, revolutionary SDs increasingly adopted this orientation. The year 1905 was widely felt by friend and foe alike to be ushering in a new historical epoch of worldwide social revolution. Pēteris Stučka proclaimed that 'the revolution can be a success only if it extends across the whole globe'.[80] And the PPS journal *Robotnik* insisted upon the 'tremendous importance' Russia's revolution had in pushing the rest of the capitalist world towards socialism.[81]

Such perspectives transformed the expectations of revolutionary social democrats concerning the potential for direct socialist transformation in Russia itself. SDKPIL leader Leo Jogiches invoked Kautsky to bolster his case that 'while the Russian revolution will be an impetus to the socialist revolution in Western Europe, the influence of the latter can allow [Russia] to proceed to socialist revolution'.[82] Both the Mensheviks and Bolsheviks adopted this perspective in 1905, thereby breaking with *Iskra*'s previous approach.[83]

Throughout the Tsarist Empire, socialist papers during the revolution were filled with extensive reports on the international solidarity actions undertaken by socialists abroad in support of Russia's revolution. Following the defeated Łódź uprising of June 1905, a proclamation by the SDKPIL emphasised that workers abroad were following the revolution in Poland and central Russia: 'We have not shed our blood in vain! The proletariat of the whole world, with admiration and adoration, watched our fearless struggle, the whole world admired our heroism'.[84]

A common agitational approach was to rouse workers by appealing to their sense of responsibility to inspire proletarians abroad, as seen in the following leaflet published by the Bund:

> Comrades! Our struggle is also accelerating the advance of socialism ... We are setting an example for the proletariat of the whole world. Our indescribable sacrifices, our mighty effort, our indestructible energy, have an

79    Kautsky 1904 [2009], pp. 218–19. Echoing Kautsky, Trotsky's *Results and Prospects* foresaw that Poland in particular could play a detonating role in the spread of social revolution to Germany and Austria (Trotsky 1906b [1969], p. 109).

80    Cited in Stučka 1976–78, Vol. 1, p. 9.

81    'Rewolucja nasza a proletarjat Europejski', *Robotnik*, 24 November 1905.

82    Jogisches 1907. See also 'Międzynarodowy socjalizm wobec naszej rewolucji', *Kurjer Codzienny*, 16 December 1905.

83    Larsson 1970, p. 307, Редакция 'Искры' 1905, and Lih 2012d.

84    'Odezwa Komitetu Łódzkiego SDKPIL' [1905] in Gąsiorowska 1957, p. 352.

incendiary impact on our comrades all over the globe. The blood flows faster in their veins, their fists clench more tightly, their hatred for the exploiters becomes fiercer. Our efforts, reflected in the peoples of Western Europe, give a powerful impetus to the nearing arrival of the international social revolution.[85]

Crucially, by conceiving of socialist revolution as a single international process, the question of the social nature of the revolution in Russia was no longer posed primarily in national terms. Like their internationalist allies across the empire, Lenin and the Bolsheviks from 1915 onwards framed the democratic revolution in Russia as an 'indivisible and integral part of the socialist revolution in the West'.[86] As left social democrat Nikolai Sukhanov noted, what united radicals of all persuasions in Russia was their conviction that 'the World War would result in an absolutely inevitable worldwide socialist revolution and that the national revolt in Russia would lay its foundations, blazing a trail not only towards the liquidation of the Tsarist autocracy, but also towards the annihilation of the power of capital'.[87]

Given the tendency of historians to assume that such hopes in world revolution were mere wishful thinking, it should be underscored that this internationalist vision became central to revolutionary Marxism precisely because of the global shock waves generated by the 1905–06 anti-Tsarist insurgency. Revolutionaries and nationalists across Africa, Asia, the Middle East, and Latin America saw the Russian Revolution as an example of the power of mass political action as well as a manifestation of the agency of non-European peoples.[88] Indian national leader Mahatma Gandhi was not alone in affirming that the revolution in Russia was 'the greatest event of the present century' and 'a great lesson to us'.[89] As one British official noted in the Iranian capital of Tehran: 'The Russian Revolution has had a most astounding effect here. Events in Russia have been watched with great attention, and a new spirit would seem to have come over the people. They are tired of their rulers and, taking examples of Russia, have come to think that it is possible to have another and better form of government'.[90] A short list of the anti-imperialist and pro-democracy revolts

---

85     '1 мая' [1906] in Савицкий 1997, p. 250.

86     Lenin 1915b [1960–65], p. 379.

87     Sukhanov 1922 [1955], p. 103. Emphasis in the original.

88     A second major factor in the development of the period's anti-colonial resistance was the example of a non-European government, Japan, defeating the Russian regime in the 1904–05 war.

89     Cited in Simha 2014.

90     Afary 1996, p. 37.

that erupted in the wake of the Russian Revolution include: India 1905–08; German East Africa 1905–07; South Africa 1906; Iran 1906–11; Turkey 1908; China 1911–12; Korea 1910–12; Indonesia 1908–13; and Mexico 1910–17.

Of all the strategic points Kautsky developed during and following 1905, one of the most important was his novel stress on the international importance of anti-colonial revolutions in the fight for world socialism. Marxists until this point had largely limited their conceptions of international revolution to the West; the prevailing perception was that the colonial world would gain its freedom in passing through the struggle of the metropolitan working class.[91] But from at least 1905 onwards, Kautsky argued that national struggles in China, India, and beyond would also be important factors in the world struggle for socialism.[92] Contrary to most socialist historiography's assumption that Lenin pioneered a Marxist case for the strategic significance of anti-imperialist movements, Kautsky's influential 1909 book *The Road to Power* stressed that the current anti-colonial uprisings against European domination would continue until they destroyed their foreign yoke. Even if not socialist in orientation, Kautsky argued, such movements could gravely weaken world capitalism.[93]

Under the impact of a rising tide of anti-imperial struggle abroad as well as Kautsky's writings, revolutionary social democrats across Russia and Europe after 1905 began to move away from their previously Eurocentric revolutionary conceptions. Like Kautsky, Polish SD Julian Marchlewski in 1907 rejected the right-wing socialist contention that 'the colonies must go through capitalism'.[94] Since the capitalist system was global in nature, an international revolutionary struggle to establish socialism did not require that undeveloped countries first pass through the same socio-economic stages as Europe.[95]

The Russian Revolution, of course, also reverberated in the West. Inspired by the workers' revolt under Tsarism, labour radicalised across Europe and the United States. Governments and bourgeois parties across Europe were justifiably scared of Russia's revolutionary contagion. In 1905, for example, barricades went up in France for the first time since the Paris Commune and socialists organised a mass campaign to protest against their government's loan to bail out the Tsarist state.[96] Like many other socialists throughout the world, lead-

---

91    See, for example, Kelles-Krauz 1898, p. 587.
92    Kautsky 1905 [2009].
93    Kautsky 1909a, p. 127. For an example of typical Lenin-centric historiography on this question, see Anderson 2007, p. 143.
94    Day and Gaido 2012, pp. 26, 38.
95    Тифлисский комитет РСДРП 1908.
96    Harison 2007, p. 34.

ers of the Dutch Social Democracy declared that the insurgency in the Tsarist state was 'the most important event of our time'.[97] Across the Atlantic, the 1905 founding congress of the Industrial Workers of the World resolved that the 'mighty struggle of the laboring class of far-off Russia ... is of the utmost consequence to the members of the working class of all countries in their struggle for their emancipation'.[98]

These hopes from below and fears from above were particularly pronounced in the European empires immediately bordering Russia: Austria-Hungary and Germany. Inspired by their revolutionary neighbours, workers and peasants across Austria mobilised and struck in unprecedented numbers. Revolutionary tensions were high in Galicia (Austrian Poland), which lay directly adjacent to insurrectionary 'Russian' Poland. Well aware of the danger of socialist contagion, the Austrian government amassed an increasing number of troops along its Polish border in the course of the year.[99] Military blockades, however, could not effectively quarantine the country, as the Russian Revolution quickly spread unrest to Austria via Polish workers and peasants.[100]

Stressing the strategic location of Poles as a political transmission belt to Austria and Germany, Austrian Marxist leader Rudolf Hilferding wrote in 1905 that,

> the collapse of Czarism is the beginning of our revolution, of our victory, that is now drawing near. The expectation, which Marx had mistakenly expressed about the movement of history in 1848, will now, we hope, be fulfilled. ... Poland would provide the strongest, most effective impulse to the 'permanent revolution'.[101]

Demonstrations for universal suffrage called by the Austrian Social Democracy brought out hundreds of thousands of workers into the streets of the empire's cities. And despite the desire of the party apparatus to prevent clashes with the state, workers frequently ignored party directions and engaged in pitched battles with the government's armed forces.

Germany, with its massive industrial working class and powerful Social Democracy, was seen by socialists across Russia and Europe as ground zero for

---

97    Cited in Naarden 1992, p. 172.
98    Cited in Day and Gaido 2009, p. 613.
99    Maciej 1985, p. 15.
100   Trotsky 1906 [1969], p. 110.
101   Cited in Day and Gaido 2009, p. 36.

the success of world socialism. And, as Kautsky had hoped, the 1905 revolution in Russia polarised German political life and imbued its working class with an unprecedented radical fervour. From 1904 to 1905, the number of strikes quadrupled. In 1905, more workers engaged in strike action than in the entire 1890s.[102] And just a few weeks after the mid-summer revolt on Russia's Battleship Potemkin, German sailors on the Frauenlob cruiser mutinied and raised the red flag. Marxists throughout the Russian Empire enthusiastically reported these developments, which seemed to confirm their hopes in the westward spread of the revolutionary wave.[103]

The German state was conscious of the danger posed. Even more than its Austrian counterpart, Germany's ruling class was particularly worried about the spread of popular insurgencies via its Polish territories. Indeed, mass strikes of Polish as well as German workers paralysed Upper Silesia and other regions of Prussian Poland.[104] And the unrest in the Baltic was no less troubling for Germany's rulers. Multiple MPs in the Reichstag openly called upon the German government to invade Russia to suppress the revolution in Latvia. On 6 December 1905, a leading German MP took the floor of the Reichstag to call for the crushing of the revolutionary movement in Russia, which was having 'very unfortunate and damaging consequences' for German interests.[105]

By late 1905, the German government had concentrated a large number of troops on its border with Russian Poland.[106] In light of these Reichstag proclamations, as well as the Kaiser's confidential July meeting with the Tsar, it was widely believed across the political spectrum that the German government was preparing to invade the Russian borderlands, were the Tsarist state to prove incapable of crushing the insurgency on its own.[107] Similarly, the conservative Russian publication *Russkii Vestnik* (Russian Herald) warned that the 'disintegration of Russia will cause the disintegration of Europe'. If Germany would have to 'divide her forces between efforts to protect her imperial unity and the occupation of insurgent regions of Russia, it would not only make an

---

102  Waldenberg 1972, p. 373 and Steenson 1991, p. 69.

103  Weill 1986, p. 443 and Stučka 1905b [1976–78], p. 138.

104  Maciej 1985, p. 32. As historian Andrzej Maciej has documented, the German government in 1905 'believed that the revolution engulfing the nearby Kingdom [of Poland in Russia], and the Polish proletariat under Prussian rule, posed a real threat of revolution in Germany' (ibid.).

105  Cited in Weill 1986, p. 425.

106  Maciej 1985, p. 15.

107  Maciej 1985, p. 18.

uprising of the German proletariat possible but also that of [Prussian] Poland and the Czechs'.[108] Kautsky, Trotsky, and many other sDs put forward similar analyses.[109]

These international shock waves left a major political imprint on revolutionary social democracy. No longer was the fight for socialism seen as a parallel and discrete battle waged inside separate countries. Without understanding this global analytical framework, and orthodox Marxism's internationalist take on state and revolution in autocratic Russia, it is impossible to make sense of the stances taken by socialists throughout imperial Russia after the overthrow of Tsarism.

Our concluding chapter and Epilogue will show that the conciliationism of moderate socialists in the empire – and across Europe – reflected, among other things, their view of class struggle as a nationally isolated process. In contrast, radicals wagered on a reciprocal international revolution.

108   Cited in Voskobiynyk 1972, p. 176.
109   Kautsky 1905b [2009], pp. 535–6; Trotsky 1906 [1969], pp. 109–10; Day and Gaido 2009, p. 36.

# The State and Revolution in Russia, Ukraine, and Poland: 1917–19

Leninism was founded on two interrelated myths about 1917. First, that the victory of the October Revolution was made possible by Lenin's successful early year push to break the Bolsheviks from the Second International's traditional stance on state and revolution. Second, that the October Revolution showed why soviet power should be fought for by socialists internationally, even in conditions of political democracy.

To challenge these twin myths, this chapter will show that continuity, not rupture, was the dominant thread for social democrats, including the Bolsheviks, in 1917. Unlike so many socialists in the decades to come, Marxists in 1917, like in years prior, understood Russia to be an exception rather than the rule for anti-capitalist rupture. And with good reason: the empire's revolutionary processes, as we will see, continued to be overdetermined by the autocratic legacy.

Building on the themes developed over the course of this book, I show that radicals in 1917 upheld revolutionary social democracy's longstanding orientation towards a proletarian-led seizure of power in Russia to win the democratic revolution and spark the international overthrow of capitalism. Conciliatory socialists, on the other hand, rejected fundamental tenets of orthodox Marxism, such as its opposition to 'ministerialism' and blocs with the bourgeoisie. Divergent governmental outcomes across Russia largely reflected inter-party competition and the political orientation of the dominant socialist party.

Our discussion begins with an analysis of the positions and practices of the empire's main moderate social democratic organisations – the Mensheviks, the Bund, the Ukrainian Social Democracy, and the Polish Socialist Party-Revolutionary Faction. Following the overthrow of Tsarism, each sought to simultaneously promote workers' independent interests without breaking an alliance with the capitalist class or those political currents subordinate to it. Often, as with the Mensheviks and the Bund, this led socialists to support or participate in coalition governments with liberals. Elsewhere, notably in Poland, Ukraine, and Georgia, this approach culminated in deals with imperialist powers.

When forced to choose between advancing proletarian struggle or maintaining a cross-class bloc, most moderate socialists ultimately chose the latter.

Though this approach eventually cost the Mensheviks and Bundists their mass influence, the Ukrainian sds and pps-fr were able to hold on to power just long enough to decisively forestall anti-capitalist revolution in their regions. The chapter then turns to an analysis of the theory and practice of the empire's revolutionary social democrats, with a focus on the Bolsheviks because they were the most influential orthodox Marxist current in 1917 and because so many non-Russian radicals merged with them over the course of the year.

According to a historiographic consensus, the Bolshevik leadership had limited itself to pressuring the Provisional Government until Lenin arrived in Russia and convinced his comrades to fight for a 'socialist', rather than 'democratic', revolution. I will show, to the contrary, that Bolshevik leaders called for the overthrow of the Provisional Government well before Lenin's arrival in April.[1] They were also already demanding that the soviets take power to end the war, meet the people's social demands, and spark international revolution. As such, the October Revolution fundamentally expressed and vindicated orthodox Marxist strategy for Russia's exceptional political context. Only after October 1917 did the Bolsheviks retroactively declare that the revolution in Russia was 'socialist' and a model for radicals in capitalist democracies.

## 1      Moderate Socialists and Dual Power in 1917

The overthrow of the Tsarist state in late February 1917 immediately transformed theoretical debates over post-autocratic power into an urgent question of practical politics. By 27 February, Tsarist authority had been swept aside by insurgent workers and soldiers. The liberal Duma was left floating in mid-air, with little support on the ground. Since the workers and soldiers looked to the new Petrograd Soviet as the legitimate authority, it likely could have taken full power had it been so inclined. During the first days of insurrection, Petrograd's radicals – Bolsheviks, the Mezhraiontsy, and Left Socialist Revolutionaries – had held the initiative. But their call on working people to gather at the Finland Station to form a soviet and establish their own provisional revolutionary government went unheeded by the insurgents.

Instead, the crowds in the capital responded to the conciliatory socialists' rival proposal to form a soviet at the Tauride Palace, where the liberal State Duma was based. Since Menshevik leaders of the Soviet were intent on a

---

1   For a pioneering work challenging the traditional historiography, see Lih 2014.

bloc with bourgeois forces, the ability of the moderate socialists to seize the movement's leadership was decisive for the particular shape of state power that replaced Tsarism. Only an alliance with liberals, they argued, could prevent a successful counter-revolution, as conditions in Russia were unripe for a working-class regime. At the first session of the Soviet, on 27 February, class-collaborationist socialists thus proposed that a purely bourgeois government be established through negotiations with Duma leaders.

At the same time, however, the Soviet leaders distrusted the Kadet Party – the main political vehicle of the Russian bourgeoisie in 1917 – and worried about losing their hold over radicalised workers and soldiers. As such, the Petrograd Soviet sought to maintain a significant amount of power in its own hands, to pressure elites to implement the people's wishes. Crucially, the Soviet's famous 'Order Number 1', issued on 1 March, declared that soldiers must only follow governmental political instructions that were also approved by the Soviet. The fruit of this approach was an ambiguous structure of 'dual power', in which neither the soviets nor the Provisional Government had a monopoly on state authority.

Menshevik and Kadet leaders met on the evening of 1 March. The latter were obliged to accept the Soviet leadership's terms for its conditional support, the most important of which were that the Provisional Government grant political freedom and legal equality for all, abolish the police and establish a people's militia, release all political prisoners, refrain from reprisals against mutinous soldiers, and convoke a Constituent Assembly as soon as possible. Significantly, withdrawing from World War One and implementing land reform were absent from the agreement. On 2 March, the Petrograd Soviet overwhelmingly accepted the leadership's resolution to support the government 'in so far as' it implemented the demands of the people.

By early March, the basic structure of dual power had been established in the capital and across the empire. The Provisional Government nominally ruled the land, but the soviets held more real power and authority. Elected by nobody, and isolated from the working class due to liberal leaders' longstanding defence of the war and the monarchy, the Provisional Government's survival depended on the support given to it by moderate socialist leaderships. In the eyes of most politically active workers and soldiers, the councils were the sole legitimate power. Michael Melancon's detailed study of local soviet resolutions in 1917, for instance, shows that 'from the very outset of the February Revolution, almost three out of four resolutions either asserted soviet primacy, ignored the Provisional Government or called for its overthrow'.[2]

---

2   Melancon 1993, p. 503.

Unlike in post-war Europe, there were no major debates at this time regarding the gradual utilisation of the parliamentary state for social transformation. The reason for this was simple: with the notable exception of Finland, no such parliament, and no such state, existed within Russia. The February Revolution had largely broken up the old Tsarist autocratic apparatus and the new Provisional Government remained a fragile, unelected body dependent on the backing of the Petrograd Soviet. Army generals and sections of the governmental bureaucracy continued to wield some significant power, but this was overshadowed by Soviet authority. Given the weak and illegitimate nature of the Provisional Government, the question of state power throughout 1917 hinged above all on whether labour leaders would uphold or break their alliance with bourgeois politicians.

True to their post-1905 strategy of strategic support for liberals, Menshevik leaders were largely responsible for establishing the new dual power regime. Though Menshevism remained a heterogeneous political tent, one fundamental point upon which virtually all wings agreed was that capitalist forces must assume the reins of power following the downfall of the autocracy. Given Russia's backward social conditions, socialist transformation was impossible and a working people's government was therefore off the table.

By 1917, most Mensheviks had long abandoned the strategy of proletarian hegemony and they viewed liberals as indispensable allies. At the same time, Mensheviks argued that the continual pressure of the independent labour movement was necessary to overcome bourgeois hesitations. Mensheviks held firm to this relatively oppositional stance for most of March, seeking to use their strength to steer the government in a progressive direction. Not surprisingly, this insistence on simultaneously supporting and confronting the Provisional Government led to ongoing clashes with liberal Kadet ministers who wanted full control of the levers of state power and who saw Mensheviks as obstructionist radicals. But lacking in popular or military authority, liberal leaders were obliged to go along with the dual power arrangement.

In line with their early strategy, Mensheviks during the spring of 1917 rejected the liberals' initial attempt to maintain monarchic rule. Instead, they asserted the Soviet's political control over the mass of soldiers, they sought to build up the body as a proletarian bastion to drive forward the revolution, and they initiated a major campaign to pressure the Provisional Government and the Allies to take concrete steps towards ending the war. In the interim, Menshevik leaders saw collaboration with the Western Allies, England and France in particular, as a necessary evil. This rapid transformation of formerly anti-war Mensheviks into open 'defencists' – despite their sincere internationalist rhetoric and long-term goals – quickly became one of the dividing lines within imperial Russia's workers' movement.

The most important non-Russian social democratic party to uphold the Mensheviks' political orientation was the Bund. Like their Menshevik comrades, Bundist leaders by 1917 rejected the strategy of proletarian hegemony and affirmed that an alliance with the Kadets was needed to defeat the counter-revolution. Insisting that 'we cannot afford a split', they argued that the bourgeois-democratic nature of the revolution precluded workers' rule: 'if the proletariat seizes power it will alienate itself from all other classes'.[3] Accordingly, early in the year the Bund's main publication affirmed 'the absolute necessity to support the bourgeois liberal government'.[4]

Bundists hoped that pressure from below would be sufficient to push the international bourgeoisie to end the war as quickly as possible; in the meantime, revolutionary Russia must defend itself against Germany.[5] Unlike some non-Russian socialists, the Bund's drift towards class collaboration cannot be attributed to a prioritisation of national struggle over proletarian independence. In fact, the Bund focused surprisingly little on the national question in 1917 – its class collaborationism was with Russian rather than Jewish liberals. Regarding Zionism, the Bund remained hostile.[6] Historian Arye Gelbard's research has shown that throughout 1917 'in the press of the Bund, the emphasis was clearly on general political issues' as opposed to the Jewish question.[7] Like their Menshevik allies, Bundist leaders in the summer and fall of 1917 began to implore Jewish workers to compromise with capital. Historian Michael Hickey notes:

> At the moment when class conflict seemed inevitable to Jewish workers, their moderate socialist leaders stepped out of alignment with the frame of class struggle. In keeping with the positions taken by the national leadership of the Bund and the other major Jewish parties, Smolensk's Jewish socialists urged workers to seek compromises with their employers, and championed the ideal of a 'class conscious, politically educated proletariat.' Shur and other Jewish Soviet and duma leaders warned workers that they must consider the 'all-state significance' of their actions, moderate their demands, and negotiate with management. But such reason and

---

3   Cited in Любовець 2010, p. 36. See also Gelbard 1982, pp. 22–3.
4   Gelbard 1982, p. 34.
5   Johnpoll 1967, p. 60. See also Gelbard 1982, p. 22.
6   See, for example, 'Избирательная платформа ЦК Бунда' [1917] in Андерсон 2010, p. 1096.
7   Gelbard 1982, p. 137.

consciousness had little appeal to workers who considered their employers intractable.[8]

The viability of the Menshevik-Bundist strategy hinged on two factors. First was the bourgeoisie's ability to continue to meet the people's urgent demands. Second was the proletariat's ability to refrain from pushing too far and too fast. But events would soon show that neither class behaved in the ways hoped for by the conciliatory socialists.

March 1917 constituted the high point of the Provisional Government's grudging acceptance of progressive measures. Despite the Soviet's campaign for peace, Russian Kadets – backed by French and English imperialism – continued the war and stated that no major social reforms would be implemented until military victory.

When news of the administration's plans to continue the war 'until victory' became public in April, anti-government demonstrations and riots broke out in the capital, against the wishes of the Soviet leadership. The April crisis made it clear that the current Provisional Government lacked sufficient popular legitimacy to govern. A restructuring of the administration – and Menshevik strategy – was required. In this context, it was impossible for Mensheviks to uphold both their principled opposition to participation in a capitalist government and also their commitment to an alliance with liberals. Faced with this practical dilemma, the Mensheviks abandoned their theory.

## 2        Moderates Join the Government

The entry of Mensheviks and SRs into the Provisional Government in the first week of May was one of the major turning points of 1917. By tying their politics to a paralysing governmental alliance with the Kadets, Russian socialists steadily alienated themselves from their mass base and set the stage for the rise of forces such as the Bolsheviks that fought for a break with the bourgeoisie. In this sense, the SRs and Mensheviks lost the revolution just as much as the radicals won it.

On 1 May, liberal ministers called upon Soviet leaders to join the administration in order to give it the necessary strength to survive. As Kautsky had warned years earlier, at moments when the direct political representatives of capital were too discredited to govern on their own, influential forces in the work-

---

8    Hickey 1998, pp. 835–6. Unlike the Mensheviks, however, the Bund did not ultimately lose its working-class base in 1917.

ers' movement would be called upon to prop up the regime. Citing the 'utterly exceptional conditions' that obliged a rupture with their own political doctrine, Tsereteli lamented that 'we tried other ways of supporting [the government], but they did not turn out. ... For all practical purposes, the government left, and we were faced with the choice of either the soviet's seizing power or our joining a Provisional Government on coalitionary principles'.[9]

Initially there was tremendous resistance in the Menshevik ranks and leadership to joining the government. One of the few doctrinal points on which all Mensheviks had previously agreed was a principled rejection of ministeralism – socialist participation in government, they had long affirmed, could only be justified during a socialist revolution.[10] One of Menshevism's most important leaders, Fyodor Dan, wrote a position paper defending the party's long-standing stance, accurately predicting the dire results that would follow from Russian 'ministerialism'.[11] Yet despite their clear assessment of the dangers of joining a capitalist administration, in the end Dan and the other leading Mensheviks within Russia opted for coalition. In the words of historian Ziva Galili y Garcia, 'where doctrine proved too limiting even in its broadest terms, they disregarded it'.[12]

The Menshevik leaders' refusal in 1917 to break with 'census society' – and their consequent attempts to hold back workers' struggles – led to a dramatic plummet in popularity. As Melancon notes,

> Suspicion toward or outright opposition to a bourgeois-oriented government or a coalitional socialist-bourgeois government did not arise in association with Bolshevik agitation but existed from the outset as part of the outlook of most socialists and their laboring constituencies. Bolshevik agitation's role was in placing that party in a position to reap organizational benefits from the existing popular attitudes toward the Provisional Government when it failed to live up to what were perceived as minimal demands made upon it and when SR and Menshevik leaders disastrously associated themselves and their parties with it.[13]

---

9    Galili y Garcia 1989, p. 178.
10   Basil 1983, p. 59 and Galili y Garcia 1989, p. 151.
11   Galili y Garcia 1989, p. 169.
12   Galili y Garcia 1989, p. 57. Apart from the Socialist Revolutionaries, the other major socialist party in the empire to consistently defend the establishment of a coalition government was the Jewish Bund; the majority of Bundists argued along the same lines as their Menshevik comrades.
13   Melancon 2004, p. 156.

When obliged by circumstances to choose between a decisive break with the capitalist class or a break with their own programme, moderate socialists in Russia and beyond almost always opted for the latter. Given the power of capital at home and abroad, this risk aversion was not unreasonable, nor was the hope to avoid civil war condemnable, as events following 1917 made clear. A leap into the unknown beyond bourgeois domination will always be a 'high-risk, high-reward' dilemma. Nevertheless, an unwillingness to take this leap in Petrograd quickly ended moderate socialism's brief ascendance in central Russia.

Joining the Provisional Government in mid-1917 did not mean that conciliatory socialists had abandoned their hopes for social transformation in Russia. They remained committed to pushing for a democratic peace, a Constituent Assembly, pro-worker economic reforms, land confiscation, national rights for oppressed peoples, and other major political measures. Their influence within the government, they hoped, together with well-organised and disciplined pressure by working people, would be sufficient to overcome the opposition of their Kadet allies. But in the concrete circumstances of Russia 1917, implementing their reform programme ultimately proved incompatible with maintaining an alliance with political representatives of the bourgeoisie.

Edward Acton notes that bourgeois 'opposition, both within and outside the cabinet, blocked Chernov's land reforms, Skobelev's labour reforms and the Soviet plan for economic regulation, and the coalition proved unable to bring about peace'.[14] The ruling circles of France, England, and Russia remained committed to waging war until victory. In the name of winning the military conflict, Russian liberals similarly opposed implementing any major social reforms, declaring that any such changes would have to wait until after the war and/or the Constituent Assembly. Fearing the socialist dominance of such a democratically elected Assembly, Kadet ministers succeeded throughout the year in postponing its convocation.

This intransigence dealt a fatal blow to moderate socialist strategy. Menshevik leader Wladimir Woytinsky later succinctly described the roots of the Mensheviks' political paralysis. He noted that an '"energetic" foreign policy led to a rupture with the allies and a separate peace', while an 'energetic' domestic orientation led to a break with the liberals and the fall of the Provisional Government. Woytinsky concluded that '[w]e wished to avoid both but did not see a way to resolve these two problems, and this led to that fatal procrastination which so characterized this period of the revolution'.[15]

---

14      Acton 1990, pp. 159–60.
15      Cited in Wade 1969, p. 73.

A disconnect between words and deeds quickly became a hallmark of right-leaning socialists in 1917. Conciliatory socialism was pushed even further to the right on the issue of war. To preserve their alliance with the Allies, the Russian Kadets, and army officers – and to put pressure on Western governments to heed their peace proposals – Menshevik leaders ended up supporting the disastrous late June military offensive against the Central Powers initiated by the Russian generals in conjunction with the Allies. Just as Mensheviks had jettisoned longstanding doctrine to join the government, so too did they drop their former insistence on a purely 'defensive' military approach. For moderate socialists and the Provisional Government, the political fall-out of this failed offensive was no less devastating than the military debacle.

Given the political imperative to incorporate and lean on forces with some credibility in the working class, intense political pressure bore down on all representatives of the workers' movement throughout 1917. Contrary to their own longstanding doctrines, many socialists across Russia found themselves playing a role they had initially neither foreseen nor desired.

## 3    Russian Moderate Socialists in the October Revolution

In early July, armed demonstrations of workers and soldiers in Petrograd calling for 'All Power to the Soviets' and an end to war clashed with the state. The Provisional Government and its socialist ministers blamed the violent unrest on the Bolsheviks. Lenin and other party leaders were falsely accused of being German agents. A whole series of repressive measures were subsequently directed against the Bolsheviks and other internationalists.

Though the impact of these confused 'July Days' hurt the radicals in the short run, the tide was swiftly turning against coalitionism and its proponents. The failed coup d'état of General Kornilov in August 1917 further revealed the political impasse of socialist-liberal collaboration. Since workers justifiably believed that the Kadets had aided and abetted the counter-revolutionary attempt, support for a bloc with the liberals precipitously dropped. Despite these developments, influential wings of Mensheviks, SRs, and Bundists up through October continued to support efforts to maintain some form of coalition government. Likewise, they sought to uphold the 'commitments' of the Russian state towards the Western Allies in the war.

Much of the drama in the months leading up to October revolved around whether the bulk of Menshevik and SR leaders would ultimately sever their links to the political representatives of the capitalist class. Significant sectors of conciliatory socialist leaders finally began to call for such a break from September onwards. To meet the people's urgent demands, many Menshevik and SR leaders now called for a 'homogenous socialist government'. By all accounts, this type of government – meant to include all wings of socialists but no bourgeois parties – remained the ideal of most workers in the empire up through October.

The official stance of the Menshevik Central Committee from 31 August onwards was against a coalition with the Kadets. In practice, however, many of the top Menshevik leaders not only failed to implement the party's official line, but in fact actively fought against it. Tsereteli helped formed a new coalition government with the liberals in late September. Despite the party's official position against such a regime, four ministry posts were occupied by leading Mensheviks.[16] Similarly, much of the SR leadership remained firmly oriented towards a bourgeois bloc.

Major differences remained between the moderate socialists' call for a homogenous socialist government and the stance of the Bolsheviks, non-Russian internationalists, and the far left of the SRs. The point of conflict was not whether the new government should be multi-party, but whether it should be based on the soviets. Though support for a soviet government was overwhelming among the working class of the main urban centres of the empire by October, Menshevik and Bundist leaders nevertheless refused to accede to this sentiment. In the fall of 1917, many Mensheviks began calling for a break with the liberals, while simultaneously rejecting the call for 'All Power to the Soviets'. These Mensheviks argued that soviets were an insufficiently broad basis for a new, non-liberal, government. Since the precise institutional mechanisms to establish such a regime were left floating in the air, its implementation became fundamentally contingent on an agreement between the different socialist leaders rather than the institutionalised democratic process of the councils.

In large part, this orientation reflected the fact that by late September 1917 it seemed very likely that the Bolsheviks would be the most influential force in any empire-wide soviet government. Right-leaning socialists seem to have adopted the slogan of a homogenous socialist government as much out of anti-Bolshevik as anti-bourgeois sentiment. Indeed, earlier in July, various left Mensheviks and Bundists had supported the call for a Soviet government. As Menshevik historian Leo Lande observes, Martov had only 'backed the motto "All power to the Soviets" … when the Bolsheviks were in the minority in most Soviets'.[17] Given this political flip-flop by Bundist and Menshevik leftists, it is

---

16    Lande 1974, pp. 22, 30–1.
17    Lande 1974, p. 24. See also Mandel 1984b, p. 78 and Mandel 1984a, pp. 354–5.

reasonable to be sceptical of their later ideological rationales for opposing the Bolsheviks' push for soviet power.

In any case, there is little reason to believe that a homogenous socialist government spanning from the far-right SRs and Popular Socialists to the Bolsheviks was a realistic alternative by the fall of 1917. The fundamental problem was that the political cleavages between the two extremes of the socialist movement were too wide to have made such a regime viable; self-identification as socialists proved to be an insufficient basis for establishing a workable government. As one left Menshevik acknowledged in January 1918, 'the most widespread illusion of our day' was a 'united socialist front'. This perspective was made unviable by the class collaborationism of moderate socialists, who had 'as much to do with real socialism, as the bourgeoisie with democracy'.[18]

In October, as in previous months, the unity of the socialist movement broke down over the issue of class independence. Had all socialists been committed to a break with the bourgeoisie, a homogenous socialist government may very well have been possible. Yet right SRs and right Mensheviks remained committed to an alliance with liberals, and refused to participate in any government with the Bolsheviks.[19]

Following the 25–26 October Second All-Russian Soviet Congress that declared the overthrow of the Provisional Government, right socialists – particularly from the SR camp – immediate launched a strike and armed struggle to depose the new Bolshevik-led Soviet government. The insistence by left Mensheviks and Bundists that these and other moderates be included in a non-liberal government, combined with their refusal to recognise the legitimacy and decisions of the Second Soviet Congress, made their homogenous socialist government proposal a non-starter. Workers overwhelmingly wanted unity among the socialists, but not if this meant sacrificing soviet power.

For their part, the Left SRs primarily blamed the intransigence of class collaborationists for the failure to establish a multi-party government at the Second Congress. Bolshevik leaders similarly affirmed that a multi-party socialist regime was necessary and possible as long as it was based on the soviets and the decisions of the Second Congress.[20] After multiple weeks of intense debate and wavering, the Left SRs, unlike their Menshevik and Bundist analogues, subsequently joined the new Soviet administration, thereby constituting an important, if minority, governmental partner of the Bolsheviks.

---

18    Cited in Гаврилов 2009, pp. 285–6.
19    Raleigh 1986, p. 293 and Rabinowitch 2007, p. 30.
20    Mandel 1984a, pp. 276–7, 357, Mawdsley 1978, pp. 103–4, Rabinowitch 2007, p. 20, and Stučka 1917b [1976–78], p. 242.

Following the October Revolution, many of the conciliatory socialists who formally rejected coalitionism in late 1917 nevertheless established or re-established blocs with wings of Russian or Western bourgeois forces, aiding their efforts to take down the new Soviet government. The Georgian Mensheviks, for instance, had throughout 1917 denounced coalition as 'the grave-digger of revolution'.[21] Yet in the wake of October, they joined a bourgeois coalition government in Transcaucasia and following the implosion of this Transcaucasian regime, they proceeded to transform Georgia into a protectorate of Germany, then Britain.[22] A similar dynamic, as we will now discuss, marked the evolution of the Ukrainian Social Democracy.

## 4      Moderate Socialists in Ukraine: 1917–18

Examining the stances of moderate Ukrainian and Polish socialists in their respective revolutionary processes will help to draw out some of the common political patterns that distinguished moderate SDs from their radical rivals across the former Tsarist Empire. Developments in Ukraine and Poland were especially significant since these were the two most strategically important regions where anti-capitalist revolutions were defeated in 1917–19.

In the borderlands, like in the imperial centre, socialists' orientation to class collaboration or proletarian hegemony was politically decisive. Though issues of state and revolution in the borderlands became inextricable in 1917 from national questions, the fight for liberation could be concretised into a wide range of distinct orientations, ranging from cross-class national unity to strident proletarian independence. It was *not* the case that an increase in national demands by socialists necessarily undermined class intransigence.

Readers will recall that the Ukrainian USDRP was politically and organisationally fractured after the defeat of the 1905 revolution. By the eve of 1917, only a few small circles of party committees were still operating inside of Ukraine. These groupings generally identified with Lev Yurkevich's leftist journal *Borotba* and they upheld an orthodox internationalist opposition to class collaboration and the imperialist war. At the same time, however, the dis-

---

21      Cited in Jones 1992, p. 254.

22      Suny 1972a, p. 175. To their credit, the Georgian SDs and their new Georgian democratic republic pursued a relatively independent and transformative course, passing a series of significant reforms such as land distribution and encouraging the growth of labour unions and producer co-operatives (Jones 1984, pp. 387–553 and Suny 1990).

persed majority of Ukrainian SD intelligentsia leaders after 1906 made a major shift to the right, immersing themselves in various cross-class political projects with Ukrainian and Russian liberals. During the war, most of these Ukrainian socialist figures supported the Russian government's military efforts.

After the February Revolution, Ukraine was immediately swept by an unprecedented upsurge in the national movement, manifest in mass rallies across urban Ukraine. With the death of the radicals' leader Lev Yurkevich en route to Ukraine and in this novel context of national 'awakening', right-leaning USDRP party leaders, in conjunction with centrist elements around Volodymyr Vynnychenko, took decisive control of the party. At the USDRP's national congress in April, Symon Petliura, Isaak Mazepa, and other open class collaborationists were elected to the party's Central Committee. Historian N.N. Popov notes that in April 1917 the USDRP made a 'quite sharp turn towards nationalism'.[23]

The party now declared that 'for working people, the right to self-government is the most urgent demand'.[24] Party leaders argued that a strong Ukrainian labour movement was impossible without national autonomy. An appeal from the Moscow USDRP branch therefore declared that 'in the interests of the class struggle and proletarian movement in Ukraine we fight to ensure the national rights of the Ukrainian people to autonomy. Without this the proletarian movement in Ukraine will be sentenced to a frail, rickety existence'.[25]

This emphasis on the fight for autonomy went hand-in-hand with the party's newly established bloc with the influential Ukrainian liberal-nationalist current, the Society of Ukrainian Progressives (TUP), which in June 1917 incongruously changed its name to the Ukrainian Party of Socialist-Federalists (UPSF). This political rebranding, however, did not change the party's underlying political liberalism: as numerous writers have noted, all Ukrainian parties vying for popular support at this time had to frame their policies through a socialistic discourse.[26]

In March, Ukrainian liberals and the USDRP initiated the Rada, a front of Ukrainian organisations to pressure the Provisional Government to grant national autonomy. In Poltava, the party signed a joint appeal with the TUP in April that declared: 'let there prevail among everyone one will, one thought: "the good of their native land and their people!" '[27] And at June's Ukrainian Mil-

23    Попов 1929, p. 117.
24    'Од централізму до федерації' [1917] in Владислав 2003, p. 96.
25    'Відозва Московського комітету УСДРП' [1917] in Владислав 2003, p. 96.
26    Винниченко 1920, Vol. 1, p. 72.
27    'Звернення до громадян Полтавщини Спільної' [1917] in Владислав 2003, p. 205.

itary Congress, Vynnychenko similarly argued that 'all our classes must unite in
the process of national revolution' – the absence of a native Ukrainian capitalist class, he claimed, meant that a strategy of national unity in the context of
Ukraine could be implemented at the service of working people.[28]

This approach marked a shift from the USDRP's official stance up until this
point. Vynnychenko later lamented that in 1917–18 he had sacrificed his commitment to socialist principles for the sake of a nationalist Ukrainian statehood
project.[29] Unsurprisingly, this turn was opposed by the left wing of the USDRP.
Radicals, however, had lost their main leader, Yurkevich, as well as their majority within the USDRP by the spring of 1917.[30]

The Ukrainian Rada had begun simply as a front to demand cultural and
political autonomy within the Russian state. As such, the Ukrainian SDs sought
an alliance with the Russian Provisional Government and refused to unilaterally proclaim national autonomy. But the allegiance of Ukrainian soldiers to
the Rada, combined with the continued crisis of Kerensky's government in
Petrograd, steadily transformed the Rada into a proto-governmental power. In
late June, Vynnychenko became the Rada's General Secretary and Ukrainian SR
head Pavlo Khrystiuk became General Chancellor; the liberal UPSF was given
the important position of Secretary of Nationalities.

Though smaller than Ukraine's SR party, the USDRP was urban based and
cadre rich, allowing it to play the leading role in the Rada throughout 1917.
Assuming partial governmental power posed new challenges to the USDRP:
Ukrainian SD leaders were in favour of agrarian reform and major social transformation, but they feared that pushing through the demands raised from
below could result in a break with the nationalists. Such a division in the
national front, in their view, would gravely impair the fight for Ukraine's
autonomy. Faced with this dilemma, party leaders prioritised their bloc with
liberal-nationalists and refused to push through any potentially polarising
social legislation.

As the year dragged on, USDRP leaders were increasingly criticised by the
Ukrainian SRs. Though it was politically heterogeneous, and included a class-
collaborationist right wing, the UPSR stood significantly to the left of the SDs
throughout 1917 and subsequent years. Nevertheless, the governmental representatives of the Ukrainian SRs acquiesced to their moderate socialist allies – at
least up through the October Revolution. Pavlo Khrystiuk, an influential SR in
the Rada, later recalled the political impasse:

28    Cited in Солдатенко 1994, p. 18.
29    Szuch 1985, p. 127.
30    Висоцький 2004, p. 73.

In glorifying the national-political struggle, the [Rada] Secretariat in fact, in its actual work, did not introduce even those socio-economic reforms expected by the Central Rada's worker-peasant majority. The old socio-economic relations were preserved virtually without change as the base for the revival of Ukrainian statehood ... This was a completely non-revolutionary position that could be easily shared by Vynnichenko with the Ukrainian [liberal] 'evolutionists'.[31]

The unwillingness of Ukrainian SD leaders to break from liberal nationalists and satisfy popular demands for socio-economic transformation is particularly striking given the weakness of the Ukrainian liberals and the virtual absence of a native Ukrainian bourgeoisie. As Vynnychenko later lamented, in the name of preserving a national front, the USDRP refused to move beyond the bounds acceptable to Ukrainian nationalist-liberals.[32] Ultimately, this approach to Ukrainian liberation proved to be counterproductive even from a purely national perspective since the Rada's refusal to grant land reform and the other urgent economic demands of working people increasingly exasperated its base. Spring's honeymoon of national collaboration quickly began to fade away.

It would be wrong to assume that the USDRP's rightwards course was an inevitable result of a desire to promote national liberation. As the experience of Finland in 1917 demonstrated, it was possible for SDs to effectively fight for self-determination from a class-struggle basis. Promoting class and national demands was not necessarily a zero-sum game. Indeed, Ukrainian SRs were more radical on *both* accounts than their USDRP allies. Up through October 1917, the USDRP called for establishing broad autonomy through negotiations with Petrograd and it remained wary of unilaterally implementing national autonomy. In contrast, the Ukrainian SRs pushed for a more intransigent course of action: in their view, it was necessary to impose federalism from below against the opposition of the Russian state as well as its conciliatory Menshevik-SR leaders.[33]

Despite the Rada's relatively modest national demands and its desire to reach an amicable accord with the Provisional Government, the strident opposition of Russian liberals to Ukrainian autonomy resulted in a deepening series of conflicts. In these battles, the top Bolshevik leadership proved to

31    Христюк 1921, p. 122.
32    Винниченко 1920, Vol. 1, pp. 21, 132.
33    On the UPSR in 1917, see Бевз 2008.

be the sole consistent empire-wide supporter of the Rada's national demands. On this terrain of struggle, Ukrainian sps often found themselves allied with the Bolsheviks, at least up through October. As the St. Petersburg USDRP committee declared in July, only the Bolsheviks 'revealed a genuine proletarian understanding of the national needs of the [Ukrainian] masses'.[34] Yet, unlike the Finnish Social Democracy, Ukrainian SDs continued to collaborate with the Russian regime and Russian moderate socialist leaders. Vynnychenko, who was especially close with Menshevik head Irakli Tsereteli, remained unwilling to declare autonomy without the Russian government's agreement.[35]

The USDRP's evolution in the fall of 1917 largely paralleled that of the Mensheviks in the imperial centre. At the party's Fourth Congress in early October, the Ukrainian Social Democracy adopted a resolution calling for an end to coalition government in the all-Russian regime, a break with the bourgeoisie, and the formation of a homogenous socialist government. Yet key leaders of the party remained firmly committed to class collaboration and the USDRP's practice basically remained the same as in previous months. Noting the gap between the party's resolutions and deeds in the fall, Vynnychenko later argued that Ukrainian SD leaders 'failed to be radicals in lived actions'.[36]

The USDRP's response to the October Revolution further revealed this disconnect. On 26 October, Ukraine's socialist-led Rada denounced the Petrograd uprising and the newly formed Soviet government. Still seeking to support an empire-wide regime, the Rada believed that the Bolsheviks could be easily cast aside; it thus immediately began working with conciliatory socialists in central Russia to replace the new Soviet government.[37]

These actions by the Ukrainian SD leadership must be underlined, since so much anti-Communist historiography has blamed the Rada-Soviet conflict purely on 'Bolshevik imperialism'. One of the few historians to challenge the dominant nationalist account is V.F. Soldatenko, whose recent study notes the 'extremely negative effects' of the Rada leadership's response to the October Revolution, which 'caused an aggravation of relations' with the new Soviet government.[38] Vynnychenko similarly observed in his 1920 self-critique that the Bolsheviks had initially sought to reach an accord with the Rada after October – in his view, blame for the spiralling conflict lay with the Ukrainian leadership.[39]

---

34    'З життя Петроградської організації усдрп' [1917] in Владислав 2003, pp. 509–10.
35    Висоцький 2004, p. 75.
36    Винниченко 1920, Vol. 1, p. 133.
37    Любовець and Солдатенко 2010, pp. 245–6 and Prymak 1979, p. 11.
38    Любовець and Солдатенко 2010, p. 285.
39    Винниченко 1920, p. 141.

In the wake of October, Ukrainian SD leaders denounced the Bolsheviks for leading the country into 'anarchy'. They again affirmed the need for a homogenous socialist government with representatives from all the different leftist parties. But as Vynnychenko eventually acknowledged, this proposal became unworkable since there was no realistic of way of maintaining unity between revolutionary SDs and right-wing socialists who supported a coalition with capitalists.[40]

With its empire-wide governmental project remaining more elusive than ever, and with Ukrainian working people rapidly pushing towards social revolution, the Rada found itself hanging in mid-air. Despite its claims to neutrality in the developing Russian Civil War, the Rada nevertheless allowed counter-revolutionary Cossack troops access through Ukraine to fight in the Don region, a centre of the anti-Soviet offensive led by Alexei Kaledin. This same right of passage, however, was denied to the Bolsheviks.[41]

Between the October Revolution and February 1918, the Rada and the Soviet government engaged in an extremely convoluted political contest. Within the local soviets and the socialist parties, including the Bolsheviks, there was a growing push to establish a Ukrainian soviet government. Marko Bojcun's important study of the working class in Ukraine's revolution convincingly demonstrates that 'for many urban councils, the real bone of contention in November was not whether there should be a Ukrainian People's Republic, but what should be the class composition of its government'.[42] Left wingers in the USDRP and a large percentage of the UPSR as a whole pushed for a break with the bourgeoisie and demanded a rapprochement with Petrograd's Soviet regime. But from November onwards, the dominant currents within the Ukrainian Social Democracy chose instead to engage in efforts to win political-military backing from Western powers. Their attempts to garner Entente support failed, but the Rada leadership's initiative to win German patronage in January 1918 ultimately proved successful.

The Bolsheviks pivoted back and forth between negotiating with the Rada, calling on it to be democratically transformed into a Soviet government, urging it to recognise and ally with the Petrograd regime, and, in the end, unsuccessfully attempting to overthrow it. By December 1917, the Bolsheviks had become the strongest current in the urban workers' movement in Ukraine and they were likewise making strong inroads among Ukrainian soldiers.[43]

---

40    Винниченко 1920, p. 131.
41    Chernev 2012, p. 473.
42    Bojcun 1985, p. 314.
43    Любовець and Солдатенко 2010, pp. 205–18.

The Rada leadership's popular base rapidly melted away from November onwards. Yet it maintained just enough armed support to cling to power in most of Ukraine up through late January 1918. One of the last acts of the Vynnychenko government was to declare martial law in Kiev and appoint as City Commandant a young soldier Mykhailo Kovenko, who promptly arrested the top radical Ukrainian SR leaders who favoured a rapprochement with the Bolsheviks.[44]

The Bolsheviks' disconnect from Ukrainian-speaking workers and peasants was another important contributing factor in the impasse of the Ukrainian Revolution. Whereas an alliance between Left SRs and Bolsheviks was critical for the success of the revolution in central Russia, an equivalent bloc with the left of the UPSR (and its peasant-soldier base) was hindered by the Bolsheviks' ethnic composition, its isolation from the national movement, and its unevenness regarding Ukrainian aspirations for federal autonomy and national-cultural affirmation. Such a bloc had been built in 1905 between the *Spilka* and the RSDRP, but Ukraine's radicals in 1917 proved unable to unite sufficiently to establish their hegemony, providing the space for Germany's military to be called in.

Of all the empire-wide political currents in Russia, the Bolsheviks as a whole were the most sympathetic to the Ukrainian movement in 1917. In particular, the top Bolshevik leadership in Petrograd supported Ukrainian national demands and actively sided with the Rada against the Provisional Government. But the stance of many Bolshevik leaders in Ukraine ranged from indifference to outright hostility towards the national movement. More important than the party's formal stance, the Bolsheviks in Ukraine, as in previous years, remained a primarily Russian and Russified current with few organic ties to the national movement or the Ukrainian countryside. In a critical balance sheet of the party's national approach in 1917, two Ukrainian Bolshevik leaders observed that 'the issue was not even that we were not fond of the slogans of autonomy, federation, and independence, and that we advocated "unity". The issue is that we completely avoided the national liberation movement'.[45]

In this context, many left Ukrainian SRs pushing for a break with capital remained wary of closely allying with Ukraine's local Bolsheviks.[46] In contrast with central Russia, where the Bolshevik-Left SR alliance was essential for establishing soviet power in late 1917, the radical Left in Ukraine remained polit-

---

44    Prymak 1987, p. 159.
45    Мазлах and Шахрай 1919 [1969], p. 165.
46    Любовець and Солдатенко 2010, p. 258.

ically and socially divided by nationality well into 1918.[47] Left SR and Bolshevik leaders later acknowledged that the latter's limitations regarding the Ukrainian national movement gave an unnecessarily strong national dimension to the socio-political conflict. As Bojcun notes, 'a major opportunity to establish [a Ukrainian worker and peasant] republic presented itself in November and December 1917'. Yet the 'opportunity was lost', he concludes, because of two main factors: the USDRP leadership's rejection of soviet power combined with the Bolsheviks' weaknesses on the national question.[48]

By January 1918, Ukrainian popular support for soviet power was reaching unprecedented levels, as was the political isolation of the Rada.[49] Most Ukrainians by then simply refused to defend the Rada politically or militarily. But the months-long delay in establishing an anti-capitalist government in Ukraine proved to have decisive consequences for the revolution's outcome. The Rada's ability to just-barely hold onto power through January 1918 gave conciliatory socialist and liberal leaders sufficient time to win over an initially hesitant German government to occupy Ukraine. These very same Ukrainian political currents had for decades been opposed to separation from Russia – and they initially upheld this position even after the October Revolution.[50] Rather than an ineluctable expression of Ukrainian national awakening, the Rada's declaration of independence on 25 January 1918 was in large part a contingent political manoeuvre aimed at winning German military backing.

Historians have detailed the catastrophic political impact of the subsequent German occupation (February–November 1918), which reversed Ukraine's push for social transformation and radically dislocated the region's already frayed socio-economic and national relations. But it is often overlooked that the overstretched German state initially had no intentions to occupy Ukraine: even after the October Revolution, Germany felt that Ukrainian lands should remain within the jurisdiction of the Petrograd regime. Indeed, the initiative for Ukraine's occupation lay entirely with a small group of moderate SD, SR and liberal leaders of the Rada who unilaterally intervened in the Brest-Litovsk negotiations, hoping to convince the German state to transform Ukraine into its military protectorate.[51]

---

47    Maistrenko 1954, p. 4.
48    Bojcun 1985, p. 343. See also Любовець and Солдатенко 2010, p. 271.
49    Портнов 2012.
50    Любовець and Солдатенко 2010, p. 312 and Prymak 1979, p. 8.
51    Fedyshyn 1971, Любовець and Солдатенко 2010, p. 311, Винниченко 1920, Vol. 1, p. 159, and Chernev 2013, p. 182.

It remained an open question for most of January 1918 whether the Rada could cling to power in Kiev long enough to sign a deal with the Germans. Negotiations went down to the wire – the German-Ukrainian pact was signed only a few hours before the Rada could no longer plausibly claim to be in full control of Ukraine.[52]

The Rada's manoeuvre undermined not only the basic principles of orthodox Marxism, but also Ukrainian national sovereignty itself. A quote from a resolution of the Ukrainian SRs in June 1918 helps underscore this point:

> The alliance of the Ukrainian government with German militarism, inexcusable and criminal from the point of view of international socialism, has discredited the Ukrainian Central Rada in the eyes of the broad masses of toilers, has compromised the very idea of the national liberation movement and the Ukrainian socialist parties, and has demoralized Ukrainian democracy, objectively leading to the liquidation of all the achievements of the revolution; it has opened a wide field in the Ukraine for the activities of international reaction.[53]

In Ukraine, like in other regions of the empire, the outcome of the revolution was determined to a significant extent by whether the dominant socialist currents were oriented to a break with the bourgeoisie. This pattern repeated itself across the empire. After the October Revolution, non-Russian socialists were confronted with a choice between allying with German (and later Anglo-French) imperialism or reaching an agreement with the Bolsheviks. Given the weakness of the native bourgeoisie in most borderlands, it was in relation to foreign intervention that the longstanding debate over proletarian hegemony was concretised as Russia descended into civil war. In Georgia, Latvia, Lithuania, Azerbaijan, and beyond, moderate socialists – hitherto universally opposed to national separatism – reversed their longstanding positions on independence from Russia in order to acquire the military-political protection of foreign states.

Separation from Russia had 'far less intrinsic appeal among the nationalities than has been customarily assumed' notes historian Ronald Suny.[54] In mid-1918, Georgian SD leaders Tsereteli and Zhordania admitted that Transcaucasia's declaration of independence 'was not motivated by demands of national self-

---

52    Prymak 1987, p. 168.
53    Maistrenko 1954, p. 266.
54    Suny 1993, pp. 81–2.

THE STATE AND REVOLUTION IN RUSSIA, UKRAINE, AND POLAND: 1917–19    363

determination' but simply by the need 'to separate from the Bolshevik power'.[55] To justify the Georgian regime's subsequent collaboration with Germany then Britain, Zhordania declared: 'I know our enemies will say that we are on the side of imperialism. There I must decisively state here: I would prefer the imperialists of the West to the fanatics of the East!'[56]

## 5    Moderate Socialism in Poland: 1918–19

Unlike the Tsarist Empire's other conciliatory socialists, the Right PPS push for national independence was not primarily a reaction to the ascent of Bolshevism in Russia – it had fought for this objective since at least 1893.

Though the PPS-FR's trajectory was distinct from other right-leaning socialist parties in the former Russian Empire, it played an analogous political role in propping up capitalism in Poland. To quote PPS leader Mieczysław Niedziałkowski, the 'merit that no one can take away from the Polish Socialist Party' was that it 'put the initial construction of the Polish state on the path of parliamentary democracy, not the dictatorship of the proletariat. This saved Poland from the fate of Russia'.[57] During the Polish Revolution of 1918–19, the PPS-FR's class-collaborationist practice was manifest primarily in its deference to Pilsudski's domestic military-nationalist bloc.

Contrary to the assumptions of decades of nationalist historiography, Polish workers' support for independence in 1918–19 did not translate into support for capitalist rule. Gendarme reports, PPS internal memos, and foreign embassy reports highlighted the radicalism of Polish workers, many of whom had directly participated in the 1917 upsurge in central Russia. Few people at the time doubted the enthusiasm of Polish proletarians for the Bolshevik Revolution or their desire for immediate social overhaul.

The downfall of moderate social democrats across Russia in 1917 impressed upon PPS-FR leaders the need to sharpen their socialist discourse and demands lest they be bypassed by the radicals. Polish socialist leader Jędrzej Moraczewski, shortly before becoming the first prime minister of the new Pol-

---

55    Tsérételli 1919 [1918], pp. 18–19.
56    Cited in Shanin 1986, p. 360. Under Martov's leadership in late 1918, the Russian Mensheviks denounced these actions of their Georgian comrades, 'which in open or secret alliance with its class enemies, are directed against the very essence of [a] revolutionary policy' (cited in Jones 1984, p. 395).
57    Cited in Holzer 1962, p. 208.

ish republic, put things bluntly in early 1918: 'One must understand the great importance of slogans and social reforms due to the need to avoid, or reduce to a minimum, the chaos and anarchy brought to the movement by the Russian Bolsheviks'.[58]

Advocates of immediately establishing working-class rule – the Polish Communist Party, plus the bulk of Polish Bundists – represented about half of the elected delegates to the hundreds of workers' councils that sprung up after the collapse of the Austro-German occupation in late 1918. Furthermore, the PPS-FR was supported from below largely because of its promises to implement deep socio-economic reforms in the interests of working people.[59] Pushing back against traditional Polish nationalist scholarship, historian Brian Porter-Szücs explains that in 1918–19 Poland 'there was a strong desire [to] achieve both national restoration and social revolution'.[60] To help understand why the latter goal was not reached requires taking a closer look at the political orientation and actions of the Polish Socialist Party-Revolutionary Faction.

By the eve of World War One, the PPS-FR's concentration on para-military separatist preparation had led it to lose its base of support in the workers' movement. But following the departure of Pilsudski in 1914, the PPS-FR made a significant turn leftwards. From 1915 onwards, the party placed an increased emphasis on proletarian struggle and it remained particularly hostile to the main bourgeois party in Poland, the far-right National Democracy, which throughout the war remained allied to the Anglo-French Entente.

Despite the PPS-FR's evolution after 1914, it nevertheless remained politically distant from revolutionary social democracy. Instead of proletarian hegemony, the PPS-FR advocated 'democratic consolidation' according to which all Polish democratic parties and currents should bloc together to win state independence. In practice, this orientation brought an unwavering allegiance to Pilsudski and his nationalist military efforts to establish Polish independence through collaboration with the Central Powers.[61] The tension between the PPS-FR's relatively militant labour orientation and its fidelity to Pilsudski – himself an open advocate of national unity – would become starkly evident as the revolutionary process unfolded.

---

58    Cited in Holzer 1962, p. 125. See also Piskała 2014, 211–12.
59    Sobczak 1970, Fiddick 1974, p. ii, Holzer 1962, pp. 43, 117–19, Holzer 1967, p. 83, Nowogrodzki 2001, pp. 22–4, and Tomicki 1982, pp. 75, 78.
60    Porter-Szücs 2014, p. 67.
61    Piskała 2014, pp. 129, 134–5, 149–50 and Holzer 1962, p. 58.

Like Piłsudski, PPS-FR leaders in November 1916 joined the puppet government created by the German-Austrian military occupiers to provide some semblance of Polish self-rule. Seeing this body as a step forward and a vehicle for the fight for full independence, the PPS-FR declared that it would 'not flinch even in the face of the heavy sacrifice of socialist participation in a bourgeois government'.[62] Party leader and theoretician Feliks Perl was quite explicit that this approach constituted a break from the radical tradition of 1905. Indeed, in an early 1917 article he implored Polish workers to break from their ultra-revolutionary heritage, in order to focus on the 'creative' work of building a new state.[63]

Since Poland remained occupied by the Central Powers up through November 1918, the February Revolution did not immediately change its political structure. But the radicalising impact of the revolution on Polish workers was profound. PPS-FR members and cadre living in the cities of central Russia were especially swept up in the ferment – they soon came to constitute the core of the party's new left-wing minority, which throughout 1918–19 called for a strict class line and an immediate proletarian conquest of political power.[64]

Foreseeing the imminence of social upheaval in Poland – termed 'a sad necessity' by Perl – and fearing that the far left would seize its leadership, the PPS-FR radicalised its practice in 1917, particularly after the October Revolution.[65] It stepped up its organisation of strikes, its attacks on the National Democrats, and its anti-capitalist rhetoric. The following PPS-FR affirmation in October 1918 was typical: 'We declare inexorable war on capitalist exploitation, we begin the fight for the abolition of the old system'.[66]

No less importantly, it resigned from the structures of the Austro-German client state and increased its mobilisations, including armed struggle, against the foreign occupation. Piłsudski, too, began to distance himself from the occupying powers, leading to his imprisonment and the strengthening of his political image as a heroic national martyr.

On 9 November 1918, revolution erupted in Germany. This upheaval combined with Polish armed uprisings brought down Austro-German rule over Poland, leaving it entirely unclear who would fill the resulting power vacuum in the war-torn region. To quote historian Wojciech Roszkowski, 'the country was

---

62    Cited in Najdus 1967, p. 239.
63    Cited in Cisek 2002, p. 141.
64    On the left wing within the PPS in 1918–19, see Holzer 1962, *passim*.
65    Cited in Holzer 1962, p. 100.
66    Cited in Cisek 2002, p. 146.

on the edge of a civil war: the growing revolutionary wave was strongly opposed by the Polish right who had every reason to fear that a social revolution with a Bolshevik internationalist would sweep away the opportunity to create an independent state'.[67]

Working-class enthusiasm for an independent Poland did not translate into support for the native bourgeoisie or for capitalism. Indeed, one of the reasons why Polish independence was so popular was that it was proclaimed in November by a socialist-led provisional government headed by moderate SD Ignacy Daszyński, leader of the Polish Socialist Party's branch in Austria-Hungary. Seeking to take the wind out of the sails of the workers' councils that were spreading across Poland, the founding declaration of the Daszyński government denounced capitalist tyranny and exploitation, called for the rule of Polish working people, and promised to expropriate some major industries and landed estates.[68] But the shallowness of the government's actual radicalism was soon made evident when it voluntarily abdicated power at the request of Jozef Pilsudski.

Hoping to avert social revolution, on 11 November the widely discredited Regency Council (the final iteration of the Austro-German client state) proclaimed Pilsudski, who had just been released from prison, Commander in Chief of the Polish army. It was upon the basis of Pilsudski's military forces that a new Polish state was eventually built. In November 1918, however, the army remained weak and fractured, precluding a military solution to the political crisis.

Pilsudski and the most conservative PPS-FR leaders such as Daszyński and Jędrzej Moraczewski aimed to form a national unity coalition government with the National Democrats. A stable government, in their view, would be hard to establish without the National Democracy, which had the support of the Polish elite, controlled major wings of the military on the Western front, and had the backing of the Entente. But such a project was shipwrecked by the mutual intransigence of the labour movement and the NDs.

Workers' councils demanding anti-capitalist action continued to rapidly spread across Poland. And in Warsaw, the PPS-FR branch led mass rallies in mid November to reject unity with the NDs and to demand the formation of a popular government. 'Working-class Warsaw was seething and boiling', reported a correspondent in the PPS-FR newspaper *Robotnik*.[69]

---

67    Roszkowski 1992, pp. 162–3.
68    'Do Ludu Polskiego. Robotnicy, Włościanie i Żołnierze Polscy!', 7 November 1918, Lublin-Kraków (Biblioteka Śląska).
69    Cited in Tymieniecka 1982, p. 10.

Pilsudski noted that the main threat to the nascent Polish government was coming from below – only a populist administration, he concluded, could hope to diffuse the revolutionary upsurge. He initiated negotiations to form an administration with the NDs, but the latter refused to take the posts offered to them. The result was that a Polish provisional government composed of conciliatory socialists and 'democratic' nationalists was formed in mid-November, with PPS-FR leader Moraczewski as Premiere.[70]

Given the militant social promises of the Moraczewski government, it is not hard to understand why workers and NDs both saw it as leading Poland towards socialism. On 21 November, the new government declared the need to nationalise the major industries of Poland, establish organised labour's right to participate in factory administration, and give the land to the peasants. Nevertheless, in line with Pilsudski's behind-the-scenes injunction that the government could not pursue any attacks on private property, Moraczewski announced that he would not immediately implement these measures. Rather, they would be submitted as proposals to a Polish parliament to be elected in early 1919. The PPS-FR leadership supported this approach, declaring that any radical socio-economic transformation must be passed through parliamentary and non-violent means.[71]

This stance, however, was not motivated purely by an ideological commitment to parliamentarism. Far from consistently deferring decisions to the future parliament, the moderate socialists did not wait for democratic elections to announce the independence of Poland or to implement a series of social reforms including democratic and trade union freedoms, the eight-hour day, and health insurance. The fledging regime and PPS-FR leaders hoped that immediately implementing these progressive measures, and promising radical change for the future, would be sufficient to improve workers' living conditions and prevent social revolution. In this spirit, the PPS-FR leadership declared that while workers' councils should defend proletarian interests, in relation to the state they must only serve as consultative and supporting organisations without any aspirations to sovereign power.[72]

It was far from clear whether the Moraczewski administration's populist gambit would extinguish or fan the flames of the revolutionary conflagration. As prominent centrist leader Wincenty Witos noted, the stance of the gov-

---

70   Roszkowski 1992, p. 163, Holzer 1962, pp. 187–8, 192, 198–9, Tymieniecka 1982, pp. 22–3, and Chełstowski 1975, p. 95.

71   Cisek 2002, pp. 155–6.

72   Tymieniecka 1982, pp. 33–4 and Karwacki 1964, pp. 407–8.

ernment 'on the one hand awakened the ever-greater desires of the mass of workers, and on the other hand strengthened the resistance of the propertied classes'.[73] December 1918 witnessed intensified urban and rural strikes and social clashes, with mass demonstrations of the unemployed shaking urban Poland and workers even beginning to occupy factories and demand their nationalisation. Communists denounced the government as a 'sham' socialist regime aiming to rescue capitalism. Radical-led workers' councils, as well as armed Red Guards calling for workers' power, continued to proliferate. Much of the Dąbrowa mining basin came under Communist control.[74]

The problems facing the regime and conciliatory socialist officials continued, with wide layers of the PPS-FR rank and file also beginning to push for immediate anti-capitalist rupture. An internal report by the government's security apparatus noted that,

> Most PPS members expected that upon taking governmental power, the party's socialist programme would be implemented at a fast pace. The young members in particular were the most revolutionary and were unreconciled to the Moraczewski government's unstable policies. They demanded that the government decree socialism through revolutionary means, to demolish the old society and bring the new society to life, to swiftly reach the final goals of socialism. These views were opposed by the older party leadership.[75]

Many of these radicalised militants, moreover, were armed. In early December 1918, the PPS-FR's militias had 6,000 organised members and another 10,000 in reserve. Under pressure from the party's ranks, the PPS-FR's Warsaw Committee in December called upon the government to immediately implement its stated radical objectives – nationalisation, agrarian reform, etc. – and take action to break the right-wing reaction. But instead of heeding this call to press the government forward, the PPS-FR leadership instead pushed back against the increased militancy of Polish workers.

In December, party leaders integrated their militias into the government's new armed forces and by July 1919 they were dissolved completely.[76] In so doing, the PPS-FR leadership sacrificed its longstanding republican demand for the

73    Cited in Chełstowski 1975, p. 90.
74    Malinowski 1967, pp. 93–6, 99–101, 107–9.
75    Tomicki 1982, p. 75 and Holzer 1962, pp. 334–5.
76    Holzer 1962, pp. 226–7, 426.

dissolution of the standing army and the creation of a popular militia. Historian Stanisław Michałowski notes that in 'the People's Militia detachments there were many people connected with the revolutionary movement, who not only refused to support the people's government but they also strove to provoke social confrontation threatening the young Polish State. For that reason, the PPS's leaders proposed to subordinate the People's Militia to the state'.[77]

Despite ongoing PPS-FR efforts to restore some semblance of order, the National Democrats believed that the Moraczewski government was facilitating Poland's descent into Bolshevik-inspired anarchy. Yet the NDs were wisely reluctant to take power on their own, fearing that doing so would immediately spark a revolutionary explosion. As such, National Democrat party chief Dmowski acquiesced to Pilsudski's provisional military authority. But the NDs nevertheless remained opposed to the Moraczewski government, which they considered dangerously radical. Throughout November and December, they led armed demonstrations across Poland against the government, often resulting in clashes with socialist workers. Even more importantly, the democratic and economic reforms of the new regime were widely sabotaged or obstructed by the NDs and the employer class. Capitalists generally refused to pay taxes or otherwise help fund the administration, hurtling it towards financial insolvency. Yet the Moraczewski government continued to reject demands from below to disarm the National Democrats or to use force to oblige the bourgeoisie to obey.[78]

Poland's crisis came to a head in the first week of 1919. On the night of 4–5 January, a group of right-wing leaders linked to the NDs and a wing of the military attempted to overthrow the Moraczewski government. Jerzy Zdziechowski, one the initiators of the coup, explained that the goal was to 'strangle internal Bolshevism'.[79] The counter-revolutionary action, however, was quickly defeated – and it pushed the nation closer to the brink of rupture. Strikes broke out across Poland, barricades went up in some neighbourhoods in Warsaw, and workers and their militias clashed with (and often disarmed) right-wing troops and militias.

PPS-FR leaders called for vigorous governmental action to disarm the Right, but Pilsudski had other plans. Seeking to restore order and reach a deal with the NDs, behind whom stood the Entente, he ordered the dissolution of the Moraczewski administration on 16 January. Soon after, Pilsudski released the coup plotters on parole.

---

77    Michałowski 2003, pp. 279–80.
78    Tymieniecka 1982, pp. 23–5, Holzer 1962, pp. 210–12, and Leslie 1980, pp. 128–9.
79    Cited in Garlicki 1977, p. 144.

For the first time, the PPS-FR leadership was obliged to make a firm choice between maintaining its allegiance to Pilsudski and upholding its strategy of 'democratic consolidation' – of which the Moraczewski government was the highest expression.[80]

In Poland, as had been the case in Ukraine and central Russia, a consistent approach to working-class independence required a willingness to break not only from capitalist parties but also from those intermediary political forces that remained committed to class collaboration.

Against the proposal of PPS-FR leftists to establish a workers' government to smash the counter-revolutionary offensive, the party leadership and its ministers, including Moraczewski, reluctantly but without protest accepted the government's disbanding. Outrage and demoralisation with this self-dissolution spread rapidly and widely among working people, including among the party's rank and file. The PPS-FR leadership responded by calling upon Polish workers to stay calm.

With the agreement of the NDs, Pilsudski proceeded to establish a centre-right administration headed by pianist Ignacy Jan Paderewski. Only the Minister of Labour post was granted to the PPS-FR.[81] Over the course of 1919, the Paderewski government – backed by the Allied governments – quickly proceeded to repress the militant labour movement, drive the Communists underground, and beat back the working-class insurgency.

Throughout the subsequent years of class struggle, the pattern of the PPS-FR's approach in January 1919 would be repeated. At moments of peak political crisis – e.g. the general strikes in 1919, the 1920 war with Russia, and the 1923 army mutinies and clashes in Kraków – the PPS-FR always proved willing to subordinate itself and the workers' movement to ensure the preservation of the existing Polish regime. In light of this dynamic, it makes sense to question historians' focus on Pilsudski's role in saving Poland from socialist overturn. According to Piotr Wróbel, for example, Pilsudski 'stopped a revolution, established a bridge between the left and the right, and helped create a compromise democratic system'.[82] Such an interpretation is not inaccurate, but it obscures a critical point: Since Pilsudski no longer had a direct base within the working class, his state-building project could not have succeeded without the active support of the PPS-FR leadership.

In Poland, and beyond, the survival of capitalist rule during the post-war revolutionary upheaval to a significant degree depended on the interventions

---

80   Holzer 1962, pp. 251–5 and Chełstowski 1975, pp. 96–7.
81   Holzer 1962, pp. 258–61 and Tymieniecka 1982, pp. 35–6.
82   Wróbel 2010, p. 119.

of moderate socialists. Given the weakness of bourgeois forces in Russia's borderlands and the absence of labour bureaucracies or real parliamentary traditions, the fact that class-collaborationist socialists frequently overcame their radical rivals was a remarkable and surprising achievement, with world-historic political consequences.

## 6    Bolsheviks and State Power: February–March 1917

There are not many points of historiographic agreement between Stalinists, Trotskyists, and liberals. One of the few exceptions is the shared argument that Lenin radically overhauled Bolshevik politics in April 1917 by convincing the party to fight for a 'socialist', rather than a 'bourgeois-democratic', revolution.

According to Trotsky's 1924 polemic *The Lessons of October*, the Bolsheviks under the leadership of Stalin and Kamenev had been mired in de facto Menshevism before Lenin 're-armed' the party with an entirely new political strategy in April 1917.[83] Specifically, he asserted that because the pre-April Bolsheviks thought that Russia was not ripe for socialist revolution, they therefore failed to see the need to seize power and accordingly sought only to pressure the bourgeoisie to meet the people's demands.[84] 'The task of conquering power', Trotsky affirmed, 'was put to the party only on 4 April, i.e., after Lenin's arrival in Petrograd'.[85]

The standard Stalinist analysis was strikingly similar, though it placed less emphasis than Trotsky on the extent of the strategic rupture and absolved Stalin of responsibility for the party's pre-April waverings.[86] With the notable exception of Lars Lih, most academic historians have likewise shared this interpretation.[87] But this consensus is factually inaccurate – and it has distorted our understanding of the 1917 revolution.

Throughout February, Bolsheviks upheld a militant, class-struggle orientation. In sharp contrast with the Mensheviks, their strategy opposed any bourgeois blocs. Bolshevik leaflets declared that a workers' and peasants' government was needed to bring peace, bread, agrarian reform, the eight-hour day,

---

83    Trotsky 1924 [2016], p. 92.
84    Trotsky 1924 [2016], pp. 92, 95.
85    Trotsky 1924 [2016], p. 96. For a recent restatement of Trotsky's 're-arming' account, see Marot 2014, p. 161.
86    Commission of the Central Committee of the C.P.S.U. (B.) 1939, pp. 183–4.
87    Slusser 1987, p. 54. Of the many other academic works that have affirmed the 're-arming' thesis, see, for example, Rabinowitch 1968, p. 46.

and a democratically elected Constituent Assembly. By taking power, they argued, Russia's working people would be able to push for an end to the war and unleash the international overthrow of capitalism.

In the first days of the February insurrection, all wings of the Bolsheviks had pushed for radicals to directly lead the overthrow of the autocracy and to take the initiative in establishing a broader revolutionary provisional government. The 27 February proclamations by the Russian Bureau and the Vyborg Committee reflected this desire to assert proletarian political hegemony, against the attempts of the liberal-oriented socialists to do the same. But the Bolsheviks and internationalists lost the battle that same day, when the Menshevik-SR leaders successfully established a soviet under their own leadership.

The specific political configuration of Russian society in March 1917 had not been foreseen by anybody. From 1905 onwards, the Bolsheviks had assumed that either workers and peasants would establish their own 'democratic dictatorship' or that Russian liberals would come to power in the framework of a constitutional monarchy. Yet the unexpected emergence of a post-Tsarist liberal government did not invalidate the Bolsheviks' basic orientation, i.e. proletarian hegemony to establish a revolutionary workers' and peasants' power to end the war and meet the people's urgent social demands.

Nevertheless, there was considerable discussion within Bolshevik ranks over how best to proceed in an unexpected post-autocratic context. To quote one Latvian Bolshevik leader, 'finding the correct tactical line in these circumstances [following the fall of the Tsar] was extremely difficult'.[88] How to engage in mass politics while avoiding sectarian isolation or excessive political compromise was no easy feat in March 1917 or, as we will see, in the months to follow.

'Old Bolsheviks' in March – like their radical allies in the SDKPIL, the Latvian SDs, and the PPS-Left – openly declared that the revolution was far from over.[89] Revolutionary social democrats had never reduced the goal of the democratic revolution to ending autocratic rule – in their view, this upheaval would only be complete once the landed estates were confiscated, the workers armed, a republic established, and a series of radical economic measures enacted. As

---

88    Dauge 1958, p. 471.
89    Reasons of space preclude a detailed discussion of the stances of these currents in early 1917. Suffice it to say that all opposed the Provisional Government and the war, all called for a break with the national and international bourgeoisie, and all argued that only under proletarian leadership could the revolution win its burning demands. And like the Old Bolsheviks, they saw the democratic revolution in Russia as a spark for the imminent international socialist revolution.

Old Bolshevik Nikolai Miliutin put it later in the month, 'our revolution is not only a political but also a social revolution'.[90]

Though such a radical-democratic transformation was not equated with socialism, it constituted a political trajectory distinct from the type of parliamentary rule prevailing in the West. In his detailed study of early-year soviet resolutions, Michael Melancon concludes that 'whatever liberals and some moderate socialists thought at the time and interested commentators think now, Russia's mass organizations – leaving aside the refractory problem of Russia's masses – did not view the February Revolution as marking the onset of liberal capitalism'.[91]

On 4 March, the Russian Bureau of the Central Committee – the top Bolshevik leadership body inside of Russia, led by Alexander Shlyapnikov and Vyacheslav Molotov – affirmed the current's strategic orientation in a resolution published in the party's central newspaper, *Pravda*:

> The present Provisional Government is essentially counter revolutionary, because it consists of representatives of the big bourgeoisie and the nobility, and thus there can be no agreement with it. The task of the revolutionary democracy is the creation of a Provisional Revolutionary Government that is democratic in nature (the dictatorship of the proletariat and the peasantry).[92]

The leftist Vyborg Bolsheviks felt that this goal was an immediate task and called upon the Soviet to declare itself the sole legitimate state authority.[93] Other Bolshevik leaders put forward a more cautious tactic: On 3 March, the Bolshevik Petersburg Committee resolved that it would 'not oppose the Provisional Government power in so far as its actions comply to the best interests of the proletariat and the broad masses of the democracy and the people'.[94] Various authors have incorrectly claimed that these Bolsheviks had thereby adopted the Mensheviks' stance of conditional support for the Provisional Government.[95] In fact, the resolution only implied that the Bolsheviks did not seek to immediately eliminate the regime and that they would support the specific progressive measures that it implemented.

---

90    Cited in Trotsky 1937, p. 247.
91    Melancon 1993, p. 504.
92    'Тактические задачи', *Правда*, 9 March 1917. On Shlyapnikov, see Allen 2015.
93    'Резолюция по текущему моменту', *Правда*, 9 March 1917.
94    'Протокол собрания от 5 марта 1917 года', *Правда*, 7 March 1917.
95    See, for example, Elwood 1974a, p. 197.

Bolshevik leaders – including Kamenev and Stalin – affirmed that they did
not support the government as such, only the particular positive actions that it
was compelled from below to implement. To quote Kamenev: 'Support is absolutely inacceptable. It is impermissible to have any expression of support, even
to hint at it. We cannot support the Government because it is an imperialist
government'.[96]

The political orientation of the Bolsheviks' Petersburg Committee – upheld
by Kamenev and Stalin upon arriving in Petrograd in mid-March – was immediately expounded in the party press. One of the more articulate explanations
came from Latvian Bolshevik leader, Pēteris Stučka, a member of the Petersburg Committee and one of the three Bolsheviks represented in the Soviet
Executive Committee. As a supporter of the Petersburg Committee's 3 March
'in so far as' resolution, Stučka elaborated on how it fit into party strategy in his
7 March article 'Our Mission'. This revealing document – overlooked in the historiography because it was published in Latvian – sought to answer 'whether
the revolution has come to an end or is just beginning' and, subsequently, how
the Bolsheviks addressed the question of state power. The article merits our
attention not because it was exceptional, but precisely because it was a standard articulation of the Bolshevik consensus.

Stučka noted that although workers and peasants in uniform had made the
revolution, the Provisional Government was run by the 'counter-revolutionary'
bourgeoisie. The new administration had been obliged by popular pressure
to take some real steps forward such as eliminating the monarchy, but it was
incapable of meeting the revolution's essential tasks: 'As soon as it loses the
support of the revolutionary people, it will fall'. He viewed this strategy as 'the
foundation which separates us from the moderate leftists' who believe that
'the fall of the Provisional Government would mean the collapse of the whole
revolution'.

In contrast, Stučka concluded that only a 'truly revolutionary provisional
government, that is, a provisional government of workers and peasants' could
lead Russia out of its crisis and meet the demands of the people, such as land to
the peasants and an end to the imperialist war. With this governmental objective in mind, the immediate task of revolutionaries was to reject 'moderation',
to raise 'direct revolutionary slogans', and to 'criticise every step' of the Provisional Government, while 'supporting only those [steps]' that did not go against
the development of the revolution.[97] In a follow-up article on 21 March, Stučka

---

96    Cited in Trotsky 1937, p. 270. Stalin's opposition to supporting the government can be seen
      in Trotsky 1937, p. 239.
97    'Mūsu uzdevums' [1917] in Stučka 1978, pp. 122–4.

went on to explicitly reject the view that anti-capitalist rupture could only take place 'many years' down the road. He argued that while 'there was little hope of putting socialism into practice within Russia's borders only, the rise of social revolution across Europe without a doubt will also drag Russia into it'.[98]

In March, and throughout the year, Marxists always framed socialist revolution as an imminent *international* process. This was true not only for the Bolsheviks, but for radical non-Russian SDs as well. In their March leaflet calling upon Polish workers to join the revolutionary struggle, for example, Petrograd's leftist Polish socialist coalition declared that '[s]ince the fall of Tsarist rule in Russia undermines the existence of all bourgeois governments, it is a harbinger of the victory of democracy internationally'.[99] On 8 March, likewise, the Bolsheviks' relatively moderate Kiev committee spelled out the consensus internationalist view that Russia must be the detonator of world socialist revolution.[100]

Bolshevik leaders in March integrated the 'in so far as' formulation – conditional support for progressive Provisional Government actions – into a distinct strategy from that of conciliatory socialists. Whereas the Menshevik leadership actively supported the establishment of capitalist rule and limited its strategic perspective to pressuring liberals, Bolsheviks rejected an alliance with the bourgeoisie and explicitly called for the replacement of the current government with a workers' and peasants' regime, to end the war and spark the international overthrow of capitalism.

To underscore the continuity of their strategy on soviet power, the editors of *Pravda*, Kamenev and Stalin, on 17 March published on the paper's front page the entire Bolshevik 1906 resolution on the soviets, which affirmed that they were 'embryos of revolutionary power' that must be 'turn[ed] into a provisional revolutionary government' through a proletarian-led uprising. The editors declared that the orientation of the resolution 'basically remains true today' even though 'today's soviets operate on a terrain that has already been cleared of Tsarism'.[101] This line was developed in *Pravda*'s 18 March issue, in which Stalin explicitly called for the establishment of an empire-wide soviet body, which must take political power – this task, he argued, was the 'first condition for the victory of the Russian Revolution'.[102] One immediate consequence of

98    'Pilsoniskā revolūcija un proletariāts' [1917] in Stučka 1978, p. 128.
99    'Do polskich robotników i żołnierzy w Rosji' [1917] in Tych 1977, p. 274.
100   'Резолюция о текущем моменте' [1917] in Манилова 1928, pp. 167–8.
101   'Советы Рабочих и Солдатских Депутатов и наша партия', *Правда*, 17 March 1917.
102   'Об условиях победы русской революции', *Правда*, 18 March 1917.

this stance was the party's consistent push for a worker-led popular militia to replace the police and the standing army.[103]

Contrary to academic and activist assumptions today, Marxists at this time did not see socialist revolution as a necessary corollary of soviet power. Looking back at the politics of the party in March, Stučka noted in 1918 that 'we, the Bolsheviks, the Petrograd executive committee, both raised the demand for all power to the soviets, but we did not yet think about immediately moving to socialism'.[104] Calls in March for a revolutionary soviet government – a dictatorship of the proletariat and peasantry – were not limited to Petrograd. In Latvia, one party committee declared that 'the only consistent expression of the workers' interests is the Soviet of Workers' Deputies, and therefore it is our duty to support it in every way, to transfer the power of the Provisional Government to it, and through this to continue the revolution until final victory'.[105] Similar proclamations were made by Bolsheviks in Moscow, Ekaterinburg, Kharkov, and Krasnoyarsk.[106]

The 3–4 April Bolshevik Moscow city-wide conference illustrates the dominant perspective on the eve of Lenin's return. Only a single person, V.I. Yahontov, opposed the fight for a new revolutionary regime, arguing that 'if the working class takes power into its own hands, it will not be able to cope with the economic breakdown'. The other delegates responded by shouting him down – 'you are a Bolshevik?' they taunted.[107] Yahontov immediately after joined the Mensheviks, as did a handful of co-thinkers in Petrograd led by Wladimir Woytinsky (who was likewise criticised and politically isolated by the Petrograd Bolsheviks).

Throughout March, liberals and right-leaning socialists attacked the Bolsheviks for opposing the war and the Provisional Government. The party's refusal to support the military effort was particularly controversial.[108] Recent

---

103    Piontkovskii 1925 [2016], p. 603.

104    Stučka 1917c [1976–78], pp. 279–80.

105    'Сообщение Руиенской социал-демократической группы' [1917] in Латвияс кп цк Партияс вēстурес институтьῷц 1963, p. 24.

106    Бурджалов 1971, pp. 33–4, 38, 197, 225, 319, 336.

107    Cited in Сахнин 2010, p. 211.

108    Шляпников 1923 [1992], p. 452 and Шляпников 1925 [1994], p. 213. Testifying to the Bolsheviks' anti-defencist consensus, Kamenev delivered the main Bolshevik speech on the war at the 29 March–3 April All-Russian Soviet conference. Denouncing the war and calling for world socialist revolution, Kamenev affirmed (as Lenin too would later) that only 'when society's working classes conquer power' would national defence be warranted (cited in Шляпников 1925 [1994], p. 232). The Bolsheviks' proposed resolution similarly declared that solely 'the transfer of power to the proletariat and the revolutionary democracy' could make Russia's involvement in the war anything other than imperial-

research by Russian scholars has detailed the consistency of the Bolsheviks' anti-war agitation in March, both among workers and inside of the army itself.[109] Moderate socialist polemics against soviet power likewise began before Lenin's return. Against their radical rivals, the Mensheviks responded that the need for an alliance with the bourgeoisie, as well as the low level of Russia's level of economic development, precluded the rule of working people.[110]

In short, Bolshevism's strategic perspective was unquestionably radical prior to Lenin's return in April. Bolsheviks rejected blocs with liberals, denounced the war, demanded land to the peasants, and called for a revolutionary government based on the Soviet, which in turn would spark world socialist revolution. The overthrow of the Tsar had not accomplished these fundamental objectives – the democratic revolution, in Bolshevik eyes, had *not* yet been completed. Adherence to the tenets outlined above constituted a red thread of political continuity between Old Bolshevism and their approach throughout the rest of the year. Up through October, the real debate within the Bolsheviks was not over whether to push for soviet power, but whether moderate socialists could be pressured to do the same.[111]

That said, revolutionary Marxists across the empire were subjected to real pressures – from conciliatory socialists and from the mass of workers – to tone down or hold back their independent line for the sake of unity. In the wake of the Tsar's overthrow, all regions were swept by a 'honeymoon' mood of euphoria and class collaboration. One Left SR recalled that 'the events of February made people forget what only a few days earlier had been their irreconcilable differences with the landowners and capitalists. It seemed like all were united'.[112] The widespread fear in early March of the immediate danger of a counter-revolutionary reaction was another important factor promoting conciliationism.[113] As David Mandel notes, 'fear of civil war, and its counterpart, the desire for broad revolutionary unity, continued to haunt the political consciousness of the working class well past the October Revolution'.[114]

The threat and risks of civil war *were* real. And events seemed to be demonstrating that Russian liberals could be pressured into making concessions. For

ist in nature ('Резолюция о войне', *Правда*, 29 March 1917). Illustrating the balance of forces inside the working class at this moment, the Bolshevik proposal was overwhelmingly defeated, 57 to 325.

109    See, for example, Тарасов 2014, pp. 39–46.
110    Шляпников 1923 [1992], p. 371.
111    This debate is examined in detail in Blanc 2017c.
112    Cited in Mandel 1983, p. 80.
113    On the moderating impact of this fear on Moscow Bolsheviks, see Бурджалов 1971, p. 87.
114    Mandel 1983, p. 84.

socialists engaged in mass politics, there were never any easy answers to political dilemmas. By 1917, most Bolshevik cadre were pragmatic radicals, whose
accumulated experience and roots in workers' movements made them hesitant to move too far, too fast. Though the Bolsheviks acquitted themselves
better than most socialists in imperial Russia, they too were subjected to the
same centrifugal forces. And they manifested many of the same vacillations.
Shlyapnikov recalled that the 'pressure was so strong that even some of those
whom we previously considered "ours" wavered and retreated'.[115]

In February and March, many Bolsheviks worked closely with moderate
socialists, who were still implementing a relatively combative approach. This
was particularly the case in the borderlands of the empire, where factional
allegiances were frail and RSDRP organisations were generally united. Such a
context contributed to the weakness of independent Bolshevik political articulation in many such locales.[116] In most regions, this wavering constituted a
break from the stance articulated by the party's Old Bolshevik leadership in
Petrograd. But such vacillations were also manifest in the capital itself.[117]

The drift towards conciliationism was not a secondary matter. Lenin's well-
known intransigence against the Mensheviks and SRs – and his exaggerated
polemical approach within the Bolshevik current in April – was in large part
aimed against the tendency of some of his comrades to bend to conciliatory
socialists, who in turn were bending to the liberal bourgeoisie. Passing radical
resolutions and making militant speeches did not guarantee that revolutionaries would avoid being swept along with the prevailing political tide. 'Whoever
wants to help the waverers must first stop wavering himself', he insisted.[118]

Yet Bolshevik vacillation in early 1917 generally took place in spite of, not
because of, the strategy of old Bolshevism. Writers have too often depicted the
actions of socialists as determined solely by ideology – according to this logic, if
Bolshevik tactics were 'wrong' before Lenin's return it must have been primarily because the party adhered to a flawed revolutionary theory. But there was no
automatic, one-to-one relation between theory and practice. All parties were
wagering on possible paths, leading many socialists in the heat of the moment
to reverse their longstanding stances or quietly refrain from fighting for them
in practice. The political whirlpool of 1917 placed intense pressures upon moderates to radicalise and on radicals to become more moderate.

---

115    Шляпников 1923 [1992], p. 367.
116    For a discussion of early 1917 Bolshevik conciliationist tendencies, see Blanc 2017d.
117    Elwood 1974, p. 197.
118    Lenin 1917b [1960–65], p. 84.

## 7    Breaking with the Bourgeoisie: April–October

Contrary to the impression one gets by looking at 1917 through the lens of Lenin's 'April Theses' or *The State and Revolution*, the major socialist debates on revolutionary power in 1917 did not revolve around the question of whether the Russian Revolution was 'democratic' or 'socialist' in nature, nor whether a soviet government was a higher form of democratic rule than a parliamentary regime. A historiographic over-focus on Lenin's writings has obscured the simplicity of the fundamental political question facing socialists in 1917: Was it necessary to ally with or break from the bourgeoisie?

It must be kept in mind that the old absolutist state was largely dismantled by the February Revolution. The new Provisional Government was a very weak institution that never possessed firm control over a repressive apparatus, let alone a monopoly of violence over society. Its tenuous popular legitimacy largely rested on the support given to it by socialist-led soviets – the sole legitimate authority in the eyes of a large percentage of soldiers, as well as workers. In these conditions, debates over state power became concentrated in the issue of whether working people should bloc with the upper class or set up some sort of independent authority to push the revolution to victory. As we have seen, Bolsheviks and revolutionary SDs generally had advocated the latter option since 1905. A non-bourgeois government, in their eyes, was a natural and necessary component of the democratic revolution.

Neither Lenin nor the Bolsheviks in 1917 equated *soviet* power as such with *workers'* power. Unlike in 1905, the soviets represented a segment of the population much larger than just the working class. As Lenin noted in April: 'in these Soviets, as it happens, it is the peasants, the soldiers, i.e., petty bourgeoisie, who preponderate'.[119] Similarly, Karl Radek explained in September that the 'transformation of the Workers' Delegates Council [of 1905] into the Workers' and Soldiers' Council [in February 1917] thus meant the transformation of a proletarian organ of struggle into an organ of revolutionary democracy, into an organ, therefore, with a predominant – and even artificially proportioned – petty bourgeois majority'.[120] By June 1917, the councils represented roughly 37 million people – only about seven million fewer than voter turnout in November's Constituent Assembly elections.[121] The defining class characteristic of the soviets was not that they were proletarian, but that they were not bourgeois.

---

119    Lenin 1917c [1960–65], p. 48.
120    Radek 1917, pp. 3–4.
121    Getzler 1992, p. 30.

Rejecting the claim that he was aiming to 'skip' the bourgeois-democratic stage, Lenin in April stressed that he was not calling for a 'workers' government' but rather for a regime of workers, agricultural labourers, soldiers, and peasants.[122] Though Lenin personally saw soviet power as the concretisation of a 'commune state', a 'step towards socialism', and 'the highest form of democracy', for a majority of workers and Bolsheviks throughout 1917 the demand for 'All Power to the Soviets' simply meant establishing a government without capitalists.[123] Lenin's particular gloss on soviet power was conspicuously absent not only in the mass agitation of the Bolsheviks, but also in the writings of most other party leaders.

Bolsheviks well after April continued to see the fight for soviet power as part of the democratic revolution. Speaking to the Moscow Soviet in the summer, one Bolshevik leader thus argued: 'When we speak of transferring power to the soviets, this does not mean that the power passes to the proletariat, since the soviets are composed of workers, soldiers, and peasants; it does not mean that we are now experiencing a socialist revolution, for the present revolution is bourgeois-democratic'.[124]

During April and throughout 1917, various Bolsheviks positively invoked Kautsky's influential 1906 argument that the Russian Revolution was a unique project situated on the border of democratic and socialist overhaul.[125] In the fall, Bolsheviks increasingly came to describe the revolution simply by the class forces involved: i.e. workers and peasants (including soldiers). The declaration announcing the Provisional Government's overthrow in Petrograd therefore concluded: 'Long live the revolution of workers, soldiers and peasants!'[126] Analogous formulations became the norm throughout imperial Russia.[127]

In Bolshevik discourse up through (and usually well past) October, invocations of socialist revolution related to the approaching social overturn in the West or the *world* revolution. Categorising the seizure of power by working people in Russia as a socialist revolution was very rare (and completely absent from the April discussions and resolutions in Petrograd and beyond). In fact, top Bolshevik leaders – including Lenin in April – explicitly rejected claims that they were calling for socialist revolution inside of Russia.[128] In virtually all

122    Lenin 1917c [1960–65], p. 48.
123    Smith 2006, p. 134 and Anweiler 1974, pp. 157–8.
124    Cited in Anweiler 1974, p. 171.
125    РСДРП (большевиков) 1917a [1958], pp. 15, 96 and РСДРП (большевиков) 1917b [1958], pp. 114, 132.
126    Lenin 1917e [1960–65], p. 236.
127    For one of many such examples, see Шаумян 1917 [1958], p. 108.
128    See, for example, Lenin 1917c [1960–65], p. 52 and Джапаридзе 1917 [1958], p. 166.

Bolshevik internal resolutions and agitation leading up to the October Revolution, as well as the documents issued by the 25–26 October All-Russian Second Soviet Congress, references to socialist revolution relate only to the international process.[129] Though a few top Bolshevik leaders began to identify Russia's revolution as socialist following the October uprising, only in early 1918 did this formulation become widely used in the party and government.[130]

Without understanding the meaning ascribed to soviet power by Bolsheviks and working people in 1917, it is hard to make sense of party stances and debates throughout the year. Consider, for example, the resolution on soviet power passed in April by the Bolshevik conference. According to the re-arming myth, this conference concretised its call for socialist revolution in the demand for a soviet regime. In reality, the conference declared that *any* majoritarian representative body, including a Constituent Assembly, could serve as the vehicle for the new revolutionary power.[131]

Since the bourgeoisie was a tiny minority of the population, the prevailing assumption was that soviets and a Constituent Assembly elected by universal suffrage would be mutually complimentary, non-capitalist institutions. To quote a resolution of Latvian riflemen, in a Constituent Assembly 'the suppressed classes naturally must have a majority'.[132] Soviets and a Constituent Assembly, in other words, would act as instruments of what was commonly referred to as the 'democracy' or 'revolutionary democracy', i.e. the worker-peasant majority. In the discourse of 1917, democracy had a distinctly anti-capitalist connotation. One liberal lamented that 'presently democracy refers only to the poor, to people without resources, that is, workers and peasants; but this is incorrect'.[133]

Workers and their mass organisations in Russia frequently portrayed the expansion of democracy as concomitant with the restriction of the rights and power of the elite.[134] Russia's leading liberals thus feared a Constituent Assembly, over which they would have little control, and postponed its convocation throughout the year. In contrast, the Bolsheviks – including Trotsky

---

129   See, for example, the documents collected in Бош 1925, Ибрагимова and Искендерсва 1957, Elwood 1974a, and Stalin 1953–55.

130   For the invocation of socialist revolution in the post-October internal debates on soviet power, see RSDRP Central Committee 1917–18 [1974]. On the general evolution of Bolshevik categorisations of the revolution after October, see White 1985.

131   'On the Soviets of Workers' and Soldiers' Deputies' [1917] in Elwood 1974a, p. 223, my emphasis.

132   Cited in Ezergailis 1983, p. 305.

133   Cited in Kolonitskii 2004, p. 81.

134   Kolonitskii 1994, p. 193.

and Lenin up through the October Revolution – consistently campaigned for both soviet power *and* a Constituent Assembly. In an internal letter to Bolshevik leaders on the eve of the October uprising, Lenin insisted that 'once power is in the hands of the Soviets' the success of the Constituent Assembly would be 'guaranteed'. The Bolsheviks, he noted, 'have said so thousands of times and no one has ever attempted to refute it. Everybody has recognised this "combined type" [of state]'.[135] Only *after* 1917 did Bolsheviks and Social Democrats alike counterpose democracy to (proletarian) dictatorship and counterpose democratic to soviet republics.

April 1917 marked a moment of tactical evolution rather than strategic rupture for Bolshevism. Though substantial opposition like that seen in Kiev was rare, the discussions in April played an important role empire-wide in cohering the Bolsheviks and overcoming their early year vacillations. Sharp attacks on the Provisional Government were stepped up after the April conference. Local Bolshevik militants across Russia began for the first time to consistently foreground the call for a soviet regime, which was henceforth much less often framed as a temporary power. The need to clearly demarcate themselves from the conciliatory socialists also became more widely accepted.

It is difficult to gauge how much of this evolution was due to Lenin's impact or to the rapidly changing political context. In March, the Provisional Government had not yet announced any major measures openly in contradiction with popular demands for change. Early Bolshevik vacillations generally reflected an adaptation to the post-February euphoria – and this mood in Russia lasted less than a month. April was marked by a massive outcry from workers in response to the revelation that the government planned to continue the war until victory.

The slogan 'All Power to the Soviets' was raised by protestors for the first time in the April demonstrations. And whereas the Soviet leadership had initially fought to push the Provisional Government forward, from early April onwards it focused on propping up the regime and dampening popular militancy – an orientation culminating in the moderate socialists' entry into the administration in early May. In the midst of an unprecedented proletarian upsurge against the Provisional Government and a steady shift to the right by the SRs and Mensheviks, it is not surprising that many Bolsheviks throughout Russia took a more militant and independent stance.

---

135   Lenin 1917d [1960–65], p. 200. This underarticulated conception of a 'combined' state based on parliamentary as well as mass democratic institutions foreshadowed later strategic elaborations by democratic socialists such as Ralph Miliband and Nicos Poulantzas. See, for example, Miliband 1989, pp. 224–34.

As the Constituent Assembly continued to be pushed by the government into the indefinite horizon, the authority and permanency of the soviets in the eyes of workers were correspondingly heightened. Given the absence of any existing national parliament or parliamentary traditions due to Russia's exceptional autocratic legacy, the soviets became the dominant democratic expression of working people, into which they invested their energy and aspirations.

Historiographic debates over the extent to which Lenin's stances marked a break from prior party strategy often overlook his relatively limited influence for most of 1917, especially outside of Petrograd. Even had he wanted to enact a major party reorientation, the loose and decentralised nature of the Bolshevik current mitigated against any such dynamic. 'Insubordination was the rule of the day whenever lower-party bodies thought questions of importance were at stake', notes Robert Service.[136] This was doubly true in Russia's borderlands and provinces, where the connection of local committees to the Petrograd-based leadership was tenuous.

Historian Hugh Phillips, for example, observes that 'Tver's archives confirm the absence of a national Bolshevik network in 1917 taking its commands from the leadership in Petrograd. In short, the city's Bolsheviks were largely on their own'.[137] Bolshevism's evolution in 1917 was driven forward by the relatively autonomous responses of party cadre at all levels to big events in political life. Despite the Bolsheviks' disconnect from the party centre, their strong commitment to a strategy of working-class hegemony served as a sufficient strategic basis to cohere the current throughout 1917.

Across Russia from late April onwards, the Bolsheviks churned out leaflet after leaflet reaffirming the same simple message: to satisfy the demands of the people, workers and their allies must break with capital and take all power into their hands. To defend and deepen the revolution required class struggle, not class collaboration. 'Our programme is the struggle with the bourgeoisie', explained one Bolshevik rank-and-file militant.[138]

Throughout 1917 it was almost always right-leaning socialists and liberals who framed the sole options for Russian development as capitalist democracy or socialism.[139] In response to such claims, Latvian Bolshevik leader Pēteris

---

136  Service 1979, p. 52. Snow likewise notes that 'a majority of those men in Siberia who called themselves Bolsheviks were successful politically, but were not Leninists' (Snow 1977, p. 16).

137  Phillips 2001, p. 7.

138  Cited in Service 1979, p. 45.

139  Galili y Garcia 1989, p. 157.

Stučka posited that erecting a rigid dichotomy between bourgeois and socialist revolution was essential for justifying their refusal to support the demand for soviet power.[140] Along these lines, Trotsky noted that the Mensheviks in February had invoked the bourgeois nature of the revolution to justify their refusal to take power; then in May they raised this same point to justify participation in a coalition government. These invocations, he concluded, were 'purely practical' measures 'to preserve the privileges of the bourgeoisie, and to assign to it in the government a role to which it is by no means entitled'.[141]

Bolshevik leaders repeatedly rejected accusations that they were trying to 'introduce socialism' as a straw-man argument that deflected attention from the real political alternative: collaboration or rupture with the capitalist class. Rather than advocate a socialist revolution in Russia, they insisted that while socialism would have to be built internationally, it was both possible and necessary to break with the capitalists. Even if one believed that the revolution was bourgeois in nature, they argued, it did not follow that this obliged the establishment of a bourgeois government. Not only would such a regime be incapable of achieving the central bourgeois-democratic goals (agrarian reform, a Constituent Assembly, etc.), but it would also be necessarily anti-democratic since most people in Russia were peasants or workers.[142]

And while the Bolsheviks were the most influential proponents of a soviet government, it is hardly the case, as John Marot has claimed, that 'no other political formation called for it'.[143] In fact, this demand was raised by the SDK-PIL, the Latvian SDs, and the Mezhraionka well before they merged with the Bolsheviks in August 1917.[144] As the SDKPIL insisted in June, either all power would pass to the soviets or the landlord-capitalist counterrevolution would prevail – 'either us or them', a party editorial concluded.[145] Calls for soviet power were also raised by parties and currents that did not affiliate with the Bolsheviks in 1917, including all (or major wings) of the Left SRs, the PPS-Left, the SR-Maximalists, left Ukrainian SRs, and anarchists.[146] In July, after the PPS-

---

140    Stučka 1917d [1976–78], p. 203.
141    Trotsky 1917 [1918], pp. 268–9.
142    Trotsky 1917 [1918], pp. 268–71.
143    Marot 2014, p. 165.
144    See, for example, Raleigh 1986, p. 328, 'Сообщение Руиенской социал-демократической' [1917] in Латвияс кп цк Партияс вēстурес институйц 1963, pp. 23–4, and Thatcher 2009, pp. 305–6.
145    Cited in Манусевич 1965, p. 220.
146    See, for example, Melancon 1997, p. 62, Любовець and Солдатенко 2010, p. 163, Шелохаев 2002, *passim*, and Сапон 2009, *passim*.

Left's call on the soviets to seize all power went unheeded, the party declared that the Soviet's Executive Committee 'felt much closer to the bourgeoisie than to the socialist working class'.[147]

Apart from the SR-Maximalists and anarchists, the aforementioned currents did not equate soviet power with socialist revolution or proletarian government. Until the Bolsheviks began winning leadership of these bodies in September, the demand for 'All Power to the Soviets' concretely meant the establishment of a government led by the Mensheviks and SRs, two currents openly opposed to direct socialist transformation in Russia. Internationalists among the Bund and Mensheviks also raised this demand in the summer, though not in the fall. Thus Rafael Abramovitch, a central leader of the Menshevik and Bundist Internationalists, argued in July 1917 that the soviets must take the reins of power.[148] He declared: 'In Russia, the bourgeois-democratic revolution must take place without the help of and even against the will of the middle or big bourgeoisie!'[149]

From May onwards, soviet power above all meant an end to coalition government with the capitalist class. In July, the Latvian Social Democracy insisted:

> Socialist ministers are incapable of carrying out truly democratic policies, but instead change themselves into active or passive supporters of the bourgeois majority's policies. The petit-bourgeois socialists are incapable of ending the imperialist war, and end up as the supporters of Russian, English, and French capitalists and the fulfillers of the tsarist embezzling treaties. The bourgeois socialist bloc is not only incapable of realizing the tasks of the revolution but, having renounced revolutionary means, they even help to deepen severely the impending industrial, financial, and food crises.[150]

As indicated above, the radicals' call for a rupture with the bourgeoisie was directed equally against the Russian and Western ruling classes. Across the empire, orthodox Marxists declared that pleading with imperialist powers to negotiate a democratic military solution was a dead-end strategy, one which had to be replaced with a direct revolutionary struggle to take political power and issue peace ultimatums to all the belligerents.[151] Rejecting the Mensheviks' plan to

---

147   Cited in Манусевич 1965, p. 239.
148   Gelbard 1982, p. 70.
149   Cited in Gelbard 1982, p. 71.
150   Cited in Ezergailis 1983, p. 203.
151   Cited in Манусевич 1965, p. 172.

end the war as unrealistic and opportunist, the PPS-Left objected to placing any hopes in either the Allies or the main socialist leaders of the West, since the latter had entered their respective governments and were 'bound ... organically to their native imperialism'.[152]

Soviet power was advocated not as a step towards socialism, nor as the establishment of a commune state, but rather as a means to achieve (or defend) the longstanding demands of the revolution that most socialists across the spectrum professed to support. And as the year dragged on, establishing soviet power increasingly came to be seen as a necessary step to defend political freedom and the revolutionary process against the Right. In this sense, Russia's revolution had more in common with Finland – and traditional orthodox Marxist strategy – than has usually been assumed.

By far the most prominent counter-revolutionary threat against the political freedoms and other conquests won since February came in the form of August's Kornilov rebellion. After General Kornilov was defeated from below, workers and radicals loudly demanded soviet power to destroy the remaining threat represented by Kerensky and the Kadets, both of whom were seen as tied to the reaction. Many feared that Kerensky, Russian liberals, and military officials would abandon St. Petersburg to the German army, in order to let it crush the popular revolution. Indeed, this was a constant motif in radical agitation up through October, particularly in borderland areas such as Latvia. As David Mandel has noted, 'October was first and foremost an act of defence of the actual and promised achievements of February in conditions where society had split into two irreconcilably hostile camps'.[153]

Though Lenin's post-August push for an insurrection against the Provisional Government points to the importance of socialist leader agency, the extent to which October was a defensive revolution has been often overlooked. The Bolsheviks and the Military Revolutionary Committee – the multi-party organisation that led the October uprising – explicitly framed all of their actions as a response to the initiatives of the Kerensky regime. Of course, the dividing line between offensive and defensive action in the class struggle remained hazy at best. But this defensive stance was not a ruse. As Michael Hickey and others have noted, '[u]ltimately, it was Kerensky's own actions to preempt the Bolsheviks on the night of 23–24 October, and not any Bolshevik plan, that launched the October Revolution'.[154]

---

152    Cited in Najdus 1967, p. 256.
153    Mandel 1984b, p. 80.
154    Hickey 2011, p. 276. See also Wade 2004, p. 232.

Throughout imperial Russia, a wide range of Marxist, SR, and anarchist organisations actively participated in the October Revolution. In central Russia, the SDKPIL and the autonomous organisations of displaced Lithuanian and Latvian SDs were integral battalions in the successful conquest of soviet power. The deeply hegemonic LSDSP easily established a new soviet government in Latvia. After a few months delay, the Bolsheviks in Baku, together with the Left SRs and the main remnants of the Muslim *Gummet*, followed suit. Bolsheviks in Estonia and Belarus likewise led successful conquests of power, though, particularly in the latter, it was with shakier support among the non-Russian population.[155]

For all the tactical and political differences that distinct contexts imposed, there was nevertheless a common political goal to the late 1917 struggle for soviet power across imperial Russia: a clean political break with the capitalist class, to implement the urgent demands of working people. In the immediate aftermath of the Petrograd uprising, for instance, Baku's Bolshevik committee made the following call for soviet power:

> Either revolution or counter-revolution. Either the power of the bourgeoisie or the power of the Soviets. ... Down with the bourgeois coalition government! Long live the Great Russian Revolution! Long live the heroic proletariat and the garrison of Petersburg! Long live the power of the Soviets of Workers', Soldiers' and Peasants' deputies![156]

Whatever criticisms one might make of Russia's radicals, the fact remains that the October Revolution did translate socialist promises into deeds. The new government broke with the bourgeoisie and it implemented the core demands

---

155   On the revolution in these regions, see Ezergailis 1974, Ezergailis 1983, Arens 1976, Suny 1972a, Najdus 1967, and Lysenko 2003. On anarchist and Left SR active participation in the fight for soviet power, see, for example, Дементьев 2013, Getzler 1983, p. 158 and Сапон 2009, *passim*. A minority of Bundists and Ukrainian SDs also supported the October Revolution (see, for example, Попов 1929, p. 148 and Любовець and Солдатенко 2010, p. 228). Members and leaders of the PPS-Left participated in the October Revolution in various cities, including in Moscow (Najdus 1967, pp. 339–40). In contrast, the PPS-Left's top representative in Petrograd, Stanisław Łapiński, continued to push for a homogenous socialist government. Unlike his Menshevik-Internationalist allies, however, he did not walk out of the Second All-Russian Congress of Soviets. By December 1917, the PPS-Left as a whole was committed to the defence of the October Revolution and the new Soviet government (Tych 1960, pp. 116–24).

156   'Ко всем рабочим Бакинского района' [1917] in Ибрагимова and Искендерсва 1957, p. 179.

for which working people had fought throughout the year, including Russia's exit from World War One, land to the peasants, workers' control of production, and the election of a Constituent Assembly.

The overthrow of the Provisional Government, of course, did not constitute the end of the anti-bourgeois struggle in Russia. Though an in-depth analysis of post-October events lies beyond the scope of our monograph, it is necessary here to briefly address the controversial question of the Bolsheviks' approach to the Constituent Assembly, since Leninists and Social Democrats alike would later insist on strategically counterposing parliaments to working-class direct democracy.

Despite the unpropitious conditions for a national popular election, the Sovnarkom (Russia's new soviet government) sanctioned elections for the Constituent Assembly. Moreover, the Sovnarkom explicitly declared itself to be a *Provisional* Workers' and Peasants' Government. As Rabinowitch notes, 'the decree establishing the Sovnarkom seemed to leave no doubt that it would soon yield its authority to the Constituent Assembly which, with the bourgeoisie swept aside, would confirm and build upon the first steps toward a bright future which the [Second Soviet Congress] delegates felt they had taken'.[157]

Elections to the Constituent Assembly took place in the last week of November. Their results punctured widespread hopes to combine soviet power with a Constituent Assembly. Though the Bolsheviks won the vast majority of workers' votes and 23.2 per cent of the general electorate, Russia's peasant majority overwhelmingly voted for the SRs, who received 40.4 per cent of the total. (The Kadets received only 4.6 per cent and the Mensheviks only 2.9, even including the votes cast for the Georgian SDs.)[158]

As has been well documented, the Assembly's results were somewhat unreflective of the political relationship of forces by late 1917 since, among other things, the Left SRs at the time of the constitution of electoral lists had not yet broken with their parent party and were underrepresented in the Assembly's elected delegates. Had the Left SRs' weight inside their party been reflected accurately in the Assembly, pro-Soviet parties would have had a clear plurality and a near majority (roughly 48 per cent). But when the Assembly finally met on 18–19 January 1918, the majority rejected the Bolshevik-Left SR proposal to sanction the legitimacy of the Soviet government and its decrees as the body's first order of business. In response, Latvian-led Soviet troops dissolved the Assembly.

---

157    Rabinowitch 2007, p. 22.
158    Protasov 2004, p. 258.

Moderate socialists and liberals – as well as their subsequent historiographic traditions – have long pointed to this dissolution as evidence for Bolshevism's anti-democratic nature. Yet such outrage was not shared by the mass of the population at the time. Even Cold War crusader Richard Pipes acknowledges that 'the dissolution of the Assembly met with surprising indifference'.[159] Similarly, historian Lev Protasov observes that in regard to political democracy and social transformation, 'most of the electorate was close to the Bolsheviks both in spirit and in methods of accomplishing their goals'.[160]

By early 1918, the civil war was underway, making intermediary options even less viable than they had been in 1917. In his study of anti-capitalist popular opinion in 1917, Kolotnitskii concludes: 'The spread of "antibourgeois" sentiments, in the formation of which the most varied and at times conflicting political forces took part, hampered the chances for a workable and durable agreement between socialists and liberals. All other alternatives, including a "unified socialist government", scarcely could have averted civil war'.[161] By October 1917, and even more so by January 1918, the social trenches carved out by the class struggle were too wide to allow for a workable all-Russian government uncommitted to one or the other side. As one Latvian Bolshevik argued right after the October Revolution: 'it is naive to speak of preventing civil war when in fact civil war has already taken over Russia'.[162]

For all their ideological commitments to notions of political democracy, it should be noted that liberals and moderate socialists did not hesitate when they felt it necessary to repress their radical rivals, resort to state-sanctioned violence against workers and peasants, or (as seen in the Finnish case) dissolve parliamentary institutions elected by universal suffrage. That the Bolshevik-Left SR government employed these same methods was not evidence of any inherent authoritarian predilections.

Though much of the common anti-Bolshevik critique is hypocritical, one need not accept Lenin's post-1917 assertions that parliamentary institutions elected by universal suffrage are forms of bourgeois rule generally incompatible with socialist transformation. Even the experience of imperial Russia itself does not confirm such claims. Finland's SDP, for instance, had won a parliamentary majority in 1916 and remained committed to universal suffrage and parliamentary democracy up through the end of its civil war. In Latvia, likewise, the LSDSP won an absolute majority of the popular vote in both

---

159    Pipes 1996, p. 163. See also Rabinowitch 2007, p. 127.
160    Protasov 2004, p. 263.
161    Kolonitskii 1994, p. 196.
162    Cited in Treijs 1977, p. 55.

the soviet and parliamentary elections in the fall of 1917. Given their social and political weight, the Latvian social democrats had the enviable opportunity in late 1917 of choosing between basing workers' rule on either of these bodies.[163] Having swept elections to many city Dumas in the fall, Russian Bolsheviks in various cities of the empire were also faced with similar opportunities on a local level.[164]

The Bolsheviks' initial hopes in the outcome of the empire-wide Constituent Assembly elections – and their related expectations for securing a solidly majoritarian social base for soviet power – proved to be over-optimistic for Russia as a whole. But it does not follow that the incompatibility of universal suffrage and a Constituent Assembly with anti-capitalist rupture in early 1918 reflected an inevitable transhistorical feature of socialist revolution. This contradiction was primarily the product of Russia's peasant majority population, which obliged socialists to choose between, rather than combine, parliamentary democracy and bottom-up organs like workers' councils.

Revolutionary social democrats in 1917 upheld and acted on their longstanding call for a government of working people to transform Russia and spark the international revolution. The October Revolution can, in hindsight, be plausibly categorised as 'socialist', but it is not factually accurate to claim that Bolsheviks or their allies saw it that way for most of 1917.

Indeed, the October Revolution did not call for the nationalisation of industry and Lenin as well as the Bolshevik leadership for months afterwards sought to reach economic arrangements with big business. Yet capitalist industrial sabotage, a wave of workers' wildcat expropriations, and the political dynamics of civil war swept the party into nationalising all major industries in the second half of 1918. 'Will this be another Paris Commune or will it lead to world socialism?', asked Bolshevik leader I. Stepanov in a 1918 pamphlet showing that the Bolsheviks had been obliged by circumstances, not ideology, to expropriate capitalist industry.[165] The Finnish Red Government after January 1918 was similarly pushed by political exigencies and counter-revolution to move significantly further down the road to socialist transformation than it had originally intended.[166]

---

163   Ezergailis 1983, pp. 92, 120.
164   See, for example, Bubnov 1925 [2016], p. 276.
165   Cited in Mandel 1984a, p. 413.
166   Since the Red Government lasted only four months, Finland's inroads into capitalist property did not go as far as in central Russia, but the trajectory was similar. On the dynamics

Though there was perhaps no other viable option in the context of a deepening civil war, this wave of Soviet nationalisations accelerated the catastrophic collapse of production as well as the massive growth of a privileged state bureaucracy.[167] As William Chamberlin notes, 'the attempt to nationalize everything from locomotive works to public baths and to provision the population through state agencies with everything from bread to mushrooms inevitably led to an enormous, unwieldy and incompetent bureaucracy, which stifled all creative initiative and often led to bungling misuse and neglect of the slender resources which the country possessed'.[168]

The real strategic break among revolutionary social democrats did not occur in April 1917. It came well after October, when the Bolsheviks began to theoretically justify their ad hoc domestic decisions and when they started to export abroad a soviet model of revolution. *The State and Revolution* soon became mandatory reading within the new Communist International, which loudly proclaimed the need in all countries to replace parliamentary rule with workers' councils by insurrectionary means. As the Comintern's 1920 'Theses on the Communist Parties and Parliamentarism' put it, in all countries 'what is at stake for us is the immediate political and technical preparations for the insurrection of the proletariat, the destruction of bourgeois power and the establishment of the new proletarian power'.[169]

This was an understandable political wager to make at a heady moment of international anti-capitalist effervescence. But moving away from revolutionary social democratic strategy minimised the distinct challenges and opportunities for Marxists operating in political democracies. The refusal of so many members of the early Communist International to seriously engage in parliamentary politics was just the tip of the resulting ultra-left iceberg, which had profound consequences for the post-war working-class upsurge.

Revising socialist strategy for bourgeois democracies went hand-in-hand with revising the history of the Russian Revolution itself. Up through late 1917, revolutionary SDs including the Bolsheviks openly insisted that Russia was an international exception rather than the norm. Indeed, this was one of the key reasons why they generally refused to call their revolution 'socialist'. Yet as historian James White's research has shown, the Bolsheviks quickly began

of capitalist expropriation and workers' control in revolutionary Finland, see Kuusinen 1919, pp. 23–4, Upton 1980, *passim* and Rinta-Tassi 1986, *passim*.

167  On the nationalisation of industry and the related political problems in Russia, see Насырин 1956 and Chamberlin 1965, Vol. 2, pp. 96–116.

168  Chamberlin 1935, p. 113.

169  Communist International 1920. See also Lenin 1920 [1960–65], p. 61 and Trotsky 1938.

changing their historical accounts of the Russian Revolution in order to better export the soviet model internationally. White documents how their new interpretation,

> held that the party, by its theoretical and organisational expertise, had led the Russian workers, overthrown the capitalist system and established the dictatorship of the proletariat. It had accomplished, in fact, what every socialist party strove to achieve, and in so doing had become an example for them all. ... [H]enceforth the history of the Russian revolution would be written in a way that did not give prominence to factors which reflected Russian national peculiarities.[170]

As we will see in the Epilogue, the Bolsheviks' retroactive decision to declare their revolution to be both 'socialist' and a model for the international proletariat would play a significant role in undercutting attempts to overturn capitalism in the imperial borderlands and the West in 1918–19.

Over the past century, radicals have continued to operate within the strategic cul-de-sac created by this tendency to overgeneralise the international relevance of the Russian Revolution. As such, rediscovering the actual experience of imperial Russia's revolutionary social democrats is not simply an academic issue. Getting this history right hardly guarantees socialist success, but it might make it more likely.

---

170   White 1985, pp. 338–9. In 1922, the Comintern somewhat ambiguously projected the possibility that electing a 'workers' government' to the existing state could be the starting point for a socialist revolution (see 'The Workers' Government' in Communist International 1922 [2011], pp. 1159–61). But this new approach only constituted a partial shift back towards revolutionary social democracy since soviet power was still declared to be the only possible form of workers' rule and since the Comintern did not retract its earlier calls to deligitimise and destroy parliamentary institutions (Communist International 1920).

# Epilogue: An International Revolution Defeated

In the wake of World War One and the Russian Revolution, capitalism stood on the edge of the abyss in numerous countries. Decades of socialist organising combined with an unprecedented military catastrophe culminated in an international revolutionary wave, whose failure was perhaps the single most important missed opportunity in twentieth century socialist politics. For radicals, it was the turning point that did not turn. Successful workers' revolutions beyond imperial Russia could have pushed history down a different course by undermining global capitalist hegemony, ending the Soviet regime's isolation, and potentially even avoiding the crystallisation of Stalinist authoritarianism.

Although a rigorous analysis of these events lies beyond the scope of our study, this Epilogue will bring in the borderlands to analyse the revolution's defeat abroad and its degeneration in Russia. By showing how the surprising setbacks in Russia's imperial periphery undercut the extension of workers' power internationally, I explore the often overlooked role of borderland socialist parties in this pivotal moment of global upsurge. In light of the history discussed in earlier chapters, there was nothing inevitable about the fact that the borderlands ended up constituting more of a barrier than a bridge to anticapitalist transformation.

## 1    Civil War and Authoritarianism

A glimpse of socialism's liberatory potential can be gleaned from the first few months of the Soviet government, as well as the Finnish Red Government. In late 1917 and early 1918, millions of workers, farm labourers, and peasants seized power in their workplaces, communities, and the state. With the overthrow of the old authorities, mass participation in virtually all facets of public life spread to an unprecedented extent. Faced with the sabotage or desertion of governmental functionaries and capitalist managers, working people stepped in to fill the vacuum. For a brief moment, multi-tendency governance and bottom-up self-management became the norm.[1]

Yet the Bolsheviks and their allies inherited a polity that was already on the verge of disintegration. Noting the imperialist encirclement of Russia, a deepening economic disaster, and active sabotage by the capitalists and intelligent-

---

1    Service 1991, p. 300, Сапон 2009, pp. 449–53, Mandel 1984a, pp. 399–413, and Rinta-Tassi 1986.

sia, Baku's Bolsheviks in November 1917 concluded that 'no other government anywhere has had to work in such complex and difficult conditions'.[2]

After the October Revolution, Bolsheviks and other radical socialists across the former Tsarist Empire immediately pushed to extend the revolution beyond Petrograd. Though they succeeded in establishing Soviet rule in central Russia, their successes in the imperial periphery were more uneven. Anti-capitalist governments were set up in Latvia, Estonia, Baku, and Finland, but by the spring of 1918 these had been toppled by foreign military invasions.[3] The early 1918 defeat of the revolution in Ukraine, and the subsequent German occupation, was an especially harsh blow since it gravely aggravated Russia's already acute food crisis.

Borderland defeats facilitated a prolonged and devastating civil war that took place primarily in the imperial periphery. 'Most of the civil war was fought over the territories of the minorities, with the Reds controlling the central Russian regions, and the Whites being based in minority areas', notes historian Nancy Stetten.[4]

Industry further imploded over the course of 1918. Ties between the city and countryside were shattered by famine, disease, and demoralisation. Conditions became almost indescribably catastrophic, making the crises of the earlier period pale in comparison. Democracy could hardly survive, let alone flourish, in such a context.[5]

For an honest contemporary description of this moment, consider the 17 July 1918 letter written by Yakov Semyonovich Sheikman, a 27-year-old Bolshevik leader stationed in Kazan, a heavily Muslim industrial town on the Volga river. Fearing that he would soon be killed in battle, Sheikman wrote the following note to his infant son in which he explained the trajectory of the struggle for which he was risking his life:

> So, dear Emi, we are surrounded. Perhaps I will have to die. Every moment danger awaits us. That's why I decided to write to you. ... You can imagine how difficult it all was [after October], since we had simultaneously to build up, to tear down, and to defend ourselves against enemies who had no shortage of furious hatred toward us. The whole country was engulfed

2  'Передовая Статья "Известий Бакинского Совета"' [1917] in Ибрагимова and Искендерсва 1957, p. 196.
3  On these governments, see Ezergailis 1983, pp. 91–169, Arens 1976, pp. 202–75, Suny 1972a,
   pp. 234–324, and Rinta-Tassi 1986.
4  Stetten 1977, p. 2. See also Acton 1990, p. 205 and Mawdsley 1987, pp. 30, 169, 181.
5  For a summary of these developments, see Acton 1990, pp. 204–7.

in the flame of the Civil War. ... The bourgeoisie and its underlings set about laying ambushes. Sabotage acquired incredible forms and reached colossal proportions. The intelligentsia, which had without complaint supported the bourgeoisie, did not want to serve the working class. As if that were not enough, it joined an alliance with the bourgeoisie directed against the working class. ... Counterrevolution struck Soviet Russia painfully. Yet Soviet power courageously repulsed the blows falling on it from all sides and soon went on the offensive. Where our enemies were prevailing, there was no mercy for us. But we also showed no mercy.[6]

The process of democratising economic and political life was quickly subordinated to military efforts to defeat the counter-revolution and feed the cities as well as the fledgling Red Army. Everything became oriented towards survival, to hold on to power as long as possible until the eruption of workers' power abroad would open up new economic and political horizons. To quote a 1918 declaration by Ukraine's Bolsheviks: 'Either we will perish, together with all our hopes for a better future for mankind, or we will hold out until that moment when the fire of the final social revolution sweeps the whole world'.[7]

As the civil war deepened, self-management was steadily submerged by authoritarianism and bureaucratisation. Noting this dynamic, Sheikman lamented that 'there is a lot of wretchedness in Soviet officials (not all, of course, are like that, but many)'.[8] Historian Vladimir Sapon's recent study of libertarian socialism in Russia paints a similar picture. Though the author is far from an uncritical defender of the Bolsheviks, he concludes that the downfall of soviet democracy in 1918 was primarily caused by the objective context: 'This idea is confirmed by the fact that in areas where the anarchists and left neo-populists consolidated their political hegemony in the period of the first Soviet government, they were no less inclined towards party dictatorship than the Bolsheviks were on a Russian-wide scale'.[9]

As Sapon observes, a comparative empire-wide analysis illustrates the determining impact of dire social circumstances on political policy. Authors arguing that the dictatorial turn of the Russian Revolution was primarily due to the Bolsheviks' inherently authoritarian politics have yet to explain why their rivals – including Russian and non-Russian liberals, nationalists, moderate socialists, and anarchists – resorted to similarly anti-democratic methods

---

6 'Private Letters from a Bolshevik Activist' [1918] in Daly and Trofimov 2009, p. 135.
7 'Воззвание Народного Секретариата' [1918] in Бош 1925, p. 252.
8 'Private Letters from a Bolshevik Activist' [1918] in Daly and Trofimov 2009, p. 136.
9 Сапон 2009, p. 470.

when faced with civil war conditions and comparable political threats to their rule.[10] Finland's Red Government also moved in an authoritarian direction in its final weeks, despite the democratic inclinations of its leaders.[11]

While conditions of social collapse and civil war pushed all major political actors towards dictatorial militarism, it is also true that the Bolsheviks made a whole host of questionable decisions and political errors after 1917. Not least of these was their tendency to theoretically codify ad hoc repressive measures imposed under duress. Bolshevism's perspectives on political democracy became increasingly authoritarian.

One-party rule, the banning of internal party factions, the elimination of civil liberties, and other repressive measures were theoretically rationalised and structurally crystallised, a process facilitated by the Bolsheviks' post-1917 break from orthodox Marxism's traditional approach to parliamentary democracy and political freedom. This tendency to make a virtue of necessity undermined the ability of party cadre to effectively challenge the growing bureaucracy. After the end of the civil war in 1921, the economy was liberalised, but the political regime was hardened.

Perhaps it would have been possible, as some have suggested, for the Bolshevik leadership to have embarked on a different road, wagering that the benefits of political democratisation outweighed the risks.[12] But there were cogent reasons why they did not take this gamble. Since the Soviet regime and the Bolsheviks by this point were so alienated from the population, including much of the working class, democratisation risked taking down the revolutionary government. In hindsight, such an outcome would have been less damaging to the world socialist movement than the rise of Stalinism – yet it would certainly also have dealt a serious blow in the short term to the morale of those struggling to overturn capitalism abroad.

## 2        International Revolution

The Bolsheviks clung on to power in Russia. And they continued through the Comintern to fight for international revolution, which they still viewed as necessary for significant socialist transformation within Russia. As was the case in the preceding years, the course of the Russian Revolution – including its abil-

---

10    See, for example, Suny 1972a, pp. 325–52, Jones 1984, pp. 426, 457, 514–16, Parsons 1987, p. 560, and Suny 1990, pp. 341, 344.
11    Rinta-Tassi 1986 and Kiiskilä 2010.
12    See, for example, Farber 1990.

ity to implement its liberatory aspirations – remained tied to politics abroad. In the words of the Polish SDs, 'the fate of the Russian Revolution is in the hands of the international proletariat and the revolution in Europe'.[13]

Was the orientation of moderate socialists in Russia and across Europe proven right by the absence of victorious social revolutions in the West? It is true that Communists underestimated the obstacles to anti-capitalist transformation in industrialised democracies. But the fact remains that there *was* a revolutionary upsurge outside of Russia after 1917. Moreover, its defeat, especially in Germany and Austria, was at least partly due to Social Democracy's conciliatory actions. As such, moderate socialist scepticism regarding international rupture with capitalism was to a significant degree a self-fulfilling prophecy.

In Austria, for example, Social Democratic leader Otto Bauer acknowledged that '[w]orkers and soldiers could have established the dictatorship of the proletariat any day. There was no power able to prevent them'.[14] Yet despite verbal commitments to orthodox Marxism, Bauer and other Austrian Social Democratic leaders refused to break with capitalist rule, arguing that such a move would leave them internationally isolated. This approach, as one critic has noted, 'proceeded from the idea of a completely isolated revolutionary movement in Austria, and was unable to conceive either the effect that an uprising such as this might have on the already battle-weary soldiers of the "imperial and royal" army, or the international implications of a revolution in Austria'.[15]

Bauer's stance marked a significant break from revolutionary social democratic strategy, which since at least 1905 had expected and oriented to a reciprocal international revolution detonated by Russia. And this is exactly what occurred in the years following 1917. The head of the German army lamented that the 'influence of Bolshevik propaganda on the masses is enormous'.[16] On the other side of the globe, Mexican revolutionary Ricardo Flores Magón exclaimed in March 1918 that the conflagration in Russia 'has to spark, whether those ingratiated with the current system of exploitation and crime like it or not, the great world revolution that is now knocking on the gates of all the peoples'.[17]

---

13    Cited in Tych 1967, p. 38.
14    Cited in Loew 1979, p. 25.
15    Loew 1979, pp. 24–5. Loew, however, fails to see that Bauer's stance – as well as the Austrian Social Democracy's subsequent participation in a bourgeois coalition government – constituted a departure from, not an implementation of, orthodox Second International Marxism.
16    Cited in Chernev 2013, p. 43.
17    Cited in Spenser 2011, p. 36.

Though it is often assumed today that the Bolsheviks' orientation towards world revolution was entirely utopian, the post-war upsurge *did* in fact threaten to topple the existing order in multiple countries of Asia and Central Europe, especially those defeated in the war. In country after country, a majoritarian desire for radical change made itself felt. Workers' and soldiers' revolutions overthrew the old imperial regimes in Germany and Austria in November 1918. Soon after, radical Marxists briefly assumed power in Hungary (1919), Bavaria (1919), and northwest Persia (1920–21). Revolutionary workers and socialists posed a credible challenge to bourgeois rule in Italy in 1919–20, Austria in 1918–19, and Germany in 1918–19 (and arguably up through 1923).

The fact that capitalist powers survived this offensive was not preordained by structural conditions. To be sure, the relationship of forces between workers and capitalists, and between radical and moderate socialists, was not as favourable abroad as it had been in Russia. Nevertheless, numerous scholars have made convincing cases that working-class struggles to radically transform society would have been sufficient to topple capitalism in various countries of Central Europe had the leadership of organised labour pushed in this direction.

Socialists were swept into power in Austria, Germany, and beyond. Yet as workers surged into action against capitalists, most Social Democratic and trade union leaders sought to restore order – all the while insisting that they were committed to socialist transformation. Regarding the German Revolution, historian Marek Waldenberg concludes that:

> An opportunity to win state power clearly faced the working class. A characteristic feature of these years was also the fact that the proletarian masses showed much stronger radicalism than the vast majority of leaders and actions of the old social democratic parties. ... [I]f the social-democratic leaders had wanted to hold on to the helm of state power and use it to initiate socialist system changes, they would have been supported by the vast majority of the proletariat and would have been able to do so because in the early days there were no social forces in Germany capable of opposing this.[18]

Of course, political responsibility for the defeat of the post-war revolutionary wave cannot be laid solely at the feet of the labour officialdom. Capit-

---

18    Waldenberg 1972, Vol. 2, pp. 460–1, 521. On Austria, see Loew 1979, pp. 24–37.

alists were economically and politically stronger in the West than in Russia, and Europe's parliamentary states had more popular legitimacy than Tsarism or the Provisional Government. Moreover, the ultra-leftism of many early Communist Parties across Europe undercut their mass influence and hampered working-class unity in action against the bourgeoisie. During the first years after 1917, the electoral arena was downplayed by all wings of the Communist movement, from Lenin and Trotsky to the most strident electoral abstentionists. Arguing that the Bolsheviks' tactics in the Tsarist Duma should be replicated abroad, the Comintern in 1920 thus insisted that the 'centre of gravity of political life has at present been removed finally and completely beyond the bounds of parliament. ... The task of the proletariat consists in breaking up the bourgeois state machine, destroying it, and with it the parliamentary institutions, be they republican or a constitutional monarchy.'

In the wake of October, caricatured understandings of the lessons of 1917 spread widely among leftists, as did tendencies to treat Russia as a political model applicable in its essentials to all countries. At this critical historic juncture, while a majority of workers attempted to use parliaments to push through radical transformation, Marxist anti-electoralism and denunciatory approaches towards political rivals led to missed opportunities for winning over moderate workers, premature clashes with the state, and repeated political defeats. Only after multiple years and heated debates did the Comintern adopt an orientation towards building a workers' united front and electing workers' governments, an approach better calibrated for the context of capitalist democracies. This political re-orientation, however, mostly came after the decline of the peak international revolutionary upsurge of 1918–19. And, this significant evolution notwithstanding, the Comintern under Lenin and Trotsky never fully broke from its international projection of the workers' council 'model'.[19]

Despite the political limitations of organised Marxists, working people came within reach of anti-capitalist revolution across the German and Austrian empires, where an explosive political mix was produced by their adjacence to Russia, their military defeats in the war, and the strong radical proletarian traditions that had arisen under each country's low inclusion constitutional monarchies. Like in 1905, it was clear by late 1918 that the revolutionary wave was quickly sweeping westward.[20]

---

19  See Communist International 1920, Communist International 1921 [2015] and Communist International 1922 [2011].

20  On dynamics in Germany and Austria, see Chernev 2013, Broué 2005, and Loew 1979.

Given the tenuous hold of the bourgeoisie and its Social Democratic allies on power in Germany and Austria, events could have taken a different turn had Russia's periphery succeeded in advancing the revolutionary domino effect begun in Petrograd. Decisive working-class victories in Ukraine or Poland, in particular, could have potentially given German and Austrian radicals sufficient momentum to overcome their rivals – a chain reaction similar to that seen when central Russia's inspiration radicalised neighbouring Finland in 1905–06.

As had been the case twelve years prior, capitalists and socialists alike wagered that the path to international socialism passed through the periphery of imperial Russia. But unlike in 1905, radicals this time lost hegemony in the most strategic parts of the Russian borderlands.

## 3      Impasse in the Imperial Periphery

Power was up for grabs in all the lands formerly ruled by Tsarism. As in Petrograd, conditions were especially favourable for advocates of anti-capitalist rupture. Unlike in most of Europe, capitalist classes across the Russian Empire's periphery were weak, there were no strong labour bureaucracies to act as buffers for bourgeois rule, and the old state machinery had been broken up. In such a context, political party articulation – particularly the growth of moderate socialism after 1905, the spread of ultra-leftism after 1917, as well as some radicals' inflexible stances on national and agrarian questions – played an outsized role in Ukraine and Poland's aborted revolutions, Georgia's transformation into a foreign protectorate, and the surprisingly rapid demise of new soviet regimes across the Baltic and Ukraine in 1919.[21]

While Petrograd was certainly the centre of political gravity in 1917, the pendulum swung back to the periphery after the October Revolution. The overthrow of the Provisional Government posed the establishment of workers' and peasants' regimes as an immediate task throughout the former Tsarist territory. All sides believed that if soviet power triumphed in imperial Russia's borderlands, it could quickly proceed to advance across Europe and Asia.[22]

---

21    Contextual factors – e.g. economic structures, strike rates, governmental repression, rural and national relations, and bourgeois strength – should also help explain why radicals lost hegemony in parts of Russia. Though I have not identified any consistent structural conditions explaining variations between regions (e.g. why radicals held sway in Latvia but not Georgia) and within regions over time (e.g. why radical Polish and Ukrainian SDS predominated in 1905 but not 1917–18), further research is warranted.

22    White 1994.

The stakes were high. As one French general warned, 'if Poland falls, Germany and Russia will combine'.[23] For their part, Latvian Bolsheviks made the following, entirely typical, declaration in early 1919:

> Latvia is the gateway through which the Russian Revolution must invade Western Europe ... This is no time for weariness or resting! We can only rest when the Red flags of the victorious Communist International wave over Berlin, Rome, Paris, and London.[24]

Though the Bolsheviks believed that the decisive battles of global anti-capitalist rupture would be fought inside the imperialist centres, they also highlighted the strategic centrality of the liberation struggles of the non-European peoples of imperial Russia and the colonial world. To quote Muslim Bolshevik leader Mirsaid Sultan-Galiev: 'The sovietization of Azerbaijan is a highly important step in the evolution of communism in the Near East. ... Soviet Azerbaijan, with its old and experienced proletariat and its already consolidated Communist Party – the Hummat Party – will become the Red lighthouse for Persia, Arabia, and Turkey'.[25]

Marxists nevertheless failed to overturn capitalism in key regions of the former Tsarist Empire – and, in other areas, they took power but were unable to hold on to it. Historian Evan Mawsdley notes that 'the failure on the periphery of the old Empire also doomed attempts to spread the revolution to other countries'.[26]

Bourgeois forces came out victorious in many regions of the Russian Empire, including Poland, Finland, and the Baltic, more often than not with the combined help of moderate socialists and imperialist military interventions. The overthrow of anti-capitalist governments in Finland, Latvia, Estonia, and Belarus during early 1918 was largely caused by German invasions and the Bolsheviks' grudging acceptance of the subsequent Treaty of Brest-Litovsk, which ceded central Russia's influence over much of the former empire. But subjective political errors also played a significant role in the downfall of borderland radicalism, particularly during the 1918–19 apex of the international revolutionary wave.

---

23    Cited in Fiddick 1974, p. i.
24    Cited in Popoff 1932, pp. 241–2.
25    Cited in Bennigsen and Wimbush 1985, p. 54. On early Communist approaches to the 'Eastern' peoples of the Russian Empire, as well as anti-colonial struggles abroad, see Riddell 1993, Smith 1999, and Riddell 2017.
26    Mawsdley 1987, p. 124.

Ultra-leftism among borderland Communists – who had become far more convinced of the revolution's 'socialist' nature than the Bolsheviks had been in 1917 – played a major part in the abortion of Poland's revolution and the downfall of the Soviet regimes set up again after November 1918 in Latvia, Lithuania, Belarus, Estonia, and Ukraine. An already difficult political and socio-economic situation for the new Soviet regimes was made much worse by their tendency to underestimate peasants' demands for land – a dogmatic stance reflecting orthodox Marxism's longstanding analysis of proper tactics for the Baltic and Poland (where rural class differentiation was stronger than in central Russia) as well as the post-1917 conversion of radicals to the view that Russia's upheaval was a 'socialist revolution'. Popular support for the borderland Marxists in power was further eroded by their sweeping nationalisations of industry, their tendency to underestimate national sentiments, and their frequently authoritarian approach towards other political currents.[27]

The basic dynamic of dashed popular enthusiasm described here in Lithuania was repeated in Belarus, Estonia, Ukraine and beyond: 'barely three weeks after [the Communists'] enthusiastic reception in January [1919], the climate of opinion had changed radically, and the sympathies for a socialist system rapidly dwindled.'[28] As the historian of Latvia's 1918–19 Communist experiment notes, 'the collapse of the Soviet regime, in late May 1919, was unexpectedly fast', a surprising outcome explained primarily by the Latvian Bolsheviks' excessive radicalism.[29]

During 1920–21, lasting Soviet rule was eventually established in Georgia and Armenia, largely through Red Army intervention. In Ukraine, Belarus, and Azerbaijan, following the overthrow of Soviet regimes established between 1917 and 1919, Communists also leaned on the Red Army to take back power in 1920–21. But the early political defeats and subsequent military morass over the years prior, exacerbated by an empire-wide economic collapse, prevented the borderlands from serving as gateways for anti-capitalist overhaul during the 1918–19 highpoint of Europe's revolutionary wave.

Given the strategic centrality of Russia's periphery for the extension of socialism abroad, these setbacks were not inconsequential episodes. As one Bolshevik leader put it in December 1917: 'Without Latvia, Finland and other

---

27  On post-1917 ultra-leftism in the Baltic and Poland, and its impact on the extension of revolution abroad, see Kowalski 1978 and White 1994. On the borderlands in the Russian Civil War, see Mawdsley 1987 and Smele 2017.

28  White 1971, p. 199. On Estonia, see Brüggemann 2008; on Belarus (which was incorporated into a joint Soviet regime with Lithuania in early 1919), see Lysenko 2003, pp. 133–40.

29  Šiliņš 2008, p. 78.

revolutionary peripheral regions, Russia cannot accomplish what is needed to establish the government of working people'.[30] Reflecting on the surprising turn of events in regions with such militant political traditions, another Bolshevik activist noted in 1927 that it 'would have seemed monstrous' in 1905 to imagine that Russia would experience ten years of workers' rule while Latvia and Poland would still be under bourgeois dictatorship.[31]

Of all the borderland setbacks, those in Ukraine and Poland were the most decisive. Ukraine was not only the largest non-Russian region of the former Tsarist Empire as well as its main breadbasket, but it also stood adjacent to Germany and Austria. Speaking for the Bolshevik leadership at the Ukrainian Communist Party's October 1918 congress, Karl Radek declared that 'the bridge to the European revolution' was the revolution in Ukraine and its adjacent nations.[32] The existence of a large Ukrainian population inside of Austria's Galicia region meant that a successful revolution in 'Russian' Ukraine would very likely seep across its borders. Indeed, this was one of the main reasons why the initially hesitant Austrian and German governments were eventually convinced by Ukrainian Rada leaders to occupy Ukraine in early 1918.[33]

As seen in the previous chapter, Ukrainian and Russian Marxists' inability to cohere a radical bloc to assume power in late 1917 had given the conciliatory Ukrainian socialist leaders just enough time to convince the German-Austrian regimes to intervene militarily. Given that moderate socialists took the initiative to summon reluctant foreign powers to invade, outside military intervention alone is insufficient to explain the revolutionary defeats in Ukraine and so many of Russia's borderlands. Reflecting on this turn of events, in May 1918 a left Ukrainian SR lamented that 'those who summoned the Germans were little interested in the revolution. They stifled our revolution and have delayed its outbreak in Germany'.[34]

But radicals in Ukraine received a second chance after the German and the Austrian revolutions in November 1918 overthrew their imperial states. In February 1919, Soviet forces took power in Kiev, with the initial support of left Ukrainian SRs (Borotbists). All of Europe was politically ablaze: it seemed as if the overthrow of capitalist rule across Central Europe might now be a matter of weeks away. Christian Rakovsky, the head of the new Soviet government, declared that 'Ukraine is truly the strategic nodal point of socialism. To create

---

30    Cited in Ezergailis 1983, p. 98.
31    Попов 1929, p. 49.
32    Cited in Graziosi 2009, pp. 20–1.
33    Kamenetsky 1977, p. 51.
34    Cited in Maistrenko 1954, p. 66; see also p. 82.

a revolutionary Ukraine would mean triggering off a revolution in the Balkans and giving to the German proletariat the possibility of resisting famine and world imperialism. The Ukrainian revolution is the decisive factor in the world revolution'.[35]

Yet at the precise moment when Soviet republics were being founded in neighbouring Hungary (March 1919) and the German region of Bavaria (April 1919), the Ukrainian Soviet government began to crumble. In marked contrast with the *Spilka*-RSDRP alliance of 1905–06, Ukraine's radicals were unable to cement a multi-national hegemonic bloc. In a context already marked by economic and social chaos, the new Soviet administration pushed a series of ill-conceived, ultra-left national and agrarian policies that especially alienated non-Russians. This difficult situation was inflamed by the reckless decision of left Ukrainian SDs to initiate an armed uprising against the Soviet regime in April, which in turn sparked rebellions by political forces well to their political right.

By the summer of 1919, Soviet rule had again been deposed. A bourgeois government headed by former Ukrainian SD Symon Petliura took power and eagerly allied itself with Pilsudski's Polish army to fight the Bolsheviks. As historian Jurij Borys notes, 'instead of advancing against Europe, the Communists were compelled to defend their capital, Moscow'.[36] A major opening for extending revolution to the West had been missed.

The inability of Marxists in Poland to lead workers to power was an even more devastating defeat for the international revolution. For many decades, Marxists had looked to Poland – Russia's second-largest borderland region – as the powder keg that could blow up the German, Russian, and Austrian regimes. Eager to gain the backing of the Entente, right-leaning Polish socialist leaders declared in April 1919 that 'only a strong Poland capable of survival can create a dam against the Bolshevik flood'.[37] Along similar lines, one French government official insisted that 'Poland is currently an essential screen between Russian bolshevism and the German revolution. She is one of the solid links in the *cordon sanitaire* which must be stretched around diseased and contagious Russia'.[38]

The inability of Polish radicals to win back hegemony in 1918–19 was an obstacle to workers' power not only in Poland, but in Germany as well.[39] The

---

35    Cited in Fagan 1980.
36    Borys 1980, p. 360.
37    Cited in Holzer 1992, pp. 374–5.
38    Cited in Bogacki 1991, p. 255.
39    Strobel 1974, pp. 670–1.

German state continued to rule over large Polish populations in Poznan and Silesia, both of which between 1918 and 1921 witnessed mass armed struggle for separation from Germany. The struggle in Silesia, a heavily proletarianised coal-mining region, was a particularly promising opening: organised nationalists were weakly implanted and the region's workers gave the national struggle a sharp anti-bourgeois content.

Polish Communists argued that Silesia would act as the bridge between the Russian and German revolutions. Yet largely due to its continued adherence to Luxemburg's anti-independence stance, the Polish Communist Party refused to support the three armed uprisings in Silesia against the German state in August 1919, August 1920, and May 1921. By 1922, Polish Communists had reoriented their approach to the national struggle, but by this time the window of opportunity had already closed.[40]

The impasse in Poland, combined with the country's continued strategic centrality, was the context for the Bolsheviks' final armed effort to expand the revolution westwards. Writing in 1920 about the 'Battle of Warsaw', Lord d'Abernon – the British government's Special Envoy in Poland at the time – argued that 'had the Soviet forces overcome Polish resistance and captured Warsaw, Bolshevism would have spread throughout Central Europe, and might well have penetrated the whole continent'.[41]

After beating back Pilsudski and Petliura's military offensive against Moscow in the spring of 1920, the Red Army was suddenly faced with the opportunity to advance upon Poland itself. With the goal of spreading workers' revolution to Germany, Lenin and a group of Polish Communist leaders in central Russia ignored the warnings of their comrades in Poland and proceeded to support the march of the army upon Warsaw. Former SDKPIL leader Joseph Unszlicht played a crucial role in feeding into Lenin's illusory hope that a Red Army invasion would be embraced by the Polish working class.[42] Such a response never materialised and the Soviet troops went down in defeat.

Invading Poland had dramatically backfired. But the action underscores that spreading the revolution abroad remained Lenin and the Bolshevik leadership's strategic north star. To quote Ronald Suny, 'the Bolsheviks used all the means available to realize their dream of international revolution. For Communists of the civil-war period, internationalism was less the servant of the Soviet state than the Soviet state was the servant of internationalism'.[43]

---

40    On the political struggle in Upper Silesia, see Hawranek 1966.
41    Cited in Croll 2009, p. 199.
42    Trembicka 1986–87.
43    Suny 1993, p. 85.

Only later was this stance replaced by Stalin's autarkic vision of 'socialism in one country'. The old axiom that the Russian Revolution would be defeated if it remained isolated was borne out. But this defeat, to the surprise of all, took the unforeseen form of Stalinism.

This book has aimed to demonstrate that an empire-wide perspective on revolutionary Russia does more than simply expand our geographic horizons. For scholars, incorporating the experience of non-Russian socialists confirms the causal importance of governmental regimes – especially the absence or presence of democratic freedoms and parliamentary institutions – for the evolution of working-class movements.[44] Dynamics in parliamentary Finland consistently diverged from the rest of the Russian Empire: absolutist conditions pushed workers' movements down a more insurgent, and less organised, path.

In short, authoritarian rule made possible the emergence of an insurrectionary working class. Conversely, legality and universal suffrage pulled workers and socialists to focus more on union organising and electoral politics – i.e. 'the democratic class struggle'.[45]

At the same time, the distinct outcomes within the lands ruled by Tsarism underscore the importance of parties for shaping the course of political life. Though they operated in circumstances not of their own choosing, workers' parties made their own history, especially in moments of revolutionary upheaval. Understanding how socialist organisations evolved strategically and competed politically is necessary, if not sufficient, for explaining why governmental outcomes diverged over space and time across imperial Russia – i.e. why moderates after 1905 won hegemony in Poland, Ukraine, Georgia, and the Jewish street but lost it in Finland.

Social structure sets the parameters for political conflicts, but it does not directly determine their results. Without the decades of socialist party organising described in this book, there is no reason to believe that the process of class formation – what orthodox Marxists called the merger of socialism and the workers' movement – would have advanced nearly as far as it did. This is a point especially worth underscoring at a moment when so few people believe that organised workers can again become the central agent for winning progressive change. But without parties today pushing to cohere workers *as workers*,

---

44    McDaniel 1988 and Goodwin 2006.
45    Korpi 1983 and Vössing 2017.

it is not surprising that such a political force has not emerged automatically. Parties do not just reflect cleavages, they help structure them by articulating class interests.[46]

Rediscovering a lost tradition of working-class politics is not the only reason left activists and organisations would do well to reassess this history. For over a century, ignoring the borderland Marxists and dismissing the politics of revolutionary social democracy has distorted the Russian Revolution and its strategic lessons. Of course, one cannot find precise answers to today's questions from studying the past. History never repeats itself exactly. Nevertheless, socialist approaches to contemporary opportunities and obstacles are always shaped by a balance sheet of the past. While the context of Tsarist Russia is different from today's advanced capitalist democracies, radicals continue to face many of the same central tasks, especially regarding how to forge class independence, build workers' unity, and root socialist organisations in the working class.

One of the goals of this book has been to help puncture myths that continue to undergird activist approaches. All too many Marxists have overgeneralised lessons from a Russian labour movement whose dynamics were determined in large part by autocratic conditions. Simplistic accounts of the Second International have played an important role in pushing generations of radicals to view the presumed innovations of the Bolsheviks as necessary components of effective socialist strategy in all countries – or to assume that the greatest risk facing socialists is always opportunism. To quote Ralph Miliband, 'warnings against the dangers of absorption into the system are ... well taken; but these dangers, it is arguable, are not greater than the dangers of permanent marginalization and impotence'.[47]

Since democratic socialism has been overshadowed for most of the past hundred years by Leninism and Social Democracy, retrieving the lost tradition of revolutionary social democracy is particularly pertinent. This book has underscored the surprising relevance of aspects of imperial Russia's political history for socialists working in legal, parliamentary conditions. Many of the goals and dilemmas of class formation confronted by socialists over a century ago remain with us today. And though there are no timeless formulas for mass politics, the long-overlooked example of Finland's Social Democracy points to the potential viability of a non-insurrectionary strategy for building working-class power and moving towards anti-capitalist rupture.[48]

---

46   Desai 2002, Desai and Tuğal 2009, de Leon, Desai, and Tuğal (eds.) 2015, and Eidlin 2016. On the agency of party leaders, see Vössing 2017.
47   Miliband 1989, p. 221.
48   For elaborations of this approach, see Miliband 1989 and Panitch, Gindin, and Maher 2020.

The experience of socialists across the Russian Empire should push us to rethink how workers' movements and revolutionary processes developed in the past – and it may even help organisers more effectively challenge capitalism in the future. In this spirit, our last word goes to Yakov Sheikman, the young Bolshevik leader in Kazan writing to his infant child in mid-1918. Penned only a few weeks before Sheikman was killed by White soldiers, the letter poignantly articulates the ethos that animated so many revolutionary social democrats across the Russian Empire. Though it was written as a personal note to his son, it can also be read as a testament to future generations:

> [Y]our mother has asked me to write you a letter. If I am killed, you will have detailed advice from your father who loves you and your mother endlessly. ... Do not be upset if I am killed. Believe me, it is not terrible. I want you, too, to be selflessly brave. Never fear death. Be faithful to yourself. Banish fright. I would hope that you will never side with the oppressors and will always stand with the oppressed, not fearing to lose your life. Work should become the foundation of your life. Do not waste time. Work. Work will give you joy. ... I am speaking with you as with a big boy. But you are still such a little one. You are probably sleeping and don't care a whit that daddy is speaking to you of revolution. Good night, my baby. I want to kiss you.[49]

---

49    'Private Letters from a Bolshevik Activist' [1918] in Daly and Trofimov 2009, pp. 134–6.

# Bibliography

This bibliography does not include archival sources, original newspaper articles, and republished documents from primary source collections. These are cited in the footnotes of the monograph. For republished texts, the date of the latest publication is included within brackets. Pseudonyms used in articles are listed within brackets.

Aatsinki, Ulla 2009, *Tukkiliikkeestä Kommunismiin: Lapin Työväenliikkeen Radikalisoituminen Ennen Ja Jälkeen 1918*, PhD Dissertation, Tampereen yliopisto.

Acton, Edward 1990, *Rethinking the Russian Revolution*, London: Bloomsbury Academic.

Adler, Victor 1954, *Briefwechsel mit August Bebel und Karl Kautsky*, edited by Friedrich Adler, Wien: Wiener Volksbuchhandlung.

Afary, Janet 1996, *The Iranian Constitutional Revolution, 1906–1911: Grassroots Democracy, Social Democracy and the Origins of Feminism*, New York: Columbia University Press.

Ailio, Jarmo 1999, *Kesken jäänyt vallankumous. Sosiaalinen mobilisaatio Helsingissä vuoden 1905 suurlakosta Viaporin kapinaan 1906*, Master's Thesis, Helsingin yliopisto.

Ахмедов, Ахмед 1926 [2002], *Азербайджанские тюрки в революции 1905 года*, Баку: Азербайджан милли Энциклопсдиясы.

Акимов, Vladimir 1904–05 [1969], *On the Dilemmas of Russian Marxism 1895–1903*, Cambridge: Cambridge University Press.

Alapuro, Risto 1988, *State and Revolution in Finland*, Berkeley: University of California Press.

Alapuro, Risto 2011, 'The Revolution of 1918 in Finland in a Comparative Perspective: Causes and Processes', in *Revolution in Nordosteuropa*, edited by Detlef Henning, Wiesbaden: Harrassowitz.

Alapuro, Risto 2018, 'Postscript to the Second Printing', in *State and Revolution in Finland*, Leiden: Brill. (Manuscript)

Allen, Barbara C. 2015, *Alexander Shlyapnikov, 1885–1937*, Leiden: Brill.

Aminzade, Ronald 1993, 'Class Analysis, Politics, and French Labor History' in *Rethinking Labor History*, edited by Lenard R. Berlanstein, Chicago: University of Illinois Press.

Anderson, Kevin 2007, 'The Rediscovery and Persistence of the Dialectic in Philosophy and in World Politics', in *Lenin Reloaded: Toward a Politics of Truth*, edited by Sebastian Budgen et al., Durham, NC: Duke University Press.

Андерсон, К.М. et al. (eds.) 2010, *Бунд. Документы и материалы 1894–1921*, Москва: РОССПЭН.

Andriewsky, Olga 1991, *The Politics of National Identity: The Ukrainian Question in Russia, 1904–12*, PhD Dissertation, Harvard University.

Anon. 1905, 'Onko toivottava, että sosialidemokratia pian pääsee voitolle?', *Sosialistinen Aikakauslehti* 1: 17–20.

Anweiler, Oskar 1974, *The Soviets: The Russian Workers, Peasants, and Soldiers Councils, 1905–1921*, New York: Pantheon Books.

Агакишиев, Исмаил Аловсат оглы 1991, *Возникновение и деятельность социал-демократической организации "Гуммет" в 1904–1911 годах*, PhD Dissertation, Московский государственный университет.

Апине, Илга 1965, *П. Стучка–революционер, мыслитель и государственный деятель*, Рига: Звайгзне.

Apine, Ilga 2005, *1905.–1907. gada revolūcija Latvijā un latviešu sociāldemokrāti*, Rīga: Zelta grauds.

Arens, Olavi 1976, *Revolutionary Developments in Estonia in 1917–18 and their Ideological and Political Background*, PhD Dissertation, Columbia University.

Ascher, Abraham 1967, 'Axelrod and Kautsky', *Slavic Review*, 26, no. 1: 94–112.

Ascher, Abraham 1972, *Pavel Axelrod and the Development of Menshevism*, Cambridge, MA: Harvard University Press.

Ascher, Abraham 1988, *The Revolution of 1905, Volume 1: Russia in Disarray*, Stanford: Stanford University Press.

Ascher, Abraham 2005, 'Introduction', in *The Russian Revolution of 1905: Centenary Perspectives*, edited by Jonathan D. Smele and Anthony Haywood, Abingdon: Routledge.

Augškalns-Aberbergs, Jānis 1929, *Latvijas socialdemokratiskā strādnieku partija: vēsturisks atskats*, Rīgā: Izd. Nakotnes Kultura.

Avrich, Paul 1967, *The Russian Anarchists*, Princeton: Princeton University Press.

A.W. 1903, 'Socyalni demokraci i socyaliści rewolucyoniści w Rosyi', *Przedświt*, 5: 192–200.

Badia, Gilbert 1975, *Rosa Luxemburg: Journaliste, Polémiste, Révolutionnaire*, Paris: Éditions sociales.

Багирова, И.С. 1997, *Политические партии и организации Азербайджана в начале XX века (1900–1917)*, Баку: ЕЛМ.

Balkelis, Tomas 2011, 'In Search of the People: The Lithuanian Intelligentsia and the Emergence of Mass Politics in the 1905 Revolution', in *Revolution in Nordosteuropa*, edited by Detlef Henning, Wiesbaden: Harrassowitz.

Basil, John D. 1983, *The Mensheviks in the Revolution of 1917*, Columbus: Slavica.

Bennigsen, Alexandre and S. Enders Wimbush (eds.) 1985, *Muslims of the Soviet Empire: A Guide*, London: C. Hurst.

Benz, Ernst 1989, *Die Revolution von 1905 in den Ostseeprovinzen Rußlands*, PhD Dissertation, Universität Johannes Gutenberg.

Beriia, L.P. 1949, *On the History of the Bolshevik Organizations in Transcaucasia: Speech*

*Delivered at a Meeting of Party Functionaries, July 21–22, 1935*, Moscow: Foreign Language Publishing House.

Berman, Sheri 2006. *The Primacy of Politics: Social Democracy and the Making of Europe's Twentieth Century*, New York: Cambridge University Press.

Bērziņš, J. 1986, 'Rīgas rūpniecības strādnieku streiku kustība 1905. gadā' in *Latvijas strādnieki un zemnieki 1905.–1907. g. revolūcijā*, edited by A. Bīrons and A. Puļķis, Rīga: Zinātne.

Bēržiņš, Valdis (ed.) 2000, *20. gadsimta Latvijas vēsture. I, Latvija no gadsimta sākuma līdz neatkarības pasludināšanai 1900–1918*, Rīga: Latvijas Vēstures Institūta.

Бевз Т.А. 2008, *Партія національних інтересів і соціальних перспектив. (Політична історія УПСР)*, Київ: ІПіЕНД іме ні І. Ф. Кураса НАН України.

Bielecki, Marian [M. Raudonas] 1904a, 'Zagadnienia Rewolucji', *Przedświt*, 24, no. 4: 152–7, 24, nos. 5–6: 200–6, 24, no. 7: 262–72, 24, no. 8: 314–22.

Bielecki, Marian [M. Raudonas] 1904b, 'Strejk powszechny jako środek walki politycznej', *Przedświt*, 24, no. 1: 11–19.

Biskupski, M.B. 1990, 'War and the Diplomacy of Polish Independence, 1914–18', *The Polish Review*, 35, no. 1: 5–17.

Blackledge, Paul 2011, 'Anarchism, Syndicalism and Strategy: A reply to Lucien van der Walt'. Accessed at: http://isj.org.uk/anarchism-syndicalism-and-strategy-a-reply-to-lucien-van-der-walt/

Blackledge, Paul 2013, 'Left Reformism, the State and the Problem of Socialist Politics Today'. Accessed at: http://isj.org.uk/left-reformism-the-state-and-the-problem-of-socialist-politics-today/

Blanc, Eric 2014a, 'National Liberation and Bolshevism Reexamined: A View From the Borderlands'. Accessed at: https://johnriddell.wordpress.com/2014/05/20/national-liberation-and-bolshevism-reexamined-a-view-from-the-borderlands/

Blanc, Eric 2014b, 'Defying the Democrats: Marxists and the Lost Labor Party of 1923'. Accessed at: https://johnriddell.wordpress.com/2014/09/10/defying-the-democrats-marxists-and-the-lost-labor-party-of-1923/

Blanc, Eric 2016a, 'Anti-Imperial Marxism: Borderland Socialists and the Evolution of Bolshevism on National Liberation', *International Socialist Review*, 100: 111–40.

Blanc, Eric 2016b, 'A Lost History'. Accessed at https://www.jacobinmag.com/2016/08/marxism-class-white-workers-socialists-race-anticolonial/

Blanc, Eric 2016c, 'Party, Class, and Marxism: Did Kautsky Advocate "Leninism"?' Accessed at: https://johnriddell.wordpress.com/2016/05/24/party-class-and-marxism-did-kautsky-advocate-leninism/

Blanc, Eric 2017a, '"Comrades in Battle" Women Workers and the 1906 Finnish Suffrage Victory', *Aspasia: The International Yearbook of Central, Eastern, and Southeastern European Women's and Gender History*, 11: 1–18.

Blanc, Eric 2017b, 'Assessing Revolutionary Social Democracy: A Response to Duncan

Hart'. Accessed at: https://johnriddell.wordpress.com/2017/07/13/assessing-revoluti
onary-social-democracy-a-response-to-duncan-hart/

Blanc, Eric 2017c, 'Did the Bolsheviks Advocate Socialist Revolution in 1917?' Accessed
at: http://www.historicalmaterialism.org/blog/did-bolsheviks-advocate-socialist-re
volution-1917

Blanc, Eric 2017d, 'A Revolutionary Line of March: "Old Bolshevism" in Early 1917 Re-
Examined'. Accessed at: http://www.historicalmaterialism.org/blog/revolutionary-li
ne-march-old-bolshevism-early-1917-re-examined

Blanc, Eric 2018, 'The Rosa Luxemburg Myth: A Critique of Luxemburg's Politics in
Poland (1893–1919)', *Historical Materialism*, 26, no. 1: 1–34.

Blanks, Ernests 1930, *1905. gada revolūcija*, Rīgā: R.L.B.-bas Nac. Pol. Audz. Nodaļa.

Blit, Lucjan 1971, *The Origins of Polish Socialism: The History and Ideas of the First Polish
Socialist Party 1878–1886*, London: Cambridge University Press.

Blobaum, Robert 1984, *Feliks Dzierżyński and the SDKPIL: A Study of the Origins of Polish
Communism*, Boulder: East European Monographs.

Blobaum, Robert 1995, *Rewolucja: Russian Poland, 1904–1907*, Ithaca: Cornell University
Press.

Bobrovskaya, Cecilia 1934, *Twenty Years in Underground Russia: Memoirs of a Rank-and-
File Bolshevik*, New York: International Publishers.

Bojcun, Jaromyr Marko 1985, *The Working Class and the National Question in the
Ukraine: 1880–1920*, PhD Dissertation, York University.

Bogacki, Anatole 1991, *A Polish Paradox: International and the National Interest in Polish
Communist Foreign Policy, 1918–1948*, Boulder: East European Monographs.

Bonnell, Victoria E. 1983, *Roots of Rebellion: Workers' Politics and Organizations in St.
Petersburg and Moscow, 1900–1914*, Berkeley: University of California Press.

Borys, Jurij 1980, *The Sovietization of Ukraine, 1917–1923: The Communist Doctrine and
Practice of National Self-Determination*, Edmonton: The Canadian Institute of
Ukrainian studies.

Бош, Е.Б. 1925, *Год борьбы. борьба за власть на Украине с апреля 1917 г. до немецкой
оккупации*, Москва, Ленинград, Госиздат.

Boshyk, George Y. 1981, *The Rise of Ukrainian Political Parties in Russia, 1900–1907: with
Special Reference to Social Democracy*, PhD Dissertation, University of Oxford.

Broido, Eva 1967, *Memoirs of a Revolutionary*, translated and edited by Vera Broido, London: Oxford University Press.

Broué, Pierre 1997, *Histoire de l'Internationale Communiste: 1919–1943*, Paris: Fayard.

Broué, Pierre 2005, *The German Revolution 1917–1923*, Leiden: Brill.

Brüggemann, Karsten 2008, '"Foreign Rule" during the Estonian War of Independence
1918–1920: The Bolshevik Experiment of the "Estonian Worker's Commune"', *Journal
of Baltic Studies*, 37, no. 2: 210–226.

Brym, Robert J. 1978, *The Jewish Intelligentsia and Russian Marxism: A Sociological*

*Study of Intellectual Radicalism and Ideological Divergence*, New York: Schocken Books.

Bubnov, A. 1925 [2016], '"The Lessons of October" and Trotskyism', in *Trotsky's Challenge: The 'Literary Discussion' of 1924 and the Fight for the Bolshevik Revolution*, edited by Frederick C. Corney, Leiden: Brill.

Bukharin, Nikolai and Evgenii Preobrazhensky 1919 [1970], *The ABC of Communism*, London: Penguin

Бурджалов Э.Н. 1971, *Вторая русская революция. Москва. Фронт. Периферия.*, Москва: Наука.

Bushnell, John 1977, *Mutineers and Revolutionaries: Military Revolution in Russiam 1905–1907*, PhD Dissertation, Indiana University.

Bushnell, John 1985, *Mutiny Amid Repression: Russian Soldiers in the Revolution of 1905–1906*, Bloomington: Indiana University Press.

Callahan, Kevin John 2001, *European Socialism and the Demonstration Culture of the Second International, 1889–1914*, PhD Dissertation, Indiana University.

Carr, E.H. 1950, *The Bolshevik Revolution, 1917–1923, Vol. 1*, London: Macmillan.

Carrère d'Encausse, Hélène 1980, 'L'Agitation Révolutionnaire en Russie de 1898 a 1904 Vue par les Représentants de la France', *Revue d'Histoire Moderne et Contemporaine*, 27, no. 3: 408–42.

Carrez, Maurice 2008, *La Fabrique d'un Révolutionnaire, Otto Wilhelm Kuusinen, 1881–1918: Réflexions sur l'Engagement Politique d'un Dirigeant Social-Démocrate Finlandais*, Toulouse: Université de Toulouse le Mirail.

Carsten, Francis Ludwig 1972, *Revolution in Central Europe 1918–1919*, London: Wildwood House.

Chamberlin, William Henry 1935, *The Russian Revolution 1917–21, Volume 1*, London: Macmillan.

Чернявский, Георгий Иосифович and Юрий Георгиевич Фельштинский 2013, *Века и страны. Б.И. Николаевский. Судьба меньшевика, историка, советолога.* Accessed at: http://www.kniga.com/books/preview_txt.asp?sku=ebooks323276

Chernev, Borislav 2012, 'Review', *Ab Imperio*, 4: 470–6.

Chernev, Borislav 2013, *'The Future Depends on Brest-Litovsk': War, Peace, and Revolution in Central and Eastern Europe, 1917–1918*, PhD Dissertation, American University.

Chełstowski Jan 1975, 'Styczniowy zamach stanu 1919 r.', *Dzieje Najnowsze*, 3: 89–98.

Chwalba, Andrzej 2007, *Sacrum i rewolucja: socjaliści polscy wobec praktyk i symboli religijnych (1870–1918)*, Kraków: Universitas.

Cielēns, Fēlikss 1961, *Laikmetu maiņā: atimņas un atziņas*, Lidingö: Memento.

Cisek, Marek 2002, *PPS przed rozłamem 1892–1921: ustrój gospodarczy w programach*, Tyczyn: Wyższa Szkoła Społeczno-Gospodarcza.

Cliff, Tony 1975, *Lenin: Building the Party (1893–1914)*. Accessed at: https://www.marxists.org/archive/cliff/works/1975/lenin1/

Cliff, Tony 1985, *Lenin 1914–1917: All Power to the Soviets*, London: Bookmarks.

Cohen, Mitchell 2017, 'What Lenin's Critics Got Right'. Accessed at: https://www.dissent
magazine.org/article/lenin-menshevik-critics-right-bolshevism-stalinism

Commission of the Central Committee of the C.P.S.U. (B.) 1939, *The History of the Communist Party of the Soviet Union (Bolsheviks), Short Course*, New York: International Publishers.

Communist International 1920, 'Theses on the Communist Parties and Parliamentarism'. Accessed at https://www.marxists.org/history/international/comintern/2nd
-congress/

Communist International 1921 [2015], *To the Masses: Proceedings of the Third Congress of the Communist International, 1921*, edited by John Riddell, Leiden: Brill.

Communist International 1922 [2011], *Toward the United Front: Proceedings of the Fourth Congress of the Communist International*, edited by John Riddell, Leiden: Brill.

Conrad, Jack 2006a, 'Programming the Russian Revolution'. Accessed at: http://weeklyw
orker.co.uk/worker/651/programming-the-russian-revolution/

Conrad, Jack 2006b, 'Kautsky, Lenin and Trotsky'. Accessed at: http://weeklyworker.co
.uk/worker/653/kautsky-lenin-and-trotsky/

Corney, Frederick (ed.) 2016, *Trotsky's Challenge: The 'Literary Discussion' of 1924 and the Fight for the Bolshevik Revolution*, Leiden: Brill.

Corr, Kevin and Gareth Jenkins 2014, 'The Case of the Disappearing Lenin'. Accessed at:
http://isj.org.uk/the-case-of-the-disappearing-lenin/

Costello, Paul 1981, 'Antonio Gramsci and the Recasting of Marxist Strategy'. Accessed
at: https://www.marxists.org/history/erol/periodicals/theoretical-review/19833101.h
tm

Croll, Kirsteen Davina 2009, *Soviet-Polish Relations, 1919–1921*, PhD Dissertation, University of Glasgow.

Czubiński, Antoni 1988, *Rewolucja Październikowa w Rosji i ruchy rewolucyjne w Europie lat 1917–1921*, Poznań: Wydawn. Poznańskie.

Daly, Jonathan W. 1998, *Autocracy Under Siege: Security Police and Opposition in Russia, 1866–1905*, DeKalb: Northern Illinois University Press.

Daly, Jonathan W. and Leonid Trofimov (eds.) 2009, *Russia in War and Revolution, 1914–1922: A Documentary History*, Indianapolis: Hackett Publishing Company.

Дан, Ф. 1904 [1905], *Из истории рабочего движения и социал-демократии в России. 1900–1904*, Санкт-Петербург.

Dauge, P. 1958, *P. Stučkas dzīve un darbs*, Rīgā: Latvijas Valsts Izdevniecība.

Davidson, Neil 2012, *How Revolutionary Were the Bourgeois Revolutions?*, Chicago: Haymarket Books.

Day, Richard B. and Daniel Gaido (eds.) 2009, *Witness to Permanent Revolution: The Documentary Record*, Leiden: Brill.

Day, Richard B. and Daniel Gaido (eds.) 2012, *Discovering Imperialism: Social Democracy to World War I*, Leiden: Brill.

Дементьев, А.П. 2013, 'Союз леворадикальных сил в Красноярске (март 1917 г.–июнь 1918 г.)', *Вестник Красноярского государственного аграрного университета*, 6: 203–9.

Desai, Manali 2002, 'The Relative Autonomy of Party Practices: a Counterfactual Analysis of Left Party Ascendancy in Kerala, India, 1934–1940', *American Journal of Sociology*, 108, no. 3: 616–57.

Desai, Manali and Cihan Tuğal 2009, 'Political Articulation: Parties and the Constitution of Cleavages in the United States, India, and Turkey', *Sociological Theory*, 27, no. 3: 193–219.

Devlin, Robert James 1976, *Petrograd Workers and Workers' Factory Committees in 1917: An Aspect of the Social History of the Russian Revolution*, PhD Dissertation, SUNY Binghamton.

Dmowski, Roman 1893 [1938], 'Nasz patriotyzm', in *Pisma*, Volume 3, Częstochowa: Gmachowski.

Donald, Moira 1993, *Marxism and Revolution: Karl Kautsky and the Russian Marxists, 1900–1924*, New Haven: Yale University Press.

Dopkewitsch, Helene 1936, *Die Entwicklung des Lettländischen Staatsgedankens bis 1918*, Berlin: H.R. Engelmann.

Dubnow, Simon 1905 [1958], 'The Moral of Stormy Days', in *Nationalism and History: Essays on Old and New Judaism*, Philadelphia: Jewish Publication Society of America.

Dūma, Līga, and Dzidra Paeglīte 1976, *Revolucionāre latviešu emigranti ārzemēs, 1897–1919*, Riga: Liesma.

Джапаридзе, П.А. 1917 [1958], 'Речь на заседании бакинского совета рабочих и военных депутатов', in *Избранные статьи, речи и письма 1905–1918 гг.*, Москва: Государственное издательство политической литературы.

Джапаридзе, П.А. 1958, *Избранные статьи, речи и письма 1905–1918 гг.*, Москва: Государственное издательство политической литературы.

E-a V-t. 1906, 'Mihin on työläisnaisen perheenäitinä pyrittävä', *Palvelijatarlehti*, 3–4: 29–30.

Edelman, Robert 1987, *Proletarian Peasants: The Revolution of 1905 in Russia's Southwest*, Ithaca: Cornell University Press.

Ehrnrooth, Jari 1992, *Sanan vallassa, vihan voimalla: sosialistiset vallankumousopit ja niiden vaikutus Suomen työväenliikkeessä 1905–1914*, Helsinki: Suomen Historiallinen Seura.

Eidlin, Barry 2016, 'Why is There No Labor Party in the United States? Political Articulation and the Canadian Comparison, 1932 to 1948', *American Sociological Review*, 81, no. 3: 488–516.

Elwood, Ralph Carter 1970, 'Trotsky's Questionnaire', *Slavic Review*, 29, no. 2: 296–301.

Elwood, Ralph Carter 1972, 'Lenin and Pravda, 1912–1914', *Slavic Review*, 31, no. 2: 355–80.

Elwood, Ralph Carter (ed.) 1974a, *Resolutions and Decisions of the Communist Party of the Soviet Union. Volume 1, The Russian Social Democratic Labour Party, 1898–October 1917*, Toronto: University of Toronto Press.

Elwood, Ralph Carter 1974b, *Russian Social Democracy in the Underground: A Study of the RSDRP in the Ukraine, 1907–1914*, Assen: International Institute for Social History.

Emmons, Terence 1977, 'Russia's Banquet Campaign', *California Slavic Studies*, 10: 45–86.

Emmons, Terence and Wayne S. Vucinich (eds.) 1982, *The Zemstvo in Russia: An Experiment in Local Self-government*, Cambridge: Cambridge University Press.

Engelstein, Laura 1982, *Moscow, 1905: Working-Class Organization and Political Conflict*, Stanford: Stanford University Press.

Esping-Andersen, Gøsta 1985, *Politics Against Markets: The Social Democratic Road to Power*, Princeton: Princeton University Press.

Ezergailis, Andrew 1967, 'The Bolshevization of the Latvian Social Democratic Party', *Canadian Slavic Studies*, 1, no. 2: 238–52.

Ezergailis, Andrew 1974, *The 1917 Revolution in Latvia*, Boulder: East European Quarterly.

Ezergailis, Andrew 1983, *The Latvian Impact on the Bolshevik Revolution the First Phase: September 1917 to April 1918*, New York: Columbia University Press.

Fagan, Gus 1980, 'Biographical Introduction to Christian Rakovsky'. Accessed at: https://www.marxists.org/archive/rakovsky/biog/index.htm

Farber, Samuel 1990, *Before Stalinism: The Rise and Fall of Soviet Democracy*, New York: Verso.

Fayet, Jean-Francois 2004, *Karl Radek (1885–1939): Biographie Politique*, Bern: Peter Lang.

Federici, Silvia 2013, 'A Feminist Critique of Marx'. Accessed at: http://endofcapitalism.com/2013/05/29/a-feminist-critique-of-marx-by-silvia-federici/

Федьков, О.М. 2007, *Політичні партії і селянство в 1905–1907 роки (діяльність партійних та непартійних організацій в селах Правобережної України)*, Кам'янець-Подільський: Абетка-НОВА.

Fedyshyn, Oleh S. 1971, *Germany's Drive to the East and the Ukrainian Revolution, 1917–1918*, New Brunswick: Rutgers University Press.

Fiddick, Thomas Charles 1974, *Soviet Policy and the Battle of Warsaw, 1920*, PhD Dissertation, Indiana University.

Figes, Orlando 1997, *A People's Tragedy: The History of the Russian Revolution*, New York: Viking.

Flis 1903, 'Strejki Południowo-Rosyjskie', *Przedświt*, 23, no. 8: 345–9.

Fountain, Alvin Marcus 1980, *Roman Dmowski, Party, Tactics, Ideology, 1895–1907*, Boulder: East European Monographs.

Frankel, Jonathan 1981, *Prophecy and Politics: Socialism, Nationalism, and the Russian Jews, 1862–1917*, Cambridge: Cambridge University Press.

Frankel, Jonathan 2009, *Crisis, Revolution, and Russian Jews*, Cambridge: Cambridge University Press.

Friedgut, Theodore H. 1994, *Iuzovka and Revolution, Vol. 2: Politics and Revolution in Russia's Donbass, 1869–1924*, Princeton: Princeton University Press.

Frölich, Paul 1940, *Rosa Luxemburg*, translated by Edward Fitzgerald, London: V. Gollancz.

Fuller, William C. 1985, *Civil-Military Conflict in Imperial Russia, 1881–1914*, Princeton: Princeton University Press.

Габдулхаков, Рамзиль Борисович 2004, *Деятельность леворадикальный политический партий на Урале в начале хх века, (1900–1917 гг.)*, PhD Dissertation, Московский городской педагогический университет.

Galili y Garcia, Ziva 1982, 'The Origins of Revolutionary Defensism: I.G. Tsereteli and the "Siberian Zimmerwaldists"', *Slavic Review*, 41, no. 3: 454–76.

Galili y Garcia, Ziva 1989, *The Menshevik Leaders in the Russian Revolution: Social Realities and Political Strategies*, Princeton: Princeton University Press.

Галоян, Жаловст 1976, *Россия и народы Закавказья: очерки политической истории их взаимоотношений с древних времен до победы Великой Октябрьской социалистичесткой революции*, Москва: Издáтельство 'Мысль'.

Garlicki, Andrzej 1977, 'Jerzy Zdziechowski o styczniowym zamachu stanu 1919 r.', *Przegląd Historyczny*, 1: 143–6.

Garlicki, Andrzej 1988, *Józef Piłsudski 1867–1935*, Warszawa: Czytelnik.

Gąsiorowska, Natalia et al. (eds) 1957, *Źródła do dziejów rewolucji 1905–1907 w okręgu łódzkim, Vol. 1*, Warszawa: Książka i Wiedza.

Гаврилов, Алсксандр Юрьевич 2009, *Меньшевизм и Российские революции начали хх века: проблемы идейной эволюции (по материалам партийной печати)*, PhD Dissertation, Федеральное государственное образовательное учреждение высшего.

Geary, Dick 1981, *European Labour Protest 1848–1939*, London: Methuen.

Geary, Dick 1987, *Karl Kautsky*, Manchester: Manchester University Press.

Gelbard, Arye 1982, *Der Jüdische Arbeiter-Bund Russlands im Revolutionsjahr 1917*, Wien: Europaverlag.

Gerber, John 1984, *Anton Pannekoek and the Socialism of Workers' Self-Emancipation: 1873–1960*, PhD Dissertation, University of Wisconsin-Madison.

Гермайзе, Осип 1926, *Нариси з історії революційного руху на Україн*, Київ: Книгоспілка.

Getzler, Israel 1967, *Martov: A Political Biography of a Russian Social Democrat*, London: Cambridge University Press.

Getzler, Israel 1983, *Kronstadt 1917–1921: The Fate of a Soviet Democracy*, Cambridge: Cambridge University Press.

Getzler, Israel 1992, 'Soviets as Agents of Democratisation', in *Revolution in Russia: Reassessments of 1917*, edited by Edith Rogovin Frankel, Jonathan Frankel, and Baruch Knei-Paz, Cambridge: Cambridge University Press.

Getzler, Israel 1994, 'Iulii Martov, the Leader Who Lost His Party in 1917: A Second Look at Martov on the 70th Anniversary of His Death', *The Slavonic and East European Review*, 72, no. 3: 424–39.

Gilcher-Holtey, Ingrid 1986, *Das Mandat des Intellektuellen: Karl Kautsky und die Sozialdemokratie*, Berlin: Siedler.

Gitelman, Zvi Y. 1972, *Jewish Nationality and Soviet Politics: The Jewish Sections of the CPSU, 1917–1930*, Princeton: Princeton University Press.

Glenny, Michael 1970, 'Leonid Krasin: The Years before 1917. An Outline', *Soviet Studies*, 22, no. 2: 192–221.

Glickman, Rose L. 1984, *Russian Factory Women: Workplace and Society, 1880–1914*, Berkeley: University of California Press.

Gluckstein, Donny 1984, 'The Missing Party'. Accessed at: https://www.marxists.org/history/etol/writers/gluckstein/1984/xx/missing.html

Gluckstein, Donny 2014, 'Classical Marxism and the Question of Reformism'. Accessed at: http://isj.org.uk/classical-marxism-and-the-question-of-reformism/

Головченко, Володимир 1996, *Від «Самостійної України» до Союзу визволення України: Нариси з історії української соціал-демократії початку XX ст.*, Харків: Майдан.

Gooderham, P. 1981, *The Anarchist Movement in Russia, 1905–1917*, PhD Dissertation, Bristol University.

Goodwin, Jeff 2006, *No Other Way Out: States and Revolutionary Movements, 1945–1991*, Cambridge: Cambridge University Press.

Graziosi, Andrea 2009, *Stalinism, Collectivization and the Great Famine*, Cambridge: Ukrainian Studies Fund.

Gronow, Jukka 2015, *On the Formation of Marxism: Karl Kautsky's Theory of Capitalism, the Marxism of the Second International and Karl Marx's Critique of Political Economy*, Leiden: Brill.

Grumolte, Inese 2013, 'Rainis' Apology of the "Basic Class": The World Revolution or the National Emancipation?', *Baltic Journal of Political Science*, 2: 98–109.

Guettel, Jens-Uwe 2012, 'The Myth of the Pro-Colonialist SPD: German Social Democracy and Imperialism before World War I', *Central European History*, 45, no. 3: 452–84.

Haapala, Pertti 1986, *Tehtaan valossa: teollistuminen ja työväestön muodostuminen Tampereella 1820–1920*, Tampere: Osuuskunta Vastapaino.

Haapala, Pertti 2014, 'The Expected and Non-Expected Roots of Chaos: Preconditions of the Finnish Civil War', in *The Finnish Civil War 1918: History, Memory, Legacy*, edited by Tuomas Tepora and Aapo Roselius, Leiden: Brill.

Haimson, Leopold H. 1955, *The Russian Marxists and the Origins of Bolshevism*, Cambridge, MA: Harvard University Press.

Haimson, Leopold H. 1964, 'The Problem of Social Stability in Urban Russia, 1905–1917 (Part One)', *Slavic Review*, 23, no. 4: 619–42.

Haimson, Leopold H. (ed.) 1987, *The Making of Three Russian Revolutionaries: Voices from the Menshevik Past*, New York: Cambridge University Press.

Haimson, Leopold H. 1989a, 'Introduction', in *Strikes, Wars, and Revolutions in an International Perspective: Strike Waves in the Late Nineteenth and Early Twentieth Centuries*, edited by Leopold H. Haimson and Charles Tilly, New York: Cambridge University Press.

Haimson, Leopold H. 1989b, 'Conclusion', in *Strikes, Wars, and Revolutions in an International Perspective: Strike Waves in the Late Nineteenth and Early Twentieth Centuries*, edited by Leopold H. Haimson and Charles Tilly, New York: Cambridge University Press.

Haimson, Leopold H. and Ronald Petrusha 1989, 'Two Strike Waves in Imperial Russia, 1905–1907, 1912–1914', in *Strikes, Wars, and Revolutions in an International Perspective: Strike Waves in the Late Nineteenth and Early Twentieth Centuries*, edited by Leopold H. Haimson and Charles Tilly, New York: Cambridge University Press.

Haimson, Leopold H. and Charles Tilly (eds.) 1989, *Strikes, Wars, and Revolutions in an International Perspective: Strike Waves in the Late Nineteenth and Early Twentieth Centuries*, New York: Cambridge University Press.

Halfin, Igal 2000, *From Darkness to Light: Class, Consciousness, and Salvation in Revolutionary Russia*, Pittsburgh: University of Pittsburgh Press.

Hallas, Duncan 1985, *The Comintern*. Accessed at: https://www.marxists.org/archive/hallas/works/1985/comintern/

Hamm, Michael F. 1993, *Kiev: A Portrait, 1800–1917*, Princeton: Princeton University Press.

Hamm, Michael F. 2002, 'On the Perimeter of Revolution: Kharkiv's Academic Community, 1905', *Revolutionary Russia*, 15, no. 1: 45–68.

Harding, Neil (ed.) 1983, *Marxism in Russia: Key Documents, 1879–1906*, Cambridge: Cambridge University Press.

Harding, Neil 2009, *Lenin's Political Thought: Theory and Practice in the Democratic and Socialist Revolutions*, Chicago: Haymarket Books.

Harison, Casey 2007, 'The Paris Commune of 1871, the Russian Revolution of 1905, and the Shifting of the Revolutionary Tradition', *History and Memory*, 19, no. 2: 5–42.

Harman, Chris 1982, *The Lost Revolution: Germany 1918 to 1923*, London: Bookmarks.

Hart, Duncan 2017, 'Lessons from Finland: Reply to Eric Blanc'. Accessed at: https://johnriddell.wordpress.com/2017/07/11/lessons-from-finland-reply-to-eric-blanc/

Hart, Duncan 2018, 'The Lost Workers' Revolution: Finland 1917–18'. Accessed at: http://marxistleftreview.org/index.php/no-15-summer-2018/152-the-lost-workers-revolution-finland-1917-18

Haupt, Georges (ed.) 1963, *Correspondance entre Lenine et Camille Huysmans, 1905–1914*, Paris: Mouton.

Haupt, Georges and Jean-Jacques Marie 1974, *Makers of the Russian Revolution: Biographies of Bolshevik Leaders*, London: Allen and Unwin.

Haustein, Ulrich 1969, *Sozialismus und nationale Frage in Polen: die Entwicklung der sozialistischen Bewegung in Kongresspolen von 1875 bis 1900 unter besonderer Berücksichtigung der Polnischen sozialistischen Partei (PPS)*, Köln: Böhlau.

Hawranek, Franciszek 1966, *Ruch komunistyczny na Górnym Śląsku w latach 1918–1921*, Wrocław: Zaklad Narodowy im. Ossolińskich.

Heikkilä, Jouko 1993, *Kansallista luokkapolitiikkaa: sosiaalidemokraatit ja Suomen autonomian puolustus 1905–1917*. Helsinki: Suomen historiallinen seura.

Heikkinen, Reijo 1980, *Joukkovoiman läpimurto. Suurlakko-yleislakko teoriassa ja käytännössä Suomessa ennen ensimmäistä maailmansotaa*, PhD Dissertation, Turun yliopisto.

Henning, Detlef 1986, *Die lettische sozialistische Bewegung. Von den Anfängen bis zur Gründung der ersten sozialistischen Parteien*, MA Thesis, Westfälischen Wilhelms-Universität.

Henriksson, Anders 1986, 'Riga: Growth, Conflict, and the Limitations of Good Government, 1850–1914', in *The City in Late Imperial Russia*, edited by Michael F. Hamm, Bloomington: Indiana University Press.

Hentilä, Marjaliisa 2013, *Sovittelija: Matti Paasivuori 1866–1937*, Helsinki: Työväen historian perinteen tutkimuksen seura.

Herzl, Theodor 1960, *The Complete Diaries of Theodor Herzl, Volume IV*, edited by Raphael Patai, New York: The Herzl Press.

Heywood, Anthony 2005, 'Socialists, Liberals and the Union of Unions in Kyiv During the 1905 Revolution: An Engineer's Perspective', in *The Russian Revolution of 1905: Centenary Perspectives*, edited by Jonathan D. Smele and Anthony Heywood, London: Routledge.

Hickey, Michael C. 1998, 'Revolution on the Jewish Street: Smolensk, 1917', *Journal of Social History*, 31, no. 4: 823–50.

Hickey, Michael C. 2011, *Competing Voices from the Russian Revolution: Fighting Words*, Santa Barbara, CA: Greenwood.

Hillis, Faith C. 2010, *Between Empire and Nation: Urban Politics, Community, and Violence in Kiev, 1863–1907*, PhD Dissertation, Yale University.

Hinkkanen, Merja-Liisa and Maija Lintunen 1997, 'Aleksandra Gripenberg: taistelija ja kansainvälinen naisasianainen', in *Yksi kamari, kaksi sukupuolta: Suomen eduskunnan ensimmäiset naiset*, edited by Pirjo Markkola and Alexandra Ramsay, Helsinki: Eduskunnan Kirjasto.

Hodgson, John H. 1967, *Communism in Finland: A History and Interpretation*, Princeton: Princeton University Press.

Hogan, Heather 1993, *Forging Revolution: Metalworkers, Managers, and the State in St. Petersburg, 1890–1914*, Bloomington: Indiana University Press.

Holmes, John Dewey 2008, *The Life and Times of Noah London: American Jewish Communist; Soviet Engineer; and Victim of Stalinist Terror*, PhD Dissertation, University of California, Berkeley.

Holzer, Jerzy 1962, *Polska partia socjalistyczna w latach 1917–1919*, Warszawa: Państwowe wydawnictwo naukowe.

Holzer, Jerzy 1967, 'Attitude of the Polish Socialist Party and Polish Social-Democratic Party to the Russian Revolution of 1917', *Acta Poloniae Historica*, 16: 76–90.

Horwitz, Maksymilian [Henryk Walecki] 1906a, *W sprawie naszej taktyki: odpowiedź c.k.r. p.p.s. na 'List otwarty' Tow. Ignacego Daszyńskiego*, Warszawa.

Horwitz, Maksymilian [Henryk Walecki] 1906b, *Przyczynek do programu p.p.s.*, Warszawa: Wydawnictwo Polskiej Partji Socjalistycznej.

Huttunen, Evert 1918, *Sosialidemokraattinen puoluejohto ja kansalaissota*, Helsinki: Osakeyhtiö Kansanvalta.

Huxley, Steven Duncan 1990, *Constitutionalist Insurgency in Finland: Finnish 'Passive Resistance' Against Russification as a Case of Nonmilitary Struggle in the European Resistance Tradition*, Helsinki: Suomen Historiallinen Seura.

Hyndman, H.M. 1901, 'La Crise Socialiste en Europe', *Le Mouvement socialiste*, 68: 449–55.

Ибрагимова, З. И. and М. С. Искендерсва (eds.) 1957, *Большевики в борьбе за победу социалистической революции в Азербайджане. Документы и материалы. 1917–1918 гг.*, Баку: Азербайджанское государственное издательство.

Ijabs, Ivars 2012a, 'Break Out of Russia: Miķelis Valters and the National Issue in Early Latvian Socialism', *Journal of Baltic Studies*, 43, no. 4: 437–58.

Ijabs, Ivars 2012b, 'The Nation of the Socialist Intelligentsia: The National Issue in the Political Thought of Early Latvian Socialism', *East Central Europe*, 39, nos. 2–3: 181–203.

International Socialist Congress at Basel 1912, 'Manifesto'. Accessed at: https://www.marxists.org/history/international/social-democracy/1912/basel-manifesto.htm

International Socialist Congress at Stuttgart 1907, 'Resolution'. Accessed at: https://www.marxists.org/history/international/social-democracy/1907/militarism.htm

Iskolats 1973, *Iskolata un tā prezidija protokoli (1917.–1918.)*, edited by A. Spreslis, Rīga: Zinātne.

Иванова, Н.А. and В.П. Желтовой 2004, *Сословно-классовая структура России в конце XIX – начале XX века*, Москва: Наука.

Ivancevich, Anthony M. 1967, *The Bolsheviks in the Russian Revolution of 1905*, Master's Thesis, Loyola University.

Jakubowski, Dawid 2007, *Julian Marchlewski – bohater czy zdrajca?* Warszawa: Instytut Wydawniczy Książka i Prasa.

Järvinen, Pekka 1983, *Edvard Valppaan kansallinen linja ja hänen suhteensa maanalaiseen toimintaan*, Master's Thesis, Helsingin yliopisto.

Jogiches, Leo 1907, 'Выступление на v съезде'. Accessed at: http://web.mit.edu/fjk/ www/Trotsky/Permanent/chapter26.html

Johnpoll, Bernard K. 1967, *The Politics of Futility: The General Jewish Workers Bund of Poland, 1917–1943*, Ithaca: Cornell University Press.

Jones, Stephen Francis 1984, *Georgian Social Democracy: in Opposition and Power 1892– 1921*, PhD Dissertation, University of London.

Jones, Stephen Francis 1992, 'Georgian Social Democracy in 1917', in *Revolution in Russia: Reassessments of 1917*, edited by Jonathan Frankel et al., Cambridge: Cambridge University Press.

Jones, Stephen Francis 2005, *Socialism in Georgian Colors: The European Road to Social Democracy, 1883–1917*, Cambridge, MA: Harvard University Press.

Judge, Edward H. 1983, *Plehve: Repression and Reform in Imperial Russia, 1902–1904*, Syracuse: Syracuse University Press.

Kalniņš, Brūno 1956, *Latvijas sociāldemokratijas piecdesmit gadi*, Stokholmā: LSDSP Ārzemju Komitejas Izdevuma.

Kalniņa, Klāra 1964, *Liesmainie Gadi, Atmiņu Vija*. Stokholmā: LSDSP Ārzemju Komitejas Izdevums.

Kałuża, Adam 2005, *Przeciw carowi!: rok 1905 w Zagłębiu Dąbrowskim*, Sosnowiec: Muzeum.

Kamenetsky, Ihor 1977, 'Hrushevsky and the Central Rada', in *The Ukraine, 1917–1921: A Study in Revolution*, edited by Taras Hunczak, Cambridge, MA: Harvard University Press.

Каменев, Лев 1907 [2003], 'Роза Люксембург О Русской Революции', in *Между двумя революциями*, Москва: ЗАО Центрполиграф.

Каменев, Лев 1912 [2003], 'Революция на востоке', in *Между двумя революциями*, Москва: ЗАО Центрполиграф.

Kanatchikov, Semën Ivanovich 1929 [1986], *A Radical Worker in Tsarist Russia the Autobiography of Semën Ivanovich Kanatchikov*, Stanford: Stanford University Press.

Kancewicz, Jan 1984, *Polska Partia Socjalistyczna w latach 1892–1896*, Warszawa: Państwowe Wydawnictwo Naukowe.

Kaplunovskiy, Alexander 2007, 'Revolutionieren oder Reformieren? Die kaufmännischindustriellen Angestellten in der Revolution 1905', in *Das Zarenreich, das Jahr 1905 und seine Wirkungen*, edited by Jan Kusber and Andreas Frings, Berlin: Lit-Verlag.

Kappeler, Andreas 2001, *The Russian Empire: A Multiethnic History*, Harlow: Routledge.

Karski, Stefan 1902a, 'Konsekwencje', *Przedświt*, 22, nos. 11–12: 406–19.

Karski, Stefan 1902b, 'Polityka niewary', *Przedświt*, 22, no. 1: 5–10.

Karwacki, Władysław Lech 1964, *Łódzka Organizacja Polskiej Partii Socjalistycznej – Lewicy 1906–1918*, Łódź: Wydawn. Łódzkie.

Karwacki, Władysław Lech 1972, *Związki zawodowe i stowarzyszenia pracodawców w Łodzi (do roku 1914)*, Łódz: Wydawn. Łódzkie.

Kasprzakowa, Janina 1965, *Ideologia i polityka PPS-Lewicy w latach 1907–1914*, Warszawa: Książka i Wiedza.

Kasprzakowa, Janina 1988, *Maria Koszutska*, Warszawa: Książka i Wiedza.

Kassow, Samuel D. 1989, *Students, Professors, and the State in Tsarist Russia*, Berkeley: University of California Press.

Kats, Mosheh 1956 [2012], *The Generation that Lost its Fear: A Memoir of Jewish Self-Defense and Revolutionary Activism in Tsarist Russia*, translated by Lyber Katz, New York: Blue Thread Communications.

Kautsky, Karl 1892 [1910], *The Class Struggle: Erfurt Program*, translated by W.E. Bohn, Chicago: Charles H. Kerr.

Kautsky, Karl 1893 [2018], 'Parliamentarism and Democracy', in *Karl Kautsky on Democracy and Republicanism*, edited and translated by Ben Lewis, Leiden: Brill. (Manuscript)

Kautsky, Karl 1896, 'Finis Poloniae?', *Die Neue Zeit*, 14, no. 42: 484–91, 14, no. 43: 513–25.

Kautsky, Karl 1898, 'Nochmals der Kampf der Nationalitäten in Oesterreich', *Die Neue Zeit*, 16, no. 23: 723–6.

Kautsky, Karl 1901, 'Die Revision des Programms der Sozialdemokratie in Oesterreich', *Die Neue Zeit*, 20, no. 1: 68–82.

Kautsky, Karl 1902 [1916], *The Social Revolution*, translated by A.M. Simons and Mary Wood Simons, Chicago: C.H. Kerr & Co.

Kautsky, Karl 1903 [2009], 'To What Extent is the Communist Manifesto Obsolete?', in *Witnesses to Permanent Revolution*, edited by Richard B. Day and Daniel Gaido, Leiden: Brill.

Kautsky, Karl 1904 [2009], 'Revolutionary Questions', in *Witnesses to Permanent Revolution*, edited by Richard B. Day and Daniel Gaido, Leiden: Brill.

Kautsky, Karl 1905, 'Differences Among the Russian Socialists', *The International Socialist Review*, 5, no. 12: 705–17.

Kautsky, Karl 1905a [2009], 'The Consequences of the Japanese Victory and Social Democracy', in *Witnesses to Permanent Revolution*, edited by Richard B. Day and Daniel Gaido, Leiden: Brill.

Kautsky, Karl 1905b [2009], 'Old and New Revolution', in *Witnesses to Permanent Revolution*, edited by Richard B. Day and Daniel Gaido, Leiden: Brill.

Kautsky, Karl 1905 [2018], 'The Republic and Social Democracy in France (1905)', in *Karl Kautsky on Democracy and Republicanism*, edited and translated by Ben Lewis, Leiden: Brill. (Manuscript)

Kautsky, Karl 1906, 'Le Droit de Suffrage pour les Femmes', *La revue socialiste*, 260: 156–65.

Kautsky, Karl 1906 [2009], 'The Driving Forces of the Russian Revolution and its Prospects', in *Witnesses to Permanent Revolution*, edited by Richard B. Day and Daniel Gaido, Leiden: Brill.

Kautsky, Karl 1908, 'Practical Work in Parliament', *International Socialist Review*, 9, no. 6: 456–60.

Kautsky, Karl 1909a, *The Road to Power*, translated by A.M. Simons, Chicago: Samuel A. Block.

Kautsky, Karl 1909b, 'Sects or Class Parties?' https://www.marxists.org/archive/kautsky/1909/07/unions.htm

Kautsky, Karl 1909 [1996], *The Road to Power: Political Reflections on Growing into the Revolution*, translated by Raymond Meyer, Atlantic Highlands, NJ: Humanities Press.

Kautsky, Karl 1920, *Terrorism and Communism: A Contribution to the Natural History of Revolution*, translated by W.H. Kerridge, London: The National Labour Press Ltd.

Казарова, Нина Акоповна 1999, *Политические взгляды и деятельность Ю. О. Мартова*, PhD Dissertation, Ростовский государственный университет.

Kelles-Krauz, Kazimierz [Ellehard Esse] 1898, 'La Politique Internationale du Prolétariat et la Question d'Orient', *Le Devenir Social*, 7–8: 565–89.

Kelles-Krauz, Kazimierz [Michael Luśnia] 1901, 'Samorząd Zaboru Pruskiego Słówko Odpowiedzi', *Przedświt*, 21, no. 10: 362–5.

Kelles-Krauz, Kazimierz 1902, 'Nasz Kryzys', *Przedświt*, 22, no. 2: 43–56, 22, no. 3: 84–94.

Kelles-Krauz, Kazimierz 1904, 'Unbewaffnete Revolution?', *Die Neue Zeit*, 22, no. 18: 559–67.

Kelles-Krauz, Kazimierz [Interim] 1905, 'Z Całej Polski', *Krytyka*, 7, no. 1: 75–9, 121–67, 250–5, 420–3.

Kelles-Krauz, Kazimierz 1905 [1907], 'Niepodległość Polski a Materialistyczne Pojmowanie Dziejów', in *Wybór Pism Politycznych*, Kraków: Nakładem Drukarni Narodowej.

Keenan, E.L. 1962, 'Remarques sur l'histoire du mouvement révolutionnaire à Bakou, 1904–1905', *Cahiers du monde russe et soviétique* 3, no. 2: 225–60.

Ketola, Eino 2017, 'Sosiaalidemokraattien ohjelma Suomen itsenäisyyden toteuttamiseksi keväällä ja kesällä 1917', in *Työväki kumouksessa*, edited by Sami Suodenjoki and Risto Turunen, Työväen historian ja perinteen tutkimuksen seura.

Kettunen, Pauli 1986, *Poliittinen liike ja sosiaalinen kollektiivisuus: tutkimus sosialidemokratiasta ja ammattiyhdistysliikkeestä Suomessa 1918–1930*, Helsinki: Suomen Historiallinen Seura.

Хомерики, Н. and Н. Рамишвили 1905, *'Большинство' или 'меньшинство'?* Женева.

Kiepurska, Halina 1967, *Inteligencja zawodowa Warszawy, 1905–1907*, Warszawa: Państwowe wydawnictwo naukowe.

Kiepurska, Halina 1974, *Warszawa w rewolucji 1905–1907*, Warszawa: Wiedza Powszechna.

Kiiskilä, Outi-Maria 2010, *Punainen Myrsky. Suomen työväenlehdistön taistelu vallankumousvuosina 1917–1918*, Master's Thesis, Jyväskylän yliopisto.

Kirby, David 1971, *The Finnish Social Democratic Party 1903–1918*, PhD Dissertation, University of London.

Kirby, David 1975, *Finland and Russia 1808–1920: From Autonomy to Independence: A Selection of Documents*, London: Macmillan.

Кирьянов, Ю.И. 1987, *Переход к массовой политической борьбе: рабочий класс накануне первой российской революции Кирьянов*, Москва: Наука.

Kmiecik, Zenon 1980, *Prasa polska w rewolucji 1905–1907*, Warszawa: Państwowe Wydawnictwo Naukowe.

Kochański, Aleksander and Ignacy Orzechowski 1964, *Zarys dziejów ruchu zawodowego w Królestwie Polskim, 1905–1918*, Warszawa: Książka i Wiedza.

Koenker, Diane P. 1981, *Moscow Workers and the 1917 Revolution*, Princeton: Princeton University Press.

Koenker, Diane and William G. Rosenberg 1989, 'Strikers in Revolution: Russia, 1917', in *Strikes, Wars, and Revolutions in an International Perspective: Strike Waves in the Late Nineteenth and Early Twentieth Centuries*, edited by Leopold H. Haimson and Charles Tilly, New York: Cambridge University Press.

Kowalski, Ronald I. 1978, *The Development of "Left Communism" Until 1921: Soviet Russia, Poland, Latvia and Lithuania*, PhD Dissertation, University of Glasgow.

Kołakowski, Leszek 1978, *Main Currents of Marxism: Its Rise, Growth, and Dissolution. Volume 2, the Golden Age*, Oxford: Clarendon Press.

Kolonitskii, Boris I. 1994, 'Antibourgeois Propaganda and Anti-"Burzhui" Consciousness in 1917', *The Russian Review*, 53, no. 2: 183–96.

Kolonitskii, Boris I. 2004, ' "Democracy" in the Political Consciousness of the February Revolution', in *Revolutionary Russia: New Approaches*, edited by Rex A. Wade, New York: Routledge.

Komunistyczna Partia Robotnicza Polski 1968 [1923], *II Zjazd Komunistycznej Partii Robotniczej Polski, 19. IX.–2.X.1923. Protokoły obrad i uchwały*, edited by Gereon Iwański et al., Warsaw: Książka i Wiedza.

Korpi, Walter. 1983. *The Democratic Class Struggle*. London: Routledge & Kegan Paul.

Korzec, Paweł 1965, *Pół wieku dziejów ruchu rewolucyjnego Białostocczyzny (1864–1914)*, Warszawa: Książka i Wiedza.

Koszutska, Maria 1918 [1961], 'Rewolucja rosyjska a proletariat międzynarodowy', in *Pisma i przemówienia*, Warsaw: Książka i Wiedza.

Kotkin, Stephen 2014, *Stalin. Vol. 1: Paradoxes of Power, 1878–1928*, New York: Penguin Press.

Kowalski, Ronald L. 1997, *The Russian Revolution: 1917–1921*, Hoboken: Routledge.

Kremer, A. and Yu. Martov 1896 [1983], 'On Agitation', in *Marxism in Russia: Key Documents 1879–1906*, edited by Neil Harding, Cambridge: Cambridge University Press.

Кремер, А.И. 1894 [2010], 'Об агитации', in *Бунд. Документы и материалы 1894–1921*, edited by К.М. Андерсон et al., Москва: РОССПЭН.

Krichevskii, B.N. 1901a [2015], 'Economics and Politics in the Russian Workers' Movement', in *The Russian Social-Democratic Labour Party, 1899–1904: Documents of the "Economist" Opposition to Iskra and Early Menshevism*, edited by Richard Mullin, Leiden: Brill.

Krichevskii, B.N. 1901b [2015], 'Principles, Tactics and Struggle', in *The Russian Social-Democratic Labour Party, 1899–1904: Documents of the "Economist" Opposition to Iskra and Early Menshevism*, edited by Richard Mullin, Leiden: Brill.

Христюк, Павло 1921, *Замітки і матеріяли до історії української революції. 1917–1920 pp. Том II*, Відень: Український Соціольоґичний Інститут

Krupskaya, N.K. 1933 [1979], *Reminiscences of Lenin*, New York: International Publishers.

Kujala, Antti 1981, 'Suomalaiset vallankumousjärjestöt ja poliittinen rikollisuus 1906–1908', *Historiallinen aikakauskirja*, 2: 106–24.

Kujala, Antti 1988, 'March Separately – Strike Together: The Paris and Geneva Conferences Held by the Russian and Minority Nationalities' Revolutionary and Opposition Parties, 1904–1905', in Motojirō, Akashi, *Rakka ryūsui: Colonel Akashi's Report on his Secret Cooperation with the Russian Revolutionary Parties during the Russo-Japanese War: Selected Chapters*, edited by Olavi K. Fält and Antti Kujala, Helsinki: Suomen Historiallinen Seura.

Kujala, Antti 1989, *Vallankumous ja Kansallinen Itsemääräämisoikeus: Venäjän Sosialistiset Puolueet ja Suomalainen Radikalismi Vuosisadan Alussa*, Helsinki: Suomen Historiallinen Seura.

Kujala, Antti 1995, *Venäjän hallitus ja Suomen työväenliike 1899–1905*, Helsinki: Suomen historiallinen seura.

Кураев, Алексей Николаевич 2000, *Партии и массовые организации в первой русской революции*, Москва: МГУП.

Kuusinen, Otto [Anon.] 1906, 'Eduskunta Taistelu on hyvä, vaikkei se yksin auta', *Sosialistinen Aikakauslehti*, 15–16: 337–9.

Kuusinen, Otto 1906 [1981], 'Oulun puoluekokouksen periaatteellinen merkitys', in Otto Wille Kuusinen, *Asian periaatteellinen puoli: valittuja kirjoituksia ja puheita vuosilta 1905–1918*, edited by Juha Ukkonen, Helsinki: Kansankulttuuri.

Kuusinen, Otto 1919, *The Finnish Revolution: A Self-Criticism*, London: Workers' Socialist Federation.

Kuusinen, Otto 1924 [2016], 'An Unsuccessful Depiction of the "German October" (Comrade Trotsky's "The Lessons of October")', in *Trotsky's Challenge: The 'Literary Discussion' of 1924 and the Fight for the Bolshevik Revolution*, edited by Frederick C. Corney, Leiden: Brill.

Кузминский, А.М. 1906, *Всеподданнейший отчёт о произведённой в 1905 году, по Высочайшему повелению, сенатором А. Кузминским ревизии города Баку и Бакинской губернии*, Санкт-Петербург: Сенатская тип.

L' internationale ouvrière & socialiste 1907, *Rapports soumis au Congrès Socialiste Inter-*

*national de Stuttgart (18–24 août 1907) par les Organisations Socialistes d'Europe, d'Australie et d'Amérique sur leur Activité Pendant les Années 1904–1907*, Bruxelles: Bureau Socialiste International.

Ładyka, Teodor 1972, *Polska Partia Socjalistyczna (Frakcja Rewolucyjna) w latach 1906–1914*, Warszawa: Książka i Wiedza.

Lambroza, Shlomo 1981, *The Pogrom Movement in Tsarist Russia, 1903–06*, PhD Dissertation, Rutgers University.

Lande, Leo 1974, 'The Mensheviks in 1917', in *The Mensheviks: From the Revolution of 1917 to the Second World War*, edited by Leopold H. Haimson, Chicago: The University of Chicago Press.

Lane, David 1969, *The Roots of Russian Communism: A Social and Historical Study of Russian Social-Democracy 1898–1907*, Assen: Van Gorcum.

Lapa, Līga 1992, 'Arodorganizāciju pirmsākumi Latvijā 1905. gadā', *Latvijas Vēstures Institūta Žurnāls*, 2: 89–106.

Larsson, Reidar 1970, *Theories of Revolution: From Marx to the First Russian Revolution*, Stockholm: Almqvist och Wiksell.

Latvijas KP CK Partijas Vēstures Institūts 1955, *Latvijas socialdemokratisko organizaciju lapiņas Krievijas pirmās revolucijas laikā*, Rīgā: Latvijas Valsts Izdevnieciba.

Latvijas KP CK Partijas Vēstures Institūts 1958, *Latvijas Komunistiskās Partijas Kongresu, Konferenču un CK Plenumu Rezolucijas un Lēmumi, 1. Dala. 1904–1940*, Rīgā: Latvijas Valsts Izdevnieciba.

Латвияс КП ЦК Партияс вēстурес институтьūц (ed.) 1963, *Коммунистическая партия Латвии в Октябрьской революции 1917. Документы и материалы (март 1917–февр. 1918)*, Рига: Латвийское гос. Издательство.

Le Blanc, Paul 2014, *Unfinished Leninism: The Rise and Return of a Revolutionary Doctrine*, Chicago: Haymarket Books.

Lenin, V.I. 1894 [1960–65], 'What the "Friends of the People" Are and How They Fight the Social-Democrats', in *Collected Works*, Vol. 1, Moscow: Progress Publishers.

Lenin, V.I. 1899 [1960–65], 'A Retrograde Trend in Russian Social-Democracy', in *Collected Works*, Vol. 4, Moscow: Progress Publishers.

Lenin, V.I. 1901 [1960–65], 'A Talk with Defenders of Economism', in *Collected Works*, Vol. 5, Moscow: Progress Publishers.

Lenin, V.I. 1902a [1960–65], 'Letter to a Comrade on our Organisational Tasks', in *Collected Works*, Vol. 6, Moscow: Progress Publishers.

Lenin, V.I. 1902b [1960–65], 'What is to Be Done? Burning Questions of Our Movement', in *Collected Works*, Vol. 5, Moscow: Progress Publishers.

Lenin, V.I. 1902c [1960–65], 'A Letter to the Northern League', in *Collected Works*, Vol. 6, Moscow: Progress Publishers.

Lenin, V.I. 1903a [1960–65], 'The National Question in Our Programme', in *Collected Works*, Vol. 6, Moscow: Progress Publishers.

Lenin, V.I. 1903b [1960–65], 'On the Manifesto of the League of the Armenian Social-Democrats', in *Collected Works*, Vol. 6, Moscow: Progress Publishers.

Lenin, V.I. 1904 [1960–65], 'One Step Forward, Two Steps Back (The Crisis in Our Party)', in *Collected Works*, Vol. 7, Moscow: Progress Publishers.

Lenin, V.I. 1905a [1960–65], 'The First Results of the Political Alignment', in *Collected Works*, Vol. 9, Moscow: Progress Publishers.

Lenin, V.I. 1905b [1960–65], 'Two Tactics of Social-Democracy in the Democratic Revolution', in *Collected Works*, Vol. 9, Moscow: Progress Publishers.

Lenin, V.I. 1905c [1960–65], 'A Militant Agreement for the Uprising', in *Collected Works*, Vol. 8, Moscow: Progress Publishers.

Lenin, V.I. 1905d [1960–65], 'Our Tasks and the Soviet of Workers' Deputies', in *Collected Works*, Vol. 10, Moscow: Progress Publishers.

Lenin, V.I. 1906 [1960–65], 'A Tactical Platform for the Unity Congress of the RSDLP', in *Collected Works*, Vol. 10, Moscow: Progress Publishers.

Lenin, V.I. 1908 [1960–65], 'Meeting of the International Socialist Bureau', in *Collected Works*, Vol. 15, Moscow: Progress Publishers.

Lenin, V.I. 1909 [1960–65], 'The Aim of the Proletarian Struggle in Our Revolution', in *Collected Works*, Vol. 15, Moscow: Progress Publishers.

Lenin, V.I. 1910 [1960–65], 'Two Worlds', in *Collected Works*, Vol. 16, Moscow: Progress Publishers.

Lenin, V.I. 1913 [1960–65], 'Comment on Kautsky's Letter', in *Collected Works*, Vol. 20, Moscow: Progress Publishers.

Lenin, V.I. 1915a [1960–65], 'The Collapse of the Second International', in *Collected Works*, Vol. 20, Moscow: Progress Publishers.

Lenin, V.I. 1915b [1960–65], 'The Defeat of Russia and the Revolutionary Crisis', in *Collected Works*, Vol. 21, Moscow: Progress Publishers.

Lenin, V.I. 1917a [1960–65], 'The State and Revolution', in *Collected Works*, Vol. 25, Moscow: Progress Publishers.

Lenin, V.I. 1917b [1960–65], 'The Tasks of the Proletariat in Our Revolution', in *Collected Works*, Vol. 24, Moscow: Progress Publishers.

Lenin, V.I. 1917c [1960–65], 'Letters on Tactics', in *Collected Works*, Vol. 24, Moscow: Progress Publishers.

Lenin, V.I. 1917d [1960–65], 'Letter to Comrades', in *Collected Works*, Vol. 26, Moscow: Progress Publishers.

Lenin, V.I. 1917e [1960–65], 'To the Citizens of Russia!', in *Collected Works*, Vol. 26, Moscow: Progress Publishers.

Lenin, V.I. 1917 [1975], 'План доклада о революции 1905 года', in *Полное собрание сочинений*, Vol. 54, Москва: Издательство Политической Литературы.

Lenin, V.I. 1920 [1960–65], '"Left-Wing" Communism: An Infantile Disorder', in *Collected Works*, Vol. 31, Moscow: Progress Publishers.

Lenin, V.I. 1960–65, *Collected Works*, Moscow: Progress Publishers.

Lenin, V.I. and Grigory Zinoviev 1915b [1960–65], 'Socialism and War', in *Collected Works*, Vol. 20, Moscow: Progress Publishers.

de Leon, Cedric, Manali Desai, and Cihan Tuğal (eds.) 2015, *Building Blocs: How Parties Organize Society*, Stanford: Stanford University Press.

Leontovitsch, Victor 2012, *The History of Liberalism in Russia*, translated by Parmen Leontovitsch, Pittsburgh: University of Pittsburgh Press.

Leslie, Robert Frank 1980, *The History of Poland Since 1863*, Cambridge: Cambridge University Press.

Levin, Vladimir 2004, 'Politics at the Crossroads – Jewish Parties and the Second Duma Elections, 1907', in *Leipziger Beiträge zur jüdischen Geschichte und Kultur*, 2: 129–46.

Levin, Vladimir 2007, *Jewish Politics in the Russian Empire During the Period of Reaction 1907–1914*, PhD Dissertation (English Abstract), The Hebrew University.

Levin, Vladimir 2008, 'The Jewish Socialist Parties in Russia in the Period of Reaction', in *The Revolution of 1905 and Russia's Jews*, edited by Stefani Hoffman and Ezra Mendelsohn, Philadelphia: University of Pennsylvania Press.

Lewis, Ben 2011, 'Kautsky: From Erfurt to Charlottenburg'. Accessed at: http://weeklywor ker.co.uk/worker/889/kautsky-from-erfurt-to-charlottenburg/

Lewis, Ben (ed.) 2018, *Karl Kautsky on Democracy and Republicanism*, Leiden: Brill. (Manuscript)

Lewis, Tom 2000, 'Marxism and Nationalism', *International Socialist Review*, 13: 48–55.

Лядов М. 1904 [1933], 'Доклад большевиков Амстердамскому международному социалистическому конгрессу 1904 г.', in *Раскол на II съезде РСДРП и II Интернационал. Сборник документов*, Москва: Партиздат.

Lih, Lars T. 2006, *Lenin Rediscovered: What Is To Be Done? in Context*, Leiden: Brill.

Lih, Lars T. 2012a, 'Falling Out Over a Cliff'. Accessed at: http://weeklyworker.co.uk/ worker/901/falling-out-over-a-cliff/

Lih, Lars T. 2012b, 'Bolshevism and Revolutionary Social Democracy'. Accessed at: http://weeklyworker.co.uk/worker/917/bolshevism-and-revolutionary-social-demo cracy/

Lih, Lars T. 2012c, 'How Lenin's Party became (Bolshevik)'. Accessed at: https://weeklyw orker.co.uk/worker/914/how-lenins-party-became-bolshevik/

Lih, Lars T. 2012d, 'Democratic Revolution in Permanenz', *Science & Society*, 76, no. 4: 433–62.

Lih, Lars T. 2013, 'Democratic Centralism: Further Fortunes of a Formula'. Accessed at: http://weeklyworker.co.uk/worker/972/democratic-centralism-further-fortunes-of- a-formul/

Lih, Lars T. 2014, 'Fully Armed: Kamenev and Pravda in March 1917', *The NEP Era: Soviet Russia 1921–1928*, 8: 55–68.

Lih, Lars T. 2016, 'Third Time's the Charm? The Project of Broad Socialist Unity, 1903– 1917', Talk at ASEEES, November.

L'internationale Ouvrière & Socialiste 1907, *Rapports Soumis au Congrès Socialiste International de Stuttgart (18–24 août 1907) par les Organisations Socialistes d'Europe, d'Australie et d'Amérique sur leur Activité Pendant les Années 1904–1907*, Bruxelles: Bureau Socialiste International Maison Du Peuple.

Loew, Raimund 1979, 'The Politics of Austro-Marxism', *New Left Review*, 115: 15–51.

Longley, D.A. 1978, *Factional Strife and Policy Making in the Bolshevik Party, 1912–April 1917 (With Special Reference to the Baltic Fleet Organisations 1903–17)*, PhD Dissertation, University of Birmingham.

Longworth, J. George 1959, *The Latvian Congress of Rural Delegates in 1905*, New York: Northeast European Archives.

Łowicki Komitet Robotniczy Polskiej Partyi Socyalistycznej 1903, 'Towarzysze Włościanie!', *Przedświt*, 23, no. 3: 116.

Löwy, Michael 1976, 'Marxists and the National Question', *New Left Review*, 96: 81–100.

Luebbert, Gregory M. 1991, *Liberalism, Fascism, Or Social Democracy: Social Classes and the Political Origins of Regimes in Interwar Europe*, Oxford: Oxford University Press.

Luxemburg, Rosa 1899, 'The Dreyfus Affair and the Millerand Case'. Accessed at: https://www.marxists.org/archive/luxemburg/1899/11/dreyfus-affair.htm

Luxemburg, Rosa 1899 [1971], 'The Militia and Militarism', in *Selected Political Writings*, edited by Dick Howards, New York: Monthly Review Press.

Luxemburg, Rosa 1900 [2004], 'Reform or Revolution', in *The Rosa Luxemburg Reader*, edited by Peter Hudis and Kevin Anderson, New York: Monthly Review Press.

Luxemburg, Rosa 1903, 'Pamięci "Proletariatu"', *Przegląd Socjaldemokratyczny*, 2, no. 1: 16–32, 2, no. 2: 49–67.

Luxemburg, Rosa 1904, 'Organizational Questions of the Russian Social Democracy'. Accessed at https://www.marxists.org/archive/luxemburg/1904/questions-rsd/index.htm

Luxemburg, Rosa 1905, 'The Revolution in Russia'. Accessed at: https://www.marxists.org/archive/luxemburg/1905/02/08.htm

Luxemburg, Rosa 1906a, 'Blanquism and Social Democracy'. Accessed at: https://www.marxists.org/archive/luxemburg/1906/06/blanquism.html

Luxemburg, Rosa 1906b, 'The Mass Strike, the Political Party, and the Trade Unions'. Accessed at: https://www.marxists.org/archive/luxemburg/1906/mass-strike/

Luxemburg, Rosa 1906c, *Rzecz o Konstytuancie i o Rządzie Tymczasowym*, Warszawa: Czerwony Sztandar.

Luxemburg, Rosa 1908, 'Likwidacja', *Przegląd Socjaldemokratyczny*, 1: 46–62, 2: 112–31.

Любовець, Олена 2010, 'Обґрунтування загальноросійськими політичними партіями курсу ліберально-демократичних реформ навесні 1917 р.', *Наукові записки*, 4, no. 48: 24–51.

Любовець, Олена and Валерій Солдатенко 2010, *Революційні альтернативи 1917 року й Україна*, Київ: Наукова Думка.

Lysenko, Irina 2003, *The Revolution in Belarus, 1917–1919*, Master's Thesis, Carleton University.

Maciej, Andrzej 1985, *Rewolucja 1905–1907 w Polsce a mocarstwa zachodnie*, Łódź: Wydawnictwo Łódzkie.

Махарадзе, Филипп 1927, *Очерки революционного движения в Закавказьи*, Тифлис: Госиздат Грузии.

Maistrenko, Iwan 1954, *Borot'bism: A Chapter in the History of Ukrainian Communism*, translated by George S.N. Luckyj, New York: Research Program on the USSR.

Malinowski, Henryk 1967, 'Charakter i formy walki polskie klasy robotnicze w latach 1918–1919', in *Rewolucja Październikowa a Polska: Rozprawy i Studia*, edited Tadeusz Cieślak and Leon Grosfeld, Warszawa: Państwowe Wydawnictwo Naukowe.

Mandel, David 1983, *The Petrograd Workers and the Fall of the Old Regime: From the February Revolution to the July Days, 1917*, New York: St. Martin's Press.

Mandel, David 1984a, *The Petrograd Workers and the Soviet Seizure of Power: From the July Days 1917 to July 1918*, Basingstoke: Macmillan.

Mandel, David 1984b, 'The Intelligentsia and the Working Class in 1917', *Critique*, 14, no. 1: 67–87.

Манилова, В. (ed.) 1928, *1917 год на Киевщине: хроника событий*, Киев: Гос. изд-во Украины.

Манусевич, А.Я. 1965, *Польские интернационалисты в борьбе за победу Советской власти в России Февраль–октябрь 1917 г.*, Москва: Наука.

Manning, Roberta Thompson 1979, 'Zemstvo and Revolution: The Onset of the Gentry Reaction, 1905–1907', in *The Politics of Rural Russia 1905–1914*, edited by Leopold H. Haimson, Bloomington: Indiana University Press,

Marchlewski, J. 1920, *Polen und die Weltrevolution*, Hamburg: Kommunistische Internationale.

Marik, Soma 2008, *Reinterrogating the Classical Marxist Discourses of Revolutionary Democracy*, Delhi: Aakar Books.

Маркарян, Александр Рафаелович 1985, *Деятельность большевиков Закавказья в период двоевластия*, PhD Dissertation, Ереванский государственный лингвистический университет имени В.Я. Брюсова.

Marot, John Eric 2012, *The October Revolution in Prospect and Retrospect: Interventions in Russian and Soviet History*, Leiden: Brill.

Marot, John Eric 2013, 'A Maverick in European Social Democracy: Trotsky's Political Trajectory Between 1905 and 1917', *Science & Society*, 77, no. 3: 412–15.

Marot, John Eric 2014, 'Lenin, Bolshevism, and Social-Democratic Political Theory: The 1905 and 1917 Soviets', *Historical Materialism*, 22, nos. 3–4: 129–71.

Martin, William Culbertson 1971, *A Sociological and Analytic Study of the Development of the Finnish Revolution of 1917–1918 in Terms of Social Structures*, PhD Dissertation, Vanderbilt University.

Martoff, L. 1910, 'Die preußische Diskussion und die russische Erfahrung', *Die Neue Zeit*, 28, no. 2: 907–19.

Martov, Iulii 1904 [2015], 'The Struggle with the "State of Siege" in the RSDLP', in *The Russian Social-Democratic Labour Party, 1899–1904: Documents of the 'Economist' Opposition to Iskra and Early Menshevism*, edited and translated by Richard Mullin, Leiden: Brill.

Martov, Julius et al. 1907, 'Платформа к съезду'. Accessed at: http://web.mit.edu/fjk/www/Trotsky/Permanent/chapter25.html

Мартынов, А. 1923, 'Великая историческая проверка'. Accessed at: http://www.magister.msk.ru/library/revolt/marta001.htm

Marx, Karl 1848, *The Communist Manifesto*. Accessed at: https://www.marxists.org/archive/marx/works/1848/communist-manifesto/index.htm

Marzec, Wiktor 2016, 'Die Revolution 1905 bis 1907 im Königreich Polen – von der Arbeiterrevolte zur nationalen Reaktion', *Arbeit – Bewegung – Geschichte*, 3: 27–46.

Marzec, Wiktor and Risto Turunen 2018, 'Socialisms in the Tsarist Borderlands Poland and Finland in a Contrastive Comparison, 1830–1907', *Contributions to the History of Concepts*, 13, no. 1: 22–50.

Matikainen, Juha 2017, 'Sosiaalidemokraattisen puolueen lehdistö keväällä ja kesällä 1917: kumouksellisuutta, eripuraa ja linjanvetoa', in *Työväki kumouksessa*, edited by Sami Suodenjoki and Risto Turunen, Työväen historian ja perinteen tutkimuksen seura.

Matiss, Vita Ingrida 2000, *Aspazija and Revolutionary Romanticism in Latvia*, PhD Dissertation, Institut universitaire de hautes études internationales (Geneva).

Matthias, Erich 1957, 'Kautsky und der Kautskyanismus', in *Marxismusstudien*, Vol. 2., edited by Iring Fetscher, Tubingen: Mohr.

Mawdsley, Evan 1978, *The Russian Revolution and the Baltic Fleet: War and Politics, February 1917–April 1918*, London: Macmillan.

Mawdsley, Evan 1987, *The Russian Civil War*, Boston: Allen and Unwin.

Mawdsley, Evan 2003, *The Stalin Years: The Soviet Union 1929–1953*, Manchester: Manchester University Press.

Мазлах, Сергій and Василь Шахрай 1919 [1969], *До хвилі*, Нью-Йорк: Пролог.

McDaniel, Tim 1988, *Autocracy, Capitalism, and Revolution in Russia*, Berkeley: University of California Press.

McKean, Robert B. 1990, *St. Petersburg Between the Revolutions: Workers and Revolutionaries, June 1907–February 1917*, New Haven: Yale University Press.

McKee, William Arthur 1997, *Taming the Green Serpent: Alcoholism, Autocracy, and Russian Society, 1881–1914*, PhD Dissertation, University of California, Berkeley.

Медем, Владимир 1904 [1906], *Социал-Демократия и Национальный Вопрос*, Санкт-Петербург: Бусселя.

Medem, Vladimir 1923 [1979], *Vladimir Medem, the Life and Soul of a Legendary Jewish Socialist*, translated by Samuel A. Portnoy, New York: Ktav Publishing House.

Megrian, Leon Der 1968, *Tiflis During the Russian Revolution of 1905*, PhD Dissertation, University of California, Berkeley.

Melancon, Michael S. 1984, *The Socialist Revolutionaries from 1902 to February 1917: A Party of the Workers, Peasants, and Soldiers*, PhD Dissertation, Indiana University.

Melancon, Michael S. 1990, '"Marching Together!": Left Bloc Activities in the Russian Revolutionary Movement, 1900 to February 1917', *Slavic Review*, 49, no. 2: 239–52.

Melancon, Michael S. 1993, 'The Syntax of Soviet Power: The Resolutions of Local Soviets and Other Institutions, March–October 1917', *The Russian Review*, 52, no. 4: 486–505.

Melancon, Michael S. 1997, 'The Left Socialist Revolutionaries and the Bolshevik Uprising', in *The Bolsheviks in Russian Society: The Revolution and the Civil Wars*, edited by Vladimir Brovkin, New Haven: Yale University Press.

Melancon, Michael S. 2004, 'From Rhapsody to Threnody: Russia's Provisional Government in Socialist-Revolutionary eyes, February–July 1917', in *Revolutionary Russia: New Approaches*, edited by Rex A. Wade, New York: Routledge.

Меленевський, М. 1923, 'До історії Української С.-Д. Спілки', *Нова Громада*, 3–4: 130–4.

Mendel, Hersh 1989, *Memoirs of a Jewish Revolutionary*, translated by Robert Michaels, London: Pluto Press.

Mendelsohn, Ezra 1965, 'Worker Opposition in the Russian Jewish Socialist Movement from the 1890s to 1903', *International Review of Social History*, 10, no. 2: 268–82.

Mendelson, Stanisław 1887, 'Biblijografija', *Walka Klas*, 2: v–xiv.

Mendelson, Stanisław 1903, 'Zasadnicza myśl polityczna Komuny Paryskiej'. Accessed at: http://lewicowo.pl/zasadnicza-mysl-polityczna-komuny-paryskiej/

Menders, F. 1959, *Domas, Darbi un Dzīve. 1903–1940, 1. Daļa, Revolūcijas Priekšlaiks*, Rk 2219, Unpublished manuscript, Akadēmiskā Bibliotēka Latvijas Universitātes.

Michałowski, Stanisław 2003, 'Polish Socialists', in *More Than Independence: Polish Political Thought: 1918–1939*, edited by Jan Jachymek and Waldema Paruch, Lublin: Maria Curie-Skłodowska University Press.

Michta, Norbert 1987, *Rozbieżności i Rozłam w SDKPIL*, Warszawa: Książka i Wiedza.

Michta, Norbert and Jan Sobczak 2004, *Zapomniany Polemista i Apostata Doktryny Róży Luksemburg–Stanisław Trusiewicz-Zalewski (1871–1918)*, Elbląg: Elbląska Uczelnia Humanistyczno-Ekonomiczna.

Miliband, Ralph 1970, 'Lenin's *The State and Revolution*', *The Socialist Register*, Vol. 7: 309–19.

Miliband, Ralph 1989, *Divided Societies: Class Struggle in Contemporary Capitalism*, Oxford: Clarendon Press.

Millers, Visvaris and Ērika Stumbiņa 1965, *Fricis Roziņš 1870–1919: dzīve un darbs*, Rīgā: Liesma.

Ter Minassian, Anahide 1983, 'Nationalism and Socialism in the Armenian Revolutionary Movement (1887–1912)', in *Transcaucasia, Nationalism and Social Change: Essays in the History of Armenia, Azerbaijan, and Georgia*, edited by Ronald Grigor Suny, Ann Arbor: University of Michigan Press.

Miške, V. 1955, *1905.–1907. gada revolucijas augstākā pakāpe Latvijā*, Rīga: Latvijas valsts izdevniecība.

Moravskis, Alfonsas 1896, 'W kwestyi taktyki ruchu robotniczego', *Przedświt*, 6: 2–10.

Morgan, Anne Dorazio 1979, *The St. Petersburg Soviet of Workers' Deputies: A Study of Labor Organization in the 1905 Russian Revolution*, PhD Dissertation, Indiana University.

Морозов, К. Н. 1998, *Партия социалистов-революционеров в 1907–1914 гг.*, Москва: РОССПЭН.

Mullin, Richard 2010, *Lenin and the Iskra Faction of the RSDLP 1899–1903*, PhD Dissertation, University of Sussex.

Mullin, Richard (ed.) 2015, *The Russian Social-Democratic Labour Party, 1899–1904: Documents of the 'Economist' Opposition to Iskra and Early Menshevism*, Leiden: Brill.

Naarden, Bruno 1992, *Socialist Europe and Revolutionary Russia, 1848–1923*, Cambridge: Cambridge University Press.

Naimark, Norman M. 1979, *The History of the 'Proletariat': The Emergence of Marxism in the Kingdom of Poland, 1870–1887*, Boulder: East European Quarterly.

Najdus, Walentyna 1967, *Polacy w rewolucji 1917 roku*, Warszawa: Państwowe Wydawnictwo Naukowe.

Najdus, Walentyna 1973, *SDKPIL a SDPRR, 1893–1907*, Wrocław: Zakład Narodowy im. Ossolińskich.

Najdus, Walentyna 1980, *SDKPIL a SDPRR, 1908–1918*, Wrocław: Zakład Narodowy im. Ossolińskich.

Насырин, В.П. 1956, 'О некоторых вопросах социалистического преобразования промышленности в СССР', *Вопросы истории*, 5: 90–9.

Nettl, J.P. 1966, *Rosa Luxemburg*, London: Oxford University Press.

Невский, В.И. 1930, *Рабочее движение в январские дни 1905 года*, Москва: Издательство Всесоюзного общества политкаторжан и ссыльнопоселенцев.

Nicolaysen, Helena M. 1990, *Looking Backward: A Prosopography of the Russian Social Democratic Elite, 1883–1907*, PhD Dissertation, Stanford University.

Nicolaysen, Helena M. 1991, 'SD Networks in Transcaucasia and Stalin: The Rise of a Regional Party Functionary (1887–1902)', International Studies Working Paper, The Hoover Institution, Stanford University.

Nowogrodzki, Emanuel 2001, *The Jewish Labor Bund in Poland 1915–1939: From its Emer-*

gence as an Independent Political Party Until the Beginning of World War II, Rockville: Shengold Books.

Offe, Claus and Helmut Wiesenthal 1980, 'Two Logics of Collective Action: Theoretical Notes on Social Class and Organizational Form,' *Political Power and Social Theory* 1(1): 67–115.

Oppenheim, Samuel A. 1972, *Aleksei Ivanovich Rykov (1881–1938): A Political Biography*, PhD Dissertation, Indiana University.

Orzechowski, Ignacy and Aleksander Kochański 1964, *Zarys dziejów ruchu zawodowego w Królestwie Polskim (1905–1918)*, Warszawa: Książka i Wiedza.

Panitch, Leo and Sam Gindin with Steve Maher 2020, *The Socialist Challenge Today: Syriza, Corbyn, Sanders*, Chicago: Haymarket Books.

Page, Stanley W. 1959, *The Formation of the Baltic States: A Study of the Effects of Great Power Politics Upon the Emergence of Lithuania, Latvia, and Estonia*, Cambridge, MA: Harvard University Press.

Parsons, J.W.R. 1987, *The Emergence and Development of the National Question in Georgia, 1801–1921*, PhD Dissertation, University of Glasgow.

Pärssinen, Hilja 1903, *Äänioikeus-asia työläisnaisten kannalta*, Helsinki: Työväen Kirjapaino.

Павко, А.І. 1999, *Політичні партії, організації в Україні: кінець XIX–початок XX століття: зародження, еволюція, діяльність, історична доля*, Київ: Іван Федоров.

Peled, Yoav 1989, *Class and Ethnicity in the Pale: The Political Economy of Jewish Workers' Nationalism in Late Imperial Russia*, London: Macmillan.

Penkower, Monty Noam 2004, 'The Kishinev Pogrom of 1903: A Turning Point in Jewish History', *Modern Judaism*, 3, no. 4: 187–224.

Pērkone, Laimdota 1992, 'Diskusijas sociāldemokrātu presē par revizionismu un oportūnismu. (1898.–1914.)', in *Vēsture. Sociālpolitiskās vēstures jautājumi*, edited by V.A. Shalda, Rīga: Latvijas. Universitātes.

Perl, F. [Rewolucjonista] 1894, 'Proletaryat inteligencyi i jego udział w ruchu socyalistycznym', *Przedświt*, 5: 2–6.

П–ра., С. 1906, 'Бібліографія', *Вільна Україна*, 4: 73–5.

Petrovsky-Shtern, Yohanan 2001, *Jews in the Russian Army: Through the Military Towards Modernity (1827–1914)*, PhD Dissertation, Brandeis University.

Petz, Barbara and Władysław Lech Karwacki 1990, 'Ruch strajkowy 1913 roku w okręgu łódzkim', in *Przemoc zbiorowa, ruch masowy, rewolucja*, edited by Elżbieta Kaczyńska and Zbigniew W. Rykowski, Warszawa: Wydawnictwa Uniwersytetu Warszawskiego.

Phillips, Hugh 2001, 'The Heartland Turns Red: The Bolshevik Seizure of Power in Tver', *Revolutionary Russia*, 14, no. 1: 1–21.

Phillips, Laura L. 1997, 'Message in a Bottle: Working-Class Culture and the Struggle for Revolutionary Legitimacy, 1900–1929', *Russian Review*, 56, no. 1: 25–43.

Piasecki, Henryk 1978, *Żydowska organizacja* PPS: *1893–1907*, Wrocław: Zakład Narodowy im. Ossolińskich.

Piatnitski, Osip 1931, *Souvenirs d'un Bolchévik (1896–1917)*, Paris: Bureau d' éditions.

Piatnitsky, Osip 1933, *Memoirs of a Bolshevik*, London: Martin Lawrence.

Pilsudski, Joseph 1937, *Pisma Zbiorowe, Vol. 1*, Warszawa: Instytut Józefa Piłsudskiego.

Piontkovskii, S.A. 1925 [2016], 'Mistakes in "The Lessons of October" by Comrade Trotsky', in *Trotsky's Challenge: The 'Literary Discussion' of 1924 and the Fight for the
Bolshevik Revolution*, edited by Frederick C. Corney, Leiden: Brill.

Pipes, Richard 1960, 'Russian Marxism and Its Populist Background: The Late Nineteenth Century', *The Russian Review*, 19, no. 4: 316–37.

Pipes, Richard 1996, *A Concise History of the Russian Revolution*, New York: Vintage.

Piskała, Kamil 2014, *Mieczysław Niedziałkowski – początki politycznej działalności i
kształtowanie światopoglądu (1893–1918)*, Warszawa: Wydawnictwa Naukowego Sem-
per.

Plekhanov, G.V. 1885, 'Our Differences'. Accessed at: https://www.marxists.org/archive/
plekhanov/1885/ourdiff/index.html

Plekhanov, G.V. 1903 [2009], '"Orthodox" Pedantry', in *Witnesses to Permanent Revolution*, edited by Richard B. Day and Daniel Gaido, Leiden: Brill.

Plekhanov, G.V. 1905, 'Еще о нашем положении: (Письмо к товарищу х)'. Accessed
at: http://web.mit.edu/fjk/www/Trotsky/Permanent/chapter21.html

Поч, Инесе Яновна 1984, *Формирование марксистско-ленинской концепции революции 1905–1907 гг. в Латвии и критика мелкобуржуазных взглядов*, PhD Dissertation, Даугавпилсский педагогический институт.

Popoff, George 1932, *The City of the Red Plague: Soviet Rule in a Baltic Town*, translated
by Robin John, London: G. Allen & Unwin.

Попов, Н.Н. 1925, *Из истории забастовочного движения в России накануне импе-
риалистической войны: Бакинская забастовка 1914 года*, Ленинград: Госиздать.

Попов, Н.Н. 1929, *Очерк Истории Коммунистической Партии (Большевиков) Украины*, Харьков: Пролетарий.

Попов, Н.Н. 1934, *Outline History of the Communist Party of the Soviet Union*, New York,
International Publishers.

Порш, Микола 1907, *Про автономію украіни*, Кіевъ: Просвѣшеніе.

Porter, Brian 2000, *When Nationalism Began to Hate: Imagining Modern Politics in
Nineteenth-Century Poland*, New York: Oxford University Press.

Porter-Szücs, Brian 2014, *Poland in the Modern World: Beyond Martyrdom*, Chichester:
Wiley-Blackwell.

Портнов, Андрій 2012, 'Ленін і більшовизм в Українській соціалістичній думці
першої третини XX століття'. Accessed at: http://www.historians.in.ua/index.php/
en/doslidzhennya/209-andrii-portnov-lenin-i-bilshovyzm-v-ukrainskii-sotsialistyc
hnii-dumtsi-pershoi-tretyny-khkh-stolittia

Post, Charles 2010, 'Exploring Working-Class Consciousness: A Critique of the Theory of the Labor Aristocracy', *Historical Materialism*, 18, no. 4: 3–38.

Post, Charles 2013, 'What is Left of Leninism? New European Left Parties In Historical Perspective', in *Socialist Register 2013: The Question of Strategy*, edited by Leo Panitch, Greg Albo, and Vivek Chibber, Pontypool: Merlin.

Potkański, Waldemar 2008, *Odrodzenie czynu niepodległościowego przez PPS w okresie rewolucji 1905 roku*, Warszawa: Wydawnictwo DiG.

Preobrazhenskii, Nikolai 2006, 'Little-known Aspects of the Russian Revolution of 1905', *Critique*, 34, no. 3: 293–314.

Prevo, Kathleen 1979, *The Revolution of 1905 in Voronezh: The Labor Movement and Political Consciousness in a Russian Provincial City*, PhD Dissertation, Indiana University.

Protasov, Lev Grigor'evich 2004, 'The All-Russian Constituent Assembly and the Democratic Alternative: Two Views of the Problem', in *Revolutionary Russia: New Approaches*, edited by Rex A. Wade, New York: Routledge.

Prymak, Thomas M. 1979, 'The First All-Ukrainian Congress of Soviets and its Antecedents', *Journal of Ukrainian Studies*, 6: 3–19.

Prymak, Thomas M. 1987, *Mykhailo Hrushevsky: The Politics of National Culture*, Toronto: University of Toronto.

Пушкарева, И.М. 2003, 'Рабочее движение в год II съезда РСДРП', *Отечественная история*, 4: 3–14.

Пушкарева, И.М. 2005, 'Рабочие и партии России в канун революции 1905–1907 годов', in *Политические партии в российских революциях в начале XX века*, edited by Г.Н. Севостьянова, Москва: Наука.

Пушкарева, И.М. (ed.) 2008, *Рабочее движение в России, 1895–февраль 1917 г.: хроника. Вып. X 1904 год, Часть II*, Москва: Институт российской истории РАН.

Пушкарева, И.М. 2011, *Трудовые конфликты и рабочее движение в России на рубеже XIX–XX вв.*, Санкт-Петербург: Алетейя.

Rabinowitch, Alexander 1968, *Prelude to Revolution: The Petrograd Bolsheviks and the July 1917 Uprising*, Bloomington: Indiana University Press.

Rabinowitch, Alexander 1976, *The Bolsheviks Come to Power: The Revolution of 1917 in Petrograd*, New York: Norton.

Rabinowitch, Alexander 2007, *The Bolsheviks in Power: the First Year of Soviet Rule in Petrograd.* Bloomington: Indiana University Press.

Radek, Karl 1916 [1984], 'The SPD: Unity or Split?', in *Lenin's Struggle for a Revolutionary International. Documents: 1907–1916, the Preparatory Years*, edited by John Riddell, New York: Monad Press.

Radek, Karl 1917, 'Der Arbeiter- und Soldatendelegiertenrat', *Bote der Russischen Revolution. Organ der ausländischen Vertretung des Zentralkomitees der Sozialdemokratischen Arbeiterpartei Russlands (Bolschewiki)*, 3: 1–5.

Radlak, Bronisław 1979, *Socjaldemokracja Królestwa Polskiego i Litwy w Latach 1893–1904*, Warszawa: Państwowe Wydawnictwo Naukowe.

Radlak, Bronisław 1988, 'Przesłanki rewolucji w koncepcjach radykalnego nurtu polskiego ruchu robotniczego w okresie zaborów', *Z Pola Walki*, 31, no. 2: 1–21.

Рафес, Моисей Григорьевич 1923, *Очерки по истории Бунда*, Москва: Московский рабочий.

Rahikainen, Marjatta 1986, *N.R. af Ursin, aatelismies Suomen työväenliikkeessä*, Helsinki: Suomen Historiallinen Seura.

Raleigh, Donald J. 1981, 'Revolutionary Politics in Provincial Russia: The Tsaritsyn "Republic" in 1917', *Slavic Review*, 40, no. 2: 194–209.

Raleigh, Donald J. 1986, *Revolution on the Volga: 1917 in Saratov*, Ithaca: Cornell University Press.

Rappaport, Herman 1960, *Narastanie Rewolucji w Królestwie Polskim w Latach 1900–1904*, Warszawa: Państwowe Wydawnictwo Naukowe.

Рашин, Адольф Григорьевич 1958, *Формирование рабочего класса России: историко-экономические очерки*, Москва: Изд-во социально-экон. лит-ры.

Равич-Черкасский, М. 1923, *История Коммунистической Партии (б-ов) Украины*, Государственное Издательство Украины.

Read, Christopher 2005, *Lenin: A Revolutionary Life*, London: Routledge.

Redakcyja [Anon.] 1905, 'Z obozu S.D. Rosyjskiej. Różdżka pokoj', *Przedświt*, 6–8: 321–3.

Редакция 'Искры' 1905, 'Революционные перспективы'. Accessed at: http://web.mit .edu/fjk/www/Trotsky/Permanent/chapter13.html

Reichman, Henry 1977, *Russian Railwaymen and the Revolution of 1905*, PhD Dissertation, University of California, Berkeley.

Reichman, Henry 1987, *Railwaymen and Revolution: Russia, 1905*, Berkeley: University of California Press.

Remeikis, Thomas 1963, *The Communist Party of Lithuania: A Historical and Political Study*, PhD Dissertation, University of Illinois.

Retish, Aaron B. 2015, 'The Izhevsk Revolt of 1918: The Fateful Clash of Revolutionary Coalitions, Paramilitarism, and Bolshevik Power', in *Russia's Home Front in War and Revolution, 1914–22: Russia's Revolution in Regional Perspective*, edited by Sarah Badcock, Bloomington: Slavica Publishers.

Ревегук, Віктор 2016, *Полтавщина в перший рік Української революції, Доба Центральної Ради (березень 1917–квітень 1918 рр.)*, Полтавський літератор, Полтава.

Rice, Christopher 1988, *Russian Workers and the Socialist-Revolutionary Party through the Revolution of 1905–07*, Basingstoke: Macmillan.

Riddell, John (ed.) 1984, *Lenin's Struggle for a Revolutionary International. Documents: 1907–1916, the Preparatory Years*, New York: Monad Press.

Riddell, John (ed.) 1993, *To See the Dawn: Baku, 1920: First Congress of the Peoples of the East*, New York: Pathfinder.

Riddell, John 2013, 'Party Democracy in Lenin's Comintern – and Now'. Accessed at: https://johnriddell.wordpress.com/2013/02/20/party-democracy-in-lenins-cominte rn-and-now/

Rieber, Alfred J. 1982, *Merchants and Entrepreneurs in Imperial Russia*, Chapel Hill: University of North Carolina Press.

Rieber, Alfred J. 2015, *Stalin and the Struggle for Supremacy in Eurasia*, Cambridge: Cambridge University Press.

Riga, Liliana 2000, *Identity and Empire: The Making of the Bolshevik Elite, 1880–1917*, PhD Dissertation, McGill University.

Riihinen, Olavi 1975, 'Ideologinen kehitys', in *Rautatieläisten liiton historia. 1. Vaikeat vuosikymmenet: kehitys vuoteen 1930*, edited by Rauno Parikka, Helsinki: Weilin & Göös.

Rinta-Tassi, Osmo 1986, *Kansanvaltuuskunta punaisen Suomen hallituksena*, Helsinki: Opetusministeriö, Punakaartin historiakomitea.

Ripa, J., and Ilga Apine 1964, *Jaunie revolucionāre uzplūdi Latvijā, 1910–1914*, Rīgā: Latvijas valsts izdevniecība.

Риш, А. 1926, *Очерки по истории Украинской социал-демократической 'Спілки'*, Харьков: Пролетарий.

Robotnik 1906 [1961], 'VIII Zjazd PPS', in *PPS-Lewica, 1906–1918 materiały i dokumenty, Vol. 1: 1906–1910, Warszawa: Książka i Wiedza*, edited by Tych Feliks, Warszawa: Książka i Wiedza.

Roobol, W.H. 1976, *Tsereteli – A Democrat in the Russian Revolution: A Political Biography*, translated by P.J.E. Hyams and Lynne Richards, The Hague: Martinus Nijhoff.

Rose, John 2015, 'Luxemburg, Müller and the Berlin Workers' and Soldiers' Councils', *International Socialism*, 147: 113–38.

Rosenberg, William 1985, 'Russian Labor and Bolshevik Power after October', *Slavic Review*, 44, no. 2: 213–38.

Roszkowski, Wojciech 1992, 'The Reconstruction of the Government and State Apparatus in the Second Polish Republic', in *The Reconstruction of Poland, 1914–1923*, edited by in Paul Latawski, Houndmills: Macmillan.

Roziņš, Fricis 1899 [1963–65], 'Ko mēs gribam', in *Rakstu izlase*, Vol. 1, Rīga: Latvijas Valsts izdevniecība.

Roziņš, Fricis 1905a [1963–65], 'Mēs varam visādi!', in *Rakstu izlase*, Vol. 2, Rīga: Latvijas Valsts izdevniecība.

Roziņš, Fricis 1905b [1963–65], 'Domas par revolūciju', in *Rakstu izlase*, Vol. 2, Rīga: Latvijas Valsts izdevniecība.

Roziņš, Fricis 1917 [1963–65], 'Sociāldemokrātijas Cīņa Pret Militārismu', in *Rakstu izlase*, Vol. 3, Rīga: Latvijas Valsts izdevniecība.

Roziņš, Fricis 1963–65, *Rakstu izlase*, Rīga: Latvijas Valsts izdevniecība.

RSDLP 1903 [1978], *Second Ordinary Congress of the RSDLP, 1903: Complete Text of the Minutes*, translated by Brian Pearce, London: New Park Publications.

RSDRP Central Committee 1917–18 [1974], *The Bolsheviks and the October Revolution: Minutes of the Central Committee of the Russian Social-Democratic Labour Party (Bolsheviks), August 1917–February 1918*, London: Pluto Press.

РСДРП 1903 [1959], *II съезд РСДРП. Июль–август 1903 года. Протоколы*, Москва: Государственное Издательство Политической Литературы.

РСДРП 1905 [1959], *Третий Съезд РСДРП. Апрель–Май 1905 Года: Протоколы*, Москва: Государственное Издательство Политической Литературы.

РСДРП 1906 [1959], *Четвертый (объединительный) съезд РСДРП, апрель–май 1906 года: протоколыт*, Москва: Государственное Издательство Политической Литературы.

РСДРП (большевиков) 1917a [1958], *Седьмая (апрельская) Всероссийская конференция РСДРП (большевиков); Петроградская общегородская конференция РСДРП (большевиков). Апрель 1917 года. Протоколы*, Москва: Госполитиздат.

РСДРП (большевиков) 1917b [1958], *Шестой съезд РСДРП (большевиков). Август 1917 года. Протоколы*, Москва: Госполитиздат, 1958.

Goldberg Ruthchild, Rochelle 2010, *Equality & Revolution: Women's Rights in the Russian Empire, 1905–1917*, Pittsburgh: University of Pittsburgh Press.

Saastamoinen, Mauri 2005, *Helsinkiläisten työväenyhdistysten jäsenistö 1905–1908: kohti ammatillista keskittymistä*, Master's Thesis, Helsingin yliopisto.

Sabaliūnas, Leonas 1990, *Lithuanian Social Democracy in Perspective, 1893–1914*, Durham, NC: Duke University Press.

Sacewicz, Karol 2014, 'Wojna na lewicy – pierwsze starcia. Walka o hegemonię w warszawskich radach delega-tów robotniczych pomiędzy KPRP a PPS (1918–1919)', in *Komuniści w międzywojennej Warszawie*, edited by Elżbieta Kowalczyk, Warszawa: Instytut Pamięci Narodowej.

Сахнин, Алексей Викторович 2010, *Внутрипартийная борьба в РСДРП(б) в конце февраля–апреле 1917 г. Механизм руководства и выработка стратегии*, PhD Dissertation, Московский государственный университет имени М.В. Ломоносова.

Шалда, В. 1982, 'О Роли Рижского Федеративного Комитета в Революции 1905–1907 Года', *Latvijas PSR Zinātņu Akadēmijas Vēstis*, 2: 28–46.

Шалда, В. 1989, *За организационное единство партии*, Рига: Авотс.

Шалда, В. and Л. Спруте 1992, 'Борьба жандярмернс против оociaчдемократии Лаааии', in *Vēsture. Sociālpolitiskās vēstures jautājumi*, edited by V.A. Šalda, Rīga: Latvijas. Universitātes.

Šalda, Vitālijs 2006, 'Latvijas sociāldemokrātijas organizatoriskās attīstības dažas tendences 1905. gada revolūcijā', in *1905. gads Latvijā: 100. Pētījumi un starptautiskas kon-

*ferences materiāli, 2005. gada 11.–12. janvāris, Rīga*, edited by Jānis Bērziņš, Rīga: Latvijas vēstures institūta apgāds.

Salkola, Marja-Leena 1985, *Työväenkaartien synty ja kehitys punakaartiksi 1917–18 ennen kansalaissotaa 1*, Helsinki: Valtion painatuskeskus.

Salvadori, Massimo L. 1979, *Karl Kautsky and the Socialist Revolution, 1880–1938*, London: Verso.

Samuś, Paweł 1975, 'Rozwój organizacyjny SDKPIL w Łodzi w latach 1905–1907', in *Rewolucja 1905–1907 w Łodzi i okręgu: studia i materiały*, edited by, Barbara Wachowska, Łódź: Wydawnictwo Łódzkie.

Samuś, Paweł 1984, *Dzieje SDKPIL w Łodzi, 1893–1918*, Łódź: Wydawn Łódzkie.

Samuś, Paweł 2009, 'Kobiety w ruchu socjalistycznym Królestwa Polskiego w latach rewolucji 1905–1907', *Rocznik Łódzki*, 56: 85–115.

Samuś, Paweł 2013, *Wasza kartka wyborcza jest silniejsza niż karabin, niż armata ...: z dziejów kultury politycznej na ziemiach polskich pod zaborami*, Łódź: Wydawnictwo Uniwersytetu Łódzkiego.

Sanders, Joseph L. 1987, *The Moscow Uprising of December 1905: A Background Study*, New York: Garland.

Сапон, Владимир Петрович 2009, *Концепция революционного освобождения общества в теоретических воззрениях и политической практике российских левых радикалов*, PhD Dissertation, Университет Лобачевского Нижний Новгород.

Sario, Jorma 1968, *Edvard Valpas: Vanhan työväenliikkeen luokkataistelija*, Master's Thesis, Helsingin yliopisto.

Савицкий, Эдуард Михайлович (ed.) 1997, *Бунд в Беларуси, 1897–1921: Документы и Материалы*, Минск: БелНИИДАД.

Schneiderman, Jeremiah 1976, *Sergei Zubatov and Revolutionary Marxism: The Struggle for the Working Class in Tsarist Russia*, Ithaca: Cornell University Press.

Schorske, Carl E. 1955, *German Social Democracy 1905–1917: The Development of the Great Schism*, Cambridge, MA: Harvard University Press.

Secrétariat Socialiste International 1904, *Sixième Congrès socialiste international, tenu à Amsterdam du 14 au 20 août 1904, Compte-rendu analytique*, Bruxelles.

Семенова, В.П. (ed.) 1913, *Россия. Полное географическое описание нашего отечества*, Санкт-Петербург: А.Ф.Девриена.

Seregny, Scott Joseph 1989, *Russian Teachers and Peasant Revolution: The Politics of Education in 1905*, Bloomington: Indiana University Press.

Service, Robert 1991, *Lenin: A Political Life: Volume 2, World in Collision*, Bloomington: Indiana University Press.

Shakhrai, Vasyl and Serhii Mazlakh 1919 [1970], *On the Current Situation in the Ukraine*, edited by Peter J. Potichnyj, Ann Arbor: The University of Michigan Press.

Shanin, Teodor 1986, *Russia as a Developing Society: The Roots of Otherness – Russia's*

*Turn of Century, Volume 2: Russia, 1905–07: Revolution as a Moment of Truth*, Basingstoke: Macmillan.

Shatz, Marshall 1989, *Jan Wacław Machajski: A Radical Critic of the Russian Intelligentsia and Socialism*, Pittsburgh: University of Pittsburgh Press.

Шаумян, С.Г. 1917 [1958], 'Ко всем товарищам солдатам Кавказской армии', in *Избранные произведения*, Vol. 2, Москва: Госполитиздат.

Шелохаев, В.В. (ed.) 2008, *Конференции РСДРП 1912 года: документы и материалы*, Москва: РОССПЭН.

Шелохаев, В.В. et al. (eds.) 2002, *Союз эсеров-максималистов: документы, публицистика, 1906–1924 гг.*, Москва: РОССПЭН.

Shlyapnikov, Alexander 1923, *On the Eve of 1917*. Accessed at: https://www.marxists.org/archive/shliapnikov/1923/eve1917/index.html

Shlyapnikov, Alexander 1923 [1992], *Канун семнадцатого года: Семнадцатый год, Т. 2*, Москва: Республика.

Shlyapnikov, Alexander 1925 [1994], *Канун семнадцатого года: Семнадцатый год, Т. 3*, Москва: Республика.

Shtakser, Inna 2007, *Structure of Feeling and Radical Identity Among Working-Class Jewish Youth During the 1905 Revolution*, PhD Dissertation, University of Texas at Austin.

Shtakser, Inna 2014, *The Making of Jewish Revolutionaries in the Pale of Settlement: Community and Identity During the Russian Revolution and its Immediate Aftermath, 1905–07*, Basingstoke: Palgrave Macmillan.

Šiliņš, Janis 2008, 'Latvian Society and the Soviet Regime in 1919: from Support to Resistance' in *Rebellion and Resistance. Power and Culture. Vol. 4* edited by Henrik Jensen, Pisa: Pisa University Press.

Sillanpää, Miina [Miina S.] 1906, 'Suurlakko, ja palvelijain muutto', *Palvelijatarlehti*, 3–4: 33–4.

Siltala, Juha 2014, 'Being Absorbed Into an Unintended War', in *The Finnish Civil War 1918: History, Memory, Legacy*, edited by Tuomas Tepora and Aapo Roselius, Leiden: Brill.

Siltala, Juha 2015, 'Dissolution and Reintegration in Finland, 1914–1932: How Did a Disarmed Country Become Absorbed into Brutalization?', *Journal of Baltic Studies*, 46, no. 1: 11–33.

Симчишин, Александр Сергеевич 2007, *деятельность бундивських організацій в правобережной Украины в начале хх века*, PhD Dissertation, Каменец-Подольський национальный университет.

Simha, Rakesh Krishnan 2014, 'How Russia Fired Up India's Freedom Movement'. Accessed at: https://www.rbth.com/blogs/2014/08/15/how_russia_fired_up_indias_freedom_movement_37555

Singleton, Fred and A.F. Upton 1998, *A Short History of Finland*, Cambridge: Cambridge University Press.

Sirola, Yrjö 1918 [1918], 'Ich klage Euch an, ihr deutschen Mehrheitssozialisten', in John Eliel, *Der Klassenkrieg in Finnland: Die Finnische Sozialdemokratie im Kampfe Gegen die Reaktion, 1905–1918*, Köpenhavn.

Skocpol, Theda 1979, *States and Social Revolutions: A Comparative Analysis of France, Russia, and China*, Cambridge: Cambridge University Press.

Slusser, Robert M. 1987, *Stalin in October: The Man Who Missed the Revolution*, Baltimore: Johns Hopkins University Press.

Smele, Jon 2017, *The 'Russian' Civil Wars, 1916–1926: Ten Years that Shook the World*, New York: Oxford University Press.

Smith, Jeremy 1999, *The Bolsheviks and the National Question, 1917–23*, New York: St. Martin's Press.

Smith, S.A. 1983, *Red Petrograd: Revolution in the Factories, 1917–1918*, Cambridge: Cambridge University Press.

Smith, S.A. 1999, 'Workers, the Intelligentsia, and Social Democracy in St. Petersburg, 1895–1917', in *Workers and Intelligentsia in Late Imperial Russia: Realities, Representations, Reflections*, edited by Reginald E. Zelnik, Berkeley: Institute and Area Studies, University of California.

Smith, S.A. 2006, 'The Revolutions of 1917–1918', in *The Cambridge History of Russia, Volume III: The Twentieth Century*, edited by Ronald Grigor Suny, Cambridge: Cambridge University Press.

Smolynec, Gregory 1993, *The Union for the Liberation of Ukraine, 1914–1918*, Master's Thesis, Carleton University.

Snow, Russell E. 1977, *The Bolsheviks in Siberia, 1917–1918*, Rutherford: Fairleigh Dickinson University Press.

Snyder, Timothy 1997, *Nationalism, Marxism, and Modern Central Europe: A Biography of Kazimierz Kelles-Krauz, 1872–1905*, Cambridge: Ukrainian Research Institute of Harvard University.

Sobczak, Jan 1970, 'Rewolucja październikowa w świetle prasy Mazowsza'. Accessed at: http://www.1917.net.pl/node/3811

Sobczak, Jan 1988, 'SDKPIL w rewolucji 1905 roku', in *Rewolucja 1905 roku w Królestwie Polskim (partie–masy–doświadczenia międzynarodowe): materiały sympozjum naukowego*, edited by Jan Sobczak, Warszawa: Akademia Nauk Społecznych PZPR.

Sobczak, Jan 1980, *Współpraca SDKPIL z SDPRR: 1893–1907: Geneza Zjednoczenia i Stanowisko SDKPIL Wewnątrz SDPRR*, Warszawa: Książka i Wiedza.

Söderhjelm, Henning 1919, *The Red Insurrection in Finland in 1918, A Study Based on Documentary Evidence*, translated by Anne I. Fausboll. London: Harrison.

Soikkanen, Hannu 1961, *Sosialismin tulo suomen; ensimmäisiin yksikamarisen eduskunnan vaaleihin asti*, Porvoo: W. Söderström.

Soikkanen, Hannu 1975, *Kohti kansanvaltaa: Suomen Sosialdemokraattinen Puolue 75 vuotta*. Helsinki: Suomen Sosialidemokraattinen Puolue, Puoluetoimikunta.

Soikkanen, Hannu 1978, 'Revisionism, Reformism and the Finnish Labour Movement Before the First World War', *Scandinavian Journal of History*, 3, nos. 1–4: 347–60.

Солдатенко, В.Ф. 1994, 'Еволюція суспільно-політичних поглядів В.К. Винниченка в добу української революції', *Український історичний журнал*, 399, no. 6: 15–26.

Солдатенко, В.Ф. 2004, *Георгій Пятаков: миттєвості неспокійної долі*, Київ: Світогляд.

Солдатенко, В.Ф. 2007, *Винниченко і Петлюра: політичні портрети революційної доби*, Київ: Світогляд.

Solzhenitsyn, Aleksandr Isaevich 1973, *The Gulag Archipelago, 1918–1956: An Experiment in Literary Investigation I–II*, New York: Harper and Row.

Spenser, Daniela 2011, *Stumbling Its Way Through Mexico: The Early Years of the Communist International*, Tuscaloosa: University of Alabama Press.

Stalin, J.V. 1901 [1953–55], 'The Russian Social-Democratic Party and its Immediate Tasks', in *Works*, Vol. 1, Moscow: Foreign Languages Publishing House.

Stalin, J.V. 1905 [1953–55], 'The Provisional Revolutionary Government and Social-Democracy', in *Works*, Vol. 1, Moscow: Foreign Languages Publishing House.

Stalin, J.V. 1906–07 [1953–55], 'Anarchism or Socialism?', in *Works*, Vol. 1, Moscow: Foreign Languages Publishing House.

Stalin, J.V. 1907a [1953–55], 'Preface to the Georgian Edition of K. Kautsky's Pamphlet The Driving Forces and Prospects of the Russian Revolution', in *Works*, Vol. 2, Moscow: Foreign Languages Publishing House.

Stalin, J.V. 1909 [1953–55], 'The Party Crisis and Our Tasks', in *Works*, Vol. 2, Moscow: Foreign Languages Publishing House.

Stalin, J.V. 1917 [1953–55], 'The Revolutionary Front', in *Works*, Vol. 3, Moscow: Foreign Languages Publishing House.

Stalin, J.V. (ed.) 1938, *History of the Communist Party of the Soviet Union (Bolsheviks): Short Course*. Accessed at: https://www.marxists.org/reference/archive/stalin/works/1939/x01/index.htm

Stalin, J.V. 1953–55, *Works*, Moscow: Foreign Languages Publishing House.

Stargardt, Nicholas 1994, *The German Idea of Militarism: Radical and Socialist Critics 1866–1914*, Cambridge: Cambridge University Press.

Стариков, Сергей Валентинович 2004, *Левые социалисты в Великой Российской революции. Март 1917–июль 1918 гг.: (на материалах Поволжья)*, Йошкар-Ола: Марийский государственный университет.

St. 1884, 'Biblijografija', *Walka Klas*, 2: 25–6.

Steenson, Gary P. 1978, *Karl Kautsky, 1854–1938: Marxism in the Classical Years*, Pittsburgh: University of Pittsburgh Press.

Steenson, Gary P. 1981, *'Not One Man! Not One Penny!' German Social Democracy, 1863–1914*, Pittsburgh: University of Pittsburgh Press.

Steenson, Gary P. 1991, *After Marx, Before Lenin: Marxism and Socialist Working-Class Parties in Europe, 1884–1914*, Pittsburgh: University of Pittsburgh Press.

Steger, Manfred B. 1997, 'Friedrich Engels and the Origins of German Revisionism: Another Look', *Political Studies*, 45, no. 2: 247–59.

Steger, Manfred B. 1997b, *The Quest for Evolutionary Socialism: Eduard Bernstein and Social Democracy*, Cambridge: Cambridge University Press.

Steinberg, Hans-Josef 1967, *Sozialismus und Deutsche Sozialdemokratie: Zur Ideologie der Partei vor dem 1. Weltkrieg*, Hannover: Verlag für Literatur und Zeitgeschehen.

Šteinbergs, Valentīns (ed.) 1977, *Apcerējumi par sabiedriskās un filozofiskās domas attistibu Latvijā: 1900–1920*, Rīga: Zinātne.

Stephens, John D. 1979, *The Transition from Capitalism to Socialism*, London: Macmillan.

Stetten, Nancy 1977, *The National Question and the Russian Civil War, 1917–1921*, PhD Dissertation, University of Chicago.

Stone, Bernard Benjamin 1965, *Nationalist and Internationalist Currents in Polish Socialism: The PPS and SDKPIL, 1893–1921*, PhD Dissertation, University of Chicago.

Стопани, А. 1923, 'Из прошлого нашей партии', in *Из прошлого*, edited by Бакуский комитет азербайджанской коммунистической партии, Баку: Бакинский рабочий.

Strobel, Georg W. 1974, *Die Partei Rosa Luxemburgs, Lenin und die SPD: der Polnische 'Europäische' Internationalismus in der Russischen Sozialdemokratie*, Wiesbaden: F. Steiner.

Stučka, Pēteris 1900 [1976–78], 'Stradnieku Biedrības', in *Rakstu Izlase*, Vol. 1, Rīga: Liesma.

Stučka, Pēteris [Anon.] 1904, 'Vienība vai Federācija', *Sociāldemokrāts*, 27: 1–10.

Stučka, Pēteris 1905a [1976–78], 'Politiska brīvība', in *Rakstu Izlase*, Vol. 1, Rīga: Liesma.

Stučka, Pēteris 1905b [1976–78], 'Patvaldības Valsts Dome', in *Rakstu Izlase*, Vol. 1, Rīga: Liesma.

Stučka, Pēteris 1906a [1976–78], 'Anarhisms vai partijas dezorganizācija?', in *Rakstu Izlase*, Vol. 1, Rīga: Liesma.

Stučka, Pēteris 1917a [1976–78], 'Pilsoniskā revolūcija un proletariāts', in *Rakstu Izlase*, Vol. 2, Rīga: Liesma.

Stučka, Pēteris 1917b [1976–78], 'Vēstule no Pēterpils', in *Rakstu Izlase*, Vol. 2, Rīga: Liesma.

Stučka, Pēteris 1917c [1976–78], 'Oktobra revolūcijas gada svētkos. 1917.–1918', in *Rakstu Izlase*, Vol. 2, Rīga: Liesma.

Stučka, Pēteris 1917d [1976–78], 'Demokrātija un kapitālisms', in *Rakstu Izlase*, Vol. 2, Rīga: Liesma.

Stučka, Pēteris 1976–78, *Rakstu Izlase*, Rīga: Liesma.

Sujecki, Janusz 1996, 'The Relation of the Polish Socialist Party-Proletariat to the Bund and the Jewish Question, 1900–1906', in *Jews, Poles, Socialists: The Failure of an Ideal*,

*Polin Vol. 9*, edited by Antony Polonsky, London: Littman Library of Jewish Civilization.

Sukhanov, N.N. 1922 [1955], *The Russian Revolution, 1917: A Personal Record*, edited and translated by Joel Carmichael, London: Oxford University Press.

Sulkunen, Irma 1990, *History of the Finnish Temperance Movement: Temperance as a Civic Religion*, Lewiston: E. Mellen Press.

Suny, Ronald Grigor 1972a, *The Baku Commune, 1917–1918: Class and Nationality in the Russian Revolution*, Princeton: Princeton University Press.

Suny, Ronald Grigor 1972b, 'A Journeyman for the Revolution: Stalin and the Labour Movement in Baku, June 1907–May 1908', *Soviet Studies*, 23, no. 3: 373–94.

Suny, Ronald Grigor 1990, 'Social Democrats in Power: Menshevik Georgia and the Russian Civil War', in *Party, State and Society in the Russian Civil War: Explorations in Social History*, edited by Diane Koenker et al., Bloomington: Indiana University Press.

Suny, Ronald Grigor 1993, *The Revenge of the Past: Nationalism, Revolution, and the Collapse of the Soviet Union*, Stanford: Stanford University Press.

Suny, Ronald Grigor 1994, *The Making of the Georgian Nation*, Bloomington: Indiana University Press.

Suny, Ronald G. and Terry Martin (eds.) 2010, *A State of Nations: Empire and Nation-Making in the Age of Lenin and Stalin*, Oxford: Oxford University Press.

Suodenjoki, Sami 2008, 'Suurlakon riitaisa yksimielisyys', in *Kansa kaikkivaltias: suurlakko Suomessa 1905*, edited by Pertti Haapala et al., Helsinki: Kustannusosakeyhtiö Teos.

Suodenjoki, Sami and Jarmo Peltola 2007, *Köyhä Suomen kansa katkoo kahleitansa: luokka, liike ja yhteiskunta 1880–1918*, Tampere: Tampere University Press.

Suodenjoki, Sami and Risto Turunen (eds.) 2017, *Työväki kumouksessa*, Työväen historian ja perinteen tutkimuksen seura.

Suomen Työväenpuolueen 1899, *Suomen Työväenpuolueen Perustavan Kokouksen Pöytäkirja Kokous Pidetty Turussa 17–20.7.1899*.

Surh, Gerald D. 1989, *1905 in St. Petersburg: Labor, Society and Revolution*, Stanford: Stanford University Press.

Sutton, Katharine 1987, *Class and Revolution in Russia: The Soviet Movement of 1905*, PhD Dissertation, University of Birmingham.

Swain, Geoff 1983, *Russian Social Democracy and the Legal Labour Movement, 1906–1914*, London: Macmillan.

Swain, Geoff 2006, *Trotsky*, Harlow: Longman.

Swietochowski, Tadeusz 1978, 'The Himmät Party: Socialism and the National Question in Russian Azerbaijan, 1904–1920', *Cahiers du Monde Russe et Soviétique*, 19, nos. 1–2: 119–42.

Szczerkowski, Antoni 1923, 'Z dziejów opozycji niepodległościowej w PPS – Lewica'.

Accessed at: http://lewicowo.pl/z-dziejow-opozycji-niepodleglosciowej-w-pps-lewi ca/

Szmidt, Bronisław (ed.) 1934, *Socjaldemokracja Królestwa Polskiego i Litwy: Materiały i Dokumenty. Vol. 1, 1893–1904*, Moskwa: Towarzystwo Wydawnicze Robotników Zagranicznych w ZSRR.

Szuch, Lubomyr Ihor 1985, *Volodymyr Vynnychenko and the Bolsheviks: A Study of the Political Evolution of a Ukrainian Revolutionary*, Master's Thesis, University of Alberta.

Tanni, Sanna 2008, *Kisällistä työväen herättäjäksi: Yrjö Mäkelinin Tampereen aika nuoruusvuosista suurlakkoon*, Master's Thesis, Tampereen yliopisto.

Тарасов, К.А. 2014, *Военная организация большевиков и борьба за власть в Петроградском гарнизоне в 1917 г.*, PhD Dissertation, Санкт-Петербургский институт истории РАН.

Тарасов, К.А. 2017, '"Левый блок" в Петроградском гарнизоне в 1917 г.' Accessed at: http://www.polithistory.ru/upload/iblock/653/6534cdf329be34465c77ac293af52f6c .pdf

Targalski Jerzy 1973, 'Geneza Polskiej Partii Socjalistycznej Proletariat', *Z pola walki*, 2–3: 39–79.

Tepora, Tuomas and Aapo Roselius (eds.) 2014, *The Finnish Civil War 1918: History, Memory, Legacy*, Leiden: Brill.

Thalheimer, August 1930, 'Rosa Luxemburg or Lenin', Accessed at: https://www.marxists .org/archive/thalheimer/works/rosa.htm

Thatcher, Ian D. 2009, 'The St. Petersburg/Petrograd Mezhraionka, 1913–1917: The Rise and Fall of a Russian Social Democratic Workers' Party Unity Faction', *The Slavonic and East European Review*, 87, no. 2: 284–321.

Тифлисский комитет РСДРП 1908, 'Листовка'. Accessed at: http://www.vostlit.info/ Texts/Dokumenty/Persien/XX/1900-1920/Iran_rev_1905_11/text.phtml?id=7779

Tikka, Marko 2009, *Kun kansa leikki kuningasta – Suomen suuri lakko 1905*, Helsinki: Suomalaisen Kirjallisuuden Seura.

Timberlake, Charles E. (ed.) 1972, *Essays on Russian Liberalism*, Columbia: University of Missouri Press.

Тютюкин, Станислав Васильевич et al. (eds.) 1996, *Меньшевики: Документы и материалы 1903–1917 гг.*, Москва: РОССПЭН.

Тютюкин, Станислав Васильевич 2002, *Меньшевизм: страницы истории*, Москва: РОССПЭН.

Tobias, Henry J. 1972, *The Jewish Bund in Russia from its Origins to 1905*, Stanford: Stanford University Press.

Tokoi, Oskari 1957, *Sisu, 'Even Through a Stone Wall': Autobiography of Oskari Tokoi*, New York: R. Speller.

Tomicki, Jan 1982, *Lewica socjalistyczna w Polsce 1918–1939*, Warszawa: Książka i Wiedza.

Transehe-Roseneck, Astaf von 1908, *Die Lettische Revolution*, Berlin: Georg Reimer.

Treijs, Rihards. 1977, '"Brīvais strēlnieks" padomju varas pirmajos mēnešos (1917.g. Oktobris–1918.g. Februāris)', in *Latvijas Komunistiskās partijas stratēģijas un taktikas problēmas, 1917. gada Oktobris*, edited by L. Malakhovska, V. Raevskiĭ, and A. Favorskiĭ, Rīga: P. Stučkas Latvijas Valsts universitāte.

Treijs, Rihards. 1981, *Pamatšķiras brīvais vārds: Latvijas marksistiskā prese 1898–1917*, Rīga: Avots.

Trembicka, Krystyna 1986–87, 'Komunistyczna Partia Robotnicza Polski wobec wojny polsko-radzieckiej w latach 1919–1920', *Annales Universitatis Mariae Curie-Skłodows ka. Sectio F, Historia*, 41/42: 169–86.

Trotsky, Leon 1904, 'Our Political Tasks.' Accessed at: https://www.marxists.org/archive/trotsky/1904/tasks/

Trotsky, Leon 1905 [2009], 'Foreword to Karl Marx, *Parizhskaya Kommuna*', in *Witnesses to Permanent Revolution*, edited by Richard B. Day and Daniel Gaido, Leiden: Brill.

Trotsky, Leon 1906a [2009], 'Kautsky on the Russian Revolution', in *Witnesses to Permanent Revolution*, edited by Richard B. Day and Daniel Gaido, Leiden: Brill.

Trotsky, Leon 1906b [1969], *The Permanent Revolution and Results and Prospects*, New York: Pathfinder Press.

Trotsky, Leon 1907 [1994], 'In Defence of the Party', *Journal of Trotsky Studies*, translated by Brian Pearce, 2: 75–223.

Trotsky, Leon 1917 [1918], 'What Next? After the July Days', in *The Proletarian Revolution in Russia*, edited by Louis C. Fraina, New York: Communist Press.

Trotsky, Leon 1924 [2016], 'The Lessons of October', in *Trotsky's Challenge: The 'Literary Discussion' of 1924 and the Fight for the Bolshevik Revolution*, edited by Frederick C. Corney, Leiden: Brill.

Trotsky, Leon 1930 [1970], *My Life*, New York: Pathfinder Press.

Trotsky, Leon 1932, *What Next? Vital Questions for the German Proletariat*, translated by Joseph Usick Vanzler, New York: Pioneer Publishers.

Trotsky, Leon 1932 [2008], *History of the Russian Revolution*, Chicago: Haymarket Books.

Trotsky, Leon 1937, *The Stalin School of Falsification*, translated by John G. Wright, New York: Pioneer Publishers.

Trotsky, Leon 1938, 'The Death Agony of Capitalism and the Tasks of the Fourth International'. Accessed at https://www.marxists.org/archive/trotsky/1938/tp/

Трусова, Н.С. (ed.) 1957, *Революционное движение в России весной и летом 1905 года*, Москва: Издательство Академии наук СССР.

Tsérételli, Irakly 1919 [1918], *Séparation de la Transcaucasie et de la Russie et Indépendance de la Géorgie*, Paris: Imprimerie Chaix.

Tuominen, Uuno 1958, 'Autonomian ajan yksikamarinen eduskunta 1907–1916', in *Suomen kansanedustuslaitoksen historia, Viides osa*, Helsinki: Eduskunnan historiakomitea.

Tych, Feliks 1960, *PPS-Lewica w latach wojny 1914–1918*, Warszawa: Książka i Wiedza.

Tych, Feliks (ed.) 1961a, *PPS-Lewica, 1906–1918 materiały i dokumenty*, Vol. 1: *1906–1910*, Warszawa: Książka i Wiedza.

Tych, Feliks (ed.) 1961b, 'La Participation des Partis Ouvriers Polonais au Mouvement de Zimmerwald', *Annali Fondazione Giangiacomo Feltrinelli*, 4: 90–125.

Tych, Feliks (ed.) 1962, *Socjaldemokracja Królestwa Polskiego i Litwy: Materiały i Dokumenty*. Vol. 2, *1902–1903*, Warszawa: Książka i Wiedza.

Tych, Feliks 1967, 'La Gauche Socialiste Polonaise et la Révolution d'Octobre', *Acta Poloniae Historica*, 16: 33–75.

Tych, Feliks 1970, 'Some Conditions and Regularities of Development of the Polish Working Class Movement', *Acta Poloniae Historica*, 22: 158–79.

Tych, Feliks 1974, *Związek Robotników Polskich, 1889–1892; anatomia wczesnej organizacji robotniczej*, Warszawa: Książka i Wiedza.

Tych, Feliks (ed.) 1975, *Polskie programy socjalistyczne 1878–1918*, Warszawa: Książka i Wiedza.

Tych, Feliks et al. (eds.) 1977, *Archiwum Ruchu Robotniczego*, Vol. 5: *Sojusz polskich i rosyjskich sił rewolucyjnych. W 60 rocznicę Rewolucji Październikowej*, Warszawa: Książka i Wiedza.

Tymieniecka, Aleksandra 1982, *Warszawska organizacja PPS 1918–1939*, Warszawa: Państwowe Wydawnictwo Naukowe.

Udrenas, Nerijus 2000, *Book, Bread, Cross and Whip: The Construction of Lithuanian Identity in Imperial Russia*, PhD Dissertation, Brandeis University.

Upton, Anthony F. 1980, *The Finnish Revolution, 1917–1918*, Minneapolis: University of Minnesota Press.

Уратадзе, Г.И. 1968, *Воспоминания грузинского социалдемократа*, Stanford: Hoover Institution on War, Revolution, and Peace.

Ury, Scott 2012, *Barricades and Banners: The Revolution of 1905 and the Transformation of Warsaw Jewry*, Stanford: Stanford University Press.

Uski, Juha 2008, *Johan Kock and the Dramatic Events of 1905 and 1906 in Helsinki*, Bachelor's degree project, Roskilde University.

Уткин, А.И. 1987, 'К вопросу о численности и составе РСДРП в 1905–1907 гг.', in *Политические партии России в период революции 1905–1907 гг. Коли-чественный анализ*, edited by А.П. Корелин, Москва: Академия наук СССР.

Valentinov, Nikolay 1968, *Encounters with Lenin*, translated by Paul Rosta and Brian Pearce, London: Oxford University Press.

Valpas, Edward 1904, *Mikä menettelytapa?: työväenliikkeen taktiikasta*, Helsinki: Työväen Kirjapaino.

Valters, Miķelis [Anon.] 1905, 'Baltijas Sociālās Demokrātijas Jautājumi', *Revolucionārā Baltija*, 2: 13–25.

Van der Linden, Marcel 2003, *Transnational Labour History: Explorations*, Aldershot: Ashgate.

Van Ree, Erik 2000, 'Stalin's Bolshevism: The Year of the Revolution', *Revolutionary Russia*, 13, no. 1: 29–54.

Васьков, Максим Александрович 2005, *Меньшевики на Дону: 1903–1914 гг. (автореферата)*. Accessed at: http://www.dissercat.com/content/mensheviki-na-donu -1903-1914-gg#ixzz4cxQS6CRd

Владислав, Верстюк et al. (ed.) 2003, *Український національно-визвольний рух. Березень-листопад 1917 року. Документи і матеріали*, Київ: Видавництво Олени Теліги.

Верстюк, В.Ф. 2004, 'Симон Петлюра: політичний портрет: (до 125-річчя від дня народження)', *Український історичний журнал*, 3: 112–26.

Voskobiynyk, Michael Hryhory 1972, *The Nationalities Question in Russia in 1905–1907: A Study in the Origin of Modern Nationalism, with Special Reference to the Ukrainians*, PhD Dissertation, University of Pennsylvania.

Vössing, Konstantin W. 2008, *The Formation of Social Democratic Parties: Degrees of Inclusion as External Constraints and the Strategic Choices of Labor Elites*, PhD Dissertation, Ohio State University.

Vössing, Konstantin, 2017, *How Leaders Mobilize Workers: Social Democracy, Revolution, and Moderate Syndicalism*, Cambridge: Cambridge University Press.

Villari, Luigi 1906, *Fire and Sword in the Caucasus*, London: T.F. Unwin.

Винниченко, Володимир 1920, *Відродження нації*, Київ: Відень.

Висоцький, О.Ю. 2004, *Українські Соціал-Демократи та Есери: Досвід Перемог і Поразок*, Київ: Основні Цінності.

Wade, Rex A. 1969, *The Russian Search for Peace: February–October 1917*, Stanford: Stanford University Press.

Wade, Rex A. 1991, 'The Revolution in the Provinces: Khar'kov and the Varieties of Response to the October Revolution', *Revolutionary Russia*, 4, no. 1: 132–42.

Wade, Rex A. 2004, '"All Power to the Soviets": The Bolsheviks Take Power', in *Revolutionary Russia: New Approaches*, edited by Rex A. Wade, New York: Routledge.

Waldenberg, Marek 1972, *Wzlot i upadek Karola Kautsky'ego: studium z historii myśli społecznej i politycznej*, Kraków: Wydawnictwo Literackie.

Warski, Adolf 1929 [1966], '20-letni spór z Leninem', in *Nowy Przegląd (Reedycja): 1929*, Warszawa: Książka i Wiedza.

Wasilewski, Leon [St. O.] 1900, 'Strejk Powszechny', *Przedświt*, 11.

Wasilewski, Leon [St. Os...arz] 1902, 'Karol Marks a Powstanie 1863 Roku', *Przedświt*, 22, no. 9: 321–4.

Wasilewski, Leon 1903, 'Strajki na południu Rosji'. Accessed at: http://lewicowo.pl/ strajki-na-poludniu-rosji/

Wasilewski, Leon 1904, *Nasi Nacjonaliści (Rzecz o Tzw. Narodowej Demokracji)*, Londyn: J. Kaniowski.

Wasilewski, Leon (ed.) 1934, *Dzieje Zjazdu Paryskiego 1892: Przyczynek do Historii Pol-*

*skiego Ruchu Socjalistycznego*, Warszawa: Instytut Badania Najnowszej Historji Polski.

Weeks, Theodore R. 2012, 'Nationality, Empire, and Politics in the Russian Empire and USSR: An Overview of Recent Publications', *H-Soz-Kult*, 29 October, www.hsozkult .de/literaturereview/id/forschungsberichte-1134.

Weill, Claudie 1977, *Marxistes Russes et Social-Démocratie Allemande 1898–1904*, Paris: Maspero.

Weill, Claudie 1986, 'La Révolution de 1905 et le Mouvement Ouvrier Allemand', in *1905, la Première Révolution Russe: Actes du Colloque International*, edited by François-Xavier Coquin and Céline Gervais-Francelle, Paris: Publications de la Sorbonne.

Weinberg, Robert Etter 1985, *Worker Organizations and Politics in the Revolution of 1905 in Odessa*, PhD Dissertation, University of California, Berkeley.

Weinberg, Robert Etter 1993, *The Revolution of 1905 in Odessa: Blood on the Steps*, Bloomington: Indiana University Press.

Weinstock, Nathan 1984, *Le Pain de Misère: Histoire du Mouvement Ouvrier Juif en Europe Tome I. L'Empire Russe Jusqu'en 1914*, Paris: La Découverte.

Weizmann, Chaim 1971, *The Letters and Papers of Chaim Weizmann, Vol. II, Series A*, edited by Barnet Litvinoff, London: Oxford University Press.

White, James D. 1971, 'The Revolution in Lithuania 1918–19', *Soviet Studies*, 23, no. 2: 186–200.

White, James D. 1985, 'Early Soviet Historical Interpretations of the Russian Revolution 1918–24', *Soviet Studies*, 37, no. 3: 330–52.

White, James D. 1990, 'Latvian and Lithuanian Sections in the Bolshevik Party on the Eve of the February Revolution', *Revolutionary Russia*, 3, no. 1: 90–106.

White, James D. 1994, 'National Communism and World Revolution: The Political Consequences of German Military Withdrawal from the Baltic Area in 1918–19', *Europe-Asia Studies*, 46, no. 8: 1349–69.

Wildman, Allan K. 1967, *The Making of a Workers' Revolution: Russian Social Democracy, 1891–1903*, Chicago: University of Chicago Press.

Williams, Beryl 2005, '1905: The View from the Provinces', in *The Russian Revolution of 1905: Centenary Perspectives*, edited by Jonathan D. Smele and Anthony Haywood, Abingdon: Routledge.

Williams, Robert Chadwell 1986, *The Other Bolsheviks: Lenin and His Critics, 1904–1914*, Bloomington: Indiana University Press.

Wojtasik, Janusz 1981, 'Problem powstania i walki zbrojnej w ujęciu PPS i SDKPIL w dobie rewolucji 1905–1907', *Studia i Materiały do Historii Wojskowości*, 24: 203–9.

Woodhouse, Charles E. and Henry J. Tobias 1966, 'Primordial Ties and Political Process in Pre-Revolutionary Russia: The Case of the Jewish Bund', *Comparative Studies in Society and History*, 8, no. 3: 331–60.

Woytinsky, Wladimir S. 1921, *La Démocratie Géorgienne*, Paris: Alcan Lévy.

Wróbel, Piotr J. 2010, 'The Rise and Fall of Parliamentary Democracy in Interwar Poland', in *The Origins of Modern Polish Democracy*, edited by M.B.B. Biskupski et al., Athens: Ohio University Press.

Wydziału Historii Partii кс рzрr 1956, *Z pola walki, Vol. 2*, Warszawa: Książka i Wiedza.

Wynn, Charters Stephen 1987, *Russian Labor in Revolution and Reaction: The Donbass Working Class, 1870–1905*, PhD Dissertation, Stanford University.

Wynn, Charters Stephen 1992, *Workers, Strikes, and Pogroms: The Donbass-Dnepr Bend in Late Imperial Russia, 1870–1905*, Princeton: Princeton University Press.

Юркевич, Лев [Л. Рыбалка] 1917, *Русскіе Соціалдемократы и Національный Вопросъ*, Женева: Изданіе Редакціи Украинской Соціалдемократической Газеты 'Боротьба'.

Żarnowska, Anna 1965, *Geneza Rozłamu w Polskiej Partii Socjalistycznej, 1904–1906*, Warszawa: Państwowe Wydawnictwo Naukowe.

Żarnowska, Anna 1991, 'Religion and Politics: Polish Workers c. 1900', *Social History*, translated by Robin Pearson, 16, no. 3: 299–316.

Заводовський, Анатолій Анатолійович 2006, *Преса української соціал-демократії та українське питання в Російській імперії на початку XX ст.*, PhD Dissertation, Кам'янець-Подільський Державний Університет.

Жордания, Ной 1968, *Моя жизнь*, Stanford: The Hoover Institution on War, Revolution and Peace.

Zimmerman, Joshua D. 2004, *Poles, Jews, and the Politics of Nationality: The Bund and the Polish Socialist Party in late Tsarist Russia, 1892–1914*, Madison: University of Wisconsin Press.

Zinoviev, Grigory 1909, 'Only One Path to Socialism'. Accessed at: http://weeklyworker .co.uk/worker/1087/only-one-path-to-socialism/

Zinoviev, Grigory 1916, 'The War and the Crisis in Socialism'. Accessed at: https://www .marxists.org/archive/zinoviev/works/1916/war/opp-index.htm

Zinoviev, Grigory and Julius Martov 1920 [2011], *Martov and Zinoviev: Head to Head in Halle*, edited and translated by Ben Lewis, London: November Publications.

# Index

CPSIA information can be obtained
at www.ICGtesting.com
Printed in the USA
JSHW051212290422
25374JS00002B/3